CALL COMMUNITIES & CULTURE

SHORT PAPERS FROM

EUROCALL 2016

Edited by Salomi Papadima-Sophocleous,
Linda Bradley & Sylvie Thouësny

esearch-publishing.net

Published by Research-publishing.net, not-for-profit association
Dublin, Ireland; Voillans, France, info@research-publishing.net

CALL communities and culture – short papers from EUROCALL 2016
Edited by Salomi Papadima-Sophocleous, Linda Bradley, and Sylvie Thouësny

Disclaimer: Research-publishing.net does not take any responsibility for the content of the pages written by the authors of this book. The authors have recognised that the work described was not published before, or that it is not under consideration for publication elsewhere. While the information in this book are believed to be true and accurate on the date of its going to press, neither the editorial team, nor the publisher can accept any legal responsibility for any errors or omissions that may be made. The publisher makes no warranty, expressed or implied, with respect to the material contained herein. While Research-publishing.net is committed to publishing works of integrity, the words are the authors' alone.

Trademark notice: product or corporate names may be trademarks or registered trademarks, and are used only for identification and explanation without intent to infringe.

Copyrighted material: every effort has been made by the editorial team to trace copyright holders and to obtain their permission for the use of copyrighted material in this book. In the event of errors or omissions, please notify the publisher of any corrections that will need to be incorporated in future editions of this book.

Typeset by Research-publishing.net
Cover design by © Easy Conferences, info@easyconferences.eu, www.easyconferences.eu
Cover layout by © Raphaël Savina (raphael@savina.net)
Photo "bridge" on cover by © Andriy Markov/Shutterstock
Photo "frog" on cover by © Fany Savina (fany.savina@gmail.com)
Fonts used are licensed under a SIL Open Font License

ISBN13: 978-1-908416-43-8 (Paperback - Print on demand, black and white)
Print on demand technology is a high-quality, innovative and ecological printing method; with which the book is never 'out of stock' or 'out of print'.

ISBN13: 978-1-908416-44-5 (Ebook, PDF, colour)
ISBN13: 978-1-908416-45-2 (Ebook, EPUB, colour)

Legal deposit, Ireland: The National Library of Ireland, The Library of Trinity College, The Library of the University of Limerick, The Library of Dublin City University, The Library of NUI Cork, The Library of NUI Maynooth, The Library of University College Dublin, The Library of NUI Galway.

Legal deposit, United Kingdom: The British Library.
British Library Cataloguing-in-Publication Data.
A cataloguing record for this book is available from the British Library.

Legal deposit, France: Bibliothèque Nationale de France - Dépôt légal: décembre 2016.

Table of contents

Preface

Salomi Papadima-Sophocleous[1]

With EUROCALL reaching its 23rd year, it has truly earned its status as an innovative conference with a mind of its own – a thought-provoking scientific gathering with high aspirations for the future. This is what we have tried to reflect in this volume of selected short papers. Short papers are an ideal forum for work in progress and late breaking results. As such, this volume captures exactly what *CALL Communities and Culture* represent: papers that are all trying to say something new and different, whether at a theoretical and practical level or in terms of research carried out in non-traditional areas or using novel methodologies.

The 23rd EUROCALL conference was organised by the Cyprus University of Technology Language Centre – the first time that EUROCALL has been held in Cyprus. More than 260 delegates representing 37 different countries attended the conference held between 24th and 27th August 2016.

The theme of the conference this year was *CALL Communities and Culture*. It offered a unique opportunity to hear from real-world CALL practitioners on how they practise CALL in their communities, and how the CALL culture has developed in local and global contexts. CALL has moved from traditional drill-and-practice programmes in the 1960s and 1970s to more recent manifestations of CALL, such as the use of interactive whiteboards, corpora and concordances, computer-mediated communication as well as the applications used in virtual learning environments and e-learning, virtual worlds, gaming and mobile-assisted language learning. Keeping an eye on the latest changes and on the future and being well informed are critical success factors for the CALL community.

Over 135 presentations were delivered and 27 posters were presented on topics related specifically to the theme and more general CALL topics. 84 of these appear in this volume.

Cyprus University of Technology, Limassol, Cyprus; salomi.papadima@cut.ac.cy

How to cite: Papadima-Sophocleous, S. (2016). Preface. In S. Papadima-Sophocleous, L. Bradley & S. Thouësny (Eds), *CALL communities and culture – short papers from EUROCALL 2016* (pp. xii-xiv). Research-publishing.net. https://doi.org/10.14705/rpnet.2016.eurocall2016.527

Our keynote speakers, who came from both within and outside the sphere of CALL, contributed greatly to fostering a greater understanding of how we might conceptualise CALL Communities and Culture, that is, the different angles we can view communities and culture within CALL practice and research. Looking into different CALL communities and cultures, building new ones and exploring their possibilities, looking into interdisciplinary communities and cultures that CALL can benefit from, these are some of the issues that our keynote speakers presented, explored and questioned.

The Graham Davies keynote speaker, Mark Pegrum, presented the possibilities of mobile learning in its various forms and the implications of this kind of learning for language learning across the various cultures. This new learning methodology adopts 21st century skills, assists in the construction of new communities and allows the various cultures to develop within their own spectrum of abilities and possibilities. Understanding how mobile learning works around the globe allows us to also develop our own learning contexts and provide the optimal kinds of mobile learning that will be beneficial for our own learners in our specific academic environments.

Panayiotis Zaphiris presented an empirical study of an online learning community that worked closely with the course design team under the participatory design process. This design process was implemented for a large online course of English speakers learning Greek and included four stages: establishing bridges with the proposed learner, identifying user needs and implementing suggestions, developing prototypes and finally providing feedback. The progress of the learners was constantly monitored and analysed throughout all stages. This participatory design methodology was based on the constructionism pedagogical theory.

Leila Kajee analysed the influence of digital technology on our everyday lives. Societies in developed countries are exposed to a massive amount of information which is available in many forms: video, text, image and audio. Even more so in the children's world, where, in their spare time they have the opportunity to retrieve information in the form of images, stories and so on. To prove her argument she presented three case studies which clearly indicate the construction of digital identity and how students engage in social networking practices. Leila Kajee used new literacy studies as a framework to provide a theory of literacy practices and the work of Hall among others to theorise identity. She also presented further implications of digital identity construction regarding teaching and learning.

Recordings of these keynote addresses, as well as the full programme and session abstracts may be found at the conference website (http://eurocall2016.org/).

We thank all of the participants of the EUROCALL 2016 conference and the presenters.

All submissions for this volume have been rigorously reviewed: submissions received an average of two external reviews and were then subjected to further meta-reviewing.

Producing this volume has been a joint effort of authors, reviewers, category co-chairs and the entire organising committee who contributed much time and effort. We would like to thank all contributors who reflect the enormous variety of topics which were addressed at this exciting event and the quality of the presentations. Without you this conference could not have taken place. We hope you will enjoy reading the volume as much as we have – the editors –, during its preparation. We hope that the essence of the EUROCALL2016 conference has been communicated to you through this volume.

Καλή Ανάγνωση! (Enjoy reading these papers!)
Salomi Papadima-Sophocleous
Conference chair of EUROCALL2016

Conference committees

Programme committee

Programme chairs
- Peppi Taalas (chair), *University of Jyvaskylä, Finland*
- John Gillespie (co-chair), *University of Ulster, United Kingdom*

Committee members
- Christine Appel, *Universitat Oberta de Catalunya, Spain*
- Androulla Athanasiou, *Cyprus University of Technology, Cyprus*
- David Barr, *Ulster University, United Kingdom*
- Becky Bergman, *Chalmers University of Technology, Sweden*
- Alex Boulton, *Atilf, CNRS & University of Lorraine, France*
- Claire Bradin Siskin, *Consultant, United States*
- Jack Burston, *Cyprus University of Technology, Cyprus*
- Monique Burston, *Cyprus University of Technology, Cyprus*
- Angela Chambers, *University of Limerick, Ireland*
- Thierry Chanier, *Universite Blaise Pascal, France*
- Suzanne Cloke, *Padova University Language Center, Italy*
- Jozef Colpaert, *Universiteit Antwerpen, Belgium*
- Piet Desmet, *KU Leuven, Belgium*
- Melinda Dooly, *Universitat Autònoma de Barcelona, Spain*
- Fiona Farr, *University of Limerick, Ireland*
- Ana Gimeno, *Universidad Politecnica de Valencia, Spain*
- Muriel Grosbois, *Université Paris Sorbonne – ESPE, France*
- Nicolas Guichon, *Lyon 2, Laboratoire ICAR, France*
- Sarah Guth, *University of Padova, Italy*
- Mirjam Hauck, *The Open University, United Kingdom*
- Trude Heift, *Simon Fraser University, Canada*
- Francesca Helm, *University of Padova, Italy*
- Phil Hubbard, *Stanford University, United States*
- Sake Jager, *University of Groningen, Netherlands*
- Juha Jalkanen, *University of Jyväskylä, Finland*
- Kristi Jauregi, *Utrecht University, Netherlands*
- Leena Kuure, *University of Oulu, Finland*

- Mike Levy, *The University of Queensland, Australia*
- Dominique Macaire, *Université de Lorraine, France*
- Teresa Mackinnon, *University of Warwick, United Kingdom*
- Liam Murray, *University of Limerick, Ireland*
- Susanna Nocchi, *Dublin Institute of Technology, Ireland*
- Robert O'Dowd, *University of León, Spain*
- Luisa Panichi, *University of Pisa, Italy*
- Antigoni Parmaxi, *Cyprus University of Technology, Cyprus*
- Hans Paulussen, *KU Leuven KULAK, Belgium*
- Pascual Pérez-Paredes, *University of Cambridge, United Kingdom*
- Elaine Riordan, *University of Limerick, Ireland*
- Shannon Sauro, *Malmö University, Sweden*
- Mathias Schulze, *University of Waterloo, Canada*
- Nicos Souleles, *Cyprus University of Technology, Cyprus*
- Oranna Speicher, *University of Nottingham, United Kingdom*
- Glenn Stockwell, *Waseda University, Japan*
- Sylvie Thouësny, *Research-publishing.net, Ireland*
- Cornelia Tschichold, *Swansea University, United Kingdom*
- Shona Whyte, *Université Nice Sophia Antipolis, France*

Local organising committee

- Salomi Papadima-Sophocleous, *Cyprus University of Technology, Cyprus*
- Fernando Loizides, *University of Wolverhampton, Wolverhampton, United Kingdom and Cyprus University of Technology, Cyprus*
- Elena Papa, *Cyprus University of Technology, Cyprus*
- Maria Victoria Soule, *Cyprus University of Technology, Cyprus*
- Elis Kakoulli Constantinou, *Cyprus University of Technology, Cyprus*
- Maro Neophytou, *Cyprus University of Technology, Cyprus*
- Anastasia Mouskou-Peck, *Cyprus University of Technology, Cyprus*

EUROCALL Executive committee 2014/2015

President and vice-president
- Françoise Blin, President, *Dublin City University, Ireland*
- Peppi Taalas, Vice-President, *University of Jyväskylä, Finland*

Members, elected and co-opted officers
- Kent Andersen, *Syddansk Erhvervsskole, Denmark*
- Alex Boulton, *University of Lorraine, France*

- Mirjam Hauck, *Open University, United Kingdom*
- Francesca Helm, *University of Padova, Italy*
- Sake Jager, *University of Groningen, the Netherlands*
- Salomi Papadima-Sophocleous, *Cyprus University of Technology, Cyprus*
- Oranna Speicher, *University of Nottingham, Nottingham, United Kingdom*

Appointed officers
- John Gillespie, Treasurer, *University of Ulster, Coleraine, Northern Ireland*
- Toni Patton, Secretary, *University of Ulster, Coleraine, Northern Ireland*

Peer-reviewing committee (full articles)

- David Alfter, *Språkbanken, University of Gothenburg, Gothenburg, Sweden*
- Christopher Allen, *Linnaeus University, Växjö, Sweden*
- Antonie Alm, *University of Otago, Dunedin, New Zealand*
- Elena Bárcena, *UNED, Madrid, Spain*
- Branislav Bédi, *University of Iceland, Reykjavík, Iceland*
- Alex Boulton, *University of Lorraine, France*
- Jack Burston, *Cyprus University of Technology, Limassol, Cyprus*
- Cristina Cervini, *University of Bologna, Bologna, Italy*
- Tatiana Codreanu, *Ecole Normale Supérieure de Lyon, Lyon, France*
- Cathy Cohen, *Université Lyon 2, Lyon, France*
- Jonás Fouz González, *Universidad Católica San Antonio, Murcia, Spain*
- Christina Nicole Giannikas, *Cyprus University of Technology, Cyprus*
- John Gillespie, *University of Ulster, Coleraine, Northern Ireland*
- Sara Guth, *University of Padova, Padova, Italy*
- Phil Hubbard, *Stanford University, Stanford, United State*
- Kristi Jauregi, *Utrecht University, Utrecht, Netherlands*
- Leila Kajee, *University of Johannesburg, Johannesburg, South Africa*
- Malgorzata Kurek, *Jan Dlugosz University, Czestochowa, Poland*
- Vera Leier, *University of Canterbury, Christchurch, New Zealand*
- António Lopes, *University of Algarve, Faro, and CETAPS, Portugal*
- Paul Lyddon, *Osaka Jogakuin College, Osaka, Japan*
- Maryam Sadat Mirzaei, *Kyoto University, Kyoto, Japan*
- Monique Monville-Burston, *Cyprus University of Technology, Cyprus*
- Neasa Ní Chiaráin, *Trinity College, Dublin, Ireland*
- Jaeuk Park, *Newcastle University, Newcastle upon Tyne, United Kingdom*
- Hans Paulussen, *University of Leuven, Leuven, Belgium*
- Maria Perifanou, *University of Macedonia, Thessaloniki, Greece*

- Müge Satar, *Bogazici University, İstanbul, Turkey*
- Shannon Sauro, *Malmö University, Malmö, Sweden*
- Oranna Speicher, *University of Nottingham, Nottingham, United Kingdom*
- Sascha Stolhans, *University of Manchester, Manchester, United Kingdom*
- Monica Ward, *Dublin City University, Dublin, Ireland*
- Ciara Wigham, *Clermont Université – LRL, Clermont-Ferrand, France*
- Nadia Yassine-Diab, *University of Toulouse, Toulouse, France*

The impact of EFL teachers' mediation in wiki-mediated collaborative writing activities on student-student collaboration

Maha Alghasab[1]

Abstract. This paper focuses on how teachers mediate wiki collaborative writing activities, and the impact of their mediations on students' collaboration. It is based on a study conducted with three English as a Foreign Language (EFL) teachers and their students (aged 17-18 years) at two government-funded girls' high schools in Kuwait. The selected groups of students, supported by their class teachers, carried out wiki collaborative writing activities over a period of eight weeks. The writing activities were tracked from conception to completion, by closely analysing the wiki discussion and edits, in order to explore the process of interaction. This was triangulated with interview data with teachers and students to gain deeper insights. The results show that, despite the fact that all groups of learners and teachers received a similar type of training and worked on the same activity, there were some variations in the level of their collaboration. Teachers played an essential role in shaping the way that learners collaborated; i.e. some teachers' behaviours promoted collaboration, while others hindered it. Although it can be acknowledged that the wiki is a powerful tool for student-centred collaborative writing, it can also be argued that the role of the teacher is indispensable, and the right kind of teacher intervention is critical to the success of collaborative writing, especially in educational contexts that are similar to Kuwaiti schools. Therefore, professional training is required in order to raise teachers' awareness of effective pedagogy in supporting wiki-mediated collaborative writing activities.

Keywords: wiki, collaborative writing, teacher mediation, student collaboration.

1. University of York, York, United Kingdom; drmahaalghasab@gmail.com

How to cite this article: Alghasab, M. (2016). The impact of EFL teachers' mediation in wiki-mediated collaborative writing activities on student-student collaboration. In S. Papadima-Sophocleous, L. Bradley & S. Thouësny (Eds), *CALL communities and culture – short papers from EUROCALL 2016* (pp. 1-6). Research-publishing.net. https://doi.org/10.14705/rpnet.2016.eurocall2016.529

1.   Introduction

The use of wiki has captured the attention of researchers because of their potential for promoting collaborative writing, which is the process whereby two or more writers compose a text (Storch, 2005). Wikis have been proposed as tools to promote collaborative interaction, i.e. interaction that is rich in reciprocal feedback, consideration of another's proposal, using a first person plural pronoun (we) throughout the activity (Li, 2013) and co-constructing the wiki text together by adding, expanding and correcting each other's text (Bradley, Lindstrom, & Rystedt, 2010). To date, studies conducted on student-student (S-S) interaction have reported mixed findings: some document a high level of collaboration (Li, 2013) whereas others observe instances of writing individually in a cooperative manner (Bradley et al., 2010), a reluctance to edit each other's texts (Lund, 2008), and unequal participation (Li & Zhu, 2011). Therefore, computer-assisted language learning researchers have called for more teacher intervention in the wiki context (e.g. Lund & Smørdal, 2006). However, previous wiki studies have not investigated this topic in depth. Given the prominent role that teachers play in promoting collaboration, as reported in other Face-To-Face (FTF) studies (e.g. Yoon & Kim, 2012), this study aims to qualitatively analyse the nature of teachers' interventions and how this influences the students' collaboration in the wiki context. The following research questions are proposed:

- How do EFL teachers mediate students' interaction in wiki-based collaborative writing activities?

- What is the impact of their mediations on the level of students' collaboration?

2.   Method

2.1.   Approach, context and participants

A qualitative multiple case study design was adopted. One embedded case, a group of four learners working together, was selected for in-depth exploration from each teacher's class. Based on students' self-reported data of the behaviours in FTF collaborative activities, representative groups – in which there was a mix of students reporting both collaborative and non-collaborative orientations – were selected for in-depth exploration. The cases refer to the interactions of three small groups of learners with their teachers, with each interaction as a bounded system.

The study was conducted in two government-funded girls' high schools in Kuwait, where English is taught as an obligatory subject five times a week. Using a convenient sampling method, three twelfth grade EFL teachers and their classes were recruited to participate in this study. All participants were non-native English speakers, their first language being Arabic. The students were all female, Kuwaiti learners of EFL, and their ages ranged from 17 to 18 years old. In the three groups, learners were asked to design a poster about Kuwait. Three PBwiki platforms were created for the purpose of the study. Each group was assigned a sub-topic, however, within each group there was no division of labour. The study was conducted in the second academic term, in February 2014, and lasted for 13 weeks. Table 1 presents the data collection timeline.

Table 1.   Data collection timeline

Weeks 1 & 2	Week 3	Weeks 4 - 11	Week 12	Week 13
Orientation/ background questionnaire and interviews. Teachers' wiki training.	Students' training.	Out of class wiki activity (designing a poster). Week 7 & 11 teachers' stimulated recall interview.	Teachers' post activity interview.	Students' post activity interview (individual interview).

2.2.   Data collection methods and analysis

Data was collected through a systematic observation of the wiki discussion and the page history, teachers' stimulated recall interviews, and semi-structured interviews with teachers and students. To characterise teachers' interventional behaviour and students' levels of collaboration, a framework was developed combining a priori (i.e. pre-established; used in previous research) and a posteriori (i.e. emerging from the data) categories. Teachers' interventional behaviours were classified into three levels: organisational, socio-cognitive, and socio-affective (Mangenot & Nissen, 2006). The three levels of interaction were also used to refer broadly to how students interacted. Within each level, in the manner of Li (2013) and Arnold, Ducate, Lomicka, and Lord (2009), contributions to the discussion were further classified according to their functions (e.g. organising the work, seeking peer feedback, expressing emotions). Previous framework categories were considered in order to analyse editing behaviours (e.g. Mak & Coniam, 2008), including adding new ideas, expanding ideas, reorganising ideas, correcting, deleting, and synthesis of information. The unit of analysis was defined as either a post to the discussion forum or an edit action. Interview data was also coded thematically according to their focus (organisational, socio-cognitive, and socio-affective levels). In order to enhance the reliability, the framework and its categories were explained to another researcher, and then the process of coding 15% randomly selected extracts was done independently by both researchers. Instances of agreement and disagreement were counted, and following Miles and Huberman's (1994) inter-coder reliability formula, the inter-rater agreement reached 86.9%. The discrepancies were resolved by discussion.

3.   Findings and discussion

Analysis of the teachers' and students' interactions in the wiki suggests that, despite the fact that all teachers and students received similar types of training and worked on a similar type of activity, there were variations in the level of collaboration across the three cases (see Figure 1), which upholds the findings of previous studies (e.g. Arnold et al., 2009; Li & Zhu, 2011). The results also show that the way in which teachers intervened in the activity had an impact on the level of collaboration among students at organisational, socio-cognitive, and socio-affective levels. For example, Case 1 teacher employed a very structured approach: she divided the work among the students, gave direct task instructions, used an authoritative tone, immediately answered students' language-related questions, and edited their wiki text. In direct contrast, Case 2 teacher only intervened in order to encourage students to participate, by suggesting ideas for the text, although she edited the students' text. She appeared to assume that the students would autonomously engage in collaborative dialogue and the co-construction of the wiki text. On the other hand, Case 3 teacher intervened in order to encourage collaboration, by establishing a wiki culture of collaboration and positioning herself as a co-learner, in an effort to promote collaborative dialogue; she asked questions about students' language use, modelled editing behaviours, and explicitly encouraged students towards such behaviour.

An examination of student-student interaction indicates that the teachers' interventional behaviours influenced how students interacted. Figure 1 shows the less collaborative group (Case 1), where the teacher structured the activity, students wrote individually, as instructed, ignored others' suggestions, rejected others' edits and depended on the teacher, with instances of seeking feedback occurring most frequently between the teacher and a student, rather than between students. In Case 2, where the teacher stepped back and intervened rarely, students failed to engage in a high level of collaboration, which supports the findings of previous research (e.g. Lund & Smørdal, 2006). Although the students' writing behaviours involved adding to and expanding on each other's ideas, they rarely engaged with each other in a collaborative dialogue by seeking and providing feedback on the text. In Case 3, the teacher's mediation of the students' interaction caused them to gradually engage in collaboration. High levels of collaborative behaviours emerged, including writing collaboratively by adding to, expanding on and correcting each other's existing texts, and engaging in a collaborative dialogue by questioning, elaborating on and suggesting alternatives to each other's language use. These collaborative behaviours have also been reported in other studies (Li, 2013), in which learners were novices individually and experts collectively.

Figure 1.   Teachers' intervention and learners' interaction

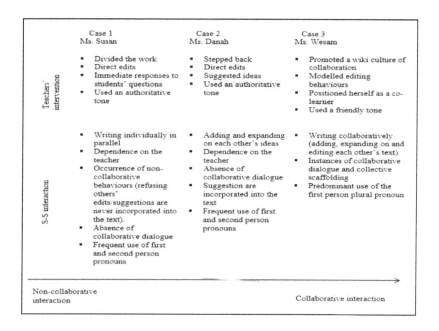

4.   Conclusion

Although wiki is a powerful tool for student-centred collaborative writing, the role of the teacher is indispensable, and the appropriate kind of teacher intervention is critical to the success of collaborative writing. This study has showcased how certain teachers' behaviours directly impact how students collaborate. Thus, professional training is required in order to raise teachers' awareness of effective pedagogy in supporting wiki-mediated, student collaborative writing.

5.   Acknowledgements

I would like to thank my supervisors, Dr Zöe Handely and Dr Jan Hardman, for their feedback and contributions. I would also like to thank all teachers and students who participated in the study.

References

Arnold, N., Ducate, L., Lomicka, L., & Lord, G. (2009). Assessing online collaboration among language teachers: a cross-institutional case study. *Journal of Interactive Online Learning, 8*(2), 121-139.

Bradley, L., Lindstrom, B., & Rystedt, H. (2010). Rationalities of collaboration for language learning in a wiki. *ReCALL, 22*(2), 247-265. https://doi.org/10.1017/S0958344010000108

Li, M. (2013). Individual novices and collective experts: collective scaffolding in wiki-based small group writing. *System, 41*(3), 752-769. https://doi.org/10.1016/j.system.2013.07.021

Li, M., & Zhu, W. (2011). Patterns of computer mediated interaction in small writing groups using wiki. *Computer Assisted Language Learning, 26*(1), 61-82. https://doi.org/10.1080/0 9588221.2011.631142

Lund, A. (2008). Wikis: a collective approach to language production. *ReCALL, 20*(1), 35-54. https://doi.org/10.1017/S0958344008000414

Lund, A., & Smørdal, O. (2006). Is there a space for the teacher in a wiki? *Paper presented at the Preceedings of the 2006 international symposium on wikis, Odense, Denmark.* https://doi. org/10.1145/1149453.1149466

Mak, B., & Coniam, D. (2008). Using wikis to enhance and develop writing skills among secondary school students in Hong Kong. *System, 38*(3), 437-455. https://doi.org/10.1016/j. system.2008.02.004

Mangenot, F., & Nissen, E. (2006). Collective activity and tutor involvement in e-learning environments for language teachers and learners. *CALICO Journal, 23*(3), 601-621.

Miles, M., & Huberman, M. (1994). *Qualitative data analysis: an expanded sourcebook* (2nd ed.). Thousand Oaks, CA: Sage.

Storch, N. (2005). Collaborative writing: product, process, and students' reflections. *Journal of Second Language Writing, 14*(3), 153-173. https://doi.org/10.1016/j.jslw.2005.05.002

Yoon, B., & Kim, H. (Eds). (2012). *Teachers' roles in second language learning: classroom applications of sociocultural theory.* Charlotte, NC: Information Age Publishing.

Towards the development of a comprehensive pedagogical framework for pronunciation training based on adapted automatic speech recognition systems

Saandia Ali[1]

Abstract. This paper reports on the early stages of a locally funded research and development project taking place at Rennes 2 university. It aims at developing a comprehensive pedagogical framework for pronunciation training for adult learners of English. This framework will combine a direct approach to pronunciation training (face-to-face teaching) with online instruction using and adapting existing Automatic Speech Recognition systems (ASR). The sample of learners chosen for the study are university students majoring in Arts, Literature or Communication at graduate and undergraduate level. These students might show an advanced mastery of grammar and syntax, but their spoken English remains heavily accented and may hinder effective communication. A considerable body of research has already investigated the efficacy of ASR systems for pronunciation training. This paper takes stock of how Computer Assisted Pronunciation Training (CAPT) software has been used and developed so far and looks at further potential improvements to address bad pronunciation habits among French learners of English.

Keywords: computer assisted pronunciation training, automatic speech recognition, CALL system design, ESL.

1.   Introduction

Pronunciation is an area of teaching which is often neglected, probably because teachers lack time and often resources to enable them to tackle phonetic and phonological competences. In most French universities, classes are overcrowded (up

1. Rennes 2 University, Rennes, France and Jean Jaures University, Toulouse, France; saandia.vanessa.ali@gmail.com

How to cite this article: Ali, S. (2016). Towards the development of a comprehensive pedagogical framework for pronunciation training based on adapted automatic speech recognition systems. In S. Papadima-Sophocleous, L. Bradley & S. Thouësny (Eds), *CALL communities and culture – short papers from EUROCALL 2016* (pp. 7-13). Research-publishing.net. https://doi.org/10.14705/rpnet.2016.eurocall2016.530

to 40 students per group) and the emphasis is placed on fluency and communication skills rather than phonetic accuracy. In addition to this observation, most teachers do not feel confident with teaching pronunciation as they often haven't received any training themselves.

Under these circumstances, students experience performance anxiety, and they only have a limited amount of time for teacher-student interaction and individualized feedback. As mentioned by Eskenazi (1999), "[l]anguage learning appears [to be] most efficient when the teacher constantly monitors progress to guide [...] remediation or advancement" (p. 450).

CAPT programs (Abuseileek, 2007) could help realise these goals by offering individual practice and feedback in a safe environment. Recent ASR based CAPT programs include Subarashii (Entropic HTK recognizer), VILTS (SRI recognizer), FLUENCY (Carnegie Mellon University SPHINX recognizer), Naturally Speaking (Dragon Systems), and FluSpeak (IBM ViaVoice recognizer).

We intend to build on these existing programs and on previous research to develop a set of tools to address bad pronunciation habits among French learners of English. In an attempt to do so, the rest of this paper will elaborate on the following questions:

- How have ASR systems been used to teach pronunciation?

- What improvements are still needed to develop an ideal pronunciation training framework for French learners of English?

2. Using ASR systems for pronunciation training: an overview of existing tools and previous research

2.1. Smartphone commercial apps

The simple act of googling 'pronunciation training apps' shows the considerable number of tools and software available to help people acquire good pronunciation. Two main types of pronunciation training apps can be found: those that target a wide variety of users ranging from students to other users, including tourists or occasional users, and those that were developed by teachers or researchers specialising in the domain of language learning and teaching. The first type of apps (see for example pronunciation checker[2], English pronunciation checker[3] or Vowel Viz[4] for iPhones) are used to check or verify the accuracy of one's pronunciation in a number of contexts. Pronunciation checker is a multilingual app based on databases of up to 1000 words for each targeted language and enables the user to listen to the production of a word, practise saying it via a recording device and then obtain an evaluation of the resulting production as a 'score'. There are two proficiency levels: easy and hard. This type of app usually lacks depth and doesn't include any linguistic or didactic information as an input or as a diagnosis, which is often limited to a numerical score.

The second kind of app is based on more in-depth linguistic and sometimes pedagogical content (see for example Sounds pronunciation apps[5] by Macmillan, English pronunciation[6] by Kepham or Speech Ace[7]). Most of these apps focus on pronunciation training at segment level and include pre-training tasks and content which revolve around interactive phonemic charts and illustrated descriptions of the articulatory features of the sounds of English. Recording facilities are also included along with diagnoses of learners' productions that can be compared with targeted productions in the chosen model (often US or UK English).

2.2. Experimental research aiming at CAPT software development

Numerous studies have tackled the question of ASR efficacy for CAPT (see e.g. Hinks, 2001). In this section, we present a brief overview of three representative studies (i.e. Elimat & Abuseileek, 2014; Escudero & Tejedor-Garc, 2015; Kim, 2006) that led to the development and testing of experimental ASR-based software for pronunciation training in English. They provide three different examples of how ASR systems and pronunciation teaching strategies can be tested and reveal the remaining challenges of current ASR technology.

Escudero and Tejedor-Garc (2015) introduce the architecture and interface of a serious game intended for pronunciation training and assessment of Spanish students of English as a second language. Android ASR and text to speech tools make it possible to discern three different pronunciation proficiency levels, ranging from basic to native. The authors use minimal pairs to promote learners' awareness

---

2. https://play.google.com/store/apps/details?id=com.app.pronunciation_checker
3. https://play.google.com/store/apps/details?id=com.eapp.pc
4. https://itunes.apple.com/us/app/vowelviz/id740035896?mt=8
5. https://play.google.com/store/apps/details?id=com.macmillan.app.soundsfree
6. https://play.google.com/store/apps/details?id=com.study.english.pronunciation
7. http://www.speechace.com/

of the potential misunderstandings and wrong meanings that can result from too approximate productions of phonemes.

Elimat and Abuseileek (2014) use the 'Tell me more performance' program to test the efficacy of ASR systems as well as various teaching techniques (i.e. individual work, pair work, group work) to train third grade learners of English. The best results were obtained with the group of students who worked individually with the ASR system.

The study of Kim (2006) resulted in the creation of Fluspeak, which is an ASR based pedagogical software used to teach US English pronunciation. It was tested with 36 university students through a hybrid teaching approach mixing Face to face teaching with individual work with the software. The study included a comparison between human scoring and automatic scoring with Fluspeak. Although Fluspeak gave good results with beginners focussing on phoneme production, it gave poor results overall for advanced learners trying to gain fluency.

On the whole and to our knowledge, most CAPT softwares show promising results and very positive impacts on the pronunciation of segmental sounds among various types of learners. Prosodic features and fluency generally speaking are areas of pronunciation training that still seem to require further research and development.

2.3. Towards enriching an ASR based pronunciation training system with linguistic and pedagogical content

Drawing conclusions from previous research and from an evaluation of commonly used CAPT software, this section provides an outline of the intended enrichment and development steps that need to be taken to develop a comprehensive pedagogical framework for pronunciation training. Three main steps were identified:

- selecting an open source ASR system to be adapted and further enriched to suit our purposes;

- enriching input data with prosodic information: selecting prosodically labelled corpora (L1 English, L1 French, L2 French);

- providing didactized content: targeted feedback, diagnosis, post-task courses and further practice.

Several open source speech recognition toolkits are available for research and development (see (Gaida et al., 2014; Povey et al., 2011). Gaida et al. (2014), for instance, compare the most commonly used open source softwares and show that the Kaldi toolkit is the most efficient and easier to adapt than the CMU sphinx toolkit for instance.

The common approach to recognize speech is to take a waveform, split it in utterances by silences and then try to recognize what is being said in each utterance. In order to do so, all possible combinations of words need to be tested and matched with the audio so as to select the best matching combination. Three models are used to complete the matching process: the acoustic model (acoustic properties for each phoneme of the target language), the phonetic model or phonetic dictionary (with the mapping from word to phone) and a language model (defining which word can follow another and restrict possible combinations).

Starting from the Kaldi toolkit, prosodic information can be added at the level of the acoustic model, which is usually based on large corpora annotated at segment level. We propose to use our own corpus developed in previous studies (see Ali, 2010; Ali & Hirst, 2009) to train Kaldi with prosodically annotated data in English. The chosen intonation model for this corpus is defined in Hirst and DiCristo (1998) and based on automatic modeling of rhythm and intonation via the Momel-Intsint algorithm (see Hirst & Espesser, 1993). Learner corpora (Diderot Longdale corpus and CIL corpus) will also be used to train the ASR system to recognize the productions of French learners of English at various proficiency levels (beginner, intermediate, advanced).

Once the recognition process has successfully taken place, pedagogical content will be added. Three kinds of tasks will be introduced:

- reading tasks based on isolated words (to assess phoneme production in monosyllabic words and word stress in polysyllabic words);

- reading tasks based on full utterances (to assess rhythm and intonation);

- conversation and guided interaction with virtual agents (to develop interaction skills, fluency and discourse level prosodic features).

Explicit feedback and diagnosis will be provided for each type of task using recording facilities along with Praat and Momel-Intsint representations to visualize productions and compare them to the target models.

3. Conclusion

Related studies such as Elimat and Abuseileek (2014) have shown that the ideal ASR software for CAPT should include at least five phases: ASR, automatic scoring on the basis of the comparison between a student's utterance and a native's utterance, error detection and error diagnosis. Starting from these essential characteristics and an evaluation of existing software, further improvements and preliminary steps were proposed in this paper in an attempt to develop a pronunciation training framework for French learners of English. The first steps mainly consist in enriching an existing open source ASR system with prosodic information to tackle the limitations of ASR tools when used to provide feedback at sentence and discourse level. This could be achieved by training ASR systems with both native and non-native speakers' prosodically labelled corpora. Further steps include the provision for enriched pedagogical content once the recognition process has successfully taken place.

References

Abuseileek, A. (2007). Computer-based pronunciation instruction as an effective means for teaching stress. *The jalt call Journal, 3*(1-2), 3-14.

Ali, S. (2010). Etude de la relation entre l'annotation des formes et des fonctions en anglais britannique contemporain. Linguistique. *Université de Provence-Aix-Marseille I. HAL Id: tel-00460431.* https://tel.archives-ouvertes.fr/tel-00460431

Ali S., & Hirst, D. (2009). Developing an automatic functional annotation system for British English Intonation. *Proceedings of Interspeech 2009, Brighton, 2207-2210.*

Elimat, A. K., & Abuseileek, A. F. (2014). Automatic speech recognition technology as an effective means for teaching pronunciation. *The JALT CALL Journal, 10*(1), 21-47.

Escudero, D., & Tejedor-Garc, C. (2015). Implementation and test of a serious game based on minimal pairs for pronunciation training pronunciation training. *Proceedings of SLaTE 2015* (pp.125-130).

Eskenazi, M. (1999). Using a computer in foreign language pronunciation training: what Advantages? *Calico Journal, 16*(3), 447-469.

Gaida, C., Lange, P. L., Petrick, R., Proba, P., Malatawy, A., & Suendermann-Oeft, D. (2014). Comparing open-source speech recognition toolkits. *Technical Report, 12.*

Hinks, R. (2001). Using speech recognition to evaluate skills in spoken English. *Working Papers, 49* (pp. 58-61). Lund University, Department of Linguistics.

Hirst, D. J., DiCristo, A. (1998). *Intonation systems: a survey of twenty languages.* Cambridge: Cambridge University Press.

Hirst, D. J., & Espesser, R. (1993). Automatic modelling of fundamental frequency using a quadratic spline function. *Travaux de l'Institut de Phonétique d'Aix 15* (pp. 75-85).

Kim, I. S. (2006). Automatic speech recognition: reliability and pedagogical implications for teaching pronunciation. *Educational Technology and Society, 9*(1), 322-334.

Povey, D., Ghoshal, A., Boulianne, G., Burget, L., Glembek, O., Goe,l N., Hannemann, M., Motlicek, P., Qian, Y., Schwarz, P., Silovsky, J., Stemmer, G., & Vesely, K. (2011). The Kaldi speech recognition toolkit. *Proceedings of the ASRU, 4.*

Digital literacy and sustainability – a field study in EFL teacher development

Christopher Allen[1] and Jan Berggren[2]

Abstract. This project introduces the concept of digital literacy at a practical level to a group of EFL teachers within the context of a single work place; a technologically well-resourced upper secondary school in Sweden. English teachers were provided with a theoretical and practical overview of the digital literacy concept as described by Dudeney, Hockly, and Pegrum (2013) before being given the task of each teaching a lesson. The teachers' reflective experiences of incorporating digital literacy into advanced level English teaching were then evaluated through a focus group interview. The results obtained show the efficacy of incorporating small scale exploratory practice research projects alongside busy teaching schedules and administrative demands as well as developing teachers' perspectives on Information and Communications Technology (ICT) in the English as a Foreign Language (EFL) classroom. In addition, the project has promoted synergies and collaboration among a school staff engaged in the long-term goal of continued professional development.

Keywords: digital literacy, exploratory practice, in-service training.

1. Introduction

1.1. In-service training and ICT

In the era of digitalization, modern language teacher training faces significant challenges in responding to the pace of technological and educational change and incorporating these developments into a coherent blueprint for classroom practice. Digital literacy, as described by Dudeney et al. (2013), offers one possible

1. Department of Languages, Linnaeus University, Växjö, Sweden; christopher.allen@lnu.se
2. Department of Pedagogy, Linnaeus University, Växjö, Sweden; jan.berggren@lnu.se

How to cite this article: Allen, C., & Berggren, J. (2016). Digital literacy and sustainability – a field study in EFL teacher development. In S. Papadima-Sophocleous, L. Bradley & S. Thouësny (Eds), *CALL communities and culture – short papers from EUROCALL 2016* (pp. 14-19). Research-publishing.net. https://doi.org/10.14705/rpnet.2016.eurocall2016.531

framework to facilitate the integration of ICT and a language subject such as English. This publication provided EFL teachers with a comprehensive framework for the incorporation of *Web 2.0* digital technology into their daily classroom routines.

This paper describes a small-scale project to introduce digital literacy to a group of EFL teachers. The teachers were first introduced to the digital literacy framework before being asked to select one or more digital learning activities which they should teach and then evaluate. The evaluation of their experiences was carried out in the form of a video recorded collegial focus group interview.

1.2. Perspectives on teaching training

Beginning in the 1980s, perspectives on professional teacher development have increasingly focused on teachers as reflective practitioners (Schön, 1983). Inspired by reflective practitioner perspectives, subsequent authors have suggested a formalization of the professional development process in the form of action research; small-scale research projects carried out by teachers in their classroom contexts in response to a perceived problem (Kemmis & McTaggart, 1982). The action research tradition has, however, tended to be individualistic, with a focus on individual teachers focusing on problems in isolation. The work of Burns (2001) puts the spotlight instead on collaborative action research initiatives with the potential for staff to learn from one another in exploiting the potential synergies of collegial efforts.

More recently within language education, Exploratory Practice (EP) was put forward as a possible method for teachers investigating solutions to educational problems (Allwright, 1993; Allwright & Bailey, 1991; Allwright & Lenzuen, 1997). This alternative approach is a recognition of the significant demands made by reflective and action research projects on the working lives of busy teachers. A central tenet of the EP framework is bringing teachers together and promoting collegiality as an activity "best served if all involved are manifestly working for each other's development as well as their own" (Allwright, 2003, p. 129 quoted in Hanks, 2015, p. 614).

1.3. Digital literacy

In a series of recent publications (Hockly, 2012; Dudeney et al., 2013), digital literacy has been put forward as a means of seamlessly integrating technology into the foreign language classroom.

Table 1. Digital literacy focus areas (adapted from Dudeney et al., 2013, p. 6)

Language focus	Information focus	Connections	(re-)design
print literacy			
texting literacy	search literacy		
hypertext literacy	tagging literacy	personal literacy	
multimedia literacy	information literacy	network literacy	
gaming literacy	filtering literacy	participatory literacy	
mobile literacy		intercultural literacy	
code literacy			remix literacy

The outline has been favourably received by the international EFL community. However, White (2015) has criticized the framework for a perceived imbalance in its focus on the receptive rather than productive skills.

2.   The study

Eight English teachers with between two and 21 years' teaching experience at a large upper secondary school in southern Sweden took part in the study. The design of the project encompassed three practical stages:

- two initial seminars/workshops offering teachers a theoretical and practical overview of the concept of digital literacy as well as outlining the teaching task;

- teaching of a digital literacy-based lesson using one of the 50 activities provided in the *Digital Literacies* resource book;

- a concluding focus group interview in which the teachers offered their experiences of integrating digital literacy into advanced level English teaching.

Each teacher taught at least one lesson based on lesson plans provided by Dudeney et al. (2013). After teaching their lessons the teachers were gathered in a focus group interview where the teachers provided their reflective experiences of (1) incorporating digital literacy into advanced level English teaching at the school, (2) the extent to which digital resources can replace or augment 'traditional' course books and finally (3) the efficacy of lesson evaluation as a form of exploratory practice. The focus interview was recorded and transcribed for further analysis.

Table 2.   Outline of teacher activities and digital literacy areas in the focus group

Teacher	Activity from resource book	Aim	Digital literacy
EL	No. 12: Sales Techniques	produce an advertisement in the form of a vodcast	multimedia
SJ	No. 27: Tree octopus	raise awareness of the importance of evaluating information on websites, by visiting a number of spoof websites	information
JK	No.3: Faking it	raise awareness of social networking profiles, online identity and identity management	personal, network
MO	No.17: Choose your own adventure	raise awareness of and implement basic game design	gaming
	No. 18: History hunt	create a local history quiz in the form of a multimedia mobile app	multimedia, gaming
DS	No. 4: Extreme Weather	raise awareness of how to convey a message via different genres of online text	print, information
	No. 6: Codeswitching	raise awareness of codeswitching	texting, print
AS	No. 12: Sales Techniques	produce an advertisement in the form of a vodcast	multimedia
	No. 44: Vox Pop	make a vodcast about culture	intercultural, multimedia
MSB	No. 6: Codeswitching	raise awareness of codeswitching	texting, print
	No. 12: Sales Techniques	produce an advertisement in the form of a vodcast	multimedia

3.   Results and discussion

The responses to the interview questions are presented below in accordance with the three focus areas outlined above.

3.1.   The teachers' reflective experiences of incorporating digital literacy into advanced level English teaching

The teachers all agreed that the integration of digital literacy into advanced level English teaching greatly stimulated interest in learning English, especially among pupils who had opted for more practical, vocationally-orientated subject combination profiles. Teachers responsible for more academically-orientated subjects in the *Technology Program* were also positive, claiming that the incorporation of digital literacy into their EFL classrooms had inspired their pupils. Staff also reported that the opportunity to work with intercultural literacy was most appreciated by the pupils involved. Pupils were offered the opportunity to explore communication in a cultural content involving people coming from other cultures, through Skype or recording a video presenting their hometown.

3.2. The extent to which digital resources can replace or augment 'traditional' coursebooks

Teachers highlighted the added multimedia dimension to their teaching which introduced a new level of creativity into their classroom practice, having previously worked with more traditional language teaching activities such as gap-filling, vocabulary lists and coursebook exercises. A number of teachers expressed that their pupils performed better when digital literacies integrated into their English teaching, since it was easier to adapt their teaching to the needs of individual pupils. It was also noted that the approach lent itself readily to the incorporation of authentic material in their classrooms, encouraging pupils to think critically about the reliability of digital information sources.

Another positive feature was the opportunity to analyse texts from different digital contexts or genres, as well as adapting texts from one digital context to another, such as converting a blog entry into a tweet, *Facebook* post, etc. These comparisons led to a heightened awareness among pupils of the differences between informal and Standard English varieties. Other pupil discussions revolved around open educational resources and *Creative Commons* digital copyright issues.

3.3. The efficacy of lesson evaluation as a form of exploratory practice (collegial learning)

Participating in the *Digital Literacy* project, teachers had an opportunity to learn and reflect upon concepts of professional relevance of digital literacies. Many teachers found that they had developed their repertoire of teaching activities in which digital literacies are integrated in advanced English language learning. Above all, this group of teachers now has access to concepts of professional relevance and an overview of digital literacies, which can be made of use in future in-service training, or collegial learning. Developing a professional language and an ability to teach digital literacies constitutes an updated professional identity for this group of teachers and is also a guarantee in itself of sustainable in-service training.

4. Conclusion

A major challenge for researchers is to bring positive change in the classroom without impinging too heavily on other professional priorities such as lesson planning, grading and assessment and pastoral considerations. The results suggest a way forward in promoting the sustainable incorporation of ICT into mainstream English language teaching and encouraging professional development on a collegial level. Future research will be directed towards building upon this collegial knowledge of digital literacy in developing greater consistency and objectivity in the assessment of digital projects.

5. Acknowledgements

The authors would like to thank the Department of Languages, Linnaeus University and *Kalmarsundsgymnasieförbund*, Kalmar Muncipality, Sweden for financial support in attending the EUROCALL 2016 conference.

References

Allwright, D. (1993). Integrating 'research' and 'pedagogy': appropriate criteria and practical possibilities. In J. Edge & K. Richards (Eds), *Teachers develop teachers research* (pp. 125-135). Oxford: Heinemann.

Allwright, D. (2003). Exploratory practice: rethinking practitioner research in language teaching *Language Teaching Research*, 7(2), 113-141.

Allwright, R., & Bailey, K. (1991). *Focus on the language classroom: an introduction to classroom research for language teachers*. Cambridge University Press.

Allwright, D., & Lenzuen, R. (1997). Exploratory practice: work at the Cultura Inglesa, Rio de Janeiro, Brazil. *Language Teaching Research*, 1, 73-79. https://doi.org/10.1177/136216889700100105

Burns, A. (2001). *Collaborative action research for English language teachers*. Cambridge University Press.

Dudeney, G., Hockly, N., & Pegrum, M. (2013). *Digital literacies*. Pearson Education

Hanks, J. (2015). Language teachers making sense of exploratory practice. *Language Teaching Research*, 19(5), 612-633.

Hockly, N. (2012). Digital literacies. *ELT J*, 66(1), 108-112. https://doi.org/10.1093/elt/ccr077

Kemmis, S., & McTaggart, R. (1982). *The action research planner* (rev. ed). Geelong: Deakin University Press.

Schön, D. (1983). *The reflective practitioner: how professionals think in action*. NY: Basic Books.

White, G. (2015). Digital literacies. *ELT J*, 69(3), 345-347.

Self-evaluation using iPads in EFL teaching practice

Christopher Allen[1], Stella K. Hadjistassou[2], and David Richardson[3]

Abstract. The relentlessly accelerating global educational demands for teaching English as a Second or Foreign Language (ESL/EFL) in multiple, diverse, and often remote geographic locations constitute new challenges for academic institutions, teacher training and preparation programs, and teachers themselves. This study describes a novel approach where five elementary school preservice teachers teaching ESL/EFL borrowed an iPad mini from their teacher training institution customized with specific apps to record a series of five teaching sequences during their teaching practice placement in elementary schools in Tanzania and Kenya. All recorded sessions were uploaded to a Moodle Virtual Learning Environment (VLE) site specially constructed for the purpose of the teaching practice course. Results indicate that, apart from their experienced instructors' feedback on their teaching practice, the recorded sessions formed constructive tools for self-reflection, self-evaluation and the pursuit of possible paths for improvement.

Keywords: iPads, ESL, EFL, pre-service teachers, teaching practice, self-evaluation.

1.   Introduction

Mobile devices, which fuse technology, culture, communication, learning and gaming, challenge some of the most salient social and cultural boundaries while at the same time inviting a discussion into their role in molding cultural expectations for teaching, learning, communication, and socialization. In ESL/EFL pedagogy and teacher preparation, scholarly research on mobile-based learning has delved into the pedagogical and learning implications of mobile devices (Goodwin-Jones, 2011; Hockly & Dudeney, 2014; Kinash, Brand, & Mathew, 2012; Kukulska-Hulme, 2009). Multiple studies have been undertaken and scholarly discussions have been built on the premise that, if mobile devices and software are exploited

1. Linnaeus University, Växjö, Sweden; christopher.allen@lnu.se
2. KIOS Research Center for Intelligent Systems and Networks, Nicosia, Cyprus; stella1@asu.edu
3. Linnaeus University, Växjö, Sweden; david.richardson@lnu.se

How to cite this article: Allen, C., Hadjistassou, S. K., & Richardson, R. (2016). Self-evaluation using iPads in EFL teaching practice. In S. Papadima-Sophocleous, L. Bradley, & S. Thouësny (Eds), *CALL communities and culture – short papers from EUROCALL 2016* (pp. 20-24). Research-publishing.net. https://doi.org/10.14705/rpnet.2016.eurocall2016.532

effectively in language learning contexts, they can expand the classroom ecology and galvanize students' learning (Vavoula, Pachler, & Kukulska-Hulme, 2010; Kinash et al., 2012). Beyond the multi-purpose nature, mobility, adaptability, and interactivity of mobile devices, scholars have also looked into the impact that mobile devices can have on language learning (Kukulska-Hulme, 2009). Kukulska-Hulme (2009) makes a call to educators constructing mobile learning activities "to enrich these types of learning and enrich them with new possibilities" (p. 160). It is not only learning but also teaching in the form of teachers' self-evaluation with recordings of their classroom performance that could be enhanced through the use of mobile devices. Previous studies, such as Bolona Lopez, Ortiz, and Allen (2015) have demonstrated that smartphones could form effective tools for assessing EFL student teachers' teaching practices in Ecuador. However, limited attention has been paid to the use of iPads as tools to record and facilitate self-evaluation among pre-service teachers on teaching practice in geographically remote locations.

2.   Method

This study aimed to investigate the role of iPads as tools to evaluate pre-service teachers' teaching practice and their perception on the integration of iPads in the self-confrontation of the teachers with video recordings of their performance. In adopting a qualitative approach, this study offered preservice teachers a level of autonomy in selecting specific parts from their practical teaching experience and the opportunity to record sessions in specific pupil age range and cultural/institutional settings. It also gave 'a voice' to preservice teachers to share their experiences throughout this process (Levy, 2015). The study was conducted during the fall of 2015. Five female primary preservice teachers enrolled in a teaching practice course at a Swedish academic institution were provided with an iPad mini for their five-week practicum. The preservice course aimed to offer preservice teachers practical teaching opportunities to teach English to primary school children in diverse locations, such as Kenya and Tanzania. All preservice teachers had previously completed their practical teaching placement in Swedish schools. Prior to their departure, they attended an orientation session with two experienced teacher trainers, the first and third authors of this paper. Both instructors specialize in computer-assisted language learning, information communication and technology, and teacher training. During the orientation session, preservice teachers were introduced to the pedagogical expectations for the practice and received tech training on relevant applications and resources to facilitate communication with the instructors and video uploading on their iPads, such as Skype and Adobe Connect and Moodle. Figure 1 below provides a screenshot of the iPad minis provided to preservice teachers.

Figure 1.   Screenshot of the iPad minis prior to departure

Students were invited to upload five shorter lesson sequence recordings on their academic institution's Moodle VLE site: (i) a brief video confirming their arrival in the host country and school site; (ii) the introduction of the subject of instruction and delivery of instructions to students; (iii) the delivery of a lesson on vocabulary, grammar, and/or pronunciation; (iv) the monitoring of group work and use of contingent feedback; and (v) the conclusion of the lesson and preparation for the next activities. These five recording sequences could be selected by the preservice teacher from any lesson during the practicum period; they did not have to be from the same lesson. The intention from the instructors' side was to provide feedback formatively following the upload of each lesson component throughout the practicum using the tools installed on the iPads. Following their return to Sweden, preservice teachers received summative feedback from their instructor and completed a written questionnaire which attempted to evaluate the learning experience through a mixture of open and fixed response questions.

3.   Results and discussion

Each preservice teacher uploaded her five recordings on the Moodle VLE site and four of them responded to the written questionnaire. Upon their return to Sweden, they met with their instructors and received constructive feedback on their teaching techniques, student group work, delivery of lesson plans, classroom management, and other classroom issues that emerged during the recordings. Unfortunately, technological contractions and challenges, such as limited or complete lack of

Wi-Fi access, inhibited the provision of feedback while students were teaching in the particular teaching context. All four preservice teachers addressed the lack of or limited Wi-Fi access in their questionnaires and considered it as a hindering mechanism in uploading their videos and receiving feedback. As Selma, a twenty-four year-old preservice teacher noted in her written response, "we couldn't upload our videos when we where [sic] away because of the internet connection".

Despite these technological challenges, all four preservice teachers perceived the use of iPads as effective tools for self-confrontation with recordings of their teaching performances. As they noted on their written questionnaires, viewing themselves in action while they were teaching and observing their teaching techniques, classroom dynamics, group work, and the delivery of their lesson plans played a central role in reflecting on their teaching practice and identifying possible ways to improve. In addition to their experienced instructors' feedback, preservice teachers critically reflected on their own teaching and pursued possible ways to improve. The use of these cultural artifacts or recordings enacted affordances for self-reflection and self-evaluation, while at the same time heightening awareness of the multiple classroom dynamics, management, and other pedagogical, instructional, and other learning constructs. For instance, as Felicia, another twenty-four year-old preservice teacher candidly admitted: "since you are able to see the recorded video after the lesson you see many things that you can improve, for example how you focus which pupils who gets your attention the most, or how you try to explain things". What they also particularly enjoyed was the flexibility and choice in selecting the recorded sessions that they felt more comfortable sharing with their instructors, which eliminated preservice teachers' level of anxiety. Selma summed it up best: "I think everybody should record themselves while teaching it feels wierd [sic] the first time you have to watch yourself but learned a lot from it! And now I am not nervous to have someone in the classroom when I teach and I am better at taking feedback".

4.   Conclusion

The findings of this study demonstrate some of the possible implications that recorded sessions on iPads could have on preservice school teachers' initial endeavors as they break into the complex arena of teaching. Teaching constitutes a complex, demanding, and at the same time rewarding profession. However, preservice teachers need not only to receive constructive feedback from experienced teacher trainers but also to be presented with their own teaching performance as a means to reflect and evaluate their own teaching practice and identify possible ways to improve. The use of iPads to record their initial teaching experiences can contribute to this process by enacting affordances for preservice students to observe their teaching in action and critically evaluate their own teaching practice.

5.   Acknowledgements

We would like to thank the Department of Language, Linnaeus University Sweden and the Kios Research Center for Intelligent Systems and Networks for financial support in attending the EUROCALL 2016 conference.

References

Bolona Lopez, M., Ortiz, M., & Allen, C. (2015). Using mobile devices and the AdobeConnect web conferencing tool in the assessment of EFL student teacher performance. In F. Helm, L. Bradley, M. Guarda, & S. Thouësny (Eds), *Critical CALL – Proceedings of the 2015 EUROCALL Conference, Padova, Italy* (pp. 77-83). Dublin Ireland: Research-publishing.net https://doi.org/10.14705/rpnet.2015.000313

Goodwin-Jones, R. (2011). Mobile apps for language learning. *Language Learning & Technology, 15*(2), 2-11.

Hockly, N., & Dudeney, G. (2014). Going mobile: teaching with hand-held devices. *Delta Teacher Development.*

Kinash, S., Brand, J., & Mathew, T. (2012). Challenging mobile learning discourse throughresearch: student perceptions of Blackboard Mobile Learn and iPads. *Australasian Journal of Educational Technology, 28*(4), 639-655. https://doi.org/10.14742/ajet.832

Kukulska-Hulme, A. (2009). Will mobile learning change language learning? *ReCALL, 21*(2), 157-165. https://doi.org/10.1017/S0958344009000202

Levy, M. (2015). The role of qualitative approaches to research in CALL contexts: closing in on the learner's experience. *CALICO Journal, 32*(3), 554-568. https://doi.org/10.1558/cj.v32i3.26620

Vavoula, G., Pachler, N., & Kukulska-Hulme, A. (Eds). (2010). Researching mobile learning: frameworks, tools and research design (2nd ed.). Bern, Switzerland: Peter Lang AG, International Academic Publishers.

Amateur online interculturalism in foreign language education

Antonie Alm[1]

Abstract. This paper discusses the animated web series *Lifeswap* as an example for 'amateur online interculturism' and investigates its potential for intercultural language education. Drawing on Dervin's (2015) discussion on the 'amateur interculturist', I suggest that online publications of personal encounters of intercultural interaction can be used to foster critical reflection in intercultural language education. To illustrate this idea, I first introduce the concept of 'amateur online interculturism' and the approach of the makers of the *Lifeswap* series. I then focus on one episode to provide an example of the series and to show how humour and cultural stereotypes can be used constructively to explore tensions in intercultural interactions. The online comments I present in the last section highlight the harmonising effect of humour but indicate that pedagogical intervention is needed to problematise intercultural issues.

Keywords: interculturalism, amateur interculturist, lifeswap, humour.

1. Introduction

Growing mobility and increased opportunities to publish and share personal impressions of encounters with people of other cultures have resulted in new resources for intercultural language education. The travel blog *matador*, for example, publishes regular posts of travellers, such as "Are Germans rude? Killing the stereotypes after living in Berlin". Shared on social networks, these personal accounts are exposed to a wide audience, natives and sojourners alike, often leading to animated discussions on incidents described by the authors.

I will refer to these accounts of personal intercultural experiences, which are shared with an online audience and discussed amongst this audience as 'amateur online interculturism'. I have borrowed the term from Dervin (2015), who associates

---

1. University of Otago, Dunedin, New Zealand; antonie.alm@otago.ac.nz

How to cite this article: Alm, A. (2016). Amateur online interculturalism in foreign language education. In S. Papadima-Sophocleous, L. Bradley, & S. Thouësny (Eds), *CALL communities and culture – short papers from EUROCALL 2016* (pp. 25-31). Research-publishing.net. https://doi.org/10.14705/rpnet.2016.eurocall2016.533

positive qualities with 'amateur', as it derives from old French, the 'lover of'. The authors and participants of 'amateur' online publications are guided by their personal and often uncritical views, yet they manifest a passion for the encountered cultures and a fascination for observed personal transformations. At the same time, these views are presented as perspectives rather than truths and invite comments for discussion. These testimonies (online publications and the ensuing conversations) lend themselves to analysis in intercultural education as they provide students with a personal point of reference (descriptions reflecting their own experiences), which can then be taken to a more critical and reflective level.

This paper discusses the animated web series *Lifeswap* as an example of 'amateur online interculturism' and investigates its potential for intercultural language education. The term 'amateur interculturalist' has been coined by Dervin (2015) in reference to Said's (1996) concept of the 'intellectual amateur'. It describes the intercultural practitioner or researcher who is not conditioned by essentialist intercultural theories and instead questions container models of culture. The 'amateur interculturist' (unlike the 'professional interculturist') is aware that people are not defined by their culture and recognises that each individual has multiple identities, which are not only context-dependent but also change over time. The object of intercultural study is therefore never only the 'other' but also the 'self' and the dialogue between the two in a specific context.

Increasing global mobility and the ability to communicate and publish online has produced another type of amateur interculturist. Equally guided by their love and passion for intercultural encounters, amateur *online* interculturists share personal experiences and observations with an online audience. It has been noted that the contact with people of different cultural backgrounds, especially in computer-mediated communication, does not necessarily lead to increased intercultural awareness and that on the contrary "can contribute to creating more stereotypes, negative and positive representations about the self and the other" (Dervin, 2014, p. 192). Yet it could also be argued that the open forum in which these reports are published can potentially create a space for critical reflection. Furthermore, the interactions on intercultural issues can be valuable material for intercultural language education.

2.   Method

With the aim of establishing an example of 'amateur online interculturalism' and of exploring its suitability for intercultural language education, the following materials have been analysed: (1) documents produced by the authors of *Lifeswap* about their web series (interviews, funding application, *Lifeswap* blog http://www. lifeswap.net/), (2) the second episode, *The Tea Towel Stinks*, and (3) comments from viewers on episode two from the *Lifeswap* blog, a Vimeo site as well as from university language students on their learner blogs.

3. Discussion

3.1. The *Lifeswap* interculturists

The producers of the series are not trained interculturists, rather they are participants and observers of intercultural encounters. The fictional characters of *Lifeswap*, Jörg from Germany and Duncan from New Zealand, represent, according to the scriptwriter William Connor, an "alter-ego duo through which we could 'earth' the various frustrations, hilarities and intriguing cultural differences we had discovered repeating themselves whenever Steffen [Kreft] and I visited each other's countries" (Ritchie, 2014, p. 19). Both Connor and Kreft had compiled 'secret mental lists' of intercultural incidents over the years. The use of humour can provide a safe place for the examination of potentially uncomfortable issues (MacIntyre, 2014) and the creation of a humorous context for their experiences allowed them to deal with these incidents in a playful manner. Each episode captures a particular 'rich point' (Agar, 1994), to which, as Kreft put it "as many specific situations, archetypes and phrases" were added to achieve "maximum funniness and recognisable idiosyncratic scenarios within a tight and manageable animation" (Ritchie, 2014, p. 19).

Humorous and exaggerated cultural stereotypes can be used constructively to identify and overcome tensions in intercultural interactions (MacIntyre, 2014). It is particularly powerful if the participants are able to laugh about themselves, and as it is the case in *Lifeswap*, if both cultures are targeted.

The episodes of the on-going series are framed by a *Skype* conversation between Duncan, who is described by the authors as "a familiar Kiwi OE candidate in his mid twenties", and Jörg, "a typically polite, well-equipped German traveller, who is passionate about 'za nature'" (Funding application, n.p.). Conner gives the characters their stereotypical language, and Kreft's illustrations support the humorous intent of the dialogues. Jörg and Duncan have *swapped lives*, or at least their flats, for a year and in their stereotyped appearance (clothing, accents) they seem oddly out of place in their equally stylised new environment: Jörg skypes from his bedroom, a room of a typical New Zealand 1920s bungalow with wooden doors and window frames, whereas Duncan sits in a very plain and tidy German living room.

3.2.   The genesis of episode two

The idea for the episode is born out of an anecdote, a personal encounter with 'German directness' (see Figure 1). The request for a new tea towel, because the old one stinks, has an unexpected effect on the Kiwi. "I was taken aback… but I was also taken aback by how taken aback I was". His emotional reaction made him reflect on his cultural conditioning, and how indirectness might appear to somebody from a different cultural background.

Figure 1.   Blog post on second episode[2]

How a smelly tea-towel inspired episode two…

Well, it all started when Steffen's mother, Margot, came to visit us in New Zealand. One afternoon we were enjoying a cross cultural dish-washing session, when all of a sudden, Margot turned to me and said:

"William, the tea towel stinks. You need a new one."

I was taken aback, not only by this wonderful example of German directness - the streamlined, teutonic "subject, verb, object" model of sentence construction - but I was also taken aback by how taken aback I was.

The fact is, life in New Zealand is generally pretty simple and easy; that is, until a problem needs confronting. At which point we Kiwis engage in a weirdly elaborate series of rituals including red-faced silences, eye-averting and all manner of verbal apologies, softeners and excuses. One feels compelled to perform a kind of musical act to avoid explaining what the problem is; it commonly involves a small jerky dance of shrugs, hand-wringing and facial contortions and a sing song of polite words.

So, in episode two of *Lifeswap*, Duncan teaches Joerg a five step method he has devised of confronting a New Zealander about a problem so as to cause only minimal offense. Watch this space!

---

2. http://www.lifeswap.net/2013/10/how-smelly-tea-towel-inspired-episode.html

3.3.   Episode 2

In the episode, Jörg commits the same faux pas as the real life Margot, telling his Kiwi flatmate Ange that he needs a fresh tea towel. He quickly realises his mistake and brings it up at their next Skype conversation. Duncan gives Jörg five unwritten rules, models the interaction (we see him instead of Jörg with Ange in the kitchen) and also makes him apply the rules in a new situation. The last scene shows Jörg mastering rule no. 2 (see Figure 2) in a different interaction with Ange.

Jörg manages to apply the five rules but neither his nor Duncan's behaviour is assimilistic. Throughout the dialogue he interjects in German (highlighting his objection). He defends his own cultural needs and after rule number four he seems to give up. He breaks out in a sweat and declares: "I think from now on I will just stay in my room". The ending indicates that he is keeping his sense of humour when applying rule number two. Duncan for his part acknowledges that he finds the directness he experiences in Germany "quite refreshing".

Figure 2.   The Tea Towel Stinks on Vimeo[3]

3.4.   Reactions

3.4.1.   Reactions from blog and Vimeo

Lifeswap is published on the producers' blog, their Facebook page and on Vimeo, providing viewers with the option of commenting and sharing the stories. Kiwis,

---

3. https://vimeo.com/81393966

Germans, bi-cultural couples and families, and German teachers in New Zealand sympathise and identify with the characters and laugh about themselves. The 'amateur online interculturist' responds to the feedback and encourages viewers to send him their own stories:

- Love this series! Episode 2 reminds me of an incident in my own house recently!

- This episode is awesome - I can def relate :) I can give you heaps of inspiration if needed - being a German married to a Kiwi, communication can get fuzzy at times :P

- Thanks. Would love to hear your experience! Fuzzy is a great word for it.

3.4.2.   Reactions from students

Used as a warm-up in a language class on intercultural mis/communication, some students of my intermediate German class wrote about the episode in their blog (weekly blogging was an integral part of this class). They related the five rules of the episode to their own observations of indirectness in their flats, one involving a dirty tea towel and the other an empty water tank (Figure 3 and Figure 4). Student A from New Zealand is now noticing a behaviour that she had not noticed before. The comment is written by an exchange student from the Czech Republic who found the indirectness irritating. The *Lifeswap* episode put these behaviours in perspective and made "the strange familiar [student B] and the familiar strange [student A]" (Byram, Gribkova, & Starkey, 2002, p. 19).

Figure 3.   Blog post from student A

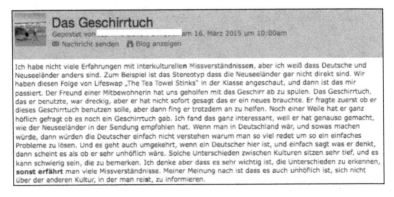

Figure 4.   Comment from student B

Kommentar von   8. März 2015 um 5:23pm

Haha, es ist so lustig, wie höflich und vorsichtig die Neuseeländer sind. Mir ist auch etwas
änliches gästern passiert. Mein Mitbewohner hat mit mir 5 Minuten gesprochen und hat mir ein
Paar komische Frage über mein Studium gestellt nur am Ende mir zu sagen, dass er kein heißes
Wasser am Abend hatte, weil ich (vielleicht) alle verbraucht habe :D ("Aber vielleich ist es mein
Schuld...") Er hat wirklich traurig ausgesehen, dass er mir fragen muss, ob ich das nächste Mal
kuerzer duschen koennte :)

4.   Conclusion

I have described the makers of the animated web series *Lifeswap* as amateur online interculturists. The intercultural interactions they portray in their episodes are based on personal anecdotes. They use humour to address intercultural differences, which has a harmonising effect. Comments indicate that viewers sympathise with the characters. For intercultural language education, however, it is crucial that these issues are problematised. The two-sided approach of *Lifeswap* (both cultures are explored) in particular invites investigations of both the 'self' and the 'other'.

References

Agar, M. (1994). *Language shock. Understanding the culture of conversation.* New York: HarperCollins.

Byram, M., Gribkova, B., & Starkey, H. (2002). *Developing the intercultural dimension in language teaching: a practical introduction for teachers.* The Council of Europe.

Dervin, F. (2014). Exploring 'new' interculturality online. *Language and Intercultural Communication, 14*(2), 191-206. http://dx.doi.org/10.1080/14708477.2014.896923

Dervin, F. (2015). *Reframing discussions a round interculturality in education.* Presentation given at University of Durham on 27 February 2015.

MacIntyre, J. (2014). *Figures of fun: humor and stereotype in Monty Python's depictions of intercultural communication* [Blog post]. https://culturematters.wordpress.com/2014/08/22/figures-of-fun-humor-and-stereotype-in-monty-pythons-depictions-of-intercultural-communication/

Ritchie, T. (2014). Germans and kiwis animated. Lifeswap series by Steffen Kreft and William Connor [Blog post]. https://thestoopthestoop.wordpress.com/2014/04/29/kiwis-and-germans-animated-lifeswap-series-by-steffen-krent-and-william-connor/

Said, E. (1996). Representations of the intellectual: the 1993 Reith lectures. Vintage.

Teaching Turkish in low tech contexts: opportunities and challenges

Katerina Antoniou[1], Evelyn Mbah[2], and Antigoni Parmaxi[3]

Abstract. Language learning has witnessed a series of changes with regards to the use of Information and Communication Technology (ICT). Recently, the digital divide has been a topic of discussion in language learning studies. Digital divide is the inequality that exists between information-poor and information-rich communities. Within the field of Computer-Assisted Language Learning (CALL), scant literature exists regarding the use of technology in poor ICT contexts. Yet, many people learn and teach language in such contexts. Egbert and Yang (2004) define low-tech context as possessing limited general access to technology, limited or no Internet access, no software, old and mandated software, and few computers and other technologies. Following action research design, we implemented a small-scale intervention using game-based quizzes in order to address the challenges encountered in teaching Turkish in a limited-tech context. Data collected included questionnaires, focus groups and participant observation in the classroom. The findings of the study informed the opportunities and challenges of teaching and learning Turkish in a technology-limited classroom.

Keywords: student response system, low-tech context, game-based quiz, Turkish language.

1.   Introduction

Language learning has witnessed a series of changes with regards to the use of ICT. At the end of the twentieth century, CALL is characterised by high speed internet connections, advances in digital technology and smaller sizes of computer hardware, laptops, multimedia mobile phones, tablets and improved learning environments such as web 2.0, etc. (Borau, Ullrich, Feng, & Shen, 2009; Parmaxi,

1. Cyprus University of Technology, Limassol, Cyprus; katiantwniou@gmail.com
2. Cyprus University of Technology, Limassol, Cyprus; evelynmbah@gmail.com
3. Cyprus University of Technology, Limassol, Cyprus; antigoni.parmaxi@cut.ac.cy

How to cite this article: Antoniou, K., Mbah, E., & Parmaxi, A. (2016). Teaching Turkish in low tech contexts: opportunities and challenges. In S. Papadima-Sophocleous, L. Bradley & S. Thouësny (Eds), *CALL communities and culture – short papers from EUROCALL 2016* (pp. 32-36). Research-publishing.net. https://doi.org/10.14705/rpnet.2016.eurocall2016.534

Zaphiris, Papadima-Sophocleous, & Ioannou, 2013). While some people have the opportunity of using the above wide range of technology in language learning, others find it difficult to access and use them. Hence, there is a demarcation between those that have access to technology and those that do not. This demarcation is referred to as a digital divide. Recently, the digital divide has been a topic of discussion in language learning studies and is defined as the divide between those who can effectively use new information and communication tools, such as the Internet, and those who cannot (Knobel, Stone, & Warschauer, 2002). Following Egbert and Yang's (2004) characteristics of low tech context as possessing limited general access to technology, limited or no Internet access, no software, old and mandated software, and few computers and other technologies, we classified the Turkish class in a public school in the Republic of Cyprus as a low tech context. It is against this background that this research sets out to investigate whether there are benefits and setbacks associated with learning Turkish in such a context. In an attempt to infuse technology in a low-tech context, we employed 'Kahoot!', a free game-based learning platform that makes it fun to learn using a collection of questions on specific topics, as an appropriate option. In the following sections, we describe the methodology employed, followed by major results and major conclusions drawn from this research.

2.   Methodology

2.1.   The setting

The study took place in a public school in the district of Larnaca, in the Republic of Cyprus. The group consisted of nine students from eight to 54 years old aiming to learn Turkish at A1 level. A questionnaire for measuring students' digital literacy and attitude towards educational technology lead to the conclusions that none of the students had used technology for educational purposes before, although they recognised its benefits. The classroom was equipped with old and new computers, slow wired Ethernet internet connection and a projector. The classroom had no Wi-Fi connection.

2.2.   Research design and data collection

The study was based on action research and data was gathered with the mixed method of participatory observation, semi-structured focus group, and discussion, in the frequency of two weekly 90 minute lessons, for a total of 13 weeks.

The instructor employed Kahoot! as a means to foster students' engagement and motivation in the language classroom. Kahoot! was selected as it was an easy solution for creating fun and interactive activities for students, with a website that was easy to use and navigate. Moreover, Kahoot! allowed for the existing technologies available in the class to be used - projector and desktop computers with slow internet connection. In this study, the instructor created quizzes in Kahoot! related to the topics of each lesson. The aim was for Kahoot! to facilitate learning, and assess students' grammar and reading skills within a friendly and comfortable environment. As there was no Wi-Fi access, students were participating in the quiz via the desktop computers. The quiz was played during the last twenty minutes of each lesson. The questions were based on the material taught during the lesson, allowing for students to playfully assess their reading and grammar skills in Turkish. A question had four possible answers, and after every question students and instructor discussed the responses since they were able to see their mistakes and correct answers. Due to low internet connectivity and insufficiency of computers, students would work in groups for replying to a Kahoot! quiz.

3.   Results and discussion

The analysis of the focus group and participant observation revealed several challenges addressed in the low-tech environment. Students' diverse personal motivations and abilities due to the age difference was an initial challenge in this study. Younger students would learn Turkish upon their parents' choice. On the other hand, students around the age of 20, chose the Turkish language as they thought it would enhance their professional development and the age bracket of 40+ would learn Turkish as a hobby. Moreover, it was observed that younger students needed more time to understand grammatical rules, compared to adult learners. Building on this challenge, and especially on students' diverse skills, interests, motivations, goals, and abilities, the instructor of this course employed a game-based quiz for providing an interactive and playful means for encouraging students to work together using the available technology in the classroom. Technology appeared to bring younger and older learners together towards a common venture; to correctly answer a Kahoot! quiz. Younger students would contribute to the use of technology and adult learners would contribute to questions related to grammatical rules. Adults who stated at first that the use of educational technology was new for them and could not realise if there would be any improvement in their language skills, were finally convinced and inspired by the younger ones who were excited and not afraid of the unknown. As stated in the focus group, the colourful environment of Kahoot! helped the visual learners remember important features of the Turkish grammar.

During the game, and after every round of questions, students were discussing their answers and gave feedback. Students noted that the feedback given after every question would help them understand and have a clear view of the new features taught during the lesson. All students agreed on the added value of technology in making their learning more interesting. They also enjoyed the fact that Kahoot! was played at the end of the lesson and it was a clever way of both assessment and learning. Simultaneously, the metacognitive ability was increased while students were trying to explore the use of technology and also find the correct answer using their language skills. Overall, students expressed enthusiasm and excitement while interacting with the game, and despite the difficulties encountered (e.g. low-internet connectivity) they successfully managed to engage with the activity.

The lack of specialised manpower was counted as an additional challenging factor, since a non-specialized on educational technology teacher integrated technology in a low-tech context. From the instructor's side, the use of technology entailed a series of concerns connected to its practical application and pedagogical grounding, regardless of audience's age and motivation. The role of the teacher was crucial in forming the activity in such a way that would convince students that technology could be an effective means of language learning. In order to do so, the instructor of this course dedicated time for managing the technology and linking it with students' interests. Kahoot! also allowed the teacher to informally assess students' performance and intervene for providing additional explanation were needed.

4.   Conclusions

The aim of this study was to evaluate challenges and opportunities in teaching Turkish in a low-context environment. This study concluded that, despite the challenges, low-techs contexts can give more opportunities than a no technology context. Evaluating the challenges and taking advantage of the opportunities by using any available technological tools, can still transform a traditional language classroom to a modern one. Challenges addressed include lack of specialised manpower, insufficient time for practice, mixed age group and diverse personal reasons for attending the course. In addressing the aforementioned challenges, the use of game-based quizzes was conceived as a playful way for bringing students closer and creating a group environment. Upon its use, several opportunities arose for enhancing students' concentration, allowing for mastery of the limited technology, an increased metacognitive ability, and adequate interaction in the classroom. This study demonstrates that despite the challenges, teachers in low-tech are encouraged to be more resourceful and be involved in in-service training in order to inform their practice with research findings.

References

Borau, K., Ullrich, C., Feng, J., & Shen, R. (2009). Microblogging for language learning: Using twitter to train communicative and cultural competence. In *International Conference on Web-based Learning* (pp. 78-87). Springer Berlin Heidelberg. https://doi.org/10.1007/978-3-642-03426-8_10

Egbert, J., & Yang, Y. F. D. (2004). Mediating the digital divide in CALL classrooms: promoting effective language tasks in limited technology contexts. *ReCALL, 16*(2), 280-291. https://doi.org/10.1017/S0958344004000321

Knobel, M., Stone, L., & Warschauer, M. (2002). *Technology and academic preparation: a comparative study.* A Report to the University of California Office of the President, Sept 15 2002. http://education.uci.edu/person/warschauer_m/docs/TAP.pdf

Parmaxi, A., Zaphiris, P., Papadima-Sophocleous, S., & Ioannou, A. (2013). Mapping the landscape of computer-assisted language learning: an inventory of research. *Interactive Technology and Smart Education, 10*(4), 252-269. https://doi.org/10.1108/ITSE-02-2013-0004

Learning Icelandic language and culture in Virtual Reykjavik: starting to talk

Branislav Bédi[1], Birna Arnbjörnsdóttir[2],
Hannes Högni Vilhjálmsson[3], Hafdís Erla Helgadóttir[4],
Stefán Ólafsson[5], and Elías Björgvinsson[6]

Abstract. This paper describes how beginners of Icelandic as a foreign and second language responded to playing the first scene in Virtual Reykjavik, a video game-like environment where learners interact with virtual characters – Embodied Conversational Agents (ECAs). This game enables learners to practice speaking and listening skills, to learn about the language and culture by solving various tasks. A mixed-method pilot study examined how six learners responded. The results were divided into how learners perceived (1) playing the game in general; (2) interaction with virtual characters; (3) multimodal behaviour of the virtual characters, in particular the speech, facial expressions, hand gestures and body movements; and (4) what the game helped them learn. In conclusion, some learners reported they learned to start speaking in Icelandic and that the spoken behaviour of virtual characters resembled real Icelanders.

Keywords: computer games, embodied conversational agents, multimodal behaviour, natural language, virtual learning experience.

1. Introduction

Virtual Reykjavik is an online language and culture training application (Vilhjálmsson, 2011) designed for beginning adult learners of Icelandic as a foreign

1. University of Iceland, Reykjavík, Iceland; brb19@hi.is
2. University of Iceland, Reykjavík, Iceland; birnaarn@hi.is
3. Reykjavik University, Reykjavík, Iceland; hannes@ru.is
4. Reykjavik University, Reykjavík, Iceland; hafdis13@ru.is
5. Reykjavik University, Reykjavík, Iceland; stefanola13@ru.is – Northeastern University, Boston, MA, United States; stefanolafs@ccs.neu.edu
6. Reykjavik University, Reykjavík, Iceland; eliasb13@ru.is

How to cite this article: Bédi, B., Arnbjörnsdóttir, B., Vilhjálmsson, H. H., Helgadóttir, H. E., Ólafsson, S., & Björgvinsson, E. (2016). Learning Icelandic language and culture in Virtual Reykjavik: starting to talk. In S. Papadima-Sophocleous, L. Bradley & S. Thouësny (Eds), *CALL communities and culture – short papers from EUROCALL 2016* (pp. 37-43). Research-publishing.net. https://doi.org/10.14705/rpnet.2016.eurocall2016.535

or second language. This video game-like environment enables learners to practice spoken language by talking to virtual characters and listening skills by listening to the virtual characters' answers. Conversational interactions are a good source for authentic language input (Krashen, 1982) and output (Swain, 2007) with potentials of developing learner's language skills (Ellis, 1991). Speaking is realised by means of Google speech recognition service for Icelandic; the speech is automatically transcribed for learners to read what has been said in a lower text window. Character responses are synthesised using the Ivona Text To Speech (TTS) system for Icelandic.

The current version uses game-based learning (Meyer, 2009), task-based learning (Ellis, 2003), and a communicative approach (Richards, 2006), supporting learning of new vocabulary through text windows of cultural information and transcribed dialogues. The main menu is in Icelandic, where learners can hover over words with a mouse cursor and see their English translation. Learners can find cultural information about selected buildings and monuments in a pop-up window when in pause or 'freeze' mode.

Figure 1.   Approaching strangers in Virtual Reykjavik

The virtual characters are designed to look and act lifelike (Prendinger & Ishuzuka, 2004). In this context, they are also called ECAs because of their embodiment within a virtual environment, taking human form, and knowing how to use their body in conversations (Cassell, 2000). They are able to "grasp situations, react to contingencies and look aware of their surroundings" (Pedica & Vilhjálmsson, 2012, p. 1). Their social and conversational behaviour is multimodal and includes speech, facial expressions, hand gestures, head, and body movement. They are designed to look natural based on research into real-life behaviour. In this way, learners can get familiar with the social behaviour and learn about culture and language remotely.

In that respect, Prada and Paiva (2014) suggest that it is important to study human social interaction in order to help create a highly interactive exchange between human users and virtual agents; the effects are stronger if the artefacts, i.e. agents, present autonomous and proactive behaviour. About 144 video recordings capturing first encounters between native and non-native speakers in the same conversational situation as in this game were collected in downtown Reykjavik and analysed. This multimodal corpus provided authentic data for a discourse modelling. Specific communicative functions and behaviours associated with those functions were implemented into the architecture of the system that the virtual characters use to generate behaviour, allowing for a more realistic human-to-agent interaction.

In the first scenario, currently including only one scene, *Týnda hljómsveitin* [The Lost Band], and one chapter, *Hvar er Hitt Húsið?* [Where is Hitt Húsið?], learners have three tasks to solve: (1) approach a virtual character, who is a native speaker of Icelandic and get his/her attention by greeting appropriately (Figure 1); (2) ask for directions to a particular place; and (3) say goodbye.

2.   Method

A mixed-method approach consisting of a questionnaire, an interview and a video recording of each participant while playing was used. The pilot study took place in a laboratory setting. Participation was anonymous and informed consent was obtained. Six learners of six different nationalities participated; four female and two male, aged 22-31; three were temporary and three permanent residents. Five were beginners and one a false beginner (intermediate); their level of Icelandic was A1 on the Common European Framework of Reference for languages.

The objectives focused on examining how learners perceived: (1) playing the game in general; (2) the interaction with virtual characters that possess communicative skills based on conversations between people in the real-life situations, because interacting with such agents may promote communication skills (Johnson et al., 2004) and facilitate learning (Shaw, Johnson, & Rajaram, 1999); (3) the multimodal behaviour of the virtual characters; and (4) what the game helped them learn.

3.   Learner's perception and learning effect

The results indicated that half of the learners found playing the game enjoyable and exciting, while two of six described it as frustrating and boring, and one as neither.

The enjoyment and excitement referred to the learners being able to talk to virtual characters and see what they were going to say. Frustration was mostly caused by the speech recognition not handling improper pronunciation of certain consonants, e.g. <ʁ> instead of <R>, and due to speaking too softly or fast into the microphone, but also by its lagging; moreover also by the lack of information about the goals of the game and not being able to ask questions other than those given in the tasks. Learners perceived boredom mostly due to the slow movement of the avatar. Two of six learners found the game easy and four as neither easy nor difficult. None of them found the game difficult.

Regarding the specific multimodal behaviour (Figure 2), spoken language was perceived as the most natural and variation was important: "[I]t wasn't just one *góðan daginn* [good day, with definite article], but also *góðan dag* [good day, without definite article] as well, so it seemed like you were actually speaking to someone". However, it was pointed out that in some cases the virtual characters did not respond adequately to all forms of greetings, such as *blessuð* [greeting a female], *blessaður* [greeting a male], etc. The reason is due to lack of informal greetings. Two learners described the facial expressions as robotic. Some learners also described the body movement as spontaneous. Hand gestures were registered only during pointing when virtual characters were giving directions or crossing their arms.

Figure 2. Perception of specific multimodal behaviour

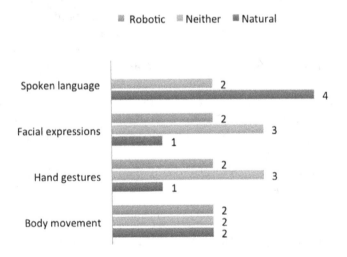

Regarding the overall multimodal behaviour (Figure 3), some learners commented that when speaking to virtual characters they had difficulties being understood;

also some virtual characters when standing on their own looked like "I-don't-wanna-talk-to-you kind of". In addition, there was a slow pace of moving around; the interaction was sometimes distracted by focusing on the red speaking button, which signalised when the learner could speak; the interaction felt natural by half, but on the other hand cold by more than a half of learners mainly due to the lack of emotion expressed by the characters.

Figure 3. Perception of the overall behaviour

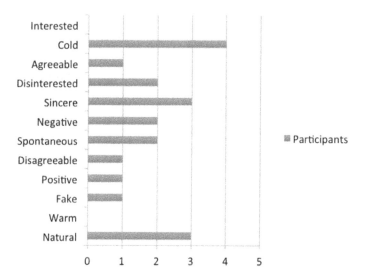

The game had a reported educational effect on five out of six learners; learning about famous places in downtown Reykjavik and to start talking in Icelandic. One learner found it pointless because of pronunciation issues and experiencing difficulty being 'not understood'. Overall, four learners stated that once the game is ready, it would help others learn about buildings and monuments and make it easier to start speaking and communicating in Icelandic. They felt that a virtual environment would be easier than learning in reality with real people face-to-face.

4. Conclusion

Five out of six learners found the game educational, of which three learners reported they learned (1) spoken language skills when initiating a conversation, and (2) about cultural sights and buildings in downtown Reykjavik. A gap between a passive and an active use of language can be bridged when learners get to practice the language in a conversation with virtual agents. Quoting from one learner: "I think it's very helpful, like when [the game] would be done, [...] especially in practicing conversations, because when you learn a language the hardest part is to start speaking". In this way, the game may help facilitate face-to-face communication in reality. The game's ultimate goal is to promote learning of language and culture based on real language use with virtual characters acting like native speakers. However, the multimodal behaviour needs to be fine-tuned yet. Adding a smile at the end of a conversation, which can also be observed in recordings from real life, can make the virtual characters friendlier. It is, nonetheless, difficult to draw a general conclusion on whether or not the design of virtual characters can have a similar effect on learners in another computer game. Since the aim of the Virtual Reykjavik project is to create lifelike virtual characters with natural multimodal behaviours, more focus must be placed on incorporating those into the system, and more research needs to be done in real-language data to reach perfection in modelling believable embodied conversational agents for language learning games.

References

Cassell, J. (2000). Nudge, nudge, wink, wink: elements of face-to-face conversation for embodied conversational agents. In J. Cassell, J. Sullivan, S. Prevost, & E. Churchill (Eds), *Embodied conversational agents* (pp. 1-27). Cambridge, MA: MIT Press.

Ellis, R. (1991). The interaction hypothesis: critical evaluation. *Paper presented at the Regional Language Seminar, Singapore, March 1991*. Eric – US Department of Education. http://files.eric.ed.gov/fulltext/ED338037.pdf

Ellis, R. (2003). *Task-based language learning and teaching*. Oxford University Press.

Johnson, W. L., Choi, S., Marsella, S., Mote, N., Narayanan, S., & Vilhjálmsson, H. (2004). Tactical language training system: supporting the rapid acquisition of foreign language and cultural skills. In *Proceedings of InSTIL/ICALL - NLP and Speech Technologies in Advanced Language Learning Systems, June 17-19, Venice*.

Krashen, S. D. (1982). *Principles and practice in second language acquisition*. Pergamon Press.

Meyer, B. (2009). Designing serious games for foreign language education in a global perspective. In A. Méndez-Vilas, J. Mesa González, J. A. Mesa González & A. Solano Martín (Eds), *Research, reflections and innovations in integrating ICT in education* (Vol. 2, pp. 715-719).

Pedica, C., & Vilhjálmsson, H. H. (2012). Lifelike virtual characters using behavior trees for social territorial intelligence (Demo/Poster). In *Proceedings of ACM SIGGRAPH'12, Los Angeles, August 5-9*. http://www.ru.is/kennarar/hannes/publications/SIGGRAPH2012_poster.pdf

Prada, R., & Paiva, A. (2014). Human-agent interaction: challenges for bringing humans and agents together. In *HAIDM – 3*rd *International Workshop on Human-Agent Interaction Design and Models held at AAMAS'2014 - 13*th *International Conference on Autonomous Agents and Multi-Agent Systems*. Paris, France.

Prendinger, H., & Ishuzuka, M. (Eds). (2004). Introducing the cast for social computing: life-like Characters. In). H. Prendinger & M. Ishuzuka (Eds), *Life-like characters: tools, affective functions, and applications* (pp. 3-16). New York, NY: Springer..

Richards, J. C. (2006). *Communicative language teaching today.* Cambridge University Press.

Shaw, E., Johnson, L., & Rajaram, G. (1999). Pedagogical agents on the Web. In *Proceedings of the third annual conference on Autonomous Agents, AGENTS'99* (pp. 283-290). New York, NY: ACM.

Swain, M. (2007). Fálagstilgátan: Kenningar og Rannsóknir. In A. Hauksdóttir & B. Arnbjörnsdóttir (Eds), *Mál málanna* (pp. 117-136). Reykjavik: Stofnun Vigdísar Finnbogadóttur í erlendum tungumálum.

Vilhjálmsson, H. H. (2011). Icelandic language and culture training in Virtual Reykjavik. The Icelandic Research Fund 2012. Project Grant - New proposal (pp. 1-13).

Investigating student choices in performing higher-level comprehension tasks using TED

Francesca Bianchi[1] and Ivana Marenzi[2]

Abstract. The current paper describes a first experiment in the use of TED talks and open tagging exercises to train higher-level comprehension skills, and of automatic logging of the student's actions to investigate the student choices while performing analytical tasks. The experiment took advantage of an interactive learning platform – LearnWeb – that integrates TED talk videos and transcripts and enriches them with tagging features and a data logging system. The data collected offered an answer to the following questions: Which of the three tasks was perceived by the students as more difficult? How was each task faced by the students? How did the logs contribute to an understanding of the students' approaches to the tasks? The experiment also suggested ideas for further development of LearnWeb's log features from a pedagogical and research perspective.

Keywords: TED talks, LearnWeb, design-based research, log analysis.

1. Introduction

LearnWeb[3] (Marenzi, 2014) is an educational platform designed for retrieving, sharing, commenting and analysing multimedia resources. This platform has recently integrated TED talks (Taibi et al., 2015) and enhanced TED transcripts with interactive features (e.g. text selections, annotations, and deletions; Bianchi & Marenzi, 2015).

This experiment tested the newly integrated features within an academic module on interpreting. The module trains core skills, which include active listening and memorization. LearnWeb was thus used to give students exercises targeting higher-level comprehension skills, and to gain insight into the student choices while

1. University of Salento, Lecce, Italy; francesca.bianchi@unisalento.it
2. L3S Research Center, Hannover, Germany; marenzi@l3s.de
3. http://learnweb.l3s.uni-hannover.de

How to cite this article: Bianchi, F., & Marenzi, I. (2016). Investigating student choices in performing higher-level comprehension tasks using TED. In S. Papadima-Sophocleous, L. Bradley & S. Thouësny (Eds), *CALL communities and culture – short papers from EUROCALL 2016* (pp. 44-49). Research-publishing.net. https://doi.org/10.14705/rpnet.2016.eurocall2016.536

performing the given tasks. The following research questions led the analysis of the data: Which of the three tasks was perceived by the students as more difficult? How was each task faced by the students? How did the logs contribute to an understanding of the students' approaches to the tasks?

Below is a brief outline of the conceptual models which informed the exercises and the analyses in the current experiment.

Discourse comprehension, memorization and summarization are fundamental skills in interpreting (Pöchhacker, 2003), and expert trainers, such as Moser-Mercer (2000), suggest that an interpreter's training should start from there. According to van Dijk and Kintsch (1983), comprehension, memorization and summarization involve the creation of three types of mental representations: *surface representations*, focusing on microstructures; *textbase representation*, containing macrostructural information; and *situation model*, integrating text information with experience of the world. Macrostructures are created by applying processes of deletion, generalization and construction. Elaborating on van Dijk and Kintsch's (1983) model, Brown and Day (1983) suggest six macrorules for text summarization: (1) deleting unnecessary information, (2) deleting redundant information, (3) substituting a list of items with a superordinate word, (4) substituting a list of actions with a word expressing a superordinate event, (5) selecting a topic sentence, and (6) inventing a topic sentence if none are available. Strategies involving substitution and construction are not used by less experienced readers (Winograd, 1983). Focus on text structure, i.e. the textbase representation, and deep understanding of the intended meaning of the text are fundamental in consecutive interpreting (Hatim & Mason, 1997).

2.   Method

The experiment involved 25 Italian natives, attending a module on consecutive interpreting in an MA curriculum for language specialists. The students – aged 21-23 (except for one student aged 47) – were B2+ or above of the CEFR in English.

The students were given three tasks revolving around the same TED video. Task 1 asked them to divide the first six minutes of the video into five sections and give them a title. This task involves the creation of a textbase representation and requires the students to verbalize it, thus gauging understanding and summary skills. Task 2 asked the students to analyse the same piece of text and distinguish key assertions from ancillary pieces of text. This task draws attention to and requires the application of one of the most basic reading and summary strategies, i.e. deletion. Finally, Task 3 required the students to mark each clause in the first three minutes of the speech with a discourse function chosen from a given list. This task draws attention to the communicative function of discourse, and involves abilities at the level of textbase representation and situation model, not to mention metalinguistic abilities. For more details, see Bianchi and Marenzi (2015).

The tasks were performed using LearnWeb's selection and annotation feature, pictured in Figure 1.

Figure 1. The annotation window

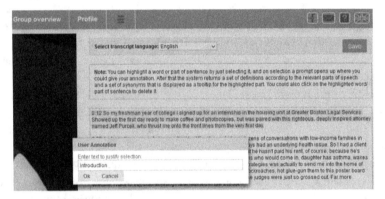

LearnWeb keeps track of the student's selections, deselections and annotations by means of a logging system and provides the teacher with a detailed log and a simple log.

3. Discussion

Due to some technical issues, only 14 resources in Task 1, 15 resources in Task 2, and 13 resources in Task 3 were suitable for analysis, along with the corresponding logs. The following paragraphs present the results, organized by research question.

3.1. Which of the three tasks was perceived by the students as more difficult?

To answer this question we used the detailed log, and manually counted the cases where a student had deselected a piece of text and subsequently changed the selection span or the annotation. The percentage of students who substantially changed at least one selection or tag was 29%, 7%, and 38% in Tasks 1, 2, and 3, respectively; the number of substantial changes recorded was, respectively, seven, one, and eight. These data suggest that Task 2 was considered much easier than the other ones. Tasks 1 and above all Task 3, on the other hand, posed problems to the students, with Task 3 recording a higher number of substantial changes across a higher percentage of students.

These results quantify and reflect the students' confidence in the given skill.

3.2.   How was each task faced by the students?

In Task 1, almost all the annotations matched Brown and Day's (1983) macrorule 6 (i.e. inventing a topic sentence), and involved strategies of substitution and creation. Furthermore, the students' annotations were structured as long phrases (47%), complete sentences (38%), or *wh* questions (15%). These techniques suggest good summary skills and are also suitable to support memorization (see e.g. Taboada & Guthries, 2006; Urlaub, 2012).

In Task 2, the students' unit of reference was the paragraph (47%), the sentence (20%), or a mix of the previous two (33%). Considering key elements entire paragraphs of a text, though theoretically possible in some contexts, is not the best approach in the current scenario. Furthermore, 13% of the students used inappropriate tags.

In Task 3, 77% selected and tagged full sentences or paragraphs instead of clauses, thus showing little sensitivity for discourse functions and limited familiarity with this type of pragmatic task. The students' deselections and changes of tag were primarily located towards the beginning of the text. These results suggest that Task 2 was actually the most difficult, while Task 1 the easiest.

3.3.   How did the logs contribute to an understanding
of the students' approaches to the tasks?

The detailed log proved fundamental to: understand whether a student had hesitations while performing the task; see the order in which selections and annotation were made; and understand the beginning and end of selections when multiple selections and tags appeared in contiguous pieces of text.

Due to the same technical issues that led to discarding some of the students' resources, the simple log could not be used in the current analyses.

4.   Conclusions

The current paper has shown a possible use of LearnWeb's interactive features and logs to gauge higher-level comprehension skills through selection and tagging exercises and the students' confidence in their own skills.

The results suggest that a large number of the students in this group had good summarising abilities – attested by their annotations in Task 1, based almost exclusively on strategies of substitution and creation –, but little awareness of the strategies and skills they automatically apply in the reading process – attested by their generally unsuitable selections in Tasks 2 and 3. Furthermore, the limited number of changes, especially in Task 2, suggest that most of the students were not aware of their limited metacognitive and analytical abilities.

The analyses were largely based on evidence that was visible in the students' final products, i.e. in the annotated resources. However, the system's detailed log played more than one important role, as summarized in Section 3.3. In particular, it gave the researchers access to the draft versions of the students work.

References

Bianchi, F., & Marenzi, I. (2015). Teaching and investigating higher-level comprehension skills in LearnWeb, an interactive platform integrating TED Talks. In *Conference Proceedings, ICT for Language Learning, Florence, Italy, 2015* (pp. 236-240). Firenze: Libreria Universitaria.

Brown, A. L., & Day, J. D. (1983). Macrorules for summarizing texts: the development of expertize. *Journal of Verbal Learning and Verbal Behavior, 22*, 1-14. https://doi.org/10.1016/S0022-5371(83)80002-4

Hatim, B., & Mason, I. (1997). *The translator as communicator*. London: Routledge.

Marenzi, I. (2014). *Multiliteracies and e-learning 2.0*. Frankfurt am Main: Peter Lang.

Moser-Mercer, B. (2000). The acquisition of interpreting skills. In L. Gran & C. Kellet Bidoli (Eds), *L'interpretazione nelle lingue dei segni: aspetti teorici e pratici della formazione. Signed-language interpretation and training: Theoretical and practical aspects* (pp. 57-61). Trieste: EUT.

Pöchhacker, F. (2003). *Introducing interpreting studies*. New York: Routledge.

Taboada A., Guthries, J. T. (2006). Contributions of student questioning and prior knowledge to construction of knowledge from reading information text. *Journal of Literacy Research, 38*(1), 1-35. https://doi.org/10.1207/s15548430jlr3801_1

Taibi, D., Chawla, S., Dietze, S., Marenzi, I., & Fetahu, B. (2015). Exploring TED talks as linked data for education. *BJET, 46*(5), 1092-1096. https://doi.org/10.1111/bjet.12283

Urlaub, P. (2012). Reading strategies and literature instruction: teaching learners to generate questions to foster literary reading in the second language. *System, 40*(2), 296-304. https://doi.org/10.1016/j.system.2012.05.002

Van Dijk, T. A., & Kintsch, W. (1983). *Strategies of discourse comprehension*. New York: Academic Press.

Winograd, P. N. (1983). *Strategic difficulties in summarizing texts*. Technical Report No. 274. http://eric.ed.gov/?id=ED228616

An evaluation of text-to-speech synthesizers in the foreign language classroom: learners' perceptions

Tiago Bione[1], Jennica Grimshaw[2], and Walcir Cardoso[3]

Abstract. As stated in Cardoso, Smith, and Garcia Fuentes (2015), second language researchers and practitioners have explored the pedagogical capabilities of Text-To-Speech synthesizers (TTS) for their potential to enhance the acquisition of writing (e.g. Kirstein, 2006), vocabulary and reading (e.g. Proctor, Dalton, & Grisham, 2007), and pronunciation (e.g. Cardoso, Collins, & White, 2012). Despite their demonstrated effectiveness, there is a need for up-to-date formal evaluations of TTS systems, specifically for their potential to promote the ideal conditions under which languages are acquired, particularly in an English as a Foreign Language (EFL) environment, as suggested by Cardoso, Smith, and Garcia Fuentes (2015). This study evaluated a modern English TTS system in an EFL context in Brazil, at a number of levels, including speech quality, opportunity to focus on form, and learners' cognitive processing of TTS-generated texts. Fifteen Brazilian EFL learners participated in the study in which they listened to both human and TTS-produced speech samples while performing the abovementioned tasks. Semi-structured interviews were used to collect data about participants' perceptions of the technology. We report an analysis of these interviews, which indicate that EFL learners have overall positive attitudes towards the pedagogical use of TTS, and that they would like to use the technology as a learning tool.

Keywords: text-to-speech synthesis, TTS, L2 pronunciation, English as a foreign language, Brazil.

1. Concordia University, Montréal, Canada; tiagobione@gmail.com
2. Concordia University, Montréal, Canada; jennica.grimshaw@gmail.com
3. Concordia University, Montréal, Canada; walcir.cardoso@concordia.ca

How to cite this article: Bione, T., Grimshaw, J., & Cardoso, W. (2016). An evaluation of text-to-speech synthesizers in the foreign language classroom: learners' perceptions. In S. Papadima-Sophocleous, L. Bradley & S. Thouësny (Eds), *CALL communities and culture – short papers from EUROCALL 2016* (pp. 50-54). Research-publishing.net. https://doi.org/10.14705/rpnet.2016.eurocall2016.537

1. Introduction

Second/foreign language (L2) learners need to be exposed to a significant amount of input in the L2 in order to acquire it. The literature suggests that the learning process is boosted when learners have access to comprehensible (Krashen, 1985) and acoustically variable input (Barcroft & Sommers, 2005) in an environment that is learner-centered and that provides multiple opportunities for self-regulation (Chapelle, 2001). However, EFL students often lack input exposure outside the classroom as they do not usually have access to proficient speakers. One way to overcome this limitation is via the pedagogical use of TTS in L2 education, which has been demonstrated to be beneficial for the development of writing (Kirstein, 2006), vocabulary and reading (Proctor et al., 2007), and pronunciation skills (Cardoso et al., 2012).

Despite their demonstrated effectiveness, there is a need for up-to-date formal evaluations of TTS systems, specifically for their potential to promote the ideal conditions under which languages are learned (e.g. via enhanced input environments – Chapelle, 2001). Recently, Cardoso et al. (2015) investigated whether TTS systems provided university-level English as a second language speakers in Canada with the opportunity to complete focus-on-form tasks, detecting English regular past tense marking (i.e. /t/, /d/ or /ɪd/) in forms such as *walked, played,* and *wanted* in both human and TTS-generated texts. Findings revealed that participants were able to identify the target forms correctly, regardless of the type of voice heard. They also examined how students perceived the quality of TTS speech in comparison with human speech, and found less favorable ratings for TTS-generated texts. They acknowledged, however, that their findings could not be generalized to 'foreign' language contexts, as their participants were native-like English speakers with vast experience with the language. The current study, therefore, addresses the following research question: What are learners' perceptions of the pedagogical use of TTS in an EFL context?

2. Method

2.1. Participants and design

Fifteen Brazilian EFL learners (university students or professionals from a variety of educational backgrounds and proficiency levels, between the ages of 16 and 32) were recruited to complete four tasks in order to evaluate the quality of TTS-generated texts: they rated speech quality, answered comprehension questions, participated in a dictation, and were asked to identify past -ed forms in what they heard. For all tasks, participants listened to speech samples alternately produced by TTS and a human. The TTS voice was Julie (by NeoSpeech), a female North American speaker, and the human was a female native-speaker of the same dialect with similar speech properties. At the end of the one hour session (one-shot design), participants were interviewed about their insights on the quality of the TTS-generated voices. This paper reports findings from the analysis of the interview data.

2.2.   Analysis

Participants' interviews were analyzed and categorized into four themes: TTS system vs. human voice, speech accuracy, comprehensibility, and potential to be used as a learning tool. Under each theme, students' opinions were labelled as positive or negative to depict their overall perception and acceptance of TTS for pedagogical purposes.

3.   Results

3.1.   TTS system versus human voice

Only four participants were able to identify the electronic/human voice opposition without prompting: "The first voice was like the Google voice, when you try to translate"; "Clearly, there was a computer voice and other that was not". Eight students only realized differences between the two types of voices when they were explicitly told that one was machine-made: "Now that you've mentioned it, yes. Actually, I hadn't stopped to think about it". The remaining three students were not able to differentiate TTS and human voices even when they were told about them: "It completely fooled me", declared a participant.

3.2.   Accuracy

At the segmental level, TTS was perceived to be as good as native voices: "For me, both were speaking as native speakers, both were super correct". However, suprasegmentals were problematic as TTS was seen as unnatural and lacking native rhythm in phrasal stress, intonation and pauses: "[the computer voice] helped my comprehension, but sometimes words have a different intonation

[...] words that should give away phrasal tone [stress]". One student noticed, however, that TTS is efficient for questions since it accurately reproduces the rising tone in interrogative clauses.

3.3.　Comprehensibility

Inaccuracy in suprasegmental production made most participants consider TTS harder to understand when compared to the human voice. Nine students stated that the pace of the TTS and consequently its intonation patterns and connected speech phenomena made it more difficult to understand: "The 'tempo' between words [in TTS] draws too much attention, because in spoken language you feel more fluidity due to different timing between word connections, grammatical constructions [...]. With computers, everything seems to have the same timing, so it creates a different perception". Five learners favored TTS because it was slower and made word boundaries more salient as it speaks "word by word".

3.4.　Potential as a learning tool

11 participants agreed that TTS technology could and should be used as a tool for language learning: they perceived that morphological features such as past -ed markings were more salient in TTS, and that it could be a source for extra input outside the classroom. Three participants suggested that TTS should only be used with beginners as more advanced learners need to experience human voice characteristics: "People will [need to] get used [to a human voice] because when they travel, they won't hear paused, word by word speech". Seven participants stated that TTS should be used for all levels as long as the human voice is not excluded from the learning process. For two students, however, TTS should not be used as a learning tool. "I don't think it is a good idea [...] it's always better when a native teacher speaks".

4.　Conclusions

This study investigated learners' perceptions of the pedagogical use of TTS in an EFL context. The findings show that participants had an overall positive impression of TTS-generated voices. TTS has evolved significantly in terms of quality in recent years to the point that most participants could not tell the difference between human voice and TTS until prompted. However, the TTS voice was still rated less favorably in terms of comprehensibility when compared to the human voice. These findings corroborate previous studies (e.g. Cardoso et al., 2015; Handley,

Tiago Bione, Jennica Grimshaw, and Walcir Cardoso

2009). On the other hand, while the low ratings for comprehensibility may appear negative, this had little impact on participants' perception of TTS as a pedagogical tool. Almost all participants recognized that TTS could and should be used for teaching purposes, and most said that it should be used regardless of students' proficiency levels. This contrasts to Cardoso et al.'s (2015) findings from a similar study conducted in a 'second' language context, wherein participants showed lower acceptance towards TTS. One reason for this high acceptance of TTS as a pedagogical tool in the current study may be due to the fact that EFL environments lack naturally occurring L2 input and access to native or proficient speakers in the target L2 outside of online environments. With TTS, language learners can gain additional exposure and have access to enhanced input environments to increase their learning opportunities (Chapelle, 2001). These findings suggest that EFL students appear to be ready to adopt TTS systems as pedagogical tools in L2 education.

References

Barcroft, J., & Sommers, M. S. (2005). Effects of acoustic variability on second language vocabulary learning. *Studies in Second Language Acquisition, 27*(3), 387-414. https://doi.org/10.1017/s0272263105050175

Cardoso, W., Collins, L., & White, J. (2012). Phonological input enhancement via text-to-speech synthesizers. *Paper presented at the AAAL Conference, Boston, U.S.A.*

Cardoso, W., Smith, G., & Garcia Fuentes, C. (2015). Evaluating text-to-speech synthesis. In F. Helm, L. Bradley, M. Guarda, & S. Thouësny (Eds), *Critical CALL – Proceedings of the 2015 EUROCALL Conference, Padova, Italy* (pp. 108-113). Dublin Ireland: Research-publishing.net. https://doi.org/10.14705/rpnet.2015.000318

Chapelle, C. (2001). *Computer applications in second language acquisition.* Cambridge, UK: Cambridge University Press. https://doi.org/10.1017/CBO9781139524681

Handley, Z. (2009). Is text-to-speech synthesis ready for use in computer-assisted language learning? *Speech Communication, 51*(10), 906-919. https://doi.org/10.1016/j.specom.2008.12.004

Kirstein, M. (2006). *Universalizing universal design: applying text-to-speech technology to English language learners' process writing.* Doctoral dissertation. University of Massachusetts, U.S.A.

Krashen, S. (1985). *The input hypothesis: issues and implications.* New York: Longman.

Proctor, C. P., Dalton, B., & Grisham, D. (2007). Scaffolding English language learners and struggling readers in a universal literacy environment with embedded strategy instruction and vocabulary support. *Journal of Literacy Research, 39*(1), 71-9.

Quantifying CALL: significance, effect size and variation

Alex Boulton[1]

Abstract. Good practice in primary research has evolved over many decades of research in applied linguistics to counter human fallibility and biases. Surprisingly, perhaps, synthesising such research in an entire field has only recently started to develop its own methodologies and recommendations. This paper outlines some of the issues involved, especially in terms of quantitative research and meta-analysis. A second-order synthesis of meta-analyses in Computer-Assisted Language Learning (CALL) provides only medium effect sizes, but the figures are interpreted in terms of realistic expectations. The inevitable variation in effect sizes can be attributed in principle either to the research methodologies (both primary and secondary) or – more interestingly – to real-world phenomena.

Keywords: meta-analysis, research synthesis, effect size, variation, CALL synthesis.

1. Primary studies and research synthesis

CALL research is often quantitative in nature, in line with the bulk of research in applied linguistics which sees measurement as a way to counter subjectivity and strive towards more 'scientific' rigour. This of course neglects the important insights that can only realistically be gleaned from qualitative studies, with their more frequent focus on emic, ecological, holistic considerations, and ability to account for complex, narrative, continuous data such as interviews which do not lend themselves easily to quantitative analysis. This is not to say that quantitative research should be abandoned, only that – like all research – it needs using and interpreting with caution.

A particular problem with primary quantitative research is that many studies adopt Null Hypothesis Significance Testing (NHST) as the standard model. NHST is

---

1. CNRS & University of Lorraine, Nancy, France; alex.boulton@univ-lorraine.fr

How to cite this article: Boulton, A. (2016). Quantifying CALL: significance, effect size and variation. In S. Papadima-Sophocleous, L. Bradley & S. Thouësny (Eds), *CALL communities and culture – short papers from EUROCALL 2016* (pp. 55-60). Research-publishing.net. https://doi.org/10.14705/rpnet.2016.eurocall2016.538

entirely subject to sample size (any difference will be significant if the sample is large enough), it doesn't tell us anything about what we're really interested in (i.e. the effect of a particular variable), and it encourages dichotomous thinking on an arbitrary basis (with p-values typically set at 95% for no good reason). NHST has been heavily criticised on all these counts, with Plonsky (2015) claiming it has done "far more harm than good" (p. 242).

More useful are effect sizes such as Cohen's d: such measures do address the real issues, and have the substantial advantage that they can be pooled across studies. For this to be effective, we first however need to begin with rigorous trawls of research in a clearly-defined field to ensure that we do in fact cover what we set out to synthesise. Traditional surveys as found in the ubiquitous 'literature review' in primary studies are notoriously inadequate if one relies on personal interpretation of serendipitous collections. This is a major issue in the complex field such as education, where "everything seems to work in the improvement of student achievement... Teachers can thus find some support to justify almost all their actions – even though the variability about what works is enormous" (Hattie, 2009, p. 6). Research synthesis and specifically meta-analysis are attempts to make the procedures more scientific and transparent (Norris & Ortega, 2000).

2.   Meta-analysis in CALL

Table 1 is an attempt to summarise meta-analyses in CALL, derived largely from Plonsky and Ziegler (2016) and Oswald and Plonsky (2010). The 12 meta-analyses show the size of the effect of CALL use in experimental groups compared to control or comparison groups. The first three give large effect sizes according Plonsky and Oswald's (2014) empirically-derived, field-specific benchmarks based on meta-analyses in Second Language Acquisition (SLA) ($d \geq .9$); the next two are medium ($d \geq .6$), followed by three small ($d \geq .4$) and four negligible effects ($d < .4$). The mean is .64, the pessimistic conclusion being that CALL work as a whole has barely a medium effect on learning. Worse, the few large effect sizes are derived from very small samples as shown in the column for k. Indeed, there is a large negative correlation ($r=-.51$) between the number of studies featuring in these meta-analyses and the effect size calculated.

This rather pessimistic discussion is based on the premise that we need to find large effect sizes for CALL. Minimally, however, what we would hope to find is that CALL is *at least as good as* traditional teaching, with an effect size of $d=0$ (or, according to Hattie, 2009, $d=.4$), which is the case here. Since most primary studies are relatively focused and short-term, they will not show other benefits which we may want to impute to CALL. These might include cost or time efficiency, motivation or enjoyment, long-term retention or appropriation, learning-to-learn or becoming 'better language learners', increased autonomy or transferable skills, etc. Such conclusions are speculative at best since these things are notoriously difficult to research, and would have to be the subject of further studies.

Table 1.   Meta-analyses in CALL (cf. Oswald & Plonsky, 2010; Plonsky & Ziegler, 2016)

study	year	source	focus	k	d
Abraham	2008	CALL	Glossing vocabulary	6	1.40
Zhao	2003	CALICO J	CALL general	9	1.12
Taylor	2006	CALICO J	Glossing reading comprehension	4	1.09
Chiu	2013	BJET	Vocabulary	16	0.75
Abraham	2008	CALL	Glossing reading comprehension	11	0.73
Chiu et al.	2012	BJET	Game-based learning	14	0.53
Taylor	2009	CALICO J	Glossing reading comprehension	32	0.49
Lin, H.	2014	LL&T	CMC	59	0.44
Yun	2011	CALL	Glossing vocabulary	10	0.37
Lin, W. et al.	2013	LL&T	SCMC	19	0.33
Grgurović et al.	2013	ReCALL	CALL general	65	0.24
Ziegler	2015	SSLA	SCMC	14	0.13

3.   Variation

Meta-analyses need interpreting with caution: in particular, it is tempting to seize on a single figure as the ultimate answer to the question: Does it work? "Professionals in CALL often find this comparison question frustrating... but in a political sense, it would be useful if CALL specialists could answer it" (Grgurović, Chapelle, & Shelley, 2013, p. 2). More realistically, we need to look at *variation* in what works: different primary studies of ostensibly of the same phenomenon will provide different effect sizes – as will different meta-analyses in a given field (cf. Table 1).

Variation in meta-analyses may derive from the studies themselves. Clearly not all primary research is of similar quality, and a synthesist has to decide how to deal with this – typically by devising *a priori* inclusion criteria (e.g. whether to include conference proceedings), or by treating quality as a variable and subsequently examining its impact on the effect sizes (e.g. to compare papers in conference proceedings against those in prestigious journal articles). This underlines the many choices that are to be made: quality is a consideration in secondary as much as in primary research. The increasing numbers of meta-analyses and the prominence given to them in such diverse places as the American Psychological Association manual or *Language Learning* editorials, along with handbooks (e.g. Cumming, 2012) and websites with methodological recommendations for good practice and increasingly sophisticated tools (cf. https://lukeplonsky.wordpress.com), may suggest that the practices are straightforward.

While SLA synthesis may have become something of a tradition in its own right, researchers have a tremendous range of options to choose from at all stages. How exactly do they define the field? What tools do they use to arrive at a (near-) exhaustive collection of studies in that field? What study types do they reject? Simply when deciding what studies to include, many meta-analyses are deliberately limited to control/experimental designs published in English in high-ranking journals in particular time periods for example, and so inevitably miss much of the field, the rationale being to increase study quality. How do they extract the data, and how do they calculate and interpret effect sizes? Primary research can be extraordinarily complex, with several experimental groups doing different things using different tools and procedures for different main objectives, and the resulting data presented in the form of raw data, descriptive statistics, *F*/*t*-scores, etc. The synthesist then has to decide the specific formula to use, and decide whether to weigh the results (e.g. for sample size) and how to deal with the extreme values for outliers. Checking is essential, usually from inter-rater reliability measures, but also in the form of funnel plots for publication bias in the studies sampled, and if possible, comparing effect sizes from different designs (control/experimental vs. pre/post-test and if possible delayed test designs).

Variation can also be examined to determine which moderator variables contribute more or less to overall effect sizes. It might be, for example, that large effect sizes only come from long-term studies, or from certain learner populations (proficiency, age, sex, cultural background, field of study, etc.), for certain linguistic objectives or tools or procedures, and so on. Promising categories therefore feature in a coding sheet, which is itself immensely complex and difficult to draw up rigorously. It is no surprise perhaps that among the main conclusions of syntheses are recommendations for better reporting practices in primary research, as it is only at this stage that it becomes really apparent how much information is missing, vague or unsubstantiated. Burston and Arispe (2016), for example, found that 50% of research articles in four major CALL journals targeting 'advanced' levels of proficiency had learner populations of B1 level only.

4.   Conclusions

Research is extremely complex, not just in terms of choices and procedures but also in terms of the field itself – language, language use and language learning. Bias is inherent in primary research, and measures need to be taken to ensure that this is not exacerbated in an overall view of the field. Quantitative studies provide essential insights but do not capture the whole picture, while narrative syntheses are "inevitably idiosyncratic" (Han, 2015, p. 411) – both are essential to provide as full an understanding as possible. Synthesists need to be rigorously transparent in designing their studies, writing up their results, and providing supplementary materials for others to check, replicate, or modify as more research becomes available.

The observations here are in large part inspired from a meta-analysis of data-driven learning, i.e. the use of corpora in language learning (Boulton & Cobb, forthcoming). In addition to the above, the main conclusions are that the many choices are often glossed over; that single-figure main effects can be misleading and need careful interpretation; and that, despite the relatively low overall effect sizes reported, there are reasons for optimism in the field. Inevitably, more research is needed in all areas.

References

Boulton, A., & Cobb, T. (forthcoming). Corpus use in language learning: a meta-analysis. *Language Learning*.

Burston, J., & Arispe, K. (2016). The contribution of CALL to advanced-level foreign/second language instruction. In S. Papadima-Sophocleous, L. Bradley & S. Thouësny (Eds), *CALL communities and culture – short papers from EUROCALL 2016* (pp. 61-68). Research-publishing.net. https://doi.org/10.14705/rpnet.2016.eurocall2016.539

Cumming, G. (2012). *Understanding the new statistics: effect sizes, confidence intervals, and meta-analysis*. New York: Routledge.

Grgurović, M., Chapelle, C. A., & Shelley, M. C. (2013). A meta-analysis of effectiveness studies on computer technology supported language learning. *ReCALL, 25*(2), 165-198. https://doi.org/10.1017/S0958344013000013

Han, Z. (2015). Striving for complementarity between narrative and meta-analytic reviews. *Applied Linguistics, 36*(3), 409-415. https://doi.org/10.1093/applin/amv026

Hattie, J. (2009). *Visible learning: a synthesis of over 800 meta-analyses relating to achievement*. New York: Routledge.

Norris, J. M., & Ortega, L. (2000). Effectiveness of L2 instruction: a research synthesis and quantitative meta-analysis. *Language Learning, 50*(3), 417-528. https://doi.org/10.1111/0023-8333.00136

Oswald, F. L., & Plonsky, L. (2010). Meta-analysis in second language research: choices and challenges. *Annual Review of Applied Linguistics, 30*, 85-110. https://doi.org/10.1017/S0267190510000115

Plonsky, L. (2015). Quantitative considerations for improving replicability in CALL and applied linguistics. *CALICO Journal, 32*(2), 232-244.

Plonsky, L., & Oswald, F. L. (2014). How big is 'big'? Interpreting effect sizes in L2 research. *Language Learning, 64*(4), 878-912. https://doi.org/10.1111/lang.12079

Plonsky, L., & Ziegler, N. (2016). The CALL–SLA interface: insights from a second-order synthesis. *Language Learning & Technology, 20*(2), 17-37.

The contribution of CALL to advanced-level foreign/second language instruction

Jack Burston[1] and Kelly Arispe[2]

Abstract. This paper evaluates the contribution of instructional technology to advanced-level foreign/second language learning (AL2) over the past thirty years. It is shown that the most salient feature of AL2 practice and associated Computer-Assisted Language Learning (CALL) research are their rarity and restricted nature. Based on an analysis of four leading CALL journals (*CALICO, CALL, LL&T, ReCALL*), less than 3% of all CALL publications deal with AL2. Moreover, within this body of research, the range of languages involved is very restricted. Three languages, English, German and French, account for nearly 87% of the studies. Likewise, in nearly 81% of the cases, the learning focus is on the written language. Attention to oral-aural skills accounts for only 18% of all AL2 CALL projects. Whatever the targeted language or linguistic focus, the most striking aspect of advanced-level L2 CALL studies is the lack of information given regarding the competency level of students and the linguistic level of the activities undertaken. The determination of these critical parameters is thus of necessity very much a highly interpretive process. Based on the available evidence, it is estimated that half of the learners in these AL2 studies were in fact within the Common European Framework of Reference (CEFR) B1 range, i.e. below what would generally be considered as advanced-level competency. So, too, half of the assigned tasks were deemed to have been below the B2 level, with 40% of these below the B1 level. This study concludes that both quantitatively and qualitatively the contribution of instructional technology to advanced-level L2 acquisition has been very limited.

Keywords: CALL, advanced, language, competence, research, CEFR, ACTFL.

1. Language Centre, Cyprus University of Technology, Limassol, Cyprus; jack.burston@cut.ac.cy
2. Department of World Languages, Boise State University, Boise, Idaho, United States; kellyarispe@boisestate.edu

How to cite this article: Burston, J., & Arispe, K. (2016). The contribution of CALL to advanced-level foreign/second language instruction. In S. Papadima-Sophocleous, L. Bradley & S. Thouësny (Eds), *CALL communities and culture – short papers from EUROCALL 2016* (pp. 61-68). Research-publishing.net. https://doi.org/10.14705/rpnet.2016.eurocall2016.539

1.   Introduction

This paper evaluates the contribution of instructional technology to AL2 over the past 30 years. It draws upon 47 Advanced-level second language papers found in four prominent journals (*CALICO, CALL, LL&T, ReCALL*), which constitutes 2.6% of their total 1840 publications from 1983 to 2015. At 5.3%, *LL&T* had the greatest proportion, with *CALICO* at 3.7%, *ReCALL* at 3.2% and *CALL* at less than 1%.

The CALL literature in this study includes only seven AL2, with English as a Foreign or Second Language (EFL/ESL) alone accounting for nearly 62% of all publications (Figure 1). This is followed in a distant second and third place by German (13.5%) and French (11.5%). Four other languages complete the inventory: Spanish (6%), Chinese (4%), and Arabic and Russian at less than 2% each.

Figure 1.   Advanced-level languages

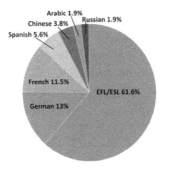

Figure 2.   Pedagogical focus

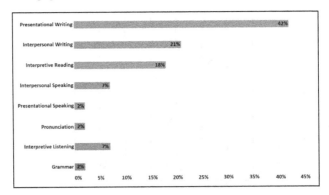

In all, nearly 81% of AL2 studies focused on the written language (Figure 2), of which presentational and interpersonal writing accounted for 63% and reading 18%. In contrast, presentational and interpersonal speaking, pronunciation and listening together were targeted in only 18% of the studies. One paper focused on basic grammar.

2.   Pedagogical focus details

2.1.   Written language

Beginning with the predominant written language paradigm, a closer inspection of the 24 AL2 studies that focus specifically on presentational writing skills reveals that 13 involve collaborative composition activities [3, 13, 14, 19, 22, 24, 27, 29, 30, 36, 39, 40, 43][3] and 11 individual writing exercises [4, 5, 6, 7, 9, 11, 23, 32, 37, 41, 47].

A number of the studies that specifically target presentational writing [29, 30, 36, 40] also involve written interpersonal communication. However, ten of the written interpersonal communication studies [1, 2, 10, 17, 25, 26, 35, 38, 42, 44] focus on text-based Computer-Mediated Communication (CMC) (i.e. chats, discussion forums, blogs) which target interaction that does not result in any formal written production. The emphasis on the written language is further extended in ten studies that target reading comprehension of online texts [12, 15, 16, 18, 20, 28, 30, 33, 34, 37].

2.2.   Other language areas

In all, only ten studies devote any attention to aural/oral skills. Only one study [30] focuses on presentational speaking, in combination with presentational writing. In all, four studies involve interpersonal speaking, three [24, 30, 36] in conjunction with presentational writing and the fourth [31] with listening comprehension. Besides the latter [31], three other studies also target listening comprehension [8, 30, 45]. The tenth aural/oral study [21] involved pronunciation correction. Lastly, one study was grammar-based [46].

---

3. In order to not encumber the text with long bibliographical citations, references in this meta-analysis are made to the number in square brackets which precedes each entry in the References section.

3. Student language competency level

The AL2 CALL publications in this study are frustratingly imprecise in identifying the language competency level of students. Of the forty-seven papers involving pedagogical implementations analysed in the present study, only nine [15, 16, 17, 21, 27, 33, 37, 46, 47] explicitly substantiate student L2 competency by reference to objective external test results (e.g. TOEFL scores). Another 12 [2, 7, 8, 10, 11, 12, 24, 28, 31, 34, 35, 39] specifically identify the competence level of their students (e.g. advanced-low, B1, etc.), but without any corroborating evidence. In the remaining 26 studies [1, 3, 4, 5, 6, 9, 13, 14, 18, 19, 20, 22, 23, 25, 26, 29, 30, 32, 36, 38, 40, 41, 42, 43, 44, 45], the competency level of students can only be determined based on circumstantial evidence (e.g. graduating L2 majors, students in an AL2 graduate course, etc.). As can be seen in Figure 3, based on the information that could be gleaned from these studies, the competence level of half the students described as advanced-level learners was in fact within the B1 range on the CEFR scale, which is to say at a level where they could at best 'communicate essential points and ideas in familiar contexts'. Only a third of the students were in the B2 range, i.e. a level generally acknowledged as advanced. The remaining 17% were at the C1 level, i.e. 'effective operational proficiency'.

Figure 3. Student L2 competency level

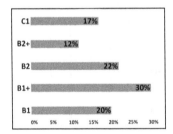

4. Language activity level

Even more so than with the definition of advanced-level competence in the description of AL2 CALL studies, identification of the linguistic level of the actual language activities undertaken by students in the projects leaves much undetermined. In fact, of the 47 implementation studies, only one [34] explicitly identified and substantiated task level with reference to an objective external metric. Three others [9, 12, 43] defined the task level explicitly, but without any substantiation. The task level of the remaining 43 (92%) could only be determined through interpretation of the activities undertaken. In all but two cases [38, 40], this nonetheless provided a reasonable estimate of task difficulty level upon which the following analysis is based.

As indicated in Figure 4, the estimated range of language activity levels in AL2 CALL studies extends from A2 to C1, of which half are below the B2 level.

Figure 4.　Task level

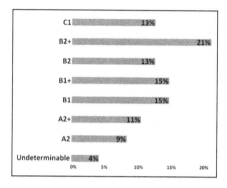

5.　Conclusion

In evaluating the contribution of CALL to advanced-level foreign/second language instruction, this study has considered a number of interrelated factors as manifested in the published research of the four most prominent CALL journals (*CALICO, CALL, LL&T, ReCALL*) over the past thirty years. As documented, AL2 barely merits a mention in the published CALL literature. Moreover, such research as exists is extremely limited in the L2 studied, with English by far being the center of attention, followed distantly by German and French and four other languages. So, too, four times as many studies focus on the written language compared to aural-oral skills. Even more seriously, AL2 CALL studies are plagued by vagueness as to what constitutes an advanced level of foreign language competence and the difficulty level of the language activities their students were required to undertake. Notwithstanding, a close analysis of these studies allows these critical parameters to be determined with reasonable accuracy. Specifically, it is shown that in half the cases student competence and their assigned tasks were advanced only to the extent that they were above the A2 level. In sum, it must be concluded that to date, CALL has contributed very little to either our understanding or practice of advanced-level foreign/second language instruction.

References

[1]Biesenbach-Lucas, S. (2005). Communication topics and strategies in e-mail consultation: comparison between American and international university students. *Language Learning and Technology, 9*(2), 60-81.

[2]Biesenbach-Lucas, S. (2007). Students writing emails to faculty: an examination of e-politeness among native and non-native speakers of English. *Language Learning and Technology, 11*(2), 59-81.

[3]Bradley, L., Lindström, B., & Rystedt, H. (2010). Rationalities of collaboration for language learning in a wiki. *ReCALL, 22*(2), 247-265. https://doi.org/10.1017/S0958344010000108

[4]Burston, J. (2001a). Exploiting the potential of a computer-based grammar checker in conjunction with self-monitoring strategies with advanced level students of French. *CALICO Journal, 18*(3), 499-515.

[5]Burston, J. (2001b). Computer-mediated feedback in composition correction. *CALICO Journal, 19*(1), 37-50.

[6]Chambers, A., & O'Sullivan, I. (2004). Corpus consultation and advanced learners' writing skills in French. *ReCALL, 16*(1), 158-172. https://doi.org/10.1017/S0958344004001211

[7]Chang, J-Y. (2014). The use of general and specialized corpora as reference sources for academic English writing: a case study. *ReCALL, 26*(2), 243-259. https://doi.org/10.1017/S0958344014000056

[8]Chang, L. (2007). The effects of using CALL on advanced Chinese foreign language learners. *CALICO Journal, 24*(2), 331-354.

[9]Chang, P. (2012). Using a stance corpus to learn about effective authorial stance-taking: a textlinguistic approach. *ReCALL, 24*(2), 209-236. https://doi.org/10.1017/S0958344012000079

[10]Chun, D. (2011). Developing intercultural communicative competence through online exchanges. *CALICO Journal, 28*(2), 392-419. https://doi.org/10.11139/cj.28.2.392-419

[11]Craven, M.-L. (1988). Evaluating CUES: some problems and issues in experimental CALL research. *CALICO Journal, 5*(3), 51-64.

[12]De Ridder, I. (2002). Visible or invisible links: does the highlighting of hyperlinks affect incidental vocabulary learning, text comprehension, and the reading process? *Language Learning and Technology, 6*(1), 123-146. https://doi.org/10.1145/506443.506515

[13]Dippold, D. (2009). Peer feedback through blogs: student and teacher perceptions in an advanced German class. *ReCALL, 21*(1), 18-36. https://doi.org/10.1017/S095834400900010X

[14]Elola, I., & Oskoz, A. (2010). Collaborative writing: fostering foreign language and writing conventions development. *Language Learning and Technology, 14*(3), 51-71.

[15]Ercetin, G. (2003). Exploring ESL learners' use of hypermedia reading glosses. *CALICO Journal, 20*(2), 261-283.

[16]Erçetin, G. (2010). Effects of topic interest and prior knowledge on text recall and annotation use in reading a hypermedia text in the L2. *ReCALL, 22*(2), 228-246. https://doi.org/10.1017/S0958344010000091

[17]Fitze, M. (2006). Discourse and participation in ESL face-to-face and written electronic conferences. *Language Learning and Technology, 10*(1), 67-86.

[18]Garrett-Rucks, P., Howles. L., & Lake, W. (2015). Enhancing L2 reading comprehension with hypermedia texts: student perceptions. *CALICO Journal, 32*(1), 26–51.

[19]Hadjistassou, S. (2012). An activity theory exegesis on conflict and contradictions in networked discussions and feedback exchanges. *CALICO Journal, 29*(2), 367-388. https://doi.org/10.11139/cj.29.2.367-388

[20]Hamel, M.-J., & Caws, C. (2010). Usability tests in CALL development: pilot studies in the context of the Dire autrement and Francotoile Projects. *CALICO Journal, 27*(3), 491-504. https://doi.org/10.11139/cj.27.3.491-504

[21]Hardison, D. (2005). Contextualized computer-based L2 prosody training: evaluating the effects of discourse context and video input. *CALICO Journal, 22*(2), 175-190.

[22]Ho, M.-C., & Savignon, S. (2007). Face-to-face and computer-mediated peer review in EFL writing. *CALICO Journal, 24*(2), 269-290.

[23]Hsieh, W.-M., & Liou, H.-C. (2008). A case study of corpus-informed online academic writing for EFL graduate students. *CALICO Journal, 26*(1), 28-47.

[24]Jauregi, K., & Bañados, E. (2008). Virtual interaction through video-web communication: a step towards enriching and internationalizing language learning programs. *ReCALL, 20*(2), 183-207. https://doi.org/10.1017/S0958344008000529

[25]Kessler, G. (2009). Student-initiated attention to form in wiki-based collaborative writing. *Language Learning and Technology, 13*(1), 79-95.

[26]Kessler, G., & Bikowski, D. (2010). Developing collaborative autonomous learning abilities in computer mediated language learning: attention to meaning among students in wiki space. *Computer-Assisted Language Learning, 23*(1), 41-58. https://doi.org/10.1080/09588220903467335

[27]Kessler, G., Bikowski, D., & Boggs, J. (2012). Collaborative writing among second language learners in academic web based projects. *Language Learning & Technology, 16*(1), 91-109.

[28]Kol, S., & Schcolnik, M. (2000). Enhancing screen reading strategies. *CALICO Journal, 18*(1), 67-80.

[29]Kol, S., & Schcolnik, M. (2008). Asynchronous forums in EAP: assessment issues. *Language Learning & Technology, 12*(2), 49-70.

[30]Leahy, C. (2004). Researching language learning processes in open CALL settings for advanced learners. *Computer-Assisted Language Learning, 17*(3-4), 289-313. https://doi.org/10.1080/0958822042000319593

[31]Lys, F. (2013). The development of advanced learner oral proficiency using iPads. *Language Learning & Technology, 17*(3), 94-116.

[32]Martínez Lirola, M., & Tabuenca Cuevas, M. (2008). Integrating CALL and genre theory: a proposal to increase students' literacy. *ReCALL, 20*(1), pp 67-81.

[33]Park, J., Yang, J.-S., & Chin Hsieh, Y.-C. (2014). University level second language readers' online reading and comprehension strategies. *Language Learning & Technology, 16*(1), 148-172.

[34]Poole, R. (2012). Concordance-based glosses for academic vocabulary acquisition. *CALICO Journal, 29*(4), 679-693. https://doi.org/10.11139/cj.29.4.679-693

[35]Rivens Mompean, A. (2010). The development of meaningful interactions on a blog used for the learning of English as a Foreign Language. *ReCALL, 22*(3), 376-395. https://doi.org/10.1017/S0958344010000200

[36]Sadler, R. (2007). Computer-mediated communication and a cautionary tale of two cities. *CALICO Journal, 25*(1), 11-30.

[37]Shei, C. (2005). Integrating content learning and ESL writing in a translation commentary writing aid. *Computer-Assisted Language Learning, 18*(1-2), 33-48. https://doi.org/10.1080/09588220500132266

[38]Söntgens, K. (2001). Circling the globe: fostering experiential language learning. *ReCALL, 13*(1), 59-66. https://doi.org/10.1017/S0958344001000611

[39]Strobl, C. (2014). Affordances of Web 2.0 technologies for collaborative advanced writing in a foreign language. *CALICO Journal, 31*(1), 1-18. https://doi.org/10.11139/cj.31.1.1-18

[40]Sun, Y.-C., & Chang, Y.-J. (2012). Blogging to learn: becoming EFL academic writers through collaborative dialogues. *Language Learning & Technology, 16*(1), 43-61.

[41]Tsai, Y.-R. (2015). Applying the Technology Acceptance Model (TAM) to explore the effects of a Course Management System (CMS)-assisted EFL writing instruction. *CALICO Journal, 32*(1), 153-171.

[42]Vandergriff, I. (2013). "My major is English, belive it or not:)" – Participant orientations in nonnative/native text chat. *CALICO Journal, 30*(3), 393-409. https://doi.org/10.11139/cj.30.3.393-409

[43]Vurdien, R. (2013). Enhancing writing skills through blogging in an advanced English as a Foreign Language class in Spain. *Computer-Assisted Language Learning, 26*(2), 126-143. https://doi.org/10.1080/09588221.2011.639784

[44]Ware, P. (2005). 'Missed' communication in online communication: tensions in a German-American telecollaboration. *Language Learning & Technology, 9*(2), 64-89.

[45]Winke, P., Susan Gass, S., & Sydorenko, T. (2010). The effects of captioning videos used for foreign language listening activities. *Language Learning & Technology, 14*(1), 65-86.

[46]Xu, J., & Bull, S. (2010) Encouraging advanced second language speakers to recognise their language difficulties: a personalised computer-based approach. *Computer-Assisted Language Learning, 23*(2), 111-127. https://doi.org/10.1080/09588221003666206

[47]Yoon, H. (2008). More than a linguistic reference: the influence of corpus technology on L2 academic writing. *Language Learning & Technology, 12*(2), 31-48.

Using instructional technology to integrate CEFR 'can do' performance objectives into an advanced-level language course

Jack Burston[1], Androulla Athanasiou[2],
and Maro Neophytou-Yiokari[3]

Abstract. The purpose of this presentation is to show how instructional technology can be exploited to effectively integrate Common European Framework of Reference (CEFR) 'Can Do' performance objectives (Council of Europe, 2001) into the syllabus and assessment of an advanced (B2) level course. The particular course that will be used for purposes of demonstration is English for Rehabilitation, an English for Specific Academic Purposes (ESAP) course offered at the Cyprus University of Technology. It is a two-semester compulsory subject for first-year students majoring in Rehabilitation Sciences, a Health Faculty discipline. The ultimate goal of the course is to increase students' linguistic competence to allow them to function professionally in English as independent learners in all four skills: listening, reading, speaking and writing. It will be shown how Internet resources, in particular YouTube and various Google applications (Google Drive, Google Docs, Google Scholar, Google Slides, Hangouts) are used to provide and organise online content as well as to support students in the production of written and oral materials based on discipline-specific input.

Keywords: instructional technology, CEFR descriptors, English for specific academic purposes.

1.   Introduction

The CEFR for Languages (Council of Europe, 2001) provides illustrative scales of 'Can Do' statements, describing foreign language proficiency at six levels, which

1. Cyprus University of Technology, Limassol, Cyprus; jack.burston@cut.ac.cy
2. Cyprus University of Technology, Limassol, Cyprus; androulla.athanasiou@cut.ac.cy
3. Cyprus University of Technology, Limassol, Cyprus; maro.neophytou@cut.ac.cy

How to cite this article: Burston, J., Athanasiou, A., & Neophytou-Yiokari, M. (2016). Using instructional technology to integrate CEFR 'can do' performance objectives into an advanced-level language course. In S. Papadima-Sophocleous, L. Bradley & S. Thouësny (Eds), *CALL communities and culture – short papers from EUROCALL 2016* (pp. 69-73). Research-publishing.net. https://doi.org/10.14705/rpnet.2016.eurocall2016.540

enable the comparability of tests and examinations across languages and national boundaries and the recognition of language qualifications. Instructional technology can facilitate the attainment of 'Can Do' skills in many ways by providing learners with an abundance of resources for both practising and producing the target language. Moreover, in Languages for Specific Academic Purposes courses, technology adds to the 'specific' and 'academic' components since it helps to develop complementary skills like online library searching, retrieving and evaluating academic and other material on the Internet, preparing assignments and presentations using digital tools, etc. Although the linguistic part of any language course can be readily aligned to the CEFR 'Can Do' statements, no such descriptors exist for related specific academic skills or the use of technology. It is, thus, the intent of this paper to help close this gap by demonstrating, within the context of an ESAP course, how instructional technology can be exploited to adapt the CEFR descriptors for B2-level competence to the teaching of both linguistic and specific academic skills.

2.   Method

The particular course that was used for purposes of demonstration is English for Rehabilitation, an ESAP at the Cyprus University of Technology. It is a two-semester compulsory subject for first-year students majoring in Rehabilitation Sciences, a Health Faculty discipline. The ultimate goal of the course is to increase students' linguistic competence to allow them to function professionally in English as independent learners in all four skills: listening, reading, speaking and writing at an advanced (B2) level. The course was implemented in collaboration with faculty members of the Department of Rehabilitation Sciences. Subject area content derives from an introductory course, simultaneously taught by this faculty in the L1 (Greek). Parts of this course were restructured to focus on the interactive use of related L2 English vocabulary and grammatical structures. Language instructors organised each semester of the ESAP course into four thematic blocks, each lasting three to four weeks.

At the beginning of each thematic block, a member of the academic staff from the Rehabilitation Sciences department gave a short lecture (30-45 minutes) in English on the block's topic. The lecture was audio-recorded in Hangouts on Air and stored in the language instructors' YouTube channel and made available to students. Over the following weeks, students undertook various tasks based on the content theme. These all involved realisations of specific B2-level 'Can Do' descriptors such as 'Listening as a member of a live audience', 'Note-taking (lectures, seminars)', 'Processing Text', and 'Sustained Monologue'.

Once the learning objectives were set, the technology tools to be used were chosen and it was decided how these were to be used in order to achieve the desired outcomes. Internet resources, in particular YouTube and various Google applications (Google Drive, Google Docs, Google Scholar, Google Slides, Hangouts) were used to provide and organise online content, as well as to support students in the production of written and oral materials based on discipline-specific input. These included listening to lectures in their field of study, taking notes and collaboratively synthesising these in written course summaries. Individual note-taking and paraphrasing of assigned disciplinary readings were also undertaken based on printed as well as web-based sources. Students were taught to take responsibility for their professional learning in English through collaborative web-based research on topics related to their discipline, for which they produced essay outlines. Communicative use of the language was practised through regular small-group interactions in class as well as through the preparation and delivery of professionally-related oral presentations using various PowerPoint functions and Prezi. Finally, students also had to provide their reflections at the end of each thematic block, which aimed to make them aware of their own learning processes and thus more independent.

Course assessment, both formative and summative, was determined in relation to students' 'Can Do' linguistic performance. The course grade was based, for both individual and group assignments, upon the extent to which students' lecture summaries, reading synopses, research outlines and oral presentations corresponded to the CEFR B2-level 'Can Do' descriptors for reading, writing, listening and speaking. As a capstone project, students produced a Google Doc-based individual e-portfolio in which they summarised the activities carried out during the course and, more generally, reflected upon their learning. The final exam, although in paper form, assessed students against the same 'Can Do' descriptors, i.e. reading a profession-related text, taking notes on it, paraphrasing some parts, summarising the whole text and showing awareness of the vocabulary learnt.

3.   Results

At the beginning of the first semester course, students were overwhelmed by the fact that they had to deal with discipline-specific material in English. Within a few weeks, however, as the lecture topics became more professionally targeted, they were not only more interested in the content, but also more engaged in the use of the language, working on summarising, synthesising, taking notes, vocabulary and language activities in English. The recurring pattern of activities in each thematic block helped students become more at ease with the assigned tasks, which they often undertook without being told.

As with the specific academic skills aspect of the course, the use of technology tools initially proved very daunting for students, most especially Google Drive. However, the support provided to students, and their own experimentation, allowed them to quickly overcome their apprehensions. After the first two thematic blocks in the first semester, students were comfortable using the various technologies and even tried out new ones (e.g. Prezi, PowerPoint) on their own. Most use of technology took place outside of class, with one student who was abroad at the time even using Skype to contribute to a group presentation in class. Above all, students had easy access to online materials and could carry out their activities via tools such as Google drive and Google docs, which were automatically saved and accessible from virtually anywhere. Ubiquitous online access to shared documents also fostered the undertaking of collaborative tasks, allowing students to easily work together to improve their English and co-construct disciplinary knowledge.

4.   Conclusions

Overall, it can be said that technology, especially Google applications, played a vital role in realising the 'Can Do' objectives of the English for Rehabilitation course. The course Google Drive allowed instructors to store and distribute course materials in digital form as well as link to a multitude of online resources. With Google Docs, students had access to their own work online at any time. So, too, the online collaborative work that the Google Drive and Google Docs made possible constituted a motivational factor for all group members in the completion of activities, as well as a means for improving linguistically, especially for lower level students. Finally, Google docs provided the platform for the e-portfolios in which students synthesised all work (assessed and non-assessed) carried out in each semester, constituting in effect each student's self-generated online textbook for the course.

5.   Acknowledgements

We would like to thank Dr Maria Kambanaros, Dr Kakia Petinou and Ms Despo Minaidou for their input in designing the specific course, and their support throughout the course.

References

Council of Europe. (2001). *Common European framework of reference for languages: learning, teaching, assessment.* Cambridge: Cambridge University Press. http://www.coe.int/t/dg4/linguistic/cadre1_en.asp

Exploiting behaviorist and communicative action-based methodologies in CALL applications for the teaching of pronunciation in French as a foreign language

Jack Burston[1], Olga Georgiadou[2], and Monique Monville-Burston[3]

Abstract. This article describes the use of instructional technology to promote, through a combination of behaviorist/structuralist and communicative/action-based methodologies, correct pronunciation of French as a Foreign Language (FFL) to native Greek-speaking false-beginner-level learners. It is based on the analysis of a teaching programme, complemented by an end-of-semester student evaluation questionnaire. Within the curriculum of the A1/A2 level French courses at Cyprus University of Technology (CUT), learners acquire the spoken language largely through communicative action-based tasks. In addition, teacher-authored preparatory exercises, created using the *Schoolshape* digital language lab system, provide the content of pronunciation exercises. Being cloud-based, *Schoolshape* allows teaching and learning to extend out of the classroom. Students can complete exercises virtually anywhere there is a broadband Internet connection and receive immediate automatic feedback as well as profit from the asynchronous online monitoring of their instructor. Moreover, the pronunciation exercises, whose substance is linked to the action-based tasks, can be meaningfully integrated into the communicative curriculum. An end-of-year survey collects feedback from students concerning the attention paid to their pronunciation in general and their use of *Schoolshape* in particular.

Keywords: phonetic correction, behaviorist methodologies, structuralist methodologies, action-based methodologies, digital language lab.

1. Cyprus University of Technology, Limassol, Cyprus; jack.burston@cut.ac.cy
2. Cyprus University of Technology, Limassol, Cyprus; olga.georgiadou@cut.ac.cy
3. Cyprus University of Technology, Limassol, Cyprus; monique.burston@cut.ac.cy

How to cite this article: Burston, J., Georgiadou, O., & Monville-Burston, M. (2016). Exploiting behaviorist and communicative action-based methodologies in CALL applications for the teaching of pronunciation in French as a foreign language. In S. Papadima-Sophocleous, L. Bradley & S. Thouësny (Eds), *CALL communities and culture – short papers from EUROCALL 2016* (pp. 74-80). Research-publishing.net. https://doi.org/10.14705/rpnet.2016.eurocall2016.541

1.   Introduction

In this article we describe the use of instructional technology to promote, through a combination of behaviorist/structuralist and communicative/task-based methodologies, correct pronunciation of FFL to native Greek-speaking false-beginner-level learners.

Computer-Assisted Language Learning (CALL) has long been valued for its potential to extend teaching out of the classroom (Reinders & Darasawang, 2012), which for oral production is essential given the practical constraints on in-class activities. CALL pronunciation programs designed for this purpose are numerous[4]. However, in attempting to exploit such online resources, teachers of FFL are confronted by two considerable shortcomings. Firstly, the majority of these websites are generic in nature and thus do not take account of L1-specific factors (here Cypriot Greek). Secondly, practice exercises are typically undertaken in isolation from communicative activities. Overcoming these obstacles requires teachers to create materials attuned to the L1 of their learners and integrated into the syllabus. In so doing, the ultimate goal is to foster the acquisition of correct pronunciation, not just in isolated exercises, but in spontaneous speech linked to meaningful discourse (Abou Haidar & Llorca, 2016). The following discussion describes how these challenges were addressed in two FFL courses at CUT.

2.   Teaching/learning spoken French
   in A1/A2 level courses at the CUT

The students involved in our study were enrolled in two courses during the 2016 Spring semester (Level 1 [CEFR A1] and Level 2 [CEFR A2]). They had studied French for four years in secondary school, or more in private institutes. In general, their speech was strongly accented to the point of preventing intelligibility, in particular at Level 1. The two courses adopt an action-based approach and aim to give students the opportunity to express themselves autonomously and authentically in situations as close as possible to those of everyday life. Learners acquire the spoken language largely through the in-class and out-of-class preparation of dialogues they create in making three short video clips which they film using their mobile phones. The work is individual and/or collective (in teams of two or three). The preparation of these clips includes the acquisition of grammar, vocabulary,

---

4. For a general discussion on CALL resources for pronunciation instruction and on their merits and limitations, see Derwing and Munro (2015).

phraseology, pragmatics and some aspects of pronunciation related to the themes of the role-plays (Level 1: getting to know someone, describing my house, giving directions; Level 2: at the market, at the restaurant, introducing oneself for an internship). From the beginning, students are made aware that pronunciation is taken into account in the evaluation of their video clips and in the midterm and final exams, which motivates them to take it seriously. There being little time for in-depth work on pronunciation in class, the great part of phonetic correction is undertaken out of class with *Schoolshape.*

3.   Using the Schoolshape digital language lab system

3.1.   Presentation of Schoolshape

Operating entirely from a remote cloud-based server, *Schoolshape* (www. schoolshape.com) is accessible from any broadband Internet connection, which facilitates its use both within and outside the classroom. The pronunciation exercises developed in *Schoolshape* are closely linked to the vocabulary, grammar and content of task-based role-play activities. Since they are audio recorded, the results of these exercises can be monitored by instructors to track student progress and more effectively target follow-up correction. The latter is done during face-to-face debriefing sessions which follow the evaluation of the role-plays.

3.2.   Types of exercises

Before starting phonetic training exercises, *Schoolshape* is used to establish a general phonological profile of each class and individual profiles for each student. This is accomplished by audio recording the pronunciation of key words containing known difficulties (e.g. front rounded vowels, nasal vowels, voiced-voiceless plosives)[5]. The purpose of these profiles is to provide more precise, better-targeted and more effective remedial work. Thanks to the flexibility of its management system, *Schoolshape* can be used to assign exercises to a class, as well as to individuals so they can work specifically on their own problems.

Aural discrimination exercises are exploited to make same/different judgements and to identify which particular sounds are heard (Figure 1).

---

5. These key words are taken from the Interphonologie du Français Contemporain corpus list (http://cblle.tufs.ac.jp/ipfc/)

Figure 1.   Aural discrimination exercises

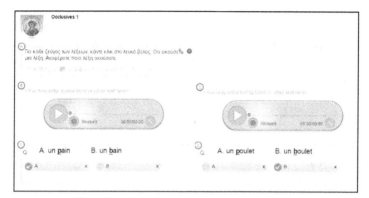

As learners gain competence in discriminating between the sounds of the L1 and the L2 as well as between L2 sounds, they also begin to notice the gap (Schmidt, 2010) between their own pronunciation and that of normative models. Listen/ repeat exercises are used to provide pronunciation practice with words and short phrases containing targeted phonological features. Written language is exploited to provide visual support for oral output and establish phonological correspondences with the orthographic system (note the underlined consonants in Figure 1).

The reading out loud and recording of model words and phrases provides both pronunciation practice and preparation for task-based role-plays (Figure 2). This is followed up with interactive communicative exercises: virtual simulated dialogues without written support in which students record their responses to oral prompts.

Figure 2.   Model words and phrases

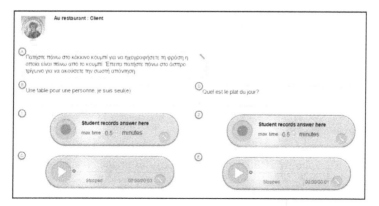

Schoolshape exercises are specifically designed to target the pronunciation difficulties of Cypriot learners (e.g. the absence of phonemic distinction between voiceless and voiced plosives – See Figure 1). Cognate French-English vocabulary also receives special attention to redress the strong contaminating effect of the L2 English pronunciation of words with similar or identical spelling in both languages (e.g. *commerce, finance, Internet*). For all exercises, the recording of students' productions allows the instructor to asynchronously monitor learners' progress and is the basis for the face-to-face sessions.

4.　　Students' evaluation of the *Schoolshape* program

All students (36) answered an end-of-semester evaluation questionnaire concerning the pronunciation teaching method used in the courses and the improvement of their pronunciation. As is attested in the following results, overall student reaction to the *Schoolshape* program was very positive. Over 93% of students felt that the exercises improved their pronunciation, 50% appreciably and 44.4% a lot (Figure 3).

Figure 3.　*Schoolshape*: improved pronunciation

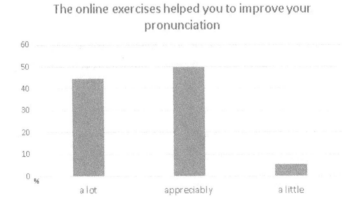

Since the purpose of the *Schoolshape* exercises was to improve the students' phonetic accuracy and speaking skills by focusing on the pronunciation of words or phrases that they would need for the creation of their filmed dialogues/presentations, they were asked about the impact of these exercises on the creation of their videos. Here again, the great majority (83%) indicated that *Schoolshape* had helped a lot (44.4%) or appreciably (38.8%) (Figure 4). The instructors observed that the

Schoolshape simulated dialogues in particular had provided effective training. The set phrases relevant to specific role-play situations that had been practiced with *Schoolshape* were internalized by students and enunciated more confidently, with phonetic features (segmental and suprasegmental) that rendered them intelligible.

Figure 4.   *Schoolshape*: video creation

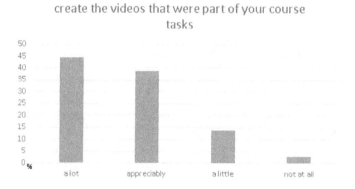

Lastly, when students were asked to indicate in what way(s) *Schoolshape* helped them to improve their pronunciation, the most frequent responses were that the exercises allowed them to listen to and repeat words/sentences (36.1%) and to become aware of what the correct pronunciation was (30.5%). A quantitative analysis of the progress made by students in their production of specific segmental phonetic features was done at the end of the semester for the Level 1 students (22). The features were: the vowels /y/ and /u/, the voiceless plosive /t/ in *étudiant* and the silent final consonant in *étudiant*. The students' productions in the initial profiles were compared to their reading aloud of short sentences during the final oral exam. Correct pronunciations improved from 15% to 54% for /y/; from 25% to 77% for /u/; from 5% to 73% for /t/. 68% of students did not pronounce the final <t> while the majority did at the beginning of the course.

5.   Conclusion

Though out of fashion, behaviorist/structuralist focus-on-form exercises (for perception and production) nonetheless remain a methodologically valid approach to L2 pronunciation training. Thanks to the cloud-based instructional technology of the type provided by *Schoolshape*, it is now possible to exploit structuralist concepts such as contrastive analysis and phonemic opposition in remedial exercises that can be undertaken anywhere a student has access to an Internet connection. Freed from the normal constraints of classroom time, the acquisition of correct pronunciation can be integrated into a communicative/action-based curriculum in a way that is motivating for students. Above all, our experience to date shows that there was substantial progress in the students' pronunciation of the phonetic features targeted during the semester.

References

Abou Haidar, L., & Llorca, R. (Eds). (2016). *L'oral par tous les sens: de la phonétique corrective à la didactique de la parole. Recherches et Applications-FDM, No 60.* Paris: CLE International.

Derwing, T. M., & Munro, M. J. (2015). *Pronunciation fundamentals – Evidence-based perspectives for L2 teaching and research.* Amsterdam: John Benjamins. https://doi.org/10.1075/lllt.42

Reinders, H., & Darasawang, P. (2012). Diversity in learner support. In G. Stockwell (Ed.), *Computer-assisted language learning: diversity in research and practice* (pp. 49-70). New York, NY: Cambridge University Press. https://doi.org/10.1017/CBO9781139060981.004

Schmidt, R. (2010). Attention, awareness, and individual differences in language learning. In W-M. Chan et al. (Eds), *Proceedings of CLaSIC 2010*, Singapore, December 2-4 (pp. 721-737). Singapore: National University of Singapore.

Mobile assisted language learning of less commonly taught languages: learning in an incidental and situated way through an app

Cristiana Cervini[1], Olga Solovova[2],
Annukka Jakkula[3], and Karolina Ruta[4]

Abstract. Learning has been moving out of classrooms into virtual and physical spaces for over a decade now (Naismith, Lonsdale, Vavoula, & Sharples, 2004). It is becoming mobile 'in space', i.e. carried across various domains (workplace, home, places of leisure), 'in time', as it encompasses different moments of the day, and in terms of 'learning purpose', which may be related to work, self-improvement or leisure (Vavoula & Sharples, 2002). In line with the principles of learning in an informal, incidental and mobile way, an open source and geolocalised application for learning foreign languages with a smartphone is being implemented within Key Action 2 of the Erasmus Plus European framework by the project called ILOCALAPP - Incidentally Learning Other Cultures and Languages – (Ceccherelli et al., 2016). ILOCALAPP will result in an app to aid in learning Finnish, Italian, Polish and Portuguese embedded within their respective cultural practices. The target group is mobility students, so the app will be situated in the university city where international students arrive, i.e. the Finnish language content will unfold in Rovaniemi, Italian in Bologna, Polish in Poznań, and Portuguese in Coimbra. The learning content will blend in the students' everyday contexts, whereby the app would be used incidentally in a game-like manner, thus providing enjoyable learning moments throughout their daily activities in an informal way.

Keywords: MALL, incidental learning, geolocalisation, multilingualism, less commonly taught languages.

1. University of Bologna, Bologna, Italy; cristiana.cervini@unibo.it
2. University of Coimbra, Coimbra, Portugal; olga@ces.uc.pt
3. University of Lapland, Rovaniemi, Finland; annukka.jakkula@ulapland.fi
4. Adam Mickiewicz University, Poznań, Poland; karuta@amu.edu.pl

How to cite this article: Cervini, C., Solovova, O., Jakkula, A., & Ruta, K. (2016). Mobile assisted language learning of less commonly taught languages: learning in an incidental and situated way through an app. In S. Papadima-Sophocleous, L. Bradley & S. Thouësny (Eds), *CALL communities and culture – short papers from EUROCALL 2016* (pp. 81-86). Research-publishing.net. https://doi.org/10.14705/rpnet.2016.eurocall2016.542

1.   Introduction

Measures on the promotion of lesser used languages in Europe have been established by the European Commission since the late 1980s. Languages spoken in the countries of ILOCALAPP partners fall within the multilingualism policies on Less Widely Used and Taught Languages in Europe (European Commission, 2011). The acknowledgement of the importance of informal learning in lifelong education within the EU, as well as the implementation of common policies for mobility by Erasmus Plus programme provide common political guidelines for the ILOCALAPP project.

Online and mobile technologies have opened up exciting new possibilities for study in higher education. Mobile learning can make boundaries between educational settings, life and work more permeable. Our app will build on mobile devices while exploiting their built-in sensors (e.g. GPS, gyroscope, accelerometer, camera), as well as an Internet connection, thus enabling to detect and identify user activities and trigger some contextual contents and activities related to specific geolocalised Points of Interest (POIs). As the user gets close to a POI, the app will upload relevant contents and activities (e.g. ordering food in a café, asking for directions). With the app, learning languages becomes more accessible in various situations, collaborative and participatory. By foregrounding cultural values and practices, it provides opportunities for authenticity, communicativeness and inclusion.

2.   Mobile technologies and learning of languages and cultures: some theoretical underpinnings

We start off from the theories of situated and incidental learning where all learning is embedded in the learners' social, cultural and historical contexts, representing interaction with their lifeworlds (Lave & Wenger, 1991). Integral to this process becomes participation in a community that shares certain cultural values, assumptions and rules, i.e. a community of practice. So in an app that supports mobility, the cultural identities of the student and surrounding community become especially important. Cultures and languages are viewed as mutually dependent – as parts of the complex language-culture nexus which is historically and ideologically situated (Risager, 2006). The app serves as an interactive device that mediates and sustains the process of discovering new cultures and languages, while learners get engaged in open and fluid social relations (Lankshear & Knobel, 2006).

The need of combining mobile technologies with language/culture learning led to creating an interdisciplinary methodological framework at the interface between multimedia design, digital literacy and language teaching/learning. The resulting framework is oriented around three interrelated thematic clusters: (1) collaborative and participatory, (2) integrated and situated, and (3) informal and incidental.

By developing a collaborative and participatory app, the ILOCALAPP team aimed to ensure an effective learner participation throughout all stages of the app development, from outlining its contents to the use and dissemination. Channels for user collaboration and participation were opened through active consultation (by carrying out surveys and focus groups with mobility students) and participant observation of users while being engaged with the preliminary app contents (through experience prototyping). The learning, use of the app and the content development are thus co-constructive (Castillo & Ayala, 2012; Traxler & Kukulska-Hulme, 2016).

The app will also be integrated and situated, so that its content is based on authentic and real-life situations, while the learning is context-aware. The context for ILOCALAPP is the daily student life in one of the partner university cities – well within the overall trend for mobile learning, which had evolved from learning with computers to being part of the ubiquitous use of mobile devices (through POIs and geolocalisation).

Finally, the app will be informal and incidental: both the contexts, contents and use of the app are situated outside the classroom and within the everyday activities of a mobility student (Laurillard, 2007; Silva, 2007). Units and exercises of formal learning are replaced by POIs, a flow of activities and game-like elements in the app contents.

3.   From theory to the content design

Factors of diverse nature contribute to the efficacy of foreign language acquisition, from internal factors such as aptitude, age, cognitive styles, motivations, etc., to external ones, like sociocultural features of the contexts learners live in. The richness and variety of the linguistic input, as well as the significance of the communicative situation learners experience, play a crucial role in the process of spontaneous acquisition. To ensure its exploitability and usability, the input should be comprehensible (Krashen, 1985), so access to written and oral texts is essential before interaction. Mapped onto the core values (collaborative/participatory, integrated/situated, and informal/incidental), the linguistic acquisition principles have guided the ILOCALAPP team in the conception of authentic contents for each town, in order to provide useful materials for students' daily life actions and interactions for language learning.

Contents will be accessible through three different points of entry: 'In the place', 'Activities', and 'Culture'. The entry 'In the place' comprises nine categories as informed by the lived experiences of an Erasmus student in a new town: (1) *Uni Life*, (2) *Getting around*, (3) *Food & Drink*, (4) *Sights*, (5) *Entertainment*, (6) *Lifestyle*, (7) *Services*, (8) *Shopping*, and (9) *Me in...* Each category includes sub-categories; for example, in 'Sights', users can explore POIs linked to the most relevant 'squares', 'monuments', and 'parks' in town, etc.

Me in... seems to be the most innovative category: an open space where users can personalise the app content by bookmarking their favourite linguistic and communicative resources. It provides the app users with a space to negotiate their own cultural identities and practices as well as find affinities with other users, thus building a community of practice.

Geolocalisation will also facilitate the content exploration thanks to active notifications about the different POIs. App users are expected to be inquiring cultural and historical information about the place, but are also encouraged to interact with other speakers in it. For this reason, the section 'Tips for talking' consists of suggestions of words and expressions useful and coherent with the local communicative situation. Simultaneously, the section 'Talk' will provide ready-made sentences in a written/audio format, followed by prototypical answers.

A robust effort has been made to let typical situations of the Erasmus students inform the app content and also to foresee their potential difficulties in understanding written and oral content, considering the following challenges:

- the app is not strictly addressed to users of a certain level of proficiency, so readjustment will be needed to ensure the materials' authenticity;

- a valid interlinguistic and intercultural model will not be easy to achieve: mobility students learning Italian and Portuguese may count on intercomprehension and positive transfer, whereas most mobility students in Poznań and Rovaniemi are beginners in Polish and Finnish, so comprehension can constitute a major challenge.

4. Final considerations and conclusion

One of the main challenges for the ILOCALAPP team resides in the fact that the app will be launched in 2018, thus needing a considerable foresight to produce an app that would still be appealing and relevant to the students' social, cultural and historical realities in 2018 and beyond. From a technical perspective, it is a multiplatform web app, designed according to human-computer interaction methodologies and built in standard technologies such as HTML5, CSS3 and standard scripting languages. Active ongoing contact with mobility students as well as their collaboration throughout all stages of the app development will be necessary to keep abreast of their lifestyle and potential changes under way. Mobile devices are ubiquitous and could be assumed to be present in everyday lives of mobility students in the future. Most importantly, the next generation of mobile learning is becoming increasingly 'context-aware' (Traxler & Kukulska-Hulme, 2016). So ideally, students would see our app as part of their everyday lives to provide a pleasant moment of informal and incidental learning amidst their mundane and institutional activities. Apart from enhancing student mobility experience, the ILOCALAPP team wants the app to pave the way both for spontaneous, motivating and context-aware language learning as well as for cultural awareness.

5. Acknowledgements

This paper is based on the work developed within the ILOCALAPP Project (www. ilocalapp.eu). ILOCALAPP (Incidentally Learning Other Cultures And Languages through an APP) is a three-year Erasmus+ project carried out by a transnational consortium of four partners: the University of Bologna (Italy), the Adam Mickiewicz University (Poznań, Poland), the University of Lapland (Rovaniemi, Finland) and the Centre for Social Studies at the University of Coimbra (Portugal). The authors wish to express their gratitude to all project partners for their active and fruitful cooperation.

References

Castillo, S., & Ayala, G. (2012). Mobile learning. In N. M. Seel (Ed.), *Encyclopedia of the sciences of learning* (pp. 2293-2295). Berlin: Springer.

Ceccherelli, A., Cervini, C., Magni, E., Mirri, S., Roccetti, M., Salomoni, P., & Valva, A. (2016). The ILOCALAPP project: a smart approach to language and culture acquisition. *The Future of Education Conference Proceedings* (pp. 270-275). Firenze: Pixel Libreria Universitaria.

European Commission. (2011). *Policy recommendations for the promotion of multilingualism in the European Union.* Brussels: Civil Society Platform on Multilingualism. http://ec.europa.eu/languages/information/language-related-tools/civil-society-platform-multilingualism_en.htm

Krashen, S. D. (1985). *The input hypothesis: issues and implications.* New York: Longman.

Lankshear, C., & Knobel, M. (2006). *New literacies: everyday practices and classroom learning.* Maidenhead: McGraw Hill.

Laurillard, D. (2007). Pedagogical forms for mobile learning. In N. Pachler (Ed.), *Mobile learning: towards a research agenda* (pp. 153-175). London: WLE Centre, IoE.

Lave, J., & Wenger, E. (1991). *Situated learning. Legitimate peripheral participation.* Cambridge: University of Cambridge Press. https://doi.org/10.1017/CBO9780511815355

Naismith, L., Lonsdale, P., Vavoula, G., & Sharples, M. (2004). Mobile technologies and learning. *Futurelab Literature Review Series, 11.* Leicester: Leicester Research Archive.

Risager, K. (2006). *Language and culture. Global flows and local complexity.* Clevedon: Multilingual Matters.

Silva, P. M. (2007). *Epistemology of incidental learning.* PhD dissertation. Virginia Polytechnic Institute and State University.

Traxler, J., & Kukulska-Hulme, A. (2016). *Mobile learning: the next generation.* New York: Routledge.

Vavoula, G. N., & Sharples, M. (2002). KLeOs: a personal, mobile, knowledge and learning organisation system. In *Proceedings of the IEEE International Workshop on Mobile and Wireless Technologies in Education* (WMTE 2002). https://doi.org/10.1109/wmte.2002.1039239

Using object-based activities and an online inquiry platform to support learners' engagement with their heritage language and culture

Koula Charitonos[1], Marina Charalampidi[2], and Eileen Scanlon[3]

Abstract. Heritage language education is distinct from the field of second language acquisition due to having the concept of identity always at its core (Leeman, Rabin, & Roman-Mendoza, 2012). This paper draws on this concept and presents an action research study focusing on the teaching and learning of Greek as a heritage language in the context of Supplementary Education in the UK. The main aim of the study is to support young learners in gaining an understanding of how language is intertwined with social and cultural aspects. The study took place in two Greek Supplementary Schools in UK during the academic year 2015-16. The participants are learners of Greek language attending pre-GCSE, GCSE and A'Level classes (13-17 years old). For the purposes of this study, the learners used mobile and web-based technologies, i.e. nQuire-It platform (http://www.nquire-it. org), to explore their environment through specific missions. The study involved a number of classroom sessions, attendance of an inter-generational object-handling workshop run by educators based at the British Museum at each of the two schools, and also participation in a museum visit. The paper presents this study and shares some preliminary findings and insights regarding the integration of mobile technologies within heritage language learning and teaching.

Keywords: heritage language learning, supplementary education, inquiry learning, mobile technologies, young people.

1. Coventry University, Coventry, United Kingdom; koula.charitonos@coventry.ac.uk
2. University of Warwick, Coventry, United Kingdom; M.Charalampidi@warwick.ac.uk
3. The Open University, Milton Keynes, United Kingdom; eileen.scanlon@open.ac.uk

How to cite this article: Charitonos, K., Charalampidi, M., & Scanlon, E. (2016). Using object-based activities and an online inquiry platform to support learners' engagement with their heritage language and culture. In S. Papadima-Sophocleous, L. Bradley & S. Thouësny (Eds), *CALL communities and culture – short papers from EUROCALL 2016* (pp. 87-93). Research-publishing.net. https://doi.org/10.14705/rpnet.2016.eurocall2016.543

1.   Introduction

At the outset of this paper is a recognition of the fundamental relationship between language and culture and an acknowledgment that this relationship is central to any process of learning another language. Especially in the context of heritage language education where the concept of identity is at its core (Leeman et al., 2012), and young learners are seen as having an emotional connection to the culture and language of the country of origin, such ideas cannot simply be seen as a body of knowledge to be taught. Rather, it is important to view learners' "lived experience" (Anderson & Chung, 2012, p. 262) of the culture and language as a framework in which learners live their lives and communicate shared meanings with each other in their communities. In other words, we draw on a view of language as a social practice (see e.g. Kramsch, 1998), hence our intention in this paper is to move beyond a view of language simply related to acquiring grammar and vocabulary. Instead, our view of language "requires learners to engage in tasks in which they create and interpret meaning, and in which they communicate their own personal meanings and develop personal connections with the new language and culture" (Scarino & Liddicoat, 2009, p. 17).

The paper presents a small exploratory study undertaken by practitioners that draws on a blended approach to learning and utilises methods of inquiry learning (e.g. observation, data collection, reflection) and mobile technologies to facilitate young people's engagement in their learning. It largely builds upon formal instruction in the language classroom and "draws attention to a learning design that blends the physical and the digital contexts [as the study] locates itself within a body of research seeking to identify more clearly a pedagogical approach to the use of technology in a learning setting" (Charitonos & Charalampidi , 2015, p. 198).

2.   Context

2.1.   Supplementary education

As discussed by Charitonos and Charalampidi (2015), community languages in the UK "are typically taught in supplementary/complementary schools. These schools offer educational support (language, core curriculum, faith and culture) and other out-of-school activities to children attending mainstream schools (Evans & Gillan-Thomas, 2015) [and] operate in community centres, youth clubs, religious institutions and mainstream schools" (p. 199).

2.2.   Participants

The participants are learners of Greek Language attending pre-GCSE, GCSE and A'Level classes (13-17 years old) in two Greek Supplementary Schools in Buckinghamshire (N=11) and Leicestershire (N=10). The participants were attending language lessons once a week for an average of three hours in total.

2.3.   nQuire-It platform

The project takes place on the online Citizen Inquiry platform nQuire-It (http:// www.nquire-it.org), which has been designed as part of the project nQuire: Young Citizen Inquiry, coordinated by the Open University in UK. The aim of the platform is to assist citizens in conducting their own science investigations, enhancing the social investigation aspect and promoting scientific thinking and exploration of the world. Two types of missions that are available in the nQuire-it platform were used in the study: (1) Spot-it missions, a user uploads pictures for the data collection and (2) Win-it missions, a user responds to a question which requires text as an answer. For the purposes of this study, and thanks to funding received, the platform was translated in Greek (see Figure 1).

Figure 1.   Screenshot of the nQuire-It platform in Greek

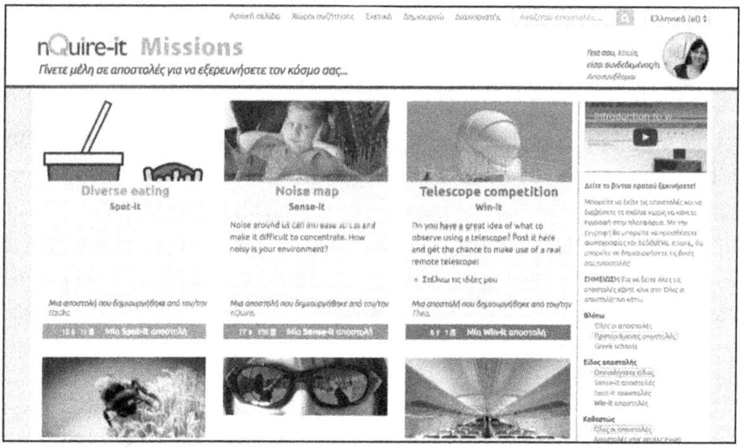

2.4.   Activities

The study consisted of a number of designed lessons involving face-to-face and online activities with specific goals that spanned over several sessions. Whole-class sessions in the classroom focused on selected aspects of the curriculum (e.g. vocabulary, i.e. nouns, connectives, adjectives; speaking, i.e. talk about routines and habits, describing objects). Additionally, the study sought to provide young learners with access to cultural experiences, hence it involved an intergenerational object-handling workshop run by educators based at the British Museum at each of the two participating schools around the theme of 'Object Journeys', and participation in a visit to the British Museum around the theme of 'People's Journeys' (Figure 2). Whereas the museum educators ran the activities in English, the participants were given the option to select any of the two languages in the tasks assigned to them and associated interactions. To ensure that all felt included, translation in both languages was provided by the teachers.

Figure 2.   Activities in the classroom

The online missions that have been created on the nQuire-It platform involved questions related to the learners' everyday life (e.g. 'ItsAHabit') or their material environment heritage (e.g. 'Looking for #AllThingsGreek', 'My very own museum'). These initial missions were initiated by the two teachers, with an aim to engage learners with aspects of inquiry learning (e.g. observation, data collection, reflection). Students were asked to use only Greek on the online platform. An example of a mission is described in the following section.

3.   Example: mission 'Looking for #AllThingsGreek'

The Spot-It mission 'Looking for #AllThingsGreek' involved participants exploring their environment and taking photographs of objects that could be associated with, or remind them of Cyprus or Greece. 17 users joined this mission on the nQuire-It platform and 18 photos were uploaded (Figure 3). The members of this mission could make comments and like other contributions and had the opportunity to win the prize for the best photograph.

Figure 3.   Mission on the nQuire-It platform: 'Looking for #AllThingsGreek'

Each mission involved preparatory and follow-up activities in the classroom. For example, prior to the mission 'Looking for #AllThingsGreek', students explored their school to spot objects that could be linked to Cyprus or Greece and provided descriptions and explanations in Greek related to their choice of particular objects. A follow-up activity took place in the classroom, where students had the opportunity to examine the whole data set of the photos uploaded on the platform, and, through group interactions and facilitated discussion with the teacher, to engage with observations, analysis and reflection. This activity is described in detail in a forthcoming publication (see Charitonos, forthcoming).

Preliminary findings from this mission point to students being engaged in this task, describing the objects and communicating their meanings around the objects that could be found in their own environments, such as souvenirs, faith items, crafts, and everyday objects. Students were able to make the connection between the physical and the digital contexts, though not all uploaded their photos online. Another finding is that students' own experiences with technology determined their engagement with the platform. For example, participants were asking for an app to directly upload pictures on the nQuire-It platform. In addition to this, it became apparent through their discussions with their teachers that a few shared some feelings of anxiety in creating and posting comments in Greek online. Issues of anxiety related to performance in the language-in-focus might have been a barrier in students' participation. Finally, schools' infrastructures (i.e. no internet connection) are seen as a limitation in students' participation in the study.

4.   Conclusions

The paper presented a small exploratory study that follows a learner-centred pedagogical approach in examining the integration of mobile and web-technologies in the language classroom in a way that allows young learners to engage in the social and cultural contexts they are embedded in. By blending the physical and the digital domains, and structuring students' engagement in and through missions, students could gather evidence, and offer descriptions and interpretations. The initial missions were initiated by the two teachers, but future plans include providing a general topic (e.g. Discovering your High Street) and giving control over the missions, the design, and how to carry out the investigation to the students. Future investigations could also draw on concepts (e.g. tradition) that emerge from data generated by students to generate new missions that will serve to challenge students' established ideas (e.g. What is tradition?).

5.   Acknowledgements

We would like to thank the British Academy for providing the funding for this study (British Academy Schools Language Awards 2015).

References

Anderson, J., & Chung, Y.-C. (2012). Community languages, the arts and transformative pedagogy: developing active citizenship for the 21st century. *Citizenship Teaching & Learning, 7*(3), 259-271. https://doi.org/10.1386/ctl.7.3.259_1

Charitonos, K. (forthcoming). Cultural citizen inquiry: making space for the 'everyday' in language teaching and learning. In. M. Sharples, E. Scanlon & C. Herodotou (Eds), *Citizen inquiry: a fusion of citizen science and inquiry learning.* London: Taylor & Francis.

Charitonos, K., & Charalampidi, M. (2015). Designs for heritage language learning: a photography project in the UK supplementary education. In T. H. Brown & H. J. van der Merwe (Eds), *The mobile learning voyage – From small ripples to massive open waters: 14th World Conference, mLearn 2015, Venice, Italy, October 17-24, 2015, Proceedings* (pp. 198-216). Communications in Computer and Information Science. Springer.

Evans, D., & Gillan-Thomas, K. (2015). *Supplementary schools. Descriptive analysis of supplementary school pupils' characteristics and attainment in seven local authorities in England, 2007/08— 2011/12*. Paul Hamlyn Foundation. http://www.phf.org.uk/publications/supplementary-schools-research-report/ 10 July 2015

Kramsch, C. (1998). *Language and culture* (1st ed.). Oxford University Press.

Leeman, J., Rabin, L., & Roman-Mendoza, E. (2012). Identity and activism in heritage language education. *The Modern Language Journal, 95*(4), 481-495. https://doi.org/10.1111/j.1540-4781.2011.01237.x

Scarino, A., & Liddicoat, A. J. (2009). *Teaching and learning languages: aguide.* http://www.tllg.unisa.edu.au/lib_guide/gllt.pdf. 20 September 2016

Urban explorations for language learning: a gamified approach to teaching Italian in a university context

Koula Charitonos[1], Luca Morini[2], Sylvester Arnab[3],
Tiziana Cervi-Wilson[4], and Billy Brick[5]

Abstract. The recent technological developments and widespread use of mobile technologies challenge traditional knowledge and skills, with language learning increasingly taking place beyond the language classroom in learners' own environments. The paper presents the ImparApp study that focuses on a pervasive and gamified approach to language teaching and learning. The study investigated language learning with mobile devices as an approach to augmenting language learning by taking learning outside the classroom into the real-world context. The paper reports on the design, development and testing of an introductory Italian Language Learning game, i.e. ImparApp, that is developed with the use of MIT's TaleBlazer authoring tool. Preliminary findings of the pre-pilot of the game prototype are drawing on data collected through participant observation of a play-test session followed by a focus group interview. The paper contributes to the field of mobile-assisted language learning with insights on pervasive and gamified approaches to teaching and learning a foreign language.

Keywords: mobile-assisted language learning, MALL, pervasive learning, game-based learning, higher education, Italian.

1. Introduction

Recent developments in mobile and web technologies bring great potential for innovation in teaching and learning, and inevitably influence language learning,

1. Disruptive Media Learning Lab, Coventry University, Coventry, United Kingdom; koula.charitonos@coventry.ac.uk
2. Disruptive Media Learning Lab, Coventry University, Coventry, United Kingdom; luca.morini@coventry.ac.uk
3. Disruptive Media Learning Lab, Coventry University, Coventry, United Kingdom; s.arnab@coventry.ac.uk
4. Language Centre, Coventry University, Coventry, United Kingdom; tiziana.cervi-wilson@coventry.ac.uk
5. Language Centre, Coventry University, Coventry, United Kingdom; billy.brick@coventry.ac.uk

How to cite this article: Charitonos, K., Morini, L., Cervi-Wilson, T., & Brick, B. (2016). Urban explorations for language learning: a gamified approach to teaching Italian in a university context . In S. Papadima-Sophocleous, L. Bradley & S. Thouësny (Eds), *CALL communities and culture – short papers from EUROCALL 2016* (pp. 94-99). Research-publishing.net. https://doi.org/10.14705/rpnet.2016.eurocall2016.544

arguing for the need to rethink practices. The paper presents a pervasive and gamified approach to teaching and learning Italian in a university context with an aim of engaging students towards a more enhanced learning experience. The study blends activities traditionally taking place in the classroom with activities enabled by the technology and draw inspiration on the built environment of a city, and utilises opportunities offered by location-based services that allow for narratives/activities to evolve via a learner's location. The paper examines this approach by outlining the development of ImparApp – a prototype mobile game for learners of Italian language.

2.   Context

2.1.   Language learning at Coventry University

Students at Coventry University can learn a foreign language by attending an Add+vantage module. These modules are credit bearing and aim to develop students' employability skills. The participants were attending an Italian Language Add+vantage module.

2.2.   ImparApp mobile game app

The ImparApp prototype game was developed with Tale Blazer, which is an open-source authoring tool, developed by MIT, for pervasive gaming to allow users to develop location-based augmented reality games (see Figure 1).

Figure 1.   Screenshots of the ImparApp prototype game (Part 1)

The ImparApp game engages learners in a range of experiences and interactions as they move around their real physical location seeking to solve a time travel mystery. Specific tasks are triggered by learners' Global Positioning System (GPS) coordinates, which prompt the users to explore the city of Coventry by providing information about its history and heritage. The tasks focus on the four language skills of listening, speaking, reading and writing. Importantly, the app allows the learners and tutors to monitor progress via a leaderboard. The design of the app and game mechanics are discussed in detail in Morini et al. (in press), where it is noted that a key aspect of the design approach is that it allows its users to experience their everyday living contexts and their course's content in a new and playful way.

2.3. Content and learning objectives

The ImparApp is designed to be used in a blended mode: learners spend one week in the classroom with a tutor, and the following week completing challenges and tasks with the app in a self-guided mode. Through the targeted use of this app in a beginners' module a student will have opportunities to practice speaking and writing short passages using appropriate grammatical structures for the task and the level. Further to this, a student should be in a position to recognise information and understand short texts with simple familiar words and phrases about themselves, their family, and concrete situations they know well.

In its current form, the ImparApp prototype game consists of four parts. Text in Part 1 is in English (see Figure 1) while Part 2 makes use of English and includes translation in Italian in brackets. Part 3 is in Italian and includes translation in English in brackets and finally Part 4 is in Italian. The four parts cover the following topics: yourself and others; work and family; routines, free time, leisure activities; and food and drinks. The app also embeds content that aims at raising students' awareness of the Italian culture.

3. Method

The development of the ImparApp aims to investigate the crossings of game-based learning and pervasive learning in support of language teaching and learning and, further, to empirically evaluate the consistency of a holistic and modular design model as a tool to guide the design process, as suggested by Arnab et al. (2015) (see Figure 2).

Figure 2.   Holistic and modular approach (Arnab et al., 2015, p. 454)

Layer 4: Technology	Interfaces	Media		Analytics	Communication	Content
Layer 3: Game design	Mechanics		Narratives		Aesthetics	UX/EX
Layer 2: Context of learning	Mode		Location		Activities	Assessment
Layer 1: Learning needs	Learners	Lesson path		Pedagogy	Learning objectives	Measures

Drawing on this model, the research team designed a pre-pilot play-test session to inform the development of the ImparApp prototype. This pre-pilot study took place in the Spring semester of 2016.

The pre-pilot play-test session involved testing Part 1 of the game. The participants were seven students (N=7) attending a Lower Intermediate Level Italian Language module at Coventry University (Common European Framework of Reference for languages Level A2). The students were selected as their knowledge of the Italian language was seen as allowing them to focus on usability and engagement aspects of the game (Layer 2/Layer 3 in Figure 2). Members of the research team accompanied the students, who were split in three groups (Figure 3).

Figure 3.   Play-test session in the city of Coventry

Data was collected through a number of open-ended questions posed to the participants at the beginning (e.g. Why did you accept taking part in this testing?; How competent do you feel in Italian/in using tech/in games?) and at the end of the play-test session (e.g. What would you change?; How do you see language learning 'working' within this app?); participant observation was conducted using a semi-structured observation sheet and a focus group interview that took place right after the session involving participants, tutors and researchers.

4.   Findings and discussion

All students appeared positive regarding the use of the ImparApp for language learning. The following comment by one participant is indicative: "I haven't seen this before. Usually is only dictionaries, translations... This is more interactive instead of sitting on a desk/with a book". One observation made by the research team during the play-test session was that the participants had limited interactions in the language-in-focus. This is seen as being largely associated with the design of Part 1 (i.e. introduction of the game, learning Italian phonetics and pronunciation), hence tests of Part 2 to Part 4 are currently planned with an aim to examine this observation further (Layer 2 - Activities, Figure 2). Additionally, most interactions in the groups were related to finding their orientation, an aspect that is seen associated with their game experience (Layer 3 - Mechanics, Figure 2). Future iterations will allow for more interactions among the users (Layer 1 - Pedagogy, Layer 2 - Activities, Figure 2), and with their built environment. Indications of incidental, non-language related learning, also emerged in the data (Layer 1 - In/non/formal, Figure 2). For example, a participant referred to a historic pub in Coventry: "Whitefriars Pub... I didn't know anything about the pub and the little alley behind the cathedral".

Furthermore in the focus group interview, students made a few suggestions (e.g. audio, video in Italian; Italian music; zoom map), which informed the development of the four parts of the app (also see Morini et al., in press) (Layer 2 - Mode, Figure 2). During the development process the team also responded to students' comments regarding the use of English and Italian, hence the language-in-focus is gradually introduced in the game's descriptions and instructions (see section *Content and learning objectives*).

Finally, issues of assessment were raised in the focus group interview (Layer 2, Figure 2). Students shared some concerns and expressed a preference for traditional methods of assessment. For example a participant said "you can go off the app and do the assessment... checking answers on a laptop. So, still you [teachers] need to do assessment in the class".

5.   Conclusions

The paper described a pre-pilot study focusing on new possibilities that emerge in language learning and teaching when pervasive approaches to learning are combined with game-based techniques. Initial findings show that the ImparApp game was positively perceived by a group of students, as it allowed them to experience their course's content in a new and playful way. Limited interactions in language-in-focus were observed, whilst indications of incidental, non-language related learning were noted. Comments on the mode of communication of the content, along with issues related to assessment were raised by the participants. Future developments include another pre-pilot blind-test study of the four parts of the app (Autumn 2016) to inform the next iteration of the app, and a pilot implementation of the ImparApp in the Absolute Beginners Italian Course in the university (Winter 2017). To conclude, the study prompts us to rethink the design and organisation of a university language course in terms of learner's experience, with an emphasis on context, learner's movement and interactions of the physical and virtual worlds that the learners find themselves in.

6.   Acknowledgements

This work was partly funded by the Disruptive Media Learning Lab. It has been also co-funded by the EU under the H2020 Beaconing project, Grant Agreement nr. 687676.

References

Arnab, S., Tombs, G., Duncan, M., Smith, M., & Star, K. (2015). Towards the blending of digital and physical learning contexts with a gamified and pervasive Aapproach. *Proceedings of Games and Learning Alliance (GALA) Conference, Rome, October 2015.* Springer.

Morini, L., Charitonos, K., Arnab, S., Cervi-Wilson, T., Brick, B., & Bellamy-Wood, T. (in press). ImparApp: designing and piloting a game-based approach for language learning. *Proceedings of ECGBL 2016, Paisley, Scotland.*

Communicate to learn, learn to communicate: a study of engineering students' communication strategies in a mobile-assisted learning environment

Li Cheng[1] and Zhihong Lu[2]

Abstract. This paper reports a 3-month study investigating engineering students' Communication Strategies (CSs) in a mobile-assisted course. 67 Chinese learners of English in this course volunteered to participate in the study. The instruments included oral communication sessions, stimulated recall interviews, WeChat exchanges, etc. Results showed that the participants used a variety of CSs when completing the academic tasks. Moreover, these CSs were closely related to the students' involvement in meaning negotiation while they were interacting to complete learning tasks. It is suggested that instructors have CS training tailored to their students' learning tasks. Future research should focus on a longitudinal investigation of the transfer of CSs across tasks.

Keywords: English education, communication strategies, mobile-assisted language learning, academic performance.

1.   Introduction

The effects of technology in English education have been investigated extensively in the past three decades. Researchers have claimed that learners in a class with Computer-Assisted Language Learning (CALL) have better opportunities for learning than those in the traditional approach of face-to-face instruction (e.g. Beatty, 2003). Mobile-learning, for example, has been found effective for second language (L2) learning because of the flexibility offered to L2 learners in and outside of the classroom (Godwin-Jones, 2011). Drawing on the recent researches in mobile-learning (e.g. Huang, 2014; Jamshidnejad, 2011; Jantjies & Joy, 2015),

1. Beijing University of Posts and Telecommunications, Beijing, China; licheng@bupt.edu.cn
2. Beijing University of Posts and Telecommunications, Beijing, China; luzhihong@bupt.edu.cn

How to cite this article: Cheng, L., & Lu, Z. (2016). Communicate to learn, learn to communicate: a study of engineering students' communication strategies in a mobile-assisted learning environment. In S. Papadima-Sophocleous, L. Bradley & S. Thouësny (Eds), *CALL communities and culture – short papers from EUROCALL 2016* (pp. 100-105). Research-publishing.net. https://doi.org/10.14705/rpnet.2016.eurocall2016.545

the present study aimed at examining the CS used by Chinese engineering students learning English in Mobile-Assisted Language Learning (MALL) settings.

The notion of CS in L2 education was first raised by Selinker (1972), followed by a series of systematic analysis of the definitions and taxonomies of CSs (e.g. Dörnyei & Scott, 1997; Færch & Kasper, 1983; Tarone, 1977). For the purpose of the study, Dörnyei and Scott's (1997) definition of CSs was used. According to Dörnyei and Scott (1997), CSs are problem solving devices used to handle three types of communication problems: (1) Own-performance problems (e.g. the strategy of 'self-repair'), (2) other-performance problems (e.g. the strategy of 'meaning negotiation'), and (3) processing-time pressure (e.g. the use of fillers, hesitation devices, etc).

Previous researches of CSs have mainly focused on the identification of learners' CSs. Few have been found investigating how Chinese learners use CSs in MALL contexts. The following were the research questions in the present study:

- What CSs do Chinese learners of English use when they are interacting to complete academic tasks?

- To what extent are the CSs used in-class communication sessions similar to or different from those used in WeChat interactions?

2.   Method

2.1.   Site and participants

This study was conducted in a joint program between a Chinese university and a university in the UK. The course of Professional Applications (PA) was offered to all the Year 2 Chinese students in this program in Beijing. In PA, students were expected to do various kinds of the tasks/projects including a 12-week project of organizing a Modal International Conference (MIC). The teaching contents were arranged with two hours' face-to face instruction every week supplemented by group discussions using WeChat on mobiles, one of the most popular social networking tools in China.

The study covered three months, from March to May of 2016. 'Organizing a Conference' was the focus of the study. The PA course was taught in English in China. 67 students volunteered to participate in this study. Among them, 35 were majoring in Telecommunications Engineering with Management and 32 in Internet of Things Engineering. These participants were divided into ten groups of six/seven. They made their own decisions as to which group to join in.

2.2.   Procedures

Two types of data served as the major sources for analysis of this study: (1) eight in-class communication sessions and 10 stimulated recall group interviews, and (2) the participants' WeChat exchanges with their group members while they were discussing their coursework. All the data were transcribed and coded by the researchers.

3.   Results and discussion

A total of eight hour communication sessions and five hour interviews were analyzed. The WeChat messages consisted of 18,241 words, 192 voice messages and 597 emoticons/pictures/videos. Based on Dörnyei and Scott's (1997) Inventory of Strategic Language Devices, the researchers analyzed the transcripts in in-class communication and identified 16 CSs over 33 CSs (See Table 1).

Table 1.   Description of CS use in the in-class communication sessions

	Category of CS	Examples of Discourse Markers	Frequency
1	Message abandonment	"MIC? Ur…It's a meeting?... Okay." ((With a puzzled facial expressions and frowns))	336
2	Message replacement	((Retrospective comments)) "I'm the char. I forgot how to say chengxuce ((conference program)). So I had to say something else".	245
3	Circumlocution	"Dress code means wearing shirts and suits…like this." ((Shows a picture of two students volunteers at Global Mobile Internet Conference 2015))	424
4	Approximation	Use of "composition" or "essay" instead of "conference paper"	245
5	Use of all-purpose words	"the thing", "something like that"	198
6	Word coinage	"unsatisfied", "unlegal"	88
7	Literal translation	"After I entered into this university…"	398
8	Foreignizing	"That's all simida" ((Use of the Korean word simida for stress))	88
9	Code-switching	"G si" and "G wu" ((Chinese equivalent for G4 and G5))	436
10	Repair	"Ladies and gentlemen. You're warmly welcomed…welcome."	195

11	Mime	"Nonverbal communication means... ((Demonstrates using hand gestures))...Is it clear?"	289
12	Use of fillers	"Well..."	165
13	Repetition	Speaker 1: "One writing mistake is redundancy." Speaker 2: "Redundancy"? Speaker 1: "Yes, redundancy."	210
14	Appeal for help	"Can you email me the IEEE paper template?"	321
15	Asking for clarification	"What do you mean?"	254
16	Expressing non-understanding	"I'm sorry. I don't understand."	132

Results of the CS use in the in-class communication sessions show high occurrences of 'Code-switching' (F=436), 'Circumlocution' (F=424) and 'Literal Translation' (F=398).

The WeChat data showed similar types of CSs used by the participants, except for Strategy 11 of 'Miming/Paralinguistic features'. Because of the absence of face-to-face communication in WeChat interactions, the participants tended to use more frequently the compensatory strategy of mobile-supported emoticons, voice messages, etc. Table 2 shows the frequency of the use of emoticons in WeChat messages. Emotions, in this study, refer to graphic representations in instant messaging sessions. They may be punctuations, facial expressions, numbers, letters, etc.

Table 2.   Frequency of the use of emoticons in WeChat interactions

	Category of CS	Explanation and/or Examples from the Data	Frequency
8	Foreignizing	Use of emoticons for stress/humor. Examples: , 纳尼?! (Japanese word 'nani' meaning 'what'), (Korean words: 'Ouba' means 'brother', and 'simida' indicates stress.	168
9	Code-switching	Use of emoticons which have both Chinese and English words. Examples:	146
14	Appeal for help	Examples: ('What was happening just now?'),	154

| 15 | Asking for clarification | Examples: , | 149 |
| 16 | Expressing non-understanding | Examples: , | 138 |

A closer look at the further contexts of the CSs in the participants' WeChat messages when they communicated to perform learning tasks revealed that they used those CSs not only for comprehension purposes but also for interpersonal communication purposes. The following extract is a WeChat example:

1. Jigang: Hi, everyone! We have reviewed all the papers. We'll soon announce the names of the students who will present at MIC.

2. Lily: Present at MIC?

3. Jigang: Yes, present at moni guiji huiyi (*Model International Conference)* simida.

4. Lily: Haosailei! ((The word haosailei means 'great' and has the pronunciation in Cantonese dialect. It is a popular Internet buzzword in China.))

5. Jigang: ((follows Lily's message and posts a smiley)) (# 176; 2016-04-27)

In the above situation, the first communicator makes an announcement. The phrase of 'Present at MIC' is repeated in the second turn, which is a signal for a problem in understanding. Jigang interprets this as a request asking for clarification. So in the third turn, he rephrases the term using the Chinese equivalent 'moni guoji huiyi'. In the fourth turn, Lily shows understanding and appreciation by using 'haosailei'. In recent years, many foreign cultures and languages have been introduced into China. That might explain why some foreign words such as the Korean word 'simida' (expressing stress) and the Japanese word of 'nani' (expressing anger and curiosity) were frequently used in the participants' oral communication and in their WeChat exchanges.

4. Conclusions and implications

In this paper, the researchers have investigated the CS use in mobile-assisted learning environments. Three conclusions can be drawn from the above discussion. First, the L2 learners used a variety of CSs in the MALL learning settings. Second, the participants used similar types of CSs in in-class communication sessions and in WeChat interactions, except for the strategy of 'Miming/Paralinguistic features'. Finally, due to the absence of face-to-face communication in WeChat interactions, the participants used emoticons more frequently in their instant message sessions. The pedagogical implication of the study is the reachability of CSs among Chinese learners of English at the tertiary level in China. Future research should focus on a longitudinal investigation of the transfer of CSs across tasks.

References

Beatty, K. (2003). *Teaching and researching computer-assisted language learning.* Harlow: Pearson Education Limited.

Dörnyei, Z., & Scott, M. L. (1997). Communication strategies in a second language: definitions and Taxonomies. *Language Learning, 47*(1), 173-210. https://doi.org/10.1111/0023-8333.51997005

Færch, C., & Kasper, G. (1983). Plans and strategies in foreign language communication. In C. Færch & G. Kasper (Eds), *Strategies in interlanguage communication* (pp. 20-60). Harlow, UK: Longman.

Godwin-Jones, R. (2011). Mobile apps for language learning. *Language Learning & Technology, 15*(2), 2-11.

Huang, R. (2014). Exploring the moderating role of self-management of learning in mobile English learning. *Educational Technology & Society, 17*(4), 255-267.

Jamshidnejad, A. (2011). Functional approach to communication strategies: an analysis of language learners' performance in interactional discourse. *Journal of Pragmatics, 43,* 3757-3769. https://doi.org/10.1016/j.pragma.2011.09.017

Jantjies M., & Joy M. (2015). Mobile enhanced learning in South Africa context. *Educational Technology & Society, 18*(1), 308-320.

Selinker, L. (1972). Interlanguage. *International Review of Applied Linguistics, 10,* 209-230. https://doi.org/10.1515/iral.1972.10.1-4.209

Tarone, E. (1977). Conscious communication strategies in interlanguage: a progress report. In H. D. Brown, C. A. Yorio & R. C. Crymes (Eds), *On TESOL '77* (pp. 194-203). Washington: TESOL.

Using a dialogue system based on dialogue maps
for computer assisted second language learning

Sung-Kwon Choi[1], Oh-Woog Kwon[2], Young-Kil Kim[3], and Yunkeun Lee[4]

Abstract. In order to use dialogue systems for computer assisted second-language learning systems, one of the difficult issues in such systems is how to construct large-scale dialogue knowledge that matches the dialogue modelling of a dialogue system. This paper describes how we have accomplished the short-term construction of large-scale and machine-readable dialogue maps that match the modelling of a dialogue system. The dialogue map is a kind of graph consisting of sub-tasks, instance-to-slots, and constraints such as 'necessary' or 'optional'. It took 5.36 months to implement a dialogue modelling in the existing dialogue system.

Keywords: dialogue map, dialogue system, dialogue system based on dialogue maps, computer assisted second language learning.

1. Introduction

A dialogue system is a computer system able to converse with a human. This system has clear potential for Computer-Assisted Language Learning (CALL) that places the second-language learner in a practical situation where a specific task has to be accomplished in the foreign language. Dialogue systems can be divided into two main classes: task-oriented and chat-bot systems. Task-oriented dialogue systems provide a framework for users to have conversations with a machine to do a task such as reserving a hotel or giving bus schedule information (Raux & Eskenazi, 2004; Young, Gašic, Thomson, & Williams, 2013). A state-of-the-art of task-oriented dialogue systems is to study a reinforcement learning based

1. Electronics and Telecommunications Research Institute, Daejeon, Korea; choisk@etri.re.kr
2. Electronics and Telecommunications Research Institute, Daejeon, Korea; ohwoog@etri.re.kr
3. Electronics and Telecommunications Research Institute, Daejeon, Korea; kimyk@etri.re.kr
4. Electronics and Telecommunications Research Institute, Daejeon, Korea; yklee@etri.re.kr

How to cite this article: Choi, S.-K., Kwon, O.-W., Kim, Y.-K., & Lee, Y. (2016). Using a dialogue system based on dialogue maps for computer assisted second language learning. In S. Papadima-Sophocleous, L. Bradley & S. Thouësny (Eds), *CALL communities and culture – short papers from EUROCALL 2016* (pp. 106-112). Research-publishing.net. https://doi.org/10.14705/rpnet.2016.eurocall2016.546

on Partially Observable Markov Decision Processes (POMDP) and Deep Neural Networks (DNN) that can make speech recognition and the language understanding robust (Henderson, Thomson, & Young, 2013; Young et al., 2013). However, task-oriented dialogue systems were not successfully deployed on a commercial scale because defining the dialogue acts was difficult. A chat-bot system does not aim at processing a task-oriented dialogue, but seeks to make a conversation with one or more human users. Also, the chat-bot system has the limit of repetitive response to the same question. To overcome this issue, a state-of-the-art of chat-bot systems is to extract the personal information from user utterances and to apply the personal information to a chat-bot conversation (Matter & Wachsmuth, 2014; Kim et al., 2015). This paper concentrates on the task-oriented dialogue system (hereafter, dialogue system) that is closely related with a dialogue-based CALL system. One of the difficult issues in these systems is to construct large-scale dialogue knowledge such as dialogue scenarios that match the modelling of a dialogue system. The existing dialogue modelling had the following weaknesses:

- Small-scale dialogue scenarios, which were manually made by professional educationists for second-language learning study.

- Difficult dialogue acts, which were defined and constructed by experts of dialogue systems.

This paper describes how we have accomplished the short-term construction of large-scale and machine-readable dialogue knowledge that matches the dialogue modelling of a dialogue system.

2. Production problem of dialogue knowledge for dialogue systems

Dialogue systems can talk with users by training knowledge through machine learning. The existing methods to build dialogue knowledge for dialogue systems can be classified into three parts: (1) extracting dialogue knowledge from real dialogue examples (Lee, Lee, & Lee, 2010), (2) building dialogue knowledge from logs of dialogue systems (Hong et al., 2009), and (3) manually making dialogue knowledge (Choi, Kwon, Jeong, & Kim, 2013).

An example of computer assisted second language learning using a dialogue system is GenieTutor (Kwon, Lee, Kim, & Lee, 2015). It was made with the purpose of English learning for Korean people and showed the correction of grammar errors and the overall feedback in fixed dialogue situations. In order to make diverse talk with Korean learners, GenieTutor needed large dialogue knowledge operable on dialogue systems. Acts were coded in the knowledge of GenieTutor. Dialogue flow was constructed by experts who know GenieTutor. It took 5.36 months to choose a task and build the whole dialogue knowledge of the task. So we could not help building a small quantity of dialogue knowledge. GenieTutor talked with Korean learners at a constricted level of dialogue and gave feedback to limited grammar error correction.

3. Construction of dialogue map and discussion

3.1. Position of dialogue map

Dialogue map is a database in which sub-tasks of a task and dialogue turns of a sub-task build a form of graph. Dialogue knowledge automatically extracted from the map is used in dialogue understanding and management. Figure 1 shows the position of the dialogue map in GenieTutor.

Figure 1.   Position of dialogue map in GenieTutor

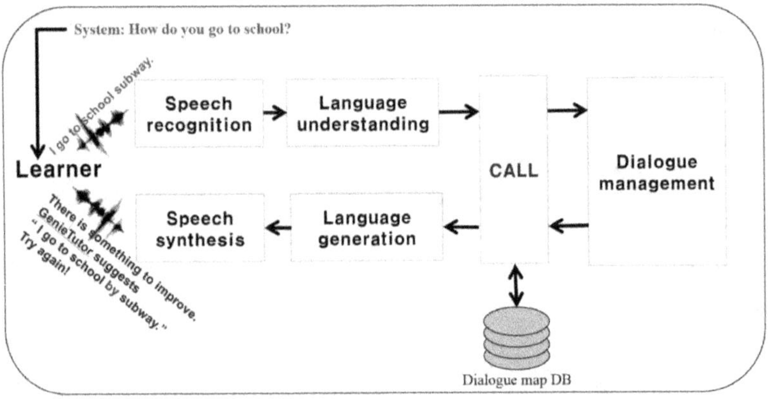

GenieTutor is a kind of hybrid system consisting of a dialogue system and a CALL system. Its dialogue system is made up of speech recognition, language understanding, dialogue management, language generation, and speech synthesis. Its CALL system is located between the language understanding module and the dialogue management module and takes charge of the second language learning. The dialogue knowledge of both the language understanding module and the dialogue management module are trained from the dialogue map database. The dialogue map database could be made by educators who do not know a dialogue system.

3.2. Configuration of dialogue map

A dialogue map consists of the following: tasks, sub-tasks that constitute a task, dialogue materials that compose each sub-task, turns including the materials, and paraphrases which are equivalent to a meaning of dialogue turn. A sub-task can have his subordinate sub-tasks. Sub-tasks can make diverse dialogue paths through constraint operators that decide whether a sub-task is necessary or optional within a task and protect reverse order among sub-tasks. Figure 2 shows a structure of a dialogue map.

Figure 2.   Structure of dialogue map

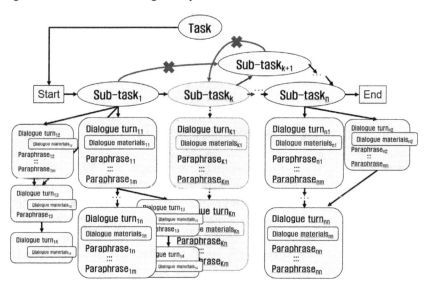

For example, let us assume a task 'ordering food'. This task can be consisted of some sub-tasks like 'Start -> greeting -> choosing main dishes -> ordering side dishes -> asking for the bill -> saying good bye -> End'. The sub-task 'choosing main dishes' would be filled with the following dialogue turns between system and user:

Task: 'ordering food'
Sub-task: 'choosing main dishes'
Dialogue materials: 'omelette', 'steak and eggs', 'French toast'
Dialogue turn:

> System: "What would you like to order?"
> User: "I would like to have the omelette."
> Paraphrase: "I'll try the omelette."
> System: "We have two kinds of omelettes, mushroom and cheese. Which one would you like?"
> User: "I would like to have the mushroom."

3.3. Method of construction of dialogue map

Professional educators build the dialogue scenarios. By using an authoring tool, they would make maps from scenarios. The authoring tool is under development.

First, dialogue scenarios can be produced by the following procedure: (1) set a task, (2) set the sub-tasks, (3) set the constraints, and (4) input dialogue turns including dialogue materials. A sub-task can also possess its subordinate sub-tasks. Sub-tasks are similar to concept of script of Schank and Abelson (1977) because scripts are structures of actions that describe a chain of events in a certain situation. Dialogue materials means core vocabularies of dialogue turns that second-language learners have to learn. Dialogue turns are sentences of talking between system and user and are constructed by dialogue materials of a sub-task. Paraphrases are built on the basis of a representative dialogue turn.

After constructing scenarios, we can make a dialogue map from the dialogue scenarios through an authoring tool with the following functions: (1) convert sentences of a scenario to the format of a dialogue map, (2) replace the materials with slot variables of the dialogue system, (3) automatically generate dialogue acts from sentences, (4) mark the command to directly move from a sentence to a sub-task, (5) show the calculus that calculates price, sums the number, and (6) visualize whole dialogue map. Figure 3 shows a sample of a dialogue map that was built from a dialogue scenario with a task 'ordering food'.

A dialogue act is automatically generated from a sentence. For example, the dialogue act of the sentence 'I would like to have the <maindishes_name>. @ maindishes_name = {'steak and eggs', 'french toast'}' is 'would_like_to_have_ maindishes (maindishes=steak_and_eggs)' which consists of a verbal phrase and a noun phrase like first order logic.

Figure 3.   A sample of dialogue map of a task 'ordering food'

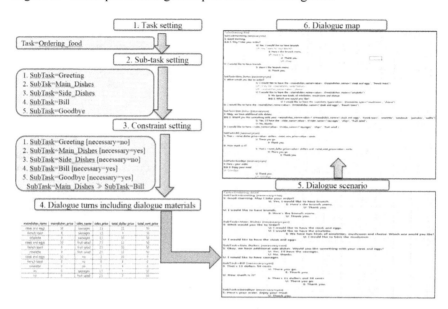

3.4.   Discussion

As mentioned in section 2, it is less time consuming to construct a dialogue map, as opposed to dialogue knowledge within an existing dialogue system. These maps connect first to a dialogue system and operate normally as a core knowledge base of dialogue-based CALL systems. The duration of constructing a dialogue map should get shorter because in the near future we will provide the educationists with an authoring tool to (1) systematically construct the dialogue scenario, (2) automatically convert a sentence into a dialogue act, (3) semi-automatically replace dialogue materials with slot variables, and (4) visualize the whole dialogue map.

4.   Conclusions

This paper describes the dialogue-based CALL system based on dialogue maps. The format and construction method of dialogue maps were detailed. The authoring tool for constructing a dialogue map is under construction. Our goal is that a duration of construction of a dialogue map is reduced from a month to two weeks. We are planning to expand the tasks of dialogue maps which are not fixed, but are free.

5. Acknowledgements

This work was supported by the ICT R&D program of MSIP/IITP [R0126-15-1117, Core technology development of the spontaneous speech dialogue processing for the language learning].

References

Choi, S. K., Kwon, O. W., Jeong, S. G., & Kim, Y. K. (2013). Method constructing dialog act tagged corpus for English dialog system for travel. *Korea Computer Congress of Korean Institute of Information Scientists and Engineers* (pp. 619-621, in Korean).

Henderson, M., Thomson, B., & Young, S. (2013). Deep neural network approach for the dialog state tracking challenge. *Proceedings of the 2013 SIGDIAL* (pp. 467-471).

Hong, G., Lee, J. H., Shin, J. H., Lee, D. G., & Rim, H. C. (2009). A study on automatic expansion of dialogue examples using logs of a dialogue system. *Human Computing Interface 2009* (pp. 257-262, in Korean).

Kim, Y. H., Bang, J. S., Choi, J. H., Ryu, S. H., Koo, S. J., & Lee, G. B. (2015). Acquisition and use of long-term memory for personalized dialog systems. *Multimodal Aanalyses enabling Artificial Agents in Human-Machine Interaction, Volume 8757 of the series Lecture Notes in Computer Science* (pp. 78-87). https://doi.org/10.1007/978-3-319-15557-9_8

Kwon, O. W., Lee, K. Y., Kim, Y. K., & Lee, Y. K. (2015). GenieTutor: a computer assisted second-language learning system based on semantic and grammar correctness evaluations. In F. Helm, L. Bradley, M. Guarda, & S. Thouësny (Eds), *Critical CALL – Proceedings of the 2015 EUROCALL Conference, Padova, Italy* (pp. 330-335). Dublin Ireland: Research-publishing.net. https://doi.org/10.14705/rpnet.2015.000354

Lee, S. J., Lee, C. J., & Lee, G. B. (2010). Example-based dialog modeling for English conversation tutoring. *Journal of Korean Institute of Information Scientists and Engineers, 37*(2), 129-136, in Korean.

Matter, N., & Wachsmuth, I. (2014). Let's personal assessing the impact of personal information in human-agent conversations. *Human-Computer Interaction, Part II, HCII, LNCS, 8511,* 450-461.

Raux, A., & Eskenazi, M. (2004). Using task-oriented spoken dialogue systems for language learning: potential, practical applications and challenges. In *STIL/ICALL Symposium 2004, Venice, Italy.*

Schank, R. C., & Abelson, R. (1977). *Scripts, plans, goals, and understanding.* London, NY: Psychology Press.

Young, S., Gašic, M., Thomson, B., & Williams J. D. (2013). POMDP-based statistical spoken dialog systems: a review. *Proceedings IEEE, 101*(5), 1160-1179. https://doi.org/10.1109/JPROC.2012.2225812

Students' attitudes and motivation towards technology in a Turkish language classroom

Pelekani Chryso[1]

Abstract. The purpose of this study is to investigate adult learners' approaches towards Turkish Language (TL) and examine learners' outlooks towards the use of digital technologies for learning. It will also evaluate the impact of the Language Lab's model on learners' language achievement. Language Lab model is a system that is used for learning languages by using technology. It comprises a teacher and student console. The role of the teacher console is to offer the control purposes while the student console is given the facility to obtain the lessons that have been recorded. They are also required to listen to the pronunciations. An example of the Language Lab is the digital language lab (Saxena, 2012).The research questions of the study were based on whether attitudes towards digital technologies varied based on different backgrounds (i.e linguistic, educational, etc). There was also an analysis of whether the implementation of Language Lab's model motivated the Turkish as a Second or Foreign Language (TSL/FL) learners of Adult Education Programs (AEP) to continue their studies. During this assessment procedure, it was identified that students used varied technological tools (Kahoot and Facebook) that motivated them to learn foreign languages in an efficient way. In conclusion, it can be affirmed that with the adoption and the execution of the above stated technological tools, the approaches of the students changed by a considerable degree in learning TL within the classroom setting. It is thus worth mentioning that the findings of this study can encourage the TL teachers to use technology in their classes in order to turn them into more autonomous, student-centered teachers using an effective language method in TL acquisition.

Keywords: Turkish language, attitudes, motivation, technology.

1. University of Cyprus, Nicosia, Cyprus; pelekani.chryso@ucy.ac.cy

How to cite this article: Chryso, P. (2016). Students' attitudes and motivation towards technology in a Turkish language classroom. In S. Papadima-Sophocleous, L. Bradley & S. Thouësny (Eds), *CALL communities and culture – short papers from EUROCALL 2016* (pp. 113-118). Research-publishing.net. https://doi.org/10.14705/rpnet.2016.eurocall2016.547

1. Introduction

The goal of this research was to investigate learners' attitudes and motivation for learning Turkish, the second official language of the Republic of Cyprus, with the help of computer technology. This is further supposed to contribute to the existing research in this particular area. In addition, an attempt has been made to evaluate the impact of Language Lab's model on learners' language achievement. The study addressed the following research questions:

- Did the implementation of Language Lab's model motivate the TSL/FL learners of AEP to continue their studies?

- What was the impact of the model on learners' TSL/FLs' skills?

2. Method

2.1. Participants and settings

TL courses offered by the Language Center (LC) with the cooperation of the Centre for Life Long Learning, Assessment and Development (KEPEAA) were designed for three different classes. These comprised Turkish B2 language level (intensive courses, Jan-May 2015), Turkish B1 language level (Sept-May 2015) and Turkish A2 language level (intensive summer courses, May-July 2015) and were delivered at the University of Cyprus (UCY) LC's labs. The study group included 26 adult learners enrolled in UCY LC AEP.

2.2. Data collection instrument

A mixed method with the inclusion of a questionnaire along with semi-structured interviews was used for collecting relevant data to be analysed and then come up with the results. The survey was contracted at the LC within the first two weeks of August 2015.

2.2.1. Questionnaire

The questionnaire was divided into two sections. The first section contained biographical information about the participants including age, gender, educational background, workplace, acquired languages and language skills.

In the second section, the participants were asked to respond to ten close-ended questions on their individual perceptions. The answers were made up of a five Likert-type scaling instrument, which comprised 62 statements.

The statements had two forms that were graded as Strongly Agree, Agree, Neutral, Disagree and Strongly Disagree and another form to be Never, Seldom, Sometimes, Often and Very Often. These questions were asked in order to clarify participants' approaches towards the TL, their learning strategies and evaluation of the effectiveness of technology in the language class (Koh, 2015).

2.2.2. Interview

The research questions of the Interview included one close-ended question and four open-ended questions. The maximum time spent for the interview was 35 minutes. The questions were:

- Why did you decide to learn Turkish? What were/are your motivations to learn this language?

- What kind of language strategies/techniques did/do you use to practice your Turkish?

- Could you please indicate how much time per week you've spent to study your Turkish?

- Which technological tools used in our class did/do you like most and why? Which of the four skills were improved more via technology?

- Which skills were improved less? Could you please give me an order from one to four with an explanation?

Their responses were accordingly recorded with an MP3 IC Recorder. To bridge the procedure of interview scheduling, two polls were conducted with the selected participants.

Three online interviews were conducted in the second week of August (10th-14th). Notably, five out of 16 interviews were conducted via Facebook, three via Skype, one via Hangouts, one via WhatsApp, five via Viber and one by phone. The analysis of the responses along with the discussion of participants' responses will be discussed in the next section of this study.

3.   Discussion

According to the results obtained, it was found that a majority of the participants (i.e. 81% of the total population) fall in the category of 19 to 25 years of age. This response eventually revealed that the generation students that are exposed to wide and new levels of technology have started learning foreign languages for finding a good job. They have also begun to understand the role played by culture when communicating with people of other ethnicities.

The factor concerning gender did not make any significant distinction in the results, as the figure of the male participants was low. The participants usually appeared from a diverse background of studies, however, there had been a significant concentration observed (42%) to Turkish Studies and (15%) to Byzantine and Modern Greek Studies and Law Studies.

The interview results showed that students usually preferred the use of computer technology in the class because with the integration of such technology, they managed to acquire better knowledge about Turkish grammar and syntax. These lessons proved very useful for them. Interestingly, students were positive on whether they learned Turkish lessons in technology-enhanced classrooms and especially, with the use of the Labs-model (Station-E Language Lab, 2011). In accordance, this particular model has been taken into consideration for discussion, as this leads towards developing the language learning procedure by various ways that entails saving much amounts of time and amplifying the participation level of the teachers and the learners in any classroom setting (Saxena, 2012). The positive effects on teaching were accordingly increasing the pace of lesson, enriching teaching and increased productivity (Grinager, 2006). Positive effects on learning thus mentioned certainly increased students' interests, along with longer attention spans, participation, understanding, performance, communication and interaction with enjoyable lessons (Shyamlee, 2012). Only few believed that the implementation of technology in class has not much effect on teaching and learning quality overall.

Regarding the effectiveness of the technological tools used in TL classes, the students stated that most of the tools used in the class were teaching aids. For instance, with the online game Kahoot, Facebook and listening materials consisting of the digital tool Vocarro, the students remained active and involved in their learning. Moreover, the Pbworks platform had an effective role in language learning. The Pbworks platform worked as a tool to develop new learning-styles and innovative methods in learning Turkish language. Students hence changed their traditional learning style and thus, integrated the Pbworks platform, which is deemed as an interactive approach with positive effects on learners, as per the results obtained.

On the other hand, the questionnaire results showed that the WiZiQ platform did not contribute a lot to TL learning. WiZiQ is regarded as a virtual classroom software that enables the learners to establish a wider connection with one another by making better use of chat options and microphones, among others (Figure 1). Some students, through their interviews, explained that within the setting of a virtual classroom, they were quite anxious and not comfortable to talk in front of the camera. Nevertheless, face-to-face classes were observed as more confident to speak and remain active throughout the language learning session.

Figure 1. Effectiveness of digital technologies

###		Average rating	Ranking between technology tools
Facebook - Group page; synchronous discussions with instructor and with peers		4.6	3
PBworks platform especially created for this class; asynchronous discussions with instructor and with peers		4.5	4
Padlet - for announcement and for sharing wishes, photos etc		4.1	6
Online diary [embedded in PBworks platform - individual page for each student]		4.0	7
Power Point Presentations		4.9	1
Kahoot - In class language game		4.8	2
Quia - online games- outside class [embedded in our PBworks platform]		4.0	7
Learning Apps. Org online games- outside class [embedded in our PBworks platform]		4.1	6
WiZiQ tests - in class self-assessment language test		3.8	8
Google form-test - in class self-assessment language [embedded in PBworks platform]		4.3	5
Viber - Our Group- synchronous discussions with instructor and with peers		4.3	5
WiZiQ - online synchronous discussion website		4.0	7
Doodle - for making a poll [embedded in our PBworks platform]		3.3	9
Makes belief Comix online task activity - in class [then embedded in our PBworks platform]		4.0	7

4. Conclusions

With the conduct of a mixed research approach by performing questionnaire surveys as well as interviews, a detailed viewpoint of the students regarding their TL experience, knowledge of technologies being used in the classrooms and their motivation level was ascertained in this study. The results of the survey and the interviews thus showcased the fact that the implementation of technology in class has enormous effects on teaching and learning the Turkish language. Such effects can be determined in distinct ways that entail learning TL grammar and syntax more quickly and communicating with others belonging to diverse cultural backgrounds in an efficient way. Thus, in conclusion, it can be inferred that the use and the integration of digital technologies, within the learning procedure, possesses the capability to improvise the learning procedures of the students and at the same time, motivate them to embrace those in making wider advancements in their future career.

References

Grinager, H. (2006). How education technology leads to improved student achievement. *Education Issues*, 2-11. https://www.ncsl.org/portals/1/documents/educ/item013161.pdf

Koh, C. (2015). *Motivation, leadership and curriculum design: engaging the net generation and 21st Century learners*. New York: Springer. https://doi.org/10.1007/978-981-287-230-2

Saxena, V. (2012). *Contemporary trends in education: a handbook for educators*. New Delhi: Dorling Kindersley. http://proquest.safaribooksonline.com/?fpi=9788131759486.

Shyamlee, S. D. (2012). "Use of technology in English language teaching and learning": an analysis. *International Conference on Language, Medias and Culture, 33*, 150-156.

Station-E Language Lab. (2011). Establishing Language Lab. http://www.station-e.com/lab-establishments.html

Vlogging: a new channel for language learning and intercultural exchanges

Christelle Combe[1] and Tatiana Codreanu[2]

Abstract. The potential for computer-supported learning in educational contexts has opened up the possibilities for learners to interact in informal contexts outside the classroom. The context of the present research is a young American individual's vlog on YouTube sharing his experiences as a learner of French. This paper focuses on the potential use of vlogs for developing language speaking skills and intercultural exchanges between users. The aim of the study is to describe and analyse informal learning communication using a vlog between one American French Language learner posting his learning experiences on YouTube and his audience. We highlight learner's opportunities in terms of speaking and intercultural skills in a vlog environment. This study is based on an empirical method of collecting ecological data on the web. The qualitative data analysis method is based on the description of the online conversation (Develotte, Kern, & Lamy, 2011) in addition to interaction analysis and technodiscursive analysis (Paveau, 2015). We discuss the qualitative findings of the research conducted on this multimodal corpus in order to highlight the vlog's potential for supporting informal language learning, speaking and intercultural exchanges between YouTube users in a globalised world.

Keywords: informal language learning, intercultural communication, social networking, vlogging.

1. Introduction

Web 2.0 tools use for online language learning and intercultural exchanges have grown significantly. Guth and Helm (2010) class Web 2.0 tools into three categories that can serve as a platform for communication and collaboration:

1. Aix-Marseille University, Aix-en-Provence, France; christelle.combe@univ-amu.fr
2. Ecole Normale Supérieure de Lyon, Lyon, France; tatiana.codreanu@univ-lyon2.fr

How to cite this article: Combe, C., & Codreanu, T. (2016). Vlogging: a new channel for language learning and intercultural exchanges. In S. Papadima-Sophocleous, L. Bradley & S. Thouësny (Eds), *CALL communities and culture – short papers from EUROCALL 2016* (pp. 119-124). Research-publishing.net. https://doi.org/10.14705/rpnet.2016.eurocall2016.548

social networks, wikis and blogs. However, media sharing communities such as Flickr and YouTube are excluded from this category. It is the latter (YouTube) that we are interested in, as it is likely to encourage online autonomous language learning (Barton & Lee, 2013) and yet is quite unexplored in the context of French language learning. Previous research highlighted learner's 2.0 skills (Guth & Helm, 2010). Our research focuses on what Herring (2015) calls emerging phenomena in digital communications: Web 2.0 platforms that support a convergence of channels or "modes" (text, audio, video, images) for user-to-user communication (Herring, 2015, p. 1).

As recalled by Blommaert and Rampton (2011), "over the past two decades, globalization has altered the face of social, cultural and linguistic diversity in societies all over the world" (p. 1). Concepts such as migration and multiculturalism have gradually been replaced by what Vertovec (2007) calls superdiversity. In this context, the emergence of new medias and technologies of communication are intensifying globalisation and are complicating the notion of superdiversity.

We discussed previously (Combe, 2014) the emergence of the vlog genre, a particular kind of vlogging as a way to practice languages online while learning.

Our study focuses on the following research question: What opportunities do a learner's vlog present in enhancing their speaking and intercultural skills? This paper is divided into three parts. Firstly we will present the theoretical and the methodological frame, then we will present the corpus of study and the results of our research.

2.   Method

2.1.   Methodological framework

The research protocol is based on an empirical method of collecting ecological data. Our research studies what Paveau (2015) defines as a 'digital' document, that is, a document natively produced online, on a website, a blog, a social network or any digital environment where speech acts take place (in this specific context the YouTube platform).

In order to analyse users' comments on YouTube, we applied Bennett's (1986, 1993) conceptual tool, the Developmental Model of Intercultural Sensitivity (denial, defense, minimisation, acceptance, adaptation, integration) to understand personal reactions and better discern the criteria of adaptation to another culture. Bennett's (1986) scale of six ranges of sensitivity to difference, aiming to underline individuals' cognitive concepts of cultural experiences, are an interesting tool for understanding emotional and conventional reactions when faced with culture shock in digital environments. The typology of the six stages is presented in a continuum: we explored to what extent the YouTube comments fall within Bennett's (1986) scale. However, the development of intercultural sensitivity follows a line of continuous progress (Bennett & Bennett, 2004). The continuum of stages is not static, as opposed to the written comments on YouTube, which once posted, if not clarified or restated by users, appear to be a definitive statement.

The qualitative data analysis method is based on Computer-Mediated Discourse Analysis (Herring, 2015) combined with recent French research on discourse and interaction analysis in digital contexts (Develotte, 2012; Paveau, 2015) and Bennett's (1986) scale of intercultural sensibility.

We adopted a semio-discursive approach in order to analyse a vlogger's discourse. Additionally, we proceeded to a preliminary heuristic analysis of the corpus of all comments based on what YouTube calls Top Comments, that is, comments YouTube users vote as the best, and have sought to manually track the number of polylogues, the number of responses they generated and the number of users who took part in the interaction.

2.2. Corpus

Given the scale of the data and the instability of the multimodal online research corpus, we selected a corpus of reference from the vlogger's 'texfrancais' channel content[3]. This corpus, determined as of 5 January, 2016, consists of 38 videos, 0:10 - 15:56 minutes published from 28 June, 2011 and the written comments they inspired.

Our corpus of study consists of three vlogs ('Unpronounceable words for us Americans', 'Differences between France and the USA' and 'American Slang') for a total of over 14 minutes and more than 7000 comments posted on YouTube.

---

3. https://www.youtube.com/user/texfrancais/videos

Table 1.   Corpus of study

Screenshots			
Title	Unpronounceable words for us Americans	The differences between France and the USA	American slang
Published	14/01/2012	09/01/2013	05/03/2015
Duration	5'09	5'34	4'48
Comments	5,386	1,628	210
Views	1,050,382	141,616	26,303
I like this	28,278	3,738	2,283
I dislike this	251	80	3

3.   Discussion

The first results of our research show that the vlogger is widely encouraged by peers (we observe strong socio-emotional aspects), exchanges take place on a multilingual environment, the vlogger is both a learner and a teacher (he practices French but also teaches American slang), and users share knowledge and comments in informal ways (without signs of stress or formality).

Vlogs offer the possibility to practice spoken production skills as recommended by the Common European Framework Reference for languages. This skill is often difficult to implement in an authentic context of communication outside the classroom. Vlogs have the potential to help develop digital literacy and speaking skills in front of a camera and encourage publication (speech acts and gestures, improving the final media product before posting it, adding text, and emoticons which illustrate speech acts). Topics such as lexicon and pronunciation generate exchanges, which lead to rich debates. Vlogging appears to be a space for collaboration and hetero-peer learning. It was observed that users often offered linguistic explanations without demonstration expertise in phonetics. Hence attempts to explain how to pronounce words appeared to be limited by both the medium (YouTube comments) and peers' knowledge of the topic. Additionally, vlogs are useful in helping negotiate the meaning of words in foreign language.

However, in contrast, intercultural issues can crystallise tensions. Vlogging space on the Internet is also conductive of exchanges on cultural issues or statements questioned by users and conflict of opinions about stereotypes. The vlogger's perceptions rise various comments in which users express their own cultural perceptions on topics that the vlogger posted, and raised reactions on a local level (France and its regions) and differences of point of view on Paris and the rest of the France, dividing users in in-groups and out-groups (Bennett, 1993). Ethnocentric attitudes of denial, defense and minimisation demonstrate some users' inter-regional cultural bias. Other users minimised their in-group and out-group division, and we also noticed some cases of acceptance and integration. One of the users in particular takes each point developed by the vlogger and positions herself with respect to these points, demonstrating the acceptance stage of Bennett's (1986) scale on topics such as the school system in France, smoking in high school, and TV channels, and gives a personal explanation on youth behaviour in France. Hence, vlogs have inherent limitations in enhancing speaking and intercultural skills.

Finally, commercial, ethical and privacy aspects of sharing on social networks need to be considered when using online interactions in pedagogical contexts.

4.   Conclusions

This study highlights the vlog's potential for supporting informal language learning and intercultural exchanges between YouTube users in a globalised world. The vlogger becomes an almost fictional character, a movie character or a digital character through the looking glass of the screen between him and his followers.

Our case study, through the example of a vlog ('texfrancais' channel), shows the potential of new multimedia and multimodal interactions for informal foreign language practicing and learning. On the one hand, vlogs offer opportunities for speaking skills, digital literacy skills, multilingual peer learning, and opinion conflicts through cultural stereotypes, and intercultural skills. On the other hand, vlogs are limited by the ethical aspects of social networks and by the linguistic skills of social network users. In a formal teaching context, 'texfrancais' channel can be a resource for teachers in order to think about the potential of a multimodal interactive platform to practice a language and develop digital literacy skills.

This case study raises important questions in the era of mass digital communication in a globalised world where the interactional reference space has diversified.

More research is needed to analyse interactions in an unstable context of production and study how language vlogs could be of interest from a pedagogical point of view.

References

Barton, D., & Lee, C. (2013). *Language online: investigating digital texts and practices*. New-York: Routledge.

Bennett, M. J. (1986). A developmental approach to training for intercultural sensitivity. *International Journal of Intercultural Relations, 10*, 179-195. https://doi.org/10.1016/0147-1767(86)90005-2

Bennett, M. J. (1993). Towards ethnorelativism: a developmental model of intercultural sensitivity. In R. M. Paige (Ed.), *Education for the intercultural experience* (pp. 21-71). Yarmouth, ME: Intercultural Press.

Bennett, J. M., & Bennett, M. J. (2004). Developing intercultural sensitivity: an integrative approach to global and domestic diversity. In J. D. Landis, J. M. Bennett & M. J. Bennett (Eds), *Handbook of intercultural training* (3rd ed.). Thousand Oaks, CA: Sage.

Blommaert, J., & Rampton, B. (2011). Language and superdiversity. *Diversities, 13*(2). http://www.unesco.org/shs/diversities/vol13/issue2/art1

Combe, C. (2014). Vlogues sur YouTube : un nouveau genre d'interactions multimodales. In I. Colon de Carjaval & M. Ollagnier-Beldame (Eds), *Actes du colloque Interactions Multimodales Par ECrans 2014, Lyon 2 au 4 juillet 2014*. http://impec.sciencesconf.org/conference/impec/pages/Impec2014_Combe_Celik.pdf

Develotte, C. (2012). L'analyse des corpus multimodaux en ligne : état des lieux et perspectives, *Actes en ligne du Congrès Mondial de Linguistique Française (CMLF)*. https://doi.org/10.1051/shsconf/20120100213

Develotte, C., Kern, R., & Lamy, M.-N. (Eds). (2011). *Décrire la conversation en ligne: le face à face distanciel*. Lyon: ENS Éditions.

Guth, S., & Helm, F. (2010). *Telecollaboration 2.0*. Bern: Peter Lang.

Herring, S. (2015). New frontiers in interactive multimodal communication. In A. Georgapoulou & T. Spilloti (Eds), *The Routledge handbook of language and digital communication* (pp. 398-402). London: Routledge.

Paveau, M.-A. (2015). L'intégrité des corpus natifs en ligne. Une écologie postdualiste pour la théorie du discours. *Cahiers de praxématique, Publications de l'Université Paul Valéry, 2015, Corpus sensibles* (pp.65-90) (hal-01185710).

Vertovec, S. (2007). Super-diversity and its implications. *Ethnic and Racial Studies, 30*(6), 1024-1054. https://doi.org/10.1080/01419870701599465

Japanese university students' self-assessment and digital literacy test results

Travis Cote[1] and Brett Milliner[2]

Abstract. Study abroad programs provide an opportunity for students to accelerate language learning and acquire cultural capital. Evaluations of returnees from study abroad programs however, have revealed that this is not always guaranteed. To promote a more positive academic and culturally-inclusive study abroad experience, one recommendation is for language teachers to focus on students' digital literacy. Given the reported levels of poor digital literacy among Japanese freshmen students, the researchers in this current study were attempting to determine if this wider trend applied to students at their private university in Tokyo. The authors surveyed first-year College of Tourism and Hospitality (CTH) students and will report on their responses to two sections of a computer literacy questionnaire originally created by Son, Robb, and Charismiadji (2011). The first section focuses on self-assessment of digital skills, while the second section reports on the results of a 10-item digital literacy test.

Keywords: digital literacy, Japanese university, CALL, English for specific purposes.

1. Introduction

This paper reports on the second phase of the researchers' investigation into how to prepare Japanese students in the CTH for a one-year study abroad program in Australia. In the initial phase, returnees from the first student cohort of the program were surveyed (Milliner & Cote, 2016). Key findings from this investigation were that students appear interested in improving their digital literacy; they recognize the necessity of digital literacy in higher education and beyond; many believed that their digital skills were inferior to their classmates in Australia; and, they reported using their computer more in Australian university classes.

1. Tamagawa University, Machida, Japan; travis@bus.tamagawa.ac.jp
2. Tamagawa University, Machida, Japan; milliner@lit.tamagawa.ac.jp

How to cite this article: Cote, T., & Milliner, B. (2016). Japanese university students' self-assessment and digital literacy test results. In S. Papadima-Sophocleous, L. Bradley & S. Thouësny (Eds), *CALL communities and culture – short papers from EUROCALL 2016* (pp. 125-131). Research-publishing.net. https://doi.org/10.14705/rpnet.2016.eurocall2016.549

In this second phase, 112 students from the 2016 freshmen cohort were surveyed on issues relating to computer ownership and accessibility, capability of performing tasks on mobile devices and PCs, personal and professional use of computers, and general interest in Computer-Assisted Language Learning (CALL). In this paper, however, student's self-assessment of digital skills and digital literacy test results are described.

Figure 1.   The Information and Communications Technology (ICT) skills review for CTH students

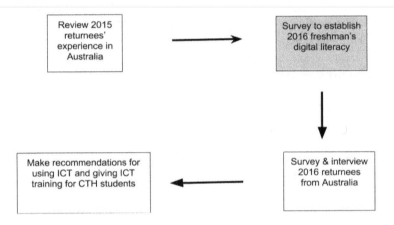

2.   Literature review

2.1.   Digital literacy

Learning to use digital technology has become a crucial step in developing literacy in the twenty-first century (Goodwin-Jones, 2000) and teachers are being asked to consider how they can effectively prepare students to develop and exercise their digital literacy skills. Corbel and Gruba (2004, p. 5) argued that students need computer skills to

- communicate effectively in society;

- interact with family and friends;

- function effectively in the workplace;

- learn new ideas and for fun and pleasure.

While traditional 'literacy' has been defined as the ability to read and write, the term 'digital literacy' appears to be more complex. The U.S. Department of Education (1996) defined digital literacy as having "computer skills and the ability to use computers and other technology to improve learning, productivity and performance" (p. 5). Barrette (2001), and Corbel and Gruba (2004) argue that digital literacy contains two core components: (1) ability to control basic computer operations, and (2) using one's understanding of computers for problem-solving and critical thinking.

2.2. Japanese student literacy

Although Japan is perceived as digitally-wired, it is well documented that digital literacy among Japanese youth is falling behind other countries. This is despite the fact that the Japanese Ministry of Education, Sports, Science and Technology (MEXT) ordered the inclusion of information computing technology in high school curriculums (MEXT, 2011). In a 2011 report by MEXT, they acknowledge that ICT utilization in Japanese schools has not been advancing at rates similar to those in other industrialized nations. In 2015, the Organization for Economic Co-operation and Development (OECD, 2015) released a critical statement on the literacy of Japanese youth, noting that 25% (age 16-29) lack basic computer skills. One explanation is that schools are not responding to the MEXT mandate to implement ICT training. In fact, contemporary reviews of freshmen Japanese university students also noted that many students did not use ICT in high school and most have low levels of digital literacy and confidence using digital tools (Gobel & Kano, 2014; Lockley & Promnitz-Hayashi, 2012; Murray & Blyth, 2011).

2.3. Digital literacy and study abroad

For CTH students studying in Australia, poor digital literacy may be limiting language-learning opportunities (Murray & Blyth, 2011), chances to engage in Australian culture (Kinginger, 2011), and their ability to function in the foreign society (Brine et al., 2015). ICT skills were identified by Jarman-Walsh (2015) as crucial for students studying abroad because they often work independently to solve personal and academic-related problems. Understanding multimedia and social networking programs have also been cited as useful approaches for students studying abroad because they can (1) access resources and strengthen relationships (Jarman-Walsh, 2015), (2) practice informal communication with peers (Kinginger, 2011), and (3) explore the communicative norms used by locals (Kinginger, 2011). While most study abroad research focuses on development of cultural awareness and language proficiency (e.g. Sato & Hodge, 2015), the examples above illustrate the role digital literacy skills can play in academic and social environments.

3. Research methods

3.1. Research questions

This study aimed to answer the following questions:

- At what proficiency level do freshmen students rank their digital literacy?

- What are the actual levels of digital literacy based on results from a digital literacy test?

3.2. Participants, demographics and computer experience

Responses from 112 freshmen students in the CTH were analysed for this study. A total of 29 males and 83 females (age 18-19) responded to the questionnaire. All (112) own a smartphone and a PC. When asked whether they used a computer daily, two thirds responded 'yes'. As a follow up, they were asked to specify where they usually used their computer. The locations identified most included: home (77), anywhere (30), and school/university (9).

3.3. Questionnaire

The 2016 freshmen cohort were asked to complete a digital literacy questionnaire adapted from a seminal survey created by Son et al. (2011). The entire survey contained 28 items, however only two sections are focused on for this report.

4. Results

4.1. Self-assessment of digital skills

When asked to self-assess their digital proficiency, the responses revealed profoundly low appraisals. Displayed below (Table 1), very few students perceived their skills as being 'above average' or 'high' for each question.

Table 1.   Self-assessment of digital skills

Question	Low	Below Average	Average	Above Average	High
How would you rate your computer skills?	30	34	39	8	1
How would you rate your Internet literacy?	29	35	41	7	0
How would you rate your typing skills?	41	26	36	8	1

4.2.   General computer knowledge

Students answered ten multiple-choice questions designed to appraise general computer knowledge. Surprisingly negative results were observed for the majority of these questions (see Table 2 below). In only four out of the ten questions, more than 50% of the responses were correct, and in six out of the ten items, 'I don't know' was selected by more than 50% of students.

Table 2.   Digital literacy test results (Son et al., 2011)

Question	Correct response %	I don't know %
What is a folder?	77%	13%
How many characters are allowed for a tweet?	69%	21%
What is a URL?	63%	12%
Which of the following is not a search engine?	55%	35%
What is the main brain of the computer?	32%	52%
What is the main function of a server in a networked environment?	31%	54%
What kind of program is used to edit a GIF file or a JPEG file?	28%	56%
How much information fits on a CD and a DVD?	16%	67%
Which of the following is considered poor email etiquette?	6%	39%
What are WAV and AIFF examples of?	7%	82%

5.   Discussion

The authors of this investigation established that freshmen in their Japanese university believe their digital literacy proficiency to be very low. These low appraisals were reinforced by poor results in the digital literacy test section. One limitation in this study is a reported tendency among Japanese students to modestly self-assess their own digital skills (Lockley & Promnitz-Hayashi, 2012). A practical test of digital tasks (e.g. analyzing a spreadsheet) may have provided a better assessment. However, the evaluation of results in the digital literacy test questions somewhat validate their own low self-assessment.

6. Conclusion

To prepare students for a study-abroad program, the authors set out to identify freshman students' level of digital literacy. The results echo other Japan-based studies, as almost all students had very low self-assessments of their digital skills, and respondents returned very poor results in the digital literacy test. Although smartphone ownership and personal computer ownership is at 100%, students do not appear to be using these devices in any depth.

After completing a more detailed report of this survey's data, the researchers will interview the second group of returnees upon returning from Australia in September 2016. The goal is to develop a training program which appropriately equips students with the digital skills that can support a more prosperous study abroad experience.

References

Barrette, C. B. (2001). Students' preparedness and training for CALL. *CALICO Journal, 19*(1), 5-36.

Brine, J., Kaneko, E., Heo, Y., Vazhenin, A., & Bateson, G. (2015). Language learning beyond Japanese classrooms: video interviewing for study abroad. In F. Helm, L. Bradley, M. Guarda, & S. Thouësny (Eds), *Critical CALL – Proceedings of the 2015 EUROCALL Conference, Padova, Italy* (pp. 91-96). Dublin: Research-publishing.net. https://doi.org/10.14705/rpnet.2015.000315

Corbel, C., & Gruba, P. (2004). *Teaching computer literacy*. National Center for English language teaching and Research Macquarie University, Sydney.

Gobel, P., & Kano, M. (2014). Mobile natives, Japanese university students' use of digital technology. In J. B. Son (Ed.), *Computer-assisted language learning: learners, teachers and tools* (pp. 21-46). Newcastle upon Tyne: Cambridge Scholars Publishing.

Goodwin-Jones, B. (2000). Emerging technologies: literacies and technology tools/trends. *Language Learning and Technology, 4*(2), 11-18. http://llt.msu.edu/vol4num2/emerging/

Jarman-Walsh, J. (2015). Preparing students for study abroad programs: tasks, skill-building and self-reflection. 安田女子大学紀要, *44*, 213-222.

Kinginger, C. (2011). Enhancing language learning study abroad. *Annual Review of Applied Linguistics, 31*, 58-73. https://doi.org/10.1017/S0267190511000031

Lockley, T., & Promnitz-Hayashi, L. (2012). Japanese university students' CALL attitudes, aspirations, motivations. *CALL-EJ, 13*(1), 1-16.

MEXT. (2011). *The vision for ICT in education: toward the creation of a learning system and schools suitable for the 21st century*. Ministry of Education, Culture, Sports, Science and Technology. http://goo.gl/KfoH0I

Milliner, B., & Cote, T. (2016). Reflections on Japanese university study abroad students' digital literacy: Is more ICT training needed? 教師教育リサーチセンター年報, *6*, 99-109.

Murray, A., & Blyth, A. (2011). A survey of Japanese university students' computer literacy levels. *The JALT CALL Journal, 7*(3), 307-318.

OECD. (2015). Graph 2.5. Youth who lack basic ICT skills: percentage of youth (16-29), 2012. In *OECD Skills Outlook 2015*. Paris: OECD Publishing. https://doi.org/10.1787/9789264234178-graph10-en

Sato, T., & Hodge, S. (2015). Japanese exchange students' academic and social struggles at an American University. *Journal of International Students, 5*(3), 208-227.

Son, J. B., Robb, T., & Charismiadji, I. (2011). Computer literacy and competency: a survey of Indonesian teachers of English as a foreign language. *CALL-EJ, 12*(1), 26-42.

US Department of Education. (1996). *Getting America's students ready for the 21st century: meeting the technology literacy challenge*. A report to the nation on technology and education. http://files.eric.ed.gov/fulltext/ED398899.pdf

Digital story (re)telling using graded readers and smartphones

Kazumichi Enokida[1]

Abstract. Extensive reading and digital storytelling can utilise 'the power of stories' effectively to enhance learners' receptive and productive skills. For the past five years, the author has been working on a classroom project combining these two activities, as a way of integrating Information and Communications Technology (ICT) into his reading-oriented English as a Foreign Language (EFL) courses. Each year the project has continually been updated and improved, reflecting the results and challenges from previous years. In this paper, the project implemented throughout the past two years (2014 and 2015) is reported on, particularly focusing on how the project improved regarding ways the story should be analysed and then how the digital stories should be created. It was found that the students were favourable to our new attempts – using smartphones for digital storytelling and retelling a story from the viewpoint of two characters. On the other hand, the way individual work and group work should be balanced has room for improvement.

Keywords: digital storytelling, MALL, extensive reading, BYOD, smartphones.

1. Introduction

There are several benefits that are expected by combining extensive reading (reading a lot of easy texts written in the target language) and digital storytelling (creating a movie clip made from text, images, sounds, and narration). First, it enables learners to input and output the target language with special attention to the structure of narrative texts. The graded readers, written or retold with a controlled range of vocabulary, could make the analysis of literary texts more approachable to learners than the authentic literary works that are often too challenging. Second, the digital stories can be easily shared and learned beyond the class – they can be stored in a repository that future students can use for their learning. Thus digital storytelling

1. Hiroshima University, Hiroshima, Japan; kenokida@hiroshima-u.ac.jp

How to cite this article: Enokida, K. (2016). Digital story (re)telling using graded readers and smartphones. In S. Papadima-Sophocleous, L. Bradley & S. Thouësny (Eds), *CALL communities and culture – short papers from EUROCALL 2016* (pp. 132-136). Research-publishing.net. https://doi.org/10.14705/rpnet.2016.eurocall2016.550

can be a communicative activity in that the creators should be conscious of the audience beyond the class and time.

The author reported at EUROCALL 2014 on his previous classroom project, where each group of students in his class was requested to choose a book from the graded readers they had studied and, based on that story, create a digital story using Microsoft PowerPoint installed in the Computer-Assisted Language Learning (CALL) room at the university campus. While the project involving story analysis and digital storytelling provided the students with deeper understanding of the narrative texts they read, the challenging process of creating a video clip on PCs made them focus on the technology rather than learning the target language; also they found it quite cumbersome to write a summary of a book as a group activity.

There were two major improvements in the classroom practice reported in this paper: First, instead of the PCs in the CALL room, Mobile-Assisted Language Learning (MALL) devices were integrated into the process. It was expected that the high penetration rate of smartphones among the college students in Japan would make it easier for them to create digital stories using a widespread-owned device. The convenience of MALL on a 'bring your own device' basis would enable them to focus more on the content of the materials rather than the technology they have to cope with. And second, instead of writing one summary in each group, they were requested to choose two characters from the book they were studying and let each of them narrate the story, so that the same story could be retold from multiple points of view.

2.   Outline

The project was conducted through an EFL reading course, 'Advanced Reading', for advanced and motivated learners at a national university in Japan, during the autumn semester of the academic years 2014 and 2015. The number of participants were 27 in total (17 in 2014 and 10 in 2015). The primary aim of the project is to direct learners' attention to the story structure while developing their reading/oral fluency.

The extensive reading activities were carried out outside the class, since it was merely a part of the 15-week-long course, covering a variety of strategies for reading different types of texts. A collection of 350 graded readers, composed of Oxford Bookworms and Macmillan Readers, were brought into the classroom every week so that the students could check them out and study outside the class. The students were encouraged to read 150,000 words or more during the 15 weeks.

At the 'Book Talk' in week five, the students talked in groups of three or four about the books they had read, and then each group chose one book that the majority of the members found interesting. Then they worked in groups to analyse the books they chose in terms of plot structure and characters, using multiple tools of analysis such as Dillingham's (2001) Visual Portrait of a Story (adapted by Ohler, 2008) and Greimas's (1966) Actantial model. Based on the analysis, they collaboratively wrote two stories, each of which were narrated by two different characters that appear in the same book.

After having their stories read by their peers and proofread by the instructor and practicing reading them orally, the writers recorded them and created video clips, adding some visual images and background sounds that might help the audience understand the story. The whole process was carried out by exploiting smartphones owned by the students; Videolicious, a free and easy-to-use digital storytelling app, was used for this purpose. Since the maximum length of a video clip that can be created with Videolicious is one minute, the students needed to plan and practice their narrations to fit it within the time limit. In order to minimise the work time on the project in the classroom, the campus learning management system ('Bb9') was used to let the students share stories they had written among other group members, and collect the digital stories they had created. The movie clips were shared and peer evaluated on Bb9.

3.   Results

A questionnaire survey, made up of ten items with a five-point Likert scale, was given at the end of the semester. There were 26 respondents in total. They were also asked to write comments on the project. The question items and results are shown in Table 1 and Figure 1.

Table 1.   Questionnaire items

1. It is meaningful to retell the book from the viewpoint of one character.
2. Summarising and recording a story help me learn English.
3. Watching digital stories of the books I haven't read makes me want to read them.
4. Choosing a book for digital storytelling at the time of the Book Talk is appropriate.
5. The period of time and the deadline given for digital storytelling are appropriate.
6. It is all right to use my smartphone for my course assignments.
7. Pair/group work helps create a digital story.
8. Structural analysis of a story helps create a digital story.
9. Structural analysis of a story helps me understand other stories.
10. Overall, creating a digital story is meaningful in this course.

Figure 1.   Survey results of Q1-10 (*N*=26)

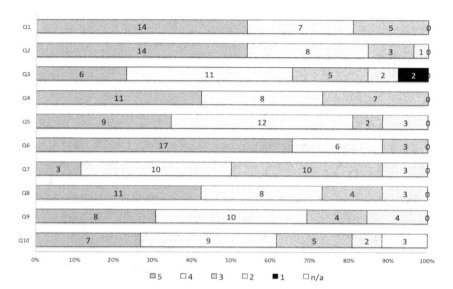

The percentages of the positive feedback (4 and 5) are as follows: 80.8% (Q1), 84.6% (Q2), 65.4% (Q3), 73.1% (Q4), 80.8% (Q5), 88.5% (Q6), 50% (Q7), 73.1% (Q8), 69.2% (Q9), 61.5% (Q10). Q3 (Learning from other digital stories), Q7 (The effects of pair/group work), and Q9 (The usefulness of structural analysis) were relatively weak. (Though Q10 also looks weak, there were 3 respondents that gave no answer. The reason being that they just missed the last question).

Among the positive comments:

- There was a lot to learn from the project, like reinterpreting the story from the viewpoint of a character and performing the character in creating the digital story.

- The whole process of digital storytelling was a new and interesting experience for me.

- It was a good opportunity to practice reading my story with the audience in mind.

And here are some of the points the students found challenging:

- Using Videolicious was challenging. I had to record a couple of times to fit my script within the time limit of one minute.

- It would be better to have more time for group discussions; I don't really feel that my group collaborated our digital story.

4.   Discussion and conclusion

The students viewed combining extensive reading and digital storytelling as an effective way to improve their four language skills and read narrative texts analytically. It was also found that overall the students were favourable to our new attempts to use smartphones for digital storytelling and then to retell the story from the viewpoint of two characters. It is also worthy to highlight that the students were extremely keen to use their own personal mobile devices for their course assignments. The convenience of creating a digital story using smartphones can be compared favourably with the technical challenges of doing so involving desktop PCs that have been previously reported on by the author.

On the other hand, the manner in which both student individual and group work should be balanced does have room for improvement. For example, more time should be spared for group discussions in the classroom throughout the whole process of the project as this will enhance the students' awareness of the project as a collaborative activity. Also, further investigation should be undertaken regarding what makes it relatively difficult for the students to learn from the digital stories shared by their classmates.

5.   Acknowledgement

This work was supported by JSPS KAKENHI Grant Number 16H03450.

References

Dillingham, B. (2001). *Visual portrait of a story: teaching storytelling* [School handout]. Juneau, Alaska.
Greimas, A. J. (1966). *Structural semantics: an attempt at a method.* University of Nebraska Press.
Ohler, J. (2008). *Digital storytelling in the classroom: new media pathways to literacy, learning, and creativity.* Thousand Oaks: Corwin Press.

HR4EU – a web-portal for e-learning of Croatian

Matea Filko[1], Daša Farkaš[2], and Diana Hriberski[3]

Abstract. In this paper, we present the HR4EU – a web portal for e-learning of Croatian. HR4EU is the first portal that offers Croatian language courses which are free-of-charge and developed by language professionals. Moreover, HR4EU also integrates bidirectional interaction with some of the previously developed language resources for Croatian. The HR4EU portal offers three general (beginner, intermediate, advanced) and two specialized (Croatian for business users, Croatian for students) Croatian language courses. Apart from language courses, the portal also offers information about Croatia presented via interactive maps, as well as other information, which can be useful to foreigners living or studying in Croatia. Moreover, HR4EU introduces users to language resources and shows them how they can efficiently be used when learning a new language on their own.

Keywords: e-learning, Croatian language, European project, language resources.

1. Introduction

In this paper, we present HR4EU, a web-portal for e-learning of Croatian (www. hr4eu.eu, www.hr4eu.hr, cf. homepage in Figure 1), developed at the Faculty of Humanities and Social Sciences in Zagreb and funded by the European Social Fund.

Since Croatian is a language with a relatively small number of speakers, its presence on the web is limited, especially when it comes to e-learning courses of Croatian. A few e-learning sites offering users the possibility to learn Croatian are either expensive or present learning material in a static manner, avoiding the usage of existing language technologies. With the HR4EU portal we aim to bridge this gap and develop a modern e-learning system which integrates bidirectional interaction

1. University of Zagreb, Zagreb, Croatia; msrebaci@ffzg.hr
2. University of Zagreb, Zagreb, Croatia; dberovic@ffzg.hr
3. University of Zagreb, Zagreb, Croatia; dhribers@ffzg.hr

How to cite this article: Filko, M., Farkaš, D., & Hriberski, D. (2016). HR4EU – a web-portal for e-learning of Croatian. In S. Papadima-Sophocleous, L. Bradley & S. Thouësny (Eds), *CALL communities and culture – short papers from EUROCALL 2016* (pp. 137-143). Research-publishing.net. https://doi.org/10.14705/rpnet.2016.eurocall2016.551

with previously developed Language Resources (LRs)[4]. This e-learning system is developed by linguists, who are native speakers and have experience in building LRs. Moreover, great efforts were made to make this portal visually attractive.

Figure 1.   HR4EU homepage

2.   HR4EU portal

The HR4EU portal is divided into four sections. The section *Courses* consists of three general (beginner, intermediate, advanced) and two specialized (Croatian for business users, Croatian for students) Croatian language courses (cf. Section 3).

The section *About Croatia* provides the cultural context for learning Croatian via nine interactive maps: borders, cities, culture, events, people, nature, wine, food, and recipes. By clicking the pins on the maps, pop-up windows appear and users can read about peculiarities related to the part of Croatia where the pin is located (cf. Figure 2).

Figure 2.   Section *About Croatia*

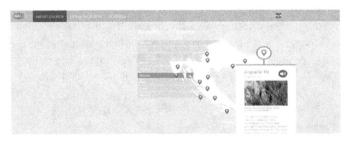

4. Cf. section 2 and 3.1. LRs are primarily used for natural language processing, but they can also be used as tools in CALL, especially in courseware engineering (cf. Colpaert, 2004, p. 17).

The section *Living in Croatia* offers useful information to foreigners in Croatia, e.g. list of important institutions (e.g. Ministry of Interior), and forms that they may be required to submit during their stay in Croatia (e.g. visa application).

The section dedicated to language resources provides users with the introduction to the Croatian LRs: Croatian National Corpus (hnk.ffzg.hr), Croatian Morphological Lexicon (hml.ffzg.hr), Croatian Wordnet (crown.ffzg.hr), Croatian Dependency Treebank (hobs.ffzg.hr), and CroDeriV – Croatian Derivational Lexicon (croderiv. ffzg.hr). These resources can be useful when learning Croatian and are used as helpful tools (so-called – HINT, cf. Figure 3) in completing assignments throughout the HR4EU courses. The section also includes a short video-tutorial for each resource and a link to the respective search interface.

Figure 3.   Using LRs in courses

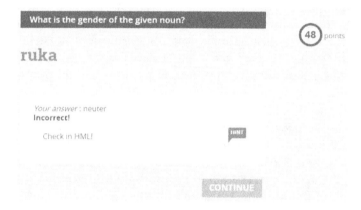

3.   Courses at HR4EU

3.1.   General courses

Although there is an extensive literature on teaching Croatian as an L2 (e.g. Barac-Kostrenčić, Kovačiček, & Lovasić, 1982; Čilaš-Mikulić, Gulešić, Machata, & Udier, 2008, 2011; Jelaska et al., 2005), authors exclusively focus on classroom teaching. We have consulted the grammar and topics they cover, but we needed to adapt it to fit a completely different approach to language learning, i.e. learning a foreign language using a language learning software. Courses available at the HR4EU portal are developed in Moodle (www.moodle.org), an open source e-learning platform, which provides course developers with numerous tools and activities that can be used in an e-learning course (e.g. interactive lessons, quizzes with multiple question types, dictionary, books, assignments). Consequently, the language material also had to be adjusted to the possibilities that this platform offers.

Each general course is divided into ten lessons: four lessons with new content are followed by a revision that covers the material learned thus far. Lessons comprise of several parts: the lesson body, grammar book, quizzes, and *Practice your writing skills* tasks. Each part focuses on the acquisition of different language skills (grammar, writing, reading, listening) and different cognitive strategies of language learning (e.g. repetition, resourcing, translation, etc., cf. Douglas Brown, 2007, p. 135).

The lesson body includes short grammar descriptions, word lists accompanied by audio tracks or illustrations or cultural peculiarities ('content pages'), and question parts ('question pages'). Content and question pages interchange in order to keep the user concentrated on the content[5]. Moreover, each lesson includes one or more short conversations or texts about the lesson topic. For the purpose of the HR4EU courses, more than 1600 audio records with vocabulary and conversations were taped[6], and over 150 digital illustrations were made that help users to learn the vocabulary[7].

The lesson body is followed by a more elaborate grammar part – *grammar book*. Grammar books follow the grammatical content from their respective lessons, but they can also be read separately, and downloaded or printed as a PDF document. The grammar books are also very useful for question parts of the lessons and for quizzes, especially due to their clear structure and large amount of examples they offer.

Each lesson consists of two quizzes – one is dedicated to practicing grammar, orthography and vocabulary, while the other is dedicated solely to practicing vocabulary. Quizzes comprise of different kinds of questions (e.g. cloze, multiple choice, matching, ordering, short answer, etc.). Just as in lesson's question pages, each question has two additional plugins: HINT and NOTE buttons. They provide users with help when they answer a question incorrectly, or with additional information about words or grammar used in the question if they answer it correctly (cf. Figure 3 and 4)[8].

---

5. Fleming (1987), according to Fahy (2004), stresses that "change and variety can help to create and sustain attention" (p. 145).
6. Newby et al. (2000) state that the combination of audio and print is a powerful alternative to reading alone.
7. According to one of Mayer's (2001, p. 68) principles that govern the impact of multimedia in teaching, students learn better when the words are combined with pictures.
8. According to Fahy (2004), users require feedback that enables "them to monitor their progress, to discover errors or misconceptions, and to recognize what they should do differently (or continue to do) to gain further proficiency" (pp. 142-147). Feedback differs according to the users' level. Therefore, we offer two-leveled feedback: (1) the information concerning the correctness of the answer, and (2) more elaborated feedback, which opens only when the user clicks the HINT or NOTE button.

Figure 4.   NOTE button

The HR4EU courses integrate bidirectional interaction with previously developed LRs. The lessons and quizzes are designed to encourage users to use LRs, e.g. to find the appropriate word form in Croatian Morphological Lexicon[9] or to learn semantically related words via Croatian Wordnet. However, our language learners often do not have a linguistic background, so some of the resources, e.g. Croatian Dependency Treebank, were modified in order to be used more easily in CALL. We have built a sub-corpus of Croatian Dependency Treebank that consists solely of the sentences from HR4EU courses and provides users with their syntactic and semantic role structure. We have also built the SynSem Visualizer[10], a tool which enables graphical representation of syntactic and semantic sentence structures.

This system is designed in a way that makes language learners helpful in the improvement of existing LRs. We will use learners' activity to enhance and enlarge existing LRs by tracking their activity yielding empty results, and adding them to the respective resources[11].

3.2.   Specialized courses

Since our main target groups of users are foreigners who are going to study or work in Croatia, we have offered two more courses at the HR4EU portal,

---

9. CML provides users with the information about the lemma of the word form, or about all possible word forms of a lemma. Cf. video-tutorial at http://www.hr4eu.hr/croatia/resources/.
10. http://hobs.ffzg.hr/en/search/
11. E.g. if the user searches for the word recept 'recipe' in CML and doesn't find it, we will add it to CML based on user's empty result.

namely Croatian for business users and Croatian for students. These courses offer specialized vocabulary related to business or education. Each course consists of four lessons that cover everyday business or student life. The final lesson of specialized courses is followed by writing assignments. Here, users can learn how to write a CV, job application or letter of motivation/recommendation in Croatian.

4.   Conclusion

In this paper, we have presented the HR4EU portal, a free-of-charge web portal for the e-learning of Croatian. It is one of few free e-learning sites that offer Croatian language courses and is developed by linguists, who are also native speakers of Croatian. The portal introduces language learners to Croatian language resources and their usefulness in learning a new language. As learners become aware of possibilities these resources offer, they can also use similar LRs in learning other languages as well, because similar resources are built and freely available for dozens of different languages.

5.   Acknowledgements

This paper and hereby presented project are fully supported by the European Union, European Social Fund, under the project grant HR.3.2.01.-0037 Mrežni portal za online učenje hrvatskoga jezika HR4EU.

References

Barac-Kostrenčić, V., Kovačićek, M., & Lovasić, S. (1982). *Učimo hrvatski: 1. stupanj: priručnik za studente.* Zagreb: Centar za učenje stranih jezika: Matica iseljenika Hrvatske.

Colpaert, J. (2004). *Design of online interactive language courseware: conceptualization, specification and prototyping. Research into the impact of linguistic-didactic functionality on software architecture.* PhD thesis. Antwerpen: Universiteit Antwerpen.

Čilaš-Mikulić, M., Gulešić Machata, M., & Udier, S. L. (2008). *Razgovarajte s nama!: A2 – B1: udžbenik hrvatskog jezika za više početnike.* Zagreb: Filozofski fakultet.

Čilaš-Mikulić, M., Gulešić Machata, M., & Udier, S. L. (2011). *Razgovarajte s nama!: B1 – B2: udžbenik hrvatskog jezika za niži srednji stupanj.* Zagreb: FF Press.

Douglas Brown, H. (2007). *Principles of Language Learning and Teaching (5th Edition).* Pearson: ESL.

Fahy, P. J. (2004). Media characteristics and online learning technology. In T. Anderson & F. Elloumi (Eds), *Theory and practice of online learning* (pp. 137-171). Athabasca University.

Fleming, M. (1987). Displays and communication. In R. M. Gagne (Ed.), *Instructional technology foundations* (pp. 233-260). Hillsdale, NJ: Erlbaum.

Jelaska, Z. et al. (2005). *Hrvatski kao drugi i strani jezik*. Zagreb: Hrvatska sveučilišna naklada.

Mayer, R. E. (2001). *Multimedia learning*. New York: Cambridge University Press. https://doi.org/10.1017/CBO9781139164603

Newby, T., Stepich, D., Lehman, J., & Russell, J. (2000). *Instructional technology for teaching and learning* (2d ed.). Upper Saddle River, NJ: Merrill.

Synchronous tandem language learning in a MOOC context: a study on task design and learner performance

Marta Fondo Garcia[1] and Christine Appel[2]

Abstract. In the context of a Language Massive Open Online Course (LMOOC), teacher interventions have to be designed into the course, since personalized teacher feedback actions are impossible due to the large number of participants. Learner autonomy, peer-feedback and task design are crucial in this course design. This paper presents a study on the task design effect on participants of a tandem MOOC (English-Spanish). The tandem MOOC takes advantage of the *massive* aspect of a MOOC to provide learners with ample opportunity for language use with native speakers of their target language, and access to peer-feedback. The tasks provide content and an objective for the conversations, turning them into episodes of meaningful language interaction. The study is conducted through observations of eight video recorded conversations by two learners of English carrying out four different tasks, eight tasks in total, with five different learners of Spanish, as it will be explained in more detail in the methodology section. The results show that task types had an effect on students' performance, but variables such as proficiency also played a role in learner interaction.

Keywords: e-tandem, MOOC, task design, student performance, student interaction.

1.   Introduction

This paper explores the effect of task design in a new web 2.0 collaborative learning environment that contributes to Synchronous Computer Mediated Communication (SCMC) and Computer Assisted Language Learning (CALL) research. The tandem MOOC (Appel & Pujolà, 2015) is an LMOOC which offers online

1. Universitat Oberta de Catalunya, Barcelona, Spain; mfondo@uoc.edu
2. Universitat Oberta de Catalunya, Barcelona, Spain; mappel@uoc.edu

How to cite this article: Fondo Garcia, M., & Appel, C. (2016). Synchronous tandem language learning in a MOOC context: a study on task design and learner performance. In S. Papadima-Sophocleous, L. Bradley & S. Thouësny (Eds), *CALL communities and culture – short papers from EUROCALL 2016* (pp. 144-149). Research-publishing.net. https://doi.org/10.14705/rpnet.2016.eurocall2016.552

speaking practice for learners of Spanish and English. It is based on the synergy of e-tandem and Task-Based Language Teaching (TBLT). In e-tandem settings, two learners of each other's language interact via videoconference in order to complete tasks together and help each other with the language learning process in their dual expert-novice roles.

This paper describes the initial findings of participants' performance and interaction analysis in relation to task design in an e-tandem setting. The aim is to explore how, and to what extent, different task designs influenced the performance of the participants in terms of communication strategies, length of conversation and immediate feedback provided during on-task time. The tasks are analysed using Robinson's (2001) Triadic Componential Framework (TCF). The data collected are the video recordings of the conversations by eight pairs of learners carrying out four different tasks in the tandem MOOC 2014.

2. Method

The setting is a six week course with a total of 36 available tasks. Learners could opt for the random tandem format in which they were paired up at random or the pre-arranged tandem format in which the interlocutor and the task were of their choice. Each week had a thematic category for all six activities: Negotiation, Quizzes, Free-talk, Problem-solving, Role-playing and Exam Preparation. All tasks had an even number of activities in English and Spanish. The tandem MOOC platform provided a videoconferencing tool which automatically records and archives the conversations, and the tandem tool which distributes the tasks to participants in real-time.

The participant sample is eight dyads, two Learners of English (LoE), B2-C1 CEFR[3] paired up with five Learners of Spanish (LoS), A2-B1 CEFR. The sample was chosen from the participants with the highest number of tasks done in the MOOC, in order to ensure a greater number of task samples available for analysis.

This study is conducted as an ex post facto observation. In order to more accurately measure the task effect on participant performance through observation, the same four tasks performed by the same two LoE were selected in order to reduce the individual differences variables. The task types used in this study, according to Pica, Kanagy, and Falodun (1993), are information gap (Quizzes 1), problem-

---

3. Common European Framework of Reference

solving (Negotiation 1, spot the difference) and opinion exchange (Free-talk 1 and Negotiation 6.3).

The task categorisation was done under the criteria of 'open-closed' solution and 'convergent-divergent' goal. Such variables are part of Robinson's (2001) TCF as interactional task conditions and have been widely studied to determine which ones ensure the optimal opportunity for conversational interaction (c.g. Duff, 1986; Long, 1981; Pica et al., 1993; Pica, Young, & Doughty, 1987). Participants' performance and interaction are measured by feedback episodes such as 1) Explicit Corrective Feedback (ECF), 2) Negotiation of Meaning (NoM) and 3) Recast. Feedback episodes are classified into successful and unsuccessful. A successful feedback episode indicates that a participant noticed the feedback and modified their output or acknowledged the correction (Table 1, sample 1). However, if a participant ignored the feedback or failed to notice the modified output then the feedback is considered to be unsuccessful (Table 1, sample 2).

Table 1.   Feedback excerpts

Successful feedback – sample 1	Unsuccessful feedback – sample 2
P: Can you see **fishes**? O: No I can't see any fish. P: I can see a lot of **fish**.	E:¿**Está una** pastel o una tarta? O:Umm creo que no, no E:Ehhh..**está**… O:En lugar de **estar es ser**, es; es dulce, no es estar, ¿es carne?, ¿es verdura?, ¿Vale?. E:¿**Está un** plato famoso en español?

3.   Discussion

According to Pica et al. (1993), Long (1996) and Duff (1986), closed solution and convergent goal tasks result in a greater amount and quality of interaction. However, in this study, such tasks (Quizzes 1 and Negotiation 1) are the ones with a lower number of feedback episodes. In contrast, in this study, the 'divergent-open' tasks, such as Free-talk 1 and Negotiation 6.3 (opinion exchange) have a longer length (Table 2).

Table 2.   Task types and length

Task	Total minutes	Pairs	Overall time
Quizzes 1	42:08	Pedro - June	17:44
		Olga - Ellen	24:24

Negotiation 1	32:10	Pedro - Oliver	18:53
		Olga - Garreth	13:17
Free-talk	78:02	Pedro - Ellen	51:47
		Olga - Christine	26:55
Negotiation 6.3	42:57	Pedro - Christine	18:49
		Olga - Christine	24:08

Divergent-open tasks have also a greater number of feedback episodes but with a high rate of unsuccessful feedback. Therefore, feedback is less effective in contrast to Negotiation 1 (closed-convergent) in which only one out of 13 feedback episodes was unsuccessful (Table 3).

Table 3.   Feedback episodes per task

Task	Total	ECB	NoM	Recast	Successful	Unsuccessful
Quizzes 1	9	1	8	0	6	3
Negotiation 1	13	3	8	2	12	1
Free-talk 1	21	6	13	2	15	6
Negotiation 6.3	12	4	7	1	10	2

In this study, proficiency and feedback are apparently closely related (Table 4). As noted by Kawaguchi and Ma (2012), "[i]t is interesting to observe that the speaker of higher proficiency level in all combinations consistently show higher frequencies of initiating recasts than the speakers of lower level while this observation is reversed with [negotiation of meaning]" (p. 8). In this study, ECF is also notably higher among the most proficient learners.

Table 4.   Feedback per participant

Participants	Proficiency	Tasks done	ECF given	NoM asked	Recast given
Pedro -NSS1	C1	4	8	1	2
Olga - NSS2	B2+	4	3	4	2
Christine-NSE1	B1	3	3	5	0
Ellen - NSE2	A2 -	2	0	12	0
Oliver - NSE3	A2+	1	1	1	1
Garreth - NSE4	A2 -	1	0	4	0
June - NSE5	B1	1	0	1	0

The most common communication strategies used during negotiation of meaning situations are language switch and ask for clarification (see Table 5). This result is analyzed in the following section.

Table 5. Communication strategies during feedback episodes

Task	Participants	Language switch	Ask for clarification
Quizzes 1	Pedro-June	1	0
	Olga-Ellen	2	0
Negotiation 1	Pedro-Oliver	2	1
	Olga-Gareth	8 (less proficient)	3
Free-talk 1	Pedro-Ellen	9 (less proficient)	1
	Olga-Christine	1	1
Negotiation 6.3	Pedro-Christine	1	2
	Olga-Christine	2	3
Total		26	11

4.   Conclusion

Task design and its effect on interaction and negotiation have been studied in different contexts in order to provide the most beneficial speaking practice to language learners. Several studies have confirmed that learners can develop their language competence through negotiation of meaning, which promotes the elicitation of modified input and output, enhances learners' comprehension and draws their attention to L2 form as well as meaning (Gass & Varonis, 1985, 1994; Long, 1996; Pica, Young, & Doughty, 1987). The results in this study have to be interpreted tentatively due to the small size of the sample, the video recording selection criteria based solely on the most active participants and the variety of tasks. Having said that, the results suggest that we cannot assume that learner performance in a tandem setting will be the same as in the Non-Native Speaker (NNS)-NNS, or novice-expert dyad configurations found in most studies in the literature of TBLT. For instance, the presence of a very high number of language switching episodes in a Native Speaker (NS)-NNS interaction (presented in Table 4) reflects the peculiarity of interaction in tandem settings, as learners know each other's language. The possibility that differences may be due to the interaction setting of a tandem conversation means that studies need to be replicated in this particular design before transferring any results. We plan to extend this study further by collecting a larger sample of data and complementing this with participant interviews in the next edition of the tandem MOOC in the fall of 2016.

5.   Acknowledgements

The tandem MOOC tools, Videochat and Tandem tool, were developed under the SpeakApps project (www.speakapps.eu) (Appel et al., 2014) within the European Lifelong Learning Program funding.

References

Appel, C., Nic Giolla Mihchil, M., Jager, S., & Prizel-Kania, A. (2014). Speakapps 2, speaking practice in foreign language through ICT tools. In S. Jager, L. Bradley, E. J. Meima & S. Thouësny (Eds), *CALL design: principles and practice. Proceedings of the 2014 Eurocall conference, Groningen, the Netherlands* (pp. 12-17). Dublin: Research-publishing.net. https://doi.org/10.14705/rpnet.2014.000187

Appel, C., & Pujolà, J. T. (2015). Pedagogical and technological issues in the instructional design of a tandem MOOC. In *Proceedings of E-Learn: World Conference on E-Learning in Corporate, Government, Healthcare, and Higher Education 2015* (pp. 1696-1705). Chesapeake, VA: Association for the Advancement of Computing in Education (AACE).

Duff, P. A. (1986). *Another look at interlanguage talk: taking task to task.* Newbury.

Gass, S., & Varonis, E. (1985). Task variation and non-native/non-native negotiation of meaning. In S. Gass & C. Madden (Eds), *Input in second language acquisition* (pp. 141-161). Rowley, MA: Newbury House.

Gass, S., & Varonis, E. (1994). Input, interaction, and second language production. *Studies in second language acquisition, 16*(3), 283-302. https://doi.org/10.1017/S0272263100013097

Kawaguchi, S., & Ma, Y. (2012). Corrective feedback, negotiation of meaning and grammar development: learner-learner and learner-native speaker interaction in ESL. *Open Journal of Modern Linguistics, 2*(2), 57-70. https://doi.org/10.4236/ojml.2012.22008

Long, M. H. (1981). Input, interaction, and second□language acquisition. *Annals of the New York academy of sciences, 379*(1), 259-278. https://doi.org/10.1111/j.1749-6632.1981.tb42014.x

Long, M. H. (1996). The role of the linguistic environment in second language acquisition. *Handbook of second language acquisition, 2*(2), 413-468. https://doi.org/10.1016/b978-012589042-7/50015-3

Pica, T., Kanagy, R., & Falodun, J. (1993). Choosing and using communication tasks for second language instruction. In G. Crookes & S. Gass (Eds), *Tasks and language learning* (pp. 9-34). Clevedon, England: Multilingual Matters. https://doi.org/10.2307/3586992

Pica, T., Young, R., & Doughty, C. (1987). The impact of interaction on comprehension. *TESOL Quarterly, 21*, 737-758.

Robinson, P. (2001). Task complexity, task difficulty, and task production: exploring interactions in a componential framework. *Applied Linguistics, 22*(1), 27-57. https://doi.org/10.1093/applin/22.1.27

What students think and what they actually do in a mobile assisted language learning context: new insights for self-directed language learning in higher education

Gustavo García Botero[1] and Frederik Questier[2]

Abstract. In an attempt to understand whether Mobile-Assisted Language Learning (MALL) could foster students' self-directed learning, this paper analyzes a self-directed learning experience by means of a language app: Duolingo. In this study, higher education language students were encouraged to use Duolingo outside of the classroom. The data collected via app tracking, surveys and semi-structured interviews reveal that the low activity in the app contrasts the high value students attribute to it. Students indicated that the low activity is due to other obligations in their lives. They also expressed the need of external motivation to finish the course. The study suggests that mentoring and modeling are still needed in the development of self-directed study skills and it highlights the importance of implementing different data collection techniques to understand what students think and do in MALL.

Keywords: data collection, Duolingo, MALL, self-directed study.

1.   Introduction

When inquiring about what students do in a computer assisted language learning environment, Stockwell (2012) hints at an over reliance on surveys as a data collection method. Likewise, Fisher (2012) states that the "use of questionnaires alone is not a reliable source of information about student use of software and should be avoided as a single source of information" (p. 27). The ubiquity and

1. Vrije Universiteit Brussel, Brussel, Belgium; Gustavo.Garcia.Botero@vub.ac.be
2. Vrije Universiteit Brussel, Brussel, Belgium; fquestie@vub.ac.be

How to cite this article: García Botero, G., & Questier, F. (2016). What students think and what they actually do in a mobile assisted language learning context: new insights for self-directed language learning in higher education. In S. Papadima-Sophocleous, L. Bradley & S. Thouësny (Eds), *CALL communities and culture – short papers from EUROCALL 2016* (pp. 150-154). Research-publishing.net. https://doi.org/10.14705/rpnet.2016.eurocall2016.553

just in time learning provided by MALL have particular implications on how users self-direct their learning and how researchers collect data on students' activity. Stockwell (2013) points out the small "amount of research examining how learners engage in mobile learning outside of the classroom" (p. 118). Little is known about what happens when students download a language application to their devices.

Conveniently, MALL applications are gradually adding features that allow quantitative measurements of app usage. One example is the free of charge application Duolingo. Through its unobtrusive tracking dashboard *Duolingo for schools*, teachers can see the languages students are practicing and their progress in the Duolingo language curriculum.

2. Method

The participants were Colombian higher education students enrolled at different levels of language courses. 574 students were given a formal lecture about Duolingo. They learned about its different features and they were encouraged to use the app at their convenience. Furthermore, students were invited to join the Duolingo dashboard where their activity would be tracked. 273 students reported to not have used Duolingo; 149 students reported having used Duolingo after the MALL lecture while 118 of these users accepted to be tracked in the dashboard.

Eight weeks after the lecture in which they were encouraged to use the app, students filled out a questionnaire on their perception of Duolingo. The questionnaire contained items measured through a Likert scale where 1 represented *totally disagree* and 5 represented *totally agree.*

Once a year had passed, students' data from the dashboard were retrieved. A stratified sampling was applied to select students for an interview about their general impressions of the app and their opinion about how to foster its use among the student population. The analysis of the sampling population resulted in the stratification of the data into three groups of students: tracked students who barely used Duolingo (students who were active ten days or less, N=73), students who had a moderate use (students who were active more than ten and less than 50 days, N=31) and students who had the most sustained use (students that were active 50 or more days, N=14). Five students in each group were randomly selected for the interview.

3.   Results

Table 1.   Questionnaire: students' perceptions about Duolingo

Duolingo item sorted from high to low score. N=149	Mean	SD
1. Duolingo encourages me to learn different languages that are not taught in the Modern Languages program	3.97	0.993
2. I would like Duolingo to be integrated as a component of independent learning (work done outside the classroom)	3.94	0.91
3. I like the game-like methodology proposed by Duolingo	3.93	0.844
4. Duolingo allows me to be independent in language learning	3.93	0.844
5. I have no problem to access Duolingo	3.93	1.101
6. I would recommend Duolingo for language learning	3.91	0.932
7. I find a connection between what I studied in Duolingo and what was taught to me by the language teachers	3.89	0.927
8. I think I can improve my vocabulary with Duolingo	3.89	0.934
9. I think Duolingo offers an organized language learning path	3.87	0.935
10. Duolingo is fun for people my age	3.87	0.903
11. I like the exercises proposed by Duolingo	3.86	0.923
12. Duolingo motivates me to study languages with my Smartphone or tablet	3.85	0.964
13. I think I can improve my grammar with Duolingo	3.83	0.918
14. I think that I can improve my listening with Duolingo	3.81	0.896
15. I think I can improve my writing with Duolingo	3.79	0.903
16. I think that I can improve my speaking with Duolingo	3.72	0.958
17. I think Duolingo can satisfy my learning needs	3.72	0.985
18. I would like my teacher to see my progress in Duolingo	3.71	1.009
19. Duolingo encourages me to go beyond what is taught in the language classroom	3.70	0.991
20. I think I can improve my reading with Duolingo	3.68	0.939
21. I would like Duolingo to be integrated inside the classroom	3.58	0.952
22. I prefer other free apps to learn languages than Duolingo	3.38	0.977

Table 2.   Duolingo dashboard: average of completed units and number of days of Duolingo use

N= 118	Mode	Range	Mean	SD	SE
Days Active	1	0- 394	15.13	45.18	3.06
Lessons completed	0	1908	56.49	169.95	11.53
Units completed*	0	78	13.55	18.47	1.25

* A unit is a set of lessons

Table 3. Course completion: verall language course completion in Duolingo

Course Group	N.	N. Students who finished the course	Language completed
English semester 1	17	1	English
English semester 2	18	1	English
English semester 3	13	3	English
English semester 4	20	2	English
French semester 1	8	0	-
French semester 2	10	0	-
French semester 3	14	2	1 English 1 French
French semester 4	18	3	3 French 1 Italian*
Total	118	12	8 English 4 French 1 Italian*

*Same student did French and Italian

4. Discussion

According to the students' questionnaire answers, Duolingo is perceived to be a useful tool for language learning. Views of Duolingo are positive as an instructional method (items 3, 7, 9, 11), motivation tool (items 1, 10, 11), promoter of self-directed learning (items 2, 4) and enabler of language skills practice items (8, 13-16, 20). These results were confirmed by the individual semi-structured interviews in which every interviewed student reported having recommended the app to peers and friends (as predicted in item 6 of the questionnaire). However, the results retrieved from the Duolingo dashboard reveal that only 12 out of the 118 tracked students (10%) managed to completely finish a Duolingo language course. Despite the considerable variability of the data, Table 2 puts into evidence the low participation of students. Different data collection techniques reveal a discrepancy between students' perception and actual use of the application. Such discrepancy is seen in similar studies (e.g. Stockwell, 2008). From the students' point of view, this is explained by their busy lives inside and outside their academic context, the lack of formal follow-up (related to the absence of a teacher), and the lack of additional motivational factors (e.g. language certificate, course grades). Our results confirm studies that take into account the relationship between students and technology (e.g. Azevedo et al., 2003) in which the difficulty of learners to self-regulate when learning is demonstrated.

5.   Conclusion

This study points out the relevance of data collection to improve the understanding of MALL outside formal educational contexts. Although tracking is not the panacea in computer-assisted language learning research to investigate student behavior (Fischer, 2007), it demonstrates the relevance of scrutinizing actual usage data because what learners indicate in surveys contradicts what they do in reality.

The combination of data collection techniques suggests that self-directed learning in MALL requires modeling and mentoring, which is why a tutor (such as a teacher) remains important. Even if students are formally introduced to an expectedly convenient and motivating app, only a small number of them make substantial extracurricular use of it. Results of the study show that for substantial MALL usage, a combination of incentives, scaffolding and curricular integration are needed. Such concepts will be investigated in follow up studies.

6.   Acknowledgements

The studies developed by Gustavo Garcia Botero are financially supported by the European Commission-Erasmus Mundus Action 2 Grant number: 2013-2591/001-001.

References

Azevedo, R., Cromley, J. G., Thomas, L., Seibert, D., & Tron, M. (2003). Online process scaffolding and students' self-regulated learning with hypermedia. *Paper presented at the annual meeting of the American Educational Research Association, Chicago, IL.*

Fischer, R. (2007). How do we know what students are actually doing? Monitoring students' behavior in CALL. *Computer Assisted Language Learning, 20*(5), 409-442.

Fisher, R. (2012). Diversity in learner usage patterns. In G. Stockwell (Ed.), *Computer-assisted language learning: diversity in research and practice* (pp.14-32). Cambridge: Cambridge University Press.

Stockwell, G. (2008). Investigating learner preparedness for and usage patterns of mobile learning. *ReCALL, 20*(3), 253-270. https://doi.org/10.1017/S0958344008000232

Stockwell, G. (2012). *Computer-assisted language learning: diversity in research and practice.* Cambridge: Cambridge University Press.

Stockwell, G. (2013). Tracking learner usage of mobile phones for language learning outside of the classroom. *CALICO Journal, 30*, 118-136.

An Audio-Lexicon Spanish-Nahuatl: using technology to promote and disseminate a native Mexican language

Rafael García-Mencía[1], Aurelio López-López[2],
and Angélica Muñoz Meléndez[3]

Abstract. This research focuses on the design of resources for both reappraising the knowledge of a native language for those who speak or have notions of Nahuatl, and getting familiar with terms for those who do not speak this language. An audio-lexicon Spanish-Nahuatl, ALEN, was developed taking advantage of new technologies, especially mobile devices and gadgets, as an opportunity to reach children and youth mainly. A beta version of ALEN has been tested by volunteers with very promising results. Examinations of knowledge of Nahuatl language before and after one week of use of ALEN have shown that most volunteers improved their vocabulary.

Keywords: native language learning, endangered languages, mobile devices.

1. Introduction

Nahuatl is a Native American language with the largest population of speakers in Mexico, nearly 1.5 million people – that represents 1.7% of the total population over five years (INEGI, 2000) speak Nahuatl. As mentioned by Monzón (1990), "Nahuatl is the result of a continuous and long history of communication creativity" (p. 11). It was the dominant language in the center of Mexico before the Spanish conquest by the mid-fourteenth century. Nowadays Nahuatl is mainly spoken by marginalised groups.

1. Universidad Autónoma de Guerrero, Chilpancingo Gro, México; menciarg@gmail.com
2. Instituto Nacional de Astrofísica, Óptica y Electrónica, Pue, México; allopez@inaoep.mx
3. Instituto Nacional de Astrofísica, Óptica y Electrónica, Pue, México; munoz@inaoep.mx

How to cite this article: García-Mencía, R., López-López, A., & Muñoz Meléndez, A. (2016). An Audio-Lexicon Spanish-Nahuatl: using technology to promote and disseminate a native Mexican language. In S. Papadima-Sophocleous, L. Bradley & S. Thouësny (Eds), *CALL communities and culture – short papers from EUROCALL 2016* (pp. 155-159). Research-publishing.net. https://doi.org/10.14705/rpnet.2016.eurocall2016.554

Diverse efforts are made around the world to preserve and disseminate endangered languages, since languages have a major role in the cultural heritage of mankind. For instance, the declaration of an International Mother Language Day by the United Nations Educational, Scientific and Cultural Organization (UNESCO), whose goal is to encourage linguistic and cultural diversity in the world and raise awareness about the 3,000 of the 6,000 languages spoken in the world that are endangered to a greater or lesser degree (UNESCO, 1999).

There are different ways to contribute to safeguarding endangered languages; from the promulgation of public policies and laws to preserve and promote minority languages to the generation of linguistic resources oriented to these minorities. This research deals with the latter effort, the design of resources for both, reappraising the knowledge of a native language for those who speak or have notions of Nahuatl, and getting familiar with Nahuatl terms for those who do not speak it.

Since this research aims to reach children, teenagers, and young adults, Nahuatl resources are developed taking advantage of new technologies, especially mobile devices and gadgets. For that, an Android based application called ALEN (from its Spanish acronym that means Audio-Lexicon Spanish-Nahuatl) has been developed and tested. ALEN comprises a database of 132 words in Spanish and Nahuatl, with both written and oral modalities, homemade illustrations and word-search capabilities.

As a preliminary step for testing with the intended users, a beta version of ALEN has been tested by volunteers, with aim of fine tuning it. These volunteers completed a Nahuatl knowledge examination twice, before and after the testing period. Volunteers also completed a test which revealed that the preliminary version of ALEN was useful to get familiar with Nahuatl notions.

2.   The Audio-Lexicon Spanish-Nahuatl

The application was created using Android Studio, the official IDE for mobile application development based on IntelliJ IDEA[4]. Overall, the ALEN application runs locally and once installed, it does not create files or require access to services and resources such as the phone network, WiFi or Bluetooth connectivity. There are more than twenty Nahuatl variants in Mexico, but the variant with the largest

---

4. Android Studio and SDK, https://developer.android.com/intl/es/sdk/index.html

number of speakers is that of the north of Veracruz. This is the Nahuatl variant included in the project.

2.1. Android app

The ALEN application has a simple interface, which allows the user to enter text in Nahuatl or Spanish. There are two buttons, one used to find the written word in the text box and the other to reproduce the pronunciation of the word when found. At the center of the screen, an image illustrating the concept related to the word is displayed. Figure 1 shows the interface of the application running on a cell phone and a tablet.

Figure 1.   ALEN interface in two devices

2.2. Experimental settings and analysis results

One dimension of the ALEN application was evaluated: how useful it is for reinforcing and acquiring vocabulary of the Nahuatl language. The procedure completed by the volunteers that participated in the study was as follows: (1) creating an access account on the website of ALEN; (2) completing an initial examination of knowledge of Nahuatl language; (3) installing the application on their mobile devices; (4) using the application as many times as possible during one week; and (5) completing a second examination of knowledge of the language.

The online examination of knowledge of Nahuatl language was specially designed for this study. Nahuatl being a native Mexican language, it has been in constant contact with Spanish, the language commonly spoken in Mexico. For that, Mexicans are familiar with some Nahuatl words and it is important to measure any notion of Nahuatl that our volunteers might have.

The examination of knowledge of Nahuatl comprised 15 questions. The first ten were aimed to achieve word pair association; in the first column Nahuatl words were listed, and in a second column Spanish words were presented, sorted in a different order. The latter five questions were intended to assess listening skills. Each question included an audio recording of a native Nahuatl speaker, and a window for writing the word heard by the user. Volunteers received one point for each question properly answered and there were no time constraints to complete the examination. The set of 132 words within ALEN was used as the battery for randomly generating the examinations of knowledge of the language.

2.3. Participants

A total of 11 volunteers participated in the evaluation of the beta version of ALEN, nine men and two women, of ages 29.6 ± 7.3 years. All the volunteers were native Spanish speakers. They gave their informed consent to participate in the study.

3. Results

Figure 2 depicts the comparison of number of points scored by volunteers in the first and second examination of knowledge of Nahuatl. Note that most users achieved clear improvement in their Nahuatl vocabulary after one week using the mobile application. In effect, 82% of volunteers improved their knowledge of Nahuatl. This result might also be related to the frequency of use of the application, with 73% of volunteers reporting the highest values of use frequency, i.e. between ten to 30 times, meaning they used ALEN at least once every day, on average.

Figure 2.   Points scored by volunteers in first and second examination

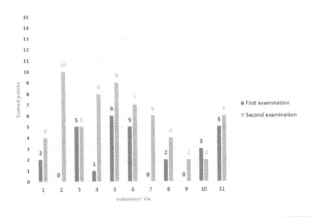

4.   Conclusions

The goal of this research is to contribute to safeguarding endangered languages, namely the Nahuatl language, by developing tools and resources for their preservation and dissemination. Also, we look to develop these resources by taking advantage of the capabilities of mobile devices that are especially popular among young people.

We have described the design of the ALEN application, an Audio-Lexicon Spanish-Nahuatl whose beta version has been evaluated by 11 volunteers with encouraging results in terms of scores of improvement of vocabulary. Most volunteer users of the ALEN application improved their Nahuatl vocabulary, and also most of them frequently used the application during the test period.

In the near future, we will extend ALEN with an option for a spoken search to improve user interaction. This extension requires the processing of audio inputs, as well as the extraction of relevant features to be compared with pre-processed models of those words in the lexicon. We will also increase the set of words of the application, and finally we will include other variants of Nahuatl.

5.   Acknowledgements

We thank Eucario Hernández Alvarado, the native speaker, and Efren Ángel García, the illustration designer.

References

INEGI. (2000). Perfil sociodemográfico de la población hablante de náhuatl. *XII Censo General de Población y Vivienda 2000*. México: Instituto Nacional de Estadística, Geografía e Informática.

Monzón, C. (1990). *Registro de la variación fonológica en el náhuatl moderno: un estudio de caso* (Vol. 34). CIESAS. México.

UNESCO. (1999). Report of Commission II at the 30th Plenary Meeting (*30 C/COM.II/3*) (Vol. 41).

The use of interactive whiteboards: enhancing
the nature of teaching young language learners

Christina Nicole Giannikas[1]

Abstract. Language teaching can be enhanced by effective uses of technology; nonetheless, there are teachers who are reluctant to integrate technology in their practice. The debated issue has resulted in a number of Ministries of Education worldwide, including the Greek Ministry, to support a transition through the introduction of Interactive Whiteboards (IWBs). This initiative was not well-received in either the public or private sector, due to the fact that teachers were not provided with any training in how to use IWBs and include them in their teaching. IWBs became intimidating to the language teacher and did not serve their intended purpose in most cases. Nonetheless, there were teachers who were intrigued by IWBs and made an effort to apply them. The present paper focuses on the development of interactive language learning and the effect the teachers' risk-taking has on pedagogy from the teachers' and students' perspectives. The outcomes of the study were that language teachers have taken charge of their own professional growth and take risks in order to help learners benefit from IWBs. However, due to lack of training, teachers and students have not reached the zenith of using IWBs.

Keywords: interactive whiteboards, young learners, teaching practices, teachers' risk-taking.

1.   Introduction

Language teaching can be enhanced by effective uses of educational technology; nonetheless, there are language teachers around the globe who are reluctant to integrate technology in their practice (Papadima-Sophocleous, Kakouli-Constantinou, & Giannikas, 2015).

---

1. Cyprus University of Technology, Limassol, Cyprus; christina.giannikas@cut.ac.cy

How to cite this article: Giannikas, C. N. (2016). The use of interactive whiteboards: enhancing the nature of teaching young language learners. In S. Papadima-Sophocleous, L. Bradley & S. Thouësny (Eds), *CALL communities and culture – short papers from EUROCALL 2016* (pp. 160-166). Research-publishing.net. https://doi.org/10.14705/rpnet.2016.eurocall2016.555

The issue has been highly debated in the field and measures have been employed to support the integration of technology in education, including financial support (DfES, 2003, 2005). Such a transition was supported by the Greek Ministry of Education through the introduction of IWBs. The Ministry of Education, with the support of MLS, a Greek leading company in educational technology, supplied and installed 3,300 IWBs in public schools across the country (http://www.skai.gr/news/technology/article/169271/diadrastikoi-pinakes-sta-ellinika-sholeia-/). This initiative inspired private language school owners to supply their teachers with IWBs as well. Due to a lack of training, this innovative and powerful technological tool was intimidating in the eye of the language teacher, and did not serve the purpose it was meant to in most cases. However, there were teachers who were intrigued by IWBs and made an effort to apply its use in their classes. These teachers were self-taught and their motivation led them into making an effort to train their peers in the process.

The present paper focuses on the self-taught language educators in question, specifically on teachers of young language learners. The effect and development of interactive language learning in a context where no training was undertaken will be discussed; additionally, the effect the teachers' risk-taking has on pedagogy are presented. The paper introduces a small-scale study with a focus on young learners.

2.   Method

2.1.   Research methods and data analysis

The current exploratory study aimed to record the use of IWBs in the young learners' classroom. The study took place in South Western Greece and focused on private language schools. For the needs of the present small-scale study, data was collected through semi-structured interviews with five language teachers, and through questionnaires completed by 50 students. ATLAS.ti 7©2013 was used to analyse and code the interview recordings. The procedure was carried out as follows (inspired by Giannikas, 2013):

- An initial reading of the transcribed interviews was conducted. This process allowed themes to emerge.

- The texts were re-read and thoughts were annotated in the margin. The text was examined closely to facilitate a micro-analysis of data.

The data from all the questionnaires were transferred onto a spreadsheet and calculated on Excel.

2.2.   Research participants and context

The study focused on young learners, aged nine to 16, who attended private language lessons after mainstream school. The teachers who participated were from the same language school and had been teaching languages for six to 25 years and four out of five held an MA in English Literature and Languages. According to the interviews conducted, four out of five teachers had been using IWBs for three to four years and one had been using it for one year. None of the teachers had official training on how to apply IWBs. They were self-taught and exchanged information regarding the use of IWBs and their features with colleagues.

3.   Discussion

Although using a PC and the Internet are a daily occurrence, integrating and mastering Information and Communications Technology (ICT) in language teaching is not a simple task, especially when no training is involved. According to interview data, all teachers claimed that IWBs had the potential to add benefits to their teaching and prompt them into becoming better pedagogists. The following figures (Figure 1, Figure 2, and Figure 3) indicate the teachers' efforts in using IWBs frequently.

Language teachers in this context have been experiencing radical transformations in their classroom environments and have been willing to take risks and expose their lack of training in the use of IWBs in order to offer as much as possible to their students. Teachers of the Greek context have been deprived of essential technical and practical guidance that would make the use of IWBs more effective.

Figure 1.   For how many years have you been using IWBs?

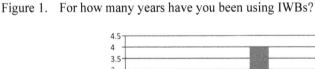
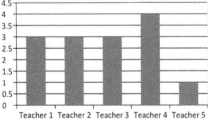

Figure 2.   How many times a week do you use IWBs?

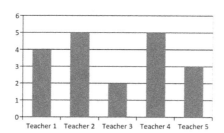

Figure 3.   How long do you use IWBs in each lesson (in minutes)?

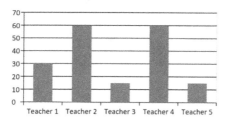

One point that was made during interviews was that three out of five teachers used the IWB more than their students did in class. More specifically, sample statements of what teachers liked least about IWBs are as follows:

"I dislike the fact that the children cannot use the IWB as much as I do" (Teacher 1).

"It requires more teaching time" (Teacher 4).

An interesting outcome of the research was that the younger teachers, who have been more exposed to technology and software, were of the impression that the IWB was mainly a tool used by the teacher rather than the students. This means that even though the IWB encourages student-centred learning, there are teachers who apply it in a teacher-centred environment due to their lack of training and/or reluctance to step out of their teacher-fronted comfort zone. The older teachers stepped back and gave students the opportunity to use IWBs more and become independent users. The teachers who embraced the student-centred environment with the help of IWBs were recorded to play more interactive games on the IWB than the younger teachers, whilst the teachers who supported a more teacher-fronted environment embraced more grammar and vocabulary tasks and avoided interactive activities.

These findings are in agreement with the outcomes from students' questionnaires as indicated in Figure 4.

Figure 4.　How often do you play games on the IWB?

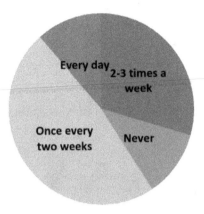

The open-ended question of what the students' favourite task on the IWB was retrieved the following sample quotes (translated from students' L1):

"Games where we learn grammar" (Student 22).

"My favourite activities are crosswords" (Students 13).

"I like playing Hangman" (Student 34).

"I like listening activities on the IWB because I can concentrate better having pictures to look at" (Student 44).

"I like fill-in the gaps activities" (Student 12).

"I like multiple-choice activities" (Student 4).

The students' responses show that students appreciate the interactive nature of the IWB and the variety it offers. The IWB has a lot to offer and the questionnaires indicate that the features of an IWB triggers all kinds of language learners. The tasks the students completed on the IWB enhance their involvement, and the hands-on tasks can give them autonomy and facilitate multisensory learning, which is evident in the students' selection of preferable tasks.

4.   Conclusions

Students' increased engagement is the main benefit of using IWBs, and this has been realised by the participant teachers who have integrated IWBs, despite the fact that they have not been officially trained to do so. They make an effort to include IWBs as often as possible in a context they can control and function. Although this may deprive them and their students of some of the interesting features IWBs have to offer, they apply the tool as much as they can. Nonetheless, teachers chose to adopt a teacher-centred environment with the use of IWBs. Had teachers been offered official technical and practical training when IWBs were introduced to the Greek education system, their approach would be different, given their openness to learning new features to language teaching and to taking risks in the classroom.

The study conducted supports that instruction with the use of IWBs can be well-received by young learners. Learners become involved and can adapt to the technological tool presented to them. It gives them many opportunities to evolve as learners and users of technology. Since IWBs already exist in most educational contexts, whether in the private or public sector, training ought to be offered to all teachers in order to enhance professional development, which will have an immediate effect on young language learners. Additionally, teachers can become more comfortable with IWB technology, being more exposed to effective pedagogical practices and teaching strategies.

The present study shows that there is potential in language learning for children with the use of IWBs, due to the teachers' willingness to integrate new technology and take risks when applying it. This attitude is a positive first step and if the correct measures are taken from policy makers and stakeholders, language teaching may advance in extraordinary ways, in the region and beyond.

5.   Acknowledgements

I would like to thank the language teachers and students who took part in the study. Their patience and excellent cooperation are very much appreciated.

References

DfES. (2003). *Towards a unified e-learning strategy. Executive summary.* London: Department for Education and Skills.

DfES. (2005). *Harnessing technology: transforming learning and children's services.* London: Department for Education and Skills.

Giannikas, C. N. (2013). *Early language learning within a Greek regional context.* PhD Thesis. London, UK: Metropolitan University.

Papadima-Sophocleous, S., Kakouli-Constantinou, E., & Giannikas, C. N. (2015). ICT in EFL: the case of Cypriot secondary education. In C. N. Giannikas, L. McLaughlin, G. Fanning, & N. Deutsch Muller (Eds), *Children learning English: from research to practice.* Reading, UK: Garnet Publishing Ltd.

A pre-mobility eTandem project for incoming international students at the University of Padua

Lisa Griggio[1] and Edit Rózsavölgyi[2]

Abstract. This study focuses on a strategic partnership with students from the University of Padua and international students coming to Padua mainly in the setting of Erasmus student mobility and exchange programs. The project is designed specifically for incoming international students to facilitate their integration into the Italian higher educational learning environment. They can practice their Italian, have practical information about Padua and its university, and get to know local students with whom they can possibly have face-to-face relationships after their arrival. The online exchange – based on the principles of tandem learning – is carried out in the setting of a one-to-one and a many-to-many interaction using different technological tools which include a dedicated institutional Moodle platform, a social Facebook area restricted to the eTandem community and other networking systems such as Skype, e-mail, chat and WhatsApp. We have found that the project helps both Italian and international students develop their digital, linguistic and intercultural competencies, boosts their critical thinking and cultivates their curiosity towards others. It facilitates international students' integration into their target country/university/culture.

Keywords: eTandem, pre-mobility, university students, international setting.

1. Introduction

New learning policies promote plurilingualism, internationalization, learner autonomy for lifelong learning and require the aptitude of young people to deal competently with the demands of linguistic and cultural diversity. To this aim, we have to rethink traditional notions and priorities of language education.

1. University of Padua, Padua, Italy; lisa.griggio@unipd.it
2. University of Padua, Padua, Italy; edit.r@unipd.it

How to cite this article: Griggio, L., & Rózsavölgyi, E. (2016). A pre-mobility eTandem project for incoming international students at the University of Padua. In S. Papadima-Sophocleous, L. Bradley & S. Thouësny (Eds), *CALL communities and culture – short papers from EUROCALL 2016* (pp. 167-171). Research-publishing.net. https://doi.org/10.14705/rpnet.2016.eurocall2016.556

Numerous educators and researchers have noted that the use of information and communication technologies in L2 teaching/acquisition seems to be the best way to cope with the challenge of internationally changing educational scenarios force upon us (e.g. Pareja-Lora, Rodríguez-Arancón, & Calle-Martínez, 2016).

It has always been an uncontroversial assumption that one of the most effective ways of improving L2 communication skills is through enabling students to engage directly with native speakers. The potential of tandem interaction in online environments is self-evident. But technology itself is only a means to an end, and the actual application of Web 2.0 tools to exploit distant peer-to-peer activities for educational purposes is far from being simple and easy. Attractive and effective foreign language learning calls for an organized and structured framework which can give students the support they need in order to make the most of the opportunities that the wide variety of communicative channels they have at hand presents.

In this study we want to exchange good practices by providing the outcomes of an eTandem project carried out at the Padua University Language Center during the winter of the 2015-2016 academic year. The project welcomed Italian students from Padua University and international students that in the framework of student mobility programs such as Erasmus were coming to Padua for the spring term of the same academic year.

Our approach was plurilingual, intercultural, inclusive and attentive to the basic e-skills which 21st century students need, i.e. strategies for effective online activities, ability to evaluate and use online sources of information, ability to use Internet applications for effective cooperation and collaboration (Dede, 2009; Fullan, 2013; Griffin, McGaw, & Care, 2012; Klimczak-Pawlak, 2014). The objectives of the project were as such manifold:

- deepening students' linguistic competence via content-related input;

- promoting their ability to perceive and mediate the relationships which exist among languages and cultures;

- supporting respect for the plurilingualism of others and the value of languages and varieties irrespective of their perceived social status;

- upholding respect for the cultures embodied in languages and the cultural identities of others.

Through the participation in this international cooperation project we wanted all students to enjoy multilingualism and not be afraid of it. Following the European educational priorities, key competences for lifelong learning (Europa, 2006) were in the forefront for better learning outcomes. By establishing a community-based learning via Facebook and by interacting and negotiating with their eTandem partners when it came to one-to-one interaction, students were engaged in meaningful communicative activities relevant to real life situations and it turned out to be creative as well as interesting for them.

2.   Description of the project

In the pre-mobility eTandem project, 78 Erasmus students and 51 Italians enrolled. Because of the different number of participants between the two groups, not only dyads but some triads were formed as well. The project took place prior to the arrival of international students to Padua and lasted eight to ten weeks. It worked as a preparatory activity to their departure, boosting both their linguistic competence and a better insight into the culture of the host country and supported personal motivation for their Erasmus program.

As most online exchanges, our project aimed to promote autonomy and reciprocity (Vassallo & Telles, 2006) in a real life language context through communication with native speakers of the target language and aspired to stimulate a deeper understanding of students' own as well as their peers' culture. Yet, our exchange offered the participants a double line of interaction: a one-to-one and a many-to-many communication mode. Besides the individual tandem in the target language with their partners, students could join our eTandem community in Facebook where different intercultural topics, either in Italian or in English used as lingua franca, were discussed. This social area implied an exchange on a wider basis: not only did it serve to put all participants in touch so that they could experience an enriching multilingual and multicultural context, but it also prevented students from dropping the exchange by creating group cohesion.

In the first week, students entered two different platforms, Moodle and Facebook. In the institutional Moodle area one was able to learn how to move the first steps in the eTandem setting and to browse some resources to support one's linguistic, digital and cultural knowledge. The project also included some theme-based asynchronous activities in Facebook on a weekly basis. Tutors proposed and moderated debates on both neutral/safe topics, like reading, traditions, food, etc., and controversial issues such as animal experimentation, legalization of soft drugs, promoting critical thinking, critical literacies and reflexivity. Any argument introduced in the social community environment could be dealt with in the individual interaction setting.

After each discussion, students were encouraged to write a diary. This type of activity served as a tool to reflect on and evaluate thoughts, ideas, feelings and students' own learning process closely following and recording their progress. The 'writing space' contributed to a growing self-awareness of students in their role of learners, but also helped tutors to have their fingers on the pulse of opinions and feelings of the eTandem community permitting a continuous adjustment of the project to students' needs, competences and suggestions.

3.   Analysis of the outcomes and conclusion

Our analysis is based on two sources: (1) feedback questionnaire outcomes and (2) the observation of the 129 participants' activity in Facebook and in Moodle. At the end of the project students were asked to fill in a feedback questionnaire in order to reflect on their linguistic, digital and social learning outcomes. Out of 129 participants, only 22 responded.

The online questionnaire was composed of 28 items and students accessed it from the eTandem Moodle platform. The great majority of the questions was closed but in some cases students were given the opportunity to express themselves freely. We wanted to know about students' eTandem management and we were curious to know if they devoted any time to corrections and if so how they delivered it. The second part of the questionnaire dealt with students' opinion about the project and students' assessment. We asked if they think their own and their partner's knowledge of language improved or was useful for them and in which areas, if they got on well with their partner(s), and if they found it useful to write diaries. Further, we investigated the topics we proposed in the e-community and which topic(s) they preferred, if they used the language resources provided in Moodle, if they would have preferred more assistance and more structured activities, if they were going to keep in touch with their partner(s) once in Padova and if after this experience they felt more confident about going abroad in the setting of a student mobility. We also asked for a global assessment of students' eTandem experience and for any suggestions to give us in order to improve the project.

Data analysis indicates that the majority of students (72%) found Facebook to be the most useful tool for interacting and used WhatsApp and e-mail equally (45%). Skype was employed by few people (36%) because of different time zones.

It emerged that all but two people considered the project very or quite useful. 21 participants declared to be willing to stay in contact with their eTandem partner once he/she is in Padua and 17 Italian students stated to be more convinced to apply for an Erasmus scholarship after this experience.

The project brought benefits to the participants. Technologically speaking, students learnt how to use Moodle and Facebook, how to search and retrieve information from the web, how to use the net and social networks in a more responsible way defending their web reputation. Linguistically, they developed informal lexicon and written and oral skills both in English/Italian used as lingua franca and their target language. Participants became more competent in social skills such as commenting, sharing and interacting online, but also active listening, understanding diversity and respect for differences. All students reflected on and learnt about their own as well as other's culture while international students felt more integrated in the host campus.

References

Dede, C. (2009). *Comparing frameworks for 21st century skills*. http://watertown.k12.ma.us/dept/ed_tech/research/pdf/ChrisDede.pdf

Europa. (2006). *Recommendation 2006/962/EC of the European Parliament and of the Council of 18 December 2006 on key competences for lifelong learning*. http://europa.eu/legislation_summaries/education_training_youth/lifelong_learning/c11090_en.htm

Fullan, M. (2013). *Stratosphere: integrating technology, pedagogy, and change knowledge*. Toronto: Pearson.

Griffin, P., McGaw, B., & Care, E. (2012). *Assessment and teaching of 21st century skills*. Dordrecht: Springer. https://doi.org/10.1007/978-94-007-2324-5

Klimczak-Pawlak, A. (2014). *Towards the pragmatic core of English for European communication: the speech act of apologising in selected Euro-Englishes*. Springer.

Pareja-Lora, A., Rodríguez-Arancón, P., & Calle-Martínez, C. (2016). Applying information and communication technologies to language teaching and research: an overview. In A. Pareja-Lora, C. Calle-Martínez, & P. Rodríguez-Arancón (Eds), *New perspectives on teaching and working with languages in the digital era* (pp. 1-22). Dublin: Research-publishing.net. https://doi.org/10.14705/rpnet.2016.tislid2014.418

Vassallo, M. L., & Telles, J. A. (2006). Foreign language learning in-tandem: theoretical principles and research perspective. *The ESPecialist, 25*(1), 1-37.

Can a 'shouting' digital game help learners develop oral fluency in a second language?

Jennica Grimshaw[1], Walcir Cardoso[2], and David Waddington[3]

Abstract. This study examines the development of oral fluency in a Computer-Mediated Communication (CMC) environment that uses a 'shouting' digital game as a pedagogical tool: Spaceteam ESL[4]. Spaceteam ESL is a game for mobile devices that involves time-sensitive aural exchanges among players (English learners), with great potential to promote fluency development (via speed) in a non-threatening environment (mediated by the game, a CMC tool). 20 high-beginner/low-intermediate English as a Second Language (ESL) learners participated in the study, divided into two groups: an experimental group (n=11), which played the game for 15 minutes as a warm-up in class for a period of six weeks, and the control group (n=9), which was engaged in 'traditional' classroom activities such as info gap, story retelling, and other interactive activities for the same period of time. The study followed a mixed-methods design with pre-, post-, and delayed post-tests to measure developments in oral fluency (measured via the computation of number of syllables per second). The results suggest that mobile games such as Spaceteam ESL have the potential to assist in fluency development, but further investigation is needed.

Keywords: MALL, digital gaming, fluency development.

1. Introduction

Fluency development, which refers to the automatization or fluidity of speech (Derwing, Munro, Thomson, & Rossiter, 2009), is largely concerned with the temporal aspects of speech. According to Nation and Newton (2008), encouraging fluency development "is important at all levels of proficiency" (p. x). Unfortunately,

1. Concordia University, Montréal, Canada; jennica.grimshaw@gmail.com
2. Concordia University, Montréal, Canada; walcir.cardoso@concordia.ca
3. Concordia University, Montréal, Canada; david.waddington@concordia.ca
4. Adapted from the original Spaceteam mobile game by David Waddington and Walcir Cardoso of Concordia University in 2015.

How to cite this article: Grimshaw, J., Cardoso, W., & Waddington, D. (2016). Can a 'shouting' digital game help learners develop oral fluency in a second language?. In S. Papadima-Sophocleous, L. Bradley & S. Thouësny (Eds), *CALL communities and culture – short papers from EUROCALL 2016* (pp. 172-177). Research-publishing.net. https://doi.org/10.14705/rpnet.2016.eurocall2016.557

because these activities do not encourage the acquisition of new language items but rather focus on practicing known items, they are often not addressed in the classroom due to time constraints (Nation & Newton, 2008). Anxiety and/or a low level of Willingness To Communicate (WTC), which often limits output production (Gregersen & MacIntyre, 2014), may further reduce chances for fluency development (Horwitz, Horwitz, & Cope, 1986).

The current study proposes the use of Spaceteam ESL, a free mobile game available on Android and iOS as a fluency development activity, and investigates its effect on fluency development. Developed by David Waddington and Walcir Cardoso, and based on the original Spaceteam mobile game created by Henry Smith of *Sleeping Beast Games* (SleepingBeastGames.com), Spaceteam ESL is an interactive digital game for mobile devices. In teams of two to four, players must engage in real-time computer-mediated interaction with other players to navigate a spaceship. Each player is presented with a unique panel of buttons and dials (labelled with randomly generated noun-verb-adjective combinations based on vocabulary frequency bands); time-sensitive orders also appear on-screen. Players must give orders to one another by reading them aloud (intelligibly) from their panels while simultaneously receiving (via listening) and interpreting commands to manipulate buttons and dials on their own panels. Players have a limited amount of time to communicate these instructions and/or carry them out (see Figure 1 for the game interface).

Figure 1.   Spaceteam ESL interface, as demonstrated on the panels of two players from the same team

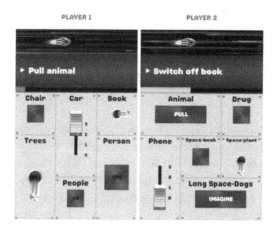

Spaceteam ESL fulfils Nation and Newton's (2008) requirements of fluency development activities: it encourages players to speed up the use of language items

(e.g. previously acquired vocabulary, phonological features such as segments) and to process a large amount of input in order to understand the interlocutor's intended meaning in an efficient, fluent manner. Results of a pilot study (Cardoso, Grimshaw, & Waddington, 2015) suggest that Spaceteam ESL may also reduce anxiety and increase WTC in learners, while encouraging higher levels of oral output. The current study focuses its attention on the development of the temporal aspects of oral fluency, such as rate of speech and pause length (operationalized here as the number of syllables a person produces per minute), as these features relate closely to Derwing et al.'s (2009) definition of fluency. Accordingly, the study asked the following research question: Does playing Spaceteam ESL affect fluency development in second language learners?

2. Method

20 students from two high-beginner ESL classes (B1-B2 based on the Common European Framework of Reference for languages) at a French-language college in Canada participated in the study. One class acted as the experimental group (n=11), which played the game for 15 minutes as a warm-up in class for a period of 6 weeks (the treatment), and the other acted as the control group (n=9), which engaged in 'traditional' but interactive classroom activities such as info gap for the same period of time.

Quantitative data were collected for all participants from the pre-, post-, and delayed post-tests. For each test, participants were recorded telling a short story about their summer vacation. Syllables Per Minute (SPM) were calculated from the recording samples collected from the participants.

3. Results

A repeated measures factorial design test was conducted to measure the difference between the treatment and control groups from pretest to two post-tests, in which the independent variable was the treatment and the dependent variable was SPM, the measure of oral fluency adopted. Results indicate that there was no significant difference in improvement between groups over time (Table 1), $p=.395$.

Paired-samples t-tests were also conducted, one for the treatment group and one for the control group. Overall, the treatment group increased their fluency performance from the pre-test ($M=108.27$, $SE=8.36$) to the post-test ($M=111.09$, $SE=8.76$).

However, this difference, −2.82, BCa 95% CI [−17.64, 12.01], was not significant $t(10)=−.42$, $p=.68$, and represented a small-sized effect, $r=0.13$. The control group, on the other hand, decreased in performance from the pre-test ($M=112.67$, $SE=10.21$) to the post-test ($M=101.78$, $SE=7.71$). As was the case with the experimental group, this difference, 10.89, BCa 95% CI [-4.71, 26.48], was also found to be not significant $t(8)=1.61$, $p=.146$, but represented a medium effect size of $r=0.5$.

Table 1.   SPM for storytelling task

Group	Pre-test		Post-test		Delayed Post-test	
	M	SD	M	SD	M	SD
Treatment	108.27	127.72	111.09	27.71	120.27	25.82
Control	112.67	30.63	101.78	23.13	123.78	29.59

While the results indicate that there was no significant difference in fluency improvement between the treatment and control group between the three tests, they do show a trend in the data. This trend suggests that although there was no significant improvement over time, the treatment group did appear to improve slightly between the pre- and post-tests, whereas the control group decreased in performance between these same tests. Participants in the treatment group continued to improve through the delayed post-test; the control group, interestingly, also improved from pre-test to delayed post-test, despite their decline in performance at the post-test. A limitation in the study may explain these results: participants had a one-week break between treatment weeks five and six. Week 6 was the final treatment session and participants had a class evaluation that same day; the post-test was also conducted during this session. Participants therefore had not practiced English for two weeks and were distracted by their evaluation. We acknowledge that this may have had an impact on their fluency (SPM) scores. Despite this, the treatment group continued to show a trend of improvement over the inconsistent results observed for the control group at the post-test. This may suggest that the use of Spaceteam ESL as a warm-up activity was a more effective 'refresher' for English after vacation than the activity the control group engaged in. The control group may have instead required more time and exposure to English to perform at their normal level.

4.   Conclusions

The study investigated the effects of playing the mobile teambuilding game Spaceteam ESL on fluency development and found that there was no significant difference between the treatment and control groups. However, evidence shows a trend in which the treatment group outperformed the control group slightly from pre-test to post-test. It is possible that these results were due to some of the limitations of the study: in addition to facing participant attrition over the six-week period (the initial participant pool consisted of over 50 participants), the researchers also experienced inconvenient timing of the post- and delayed post-tests, as discussed in the previous section. Further research under more controllable conditions and a longer period of treatment is needed to determine how much the game can truly influence the development of oral fluency.

Interviews with participants revealed that the treatment group's improvement may be due to an increased motivation that results from game play, as observed in the literature (Wang, Khoo, Liu, & Divaharan, 2008). Oral production is a vital component of fluency development (Nation & Newton, 2008); however, students are less likely to participate orally due to high levels of anxiety and low levels of WTC (Gregersen & MacIntyre, 2014), reducing opportunities for relevant oral interactions (Horwitz et al., 1986). Spaceteam ESL, on the other hand, requires a significant amount of oral production in a limited amount of time in order for teams to be successful. According to one student, his oral production was considerably higher during a 15-minute gaming session than in a three hour class: "more English in more small time... because in class I never speak because I don't like [sic]". Regarding anxiety and WTC, another participant reported that, while playing, he "didn't pay attention about [his] nervosity in English", which allowed him to focus on his speaking skills. Spaceteam ESL therefore creates a favourable environment for oral fluency development, one which will be investigated in further research.

To summarize, Spaceteam ESL offers a combination of features to encourage fluency development, addressing the requirements for it to occur, as outlined by Nation and Newton (2008). The game also offers a fluency development activity that is pre-prepared and ready for use in the language classroom, requiring little preparation from the classroom teacher. Although results between the treatment and control groups were not significant, the data suggest that playing Spaceteam ESL as a warm-up activity has the potential to positively influence the development of oral fluency in L2 learners.

5. Acknowledgements

We would like to thank the people who were involved in different aspects of this study: Henry Smith, Elisabeth Maegerlein, Eric Dahl, Alexandre Dion, Stef Rucco, Nina Padden, George Smith, Lauren Strachen, Tiago Bione, and Kym

Taylor. Finally, we would like to acknowledge the invaluable contribution of the participants and judges.

References

Cardoso, W., Grimshaw, J., & Waddington, D. (2015). Set super-chicken to 3! Student and teacher perceptions of Spaceteam ESL. In F. Helm, L. Bradley, M. Guarda & S. Thouësny (Eds), *Critical CALL – Proceedings of the 2015 EUROCALL Conference, Padova, Italy* (pp. 102-107). Dublin Ireland: Research-publishing.net. https://doi.org/10.14705/rpnet.2015.000317

Derwing, T. M., Munro, M. J., Thomson, R. I., & Rossiter, M. J. (2009). The relationship between L1 fluency and L2 fluency development. *Studies in Second Language Acquisition, 31*(4), 533-557. https://doi.org/10.1017/S0272263109990015

Gregersen, T., & MacIntyre, P. D. (2014). *Capitalizing on language learners' individuality: from premise to practice*. Bristol: Multilingual Matters.

Horwitz, E. K., Horwitz, M. B., & Cope, J. (1986). Foreign language classroom anxiety. *The Modern language journal, 70*(2), 125-132. https://doi.org/10.1111/j.1540-4781.1986.tb05256.x

Nation, P., & Newton, J. (2008). *Teaching ESL/EFL listening and speaking*. New York: Routledge.

Wang, C., Khoo, A., Liu, W., & Divaharan, S. (2008). Passion and intrinsic motivation in digital gaming. *Cyber Psychology and Behavior, 11*(1), 39-45. https://doi.org/10.1089/cpb.2007.0004

Feedback visualization in a grammar-based e-learning system for German: a preliminary user evaluation with the COMPASS system

Karin Harbusch[1] and Annette Hausdörfer[2]

Abstract. COMPASS[3] is an e-learning system that can visualize grammar errors during sentence production in German as a first or second language. Via drag-and-drop dialogues, it allows users to freely select word forms from a lexicon and to combine them into phrases and sentences. The system's core component is a natural-language generator that, for every new word the user wishes to attach to the current string (as an extension of this string or as a replacement of a substring), checks whether this tentative attachment is grammatically well-formed or not. On this basis, the system can compute and display online the grammatical structure of input strings in the form of syntactic trees, and identify and diagnose input errors. In the following, we focus on the crucial question of how to present the feedback to the learner. We propose tutored visualizations with animations of pedagogical agents. We briefly report the results of a preliminary user evaluation study in which the participants judged the well-formedness of prefabricated input sentences. The data, collected by means of eye-tracking and a questionnaire, show that L1 learners who are exercising an unfamiliar and error-prone grammatical structure, pay due attention to, and can profit from, this type of visualized error feedback.

Keywords: ICALL, grammar teaching, natural-language generation, personalized feedback, evaluation.

1. Introduction

Automatically generating personalized, reliable and immediate learner feedback is an important prerequisite for effective learning in Intelligent Computer-Assisted

1. University of Koblenz-Landau, Koblenz, Germany; harbusch@uni-koblenz.de

2. University of Koblenz-Landau, Koblenz, Germany; ahausdrfer@uni-koblenz.de

3. COMPASS stands for COMbinatorial and Paraphrastic Assembly of Sentence Structure (for more information see: https://userpages.uni-koblenz.de/~harbusch/COMPASS/index.html).

How to cite this article: Harbusch, K., & Hausdörfer, A. (2016). Feedback visualization in a grammar-based e-learning system for German: a preliminary user evaluation with the COMPASS system. In S. Papadima-Sophocleous, L. Bradley & S. Thouësny (Eds), *CALL communities and culture – Short papers from EUROCALL 2016* (pp. 178-184). Dublin: Research-publishing.net. https://doi.org/10.14705/rpnet.2016.eurocall2016.558

Language-Learning (ICALL). Molloy and Boud (2014) point out that "[f]eedback is a key process in learning, providing information on actual performance in relation to the goal of performance. [...] There is mounting survey data to suggest that students are dissatisfied with feedback" (pp. 413-414); see Narciss (2008) for a thorough overview of feedback strategies in language learning. In the area of German as a second language, studies by Diehl et al. (2000; native speakers of French at various high school levels) and Ballestracci (2005; native speakers of Italian at university level) underscore the importance of feedback tuned to the learner's current performance level and his/her understanding of the explicitly presented grammar rules (see also Kartchava, 2012; van der Kleij, 2013; Varnosfadrani & Ansari, 2011).

In this paper, we focus on automatic feedback presentation in COMPASS, an e-learning system for German as a first and second language (described in several papers by Harbusch & Kempen, 2011; Harbusch, Härtel, & Cameran, 2013; Harbusch, Cameran, & Härtel, 2014). It confronts the learners only with errors they could have avoided, given their current proficiency level and their current understanding of the grammar rules. The relevant feedback calculated according to the learner's proficiency level is provided by an animated tutor pointing out which problem COMPASS has identified and where it is located in the syntactic structure. In a user study we explore how the feedback visualization is perceived by test subjects.

In Section 2, we argue for tutored visualizations with an animated pedagogical agent. Section 3 describes a preliminary user study with L1 learners as participants who judged the well-formedness of prefab input sentences that provided unfamiliar and error-prone grammatical structures. In the final Section 4, we draw some conclusions and address future work.

2.   Feedback in COMPASS

In COMPASS, the user selects word forms from a lexicon and combines them into phrases and sentences via drag-and-drop dialogues. In response to each user action, the system displays the grammatical structure of the resulting word-form string in the form of a syntactic tree (see Figure 1). The system provides feedback on the (un)grammaticality of the string. In the example, both noun phrases are syntactically licensed as subject, although, 'der Stein' is semantically not an appropriate actor. However, none of the two can become the direct (cf. grammatical function OA[4]=accusative object) or indirect object (cf. DA(=dative object) node) of the verb 'sieht' due to case mismatch.

Figure 1.   A snapshot of the COMPASS workspace illustrating a scenario where the learner has selected the verb form 'sieht' *sees*. Moreover (s)he has assembled and word ordered the two noun phrases 'der Mann' *the man* and 'der Stein' *the stone*. (N.B. linearization checking is activated by drawing nodes into the grey boxes around grammatical functions provided by each Kopf/head; outside the boxes only the hierarchical structure – relations between nodes – is validated)

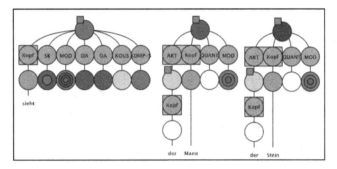

As mentioned by Harbusch et al. (2013),

> "the grammar formalism underlying COMPASS is *Performance Grammar* (Kempen & Harbusch, 2002), which uses separate rules for the hierarchical *structure* of a sentence and the *linear order* of its constituents. This split allows the student to divide a sentence construction exercise into relatively small parts. For instance, the learner can select a word, and inflect it as required by the intended grammatical function, without simultaneously considering the linear position of the constituent in the sentence under construction. At any time during this 'scaffolded' sentence construction process, the syntactic tree built so far remains visible on the screen, ready to be expanded or modified with additional words or phrases. Any sentence construction step can be undone and replaced online" (p. 105).

Another advantage arises from the generation-based approach of COMPASS, where the learner and system assemble an unambiguous syntactic tree together. Compared to other systems that allow free sentence construction by the user but

---

4. The annotations in trees resemble the ones in the TIGER corpus (Brants et al., 2004; e.g. KOUS=Unterordnende Konjunktion /subordinating conjunction).

rely on natural-language parsing, the feedback in a generation-based system is not hampered by ambiguous syntactic structures, meaning that feedback can be precise and exhaustive. However, as outlined in Section 1, it is desirable to highlight only those errors against rules the student is supposed to have mastered. COMPASS uses underspecification of grammar rules to accomplish this (cf. Harbusch et al., 2014; in the example in Figure 1, beginners might attach any of the two NPs as SB/OA/DA as case agreement is 'overlooked' by COMPASS on that proficiency level).

The question we deal with in this paper concerns the format in which to present the feedback. Widely practiced in e-learning systems are animated tutors that interact with the user in a socially engaging manner (for a recent overview, see, e.g. Govindasamy, 2014). Adopting this format, we have chosen an owl – portrayed as intelligent and wise in Aesop's fables – as a character capable to attract and motivate children as well as young adults. The user can select feedback at two levels of detail:

(1) In *verbose mode*, if COMPASS spots an error, the owl shows up at the word or phrase the learner has just attached erroneously, and displays a box with information about the error type (see left panel in Figure 2 for an example of missing subject-verb agreement).

(2) In *concise mode*, the owl has green eyes, sitting in a green box at the upper right corner as long as the user is building grammatically correct structures (right panel in Figure 2). In case of an error the color changes to red.

The user can switch off feedback if desired.

Figure 2.   Syntactic structures with feedback. Left image: verbose feedback presented after a subject-verb agreement error. Right image: concise feedback after a correct attachment

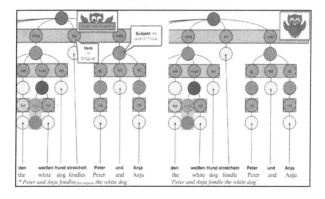

3.   A preliminary system evaluation using eye-tracking

In order to find out whether the feedback was sufficiently salient and informative to attract the attention of the users, we performed an eye-tracking experiment with 20 adult native speakers of German (university students) who were instructed to judge the grammatical correctness of displayed sentences. We also asked the participants to express in a questionnaire their subjective impression of the usefulness of the feedback.

The experiment comprised two phases. In Phase I, the participants familiarized themselves with COMPASS by freely composing syntactic trees in drag-and-drop dialogues with the system. Then, in Phase II, they were presented with prefabricated sentences featuring correct or incorrect subject-verb agreement (adapted from an experiment by Bock & Miller, 1991), allowing them to exercise relatively rare and error-prone agreement cases. In addition to these experimental sentences, there were filler sentences that were either grammatically correct or contained other types of errors. In one experimental condition, the participant delivered his/ her grammaticality judgment, and the owl indicated the (un)grammaticality of the input sentence in the manner illustrated in Figure 2. All sessions were video-recorded and transcribed.

Figure 3.   'Heat maps' representing fixation durations for the images in Figure 2. Green spots: short fixations; fixation durations increase via yellow to red. Left image: fixation pattern in case of a subject-verb agreement error; right image: fixations in case of positive feedback

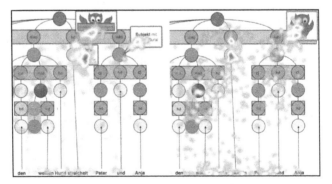

As indicated by the 'hot spots' in the heat maps (Figure 3), the participants did pay attention to the feedback agent. The percentage of correct answers increases from 52% in the control condition (no tree, no feedback) to 67% in the experimental

condition with syntactic trees (more precisely, in the experimental subcondition without feedback where the owl did not give away the correct answer). This suggests the feedback was not only perceived but also yielded a learning effect. The questionnaire data showed that several participants (5 out of 20) found the trees baroque and confusing rather than helpful. These participants did not profit from the feedback.

4.   Conclusions

The results of our preliminary user evaluation experiment suggest that our way of presenting feedback via an animated pedagogical agent is promising. However, the questionnaire revealed considerable dissatisfaction with the level of detail of the linguistic information provided by COMPASS. The participants' complaints ranged from too many colors to too much linguistic sophistication. We take these results as recommendations to continue with feedback presentation in the form of animated tutors and with syntactic trees, but also to simplify the tree format considerably.

5.   Acknowledgements

We would like to thank Kashif Arshad who conducted the experiment. Moreover, we are indebted to Gerard Kempen for valuable comments on earlier versions of the paper.

References

Ballestracci, S. (2005). *Zum DaF-Erwerb ausgewählter grammatischer Strukturen der deutschen Sprache bei italophonen Studierenden der Pisaner Facoltà di Lingue e Letterature Stranieret.* Doctoral dissertation. Università di Pisa, Italy.

Bock, K., & Miller, C. A. (1991). Broken agreement. *Cognitive Psychology, 23*(1), 45-93. https://doi.org/10.1016/0010-0285(91)90003-7

Brants, S., Dipper, S., Eisenberg, P., Hansen-Schirra, S., König, E., Lezius, W., Rohrer, C., Smith, G., & Uszkoreit, H. (2004). TIGER: linguistic interpretation of a German corpus. *Research on Language and Computation, 2*(4), 597-620. https://doi.org/10.1007/s11168-004-7431-3

Diehl, E., Christen, H., Leuenberger, S., Pelvat, I., & Studer, T. (2000). *Grammatikunterricht: Alles für der Katz?* Tübingen: Niemeyer.

Govindasamy, M. K. (2014). Animated pedagogical agents: a review of agent technology software in electronic learning environments. *Journal of Educational Multimedia and Hypermedia, 23*(2), 163-188.

Harbusch, K., Cameran, C.-J., & Härtel, J. (2014). Feedback to grammatical errors in German as second language focused on the learner's personal acquisition level. In S. Jager, L. Bradley, E. J. Meima & S. Thouësny (Eds), *CALL design: principles and practice* (pp. 140-145). Dublin: Research-publishing.net. https://doi.org/10.14705/rpnet.2014.000208

Harbusch, K., Härtel, J., & Cameran, C.-J. (2013). COMPASSIII: teaching L2 grammar graphically on a tablet computer. *Proc. of SLaTE 2013, Grenoble, France.*

Harbusch, K., & Kempen, G. (2011). Automatic online writing support for L2 learners of German through output monitoring by a natural-language paraphrase generator. In M. Levy, F. Blin, C. Bardin Siskin & O. Takeuchi (Eds), *WORLDCALL* (pp. 128-143). New York: Routledge.

Kartchava, E. (2012). *Noticeability of corrective feedback, L2 development and learner beliefs.* PhD Thesis. Université de Montréal, Canada.

Kempen, G., & Harbusch, K. (2002). Performance grammar: a declarative definition. In M. Theune, A. Nijholt & H. Hondorp (Eds), *Computational linguistics in the Netherlands 2001.* Amsterdam: Rodopi. https://doi.org/10.1163/9789004334038_013

Molloy, E. K. & Boud, D. (2014). Feedback models for learning, teaching and performance. In J. M. Spector, M. D. Merrill, J. Elen & M. J. Bishop (Eds), *Handbook of research on educational communications and technology* (pp. 413-424). New York: Springer.

Narciss, S. (2008). Feedback Strategies for Interactive Learning Tasks- In J. M. Spector, M. D. Merrill, J. J. G. van Merriënboer, & M. P. Driscoll (Eds.), *Handbook of Research on Educational Communications and Technology* (pp. 125-144). Mahwah, NJ: LEA

Van der Kleij, F. M. (2013). *Computer-based feedback in formative assessment.* PhD Thesis. University of Twente, Enschede, the Netherlands.

Varnosfadrani, A. D., & Ansari, D. N. (2011). The effectiveness of error correction on the learning of morphological and syntactic features. *World Journal of English Language, 1*(1), 29-40. https://doi.org/10.5430/wjel.v1n1p29

The multimodality of lexical explanation sequences during videoconferenced pedagogical interaction

Benjamin Holt[1]

Abstract. This study aims to identify and analyze the ways in which semiotic resources are orchestrated by teacher-trainees during videoconferenced French foreign language teaching. Our corpus is made up of six weeks of interaction between seven teacher trainees enrolled in a master's program at Université Lumière Lyon 2 in France and 12 undergraduate business students at Dublin City University in Ireland. 15.5 hours of video data were transcribed using ELAN, and 195 lexical explanation sequences were identified. These sequences were categorized according to whether the lexical problem came from an inability to understand or an inability to speak, and were then split into phases according to a three-step canonical model (Lauzon, 2008). During each phase we look at which semiotic resources were used, combined and co-contextualized by the teacher trainees. Our methodology, which will be used to complete our PhD project, is outlined here as well as preliminary results.

Keywords: videoconferencing, lexical explanation, multimodality.

1. Introduction

It has been shown that during native-non-native and non-native-non-native interaction, negotiation sequences are most commonly initiated by lexical triggers (Nicolaev, 2010; Smith, 2003). Various models for negotiation sequences have been proposed (Smith, 2003; Varonis & Gass, 1985) to describe how a negotiation sequence unfolds in time. Lauzon (2008), for example, presents a three-step canonical model specifically for lexical explanation sequences during teacher-student interactions. A lexical explanation sequence occurs when the normal progression of a conversation or activity comes to a halt and participants orient

1. Université Lumière Lyon 2, Lyon, France; Benjamin.Holt@univ-lyon2.fr

How to cite this article: Holt, B. (2016). The multimodality of lexical explanation sequences during videoconferenced pedagogical interaction. In S. Papadima-Sophocleous, L. Bradley & S. Thouësny (Eds), *CALL communities and culture – short papers from EUROCALL 2016* (pp. 185-189). Research-publishing.net. https://doi.org/10.14705/rpnet.2016.eurocall2016.559

their focus towards a lexical item that a learner fails to understand or fails to produce. In the first case, the non-understood lexical item comes from the teacher's discourse or from a pedagogical support such as a video, audio track, text or image. In the second case, failure to produce a lexical item hinders the learner's foreign language output. The teacher must intervene to explain the non-understood lexical item or provide a sufficient one in order for communication to resume. In Lauzon's (2008) three-phase canonical model, there is an opening, a nucleus, and a closing. During the opening phase, the lexical item that is either misunderstood or searched for by the learner is recognized by the participants and problematized. During the nucleus, the teacher attempts to explain the non-understood word or provide the correct word that is being searched for by orchestrating various linguistic and multimodal resources. During the closing phase, the learner's comprehension or ability to properly use the just-provided word is evaluated or ratified by the teacher.

Of interest to us are the ways in which the different phases are multimodally orchestrated by the participants. A multimodal phase (Baldry & Thibault, 2006) is defined by semiotic coherence. During each phase, different modes (voice, eye contact, posture, proxemics, head movements, facial expressions, gestures, written text, etc.) work together in synergy to make meaning, with the hierarchy of modes constantly being rearranged and renegotiated by the participants (Norris, 2004). According to Norris (2004), a mode has high modal density if it carries most of the meaning at a given time or if communication would come to a halt if it were removed. In a videoconferencing environment such as *Visu* (Guichon, Bétrancourt, & Prié, 2012), these modes are channeled through the affordances of the platform. In our case, *Visu* offers a video channel, an audio channel, a text chat channel, and the ability to send prefabricated instructions and multimedia documents such as images and links to external websites. The aim of this study is to identify what modes are used for what purposes during each phase of lexical explanation sequences and to explore the ways in which the modes interact with each other.

2. Method

2.1. Corpus

Our corpus, which is part of the ISMAEL project (Guichon, Blin, Wigham, & Thouësny, 2014), consists of six weeks of videoconferenced interactions mediated by *Visu* during the fall semester of 2013 between seven future teachers of French enrolled in a master's program for teaching French as a foreign language at

Université Lumière Lyon 2 in Lyon, France, and 12 undergraduate learners of French at Dublin City University in Dublin, Ireland. These undergraduate business students had a level B1-B2 in French and were preparing to complete an internship the following year in Reims, France. The 40-minute interactions were specifically engineered for business purposes and were centered around themes such as paid vacation, strikes, coffee breaks, professional experience, project management, job interviews, etc. The 28 interactions that were collected have a total time of 15.5 hours and were transcribed using ELAN (Wittenburg et al., 2006).

The verbal and text chat channels were transcribed for all participants for the entire corpus. Next, we identified 195 lexical explanation sequences and split each one into phases using the model mentioned above. The lexical explanation sequences were then divided almost evenly into two main categories: sequences resulting from a comprehension problem and those resulting from a production problem.

3.   Preliminary results and discussion

Each multimodal environment has a unique palette of semiotic resources, which makes direct comparisons difficult. For this particular multimodal environment, our phase-by-phase preliminary analysis shows that a diverse range of semiotic resources was used during the opening, nucleus and closing phases for different purposes.

Gestures, which play a critical role during classroom foreign language teaching (Tellier, 2008), were put to use during some lexical explanation sequences. In particular, during word searches, teachers sometimes used gesture to verify their own comprehension of the word being searched before providing it. For example, when asked by a learner how to say 'yawning' in French, one teacher trainee, unsure of her own comprehension of the English word, used a gesture to verify it before providing the French translation (see Figure 1, left). For sequences triggered by incomprehension, gestures were used to describe actions, concepts, concrete objects, and even explanation strategies. For example, when explaining the verb 'to strike', one teacher-trainee illustrated the act of chanting slogans by moving his arm up and down in front of the webcam (see Figure 1, center). On many occasions, gestures carried high modal density because they were produced in the absence of speech (such as in the 'yawning' example) and/or deliberately placed directly in front of the webcam. The third teacher-trainee pictured below (see Figure 1, right) rarely made gestures visible to the webcam, but in this case made an effort to make her emblematic gesture visible when illustrating the concept of adding a zero to a monthly paycheck.

Figure 1.   Gestures produced by teacher-trainees during lexical explanation
sequences

The text chat was used during all three phases. Before incomprehension was manifested, teacher-trainees often anticipated the difficulty of a word by typing it in the text chat window. During the nuclei and closing phases, teacher-trainees used the text chat to type the word that was either just explained or provided in order to offer a visual representation and reinforce memorization. Text messages were not always redundant, often obtaining high modal density when produced in the absence of oral speech. Multimedia documents were also sent during all three phases of lexical explanation sequences having to do with incomprehension, either to present learners with a visual representation before, during or after the explanation.

Finally, we have found synchronization and co-contextualization of resources. The text chat was often co-contextualized by other resources: teacher-trainees regularly said, "I'm putting it in the chat window" or made gestures pointing to the chat window. The sending of documents was similarly co-contextualized by the verbal channel. Teacher-trainees tended not to make hand gestures and send written messages simultaneously due to the difficulty of typing and making gestures at the same time.

4.   Conclusions

More data must be analyzed in order to proceed to any sort of statistical analysis. Furthermore, facial expressions, eye movements, eyebrow movements and posture, which are important meaning-making resources in face-to-face interaction, still need to be analyzed. For our PhD project, by using the methodology outlined above, we will analyze the entirety of our 195-sequence corpus in order to spot patterns, explore variation between the participants, and eventually propose a structural model for videoconferenced lexical explanation sequences similar to the one proposed by Smith (2003) for synchronous text-based negotiation sequences.

5.   Acknowledgements

We would like to thank the ASLAN project (ANR-10-LABX-0081) of Université de Lyon, for its financial support within the program 'Investissements d'Avenir' (ANR-11-IDEX-0007) of the French government operated by the National Research Agency (ANR).

References

Baldry, A., & Thibault, P. (2006). *Multimodal transcription and text analysis*. London; Oakville, CT: Equinox Publishing.

Guichon, N., Bétrancourt, M., & Prié, Y. (2012). Managing written and oral negative feedback in a synchronous online teaching situation. *Computer-Assisted Language Learning, 25*(2), 181-197. https://doi.org/10.1080/09588221.2011.636054

Guichon, N., Blin, F., Wigham, C., & Thouësny, S. (2014). *ISMAEL learning and teaching corpus*. Dublin, Ireland: Centre for Translation and Textual Studies & Lyon, France: Laboratoire Interactions, Corpus, Apprentissages & Représentations.

Lauzon, V. F. (2008). *Interactions et apprentissages dans des séquences d'explication de vocabulaire*. https://libra.unine.ch/export/DL/Evelyne_Pochon-berger/20434.pdf

Nicolaev, V. (2010). Les négociations de sens dans un dispositif d'apprentissage des langues en ligne synchrone par visioconférence. *Les Cahiers de l'Acedle, 7*, 169-198.

Norris, S. (2004). *Analyzing multimodal interaction: a methodological framework* (1st ed.). New York: Routledge.

Smith, B. (2003). Computer-mediated negotiated interaction: an expanded model. *The Modern Language Journal, 87*, 38-57. https://doi.org/10.1111/1540-4781.00177

Tellier, M. (2008). Dire avec des gestes. *Le Français Dans Le Monde: Recherche et Application*, 40-50.

Varonis, E. M., & Gass, S. (1985). Non-native/non-native conversations: a model for negotiation of meaning. *Applied Linguistics, 6*(1), 71-90. https://doi.org/10.1093/applin/6.1.71

Wittenburg, P., Brugman, H., Russel, A., Klassmann, A., & Sloetjes, H. (2006). Elan: a professional framework for multimodality research. In *Proceedings of LREC* (Vol. 2006, p. 5).

Automatic dialogue scoring for a second language learning system

Jin-Xia Huang[1], Kyung-Soon Lee[2],
Oh-Woog Kwon[3], and Young-Kil Kim[4]

Abstract. This paper presents an automatic dialogue scoring approach for a Dialogue-Based Computer-Assisted Language Learning (DB-CALL) system, which helps users learn language via interactive conversations. The system produces overall feedback according to dialogue scoring to help the learner know which parts should be more focused on. The scoring measures are presented, including task proficiency, grammar accuracy, vocabulary knowledge, and syntactic ability, to assess the user performance during the dialogue. A user evaluation is performed on the automatic dialogue scoring results and the generated feedback to collect the feedback from real learners, and to see if the measures are helpful and proper. A discussion is also held about the difference between the automatic dialogues scoring from essay scoring based on the user evaluation.

Keywords: computer-assisted second-language learning system, dialog-based CALL, automatic dialogue scoring, feedback for L2, automatic essay scoring.

1.   Introduction

A DB-CALL system usually provides grammar correction feedback with a grammar checker, and discourse feedback via a semantic checker. We have developed GenieTutor (Kwon, Lee, Kim, & Lee, 2015a; Kwon et al., 2015b), which is a DB-CALL system for English learners in Korea. GenieTutor leads dialogues by asking questions on different topics according to given scenarios, language learners answer questions orally, and the system recognises the speech,

1. Electronics and Telecommunications Research Institute / Chonbuk National University, Daejeon, Korea; hgh@etri.re.kr
2. Chonbuk National University, Jeonju, Korea; selfsolee@chonbuk.ac.kr
3. Electronics and Telecommunications Research Institute, Daejeon, Korea; ohwoog@etri.re.kr
4. Electronics and Telecommunications Research Institute, Daejeon, Korea; kimyk@etri.re.kr

How to cite this article: Huang, J.-X., Lee, K.-S., Kwon, O.-W., & Kim, Y.-K. (2016). Automatic dialogue scoring for a second language learning system . In S. Papadima-Sophocleous, L. Bradley & S. Thouësny (Eds), *CALL communities and culture – short papers from EUROCALL 2016* (pp. 190-195). Research-publishing.net. https://doi.org/10.14705/rpnet.2016.eurocall2016.560

evaluates if the answers are semantically proper for given questions, and checks grammatical errors and provides feedback (Lee, Kwon, Kim, & Lee, 2015). The dialogues normally consist of two to four turns, and the system provides semantic and grammar error feedback in each user utterance, deciding if the dialogue can move to the next turn. During the development and user tests, we noticed that users would like to know their overall scoring and level after finishing a whole dialogue.

In this paper, we investigate the dialogue scoring measures for the GenieTutor system. The measures include task proficiency, grammar accuracy, utterance length and complexity, vocabulary level and diversity. Synonyms are also provided as suggestions to improve user vocabulary.

2.   Measures for automatic dialogue scoring

Speech scoring has focused on restricted and highly predictable speech, mainly evaluating aspects of speaking related features, including pronunciation, intonation, rhythm, and fluency, such as speaking rate or length and distribution of pauses. For automated scoring of unrestricted spontaneous speech, more speaking content related features are adopted, including grammatical accuracy, syntactic complexity, vocabulary diversity, and spoken discourse structure (Chen & Zechner, 2011; Xie, Evanini, & Zechner, 2012). These speaking content related measures are similar to the essay scoring, because they both intend to assess communicative competence (Attali & Burstein, 2004).

Our DB-CALL system has expected user answers for each system utterance, similar with the restricted speech scoring. However, considering it is a dialogue system, some factors of unrestricted spontaneous speech should also be considered in the scoring.

The first measure investigated for dialogue scoring is dialogue proficiency, indicating how fluently the conversation has been maintained. It consists of task turn pass ratio and user utterance pass ratio, where task turn pass ratio is the ratio of the passed turns out of all task turns. For example, there are 3 turns predefined for the scenario, if the learner passes two turns and gives up in the final turn, than the task turn pass ratio is 66.7%.

User utterance pass ratio is the ratio of the passed user utterances out of all user utterances. For example, for a dialogue with two task turns, the learner finished it with five utterances. Then, there are two task turns, two passed user utterances out of all five user utterances, then the user utterance pass ratio is 40% while the task turn pass ratio is 100%. If a user utterance passes, the task turn is performed by the semantic correctness module (Kwon et al., 2015a).

The second measure is grammar accuracy. Grammar checks have been performed by grammatical error correction modules in each turn (Lee et al., 2015). What dialogue scoring needs to do is compute the accuracy according to the weighted number of grammar errors, dividing this by the total number of words in all user utterances. This measure is the same with essay scoring (Attali & Burstein, 2004).

The third measure is vocabulary, including vocabulary level and diversity. Vocabulary level has five categories, from primary school level to university level. Vocabulary level estimates the user word level according to the word distributions by dividing the number of user words in ith category ($n$uw,i) to the number of user words ($n$uw), and compares it with the vocabulary level of the scenario – a scenario which provides correct references from native speakers. Each category has different a weight wi. The vocabulary level would be set to one if the dividing result is higher than one.

Vocabulary diversity is the ratio of number of word types to tokens in the user utterances (Attali & Burstein, 2004). However, different from essay scoring, the ratio should be a relative one compared with the vocabulary diversity of the scenario. For example, in user utterances "Movies interest me a lot", "I'm interest in Action Movies a lot", there are nine word types, "movies, interest, me, a, lot, I, am, in, action" and 13 tokens, so the diversity is 0.69 (9/13). Again, it is also divided into the vocabulary diversity of the scenario, which would be set to one if the dividing result is higher than one.

The system provides synonyms and similar expressions to improve user vocabulary if the same word is adopted several times in the user utterances. For above cases, GenieTutor will suggest 'See also these similar expressions: interest → fascinate, attract, entertain'.

Syntactic ability includes utterance length and syntactic complexity, the former relates with the utterance lengths, while the complexity considers the syntactic structure of the utterances. Utterance length compares the lengths of user sentences to the length of references in the scenario, and syntactic complexity gives relative complexity scores by considering the length of the utterances and the number of conjunctions.

Dialogue score is the weighted average of all above measures. The system provides overall feedback according to the dialogue score (Figure 1).

Figure 1.   Overall feedback of GenieTutor

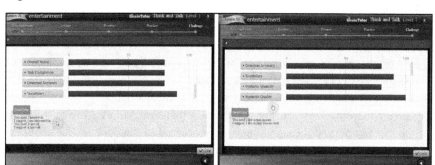

3.   Survey and discussion

A survey on the GenieTutor overall feedback are performed involving 30 human evaluators, 14 of them elementary English learners, and 16 intermediate learners. They are asked five questions, from range one to five, from 'Strongly disagree' to 'Strongly agree', respectively. The evaluators needed to pick at least one item for the final question.

Table 1.   User evaluation on the overall feedback generated from dialogue scoring

Idx	Questions		Score
1	Do you think overall feedback would be helpful to improve your conversation level?		3.53
2	Do you think overall feedback would be helpful to motivate your learning?		3.67
3	Do you think the evaluation items of the overall feedback are proper?		3.97
4	Do you think the overall score and the final feedback are proper?		3.50
5	Which evaluation item(s) do you think unnecessary among the overall feedback? You can pick one or more from following items :	A. Overall score	4
		B. Task proficiency	8
		C. Grammar	1
		D. Vocabulary	1
		E. Syntactic	17

From Table 1, we can see that the human evaluators considered the overall feedback *tend to be helpful* to their English learning (average scores=3.53/3.67 for the first and second questions). About the evaluation items of the overall feedback, the users think measuring items are proper (average score=3.97 for the 3rd question). However, the scoring of the items are considered as just *tend to be proper* (average score=3.50 for the 4th question), implying that the scoring approach still needs to be fine-tuned to reflect the learner's performance more accurately.

Interestingly enough, more than half of the evaluators think the measure *Syntactic* is less necessary (17 votes out of 30 evaluators), while *Vocabulary* and *Grammar* measures get only one vote, respectively. It indicates dialogue scoring should be different from essay scoring considering that the *Syntactic* measure is one of the most important measures in essay scoring. The dialogue in GenieTutor is restricted and predictable, which is very different from the essay. For example, the learner already learns the dialogue "what kind of movies do you like? → I like Action Movies" from the given class (scenario). However when the learner utters the same sentences in the practice, the syntactic complexity measure would give a lower score to the user utterance, and suggest *try to practice longer expressions: I'm interested in Action Movies a lot*. The task proficiency gets eight votes mostly from the speech recognition problem – the learner complains that, when the speech is not recognised correctly, the user utterance would get failure in semantic check, it reduces turn pass ratio and reflects the accuracy of task proficiency. It means the performance of the speech recognition could impede the participants' views.

4.   Conclusion

This paper investigated the measures for automatic dialogue scoring and performed user evaluation on the overall feedback. The result showed that the overall feedback after a dialogue tended to be helpful to the language learner, even if there were already turn-by-turn feedback provided for semantic and grammar error correction. The user evaluation result also showed that the dialogue scoring for a DB-CALL system should be different from automatic essay scoring in some measures – in our case, the syntactic ability measure was considered less helpful than others, while grammar and vocabulary measures were considered necessary with the overall score.

5.   Acknowledgement

This work was supported by the ICT R&D program of MSIP/IITP [R0126-15-1117, Core technology development of the spontaneous speech dialogue processing for language learning].

References

Attali, Y., & Burstein, J. (2004). Automated essay scoring with e-rater V.2.0. *Paper presented at the Annual Meeting of the International Association for Educational Assessment, Philadelphia, PA.* https://doi.org/10.1002/j.2333-8504.2004.tb01972.x

Chen, M., & Zechner, K. (2011). Computing and evaluating syntactic complexity fetures for automated scoring of spontaneous non-native speech. In *Proceedings of the 49th Annual Meeting of the Association for Computational Linguistics* (pp. 722-731).

Kwon, O.-W., Lee, K., Kim, Y.-K., & Lee, Y. (2015a). GenieTutor: a computer assisted second-language learning system based on semantic and grammar correctness evaluations. In F. Helm, L. Bradley, M. Guarda, & S. Thouësny (Eds), *Critical CALL – Proceedings of the 2015 EUROCALL Conference, Padova, Italy* (pp. 330-335). Dublin Ireland: Research-publishing.net. https://doi.org/10.14705/rpnet.2015.000354

Kwon, O. W., Lee, K., Roh, Y.-H., Huang, J.-X., Choi, S.-K., Kim, Y.-K., Jeon, H. B., Oh, Y. R., Lee, Y.-K., Kang, B. O., Chung, E., Park, J. G., & Lee, Y. (2015b). GenieTutor: a computer assisted second-language learning system based on spoken language understanding. In *Proceedings of the 2015 International Workshop on Spoen Dialogue Systems (IWSDS).* https://doi.org/10.1007/978-3-319-19291-8_26

Lee, K., Kwon, O.-W., Kim, Y.-K., & Lee, Y. (2015). A hybrid approach for correcting grammatical errors. In F. Helm, L. Bradley, M. Guarda, & S. Thouësny (Eds), *Critical CALL – Proceedings of the 2015 EUROCALL Conference, Padova, Italy* (pp. 362-367). Dublin Ireland: Research-publishing.net. https://doi.org/10.14705/rpnet.2015.000359

Xie, S., Evanini, K., & Zechner, K. (2012). Exploring content features for automated speech scoring. In *Proceedings of the 2012 Conference of the North American Chapter of the Association for Computational Linguistics: Human Language Technologies* (pp. 103-111).

Effects of task-based videoconferencing on speaking performance and overall proficiency

Atsushi Iino[1], Yukiko Yabuta[2], and Yoichi Nakamura[3]

Abstract. The purpose of this study is to find the effects of using Videoconferencing (VC) as a tool for foreign language instructions in a semester long research study. The research questions focus on the effects of VC (1) on speaking skills, and (2) on general proficiency scores. English as a Foreign Language (EFL) learners in a university in Japan were divided into an Experimental Group (EG) with weekly VC outside the classroom, and a Control Group (CG) provided with 'shadowing practice' and written assignments instead of VC. Both groups spent eight weeks under the treatments with pre and post measurements. The results showed improvement in holistic ratings and temporal measurement in transcribed speech data, but not statistically significant in interaction between time and treatments. Speaking performance of the EG showed statistically more significant progress in fluency and lexical variation, and in general proficiency. The results suggest that using VC with tasks in a blended manner with classroom instruction develops balanced L2 competence and performance.

Keywords: videoconferencing, task-based language learning, speaking, proficiency.

1.   Introduction

It is not easy to find regular opportunities for interaction in English with fluent English speakers in an EFL context such as Japan. Even some learners who attend conversation classes in universities cannot be given sufficient time to talk in English with English speaking instructors due to large class sizes. This situation leads to the fact that many learners in Japan cannot communicate sufficiently in English, particularly in speaking (MEXT, 2016). This fact also leads to an increasing number

1. Hosei University, Tokyo, Japan; iino@hosei.ac.jp
2. Seisen Jogakuin College, Nagano, Japan; yabuta@seisen-jc.ac.jp
3. Seisen Jogakuin College, Nagano, Japan; youichi@seisen-jc.ac.jp

How to cite this article: Iino, A., Yabuta, Y., & Nakamura, Y. (2016). Effects of task-based videoconferencing on speaking performance and overall proficiency. In S. Papadima-Sophocleous, L. Bradley & S. Thouësny (Eds), *CALL communities and culture – short papers from EUROCALL 2016* (pp. 196-200). Research-publishing.net. https://doi.org/10.14705/rpnet.2016.eurocall2016.561

of people counting on English language programs through VC (Yano Economic Research Institute, 2015).

However, one problem with commercial programs using VC for language learning is that the content dealt with in sessions seems not to expand learners' L2 competence but just to the extent that the learners manage to develop fluency in daily conversation. Therefore it appears necessary to introduce frameworks from Second-Language Acquisition (SLA) such as task-based language learning, which facilitates L2 development (González-Lloret & Ortega, 2014).

As a solution to such issues, we have implemented interaction-based instruction with the goal of role-play tasks through VC with English speakers. Hence, the purpose of the study is to find the effects of using VC as a tool of foreign language instructions in a semester long research project. The aim of this study is to investigate the effects of the instruction that includes VC as its communicative goal (1) on speaking skills, and (2) on general proficiency consisting of vocabulary, reading and listening.

2.   Method

2.1.   Participants and instructional conditions

The EG, consisting of 22 university level learners of English in Japan experienced eight role-play task sessions through VC over the course of one semester. The weekly VC sessions were held with English teachers living in the Philippines. The teachers had experience in teaching English in a language school in the Philippines, so they were familiar with how to handle a discussion class with two learners. Each session was 45 minutes long. We gave the teachers a brief scheme for the 45 minute sessions: ten min. for warm-up, 25 min. for a role-play task and ten min. for cross-cultural questions which the learners prepared in order to learn about the situation in the Philippines in accordance with the topic they discussed in the role-play task.

The issues for VC sessions were from a listening course book with which the learners do listening comprehension and dictation on their own before a preparatory class, a 90 minute regular class. In the class, being conducted by a Japanese teacher of English, the following five steps were taken: (1) free discussion between the learners on the issue; (2) sharing of words and expressions as 'gaps' they noticed – the teacher provided L2 expressions equivalent to L1 based on the notes of 'what they wanted to say but could not'; (3) presentation by an assigned group of learners on the issue in order to stretch their content knowledge; (4) re-discussion on the same issue to incorporate their learning in Step 2 and 3 with different learners; and (5) role-play practice in triads among the learners, in which they could switch roles in order to prepare for any role in the task. After the preparatory class, paired learners experienced the same role-play task through VC with the teachers in the Philippines. As a post task, the learners were given a writing assignment.

The CG, consisting of 27 learners in the same university, were provided with the same listening pre-task as EG before their weekly 90 minute classes. They used the same materials, and experienced the same steps in the classroom up to the part of a role-play among the learners. Instead of VC, however, they were assigned to do 'shadowing practice', i.e. repeating or reproducing aloud the sound of the listening material for ten minutes daily and to keep a record of it. They were assigned to write a short essay on the same topic as well.

2.2.   Data collection tools and procedures

The test followed the style of the TOEFL Speaking Section Part 1. Learners were asked, for example, 'Some students prefer to work on class assignments by themselves. Others believe it is better to work in a group. Which do you prefer? Explain why'. The teacher read aloud the question and provided 15 seconds for planning, then had the learners talk in the microphone in a computer-assisted language learning system for 45 seconds. The learners' oral production was recorded and rated up to four points by three raters, including the authors using the TOEFL Independent Speaking Rubric (a=.94). The spoken language was manually transcribed and analyzed quantitatively.

The Eiken IBA is a multiple choice question style standardized proficiency test consisting of listening and reading parts. Each part consisted of 50 questions; the reading part included 15 vocabulary featured questions. We used the score percentage in each section to compare the progress of the CG and EG.

3.   Results and discussion

In order to make the two groups homogenous in the initial evaluation score in the TOEFL style test, the number of the participants became 30, that is 15 in each group by cutting the top learners in the EG and the bottom layer of the CG.

For the TOEFL style speaking test, the result of two-way ANOVA repeated measurements showed no significant interaction ($F(1,28)$=2.66, p=.114, $\eta2$=.02,) but a significant difference between pre- and post-tests (Time : $F(1,28)$=28.78, p<.001, $\eta2$=.24,). Regarding the quantitative analysis of temporary measurement based on the transcribed data, significant interactions indicating EG>CG were observed in two variables: fluency by word per minute ($F(1,28)$=9.49, p=.004, $\eta2$=.05), and lexical variation by type-token ratio in the Giraud Index ($F(1,28)$=8.99, p=.006, $\eta2$=.04).

For the results of the *Eiken* IBA proficiency test, the EG outperformed the CG with a significant interaction ($F(1,28)$=6.11, p=.019, $\eta2$=.04). Hence it can be said that VC brought about more L2 development in overall proficiency. These positive results for VC are in accordance with effects of interaction in SLA.

4.   Conclusions

In this research, we found that providing task-based interaction using VC to EFL learners improved their speaking ability in fluency and lexical variation. The instruction also improved listening and reading proficiency. These findings add more evidence of positive effects of using VC in a sequence of L2 instruction.

In conclusion, since the CG also showed improvement in speaking, creating opportunities for L2 interaction with role-play tasks particular in EFL contexts can be a necessary condition, and VC session as a goal of interaction can be regarded as a satisfactory condition to enhance further L2 development in fluency and complexity.

5.   Acknowledgements

This research is partially supported by the Ministry of Education, Science, Sports and Culture in Japan, Grant-in-Aid for Scientific Research (C), 2014-2016 (26370675, Atsushi Iino). The authors appreciate the members of the project for their valuable advice and help: Professor Hideo Oka (Professor Emeritus, the Tokyo University), Dr. Akiko Fujii (International Christian University), and Ms. Heather Johnson (Hosei University). We also thank the teachers in the Philippines, Mr. Marvin Dimatulac and Ms. Grace Dizon for their cooperation in VC sessions, and Ms. Maria Rosario Magat for transcribing spoken data.

References

González-Lloret, M., & Ortega, L. (2014). Towards technology-mediated TBLT: an introduction. In M. González-Lloret & L. Ortega (Eds), *Technology-mediated TBLT: researching technology and tasks* (pp. 1-22). Amsterdam, the Netherlands: John Benjamins. https://doi.org/10.1075/tblt.6

MEXT. (2016). *Heisei 27 nendo eigo ryoku chousa houkoku (3rd grade in high school) sokuho.* Ministry of Education, Culture, Sports, Science and Technology. http://www.mext.go.jp/b_menu/shingi/chousa/shotou/117/shiryo/icsFiles/afieldfile/2016/05/24/1368985_8_1.pdf

Yano Economic Research Institute. (2015). Gogaku business shijo ni kansuru chosa kekka 2015 (Press released digest in Japanese). https://www.yano.co.jp/press/press.php/001415

Telecollaborative games for youngsters: impact on motivation

Kristi Jauregi[1]

Abstract. The present paper describes a case study on the effects of telecollaborative games on learners' motivation. 12 learners from a Dutch and a British secondary school participated in the study. Different games, which included gamification elements, were developed on OpenSim. The overall educational goals of the games were to enhance cultural awareness and intercultural communication of German as a foreign language. Three different cross-cultural groups played the telecollaborative games in two different sessions. Data from pre- and post-surveys were gathered for measuring the impact of telecollaborative games on learners' motivation. At the end of the game sessions, focus group discussions were organised for evaluating the experience. The results indicate that telecollaborative games have a positive impact on learners' motivation.

Keywords: virtual worlds, gamification, telecollaboration, motivation, youngsters.

1.   Introduction

Video games and virtual worlds are viewed as relevant educational tools not just for their potential for entertainment, but also for promoting learning (Prensky, 2007). This is mostly due to game techniques that seem to promote user engagement and motivation. These techniques are increasingly being employed in so-called serious games: games whose main purpose is to educate while entertaining their users. Recently, a growing awareness of the learning potential of games and virtual worlds has been observed in the computer-assisted language learning field (Cornillie, Thorne, & Desmet, 2012; Jauregi et al., 2011; Panichi & Deutschmann, 2012; Reinders, 2012; Sykes & Reinhardt, 2012). This paper presents the results of a case study on the effects of telecollaborative games on learners' motivation, who

---

1. Utrecht University, Utrecht, Netherlands; k.jauregi@uu.nl

How to cite this article: Jauregi, K. (2016). Telecollaborative games for youngsters: impact on motivation. In S. Papadima-Sophocleous, L. Bradley & S. Thouësny (Eds), *CALL communities and culture – short papers from EUROCALL 2016* (pp. 201-207). Research-publishing.net. https://doi.org/10.14705/rpnet.2016.eurocall2016.562

are learning German as a foreign language in secondary schools. Different cultural games were developed on OpenSim which included several gamification elements. In order to achieve game goals pupils were required to collaborate with peers. They all used German as a *lingua franca*. The games were played cross-culturally in a virtual international setting. Our approach to the analysis of motivation is based on the self-determination theory framework (Ryan & Deci, 2000).

2. Method

The main research question we address in the present case study is: How do cultural games played cross-culturally in OpenSim influence learners' motivation?

2.1. Subjects

12 learners from a Dutch and a British[2] secondary school participated in the study: ten boys and two girls. They were between 14 and 15 years old. Three cross-cultural teams with two Dutch and two British pupils each were created to play the games. The pupils learned German as a foreign language at their school. Their proficiency level ranged between A1 and A2. The experience was carried out within the framework of the European TILA project[3].

2.2. Games

Two series of games[4] were developed in the TILA grid of OpenSim, an open source 3D virtual environment, where users represented as *avatars* can communicate using textual chat or voice, move around, interact with objects and engage in action. The games had a German cultural focus. All quizzes, hints and explanations were in German. The gamification elements included both time and point counts.

Each game cycle had five different spaces with a different game in each space. In the first room (see Figure 1), each team member received hints (example of hints: *It is a German city. Carnaval is celebrated here. It is in the west)* when sitting down around a table. Together the pupils had to be able to create the password that when being written in the chat box would open the door to the next game space.

---

2. Secondary schools: The Ashcombe School, Dorking, United Kingdom. Pleincollege Nuenen, Nuenen, The Netherlands.
3. Telecollaboration for Intercultural Language Acquisition: www.tilaproject.eu
4. The games were developed by the collaborating teachers at both schools: Helen Meyer and Bart Pardoel. Nick Zwart developed the games in OpenSim.

Figure 1. First room in the cultural German game

Figure 2. Pupils playing the game on the German cultural quizzes

In the second room the hints appeared in the walls when standing on specific yellow plates (examples *First day of the week... The opposite of west... The opposite of north... No right hand...*). The team members had to discover a five-letter word (example: the name of a German river). In the third game room the group split up into two dyads. The two dyads had to cooperate to build a bridge with the blocks floating on the water and be able to cross the water to continue with the last games. The builders had to communicate purposefully with the other dyad, as these were the ones who could move the blocks by following the directions provided by the builders and the other way round. In the fourth game room there were four quiz chairs. When sitting on the chair the pupils got the quiz in the form of multiple choice questions (example of questions: *In which country is German not an official language? In which city was the wall? How many inhabitants has Germany?*). If they knew the right answer they got a point and the chair raised automatically (see Figure 2). All team members had the same quiz questions and were expected to discuss and share the answers in order to be able to get the highest amount of points with the whole team.

In the final game room, the pupils had to find the right ingredients for two different German recipes displayed on the walls. If they clicked on the wrong ingredient they got a point deducted. When clicking on the right ingredient they received a point. The winner was the team with the most points in the shortest period of time.

2.3. Motivation surveys

Several surveys were developed:

- A background survey, that included biographic information and language learning experience. It was filled by all participants before playing the games.

- The user experience survey gathered information about the game and was filled in after each game session.

- A post-survey on the general experience was filled in after the second game session.

In this short paper we will be presenting the results of the user experience survey and will compare the results per game and pupil cluster. For the closed items a five-point Likert scale was used with low values indicating non agreement and high values total agreement.

3. Results

Mean and Standard Deviation (SDev) values were calculated for the different items. The pupils enjoyed the German cultural game being played cross-culturally among Dutch and British pupils. Technically, they found it easy to play the game and the sound and video quality were very good, particularly in the second game session (see Table 1).

Table 1. SDev values on technical issues for the British and Dutch pupils playing Games

Item	British				Dutch			
	Game 1		Game 2		Game 1		Game 2	
Technology	Mean	SDev	Mean	SDev	Mean	SDev	Mean	SDev
It was easy to USE the game	3.6	0.5	4.2	0.8	4.2	0.4	4.5	0.5
SOUND was good	3.8	0.4	3.8	0.8	3.6	0.9	4.5	0.5
VIDEO was good	3.5	0.6	4.3	0.5	4.4	0.5	4.7	0.5

Pupils liked very much to communicate and interact in the game environment with pupils from other countries (see Table 2). They liked the game environment and being an avatar. Interestingly, the scores of the British pupils in the second game are much higher than in the first game session, while for the Dutch ones the scores on the second game were a little bit lower than in the first game, but still very high (mean values above 4.0).

Table 2. Values for pupils' preferences and likes

Item	British				Dutch			
	Game 1		Game 2		Game 1		Game 2	
Preferences & Likes	Mean	SDev	Mean	SDev	Mean	SDev	Mean	SDev
I like to communicate and interact in this game environment	3.8	0.4	4.5	0.5	4.6	0.5	4.2	0.8
I like to meet students from other countries in this game environment	4.2	0.8	4.7	0.5	4.6	0.5	4.2	0.8
I like to learn in this game environment	4.0	0.0	4.5	0.8	4.4	0.5	4.0	0.9
I like to be an avatar	4.6	0.5	4.5	0.5	4.4	0.5	4.3	0.8

As to satisfaction and ease factors, British pupils seem to have felt more comfortable and co-present in the second game than in the first one, scores reaching very high values. The Dutch pupils felt very positive about the games but the scores in the second were slightly lower (see Table 3).

Table 3. Values for pupils' satisfaction and ease issues

Item	British				Dutch			
	Game 1		Game 2		Game 1		Game 2	
Feel	Mean	SDev	Mean	SDev	Mean	SDev	Mean	SDev
I felt comfortable during the game	3.8	0.4	4.7	0.8	4.2	0.4	4.2	0.8
I felt I was in the same place with the others	3.8	0.4	4.2	1.3	4.2	0.4	3.7	1.0
I felt satisfied with the way I communicated	3.8	0.4	4.0	0.9	4.0	0.0	3.8	1.0
I felt the game environment affected in my communication positively	4.0	0.0	4.5	0.8	4.2	0.4	4.0	1.1
I felt part of a group	4.0	0.0	4.2	1.3	4.0	0.7	4.3	0.5

Finally, pupils were very enthusiastic about the game and the possibility to play it with pupils from another country. They would recommend to other pupils to play these games and they would themselves like to engage in these kinds of games more frequently (see Table 4). All values were very positive. Yet it was remarkable that the scores of British pupils were considerably higher in the second game than in the first one.

Table 4.   Overall game experience

Item	British				Dutch			
	Game 1		Game 2		Game 1		Game 2	
Game	Mean	SDev	Mean	SDev	Mean	SDev	Mean	SDev
I enjoyed communicating with students from another country	4.2	0.4	4.7	0.5	4.2	0.4	4.0	1.1
I enjoyed the game	4.0	0.0	4.4	0.9	4.6	0.5	4.7	0.5
Because there was interaction with pupils from other countries...	4.0	0.0	4.6	0.5	4.6	0.5	4.7	0.5
I found the game useful for my language learning	4.0	0.0	4.6	0.5	4.4	0.5	4.2	0.8
I would suggest to a friend to take part in this kind of international games	4.0	0.0	4.6	0.5	4.6	0.5	4.2	0.8
I would like to use games with pupils from other countries more often	4.0	0.0	4.6	0.5	4.6	0.5	4.3	0.5

4.   Conclusions

Pupils greatly enjoyed playing the cultural games with peers from another country. Interestingly, Dutch pupils were very positive about the telecollaborative game experience from the very beginning, while the British pupils started quite cautiously in the first game but grew considerably in self-confidence and satisfaction in the second game. This case study seems to indicate that serious games played telecollaboratively can contribute to boost the learners' motivation to learn foreign languages meaningfully and playfully. Additional research is needed to confirm these initial findings.

5.   Acknowledgements

We would like to thank the pupils, the teachers (H. Meyer & B. Pardoel), the OpenSim expert, N. Zwart, and the TILA project.

References

Cornillie, F., Thorne, S. L., & Desmet, P. (2012). ReCALL special issue. Digital games for language learning: challenges and opportunities. *ReCALL, 24*(3), 243-256.

Jauregi, K., Canto, S., De Graaff, R., Koenraad, T., & Moonen, M. (2011). Verbal interaction in Second Life towards a pedagogic framework for task design. *Computer Assisted Language Learning Journal, 24*(1), 77-101. https://doi.org/10.1080/09588221.2010.538699

Panichi, L., & Deutschmann, M. (2012). Language learning in virtual worlds: research issues and methods. In D. Melinda & R. O'Dowd (Eds), *Researching online foreign language interaction and exchange: theories, methods and challenges* (pp. 205-232). Bern: Peter Lang Publishing Group.

Prensky, M. (2007). *Digital game-based learning.* Paragon House.

Reinders, H. (Ed.). (2012). *Digital games in language learning and teaching.* Palgrave McMillan.

Ryan, R. M., & Deci, E. L. (2000). Self-determination theory and the facilitation of intrinsic motivation, social development, and well-being. *American Psychologist, 55*(1), 68-78.

Sykes, J., & Reinhardt, J. (2012). Language at play: digital games in second and foreign language teaching and learning. In J. Liskin-Gasparro & M. Lacorte (Eds), *Second language classroom instruction. Series on theory and practice.* Pearson-Prentice Hall.

The Exercise: an Exercise generator tool for the SOURCe project

Fryni Kakoyianni-Doa[1], Eleni Tziafa[2], and Athanasios Naskos[3]

Abstract. The Exercise, an Exercise generator in the SOURCe project, is a tool that complements the properties and functionalities of the SOURCe project, which includes the search engine for the Searchable Online French-Greek parallel corpus for the UniveRsity of Cyprus (SOURCe) (Kakoyianni-Doa & Tziafa, 2013), the PENCIL (an alignment tool) (Kakoyianni-Doa, Antaris, & Tziafa, 2013), and the Synonyms and the Library tools. These are designed as freely available resources for language processing, easy to use by teachers and learners. The Exercise tool enables teachers to create either online activities or print out paper-based worksheets, including a variety of texts and activities on topics, in a variety of exercise types (e.g. multiple choice, word, phrase or sentence matching, filling the gaps with missing words/phrases, text reconstruction, listening, etc.).

Keywords: exercise generator, computer-based language testing, teachers' tool, language acquisition.

1.   Introduction

The SOURCe project aims at providing a whole platform of tools to assist the French language teachers in the classroom. In this paper we present the latest tool called Exercise, an Exercise generator in the SOURCe project. This is the fifth tool of the SOURCe project, which consists of:

- The Source[4] Corpus tool, which is a search engine for the searchable online French-Greek parallel corpus for the university of Cyprus (Kakoyianni-Doa & Tziafa, 2013).

---

1. University of Cyprus, Limassol, Cyprus; frynidoa@ucy.ac.cy
2. University of Cyprus, Limassol, Cyprus; tziafa.eleni@ucy.ac.cy
3. Aristotle University of Thessaloniki, Thessaloniki, Greece; anaskos@csd.auth.gr
4 The Source Corpus is referred to as Source, while the project as a whole is referred to as SOURCe.

How to cite this article: Kakoyianni-Doa, F., Tziafa, E., & Naskos, A. (2016). The Exercise: an Exercise generator tool for the SOURCe project. In S. Papadima-Sophocleous, L. Bradley & S. Thouësny (Eds), *CALL communities and culture – short papers from EUROCALL 2016* (pp. 208-214). Research-publishing.net. https://doi.org/10.14705/rpnet.2016.eurocall2016.563

- The PENCIL tool, an alignment tool for translators, teachers and learners, which enables the creation and customisation of web-based corpora, by uploading and aligning French and Greek texts (Kakoyianni-Doa et al., 2013).

- The Synonyms tool, which provides a search engine for synonyms, based on machine translation or dictionary searches.

- The Library tool, which showcases a part of the SOURCe project corpus.

- The Exercise tool (presented in the following sections), which enables teachers to create online activities and/or print out paper-based worksheets.

Following Kakoyianni-Doa and Tziafa's (2013) methodology, "all these tools and functionalities are designed as freely available resources for language processing, along with the data to be processed, in usable formats for both teachers and learners" (p. 2) (Figure 1). As regards the parallel corpora, "the translations included are based on human understanding of textual relations, which is not the case for machine translation (yet), despite the fact that students tend to rely more and more on it" (Kakoyianni-Doa & Tziafa, 2013, p. 3). The time period covered by the corpus spans over six centuries, from the 15th to 21st century. The texts under study are instances of different domain-specific registers, so that students may compare the results and the use of each word or phrase in different contexts. The corpus consists of a fiction and a non-fiction part of 720,282 aligned sentences.

Figure 1.   The SOURCe project's home page

In the following sections we focus on the construction and composition of the Exercise tool, based on a parallel corpus, "the content, annotation, encoding and availability of which are meant to serve the needs of teachers and students of French or Greek as a foreign language and also to facilitate future linguistic research" (Kakoyianni-Doa & Tziafa, 2013, p. 1). Moreover, we outline its future perspectives and applications.

2. Method

2.1. The Source Corpus as a basis

Following Kakoyianni-Doa and Tziafa (2013) methodology, the core of the project is a collection of parallel corpora, either already existing or created by the participating researchers, and aligned (at sentence level) original and translated texts, in French and Greek. The corpus development is an ongoing process, with new texts constantly added. According to previous research, "the use of corpora in the classroom can have remarkable results as regards foreign language learning" (Kakoyianni-Doa & Tziafa, 2013, p. 2; see also Hadley, 2002). Moreover, as Kilgarriff (2009) suggests, parallel corpora are easier to be disguised as dictionaries and be brought for use in the classroom. The corpus consists of different registers (Biber, 1993), in order to facilitate comparison of the results and to study the use of each word or phrase in a different context (e.g. literature, scientific, official, technical and journalistic language). Commonly used parallel corpora, mainly EUROPARL (Koehn, 2005) and the JRC Acquis corpus (Steinberger et al., 2006) from the Opus open parallel corpus (Tiedemann, 2012) were also used, as were literary works available from Project Gutenberg, or scanned, mainly from the local historical library Severeios.

2.2. The Exercise tool construction

In order to support the use of corpus linguistic tools by teachers and learners with no previous expertise, we designed a simple interface through which the user may search existing corpora, upload texts, and work online with interactive exercises. The Exercise tool enables teachers to create either online activities or print out paper-based worksheets, including a variety of texts and activities on topics, in a variety of exercise types (e.g. multiple choice, word, phrase or sentence matching, filling the gaps with missing words/phrases, text reconstruction, listening, etc.). Throughout the SOURCe project, and especially in the Exercise tool, we used Java

(Enterprise Edition) for the backend and HTML5, CSS3 and Javascript for the frontend and Apache Solr for indexing, searching and sentence fetching based on a given similarity distance (used in the multiple choice exercise for the automated text selection feature, presented in the next section).

3.   The Exercise tool

On the main page of the tool (Figure 2) there is a table listing the existing exercises and four buttons to create a new exercise (if the user is a teacher or administrator) or to filter the listed exercises in the table according to the exercise type (if the user is a student).

Figure 2.   The exercises page (from the teacher homepage)

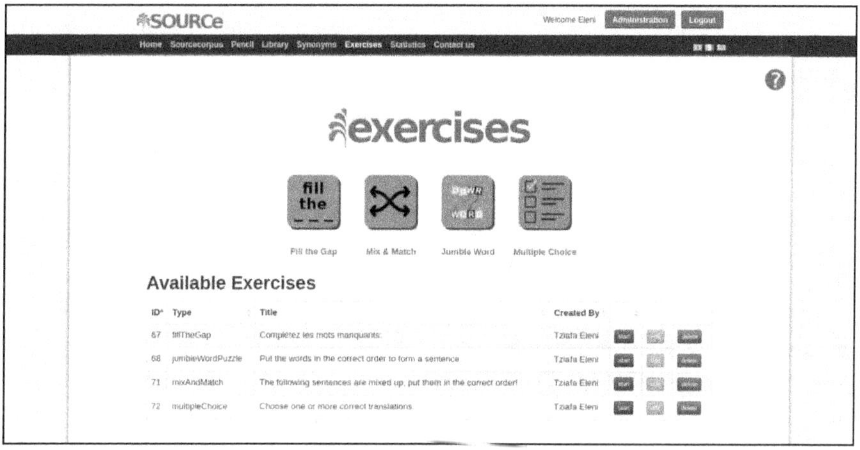

All the exercises offer (1) a common construction interface to provide the title of the exercise (in Greek and French), (2) a description, which is available only to the creator of the exercise, to take notes about the specific exercise, and (3) an automated text selection feature, which automatically fetches text from the parallel corpora collection, based on the user selection. The difference in the common automated text selection interface is that in the multiple choice exercise the teacher can select the number of suggested returned translations of every sentence based on a distance metric provided by the Apache Solr tool. The user can edit the automatically fetched text of the exercise or provide the text manually with a simple interface. All the exercises can be combined with an audio file, to produce a listening exercise. The user selects an MP3, OGG or WAV audio file and the number of the allowed replays. The exercises can be solved either online or be given as a printout (even in cases that an audio file is attached, in order to accompany the audio file played in classroom). The combinations are innumerable. We can edit the French part, the Greek part or both, thus providing scalable difficulty levels.

When students are solving the exercise, they are able to check the results or have the solution displayed (Figure 3).

Figure 3.   Solution display when the student solves a jumble words puzzle

4.   Conclusions

In this paper we have presented the latest tool of the SOURCe project, the Exercise tool, which offers to French language teachers a friendly interface for online or printout exercise creation, and to students an online platform for practice. There are plenty of online exercise generators available, but they apply mostly in high-resourced languages, like English, in monolingual texts, and most of them are not free. There are very few proposals which apply on other languages (e.g. Swedish: Volodina & Borin, 2012).

Unlike other tools, the Exercise tool supports the low-resourced French and Greek languages in aligned texts. Moreover, it offers an online practice platform for students solving exercises online and checking their results in an automated manner. Finally, it is offered freely (registration required) and its source code and its assets are available under the Creative Commons license.

Our future plans include the addition of more types of texts and also exercises, along with experimental evaluations and questionnaires, in order to testify the attitude of users toward the provided tools and also encourage teachers and students to use these resources in the classroom or beyond.

Our objective is to develop a whole platform of tools that will assist teachers to find out about, adapt and apply new tools in the classroom. To overcome the well-known problem of the existing natural language processing tools and resources not actually being included in the language learning procedure, despite their potential as learning and research tools, the main goal of the proposed project is to provide language instructors and learners with ready-made corpora and corpus-based exercises, available for use in a new learning environment. The platform provides innovative corpus-based learning activities and interactive exercises. This study could also serve as a pilot study for the creation of multilingual resources in the form of parallel corpora. This project is thus intended not only to fill a gap in the literature on corpora used in the classroom, but also to make available valuable resources, especially for a low resourced language such as Greek.

5.   Acknowledgment

This project is led by Fryni Kakoyianni-Doa and is fully funded by the University of Cyprus.

References

Biber, D. (1993). Representativeness in corpus design. *Literary and Linguistic Computing, 8*(4), 243-257. https://doi.org/10.1093/llc/8.4.243

Hadley, G. (2002). Sensing the winds of change: an introduction to data-driven learning. *RELC Journal, 33*(2), 99-124. https://doi.org/10.1177/003368820203300205

Kakoyianni-Doa, F., Antaris, S., & Tziafa E. (2013). A free online parallel corpus construction tool for language teachers and learners. *Procedia - Social and Behavioral Sciences, 95*(25), 535-541.

Kakoyianni-Doa, F., & Tziafa, E. (2013). Source: building a searchable online French Greek parallel corpus for the University of Cyprus. *Revista Nebrija de Lingüística Aplicada 13* (número especial). http://www.nebrija.com/revista-linguistica/files/articulosPDF/articulo_5326df173f8bc.pdf

Kilgarriff, A. (2009). Corpora in the classroom without scaring the students. *Proceedings of the 18th International Symposium on English Teaching and Learning in the Republic of China.* Taipei: National Taiwan Normal University. http://www.kilgarriff.co.uk/Publications/2009-K-ETA-Taiwan-scaring.doc

Koehn, P. (2005). Europarl: a parallel corpus for statistical machine translation. *Proceedings of the 10th Machine Translation Summit, Phuket, Thailand* (pp. 79-86).

Steinberger, R., Pouliquen, B., Widiger, A., Ignat, C., Erjavec, T., Tufis, D., & Varga, D. (2006). The JRC-Acquis: A multilingual aligned parallel corpus with 20+ languages. *5th Language Resources and Evaluation Conference (LREC), Genoa, Italy* (pp. 2142-2147).

Tiedemann, J. (2012). Parallel data, tools and interfaces in OPUS. *8th International Conference on Language Resources and Evaluation (LREC)* (pp. 2214-2218). http://lrec.elra.info/proceedings/lrec2012/pdf/463_Paper.pdf

Volodina, E., & Borin, L. (2012). Developing an Open-Source Web-Based Exercise Generator for Swedish. In L. Bradley & S. Thouësny (Eds), *CALL: Using, Learning, Knowing, EUROCALL Conference, Gothenburg, Sweden, 22-25 August 2012, Proceedings* (pp. 307-313). Dublin Ireland: Research-publishing.net. https://doi.org/10.14705/rpnet.2012.000072

Students' perceptions of online apprenticeship projects at a university

Hisayo Kikuchi[1]

Abstract. The purpose of this study is to examine the impact of a hybrid apprenticeship model in the context of university level English education in Japan. The focus is on freshman perceptions and attitudes toward their English learning. For this study, seniors were asked to create brief videos in English sharing study strategies, helpful student life tips, and advice regarding study abroad programs. The study examined (1) the improvement of the freshmen's smartphone video assignments before and after they viewed the seniors' videos discussed above, and (2) pre- and post-questionnaires with four Likert-scale items and one open question. These results show that the apprenticeship videos can not only serve as modeling but also foster scaffolding outside of the classroom.

Keywords: apprenticeship, university, Japan, smartphone.

1.   Introduction

Throughout history, apprenticeship has been a primary mechanism for teaching and learning. However, in Japanese universities, the apprenticeship model, in the context of English education, has been difficult for three primary reasons. In general, Japanese young adults over age 25 generally do not attend universities. Recent statistics show no more than 1.9% of Japanese university students are over 25 years old, which is low compared to the world average (19.6%) (MEXT, 2011; OECD, 2014). Thus, there is a statistical shortage of 'mentor' students who have accumulated enough life experience to provide more meaningful tutelage to younger students. Furthermore, new students often do not have opportunities to make strong connections with more senior students. Individual English classes are generally comprised of students at the same education level, so freshmen are not

1. Aoyama Gakuin University, Tokyo, Japan; hisayo@t07.itscom.net

How to cite this article: Kikuchi, H. (2016). Students' perceptions of online apprenticeship projects at a university. In S. Papadima-Sophocleous, L. Bradley & S. Thouësny (Eds), *CALL communities and culture – short papers from EUROCALL 2016* (pp. 215-220). Research-publishing.net. https://doi.org/10.14705/rpnet.2016.eurocall2016.564

likely to mix with seniors in the course of regular class activities. Thus, vertical connections between different class years are improbable.

Finally, when newer students have chances to interact with older students, they may hesitate to ask for advice. This may be traceable to traditional Japanese societal paradigms, which assign roles of superiority and inferiority to senior and junior positions, respectively (Mosk, 2007). In addition, in English as a foreign language settings like Japan, it can be hard to find a role model. In many cases, teachers who are native English speakers are likely to become students' role models. However, this is not always beneficial, according to Vygotsky's (1978) zone of proximal development. If the role model is too far removed from the learner, in terms of skills, the learners may lose their motivation. Murphey (1998) recommends that for the purpose of modelling, we focus on various desirable attitudes and practices of some "lesser gods, closer to home" such as the students' "Near Peer Role Models" (NPRMs)" (p. 202).

2.   Literature review

Examining NPRMs (Murphey & Arao, 2001) provides useful information for this study. Murphey and Arao (2001) defines NPRMs as "peers who are close to one's social professional, and/or age level, and whom one may respect and admire" (p. 2). Long and Porter (1986) examined the language produced by adult learners whose first language was Spanish. Intermediate learners talked with a speaker from each of the three levels: intermediate, advanced, and native speaker of English. They found that the learners talked most with advanced level speakers. This means that an apprenticeship relationship may be most effective if the ability gap between the mentor and the learner is not too wide. The study of Choi and Ishiwata (2016) found that in Australia, adult low pro-proficiency learners of English had greater language learning success when they were grouped with high-proficiency learners as opposed to other low-proficiency learners.

3.   Method

3.1.   Participants

The participants of this study were 28 freshmen in an English class at a university in the Kanto area (16 male students and 12 female students). Their collective English level was B1 according to the Common European Framework of Reference for languages (CEFR). All of them were non-English majors and taught by a Japanese teacher who used both English and Japanese in class. The class was held once a week for three months (90 minutes per class session).

3.2. Procedures

For the study's mentors, I asked a successful second-year class (CEFR B2-C1) consisting of ten students (four male and six female students) to participate in this study. I explained to them that their learning techniques and university survival skills would be accessed and leveraged to help freshmen. I asked them to discuss their experiences and decide upon one topic individually, avoiding overlaps. They created brief instructional videos using their own smartphones. The length of each video was about one minute. The topics were:

- How to effectively use time.
- How to find opportunities to use English outside of class.
- How to stay in good physical shape.
- What my first year schedule looked like.
- How club activities help me.
- Why it is important to join university union projects.
- What part-time job or internship I did.
- How I improved my English.
- How I improve my test scores.
- What classes I took.

3.3. Questionnaire

At the first class the freshmen responded to the pre-questionnaires. The questionnaire items were adopted from Murphey and Arao (2001). About one month later, these freshmen watched the videos created by seniors and posted their opinions on our closed webpage in either Japanese or English. They also answered the post-questionnaire. The pre- and post-questionnaires featured the same elements with a five point Likert Scale (1=Strongly disagree, 2=disagree, 3=neither agree nor disagree, 4=agree, and 5=strongly agree), followed by an open question.

- Making mistakes in English is OK.
- It is good to have goals in learning English.
- Speaking English is fun.
- Japanese can become good speakers of English.

- What did you learn from the seniors' videos?

4. Results

First, the scores of the questionnaire items increased across the board after the freshmen viewed the mentoring videos (Table 1). Second, in particular, those who did not have prior successful English learning experiences, or who had low confidence, showed greater positivity in terms of responses. Third, the freshmen's videos were more creative and more relatable to their daily life.

The online comments posted on our closed website were basically short, such as "Great!", "Cool!" and "I want to speak like them". These comments were in keeping with the results from Murphey and Arao's (2001) study. There were no comments regarding the content, including further questions about learning skills or strategies.

When I asked the apprentice group of younger students to write follow-up questions to the mentoring seniors, they wrote questions such as the following (in Japanese):

- What kind of practice do I need?
- How did you improve your pronunciation?
- What practice do you usually do at home?
- How much did you study English?

Table 1. The mean ratings before and after the freshmen viewed the seniors' video

	before	after
1. Making mistakes in English is O.K.	3.8	4.2*
2. It's good to have goals in learning English.	3.7	4.5**
3. Speaking English is fun.	3.2	3.7**
4. Japanese can become good speakers of English.	3.7	4.1*

*significant changes at $p<0.05$, ** significant changes at $p<0.01$

In response to the open question: *What did you learn from the seniors' videos?*, the freshmen did not mention the 'academic' content of the mentoring videos (such as learning skills or strategies). The apprentice students were instead focused on the presentation aspects of the instructional videos. Responses included:

"I think I should speak faster".

"Seniors used easier vocabulary than I thought. I always thought I needed to use difficult words, but I think easy words should be better and more understandable".

"I cannot believe the length of the presentation in the video was only around one minute. There was a lot of content even though it was only one minute".

The study protocol included freshmen preparing their own videos. In their first videos, they were likely to read from pre-prepared scripts and be quite short. However, after watching the seniors' mentoring videos, freshmen's confidence appeared to increase, and they were inclined to speak in more impromptu and creative ways.

After this study, I created an opportunity for the freshmen and the sophomores to meet face-to-face at a luncheon. Five sophomore 'mentor' students and nine freshmen participated. My observations included the following: (1) both freshmen and sophomores willingly helped each other, (2) they talked about the video content, and further asked about it in Japanese, and (3) the sophomore students were very proud of themselves.

5.   Conclusions

The study established the following three points: first, it is very useful to provide video apprenticeship features for newer students. Second, structured apprenticeship programs, such as the smartphone video apprenticeship program used in the study are helpful in fostering the apprenticeship model. Without this kind of structured interaction, it can be rare for freshmen to have opportunities to meet older students at universities in Japanese English class. Third, as observed in NPRMs (Murphy, 1996), a one or two-year gap between student groups is suitable. Based on my observations throughout the study, the freshmen's awareness of the fact that successful mentor students were only one year older appeared to be a factor in engendering confidence in the younger students.

6.   Acknowledgements

This work was supported by JSPS KAKENHI Grant Number JP 15H06577. I extend my sincere gratitude to all of the students who participated in this study.

References

Choi, H., & Ishiwata, N. (2016). Interactional behaviours of low-proficiency learners in small group work. In M. Sato & B. Susan (Eds), *Peer interaction and second language learning: pedagogical potential and research agenda* (pp. 113-134). John Benjamins Publishing. https://doi.org/10.1075/lllt.45.05cho

Long, M. H., & Porter, P. (1986). Group work, interlanguage talk, and second language acquisition. *TESOL Quarterly, 19*(2), 207-228. https://doi.org/10.2307/3586827

MEXT. (2011). *Shakaijin ryugakusei no jokyo* (in Japanese). Ministry of Education, Culture, Sports, Science and Technology. http://www.mext.go.jp/b_menu/shingi/chousa/shougai/031/shiryo/__icsFiles/afieldfile/2014/06/05/1348400_09.pdf

Mosk, C. (2007). *Markets, norms, constraints. Japanese economic development: markets, norms, structures*. Taylor & Francis e-Library. https://doi.org/10.4324/9780203935873.pt1

Murphey, T. (1996). Near peer role models. *Teachers talking to teachers, 4*(3), 21-22.

Murphey, T. (1998). Motivating with near peer role models. *On JALT '97: Trends & Transitions* (pp. 201-204).

Murphey, T., & Arao, H. (2001). Reported belief changes through near peer role modeling. *TESL-EJ, 5*(3), 1-14.

OECD. (2014). *Education indicators focus 23*. https://www.oecd.org/education/skills-beyond-school/EDIF_23%20eng%20(2014)EN.pdf

Vygotsky, L. S. (1978). *Mind in Society*. Cambridge, MA: Harvard University Press.

The effects of multimodality through storytelling using various movie clips

SoHee Kim[1]

Abstract. This study examines the salient multimodal approaches for communicative competence and learners' reactions through storytelling tasks with three different modes: a silent movie clip, a movie clip with only sound effects, and a movie clip with sound effects and dialogue. In order to measure different multimodal effects and to define better delivery modes, three one-shot commuter-based tests for each mode and one survey were conducted. Three tasks were administered on the websites specially designed for the study using Flying Popcorn 7.0, a web authoring programme. After viewing each movie clip, participants were asked to immediately record a one-minute story. There were 90 Korean English learners who attended academic English classes at a university located in South Korea. The results showed that there was a significant difference in their speaking performance when using the movie clip with sound effects and dialogue. In the survey, participants responded that the movie clip with sound effects and dialogue provided a good way to assess speaking and listening within a given time frame.

Keywords: storytelling, multimodal learning, media effects, speaking assessment.

1. Introduction

Multimodality can refer to a new form of communication that provides learning experiences for language learners. It is composed of more than one medium and is defined as the learner's use of more than one sense (Mayer & Sims, 1994). Multimodal modes include more than language, enabling language learners to perceive and understand differently, based on their language proficiency and their cognitive processes used to interpret media. Moreover, using a variety of modes can also lead to the development of integration skills, allowing language learners to interpret multiple modes simultaneously. In order to investigate multimodal

---

1. Korea University, Seoul, South Korea; grinplus@gmail.com

How to cite this article: Kim, S.H. (2016). The effects of multimodality through storytelling using various movie clips. In S. Papadima-Sophocleous, L. Bradley & S. Thouësny (Eds), *CALL communities and culture – short papers from EUROCALL 2016* (pp. 221-224). Research-publishing.net. https://doi.org/10.14705/rpnet.2016.eurocall2016.565

---

effects, this study used different movie clips for a storytelling task on computer-based tests to find salient media effects. Since using a movie clip draws attention for active viewing, encourages discussion among language learners, and develops opinions and literature skills (Kim, 2014; Scheibe & Rogow, 2008), a storytelling task with a movie clip can be an effective medium to assess language learners' media effects. This study explores how English learners interact differently with media, a movie clip, and attitudes towards different modes.

2. Method

2.1. Participants

The participants in the present study were 90 university students (53.3% male, $n=48$; 46.7% female, $n=42$) who attended academic English classes to fulfill their graduation requirements in South Korea. There were 59 freshmen, 25 sophomores, four juniors, and two seniors. The Test of English for International Communication (TOEIC) scores ranged from 325 to 940. Overall, they had studied English in Korea between two and 16 years and had studied in English-speaking countries between zero and five years.

2.2. Research questions

This research explores the impact of effective media learning environments on the development of oral proficiency, as well as exploring guidelines for language teachers for effective learning through media teaching. To address this, the study had the following two research questions: (1) How does the participants' speaking performance differ relative to the three various modes through storytelling? (2) What specific interactions are related to the three different modes for oral performance?

2.3. Materials and methods

This study investigates the language learners' attitudes towards different modes and speaking performances through storytelling on three online computer-based tests. After viewing each movie clip, participants were asked to record a one-minute story based on what they had seen. Three tests were developed using the Flying Popcorn 7.0 web software programme that allows test-takers to record oral performance for the movie clip task and saves their recorded files on the computer.

All participants were required to write their names on the first screen and then they were able to watch each movie clip in order to record their stories.

The first task used the movie clip with sound effects: Charlie Chaplin's 'The Coffee'. The second task featured the silent movie clip: Charlie Chaplin's 'Hotel Evergreen'. The last task used the movie clip with sound effects and dialogue, 'Turbo Diner' from the Wallace and Gromit movie. All the movie clips were under two minutes long.

The participants' oral proficiency was assessed holistically and analytically with four criteria: discourse, vocabulary, grammar, and sentence complexity. The Common European Framework of Reference (CEFR) scores from one to six were used as the holistic rubric. The analytical rubric was based on the Communicative Language Ability (CLA) model and was adapted into four categories in order to measure discourse, vocabulary, grammar, and sentence complexity (Kim, 2014). Each category is scored from one to five. T-tests, ANOVA and Chi-Square tests were used to examine recording and questionnaire data. Participants' TOEIC listening comprehension scores were compared with speaking performance in order to determine if there were any differences for the three modes.

3. Results and discussion

Three native speakers – two British and one American – assessed participants' oral performance, and the inter-rater reliability of Cohen's Kappa coefficient was .885. The results revealed that Task 3, Task 2, and Task 1 had higher scores respectively on both the holistic and discourse scores. In line with this, there were significant differences for holistic scores between Task 1 and Task 3 ($p<0.05$) and discourse scores between Task 1 and Task 2 ($p<0.05$), as well as between Task 1 and Task 3 ($p<0.05$).

Moreover, there was no significant difference between participants' preferences or level of difficulty in their speaking performance relative to the three movie clips when creating a story. There was, however, significant difference between how easy participants founded the tasks and their speaking performance ($p<0.05$) as well as grammar scores ($p<0.05$) for Task 3.

In the survey, participants answered that Task 3 was a good test to assess their listening and speaking skills over a short time period. They also felt that a movie clip without dialogue can offer freedom to make a story.

4.   Conclusions

This study concluded that the participants' oral performance was substantially different for holistic and discourse scores for the three tests. Moreover, they had different interpretations towards different modes.

This study investigated multimodal effects through storytelling with various media modes for oral proficiency, but a longevity study with different types of movie clips and an investigation of learners' preference for various movie clips for storytelling still need to be conducted for media literacy.

5.   Acknowledgements

I would like to thank my colleague Gary Young for his kind contributions to the data collection in this study.

References

Kim, S. H. (2014). The effects of using storytelling with a Charlie Chaplin silent movie clip on oral proficiency development. *The Society for Teaching English through Media, 15*(1), 1-20.

Mayer, R. E., & Sims, V. K. (1994). For whom is a picture worth a thousand words? Extensions of a dual-coding theory of multimedia learning. *Journal of Educational Psychology, 86*(3), 389-401.

Scheibe, C. L., & Rogow, F. (2008). *Basic ways to integrate media literacy and critical thinking into any curriculum* (3rd ed.). New York Ithaca College.

Collaboration through blogging: the development of writing and speaking skills in ESP courses

Angela Kleanthous[1] and Walcir Cardoso[2]

Abstract. There has been a growing interest in incorporating social media in education and in language teaching in general. From a pedagogical perspective, as mentioned in Kleanthous (2016), blogs (or weblogs) appear to be effective in enhancing writing and/or reading skills, as their interactive platforms enable learners to exchange comments and offer feedback to each other, thus allowing learners to reflect on their own work and the learning process. Following our previous research (Kleanthous, 2016), this study proposes a research agenda for the effectiveness of collaboration through peer feedback in order to enhance the writing and speaking skills of English for Specific Purposes (ESP) students in online settings. A preliminary analysis of data collected suggests that the interactive use of blogs in the ESP classroom has a positive impact on students' writing and speaking skills. The discussion of our results highlights the importance of social media in promoting language learning within a collaborative environment that is essentially learner-centered and teacher facilitated, as recommended by Computer-Assisted Language Learning (CALL) researchers (e.g. Chapelle, 2001).

Keywords: blogs, collaborative learning, peer feedback, social media.

1.   Introduction

Collaboration among students is believed to be beneficial because it encourages them to become motivated and engaged in the learning process, as attested by recent research. For example, Fernández Dobao (2012) investigated the effect of pair and group work in written accuracy, fluency and complexity, as well as the frequency and nature of language related episodes. Her study indicated that

1. University of Cyprus, Nicosia, Cyprus; angela@ucy.ac.cy
2. Concordia University, Montreal, Canada; walcir.cardoso@concordia.ca

How to cite this article: Kleanthous, A., & Cardoso, W. (2016). Collaboration through blogging: the development of writing and speaking skills in ESP courses. In S. Papadima-Sophocleous, L. Bradley & S. Thouësny (Eds), *CALL communities and culture – short papers from EUROCALL 2016* (pp. 225-229). Research-publishing.net. https://doi.org/10.14705/rpnet.2016.eurocall2016.566

collaboration, either in pairs or in small groups, produced more grammatically and lexically accurate written materials.

Similarly, collaborative assessment in e-learning environments suggests that active collaboration among students makes them more motivated and engaged in the process of learning (McConnell, 2002). Knowing that there is an audience of readers or listeners seems to make students more motivated and, accordingly, they are more willing to put effort into assigned activities and thus do their best to perform well. Providing and receiving feedback by both their peers and instructor via this collaborative process can also be beneficial, especially in improving the students' writing and speaking skills, and their overall language development.

The focus of this paper is on the productive skills of writing and speaking because these are more easily implemented in a blog environment due to its message posting features. This paper is part of the first author's PhD research, and it aims to set out a research agenda for the effectiveness of collaboration through peer feedback in order to enhance the writing and speaking skills of ESP students in online settings. As such, the study aims to answer the following two research questions: (1) what impact does the use of blogs have on written and spoken language development in ESP contexts?, and (2) what are the students' perceptions on whether collaboration through peer feedback helps improve personal writing and speaking skills in ESP?

2.   Method

2.1.   Participants

43 first-year Computer Science undergraduate students at the University of Cyprus participated in this study. They were 19 to 22 year old Cypriots enrolled in the compulsory *English for Computer Science* course.

2.2.   Procedure and instruments

The instructor/researcher created a class blog using Blogger (www.blogger.com) in which students became both followers and authors. Two writing tasks and two speaking tasks were uploaded throughout the semester. Students had to complete each task by a specific deadline and then comment on each other's posts as a follow-up activity after each task. The instructor monitored all comments and facilitated the discussion if some comments were not clear.

In general, students offered more comments related to the content, format and style of the written tasks, and less on correcting grammar, vocabulary and spelling errors. With respect to the speaking tasks, students provided oral comments expressing agreement/disagreement or personal views on the specific task at hand. These recordings were conducted using Vocaroo (www.vocaroo.com), in the form of podcasts, which were then uploaded to the course blog for peer feedback.

2.3.   Data collection

The methods used to answer the two research questions included the collection of qualitative data such as writing samples from the learners' blog. Apart from their own posts, learners were encouraged to comment on their classmates' work by giving constructive feedback based on a set of pre-established criteria. By using their peers' feedback, students had to revise their assignments and upload the final drafts so that the instructor could evaluate them.

Following the students' initial posts, seven volunteers were interviewed in two focus-group sessions in which they were asked to report and answer questions about their perceptions and attitudes towards the use of blogs, as conceptualized in the study. The same number of students was interviewed again in the same focus groups at the end of the semester, after they had completed all blog-related assignments. Finally, participants were interviewed individually at the end of the study.

3.   Results and discussion

With respect to the impact of blogs on the development of the students' writing and speaking skills in an ESP course, an analysis of the data, which included extracts from blog posts and comments, reveals a perceived improvement in the students' performance, especially in writing. A comparison was made between the blog posts and their comments (which constituted their first attempt at writing a memo on the blog), against their performance in the subsequent memo assignment, midterm and final exams. The participants' writing mistakes noted on the first task were not repeated in subsequent exams and they further improved their memo-writing skills. Regarding the students' speaking skills, due to students' hesitation to record their own speech and upload it to the blog, only one third of the students performed these tasks, therefore additional data need to be gathered to draw reliable conclusions.

An analysis of the data also revealed the students' positive attitudes towards the use of blogs for improving their writing skills. They felt it was an innovative and interesting way to do their homework: "interesting, a different way to give my papers and get in contact with my teacher; [...] helpful; reading others' posts helps understand the task better if I have difficulty". They also stated that the interactive feature blogs, through which they could exchange feedback on their work, helped them improve their writing, and made them pay attention to their peers' comments. Some participants stated that "getting comments is motivational; I didn't repeat the mistake; it's more helpful to the instructor's comments because you just read the teacher's comments and forget them, but your classmates' comments you cannot forget". Even though some participants felt uncomfortable giving comments and feedback to peers, as they felt that their classmates might be offended, they recognized in the end that by identifying errors in their classmates' work, they helped each other identify errors in their own writing, and this prevented them from making the same mistakes again: "I felt good about giving comments because I felt I was helping someone get better and it helped me express myself when I commented on others' work and it improved my writing as well". They also stated that using the blog positively affected their motivation, as they would constantly log in to check whether someone had posted a comment on their writing or speaking tasks.

With regards to the participants' speaking tasks, they stated that using Vocaroo was easy, and that completing the tasks did not take a considerable amount of extra time. However, some felt nervous about recording their voice and sharing it with their classmates, since it was something they had never done before. Finally, according to their responses, speaking tasks that take place on a blog may be more helpful for preparing a presentation, since they can be rehearsed before they are recorded: "[blogs] improved my speaking skills mostly because I had to record myself, tried more than once to have a good result [...]; similar to giving a presentation, so I practiced that skill".

4.   Conclusion

To conclude, the results reported here reveal that the participants perceive blogs as important tools to promote language learning within a collaborative environment that is essentially learner-centered and teacher-facilitated, as recommended by CALL researchers (Chapelle, 2001). In particular, participants felt that they improved in their writing, speaking and reading skills, especially through the exchange of feedback, although they felt hesitant and anxious about recording and sharing their own speech. Finally, they perceived blogs as motivating and fun tools that enhanced their overall language learning experience.

5.   Acknowledgements

We would like to thank Angela's supervisors, Prof. Vic Lally and Prof. Fiona Patrick at the University of Glasgow, for their support throughout this research.

References

Chapelle, C. (2001). *Computer applications in second language acquisition: foundations for teaching, testing, and research.* Cambridge: Cambridge University Press. https://doi.org/10.1017/CBO9781139524681

Fernández Dobao, A. (2012). Collaborative writing tasks in the L2 classroom: comparing group, pair, and individual work. *Journal of Second Language Writing, 21*(1), 40-58. https://doi.org/10.1016/j.jslw.2011.12.002

Kleanthous, A. (2016). Collaboration through blogging to develop writing and speaking skills in english for specific purpose (ESP) courses. *EDULEARN16 Proceedings* (pp. 1110-1118). https://doi.org/10.21125/edulearn.2016.1230

McConnell, D. (2002). The experience of collaborative assessment in e-learning. *Studies in Continuing Education, 24*(1), 73-92. https://doi.org/10.1080/01580370220130459

Cultivating a community of learners in a distance learning postgraduate course for language professionals

Angelos Konstantinidis[1] and Cecilia Goria[2]

Abstract. The purpose of this contribution is to share reflections and practices in cultivating a community of learners in the context of a professional development programme at Master's level for language teachers. The programme implements a highly participatory pedagogical model of online learning which combines the Community of Inquiry (CoI) model (Garrison, Anderson, & Archer, 1999) with the Community Indicator Framework (CIF) (Galley, Conole, & Alevizou, 2012). The tangible outcome of our revised interpretation of the two models is a cohesive community characterised by a strong sense of commitment towards the learning of the individuals as well as that of the group. This affects the quality of the learning experience, enhances academic achievements, and increases student retention.

Keywords: online community, language teachers, distance learning.

1.   Introduction

Online and distance learning is increasingly used in teacher education programmes since it affords access to course materials anytime/anywhere, participation from disperse geographical locations, and a flexible schedule. At the same time, it faces a number of challenges such as effective use of technology, students' personal commitments affecting engagement with the course, and students' feelings of isolation affecting their participation.

The Master of Arts in Digital Technologies for Language Teaching (MA in DTLT), University of Nottingham, is a two-year part-time online distance learning

---

1. University of Nottingham, Nottingham, United Kingdom; Angelos.Konstantinidis@nottingham.ac.uk
2. University of Nottingham, Nottingham, United Kingdom; Cecilia.Goria@nottingham.ac.uk

How to cite this article: Konstantinidis, A., & Goria, C. (2016). Cultivating a community of learners in a distance learning postgraduate course for language professionals. In S. Papadima-Sophocleous, L. Bradley & S. Thouësny (Eds), *CALL communities and culture – short papers from EUROCALL 2016* (pp. 230-236). Research-publishing.net. https://doi.org/10.14705/rpnet.2016.eurocall2016.567

programme that targets qualified teachers interested in developing their theoretical and practical expertise in the field of digital technologies with a specific focus on the learning and teaching of foreign languages. The programme addresses the aforementioned challenges by leveraging course design as well as a series of Web 2.0 tools to cultivate a strong sense of learners' community and increase students' commitment to the programme.

In the following section we present the development of our pedagogical framework and reflect on its design. Next, we briefly discuss its implementation and, lastly, we list the most important outcomes.

2.   The development of our framework

In creating our framework for designing and implementing the programme, we laid two cornerstones. The first is the CoI by Garrison et al. (1999). The CoI posits that valuable educational experiences are embedded within a CoI consisted of teachers and students, where learning occurs through the interaction of three core elements, namely *cognitive* presence, the extent that participants are in position to construct meaning through communication; *social* presence, the participants' ability to project their socioemotional traits into the community; and *teaching* presence, which relates to the design and facilitation of the educational experience.

Our second cornerstone is the CIF by Galley et al. (2012), a tool for monitoring, observing and supporting collaborative activities in online communities of practice. The CIF identifies four fundamental aspects of experience: *participation,* the ways in which individuals engage in activity; *cohesion,* the ties between individuals and the community as a whole; *identity,* how individuals perceive the community and their place within it; and *creative capability,* the ability of the community to create shared artefacts and knowledge (Goria & Lagares, 2015, p. 224).

CoI and CIF differ in two ways. Firstly, CoI provides a framework for computer mediated communication for closed educational settings, while CIF is informed by the principles of open education and focuses on open social networks for education professionals. Secondly, CoI supports purposely designed educational experiences, while CIF supports community development in an open social network site. Given that the MA in the DTLT programme sits within an institutionally closed online educational context and yet employs open pedagogies based on the wider social web and its students' online communities, we attempted to reconcile the two models to develop a framework (Figure 1) for monitoring and supporting the development of our learning community. What follows is a brief description of this process.

Figure 1. 'Learning in online communities' framework adapted from CoI and CIF

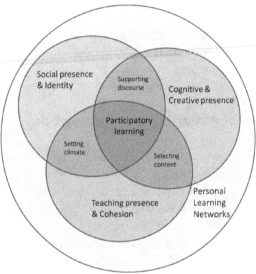

Firstly, we associated *social* presence with *identity* since both are related to the social characteristics of a community. Next, we placed *cohesion* along with *teaching* presence, since we believe it is a primary function of the teacher to establish ties between members. We placed *creative capability* in the *cognitive* sphere, since it is related to the ability of the community to engage in productive activities. Lastly, we positioned *participation* in the centre since it is related to the whole operation of the community.

We included participants' Personal Learning Networks (PLNs) into the model for three reasons. Firstly, each participant's PLN is significantly enhanced through his/her participation to the programme. Secondly, learning outputs of each participant's PLN affects the learning experience of the community. Thirdly, the pedagogical approach implemented with our programme actively scaffolds the development of our students' PLNs. Hence, there is a reciprocal exchange between each student's PLN and the community. We considered that such a relation would best be illustrated by drawing a surrounding circle that encapsulates the community and its participants.

3. Implementation of the framework

3.1. Social presence

Three methods are employed for enhancing social presence:

- *Welcoming new students.* Part of our induction process, we invite new students to join a closed group and engage them in a series of warm-up activities.

- *Celebrating social events.* We use various web tools and ways to celebrate social events in which our students are invited to participate.

- *Synchronous meetings.* We schedule online synchronous meetings regularly.

3.2. Identity

We employ four methods to promote group identity:

- *Addressing students as a group.* We cultivate a culture of shared responsibility in studying and doing the activities.

- *Peer-feedback.* We constantly encourage peer-feedback.

- *Group tasks.* During each year students have to complete at least one group task.

- *Dissertation Show.* Every summer all community members are invited to the dissertation show, an online event where second-year students present ongoing work on dissertations. Since dissertations are the most important assignments that students undertake, this event helps them feel that they are all in the same boat.

3.3. Cognitive presence

We followed the critical inquiry model (Garrison et al., 1999) in the design and implementation of our overall strategy and the individual learning tasks to enhance cognitive presence:

- *Triggering event.* Integration of web tools in the activities positively affects their reception from students.

- *Exploration phase.* Students are encouraged to employ their PLN in their quest for information.

- *Integration and resolution phases.* We design tasks that challenge students to step out from the exploration phase and reach the integration and subsequently the resolution phases.

3.4.   Creative presence

The focus of our efforts is on ways of establishing a conducive context for creative processes. Our strategy is built on four pillars:

- *Spirit of collaboration.* This is not to suggest that creativity can only be expressed through collaborative practices, rather that members should sense that there is a shared goal and that reaching this goal necessitates collaborating with others instead of antagonising.

- *Spirit of openness.* We hold that open education can be realised in many ways. One of these ways is to cultivate the identity of 'open scholar' to the members of the community (Weller, 2012). Indeed, our community members develop most of the practices described as the characteristics of open scholar.

- *Spirit of problem-based learning.* Rather than lecturing about the weekly topics, we prepare tasks that resemble real-world problems.

- *Spirit of technology integration.* We consider technology integration important for a number of reasons, such as authenticity in tasks, collaboration, etc.

3.5.   Teaching presence

The role of the teacher can be acquired by any community member, so the following ways of establishing teaching presence should be approached with this premise in mind:

- *Peer interaction.* We encourage peer-to-peer interaction since it is the first step for adopting teacher's role by students. Accordingly, use of different platforms that we support in the programme provides multiple opportunities for interaction.

- *Shifting roles.* We actively encourage students to acquire the role of the teacher in several occasions (i.e. sharing expertise).

3.6. Cohesion

We consider group cohesion not as something static, but rather as constantly evolving and changing depending on the member who acquires the role of the teacher at any given moment. Although this may seem challenging in maintaining a coherent community, we employ the following strategies to cultivate a cohesive atmosphere:

- *Non-hierarchical relations.* We establish a mutual relationship with tutors and students alike. The use of the inclusive 'we' is a feature of the way groups are addressed.

- *Casual language and environments.* We eschew formalities both in language and in online environments.

- *Self-disclosure.* Self-disclosure helps members to build friendly relations. We facilitate self-disclosure through online social games.

4. Outcomes

The tangible outcome of our revised interpretation of the two models is an active and cohesive community characterised by a strong sense of commitment towards the learning of the individuals as well as that of the group. This affects the quality of the learning experience, enhances academic achievements, and increases student retention.

5. Conclusion

In this paper we discussed and reflected on the development of the pedagogical framework for cultivating an online community of learners at the online distance learning MA in DTLT. We presented an array of strategies that we employ and we consider important for the success of the framework. We perceive that the proposed framework offers to our programme, as well as to other educators who organise and facilitate similar online courses, a valuable tool to monitor and support the development of a learning community.

References

Galley, R., Conole, G., & Alevizou, P. (2012). Community indicators: a framework for observing and supporting community activity on Cloudworks. *Interactive Learning Environments, 22*(3), 373-395. https://doi.org/10.1080/10494820.2012.680965

Garrison, D., Anderson, T., & Archer, W. (1999). Critical inquiry in a text-based environment: computer conferencing in higher education. *The Internet and Higher Education, 2*(2-3), 87-105. https://doi.org/10.1016/S1096-7516(00)00016-6

Goria, C., & Lagares, M. (2015). Open online language courses: the multi-level model of the Spanish N(ottingham)OOC. In F. Helm, L. Bradley, M. Guarda, & S. Thouësny (Eds), *Critical CALL – Proceedings of the 2015 EUROCALL Conference, Padova, Italy* (pp. 221-227). Dublin Ireland: Research-publishing.net. https://doi.org/10.14705/rpnet.2015.000337

Weller, M. (2012). The openness-creativity cycle in education. *Journal of Interactive Media in Education JIME, 2012*(1), 2. https://doi.org/10.5334/2012-02

Task-oriented spoken dialog system
for second-language learning

Oh-Woog Kwon[1], Young-Kil Kim[2], and Yunkeun Lee[3]

Abstract. This paper introduces a Dialog-Based Computer Assisted second-Language Learning (DB-CALL) system using task-oriented dialogue processing technology. The system promotes dialogue with a second-language learner for a specific task, such as purchasing tour tickets, ordering food, passing through immigration, etc. The dialog system plays a role of a ticket agent, a waiter, or an immigration officer at each task and the learner completes the task through talking with the system in the second-languages. The system gives a new situation of the task at every trial, so that the learner could have a different experience and learn various expressions in the same task. Our DB-CALL system is based on a task-oriented dialog system consisting of a language understanding module using a structural support vector model and a dynamic dialog graph based dialog management module. Our task-oriented dialog system is trained from the intention-annotated real dialog scripts. The experiments for the performance of our proposed dialog system show the average task success rate of 85.52%, the average turn success rate of 85.32%, and the average turn length of 14.61. In a satisfactory survey targeting the subjects, the subjects agreed that our system makes them learn the second-language more efficiently and with less effort.

Keywords: computer-assisted second-language learning system, dialog-based CALL, task-oriented dialog system, language understanding, dynamic dialog graph based dialog management.

1. Introduction

Many methods from the field of natural language processing and dialog processing have been employed in CALL (Johnson & Valente, 2009; Kwon, Lee, Kim, & Lee,

1. Electronics and Telecommunications Research Institute, Daejeon, Korea; ohwoog@etri.re.kr
2. Electronics and Telecommunications Research Institute, Daejeon, Korea; kimyk@etri.re.kr
3. Electronics and Telecommunications Research Institute, Daejeon, Korea; yklee@etri.re.kr

How to cite this article: Kwon, O.-W., Kim, Y.-K., & Lee, Y. (2016). Task-oriented spoken dialog system for second-language learning . In S. Papadima-Sophocleous, L. Bradley & S. Thouësny (Eds), *CALL communities and culture – short papers from EUROCALL 2016* (pp. 237-242). Research-publishing.net. https://doi.org/10.14705/rpnet.2016.eurocall2016.568

237

2015; Wilske, 2015). The approaches engage the learner in a dialog and provide educational feedback, focusing on either form-based instruction or meaning-based instruction. Focus-on-form approaches tend to allow for relatively constrained input to provide more explicit feedback of linguistic forms and formal correctness about the learner's utterance (Kwon et al., 2015), whereas focus-on-meaning approaches tend to allow the learner to freely speak for providing opportunities for communication in the real world, but provide the less informative feedback (Wilske, 2015).

In this paper, we introduce a task-oriented spoken dialog system for providing the opportunities to use English in a situation that is similar to situations in real-life. A task-focused CALL system gives learners rich and realistic opportunities to practice achieving those tasks (Johnson & Valente, 2009). Our task-oriented spoken dialog system allows the learners to speak freely without a fixed scenario in a given task, then the learners can change the system initiative dialogue to their initiative dialogue. Our system provides no grammatical feedback and only provides the next recommended utterances for the learners after each system response. The proposed DB-CALL system focuses on meaning-based second language learning for the learners being familiar with English forms.

2. Task-oriented spoken dialog system for second-language learning

The system consists of Automatic Speech Recognition (ASR), task-oriented dialog processing, and Text-To-Speech (TTS) as shown in Figure 1. The ASR is optimized to recognize the English utterances of Korean learners as well as native speakers' utterances (Kwon et al., 2015) using a commercial English TTS engine to generate voices from system responses.

Our task-oriented dialog processing consists of a language understanding module using a Structural Support Vector Model (SSVM) (Lee & Jang, 2009) and a dynamic dialog graph based dialog management module. Our task-oriented dialog system uses the knowledge, which is trained from intention-annotated dialog scripts. Every dialog script is a real dialog between two persons who play a role of native (system) and learner (user) to accomplish the predefined task goal. We annotated every system and learner utterance with its intention using predefined dialog acts and slots. To classify user utterance with the predefined dialog acts and slots, the language understanding module trained dialog act classification model and slot classification model from user utterances of the intention-annotated corpus using SSVM, respectively. The dialog management model automatically constructs the task-oriented dialog-graph from the intention-annotated corpus. The task-oriented dialog-graph consists of user and system intention nodes having slot history vectors and direct links between nodes with weights. The user and system nodes of the graph corresponds to the user and system intention of the dialog scripts. The edges between nodes present the dialog flow of the dialog scripts. The dialog management module finds the best user node similar to the intention of current user's utterance in the current dialog history, and then selects dynamically one among the system nodes linked by the best user node according to the level of difficulty for learning. We define the longer the length of dialogue is, the more difficult the level. Therefore, the management selects the system node on the shorter path into the terminal nodes when the level is easier. The dialog management module generates system responses using the example sentence of the selected system node. The management module memorizes the used frequency of each node during communication with a learner and selects the system node having the least frequency to provide the learner new situations.

Figure 1.   Schematic diagram of the proposed task-oriented dialog system for second-language learning

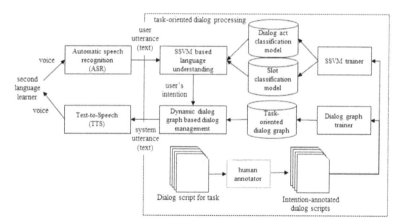

3.   Results and discussion

For the experiments, we constructed two task-oriented dialog systems, purchasing city tour bus tickets and passing through immigration. For each task, we firstly set up several situations, next gathered 100 dialog scripts between an English native (system) and a Korean English teacher (user), then English natives proofread the utterances of Korean teachers. Figure 2 shows an example of dialog script for purchasing city tour bus tickets. Next, we annotated the utterances with system or user intentions. Finally, our task-oriented dialog system was trained from the intention annotated scripts.

Figure 2.   Example of dialog script for purchasing city tour bus tickets

```
Task: Buying city tour bus tickets
Goal: Buy New York City Bus Tour tickets
Scenario condition: (1) 1 adult, 1 child (5 years old); (2) Take daytime tour; (3) Get two-day
ticket; (4) Visit Statue of Liberty; (5) Get 1 audio guide, 1 Korean tour booklet; (6) Spend
$120 or less

S:      Hi there. Welcome to the New York City Bus Tour Center.
U:      I want to buy tickets for me and my child.
S:      What kind of tour would you like to take?
U:      We would like to go on a tour during the day.
S:      We have two daytime tours: the Downtown Tour and the All Around Town Tour.
U:      Which tour goes to the Statue of Liberty?
S:      You can visit the Statue of Liberty on either tour.
U:      Can we get two-day tickets?
S:      You can get two-day tickets for the All Around Town Tour.
U:      Do you provide any guide materials?
S:      We have an audio guide for 10 dollars and free tour booklets.
U:      Do you have tour booklets in Korean?
S:      Yes, we have Korean tour booklets.
U:      How much are tickets for the All Around Town Tour?
S:      Adult tickets are 60 dollars.
U:      How much are tickets for children?
S:      Children 5 years old and under pay 50 dollars.
U:      Okay. I would like one adult ticket and one child ticket.
S:      Is your child 5 years old?
U:      Yes. I would like also an audio guide and a Korean tour booklet.
S:      Okay. That will be 120 dollars.
U:      Here you go.
S:      Thank you. Enjoy the tour.
```

To evaluate the performance of the systems, we recruited 20 subjects: Group A with low proficiency levels (five subjects with Test of English for International Communication (TOEIC) scores lower than 500), Group B with middle proficiency levels (ten subjects with TOEIC scores between 500 and 800), and Group C with high proficiency levels (five subjects with TOEIC scores higher than 800). Each subject had a dialogue with the system to achieve a given mission. In the experiments, the subjects tried four missions for each task. If there are ASR errors, the subjects corrected the ASR errors by typing to only evaluate our proposed task-based dialog processing engine without ASR errors. Table 1 shows the results of the experiments. The experiments show the average task success rate of 85.52%, the average turn success rate of 85.32%, and the average turn length of 14.61. Contrary to our expectations, the success rates of Group C are lower than Group A and B. The reason is that the subjects of Group C tried the communication and intelligence abilities of the dialog system by speaking various utterances and driving the system to an unexpected situation, while the subjects of Group A and B made utmost efforts to accomplish their goals.

Table 1.   The results of the experiments to evaluate the task-oriented dialog system

Measure	Subject group			
	Group A	Group B	Group C	All subjects
Avg. Task Success Rate (%)	93.75	89.90	72.92	**85.52**
Avg. Turn Success Rate (%)	86.71	87.09	82.17	**85.32**
Avg. Turn Length	14.71	13.80	15.32	**14.61**

We also investigated a satisfactory survey targeting the subjects about the second-language usefulness and efficiency. Table 2 shows the survey questionnaires and the average satisfactory scores of the subjects. The subjects indicated their level of agreement on each of the questionnaires. The levels of agreement are scored from one (strongly disagree) to six (strongly agree). From the results of the survey, most subjects agreed to that our system helps them learn English more efficiently and with less effort. Although the subjects of Group C did not faithfully take part in the experiments, the survey gained a better satisfaction score from Group C than those of the Group A and B. We assumed the reason is that our proposed task-oriented dialog system meets the requirement of the learners with high proficiency levels who want to exercise and acquire English through communicating spontaneously in authentic social situations.

Table 2.   The results of a satisfactory survey

Survey questionnaires	Level of agreement (1 through 6)			
	Group A	Group B	Group C	All
Q1) The naturalness of the dialogue made the system so true to life.	4.20	4.42	4.63	4.41
Q2) The hints and suggestions are appropriate for the dialog context.	4.95	4.67	4.75	4.76
Q3) The dialog system helps you learn English more efficiently.	4.65	4.92	5.13	4.90
Q4) The ASR function helps you learn English more efficiently.	5.05	5.08	5.38	5.15
Q5) The TTS function helps you learn English more efficiently.	4.80	4.67	4.63	4.69
Q6) The system has some good features to help us learn English more efficiently and with less effort, compared to the previous methods.	5.15	5.25	5.25	5.23
Total	**4.80**	**4.83**	**4.96**	**4.86**

*Level of agreement : 1- strongly disagree, 2 - disagree, 3 - somewhat disagree, 4 - somewhat agree, 5 - agree, 6 - strongly agree

4.   Conclusions

This paper described a DB-CALL system using a task-oriented dialog processing technology. The task-oriented dialog understanding and managing knowledge are automatically trained from the intention-annotated real-dialog scripts for accomplishing the task. In the experiments, the system showed a good performance with the average task success rate of 85.52% and the average turn success rate of 85.32%. Also, from the result of a satisfactory survey, we expected that our task-oriented dialog system might satisfy the needs of the second-language learners with high proficiency levels who want to communicate with natives in real-life situations.

5.   Acknowledgements

This work was supported by the ICT R&D program of MSIP/IITP [R0126-15-1117, Core technology development of the spontaneous speech dialogue processing for language learning].

References

Johnson, W. L., & Valente, A. (2009). Tactical language and culture training systems: using AI to teach foreign languages and cultures. *AI Magazine, 30*(2), 72-83.

Kwon, O.-W., Lee, K., Kim, Y.-K., & Lee, Y. (2015). GenieTutor: a computer assisted second-language learning system based on semantic and grammar correctness evaluations. In F. Helm, L. Bradley, M. Guarda & S. Thouësny (Eds), *Critical CALL – Proceedings of the 2015 EUROCALL Conference, Padova, Italy* (pp. 330-335). Dublin Ireland: Research-publishing. net. https://doi.org/10.14705/rpnet.2015.000354

Lee, C., & Jang, M.-G. (2009). Fast training of structured SVM using fixed-threshold sequential minimal optimization. *ETRI Journal, 31*(2), 121-128. https://doi.org/10.4218/etrij.09.0108.0276

Wilske, S. (2015). *Form and meaning in dialog-based computer-assisted language learning.* Ph.D. thesis. Saarland University.

Promoting multilingual communicative competence through multimodal academic learning situations

Anna Kyppö[1] and Teija Natri[2]

Abstract. This paper presents information on the factors affecting the development of multilingual and multicultural communicative competence in interactive multimodal learning environments in an academic context. The interdisciplinary course in multilingual interaction offered at the University of Jyväskylä aims to enhance students' competence in multilingual and multicultural academic communication by promoting the use of their entire linguistic repertoire in various learning situations. Throughout the course, we observed the students' engagement in multilingual and multicultural activities. These observations suggest that simultaneous use of multiple languages in synchronous and asynchronous learning environments has evident impact on the development of learners' multilingual and multicultural competences as well as increases their multicultural awareness. Learners' experiences, collected through learning journals and reflective feedback, suggest that the use of multimodal interactive learning environments may support multilingual and multicultural learning and enhance learner agency.

Keywords: multilingual communication, multicultural communication, multilingual and multicultural academic communication competence, multicultural awareness, learner agency.

1. Introduction

This empirical study presents information about affordances for the development of learners' multilingual and multicultural communicative competence in interactive multimodal learning environments. The context of the study is an interdisciplinary course in multilingual interaction aimed at enhancing students' competence in multilingual and multicultural academic communication by promoting the use

1. University of Jyväskylä, Jyväskylä, Finland; anna.kyppo@jyu.fi
2. University of Jyväskylä, Jyväskylä, Finland; teija.natri@jyu.fi

How to cite this article: Kyppö. A., & Natri, T. (2016). Promoting multilingual communicative competence through multimodal academic learning situations. In S. Papadima-Sophocleous, L. Bradley & S. Thouësny (Eds), *CALL communities and culture – short papers from EUROCALL 2016* (pp. 243-247). Dublin: Research-publishing.net. https://doi.org/10.14705/rpnet.2016.eurocall2016.569

of their entire linguistic repertoire in various social learning situations. A major source of inspiration is the MAGICC project of the EU Lifelong Learning Programme 2012-2014 (http://www.magicc.eu), which emphasises the role of languages and communication as part of academic expertise. Of similar importance is Blommaert's (2010) perception of multilingualism as a complex of semiotic resources and a repertoire of varying language abilities. The focus is on various aspects of multilingual and multicultural communication. Due to the multilingual character of the course, students are required to have partial competence in at least two languages other than their L1. Furthermore, the presence of four to five teachers with various linguistic repertoires facilitates the creation of multilingual social space. To enhance learner agency and increase learners' multilingual agility, task-based learning is employed. Multiple languages in synchronous and asynchronous learning environments are used simultaneously, an approach which results in multidirectional teacher–learner interaction and the enhancement of multicultural skills.

2.   Method

Even though the concepts of multilingualism and multilingual competence have been explored from various perspectives, our focus is on learning. Our theoretical background, therefore, is to be found in Blommaert's (2010) definition on multilingualism (see above) and in theories related to translanguaging (Garcia, 2009; Park, 2013; Swain & Watanabe, 2012). The purpose is to promote the development of learners' multilingual communicative competence through multilingual mediation and meaning-making. Learners' multilingual repertoires are activated through various interactive scenarios. In these they are expected to employ their problem-based learning strategies to find a solution or to act in a situation that is close to real life. The lessons are in line with scenario-based e-learning (Pappas, 2014), which gets learners involved in 'real-life simulations' and provides them with learning experiences aimed at gathering skills which may be useful for their future working life. Through the lessons, various aspects of multilingual and multicultural communication are addressed, including non-verbal communication, various mediation activities such as intercomprehension, activation of receptive skills between typologically related yet different languages (Berthele, 2007), and persuasion and negotiation in multicultural settings. In mediation activities, one or more languages are used for reading or listening and one or more other languages for speaking or writing. To enhance learners' collaborative social skills, the educational mobile platform REAL, developed by the Jyväskylä University of Applied Sciences, is used in scenario-based assignments, while the web-based learning platform Optima serves as the course workspace. Optima further acts as a uniting factor facilitating the common learning experience. Learner logs have been used to obtain information on the usefulness of tasks, technology choices and the achievement of learning outcomes. In addition, a final survey on learner agency – on their commitment to and engagement in the learning process (Mercer, 2012) – was conducted.

3.   Discussion

The course aim was to activate learners' overall linguistic repertoires. Students found that the course helped to develop their linguistic agility and viewed it as a safe learning environment in which to share their ideas on various aspects of linguistic and cultural identity.

> "this class gave an important opportunity to reflect upon my recent and not-so-recent experiences in multilingual and multicultural environments... I had the chance to make sense and understand on a deeper level some of the things that I had encountered in the real world. Also, this class helped to break the barriers we tend to build between languages. It helped me understand that my language skills reach over the boundaries of languages, I understand and speak languages that I don't officially understand or speak. That is an important discovery that everyone should get the chance to make already in high school, for example" (Student learner log, unedited).

The feedback on the task design and use of the mobile platform received from students' learner logs and course feedback forms was very significant, especially for the teachers. The mobile platform REAL was tested in scenarios related to the concept of culture and receptive multilingualism. The tasks consisted of communicative assignments, such as searching for information, negotiation and decision-making. Students were obviously not only aware of the *raison d'être* of scenarios, but they were also excited by the use of this particular platform due to its flexibility and the user-friendly mobile application.

> "This app [REAL] is innovative, functioning... it enables sharing the ideas... The chat is quick and dynamic, and what is best, it is accessible from more than one device. It is near to us, young people's lifestyle, since we master the technology..." (Student learner log, unedited).

Students felt that they were free to express their opinions via REAL and preserve their privacy at the same time. Voting and commenting was considered to be attractive and to increase participants' engagement in discussions. From the teachers' viewpoint, the use of new technology offers not only a unique opportunity to document the flow of discussion, but also the possibility to pinpoint some ideas or recurrent themes in students' discussions by means of word clouds and other visual tools.

While student reflections and feedback collected through learner logs generally referred to the task design and the use of the mobile platform, the end-of-course survey provided information on students' learner agency, that is, on their activity and initiative as well as their personal engagement in the learning process. According to Mercer (2012), agency reflects not only the learners' attitudes and observable actions, but also their behavior, beliefs, thoughts and feelings, which may not be observable through the feedback and learner logs. The survey reveals that the majority of students took responsibility for shared learning situations and perceived the co-students as a resource for learning. The technological solutions used on the course were regarded as supportive for teamwork. Furthermore, they were perceived as providing a meaningful learning experience.

4.   Conclusions

As the challenges of international and multicultural working life have increased, the need for multilingual and multicultural courses at the university level has grown. Courses in multilingual and multicultural communication may enhance learner agency and provide students with tools and strategies that will be useful in their professional careers. Furthermore, the integration of multiple languages into subject studies and the use of multimodal interactive online resources are essential because they present an integrated part of people's professional frameworks.

The experiences of learners and teachers collected on this course reveal a range of issues that would be important for further study: interactive multimodal learning environments, which seem to be a major affordance for both parties; the development of multidirectional networking skills and the acquisition of multilingual/multicultural communication competences.

5.   Acknowledgements

We would like to thank the students and colleagues who have worked with us on the course as well as Peppi Taalas (PhD), Language Centre Director, who has paved the way for the development of multilingual and multicultural teaching at the University of Jyväskylä.

References

Berthele, R. (2007). Zum Prozess des Verstehens und Erschließens. In B. Hufeisen & N. Marx (Eds), *EuroComGerm—Die sieben Siebe: Germanische Sprachen lesen lernen* (pp. 15-26). Aachen, Germany: Shaker Verlag

Blommaert, J. (2010). *The sociolinguistics of globalization*. Cambridge: Cambridge University Press. https://doi.org/10.1017/CBO9780511845307

Garcia, O. (2009). *Bilingual education in the 21st century: a global perspective*. Oxford: Wiley-Blackwell.

Mercer, S. (2012). The complexity of learner agency. *Apples – Journal of Applied Language Studies, 6,* 41-59.

Pappas, C. (2014). Scenario-based e-learning to improve learners' engagement [Blog post]. https://elearningindustry.com/the-basics-of-scenario-based-e-learning

Park, M. S. (2013). Code-switching and translanguaging: potential functions in multilingual classroom. *Working Papers in TESOL & Applied linguistics, 13*(2), 50-52.

Swain, M., & Watanabe, Y. (2012). Languaging: collaborative dialogue as a source of second language learning. In C. Chapelle (Ed.), *The encyclopedia of applied linguistics*. Oxford: Blackwell Publishing. https://doi.org/10.1002/9781405198431.wbeal0664

Teacher professional learning:
developing with the aid of technology

Marianna Kyprianou[1] and Eleni Nikiforou[2]

Abstract. Education is a field that constantly changes, which dictates the need for continuing teacher professional learning and development. Teacher professional learning and development can be divided into two categories: formal learning/development and informal learning/development. This paper focuses on the experience of the presenters as coordinators of a large language section in a tertiary education institution, as this gave them the chance to develop professionally through informal learning, without attending any formal training sessions. Both coordinators did not have any previous experience in coordination, but they decided to keep a positive outlook on challenges and weaknesses, turning them into opportunities and strengths with the aid of technology. The experience of coordination will be presented using a Strengths, Weaknesses, Opportunities, and Threats/challenges (SWOT) framework of analysis. The present paper will report on this experience and how it helped the presenters develop professionally, and will also discuss the role of the use of online tools in the process.

Keywords: continuing professional development, CPD, informal learning, SWOT, technology.

1.   Introduction

The current project is an example of informal learning, reflecting on the experience of the authors as coordinators of a large language section in a tertiary educational institution in Cyprus. The authors assumed coordination duties in July 2014 and decided to take a reflection in-action and reflection-on-action approach in order to collaborate in the best possible way so that they could carry out their duties as coordinators. The application of the SWOT framework enabled them to formally

1. University of Cyprus, Limassol, Cyprus; kyprianou.marianna@ucy.ac.cy
2. University of Cyprus, Limassol, Cyprus; eleninik@ucy.ac.cy

How to cite this article: Kyprianou, M., & Nikiforou, E. (2016). Teacher professional learning: developing with the aid of technology. In S. Papadima-Sophocleous, L. Bradley & S. Thouësny (Eds), CALL communities and culture – short papers from EUROCALL 2016 (pp. 248-253). Research-publishing.net. https://doi.org/10.14705/rpnet.2016.eurocall2016.570

examine their experience and reflect on their own professional development through informal learning.

2.   Literature review

Continuing Professional Development (CPD) has been defined in the literature as "a commitment by members to continually update their skills and knowledge in order to remain professionally competent and achieve their true potential" (CAE, n.d.). In education, CPD carries connotations of teacher quality, reflecting on the quality of learning received by students (Borg, 2015). UNESCO (2014) proclaims that "an education system is only as good as its teachers" (p. 9), stressing the need for CPD in order to improve teaching and learning.

When CPD is cited in the literature, it is often linked to obvious examples of structured learning, such as seminars and conferences (see, for example, Villegas-Reimers, 2003). While these are excellent examples of CPD, there are also other, not so obvious activities which count as well, such as sharing and collaborating with colleagues, private study etc. CPD can be divided in two categories: formal and informal learning. For the purposes of the current paper, we will follow the definition provided by Levenberg and Caspi (2010, p. 324):

> **Formal learning** is learning supported by an educational or training institution, structured [… and] controlled by a teacher or a guide, resulting in a certificate.

> **Informal learning** is not supported by an educational or training institution. It is controlled primarily by the learner.

3.   Method

The coordination project was conducted over a period of two years, starting in July 2014 and ending in August 2016. A SWOT framework was employed to identify and analyse the internal and external factors that can influence the viability of the project, following Rouse (2013). The SWOT analysis focuses on the following four elements: Strengths (S), Weaknesses (W), Opportunities (O) and Threats/challenges (T). Rouse (2013, para. 3) defines them as follows:

- Strengths: the internal attributes and resources that support a successful outcome.

- Weaknesses: the internal attributes resources that work against a successful outcome.

- Opportunities: the external factors the project can capitalize on or use to its advantage.

- Threats/Challenges: the external factors that could jeopardize the project.

The English section is the largest language teaching unit at the Language Centre of the University of Cyprus. Over 2000 undergraduate students from 22 departments register to around 100 courses every year. Approximately 20 instructors (both full-time and part-time) teach the various English courses that are currently on offer (13 different courses, English for academic purposes and English specific purposes).

The coordinators of the English section work closely with the various university services in terms of scheduling and allocating courses, overseeing courses and course supervisors, establishing communication within and outside the section, examining and granting course equivalences/exemptions and generally dealing with any issues relating to the English section. The current authors had no previous experience in coordination, but nevertheless made a choice to see this as an opportunity to develop professionally by keeping a positive outlook on threats/challenges and weaknesses and turning them into opportunities and strengths during this coordination project.

4.   Results

4.1.   Strengths

The authors identified the following strengths on which they could rely throughout the duration of their coordination: (a) they both had previous experience as course supervisors which helped them understand the structure of the section in depth as well as the characteristics each role had i.e. the role of the supervisors and the role of the coordinators; (b) they both had long teaching experience at the University of Cyprus which translates into in-depth knowledge of not only the structure of the English section and the courses it offers but also the structure of the Language

Centre and the University of Cyprus; (c) they collaborated well with each other on various projects; (d) they have good organisational skills; (e) they are both adept in using technology; (f) they are both highly motivated individuals who always strive for the best possible outcome in whatever endeavour they follow, and finally (g) they are very keen on reflective practice as a means of developing professionally.

4.2. Weaknesses

In undertaking coordination, the researchers identified the project's weaknesses so that they could approach them in the most effective way. First of all, a mentoring scheme was not in place, which means that the new coordinators needed to familiarize themselves with the task at hand on the job. Secondly, they had to deal with heavy teaching workloads. Moreover, there is a lot of paperwork involved in the coordination of a section of this size. Finally, there was lack of online databases. To deal with all these issues the use of technology was adopted, which helped make tasks less time-consuming, assisted online collaboration, supported the creation of online databases, and helped support each other throughout the duration of the coordination.

4.3. Opportunities

As aforementioned, the authors undertook the project with a positive outlook and the determination to turn weaknesses into strengths and challenges into opportunities. For example, they saw an opportunity to create an online database for the accreditation of external exams which would make the process easier for those involved (students, coordinators, administrative staff). They also took the initiative to create databases for syllabi, to develop handbooks for the English language instructors, to revise the descriptions of the English language courses in collaboration with colleagues. They collaborated with all the departments of the university closely to improve the existing schedule. Furthermore, they suggested the establishment of a mentoring scheme for new coordinators. They increased sharing and collaboration with colleagues through the use of technology. Finally, they increased the visibility of the English section with their active participation in events and conferences, as well as with their involvement in the organisation of events and conferences.

4.4. Threats/challenges

The challenges faced during the coordination project included budget constraints and tight deadlines. These external factors are commonly found in Higher Education institutions (see, for example, Yuan & Powell, 2013 on budget constraints).

4.5. The role of technology in the SWOT

The application of technology during the coordination project made it feasible for the coordinators to collaborate efficiently, enabled them to reflect upon their work, kept them motivated, and helped them be organised. The tools used were the following: Dropbox, with which the authors collaborated in creating and editing the materials relating to the coordination of the section; Viber, Skype and emails for their communication; Microsoft Office (especially Excel and Word) for data analysis, development of materials, and creation of databases; and an online shared calendar to organise and manage tasks.

5. Conclusions and reflections

The authors, upon reflection through the application of the SWOT framework, came to realize that in dealing with weaknesses and threats/challenges, they should be well-informed in order to both pursue what was best for the English section but also to be able to work together on the various issues at hand. Especially in relation to weaknesses, it became evident that hard work was needed in order to be able to execute their duties well. It was also apparent that they needed to make suggestions to improve the situation in the future, for example they made a suggestion for a mentoring scheme for future coordinators. When it comes to threats/challenges, the authors realized that they needed to be informed on the policies and regulations pertaining to the budget issues and deadlines.

Following a reflection-in-action and reflection-on-action approach during the coordination project, the authors were successful in developing themselves professionally through informal learning. Following this approach, they took numerous initiatives to improve practice and to create a more efficient working environment for themselves and their section during their coordination. The role of technology in this was paramount, as it supported them in creating an online space where they could work collaboratively to coordinate the English section.

References

Borg, S. (2015). *Contemporary perspectives on continuing professional development*. Teaching for Success. British Council.

CAE. (n. d.). *What is CPD?* Cambridge Association of Entrepreneurs. http://cae-org.co.uk/cpd/

Levenberg, A., & Caspi, A. (2010). Comparing perceived formal and informal learning in face-to-face versus online environments. *Interdisciplinary Journal of E-Learning and Learning Objects,* *6*(1), 323-333. http://www.ijello.org/Volume6/IJELLOv6p323-333Levenberg706.pdf

Rouse, M. (2013). *SWOT analysis (strengths, weaknesses, opportunities and threats analysis) definition.* http://searchcio.techtarget.com/definition/SWOT-analysis-strengths-weaknesses-opportunities-and-threats-analysis

UNESCO. (2014). Teaching and learning: achieving equality for all. *11th EFA global monitoring report.* Paris: UNESCO.

Villegas-Reimers, E. (2003). *Teacher professional development: an international review of the literature.* UNESCO: International Institute for Educational Planning. http://unesdoc.unesco.org/images/0013/001330/133010e.pdf

Yuan, L., & Powell, S. (2013). MOOCs and open education: implications for higher education. *JISC Centre for Educational Technology and Interoperability standards (CETIS).*

Quizlet: what the students think – a qualitative data analysis

Bruce Lander[1]

Abstract. The immediate area of interest in this study is the primary building block of all foreign languages: vocabulary acquisition. Due to recent updates and innovations in educational software, foreign language educators now have a huge supply of ever improving tools to help enhance, transform and completely modify learning. Despite this surge in interest of recent times, there is very little physical evidence that indicates an overall sign of approval from learners. This empirical study used the now well-known digital flashcard tool Quizlet to help a large group of lower intermediate students to improve their vocabulary and ultimately raise their English comprehension levels at a medium sized private university in Japan. They were encouraged to use the said tool throughout the duration of the year-long course and were asked for their feedback about it in the final class. This study helps to reinvigorate the notion that technology can and does help the modern day language learner and can be approved in a positive manner by the majority stakeholder; the student.

Keywords: Quizlet, digital flashcards, blended learning, qualitative data analysis.

1.   Introduction

This paper will provide empirical evidence of what students think about using Quizlet. This tool was first released in 2007 and provided a contemporary alternative to traditional, paper flashcards. Quizlet has since undergone considerable changes and now provides near perfect text-to-speech pronunciation of words entered, has an in-built dictionary, and allows users to add visual aids in the form of all jpeg or gif files publicly available on flickr (flickr.com). These functions provide users with a tool far superior to their analogue paper flashcard counterparts. There are

1. Matsuyama University, Matsuyama, Japan; bruce.w.lander@gmail.com

How to cite this article: Lander, B. (2016). Quizlet: what the students think – a qualitative data analysis. In S. Papadima-Sophocleous, L. Bradley & S. Thouësny (Eds), *CALL communities and culture – short papers from EUROCALL 2016* (pp. 254-259). Research-publishing.net. https://doi.org/10.14705/rpnet.2016.eurocall2016.571

now several competitors. However, the widespread use of Quizlet with its clever, interactive interface remains in language learning.

Many emerging educational software programmes are now providing links to Quizlet and its user-friendly interface thanks to its increasing popularity the past two years in Japan and abroad. Ashcroft and Imrie (2014) gave a practical account of Quizlet and its full functionality at that time. They focused their account of Quizlet on the Puentedura's (2013) Substitution Augmentation Modification Redefinition (SAMR) model. Although their account provided a highly practical outlook on the various functions available, it did not provide any factual data to disclose its approval with students. Barr (2016) classified users of Quizlet into three types, non-users who only use in class, visual and kinesthetic users. However, no evidence was given on student opinion on the tool.

This begs the following questions: (1) what do students think of Quizlet and its digital flashcard format?; (2) do they prefer it to more traditional methods of learning vocabulary?; and perhaps more importantly, (3) is it effective? This study will introduce two sets of qualitative data obtained over a two-year time span in a test-based English language class and aims to answer these three questions.

2.   Method

Quizlet was introduced to two sets of lower intermediate students in an introductory Test Of English for International Communication (TOEIC) course at a university in Japan. The first set comprised of 450 students varying in age and gender from ages 19-21 years old. This group was instructed from April 2013 to January 2014 over the course of two 15-week semesters. The second set comprised of a smaller group of 380 students from April 2014 to January 2015, bringing the total sample size of this study to 830 subjects. No student within this group had any prior experience with Quizlet or any other digital flashcard tool to date.

Although Quizlet was not the entire focus of this course, it played a large part in the internal and external running of the class. Each student within both groups was required to create their own word list in class and to review words out of class. All classes were conducted in computer classrooms with one computer per student. Students were encouraged and expected to review words autonomously at home either by computer or through the freely available smartphone application.

All lists were accessible by members of each class, creating a profoundly collaborative nature of learning.

In the final class of the second term, students were required to answer two simple questions. The first question involved students giving their opinion in a 6-point Likert scale format, (1=strongly disagree, 2=disagree, 3=somewhat disagree, 4=somewhat agree, 5=agree, 6=strongly agree) on the following construct: "I think smartphone apps can be effective for learning English" (Construct 1).

Students were also asked to give their opinion on Quizlet through the following question: "Do you think Quizlet is a useful learning tool? If so why?" (Question 1).

Both the construct and the question[2] were conducted online using *surveymonkey*. Questions were written in Japanese and English. Data was analysed with a text-mining tool called '*Wordminer*', version 1.5 by Fujitsu.

3. Discussion and results

Table 1. Qualitative data obtained

	Phase 1 (n=432)	Phase 2 (n=371)
Total Japanese characters	8,990	11,325
Average length of answer	20.8	30.5
Retrieved	676	1,029
Repeated	50	86
No. of clusters	7	9

Table 1 shows the volume of data obtained from both data collection phases. Altogether, 803 students responded. Of this total there were 788 respondents who answered in Japanese, while 15 answered in English. All English answers were translated into Japanese. This gave an average length of almost 21 characters per answer in Phase 1 and about 30 for Phase 2. Designed specifically for Japanese, *Wordminer* analyses repeatedly used phrases or text within a qualitative dataset. All redundant phrases are omitted by this tool, giving researchers the choice to choose between the number of repetitions in each dataset. This number was set at five or more for this study. Construct 1 and Question 1 above were compared and collated.

---

2. The author carried out a similar study to this one in 2014 (Lander, 2015). However, that study analysed a different, and smaller set of data.

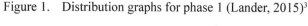

Figure 1.   Distribution graphs for phase 1 (Lander, 2015)[3]

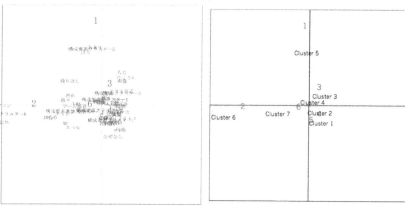

Figure 1 shows all 50 of the phrases that were repeated five times or more on the left and then in a more comprehendible manner on the right. Figure 2 shows all of the 86 repeated phrases for Phase 2. The bold red numbers indicate the Likert-scale choice subjects chose for Construct 1. The cluster number demonstrates the typical pattern of text choice to describe Question 1.

Figure 2.   Distribution graphs for Phase 2

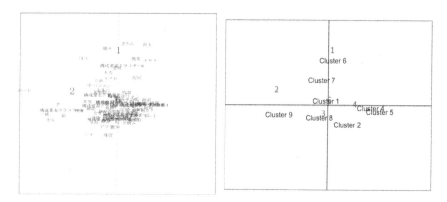

These distribution graphs indicate that the majority of subjects in this study gave positive comments. This point is demonstrated by the relative position of clusters in the central zone, which is true of both figures, but accentuated in Figure 2. Three

---

3. Republished with kind permission from Emerald

student answers to Question 1 are highlighted below. All comments were translated into English from their original for this paper.

> "I think Quizlet is a very useful learning tool. With Quizlet we can upload our own word list, review words and take tests as many times as we want. It also provides us with the correct pronunciation of words which is very helpful when having trouble reading" (Student 1).

> "I think it is useful, it provides many more ways to learn words than normal. Quizlet helps us to keep focused and not lose interest" (Student 2).

> "No, I don't. I think using a regular dictionary for learning new words is more efficient" (Student 3).

Students 1 and 2 give a clear indication that Quizlet provided a novel and enjoyable way to learn vocabulary. Critical comments although in the minority, were evident as is revealed by the comment made by student 3. By analysing qualitative, empirical data in this way, repeated words can be highlighted and easily identified. Table 2 shows a selection of words and phrases that were repeated five times or more. It is again possible to draw further conclusions through closer observation of the words obtained in this table.

Table 2. Repeated words and phrases obtained

Words, phrases	No. of repetitions
Our own pace	12
Correct spelling	18
Pronunciation	13
Countless times	15
Simple and easy to use	11
Various ways	8
Test function	9
Effective	8
Simple and convenient	7
Not really	5

4.   Conclusions

By using highlighted phrases and word items selected by a text-mining tool like *Wordminer*, it is much easier to see overall opinion of a blended learning tool such as Quizlet. Students in this study have shown a resounding approval of digital flashcards, but clearly some students prefer more traditional methods of learning vocabulary. Lander (2015) conducted a more detailed study to this one, and discovered that test scores in students who extensively used Quizlet can be boosted by 6% compared to those who did not. New additions to Quizlet and further improvements from competitors are inevitable. It is our duty as educational researchers to make use of such tools, to enhance and redefine the way our students learn vocabulary with technology such as this.

References

Ashcroft, R. J., & Imrie, A. C. (2014). Learning vocabulary with digital flashcards. In *JALT2013 Conference Proceedings.* Tokyo: JALT.

Barr, B. (2016). *Checking the effectiveness of Quizlet® as a tool for vocabulary learning* (Doctoral dissertation). The Centre for ELF Journal, Tamagawa University, Tokyo.

Lander, B. (2015). Lesson study at the foreign language university level in Japan: blended learning, raising awareness of technology in the classroom. *International Journal for Lesson and Learning Studies, 4*(4), 362-382. https://doi.org/10.1108/IJLLS-02-2015-0007

Puentedura, R. R. (2013, May 29). *SAMR: Moving from enhancement to transformation.* http://www.hippasus.com/rrpweblog/archives/000095.html

'Just facebook me': a study on the integration of Facebook into a German language curriculum

Vera Leier[1] and Una Cunningham[2]

Abstract. Student and teacher activity in a closed Facebook group for a tertiary German class was observed during a 12-week teaching semester. This was complemented by questionnaires, semi-structured interviews with students, and teacher reflections in a researcher journal. Collected data were analysed using an inductive thematic analysis followed by a deductive Activity Theory (AT) analysis to explore the tensions between student and teacher expectations of the Facebook component of the course. The analysis showed individual variation in Facebook behaviours. A number of students were reluctant to write in the target language, German, reporting that they felt anxious when required to do so. It became evident that students differentiated sharply between their private Facebook interactions and their interactions in the Facebook group. Students adopted the Facebook group as an authentic language platform and continued to use the page after the course had ended. The Facebook group facilitated high quality meaning-focused target language production within the class group, and the participants were overwhelmingly positive towards their Facebook experience.

Keywords: Facebook, German language learning, activity theory.

1. Introduction

The aim of this study is to understand the practices and perspectives of students and teachers using Facebook as part of the curriculum in a German language class at tertiary level in New Zealand. Facebook-based activities were introduced into the German intermediate class in an attempt to make German language study more authentic and more learner-centred for English-speaking learners.

1. University of Canterbury, Christchurch, New Zealand; vera.leier@canterbury.ac.nz
2. University of Canterbury, Christchurch, New Zealand; una.cunningham@canterbury.ac.nz

How to cite this article: Leier, V., & Cunningham, U. (2016). 'Just facebook me': a study on the integration of Facebook into a German language curriculum. In S. Papadima-Sophocleous, L. Bradley & S. Thouësny (Eds), *CALL communities and culture – short papers from EUROCALL 2016* (pp. 260-264). Research-publishing.net. https://doi.org/10.14705/rpnet.2016.eurocall2016.572

This article will report the experiences of the 12-week period of Facebook integration.

2.   Facebook in language learning environments

When Facebook first started to become mainstream in 2007, it seemed to be a platform soon to be replaced by the next wave of social media. Nonetheless, at the time of writing in 2016, Facebook remains the most used communication channel in the world amongst students and young people (Duggan, 2016). Facebook offers easy uploading mechanisms for photos and videos and its interface can be set to over 70 foreign languages, so it is a tool well suited for use in a foreign language classroom. Through Facebook, students can be immersed into the target language whilst simultaneously developing cultural knowledge and sharing German artefacts. Previous work using Facebook in the foreign language classroom includes Mills (2011), who used a Facebook group to make her French class more authentic. Blattner and Fiori (2009) saw great potential in Facebook groups as a platform for building telecollaborative communities in their Spanish language classes, since it was readily available and user friendly. Their learners were able to connect via Facebook with native speakers of Spanish. Blattner and Fiori (2011) used a Facebook site as part of their assessment in their intermediate Spanish class and found that through interaction with authentic Spanish speakers, the students gained a better socio-pragmatic understanding of the language.

3.   Methods

3.1.   Context

A Facebook group was designed and all students of the language class joined the group (N=21). The instructor of the class started a closed Facebook group and sent out the link to the class and asked them to join the group. The students joined the group and were made administrators of the group. The teacher retreated into an observer role and left the students to construct the platform autonomously. The students were asked to make five posts about various German related topics. The posts had to include three complete sentences written in German. The focus was on meaning and only minor corrections on form were made by the teacher. The posts were not graded, rather they were marked on a pass/fail basis which represented just 2% of the overall mark.

3.2. Data collection

The study used an ethnographic research method suitable for gaining rich data from this relatively uncharted platform (Beaulieu, 2004; Hine, 2005; Markham, 2011). Data collected during the semester included pre- and post- questionnaires, interviews (n=10), a research journal which the first author filled in every day as a participant observer and the archive of the Facebook site containing all the contributions of the students and teachers.

3.3. Data analysis

The data were transcribed and coded using four cycles of inductive thematic analysis (cycles 1 and 3) and deductive coding using AT as a lens (cycles 2 and 4). The data were first coded manually and then NVivo was used for further focus of the data. In the initial stage, the first cycle of coding was of an exploratory nature. The data was fragmented and codes were identified (Corbin & Strauss, 2008). After the initial inductive cycle, a deductive cycle of analysis was applied to the data, with AT elements using Engeström's (1987) model of subject, object, community, rules, division of labour, tool/artefacts, and outcome (Figure 1). The data was entered into NVivo as predetermined nodes (Ezzy, 2002). The third cycle of coding was conducted inductively to step back from the pre-defined AT elements and to keep an open mind about the data. The final cycle of coding returned to AT components to identify patterns and emerging categories within the AT elements.

Figure 1.   Activity system[3], based on Engeström's (1987) activity model

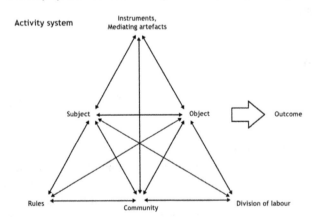

3. © Matt Bury, 2012 - CC BY-SA 3.0, https://commons.wikimedia.org/w/index.php?curid=18600235

4.   Results and discussion

The use of a Facebook group in a German classroom was well received but the students did not actively contribute to the group more than minimally. The data showed that the students enjoyed reading other students' comments to improve their vocabulary but otherwise preferred to simply observe the activity in the group. Students reported enjoying the platform, and they found it easy to use and familiar, but they also felt anxious about producing posts. Students were conscious of fellow students being able to read their posts and judge their spelling and grammar. Most students were keen users and contributors in the beginning and also towards the end of the semester when the assignment task had to be completed. They did not spontaneously post in the group.

AT analysis revealed three contradictions within the class activity system. The first contradiction was between the subjects and rules and between the subjects and the object: the students resisted the rules for using Facebook as a learning tool. They needed to be reminded to post their required posts. They did not use the Facebook group for spontaneous communication commenting, for example, "Facebook group was not a familiar educational environment for me" and "Facebook intruded into my personal Facebook use".

The second contradiction occurred between subject and tools. Students commented that "Facebook for learning was too forced" and "I could not read all the comments, it was too time-consuming, I preferred looking at the photos". In interviews, students report preferring to use Facebook for sharing pictures.

The third contradiction was between subject and division of labour. The teacher was trying to keep a low profile to make the environment more natural, but the students expected more feedback; they commented, "I felt a bit left out that I did not receive feedback". Still the Facebook group was perceived by the students as part of their educational environment; it did not develop into a social communication group. Students commented that "Facebook means leisure time for me, this was too much work".

5.   Conclusions

The findings of this study raise many issues relating to the use of Facebook in a language class. In this study, although popular with students, Facebook did not lead to the anticipated extensive informal use of German. Some changes may improve the results. The teacher as the designer of the assignment and also the person who assigns course grades is in a position of power. It may be better to assign the role of a facilitator of the Facebook group to a student, or a student teacher if available, as this may lead to the posts being more spontaneous. Perhaps Facebook communication would be richer if the posts were not part of the final course grade. To ease anxiety about performance in the target language, it may be beneficial if students worked in groups to produce posts for the Facebook group page. With regards to the design, rules and instructions for how to use the group for the assignment need to be explicit and clearly stated. Future developments in social media will doubtless offer new opportunities for extensive free production in a target language.

References

Beaulieu, A. (2004). Mediating ethnography: objectivity and the making of ethnographies of the internet. *Social Epistemology, 18*(2-3), 139-163. https://doi.org/10.1080/0269172042000249264

Blattner, G., & Fiori, M. (2009). Facebook in the language classrrom: promises and possibilities. *International Journal of Instructional Technology and Distance Learning, itdl, 6*(1). http://www.itdl.org/journal/jan_09/article02.htm

Blattner, G., & Fiori, M. (2011). Virtual social network communities: an investigation of language learners' development of sociopragmatic awareness and multiliteracy skills. *CALICO, 29*(1), 24-43. https://doi.org/10.11139/cj.29.1.24-43

Corbin, J., & Strauss, A. (2008). *Basics of qualitative research: techniques and procedures for developing grounded theory* (3rd ed.). Thousand Oaks: Sage. https://doi.org/10.4135/9781452230153

Duggan, M. (2016). *The demographics of social media users*. PewResearcCenter. http://www.pewinternet.org/2015/08/19/the-demographics-of-social-media-users/

Engeström, Y. (1987). *Learning by expanding: an activity-theoretical approach to developmental research*. http://lchc.ucsd.edu/mca/Paper/Engestrom/expanding/toc.htm

Ezzy, D. (2002). *Qualitative analysis*. Crows Nest, NSW: Allen & Unwin.

Hine, C. (2005). *Virtual Methods*. Oxford: Berg.

Markham, A. (2011). Internet research. In D. Silverman (Ed.), *Qualitative research* (3rd ed) (pp. 111-127). Thousand Oaks: Sage.

Mills, N. (2011). Situated learning through social networking communities: the development of joint enterprise, mutual engagement, and a shared Repertoire. *CALICO, 28*(2), 1-24. https://doi.org/10.11139/cj.28.2.345-368

A survey on Chinese students' online English language learning experience through synchronous web conferencing classrooms

Chenxi (Cecilia) Li[1]

Abstract. The online education industry has had a rapid economic development in China since 2013, but this area received little attention in research. This study investigates Chinese undergraduate students' online English learning experiences and online teacher-learner interaction in synchronous web conferencing classes. This article reports the findings from a pilot questionnaire survey in December 2015. It is found that synchronous online English classes are often oversized (more than 50 students). However, students report a high level of online teacher-learner interaction. Further investigation is necessary to reveal what actual online learning and teaching activities are going on in synchronous web conferencing English classrooms in China.

Keywords: synchronous web conferencing, SCMC, English language teaching, online interactions, China.

1. Introduction and literature review

Computer Assisted Language Learning (CALL) has become increasingly popular in China since 2013. According to the 2014 China Online Language Education Industry Report (iResearch, 2015), the market value of online language education in China is around 3 billion USD and the amount of online language learners reached 14.8 million in 2014 (iResearch, 2015). However, little is known about the recent developments and current problems of the Chinese CALL community. Behind the massive economic development, what are the real online teaching and learning activities going on? This study aims to investigate Chinese undergraduate

1. The Open University, Milton Keynes, United Kingdom; Cecilia.Li@open.ac.uk

How to cite this article: Li, C. (2016). A survey on Chinese students' online English language learning experience through synchronous web conferencing classrooms. In S. Papadima-Sophocleous, L. Bradley & S. Thouësny (Eds), *CALL communities and culture – short papers from EUROCALL 2016* (pp. 265-270). Research-publishing.net. https://doi.org/10.14705/rpnet.2016. eurocall2016.573

students' online English language learning experience and online teacher-learner interactions in synchronous web conferencing English classes in the private sector in China using a questionnaire survey, interviews and a content analysis of the video recordings of synchronous web conferencing English classes.

To explore the online learning and teaching activities in synchronous web conferencing English classes, the author focuses on online teacher-learner interaction. Moore (1989) defines learner-teacher interaction as the "dialogue between learners and the subject expert, which is regarded [essentially by] many educators and highly desired by distance learners" (p. 2). Synchronous web conferencing technology can afford synchronous interaction between online teachers and learners. Consequently, it is possible to look into how English is taught and learned online through studying the teacher-learner interactions in synchronous web conferencing English classes. Therefore, the research questions are:

- What are Chinese undergraduate students' online language learning experiences through synchronous web conferencing classes?

- To what extent and about what content do online English language teachers and learners interact with each other in synchronous web conferencing classes?

The first question aims to explore some basic information about students' synchronous online learning experiences including the reasons for learning languages online, the types of technology used for language learning, the length, size and content of online language classes, etc. The second question mainly focuses on online teacher-learner interaction, the amount and the content of online interactions in synchronous web conferencing English classes.

2.   Research methods

The questions in the survey are developed based on the relevant literature (e.g. iResearch, 2014; Li et al., 2014; Murphy, 2015; Tan, 2013; Zhang & Rong, 2013). The questionnaire is designed in English and translated into Chinese to avoid misunderstandings and attract more replies. The questionnaire was distributed through popular social networks in China (e.g. WeChat and QQ). The data collection follows a chain referral sampling method (Biernacki & Waldorf, 1981) because one student who had taken synchronous web conferencing English classes can answer the questionnaire and share its link to more people with such experiences.

In total, there are 221 replies on general online language learning experiences and 42 replies on synchronous web conferencing language learning experience. This paper reports key findings on synchronous web conferencing English language learning experience because synchronous web conferencing classes can support online interaction, which is key to language learning (Ellis, 1991).

3.   Findings

At the beginning of the survey, students are asked about their online English language learning experience through different types of technology. There are 42 participants (42 out of 221, p=19%) who have taken synchronous English language classes through web conferencing classrooms. The following reports on participants' online English language learning experiences and on online teacher-learner interaction through synchronous web conferencing English classes. The findings presented below are all results from multiple choice questions.

3.1.   Online learners' experiences

Regarding content of synchronous web conferencing English classes, 57% of participants have taken English test preparation classes (e.g. IELTS/TOEFL). Almost half (48%) of the respondents have taken English language proficiency courses to improve their speaking and listening skills, and one third of participants have learned grammar, vocabulary, reading and writing skills in synchronous online classes.

In terms of how many hours of online classes participants have taken, while some (29%) have taken more than 30 hours of synchronous web conferencing English classes, almost half of them have taken less than ten hours of online classes.

As for the size of synchronous web conferencing English classrooms, 60% of respondents report to have more than 50 in the online classes. However, there are also some smaller classes with less than ten students (p=22%) or even only one student (p=12%).

Most participants (88%) choose to take synchronous web conferencing English classes instead of learning in face-to-face classrooms because they do not have to travel, which is very convenient and efficient. There are also many respondents who choose online classes because of their lower prices. A few (24%) participants believe they study English more effectively in synchronous web conferencing classes while those (24%) who take one-to-one online classes through synchronous web conferencing tools highlight the personalized learning opportunities.

3.2.   Online teacher-learner interactions

This section reports findings on questions regarding online teacher-learner interaction through synchronous web conferencing English classes.

Participants take online English courses from different online teaching platforms with different technological affordances. In this survey, it is found that 79% of participants can post text chat messages in the synchronous web conferencing classroom so that they can have synchronous and ongoing conversations with their online teachers. Moreover, almost half (45%) of respondents are allowed to use audio channels to practice speaking skills with their online teachers and 19% can even use video cameras in their synchronous English classes.

When an online teacher presents content knowledge, very often (83%) there are students who raise questions about the course content, and sometimes (57%) some students report technical issues. Furthermore, sometimes (45%) there are interactions among students themselves about the course content being presented by the teacher.

When an online teacher asks questions, very often (79%) students answer the questions through text chat messages. However, some students complain that occasionally (21%) the teacher moves on before they finish typing their answers. And a few students (17%) report having little or no 'Questions and Answers' interaction between online teachers and learners in their synchronous web conferencing English classes.

4.   Discussions and conclusions

4.1.   What are Chinese undergraduate students' online language learning experiences through synchronous web conferencing classes?

Generally speaking, students' online English language learning experience vary among individuals, but there are some general trends. First, in terms of the course content, synchronous web conferencing English courses on exam preparation and communicative skills (e.g. speaking and listening skills) are most popular among students. Second, the size of synchronous web conferencing English classes is usually large (more than 50 students). Third, convenience and good price are two main reasons for students to choose synchronous online classes over face-to-face classes.

4.2. To what extent and about what content do online English language teachers and learners interact with each other in synchronous web conferencing classes?

In terms of technological availability/affordances, most respondents are able to participate in synchronous interaction with their online English teachers in synchronous web conferencing classrooms; some can even use audio and video channels for more multimodal teacher-student interaction. Participants also report a relatively high level of online learner-teacher interaction in both cases when an online teacher presents content knowledge and also when the teacher asks students questions.

However, some findings from the questionnaire are still not clear and can even be potentially contradictory. For example, most students (60%) report having an online class of more than 50 students. Meanwhile, they report to have a good amount of online teacher-learner interactions. So, the question is how can online English teachers take care of so many students in one synchronous web conferencing classroom and yet still be able to have sufficient teacher-learner interactions. Clearly, more investigation is needed to further reveal what online teaching and learning activities are actually going on in synchronous web conferencing English classes in China. The author intends to interview online English teachers and learners, and conduct a content analysis of video recordings of synchronous web conferencing English classes to find more answers to this question.

References

Biernacki, P., & Waldorf, D. (1981). Snowball! sampling: problems and techniques of chain referral sampling. *Sociological Methods & Research,10*(2), 141-163.

Ellis, R. (1991). The interaction hypothesis: a critical evaluation. In E. Sadtono (Ed.), *Language acquisition in the second/foreign language classroom* (Anthology Series 28, pp. 179-211). Singapore: SEMEO, Regional Language Centre.

iResearch. (2015). 2014 China online language education industry research report. http://www. iresearch.com.cn/report/2326.html

Li, S., Zhang, Y. X., Chen, L., Zhang, J. J., & Liu, Y. Q. (2014). Wang luo jiao yu shi dai kai fang da xue ke cheng fu dao jiao shi jue se ding wei yu zhi neng zhuan bian shi zheng yan jiu [An empirical study on the changing roles of assistant online teachers in open university in the e-learning age]. *Zhong guo dian hua jiao yu* [China Educational Technology], *9,* 50-57.

Moore, M. G. (1989). Editorial: three types of interaction. *American Journal of Distance Education, 3*(2), 1-7. https://doi.org/10.1080/08923648909526659

Murphy, L. (2015). Online language teaching: the learner's perspective. *Developing Online Language Teaching: Research-Based Pedagogies and Reflective Practices, 45.*

Tan, X. (2013). Ji yu YY ruan jian de wang luo ying yu jiao xue fa yan jiu [Research on pedagogical approaches for English language teaching through YY Edu online teaching platform]. *Jiao xue yan jiu* [Research in teaching], *36*(7), 36-40.

Zhang, Y., & Rong, H. L. (2013). Jiao shi zai yuan cheng ying yu zi zhu xue xi zhong de yu qi jue se he shi ji xing wei yan jiu [A study on online teachers' expected roles and actual behaviors about learner autonomy in distance English teaching]. *Zhong guo yuan cheng jiao yu* [Distance Education in China], *4,* 83-88.

Identifying and activating receptive vocabulary by an online vocabulary survey and an online writing task

Ivy Chuhui Lin[1] and Goh Kawai[2]

Abstract. Seeking to identify and activate the Receptive Vocabulary (RV) of English Language Learners (ELLs), we designed (1) an online five category multiple-choice vocabulary survey that more quickly measures vocabulary knowledge, and (2) an online creative writing task where ELLs chose RV items identified in step (1). While RV items of highly proficient ELLs cause difficulties in language production, writing tasks promote active vocabulary use and knowledge (Laufer, 2013). We designed a four stage, five week writing task based on task-induced involvement constructs where vocabulary acquisition involves need, search and evaluation (Laufer & Hulstijn, 2001). Results show (1) 74% of RV items were activated, (2) ELLs' Productive Vocabulary (PV) increased from 21% to 37%, and (3) unknown vocabulary items decreased from 25% to 14%. In future work we will measure the individual and presumably diverse use of RV.

Keywords: vocabulary measurement, receptive vocabulary, corpus-based vocabulary, online creative writing.

1.   Introduction

The large number of vocabulary items that are in the RV but not in the PV of highly proficient ELLs causes difficulties in language production (Laufer, 2013). While existing tools mostly measure the properties of RV and PV, and RV-PV ratios, only few studies focus on the learning process of PV (e.g. Pignot-Shahov, 2012).

1. Hokkaido University, Sapporo, Japan; chuhuichu@gmail.com
2. Hokkaido University, Sapporo, Japan; goh@kawai.com, http://goh.kawai.com/

How to cite this article: Lin, I. C., & Kawai, G. (2016). Identifying and activating receptive vocabulary by an online vocabulary survey and an online writing task. In S. Papadima-Sophocleous, L. Bradley & S. Thouësny (Eds), *CALL communities and culture – short papers from EUROCALL 2016* (pp. 271-276). Research-publishing.net. https://doi.org/10.14705/rpnet.2016.eurocall2016.574

Writing activities have been said to promote the development of vocabulary knowledge (Laufer, 2013). Unknown vocabulary items that are unfamiliar to ELLs might require more training before they become RV. RV items, on the other hand, are prime candidates for activation because the items' phonology, morphology, and syntax are already known to the ELL. As such, RV items need to be identified because they should be activated through explicit instruction to become PV(Lee & Muncie, 2006).

To observe how RV changes to PV among groups of ELLs, we ran a two phase study. In Phase 1, to identify the ELLs' RV, we designed and administered a five category multiple-choice online vocabulary survey. In Phase 2, we ran a four stage online creative writing task to improve the ELLs' PV knowledge. ELLs used at least 20 out of 148 RV items that we grouped into ten thematic categories. ELLs received corrective feedback on their RV activation.

2.   Method

2.1.   Phase 1: five category multiple-choice online vocabulary survey

Existing tools for measuring vocabulary knowledge include the following: (1) the productive vocabulary level test (Laufer & Nation, 1999), which measures lexical knowledge, but does not necessarily measure vocabulary production (Lee & Muncie, 2006); (2) the English as a foreign language vocabulary test (Meara, 1997), which is fast but lacks reliability (Schmitt, 2014); and (3) the vocabulary knowledge scale (Paribakht & Wesche, 1997), which asks examinees to write sentences, thus improving the reliability of PV measurements but requires more testing and grading time per vocabulary item.

To avoid impeding upon our other learning activities, we needed to measure the levels of vocabulary knowledge of 300 vocabulary items within 15 minutes. Since no existing technique measures at this rate, we developed a radio-button style online survey that ELLs respond to in less than three seconds per vocabulary item.

For each vocabulary item, ELLs chose from five statements: (1) *I never saw this word before*, (2) *I forgot what this word means*, (3) *I can guess what this word means*, (4) *I know what this word means*, and (5) *I use this word when I write or talk*. The choices were based on self-introspection. Items with mean scores between three to four were considered RV items. This survey was conducted two times with a 13-week interval.

The vocabulary items were selected from the college entrance examination stratum of the Hokkaido University English Vocabulary List (Sonoda, 1996). This list stratifies vocabulary items into five levels, from middle school to advanced college. The entrance examination level consists of 2,096 items. Based on our vocabulary survey, we chose thematically-grouped 148 RV items that were likely to belong to the RV of the majority of our 134 ELLs.

2.2.   Phase 2: four stage online creative writing task

Laufer and Hulstijn (2001) proposed a task-induced involvement construct, where the more cognitively involved ELLs are, the deeper vocabulary knowledge can be acquired. Kim (2011) and Lee and Muncie (2006) both reported positive effect on the development of vocabulary through the adaptation of task-induced involvement in writing activities.

Our ELLs engaged in a four stage online creative writing task over a five week period:

- Stage 1 (preparatory): ELLs wrote an approximately 150-word story on an online forum that was viewable by all 134 ELLs, and read the story aloud to classmates.

- Stage 2 (design): ELLs designed a story by using a template to specify characters, settings, events, and ending.

- Stage 3 (write and activate RV): the 148 target RV items were presented in 10 categories to facilitate ELLs writing task. ELLs wrote a 400 to 600-word story that included at least 20 out of 148 RV items.

- Stage 4 (rewrite): ELLs received corrective feedback, improved writing, and read story aloud to classmates.

The 148 RV items were presented in ten thematic categories to facilitate the ELLs' writing tasks, which are emotion, action, personality, settings, solutions, problems, objects, events, situations, and jobs.

3. Discussion and conclusion

Figure 1 shows that between the pre- and post-surveys PV items increased from 21% to 37%, unknown-vocabulary items decreased from 25% to 14%, and RV items stayed mostly constant at 52 % and 49%. Our results are consistent with Laufer and Goldstein (2004), which states that RV is about 50% of total vocabulary. This suggests that the 700 items that were used in our survey seem to have been appropriately familiar to our ELLs. Moreover, the fact that RV items remain the same also implies that the process of vocabulary knowledge is a developmental continuum (Schmitt, 2014), RV activation is unlikely through one-time practice.

Figure 1.   Percentages of the number of mean response values within four ranges for each of the 700 vocabulary items in the five category multiple-choice online vocabulary survey (the five categories are: (1) *I never saw this word before*, (2) *I forgot what this word means*, (3) *I can guess what this word means*, (4) I *know what this word means*, (5) *I use this word when I write or talk*)

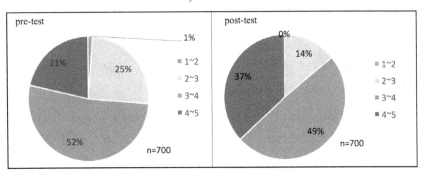

Figure 2.   Percentages of the number of 148 RV items having mean response values in the three to four range or four to five range after the online creative writing task

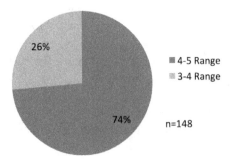

Figure 2 shows that for 74% of RV items the mean response values increased from the three to four range to the four to five range after the online creative writing task. This suggests an increase in vocabulary knowledge. We also observed that the items with large increases occurred frequently in ELLs' writing corpus.

Based on informal interviews conducted after the fourth stage of the writing task, ELLs stated that the writing task was time-consuming, and that writing using the required RV items was a challenge.

For the sake of teaching a group of students uniformly, we assumed that ELLs shared the same 148 RV items. Although results do show that these RV items were activated to PV for our group of students, in future research we might measure individual gains using tools such as Lexinote (Tanaka, Yonesaka, Ueno, & Ohnishi, 2013) that tracks vocabulary acquisition of individuals over time.

With the developmental nature of vocabulary acquisition (Schmitt, 2014), observing PV gains over multiple learning sessions is desirable. We relied on ELL self-introspection to determine vocabulary knowledge. While this technique may be suited for assessing passive memory recall of RV, a more reliable measurement is desired for active memory recall of PV.

ELLs' PV remain small compared to their RV. Though our method may assist instructors in identifying RV items and activating them through writing tasks, the gains of ELLs' PV knowledge remain unclear. A more direct approach to promote ELLs' PV knowledge may be required for future research.

References

Kim, Y. (2011). The role of task-induced involvement and learner proficiency in L2. *Language Learning, 61*(1), 100-140. https://doi.org/10.1111/j.1467-9922.2011.00644.x

Laufer, B. (2013). Vocabulary and writing. In C. A. Chappell (Ed.), *The Encyclopaedia of Applied Linguistics.* https://doi.org/10.1002/9781405198431

Laufer, B., & Goldstein, Z. (2004). Testing vocabulary knowledge: size, strength, and computer adaptiveness. *Language Learning, 54*(3), 399-436. https://doi.org/10.1111/j.0023-8333.2004.00260.x

Laufer, B., & Hulstijn, J. (2001). Incidental vocabulary acquisition in a second language: the construct of task-induced involvement. *Applied Linguistics, 22*(1), 1-26.

Laufer, B., & Nation, P. (1999). A vocabulary-size test of controlled productive ability. *Language Testing, 16*(1), 33-51. https://doi.org/10.1177/026553229901600103

Lee, S., & Muncie, J. (2006). From receptive to productive: improving ESL learners' use of vocabulary in a post-reading composition task. *TESOL Quarterly, 40*(2), 295-320. https://doi.org/10.2307/40264524

Meara, P. (1997). Towards a new approach to modelling vocabulary acquisition. In N. Schmitt & M. McCarthy (Eds), *Vocabulary: description, acquisition, and pedagogy* (pp. 109-121). Cambridge, UK: Cambridge University Press.

Paribakht, T. S., & Wesche, M. (1997). Vocabulary enhancement activities and reading for meaning in second language vocabulary acquisition. In J. Coady & T. Huckin (Eds), *Second language vocabulary acquisition* (pp. 174-200). Cambridge, UK: Cambridge University Press.

Pignot-Shahov, V. (2012). Measuring L2 receptive and productive vocabulary knowledge. *Language Studies working Papers, 4*, 37-45.

Schmitt, N. (2014). Size and depth of vocabulary knowledge: what the research shows. *Language Learning, 64*(4), 913-951. https://doi.org/10.1111/lang.12077

Sonoda, K. (1996). *Hokkaido University English vocabulary list.* English Department, Hokkaido University.

Tanaka, H., Yonesaka, S., Ueno, Y., & Ohnishi, A. (2013). Developing e-portfolio to enhance sustainable vocabulary learning in English. In *WorldCall conference proceeding* (pp. 341-344). Glasgow.

Exploring learners' perceptions of the use of digital letter games for language learning: the case of Magic Word

Mathieu Loiseau[1], Cristiana Cervini[2], Andrea Ceccherelli[3], Monica Masperi[4], Paola Salomoni[5], Marco Roccetti[6], Antonella Valva[7], and Francesca Bianco[8]

Abstract. In this paper, we present two versions of a learning game developed respectively at the Grenoble Alpes and Bologna University. This research focuses on a digital game aimed at favouring the learners' *playful attitude* and harnessing it towards *accuracy* aspects of language learning (lexicon and morphology, here). The game, presently available for English, French and Italian, could be described as a letter game stemming from the archetypal example of Turoff's Boggle. Avatars of this game genre both exist as commercial off the shelf games and as learning games. We explain in this paper how our two versions respectively tackle two different aspects of language learning. We conducted an experiment in which all students tried both versions to study their perceptions of both games contrastively in order to prepare for the development of subsequent versions of the game.

Keywords: game based learning, Italian as a foreign language, learner perceptions, lexicon, morphology.

1. Université Grenoble Alpes – LIDILEM, Innovalangues, Saint Martin d'Hères, France; mathieu.loiseau@univ-grenoble-alpes.fr
2. Università di Bologna – LILEC Department, Innovalangues, Bologna, Italy; cristiana.cervini@unibo.it
3. Università di Bologna – LILEC Department, Bologna, Italy; andrea.ceccherelli@unibo.it
4. Université Grenoble Alpes – LIDILEM, Innovalangues, Saint Martin d'Hères, France; monica.masperi@univ-grenoble-alpes.fr
5. Università di Bologna – Department of Computer Science and Engineering, Bologna, Italy; paola.salomoni@unibo.it
6. Università di Bologna – Department of Computer Science and Engineering, Bologna, Italy; marco.roccetti@unibo.it
7. Università di Bologna – LILEC Department, Bologna, Italy; antonella.valva2@unibo.it
8. Università di Bologna – Innovalangues, Bologna, Italy; francesca.bianco6@studio.unibo.it

How to cite this article: Loiseau, M., Cervini, C., Ceccherelli, A., Masperi, M., Salomoni, P., Roccetti, M., Valva, A., & Bianco, F. (2016). Exploring learners' perceptions of the use of digital letter games for language learning: the case of Magic Word. In S. Papadima-Sophocleous, L. Bradley & S. Thouësny (Eds), *CALL communities and culture – short papers from EUROCALL 2016* (pp. 277-283). Research-publishing.net. https://doi.org/10.14705/rpnet.2016.eurocall2016.575

1.   Game based (accuracy) learning[9]

Many researchers see various advantages in game based learning (e.g. Oblinger, 2004). Some see games as consistent with the central notion of tasks (Cornillie, Thorne, & Desmet, 2012). Yet the emergence of a *playful attitude*, considered productive in games in terms of (language) learning (Silva, 2008), is far from being systematic in learning games. In the hope of favouring its emergence, we resort to the *metaludic* rules (pertaining to a game genre) (Silva, 1999) of successful and repeatable games (digital or board games, which do not rely on a plot).

Our research could be described as 'design based', which is inseparable from iterative development (Harvey & Loiselle, 2009). To prepare for subsequent iterations, we implemented two versions of the same game with a view to comparing the responses of learners to both. Each version has its own pedagogical approach but both address *accuracy* – micro-operations and language correction – as opposed to *fluency* (Portine, 2013). The first prototype was conceived and implemented at the Grenoble Alpes University (Loiseau, Zampa, & Rebourgeon, 2015), within the Innovalangues project (Masperi & Quintin, 2014), while the second was developed by the University of Bologna within the context of the 'E-LOCAL for all' project (Ceccherelli & Valva, 2016).

2.   The prototypes

Despite adopting different points of view, both versions of our digital letter game, called Magic Word, are based on the same metaludic rules that could be exemplified by the well-known example of Boggle[10], where the user is presented with a 4×4 letter grid and can create inflected forms ('example' and 'examples' are considered two separate words) using contiguous letters, in every direction, using each letter cell at most once per word form.

The Grenoble prototype was implemented in 2014[11]. Available in French, English and Italian, it aims at harnessing *normative* rules – rules adopted by advanced players of the game (Silva, 1999) – to work on morphological aspects of the language. It is inherent to the game, especially for languages with rich inflexion mechanisms, that the player should exhaustively seek all forms stemming from

---

9. Our approach is consistent across projects, this re-uses parts of Loiseau, Hallal, Ballot, and Gazidedja (2016, this volume) rather than artificially paraphrasing it, but also completes it.
10. Designed by Turoff in 1972, see https://en.wikipedia.org/wiki/Boggle.
11. http://gamer.innovalangues.net/magicword/ / https://github.com/InnovaLangues/Magic-Word-game

found words (Loiseau et al., 2015). In Figure 1, for instance, if both players found '*mia*' ('my', fem. sing.), the player who realises that its masculine ('*mio*') and plural feminine ('*mie*') forms are also in the grid will have an advantage over the opponent. Even if a player finds a form by luck, the competitive nature of this version provides an incentive to infer the category of the word in order to see if the grid does not contain other forms. Games are played one-on-one (asynchronously) in three sets. While the lexical nature of the game is mainly addressed through the existence of a personal lexicon for each learner, called a 'wordbox', stemming mechanisms are at the core of the rules.

Figure 1.   Screen captures of both versions of the game (left: Grenoble / right: Bologna)

The Bologna prototype[12], solely in Italian, is to be interfaced with the 'E-LOCAL for all' project. Dedicated to helping student mobility and multilingualism, the project proposes eight core units built around a main theme linked to a possible real-life situation (Ceccherelli & Valva, 2016). This thematic progression calls for a focus on vocabulary that the Grenoble version could not provide. Creating grids containing certain forms is a complex algorithmic problem. This version provides a solution able to produce a grid containing a significant number of E-LOCAL terms (Roccetti et al., 2016). Each grid in this prototype has a specific cultural background concerning Italy and specifically Bologna; graphics were adapted through pictures linked to each theme to convey that cultural focus.

3.   Experiment protocol

Following design based research principles, we took advantage of these two versions to gather learner reactions to each prototype's specificities: different

_____
12. http://www.lilec-linguistica.it/magicword/page.html / https://github.com/giacomo-mambelli/magicword

learning objectives (morphology vs lexicon) sought after through different game structures (speed and competition vs completion of lexical puzzles), with different input modalities (sliding vs successive clicks) and layouts.

The experiment was conducted for Italian as a foreign language over 20 groups of learners from the Université Grenoble Alpes and the Università di Bologna (group levels A1 to C1). It took place in March and April 2016 during the classes of eight different teachers. The project and games were introduced briefly. Around 40 minutes were then left to the 148 learners[13] surveyed to test both games and 20 minutes to fill out the questionnaires presented to them (in English, French or Italian). To make sure that results were not influenced by which game was presented first, some groups started with the Bologna version while others with Grenoble's. A third of the students (59) were given a self-assessing pre-test. Students were to tick the words they knew from a list. It meant to get an indication of their lexical knowledge, but also to see whether reading some words present in the Bologna grids before playing would help them solve the puzzles. Such short exposure to the games will not allow us to draw any conclusions concerning their learning outcomes (Girard, Ecalle, & Magnan, 2013); we focused on the students' reactions and expectations.

4. Results

We are interested in the learners' perceptions of the game and their inclination to play them again. After the experiment, we asked them whether they would like to play (any) Magic Word during their Italian language class, nearly 85% of the students answered positively.

The students were also asked to answer on a four-level Likert scale various questions, including concerning their appreciation of the games (how much fun they had playing and whether they would like to play again) and if they felt they could learn while playing them. Considering the two upper levels of the Likert scale as positive outcomes, about 80% of the students found the Bologna version fun and more than 75% wanted to play it again, while more than 85% found the Grenoble version fun and 85% wanted to play it again.

Attributing a number (one to four) to every level of the scale allowed to perform inferential statistics[14]. The following results always use such data with questions

---

13. 75% female, 90+% between 18 & 24 years old.
14. The tests performed were paired samples t-tests, Welch two samples t-tests, Pearson's Chi-squared test with Yates' continuity correction and Pearson's product-moment correlation (Norman, 2010).

directly targeting each feature described. For instance, the differences above were significant (Fun: $t(147)=-4.3533$, $p<.001$; Play again: $t(147)=-3.5961$, $p<.001$), even though the students significantly preferred the graphics of the Bologna version (92.5% favorable opinion for Bologna vs 83% for Grenoble – $t(147)=3.2286$, $p<.005$). This difference could be linked to the fact that 93% viewed competition positively (Grenoble) against 79% appreciating being able to play without the pressure of a timer (Bologna).

The learners found the Bologna version slightly, yet significantly, more relevant for learning than the Grenoble version (75% favorable opinion for Bologna vs 71% for Grenoble ($t(147)=2.5376$, $p<.05$), thus echoing the teachers preference for the lexical dimension of the game.

Finally, results to the pre-test did not yield effect on other variables, taking it did not influence the players' achievements. However, its mere presence underlined the importance of the 'ludic context'; learners who were administered the tedious pre-test (checking long lists of words) showed less inclination towards playing either game again (Reusing MW in class: $\chi^2(1)=4.0281$, $p<.05$; Play again - Grenoble: $t(92.5)=2.9759$, $p<.005$; Play again - Bologna: $t(102)=1.7607$, $p<.05$).

5.   Discussion, future works and conclusion

Our experiment, testing two versions of Magic Word, shows positive reception of both versions in terms of game characteristics and expected learning outcomes. Though the fact that the games were played for less than an hour should be taken into consideration when interpreting the results, this reception is encouraging. Learners display a certain preference for the Grenoble version, though the Bologna version is perceived as more likely to result in learning. We also know its rules are more favoured by teachers, which could be linked to the level of rules at which the 'learning' component is integrated (constitutive or even metaludic for lexicon vs normative for morphology). Thus, future versions of the game should (1) adapt the Bologna rules to introduce a competition element, and (2) make the normative rules of the Grenoble version more perceivable by beginner players.

Consequently, the algorithm conceived in Bologna is of the utmost importance for both institutions as it will facilitate the integration of the game in classes. Completing these results, a focus groups showed that teachers are more prone to using Magic Word for lexical acquisition. The algorithm thus opens doors for customisation of the content by teachers, one of their central needs (Hallal, 2015).

Thanks to the open-source nature of both prototypes, a new version is being implemented in Grenoble. Though this work is mostly focused on the ludic structures, the response of the students who took the pre-test also underlines the influence of the ludic context on the reception of the game, highlighting Silva's (2008) point of view. Finally, it is worth mentioning that neither the proficiency level of the students, nor their gaming experience or gender yielded any significant difference in their appreciation of either game.

6.   Acknowledgements

We would like to thank the Innovalangues and 'E-LOCAL for all' projects for allowing this research. We also thank all those who contributed to it (especially the upcoming version) including: Pauline Ballot, Racha Hallal, Virginie Zampa, Pauline Rebourgeon, Giacomo Mambelli, Christine Lutian, Maryam Nejat, David Graceffa, Richard Boualavong, Agnès Montaufier, Benjamin Abrial, Arnaud Bey and all the teachers and learners who tried it.

References

Ceccherelli, A., & Valva, A. (2016). Fostering multilingualism and student mobility: the case of E-LOCAL for all. In C. Cervini (Ed.), *Interdisciplinarità e apprendimento linguistico nei nuovi contesti formativi. L'apprendere di lingue tra tradizione e innovazione* (pp. 21-39). Bologna: CeSLiC. https:doi.org/10.6092/unibo/amsacta/5069

Cornillie, F., Thorne, S. L., & Desmet, P. (Eds). (2012), Digital games for language learning: challenges and opportunities. *ReCALL special issue, 24*(3), 243-256.

Girard, C., Ecalle, J., & Magnan, A. (2013). Serious games as new educational tools: how effective are they? A meta-analysis of recent studies. *Journal of Computer Assisted Learning, 29*(3), 207-219. https://doi.org/10.1111/j.1365-2729.2012.00489.x

Hallal, R. (2015). *La conception d'un jeu numérique pour l'apprentissage des langues — Considérations théoriques et empiriques*. Masters thesis. Université Stendhal Grenoble 3. http://dumas.ccsd.cnrs.fr/dumas-01236245

Harvey, S., & Loiselle, J. (2009). Proposition d'un modèle de recherche développement. *Recherches qualitatives, 28*(2), 95-117.

Loiseau, M., Hallal, R., Ballot, P., & Gazidedja, A. (2016). Game of Words: prototype of a digital game focusing on oral production (and comprehension) through asynchronous interaction. In S. Papadima-Sophocleous, L. Bradley & S. Thouësny (Eds), *CALL communities and culture – short papers from EUROCALL 2016* (pp. 284-289). Research-publishing.net. https://doi.org/10.14705/rpnet.2016.eurocall2016.576

Loiseau, M., Zampa, V., & Rebourgeon, P. (2015). Magic Word : premier jeu développé dans le cadre du projet Innovalangues. *ALSIC, 18*(2). https://doi.org/10.4000/alsic.2828

Masperi, M., & Quintin, J.-J. (2014). L'innovation selon Innovalangues (E. D. Col, Ed.). *Lingua e nuova didattica, 1*, 6-14.

Norman, G. (2010). Likert scales, levels of measurement and the « laws » of statistics. *Advances in Health Sciences Education, 15*(5), 625-632. https://doi.org/10.1007/s10459-010-9222-y

Oblinger, D. G. (2004). The next generation of educational engagement. *Journal of Interactive Media in Education, 2004*(1), 10. https://doi.org/10.5334/2004-8-oblinger

Portine, H. (2013). L'ingénierie linguistique : des technologies au service d'une didactique intégrant la cognition ? In C. Ollivier & L. Puren (Eds), *Mutations technologiques, nouvelles pratiques sociales et didactique des langues* (pp. 159-168). Clé International.

Roccetti, M., Salomoni, P., Loiseau, M., Masperi, M., Zampa, V., Ceccherelli, A., Cervini, C., & Valva, A. (2016). On the design of a word game to enhance Italian language learning. *Presented at the 2016 International Conference on Computing, Networking and Communications (ICNC 2016) — 12th IEEE International Workshop on Networking Issues in Multimedia Entertainment (NIME 2016), Kaui: IEEE Communications Society* (pp. 1-5). http://dx.doi.org/10.1109/ICCNC.2016.7440546

Silva, H. (1999). *Poétiques du jeu. La métaphore ludique dans la théorie et la critique littéraires françaises au XXe siècle.* PhD thesis. Paris: Université Paris 3, Sorbonne Nouvelle. http://lewebpedagogique.com/jeulangue/files/2011/01/PoetiquesLud.pdf

Silva, H. (2008). *Le jeu en classe de langue.* Techniques et pratiques de classe. Paris: CLE International.

Game of Words: prototype of a digital game focusing on oral production (and comprehension) through asynchronous interaction

Mathieu Loiseau[1], Racha Hallal[2],
Pauline Ballot[3], and Ada Gazidedja[4]

Abstract. In this paper, we present a learning game designed according to a strategy focusing on favouring the learners' *playful attitude*. The game's modalities pertain to what we might call 'guessing games'. The chosen avatar of such guessing games both exists as learning and Commercial Off The Shelf (COTS) board games. We explain in this paper how we adapted them into a digital game, taking decisions prompted by language learning but also addressing technical and contextual issues. We resort to the literature on communicative strategies to justify the expected outcomes of using this game and describe certain feedback stemming from self enrolling user tests performed by language teachers in early 2016. We conclude by describing the next steps in this research.

Keywords: game based learning, strategic competence, oral production, oral comprehension.

1. Guessing game based learning[5]

Many researchers see various advantages in resorting to game based learning. In the field of language learning, some see in games an opportunity to overcome excessive *self consciousness* impeding involvement in tasks (Villez, 2006). Yet the emergence of a *playful attitude* considered productive in games in terms of (language) learning is far from being systematic in learning games (Lavigne,

---

1. Université Grenoble Alpes, LIDILEM, Innovalangues, Grenoble, France; mathieu.loiseau@univ-grenoble-alpes.fr
2. Télécom SudParis — Institut Mines-Télécom, Paris, France; racha.hallal@telecom-sudparis.eu
3. Claroline.com, Grenoble, France; pauline.ballot@claroline.com
4. Università di Bologna, Innovalangues, Bologna, Italy; ada.gazidedja@studio.unibo.it
5. Our approach is consistent across projects, see Loiseau et al. (2016, this volume), for more bibliographic references.

How to cite this article: Loiseau, M., Hallal, R., Ballot, P., & Gazidedja, A. (2016). Game of Words: prototype of a digital game focusing on oral production (and comprehension) through asynchronous interaction. In S. Papadima-Sophocleous, L. Bradley & S. Thouësny (Eds), *CALL communities and culture – short papers from EUROCALL 2016* (pp. 284-289). Research-publishing.net. https://doi.org/10.14705/rpnet.2016.eurocall2016.576

2013). The metaphor of 'chocolate coated broccoli' for serious games has even been used in various publications (see Söbke, Bröker, & Kornadt, 2013). To avoid this type of reaction, we have adapted Söbke et al.'s (2013) design suggestions. Though they advocate for directly using COTS, they acknowledge that COTS that can be enriched with educational content are rare (Söbke et al., 2013). Consequently, we have chosen to design games by resorting to *metaludic rules* (pertaining to a game genre) (Silva, 1999) of successful games. Additionally, we have so far designed games that offer the student the possibility to repeat games (in a casual game manner) rather than resorting to an elaborate one time play scenario.

In this paper, we aim to introduce a game prototype designed and developed within the GAMER work package of the Innovalangues project. We focus on *Game of Words*[6], which could be described as a guessing game. The metaludic rules are as follows:

- one player/team holds a knowledge (often a word, sometimes an expression or a person);

- one player/team ought to guess this knowledge;

- specific modalities are defined as to how this knowledge is to be transmitted between the two entities.

Depending on the said modalities, such communication games seem to be a way by which learners might be led to work on the appropriate use of the 'strategic competence'. Each such set of modalities defines another avatar of guessing games.

2.   Strategic competence

Canale and Swain (1980) define the strategic competence as "verbal and non-verbal communication strategies that may be called into action to compensate for breakdowns in communication due to performance variables or to insufficient competence" (p. 30). Many authors concur in dividing those strategies into two categories (sometimes bearing different names depending on the author): *message adjustment strategies* and *resource expansion strategies* (CECRL, 2000; Dörnyei & Thurrell, 1991; Mariani, 1994).

---

6. http://gamer.innovalangues.net/gameofwords / and https://github.com/InnovaLangues/GameOfWord

While the Common European Framework of Reference for languages (CEFR or CECR in French) does not formally define the strategic competence, it stresses the importance of strategies (be they communicative or learning strategies) (CECRL, 2000), thus highlighting the point made earlier by Dörnyei and Thurrell (1991). Additionally, Mariani (1994) mentions that the acquisition of *resource expansion strategies* are by definition more profitable to the learner, as they do not rely on their avoiding difficulties.

In this paper, we focus on verbal production strategies as they are at the core of our game's ludic structures, and more precisely on *resource expansion strategies*.

3. Our prototype

The avatar of guessing games we chose for the first version of this prototype is based on the well-known modalities of *taboo*[7]: in order to convey their knowledge (a word) the first team can neither use that word, nor a list of words deemed by the designer of the game as useful to describe the word. By essence, these rules force the learner to find ways to have other players find a specific word without ever mentioning it. Indeed one can link the task performed in the game to the one used by Paribakht (1985) in her experiment meant to establish a taxonomy, where she would ask the student to communicate a lexical item (concrete or abstract) to a (native) student, without using the word.

The chosen rules are also consistent with some of Dörnyei and Thurrell's (1991) suggestions for strategic competence focused learning tasks. These rules are also consistent with games used in class by teachers of English, French and Italian as foreign languages, according to interviews we performed.

One of the advantages of using a digital game is that it can be used both in and out of the classroom, but it also comes with constraints, especially when devising a first prototype. We implemented our prototype according to two such constraints:

- the game was to focus on oral production and comprehension;

- the game is asynchronous in its modalities.

---

7. Designed by Hersch & Bougrèle (1990), see https://en.wikipedia.org/wiki/Taboo_(game).

The oral component is a priority due to its relative under-representation in CALL, but we only handle audio, both to make the development faster and because video would require a lot more space on the server. But this discards one of the four approaches identified by Paribakht (1985) in her taxonomy, which is non-verbal (mime as opposed to linguistic, contextual, and conceptual approaches).

The asynchronous aspect rather emerged from the game mechanics. Such guessing games induce that three persons are required to make the game playable, which can be an issue. Using synchronous modalities, the lack of players can result in players spending most of their playing time waiting for other users. On the other hand, in asynchronous modalities, we can ensure that the player can have some activity anytime they connect. But the downside of this decision is that it cuts interaction down to the minimum, and needs to be orchestrated.

In a role playing game fashion, we associated each role to a trade: *druid, oracle,* and *augur* (cf. Figure 1). The *oracle*'s role is to record a riddle meant to allow other players to find the explained word ('Coffee' in Figure 1) without using any word displayed on the 'card' provided (see 'Input' in Figure 1). The *druid* makes sure that the recording is technically audible and that the oracle did not use any forbidden word. Finally, if the recording is adequate, it is submitted to the *augur* whose goal is to interpret the *oracle*'s riddle.

Figure 1. Roles, tasks and data lifecycle in *Game of Words*

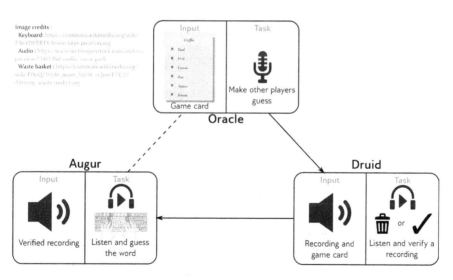

Each role is associated to a scoring category in order to motivate players to play all roles, as the playability of the game directly relies on people adopting every role. Indeed, if no one verifies, as a *druid*, that oracles follow the rules, there will never be recordings for *augurs*, and the *oracle*'s activity will remain pointless. Yet to provide more game opportunities, a given recording can be served to various *augurs*.

Players can also earn *druid* points by creating new cards (a *word to guess* associated with one or more *forbidden words*[8]). Resorting to user generated content makes the game playable in any language that can be written using UTF-8 characters and verbalised (sign languages cannot be handled thus far, for instance).

4.   Experiments, future works and conclusion

The first development cycle led to a testable game prototype. In order to prepare for the following iteration, a user test was set up with teachers and language students. The game was made available to the public and submitted to teachers and learners to use autonomously with no other guidance than a short explanation of the functionalities. Users could later fill a questionnaire. Qualitative analysis of our data allowed us to identify some bugs and to enrich the database with new 'game cards' created by teachers and learners. The test also raised some specific needs of teachers to improve the functionalities: mainly to allow to delete content. As a learning task, one teacher had his student create cards to play later. In this process, he wanted to be able to validate the cards.

The resulting prototype is still in alpha stage, but playable, and we plan to carry out an experiment in the winter to both evaluate Game of Words from the standpoint of game structures – do the students adopt a playful attitude? What prevents them from acquiring it? – and of the strategies invoked. As such, we hope to collect enough recordings to compare the students' productions with existing strategic competence taxonomies.

These results will allow us to implement a first version of the game, which will in turn allow the evaluation of the learning outcomes of the game. More game modes might be included. Some modes might offer new knowledge transmission rules, based on other such activities (Dörnyei & Thurrell, 1991) or exploring multimodality. Finally, other game modes might build on L1 based strategies and the growing body of literature regarding intercomprehension.

---

8. The number of forbidden words varies depending on the level of the player (as teachers we interviewed do in class).

5. Acknowledgements

We would like to thank the Innovalangues project for allowing this research and all those who contributed to it: Virginie Zampa, Chloe Cimpello, Justine Reverdy, Maryam Nejat, David Graceffa, Benjamin Abrial, Arnaud Bey and all the teachers and learners who tried Game of Words.

References

Canale, M., & Swain, M. (1980). Communicative approaches to second language teaching and testing. *Applied Linguistics*, *1*(1), 1-47. https://doi.org/10.1093/applin/1.1.1

CECRL. (2000). *Cadre européen commun de référence pour les langues: apprendre, enseigner, évaluer*. (Conseil de la coopération culturelle — Comité de l'éducation — Division des langues vivantes, Ed.) (Édition française). Strasbourg ; Paris: Conseil de l'Europe. http://medias.didierfle.com/media/contenuNumerique/007/4140016745.pdf

Dörnyei, Z., & Thurrell, S. (1991). Strategic competence and how to teach it. *ELTJ*, *45*(1), 16-23. https://doi.org/10.1093/elt/45.1.16

Lavigne, M. (2013). Pertinence et efficacité des serious games — Enquête de réception sur neuf serious games (S. Leleu-Merviel & K. Zreik, Ed.). *Revue des Interactions Humaines Médiatisées*, *14*(1), 99-123.

Loiseau, M. et al. (2016). Exploring learners' perceptions of the use of digital letter games for language learning: the case of Magic Word. In S. Papadima-Sophocleous, L. Bradley & S. Thouësny (Eds), *CALL communities and culture – short papers from EUROCALL 2016* (pp. 277-283). Research-publishing.net. https://doi.org/10.14705/rpnet.2016.eurocall2016.575

Mariani, L. (1994). Competenza strategica e interazione orale. In D. Corno & M. G. Dandini (Eds), *La voglia di insegnare* (pp. 145-152). Presented in VIIIe colloque « teaching & learning », Turin: Regione Piemonte Assessorato Istruzione. http://www.learningpaths.org/Articoli/competenzastrategica.pdf

Paribakht, T. (1985). Strategic competence and language proficiency. *Applied Linguistics*, *6*(2), 132-146. https://doi.org/10.1093/applin/6.2.132

Silva, H. (1999). *Poétiques du jeu. La métaphore ludique dans la théorie et la critique littéraires françaises au XXe siècle*. (Thèse). Université Paris 3 — Sorbonne Nouvelle, Paris. http://lewebpedagogique.com/jeulangue/files/2011/01/PoetiquesLud.pdf

Söbke, H., Bröker, T., & Kornadt, O. (2013). Using the master copy — Adding educational content to commercial video games. In P. Escudeiro & C. V. de Carvalho (Eds), *The Proceedings of The 7th European Conference on Games Based Learning* (Vol. 2, pp. 521-530). Reading: Academic Conferences and Publishing International Limited. http://issuu.com/acpil/docs/ecgbl2013-issuu_vol_2

Villez, B. (2006). Objectifs spécifiques d'apprentissage en langues étrangères à l'Université. (Y. Ayme, Ed.). *Cahiers pédagogiques, 448*, 51-53.

PETALL in action: latest developments and future directions of the EU-funded project Pan-European Task Activities for Language Learning

António Lopes[1]

Abstract. The Common European Framework of Reference (CEFR) proposes Task-Based Language Teaching (TBLT) as an important strategy to develop the learners' linguistic competences along with their communicative skills. Since it is learner-centred and relies mostly on engaging learners in meaningful communicative interchanges in a foreign language, it allows for greater interaction and collaboration between them in the development of products, in problem-solving processes and in the construction of knowledge. Nevertheless, teachers have revealed some resistance to this approach. Pan-European Task Activities for Language Learning (PETALL) is a project involving ten countries and seeks to address these problems by constructing a transnational strategy for Information and Communications Technology (ICT)-based task design management. It aims to produce tasks that can be implemented in different educational contexts, and offer training courses to help teachers build their confidence in TBLT. This presentation seeks to offer an overview of the project, including its objectives, underlying principles and deliverables (samples of good practices, the website, the courses, and the international conference).

Keywords: task-based language teaching, TBLT, ICT, CEFR, teacher training.

1.   Introduction

PETALL is a project co-funded by the former EU Life-Long Learning Programme. The project seeks to address three specific objectives of the programme (European Union, 2006), namely the promotion of language learning and linguistic diversity, the support to the development of ICT-based resources and the improvement of

1. University of Algarve, Faro, and CETAPS, Portugal; alopes@ualg.pt

How to cite this article: Lopes, A. (2016) PETALL in action: latest developments and future directions of the EU-funded project Pan-European Task Activities for Language Learning. In S. Papadima-Sophocleous, L. Bradley, & S. Thouësny (Eds), *CALL communities and culture – short papers from EUROCALL 2016* (pp. 290-294). Research-publishing.net. https://doi.org/10.14705/rpnet.2016.eurocall2016.577

their quality by encouraging "the best use of results, innovative products and processes" along with the exchange of good practice "in order to improve the quality of education and training" (p. 49).

The project consortium, constituted of twenty institutions from ten countries across Europe, is coordinated by the University of Algarve, Portugal.

Its main purpose is to encourage teachers to make use of ICT-resources in task-based language teaching, an approach to which the CEFR (Council of Europe, 2001) dedicates a whole chapter; 'Tasks and their role in language teaching'.

The project, which should have started in 2013, only had its kick-off meeting in June 2014 due to a series of institutional cutbacks, and is to end in June 2016. After the first year of implementation, the paper discusses the need for teacher training in technology-mediated TBLT, and looks at what has been achieved so far and how things are expected to evolve in the near future.

2. Meeting practical challenges

In several teacher training courses run by the higher education institutions that participate in the project, it has become evident that for the majority of trainees the principles and practices of TBLT still remain a challenge, despite the fact that most agree on the benefits of this approach at different proficiency levels and across different age groups, including adult education. A survey undertaken within the scope of the European Task-based Activities in Language learning: A Good practices Exchange (ETALAGE), another EU co-sponsored project, showed that teachers considered the lack of training opportunities, the absence of material and practical conditions, or even the difficulty in finding resources for developing materials and planning lessons, to be the major obstacles to an effective implementation of TBLT in schools (Lopes, 2012). Their reluctance is aggravated not only by their dependence on traditional methods, but also by the fact that examples of good practices that they can easily tailor to their needs – even more so if it involves ICT – are not easy to come by.

PETALL is precisely trying to tackle these problems by (a) providing teachers with samples of good practices that can be used regardless of the language taught and of the age group being targeted, (b) offering teacher training courses in all the countries of the consortium, (c) disseminating the theory and practice of TBLT in schools, and (d) providing a virtual space to help teachers discuss and share ideas.

In addition to this, one of the project's concerns is to make sure that the proposed samples can travel well from one country to the next and from one educational context to another without losing their pedagogical efficacy. That is why the project relies heavily on the transnational collaborative work between teachers, all of them coming from different cultural backgrounds, working within different education systems and teaching different languages. In order to facilitate such cross-cultural dialogue, the project has resorted to the CEFR as the conceptual tool that best provides a common ground for mutual understanding and for bridging the gaps that exist between education systems.

3.   Relevant literature

The integration of ICT into TBLT is now receiving the attention of an increasing number of researchers. Little more than a decade ago, authors like Willis and Willis (2001), Ellis (2003), and Nunan (2004) laid down the theoretical and methodological foundations of TBLT. However, exploring the potential of technology was not their primary concern back then. The rapid evolution of ICT and its growing importance in everyday life have changed the ways in which human beings not only work and communicate, but also socialise and engage in new experiences. If, according to Ellis (2003), "a task is intended to result in language use that bears a resemblance, direct or indirect, to the way language is used in the real world" (p. 16), then the tasks proposed to the learners cannot be overlooked as the growing prevalence of ICT in their lives. Tasks, practical as they are, must emulate these ever-evolving technology-mediated contexts. One of the first volumes of studies on the integration of ICT and TBLT, Thomas and Reinders, appeared in 2010. It covered a wide variety of topics (use of computer-mediated communication in intercultural exchanges, network-based computer-assisted language learning, teacher training, and virtual-world learning environments). More recently, González-Lloret and Ortega (2014) edited another volume dedicated to the use of ICT in TBLT activities. As they argue, "the canonical principles of task-based language teaching (TBLT) can be fitted integrally into the new language education and digital technology realities" (p. 1).

4.   Latest developments in the project and conclusion

Each national tandem, formed by a practice school and a teacher training institution, has until now produced four tasks (40 *in toto*), which have already been trialled in the practice schools pertaining to the tandems of neighbouring countries. With the results of the trial (obtained from direct observation in school settings, analysis of outputs, evaluation by end users), the tandems have been carefully revising the tasks before submitting them to a team of independent reviewers. The latter will evaluate them according to a series of pre-defined criteria (including its compliance with the CEFR, functionality, quality of planning, availability of resources, and clarity of the assessment procedures) (see also Lopes, 2015). Recommendations for improvement will then be incorporated into the tasks before they are translated into the consortium languages and made available in the project website at http://petallproject.eu.

Besides a thorough description of each of the ten national courses offered by the teacher training institutions, the website will also feature all the products of dissemination and exploitation activities carried out to date by the consortium members. They include presentations at national and international conferences, papers published in journals, theses produced in the context of the project, and reports on meetings with the teaching staff of schools and university departments.

Since one of the goals of the project is to foster transnational collaboration, the website also hosts a forum for teachers and trainees to exchange ideas, discuss practical issues and submit their own proposals of tasks to be added to the online project repository. On the other hand, national courses are also going to be scheduled in such a way as to allow trainees to engage in collaborative work with colleagues abroad. Common projects resulting from this work will be added to the repository.

Another equally important initiative is the 2016 international conference at Granada University (Spain). It aims to (a) disseminate the project products amongst practitioners, through hands-on workshops and practical sessions, (b) discuss the latest investigation in the field, and (c) promote a debate between stakeholders involved in the design of language education policies not only in each country of the consortium, but also at European level. The starting point of the debate is a study based on an online survey to be carried out at European level aiming to ascertain:

- the teachers' perceptions of TBLT;
- how willing they are to implement technology-mediated TBLT;
- how much they know about the CEFR;
- how much they still rely on more traditional approaches;
- their training needs in this area.

Only by the end of the project will it be possible to measure its reach and impact. However, from the preliminary results of its implementation, exploitation and dissemination, as well as from the feedback from stakeholders and end users, the consortium expects to achieve the objectives successfully and to open new avenues for further research and actions.

References

Council of Europe. (2001). *Common European framework of reference for languages: learning, teaching, assessment.* Cambridge: Cambridge University Press.

Ellis, R. (2003). *Task-based language learning and teaching.* Oxford: Oxford University Press.

European Union. (2006). European decision No 1720/2006/EC of the European Parliament and of the Council of 15 November 2006 establishing an action programme in the field of lifelong learning. *Official Journal of the European Union.* 24 November, L 327, 45-68. http://eur-lex.europa.eu/legal-content/EN/TXT/?uri=celex:32006D1720

González-Lloret, M., & Ortega, L. (Eds). (2014). *Technology-mediated TBLT: researching technology and tasks.* Amsterdam: John Benjamins. https://doi.org/10.1075/tblt.6

Lopes, A. (2012). Changing teachers' attitudes towards ICT-based language learning tasks: the ETALAGE Comenius project (the Portuguese case). *The EUROCALL Review, 20*(1), 100-103.

Lopes, A. (2015). Critical issues in the evaluation of an international project dedicated to technology-mediated TBLT (PETALL). *TEwT - The Journal of Teaching English with Technology, 15*(2), 4-18.

Nunan, D. (2004). *Task-based language teaching.* Cambridge: Cambridge University Press. https://doi.org/10.1017/CBO9780511667336

Thomas, M., & Reinders, H. (Eds). (2010). *Task-based language learning and teaching with technology.* London & New York: Continuum.

Willis, D., & Willis, J. (2001). Task-based language learning. In R. Carter & D. Nunan (Eds), *The Cambridge guide to teaching English to speakers of other languages* (pp. 173-179). Cambridge: Cambridge University Press. https://doi.org/10.1017/CBO9780511667206.026

Exploring EFL learners' lexical application in AWE-based writing

Zhihong Lu[1] and Zhenxiao Li[2]

Abstract. With massive utilization of Automated Writing Evaluation (AWE) tools, it is feasible to detect English as a Foreign Language (EFL) learners' lexical application so as to improve their writing quality. This study aims to explore Chinese EFL learners' lexical application to see if AWE-based writing can bring about positive effects of lexicon on linguistics features, especially in word count, word frequency and word density in their writing texts across a series of tracked revisions in University English classrooms and beyond. The findings from both classroom observations and learners' responses to a post-test questionnaire survey reveal that they showed very positive perceptions of AWE-based writing in which they were greatly encouraged to make modifications in each writing task. It shows from data analysis of the writing texts that learners tended to replace simple lexical terms with more academic and concrete ones in revisions. The results signify implications for EFL learning of lexicon and writing, and also for AWE developers. However, it implies from the analytic features of lexicon that learners' lexical modification was limited. This perhaps suggests for further research on learners' lexical modification in AWE-based writing context to see if there is any difference across genders and different levels of achievers.

Keywords: AWE, lexical application, modification, *Pigai* system.

1. Introduction

Learners' writing proficiency partly depends on their lexical ability in terms of writing improvement, as writing consists of 'grammaticalized lexis' (Lewis, 1993). Lexicon, not merely a list of words, is conceived as "a set of lexical resources, including the morphemes of the language, plus the processes available in the

1. Beijing University of Posts and Telecommunications, Beijing, China; luzhihong@bupt.edu.cn
2. Beijing University of Posts and Telecommunications, Beijing, China; briannalee@163.com

How to cite this article: Lu, Z., & Li, Z. (2016). Exploring EFL learners' lexical application in AWE-based writing. In S. Papadima-Sophocleous, L. Bradley & S. Thouësny (Eds), CALL communities and culture – short papers from EUROCALL 2016 (pp. 295-301). Research-publishing.net. https://doi.org/10.14705/rpnet.2016.eurocall2016.578

language for constructing words from those resources" (Trask, 1999, p. 111). In this study, lexical application ability refers to learners' effective use of lexical items, including words and phrases, frequent collocations, institutionalized utterances, sentence frames and heads (Lewis, 1993). Previous research has proved a positive relationship of lexicon on language learners' writing quality in terms of word range, word diversity, word frequency, and polysemy (Engber, 1995; Hu, 2015; Qin & Wen, 2007; Laufer & Nation, 1995).

Recently, massive application of AWE tools has been expanded to language teaching and learning purposes, which has provided great potential possibilities for EFL learners to proceed with their writing tasks at their own rate with real-time feedback. Much research is reportedly promising and positive, where the utilization of AWE tools can be realized in terms of time efficiency, reduction of teachers' workloads, increased learner autonomy (Sherimis & Burstein, 2013) and improved writing skills (Scharber & Dexter, 2008). This study aims to explore EFL learners' lexical application to see if AWE-based writing has positive effects of lexicon on linguistic features based on their writing tasks on a web-based AWE tool, the *Pigai* system (http://www.pigai.org), which makes it accessible to keep precise track of any step in the creation of writing with real-time feedback in terms of vocabulary use, grammar, cohesion, and content relevancy.

2. Method

2.1. Research questions

This study is driven by the following questions:

- Is the AWE tool, the *Pigai* system, helpful for students to improve their writing skills, especially in terms of lexical application?

- If yes, to what extent does the AWE-based writing affect students' lexical application? If not, what are the causes?

2.2. Teaching and research design

The study was carried out in one-week intervals from September 2015 to January 2016 and it involves 26 second year non-English majors in Beijing University of Posts and Telecommunications' English Audio-Video Speaking

Course (EAVSC), with a pre- and post-test design coupled with follow-up questionnaires in a digital lab. All of the students had passed CET-4[3] before taking the course but were still required to take a test of the same format of content-based integrated listening-speaking tasks through a self-developed web-based English language skills training system at the beginning and the end of the semester. During the whole semester, classes were conducted using the following pattern: students began every class by watching a video clip; next, engaged in synchronous computer-mediated group and pair discussions on the given topics; then proceeded with a ten minute online writing task on the same topic using the *Pigai* system; finally, performed a one minute recorded personal statement task on the same topic. The AWE-based ten minute writing task in class with an assigned topic each week served as an embedded task on a regular basis and students were allowed to revise their writing after class before a deadline set by the instructor.

Figure 1. A screenshot of students' writing submissions on the *Pigai* system

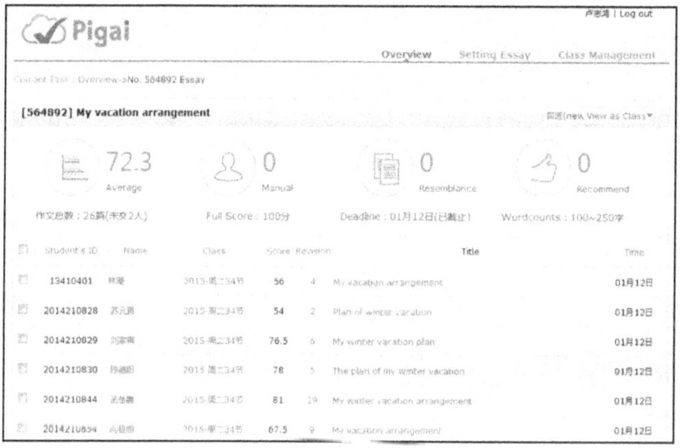

2.3.   Data collection

The questionnaires and interviews following pre- and post-tests were conducted and collected through the adopted system, which would provide insights into students' perceptions of the *Pigai* system, particularly their feedback in terms of vocabulary, grammar, content and cohesion. All of the students submitted their pre-test questionnaire, but one missed the post-test questionnaire. All the students' writing texts were collected and each modification or reconstruction was tracked through the *Pigai* system.

---

3. CET is the abbreviated form of 'College English Test'. The national College English Test Band Four—CET-4 in China aims to evaluate non-English majors' comprehensive language proficiency. Apart from CET-4, there is also CET-6, which is widely used to evaluate above-average college students' English language proficiency.

2.4.   Data analysis

There were 11 writing tasks during the whole semester which covered a variety of social issue topics, including job hunting, the relationship between tourism development and environmental protection, e-games, etc.

In order to explore the students' lexical application and the effectiveness of lexical modification in AWE-based writing, the multiple writing scores and lexical features of the three writing tasks (the first, sixth, and final ones) were selected as the research samples in the current study. The scores data were processed using SPSS 22.0 to see if there is a significant difference in the first and final draft in each of the three writing tasks.

To investigate students' lexical application across multiple drafts and their lexical modification in AWE-based writing, the Coh-metrix tool (Graesser, McNamara, Louwerse, & Cai, 2004) was employed as a complementary tool for analytic features on texts.

The web-based Coh-metrix, developed by the University of Memphis, automates over 200 measures of language, discourse and cohesion through extracting information from texts. Change in lexicon use can be seen from the measured scores of texts calculated with Coh-metrix, including word count, word length, word frequency, and lexical richness across multiple writing results.

3.   Results and discussion

3.1.   Analysis of AWE-based writing scores

The average number of revision times of the 11 writing tasks is 5.12 to 13.42 (in the seventh task). Although it drops to 6.81 in the final task after 12.69 for the tenth task (probably because it was close to the final exam session), as shown in Table 1, students in the mid and final writing tasks still conducted more revisions than they did in the first task.

The results of the students' writing scores basically fit the normal distribution and paired sample t-tests revealed a significant difference in scores between the first and the final drafts for all of the three writing tasks in the study ($t$first task= -6.06, p <0.05; $t$sixth task= -5.50, p<0.05; $t$final task= -7.34, p<0.05).

Table 1.   Paired sample *t*-test of scores for students' drafts

	N	Average times of revision drafts	Mean Scores				MD	t
			First draft		Final draft			
			M	SD	M	SD		
First writing task	26	5.12	70.06	9.78	75.90	8.11	-5.84	-6.06*
Sixth writing task	26	7.31	69.04	12.74	78.50	8.22	-9.46	-5.50*
Final writing task	26	6.81	63.83	7.28	72.25	7.45	-8.42	-7.34*

Analytic features of students' perceptions

With respect to how students perceive the *Pigai* system in affecting their writing quality, from the questionnaire feedback, 84% students considered that for each revision they valued the score provided by the system, and only 20% of them thought they would cease modification if they get a lower score after their modification. 68% of them showed gratitude to the real-time and multiple comments which helped them realize their weaknesses and pushed them to rewrite or revise.

3.2.   Analytic features of lexicon

As is shown in Table 2, the paired sample *t*-test results revealed that there was no significant difference between the first and the final draft both in average word count (*t*=-1.89, *p*>0.05) and word frequency (*t*=0.67, *p*>0.05). The word frequency count was based on CELEX, the database from the Dutch Centre for Lexical Information (Baayen, Piepenbrock, & Gulikers, 1995). For the average word length, students chose longer words in their final drafts than those in their first drafts (*t*= -4.44, *p*<0.05), indicating that they possibly used more academic or formal words in the process of revision.

Table 2.   Analytic features of the final writing task

Linguistic features	N	Drafts for the final writing task			
		First draft	Final draft	MD	t
Average word count	26	138.80	159.35	-20.54	-1.89
Average word length	26	4.14	4.26	-0.12	-4.44*
Word frequency	26	3.08	3.07	0.01	0.67
Type-token ratio	26	0.62	0.60	0.02	1.49
Connective incidence	26	103.63	1.09.39	-5.75	0.013*

Note: *p<0.05

Type-token ratio is very important to measure the lexicon richness, for a low ratio usually indicates that words are repeated many times. Table 2 shows that type-token ratios of the first and the final draft had no significant difference ($t=1.49$, $p>0.05$). However, the results revealed a significant difference in connective incidence ($t=0.013$, $p<0.05$). The higher the incidence of connectives, the more it is assumed that students applied connective words and phrases in their final drafts.

4.   Conclusions

The findings from the research showed that students appreciated and valued the real-time feedback provided by the *Pigai* system and they were highly motivated and encouraged to make modifications for each writing task. They tended to replace simple lexical items with more academic and concrete ones. Nevertheless, the analytic features of lexicon implied that their writing improvement was limited, and this perhaps requires for a further study on textual analysis in depth so as to better explore their modification tracked by the *Pigai* system to see if there is any difference across genders and among different English levels of students.

5.   Acknowledgements

This study is part of the humanities and social sciences project 'Research on Multidimensional Assessment for a Web-based English Audio-video Speaking Course' (12YJA740052), supported by the Ministry of Education in China. We would like to thank Mr. Zhang Yue and his *Pigai* company for their technical support in the course of the study.

References

Baayen, R. H., Piepenbrock, R., & Gulikers, L. (1995). *The CELEX lexical database (CD-ROM)*. Philadelphis: University of Pennsylvania, Linguistic Data Consortium.

Engber, A. C. (1995). The relationship of lexical proficiency to the quality of ESL compositions. *Journal of Second Language Writing, 4*(2), 139-155. https://doi.org/10.1016/1060-3743(95)90004-7

Graesser, A., McNamara, D. S., Louwerse, M., & Cai, Z. (2004). Coh-Metrix: analysis of text on cohesion and language. *Behavioral Research Methods, Instruments, and Computers, 36*(2), 193-202. https://doi.org/10.3758/BF03195564

Hu, X. (2015). Effects of online self-correction on EFL students' writing quality. *Computer-Assisted Foreign Language Education, 163*, 45-49.

Laufer, B., & Nation, P. (1995). Vocabulary size and use: lexical richness in L2 written production. *Applied Linguistics,16*(3), 307-322. https://doi.org/10.1093/applin/16.3.307

Lewis, M. (1993). *The lexical approach: the state of ELT and the way forward.* Hove, England: Language Teaching Publications.

Qin, X., & Wen, F. (2007). *EFL writing of college English majors in China: the developmental perspectives.* China Social Science Press.

Scharber, C. S., & Dexter, R. E. (2008). Students' experiences with an automated essay scorer. *The Journal of Technology, Learning, and Assessment, 7*(1), 1-45.

Sherimis, D. M., & Burstein, J. (2013). *The handbook of automated essay evaluation current applications and new directions.* New York: Routledge.

Trask, L. R. (1999). *Key Concepts in language and linguistics.* Routledge.

Mobile-assisted language learning and language learner autonomy

Paul A. Lyddon[1]

Abstract. In the modern age of exponential knowledge growth and accelerating technological development, the need to engage in lifelong learning is becoming increasingly urgent. Successful lifelong learning, in turn, requires learner autonomy, or "the capacity to take control of one's own learning" (Benson, 2011, p. 58), including all relevant decisions about what, when, where, and how to learn. Mobile technologies, as not only potential means for learning anywhere and anytime but also conduits to rich, multimodal content, provide unprecedented opportunities for the development of learner autonomy. However, even when learners possess adequate training in mobile technology use and autonomy itself, implementation of mobile learning devices in the classroom often seems to engender little additional autonomous behavior. This paper highlights the differing constraints on learner autonomy in formal and informal learning environments. It then proposes an approach to encouraging greater demonstration of autonomy through an explicit linking of institutional requirements associated with routine lesson assignments and the achievement of personally meaningful, individually determined learning goals. Finally, it suggests the role that mobile technology can and properly ought to play in capacitating consistently high levels of demonstrated autonomy both inside and outside the classroom.

Keywords: lifelong learning, mobile technology, learner training, learning context.

1.   Introduction

As the rate of technological advancement continues to accelerate, the exponential growth and rapid dissemination of new knowledge now makes many traditional academic courses of study out-of-date almost as soon as they reach completion. As such, lifelong learning can no longer be considered the recreation of an exceptional

1. Osaka Jogakuin College, Osaka, Japan; lyddon@wilmina.ac.jp

How to cite this article: Lyddon, P. A. (2016). Mobile-assisted language learning and language learner autonomy. In S. Papadima-Sophocleous, L. Bradley, & S. Thouësny (Eds), *CALL communities and culture – short papers from EUROCALL 2016* (pp. 302-306). Research-publishing.net. https://doi.org/10.14705/rpnet.2016.eurocall2016.579

few who happen to possess the necessary resources and disposition, but an absolute imperative for all who wish to be gainfully employed for the duration of their working years. For lifelong learning to be successful, however, learners need to possess a high degree of autonomy, in other words, the capacity to take control of their own learning (Benson, 2011, p. 58). This capacity includes determining learning objectives, defining scope and sequence, selecting methods and techniques, setting locations and schedules, and evaluating outcomes (Holec, 1981).

The invention and spread of Internet-capable mobile devices such as smartphones and tablet computers has certainly opened up new possibilities in terms of learner autonomy by providing not only a potential means of learning anytime and anywhere, but also access to a virtually endless variety of rich, multimodal content. However, a means in itself is insufficient. At a minimum, it also requires the ability to use it. Consequently, countless learner training programs have now been put in place, and many of these include mobile technologies as a key component.

Possession of mobile learning devices and demonstrated ability to create and successfully complete individualized learning plans entailing their use outside of class notwithstanding, learners often fail to exhibit similar levels of autonomy inside the classroom. For instance, in an activity where a simple image search might help them either understand or express an essential concept during a class discussion, they inexplicably choose instead to flounder. The purpose of this paper is to suggest a plausible reason for the inconsistent display of autonomous behavior between formal and informal contexts and to propose an approach to rectifying this apparent discrepancy.

2.   Background

Though their exact origins are difficult to pinpoint, discussions of autonomy in education greatly intensified in the wake of the social and political turmoil immediately following World War II (Gremmo & Riley, 1995). By the early 1970s, initiatives such as the Council of Europe's Modern Language Project had emerged to provide opportunities and support for lifelong learning so as to nurture individuals' abilities to responsibly participate in the affairs of modern society (Benson, 2011). Given the rapid pace of technological change in the current digital age, the need for learner autonomy is now crucial, for students must now be prepared for "jobs that don't yet exist, using technologies that haven't been invented, in order to solve problems we don't even know are problems yet" (mesjms, 2016).

The adoption of mobile devices such as smartphones and tablet computers has largely eased restrictions on where and when learners can learn as well as introduced a host of previously unavailable options in terms of modality and content. Moreover, inasmuch as they are technological artifacts, these devices might even be qualified as extensions of our mental and physical faculties (Brey, 2000). Just as glasses improve our ability to see, smartphones and tablets have the potential to help us observe and recall things better, fill gaps in our knowledge, and enhance our ability to communicate. As such, with the inclusion of training on how to take advantage of them in learner training programs, these powerful technologies should additionally lead to greater learner autonomy. However, the results are not always consistent, and the question is why.

3. Discussion

True learner autonomy, in the sense of self-determination, would include not only what, where, when, and how to learn, but whether to learn at all. While it is true that students cannot choose whether to learn if they do not know how, it must also be admitted that most formal language learning is compulsory and that many students might indeed opt out if given the choice. Despite the Common European Framework of Reference for languages (CEFR)'s explicit acknowledgment of the importance of learner autonomy, the Council of Europe (2014) explains the framework's overall purpose as "to provide a transparent, coherent and comprehensive basis for the elaboration of language syllabuses and curriculum guidelines, the design of teaching and learning materials, and the assessment of foreign language proficiency" (para. 1). In other words, learners are not, in fact, free to simply learn whatever they like, at least not if they wish to meet international program standards.

Learner autonomy in most formal learning contexts is limited in a number of other important ways as well. Among the most evident are time and place, ironically the two constraints that mobile technologies are touted to overcome. Perhaps the most serious additional impediment of formal learning contexts with respect to learner autonomy, however, is that of tool use itself. While no teacher would likely prohibit students from wearing glasses in class, it is largely because the intended purpose of glasses is clear and the potential for its perversion is slight. The purpose of versatile tools such as mobile devices, on the other hand, is ambiguous and, thus, invites misuse in the form of off-task student behaviors. Thus, it is for this reason, I would argue, that many instructors do not allow the use of mobile devices in their classrooms. Moreover, the mindset of formal schooling is so strong that even in classrooms where teachers do not expressly prohibit their use, students are conditioned to assume prohibition unless explicitly told otherwise. Consequently, despite having the means and ability, they fail to demonstrate autonomy out of a perceived denial of permission.

Not to challenge the notion of standards-based education, I simply wish to acknowledge the constraints of formal learning contexts and suggest a way of working within them. In any context, learner autonomy consists more of interdependence than independence, but especially in a formal context, I would contend that autonomous learners should possess the following five characteristics: *compliance, competence, cognizance, introspection*, and *diplomacy*.

These five characteristics can be imagined on a horizontal cline, with increasingly autonomous learners exhibiting more of them from left to right. The least autonomous students are non-compliant, that is, they choose not to participate in assigned learning activities. Those who are *compliant* but incompetent participate but may not follow the prescribed requirements out of lack of understanding and failure to seek clarification. Those who are only additionally *competent* follow the assignment directions to the letter while sometimes awkwardly violating the intended pedagogical purpose. Those who are additionally *cognizant* also understand the teacher's rationale, those who are *introspective* can see the personal value of the assignment, and those who are *diplomatic* can negotiate task completion accordingly.

After clearly highlighting to students the necessarily limited nature of learner autonomy in the formal learning context, the first step in developing it is to inculcate these expected characteristics, for instance by engaging learners in regular self-reflection on their level of conscious involvement in the completion of required learning assignments. It is only at this point that the role of mobile technology in bolstering learner autonomy can truly be addressed, for only then can students begin to see the value of the technology in helping them to achieve their personal goals, understand how use of the technology is consistent with instructional, institutional, or societal goals, and use the technology conscientiously to mediate these two sometimes competing ends.

4. Conclusion

As technological artifacts can be considered extensions of our physical and mental faculties, mobile technologies open up promising new possibilities in terms of the exercise of learner autonomy. However, compulsory learning in formal contexts may inhibit their full exploitation in the classroom. To help learners overcome their inhibition, teachers should explicitly acknowledge the limited nature of autonomy in formal learning contexts and inculcate expectations of learner characteristics aimed at linking the institutional requirements associated with routine lesson assignments to the achievement of personally meaningful, individually determined learning goals. Finally, they should encourage the development of a new type of self-awareness and self-discipline that embodies mobile technologies and, thus, enables them to be effectively employed to further this purpose.

References

Benson, P. (2011). *Teaching and researching autonomy* (2nd ed.). Harlow, UK: Pearson Education.

Brey, P. (2000). Theories of technology as extension of human faculties. In C. Mitcham (Ed.), *Metaphysics, epistemology, and technology: research in philosophy and technology, vol. 19* (pp. 59-78). London, UK: Elsevier/JAI Press.

Council of Europe. (2014). *Common European framework of reference for languages: learning, teaching, assessment (CEFR)*. http://www.coe.int/t/dg4/linguistic/cadre1_en.asp

Gremmo, M.-J., & Riley, P. (1995). Autonomy, self-direction and self-access in language teaching and learning: the history of an idea. *System, 23*(2), 151-164. https://doi.org/10.1016/0346-251X(95)00002-2

Holec, H. (1981). *Autonomy in foreign language learning*. Oxford: Pergamon.

mesjms. (2016, January 18). Did you know 2016 [Video file]. https://youtu.be/uqZiIO0YI7Y

YELL/TELL: online community platform for teacher professional development

Ivana Marenzi[1], Maria Bortoluzzi[2], and Rishita Kalyani[3]

Abstract. The community platform *Young/Teen English Language Learners* (YELL/ TELL), as mentioned by Bortoluzzi and Marenzi (2014) was "developed to respond to the needs of collaboration and sharing among trainee teachers, school teachers, teacher trainers and researchers in the field of language learning for English [as a Foreign or Second Language (FL/SL)]" (p.182). The current study focuses on ethnographic observation and data gathered during a workshop for professional development organised for experienced teachers. We compare the evidence of the teachers' actions, with the analysis of their perception about their professional use of the online environment and their critical reflection about the experience.

Keywords: teacher professional development, lifelong learning, collaboration, evaluation-driven approach.

1. Introduction

The social community YELL/TELL, supported by the LearnWeb[4] social platform, has the aim of encouraging professional collaboration among teachers of different school levels and backgrounds. Lifelong learning and peer-teacher education are promoted on the basis of sharing resources and commenting and reflecting on them in the spirit of co-construction of knowledge through open-educational practices and resources for teaching English as a FL/SL.

This paper is based on an ethnographic observation and qualitative study of the activities carried out in the online community during a blended professional development workshop for experienced school teachers in Italy. The research

---

1. Leibniz University of Hannover, Hannover, Germany; marenzi@L3S.de
2. University of Udine, Udine, Italy; maria.bortoluzzi@uniud.it
3. Leibniz University of Hannover, Hannover; kalyani@L3S.de
4. http://learnweb.l3s.uni-hannover.de

How to cite this article: Marenzi, I., Bortoluzzi, M., & Kalyani, R. (2016). YELL/TELL: online community platform for teacher professional development. In S. Papadima-Sophocleous, L. Bradley, & S. Thouësny (Eds), *CALL communities and culture – short papers from EUROCALL 2016* (pp. 307-312). Research-publishing.net. https://doi.org/10.14705/rpnet.2016. eurocall2016.580

---

aim is two-fold: (1) investigating how a group of experienced teachers perceive the participation in a professional online community for their professional development, and (2) identifying the affordances of the platform that enhance professional development and improve on the system design.

The study followed the progress of 16 experienced teachers of primary and lower secondary schools during a blended workshop in which the current version of the platform was used to share open access resources and practices, collaborate online and improve on the professional digital skills of searching, selecting, annotating, customising and uploading online resources for English language learning and plurilingualism. The evidence of the teachers' actions within the online environment (logs) were analysed in context along with their discussions about the use of the system and their critical reflection on the experience (comments on the forum and the final questionnaire).

2.   Method

2.1.   The online platform and community

The YELL/TELL community platform allows users to share and collaboratively work on resources collected from the web or teacher-generated; resources can be bookmarked, tagged, rated, and discussed by all users who join the different interest groups (Marenzi & Zerr, 2012). Users can create folders "to bundle resources that belong to the same learning context, [… hence,] collaboratively identify the best learning resources for specific learning domains" (Abel, Marenzi, Nejdl, & Zerr, 2009, p. 158; see also Bortoluzzi & Marenzi, 2014). Different groups of users have been involved in the co-design of the platform (Wang & Hannafin, 2005) from the start (2012), which allows us to carry out throughout the years an *iterative evaluation-driven design-based research approach* (Marenzi, 2014; Mirijamdotter, Somerville, & Holst, 2006).

The online community supported by the platform is an inclusive, boundary-crossing professional community used for pre-service, in service and lifelong language teacher education for teachers of nursery, primary and secondary schools. Participants also include teacher educators, university lecturers and computer developers. The community was developed within a flexible socio-constructivist framework as a technology-supported community to contribute to the quality of the teaching profession "by encouraging collaboration and knowledge exchange"

(Vuorikari et al., 2012, p. 7), to multiliteracy for teachers (Cope & Kalantzis, 2009) and to enhancing reflection on practice and theory (Edge, 2011).

2.2.   The blended in-service professional development workshop

The workshop was organised in Pordenone (Italy) and lasted from September to December 2015 for a total of 14 contact hours and tasks for individual online work. Participants were primary and lower secondary school experienced teachers and had very diversified digital skills (from beginners to competent). None of them had ever used the YELL/TELL platform before and the majority were new to digital assistance as a teaching aid. Tasks were designed to get the teachers to do hands-on work: post materials online, share resources and teaching experiences, discuss teaching practices and the affordances of the platform.

The general aim of the workshop was to reflect on online collaboration for teaching and plurilingual education. From the technical point of view, the research goal was to collect information about teachers' online practices (such as searching, selecting, annotating and customising online resources) and improve on the system interface in support of teaching scenarios.

2.3.   Data analysis

The data gathered is both hard evidence of actions (logs) and qualitative ethnographic observation as well as qualitative evaluation in context (forum participation, task completion and final questionnaire). In fact, we found a contrast between these two sets of data: whereas the first (1. below) would point towards a rather limited use of the platform, the second (2. below) yields a rich, involved and personalised use of the platform.

> 1. Activity logs were used to study the search behaviour: how teachers refined their search queries, whether they liked the resource pool returned by the system and whether they encountered some problems while working with the system. A quantitative analysis of the logs showed that teachers issued 840 search queries across the search types Image, Web and Video. Teachers uploaded 262 resources out of which 66% from their personal workstation and 34% added through searching on the platform. 30% of the resources added through search were found in the YELL/TELL platform (not on the Web) as they had been previously added by other users, and were appreciated by the teachers as valuable to be reused in their learning/ teaching context. We know from the feedback questionnaires (2. below)

that one of the reasons why several teachers were more inclined to share resources from their own desktop was that they felt more confident while sharing a familiar resource, because they had already used and tested it in their teaching practice. Search logs show that sometimes teachers searched for the same query multiple times by either refining the search query itself or by using various search filters. Based on the logs analysis, a few improvements were suggested, and a questionnaire was designed to investigate the observed patterns better.

2. Forum participation and task completion demonstrated the group and individual commitment in using the platform and its affordances: experienced teachers appreciated to be part of a community of like-minded people with whom they could share resources, practices and discuss problems. They praised the fact that resources they can find on the platform are already qualitatively selected and organised by teachers like them and educational experts. They discussed how to tag and annotate resources collaboratively in order to sort and find resources easily, suggesting that a more professionally related tagging system should be put in place. Teachers appreciated the social aspect of the online community and the ease with which it is possible to share and collaborate through commenting, discussing in the forum and creating documents collaboratively.

3.   Discussion

On the one hand, the hard evidence of logs is limited in range and shows repetitive or incomplete actions: teachers searched for resources, but then uploaded new ones mainly from their desktop; and some uploaded many times the same resource or keyed in strings with errors to search for resources. On the other hand, the 'soft evidence' and ethnographic observation (participation in the discussion online and offline, forum, quality of tasks and final questionnaire) show, instead, a very involved, motivated, personalised and creative group of teachers who explored and critically discussed resources (for teaching or professional improvement), and provided useful remarks and suggestions for platform improvement such as pre-designed categorisation of resources, improved group design, and system documentation. Their suggestions were so relevant that we are currently implementing new features in the system: better search categorisation, a tagging system suited to the professional community of teachers, and *My resources* as a space that functions as a personalised laboratory and sandbox.

The difficulties with handling platform functionalities, which resulted in limited log data, were due to the general low level of digital skills and lack of experience as members of a professional online community. Practical difficulties were overcome thanks to the high level of motivation and involvement. The platform design will profit from the teachers' constructive and professional feedback.

4.   Concluding remarks and further developments

The two-fold aims of the study were met beyond expectations: the experienced teachers who participated in the workshop confirmed the relevance of professional development through online collaboration in a community for professional development. Experienced teachers gained confidence in digital skills, in their professional competence, and actively contributed to improving the system design and the use of the platform. The participants also decided to organise teacher-training meetings in their different schools to share the experience and the expertise they acquired during the workshop. Thus, these experienced teachers have become teacher educators and will promote digital and professional competence through the online community.

Research and practice on the YELL/TELL platform and community are ongoing; we aim to promote internationally this expanding teacher community.

References

Abel, F., Marenzi, I., Nejdl, W., & Zerr, S. (2009). Sharing distributed resources in LearnWeb2.0. In U. Cress, V. Dimitrova, M. Specht (Eds), *Learning in the synergy of multiple disciplines, 5794*, 154-159. https://doi.org/10.1007/978-3-642-04636-0

Bortoluzzi, M., & Marenzi I. (2014). YELLing for collaborative learning in teacher education: users' voices in the social platform LearnWeb2.0. *IJSMILE*, 2(2), 182-198. https://doi.org/10.1504/IJSMILE.2014.063402

Cope, B. and Kalantzis, M. (2009). Multiliteracies: new literacies, new learning. *Pedagogies: An International Journal, 4*(3), 164-195. https://doi.org/10.1080/15544800903076044

Edge, J. (2011). *The reflexive teacher educator in TESOL*. London: Routledge.

Marenzi, I. (2014). *Multiliteracies and e-learning 2.0. Foreign language pedagogy content- and learner-oriented* (Vol. 28). Frankfurt am Main: Peter Lang.

Marenzi, I., & Zerr S. (2012). Multiliteracies and active learning in CLIL: the development of LearnWeb2.0. *IEEE Trans. Learning Technologies (TLT), 5*(4), 336-348. https://doi.org/10.1109/TLT.2012.14

Mirijamdotter, A., Somerville, M. M., & Holst, M. (2006). An interactive and iterative evaluation approach for creating collaborative learning environments. *EJISE, 9*(2), 83-92.

Vuorikari, R. et al. (2012). *Teacher networks. Today's and tomorrow's challenges and opportunities for the teaching profession.* Brussels, Belgium: European Schoolnet.

Wang, F., & Hannafin, M. J. (2005). *Design-based research and technology-enhanced learning environments. ETR&D, Wilson, 53*(4), 5-23. https://doi.org/10.1007/BF02504682

Leveraging automatic speech recognition errors to detect challenging speech segments in TED talks

Maryam Sadat Mirzaei[1], Kourosh Meshgi[2], and Tatsuya Kawahara[3]

Abstract. This study investigates the use of Automatic Speech Recognition (ASR) systems to epitomize second language (L2) listeners' problems in perception of TED talks. ASR-generated transcripts of videos often involve recognition errors, which may indicate difficult segments for L2 listeners. This paper aims to discover the root-causes of the ASR errors and compare them with L2 listeners' transcription mistakes. Our analysis on the ASR errors revealed several categories, such as minimal pairs, homophones, negative cases, and boundary misrecognition, which are assumed to denote the challenging nature of the respective speech segments for L2 listeners. To confirm the usefulness of these categories, we asked L2 learners to watch and transcribe a short segment of TED videos, including the above-mentioned categories of errors. Results revealed that learners' transcription mistakes substantially increase when they transcribe segments of the audio in which ASR made errors. This finding confirmed the potential of using ASR errors as a predictor of L2 learners' difficulties in listening to a particular audio. Furthermore, this study provided us with valuable data to enrich the Partial and Synchronized Caption (PSC) system we proposed earlier to facilitate and promote L2 listening skills.

Keywords: automatic speech recognition, listening skill, error analysis, partial and synchronized caption.

1. Introduction

Among the four skills that play crucial roles in L2 learning, listening is of paramount importance for being a prerequisite of speaking and for providing the language input (Rost, 2005). Mastery in listening needs exposure to authentic

1. Kyoto University, Kyoto, Japan; maryam@sap.ist.i.kyoto-u.ac.jp
2. Kyoto University, Kyoto, Japan; meshgi-k@sys.i.kyoto-u.ac.jp
3. Kyoto University, Kyoto, Japan; kawahara@i.kyoto-u.ac.jp

How to cite this article: Mirzaei, M. S., Meshgi, K., & Kawahara, T. (2016). Leveraging automatic speech recognition errors to detect challenging speech segments in TED talks. In S. Papadima-Sophocleous, L. Bradley & S. Thouësny (Eds), *CALL communities and culture – short papers from EUROCALL 2016* (pp. 313-318). Research-publishing.net. https://doi.org/10.14705/rpnet.2016.eurocall2016.581

audio/visual input, which in turn makes the listening process more difficult. The main reason lies in the fact that listening is a complicated process, from perceiving the speech to comprehending the content, and when using authentic materials, L2 listeners are more likely to encounter difficulties and make recognition mistakes (Gilmore, 2007).

Despite a body of work (Bloomfield et al., 2010; Révész & Brunfaut, 2013) on L2 listening difficulties, there is no reliable resource to detect those segments of an audio/visual material that cause recognition difficulties for L2 listeners. Motivated by this demand, we decided to find a means for discovering these difficulties in order to scaffold the language learners. Undoubtedly, L2 learners, in accordance with their language proficiency level and individual skills, may encounter different types of problems in recognizing speech. However, certain factors are more likely to result in misrecognition for the majority of L2 learners.

Detecting difficult words and phrases in audio/visual material is initially developed in our work (Mirzaei, Meshgi, Akita, & Kawahara, forthcoming), the PSC system. PSC identifies difficult words in TED talks and presents them in the caption while hiding easy ones to encourage listening over reading. The PSC system detects difficult words based on high speech rate, low word-frequency, and specificity (specific or academic terms). Nevertheless, these factors alone may not encompass all problematic speech segments in different videos.

To consider other factors, this study aims to establish the viability of using ASR as a predictor of L2 listeners' problems. ASR systems can generate transcriptions of spoken language, but this transcript often involves some errors. Despite common criticisms that regard these errors as major drawbacks of ASR systems, this paper investigates their usefulness to discover challenging speech segments of TED talks and to seek means for enhancing the PSC system.

2.   Method

The Julius ASR system was used to transcribe 72 TED talks; the ASR errors were derived from the system and given to a linguist expert to perform a root-cause analysis. These errors were then compared with PSC's selected words to show in the caption. Since PSC also chooses difficult words for L2 listeners based on speech rate, frequency and specificity factors, some overlaps are anticipated, while some mismatches can also be detected (Figure 1). These mismatches are automatically extracted and further analysed by the expert to discover the challenging speech segments that are not yet handled by the PSC system (dashed area in Figure 1).

Figure 1.　Diagram of the PSC shown words vs. ASR error categories: dashed area presents the scope of analysis

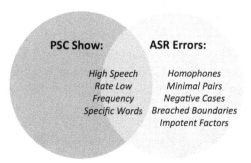

Expert analysis on these ASR errors revealed several clusters, four of which seemed to be the prudent sources of listening difficulties for L2 learners: homophones, minimal pairs, negative cases and breached boundaries.

Homophones (e.g. plain/plane) and minimal pairs (e.g. face/faith) hinder recognition processes by activating several word candidates (Weber & Cutler, 2004) and imposing high-level semantic analysis to select the right choice. Moreover, the wrong choice of words may thoroughly change the meaning of the sentence and deteriorate the comprehension. The same argument can be made for negative cases (e.g. can/can't). Finally, breached boundary (i.e. wrong lexical segmentation) is perhaps the most important category of errors that are very likely to arise when L2 learners watch a video, identifying word or phrase boundary is a challenging part of L2 listening (Field, 2009). A number of factors can be responsible for wrong lexical segmentation, including, assimilation, stress patterns, frequency rule and resyllabification (Cutler, 1990; Field, 2003). Regardless of their causes, breached boundary occurrences are hard to be predicted. ASR errors, however, provide helpful clues to detect such kinds of potentially misrecognized boundaries.

3.　Experiment

A transcription experiment is conducted to verify whether these four categories of ASR errors are actually problematic for L2 listeners. The data from this experiment allows comparing ASR errors to those of L2 learners' recognition mistakes.

The participants of this study were 11 Japanese and 10 Chinese students who were undergraduates and graduates majoring in different fields. All participants were intermediates with TOEIC scores (or equivalents) of above 650. There were 8 female and 13 male students.

The material of this experiment included twenty talks selected out of 72. The selected videos were delivered by native American English speakers in order to exclude the effect of other accents (e.g. British English). Two segments were chosen from each video:

- one including four ASR error categories which PSC hid ('difficult' cases that PSC failed to predict);

- one including ASR correct cases which PSC hid ('easy' cases both for ASR and PSC).

The former involved minimal pairs, homophones, negative forms, and breached boundaries and were tested to identify the difficulty-level of these categories. The latter were chosen to compare the performance of L2 listeners on transcribing easy versus potentially difficult speech segments.

Each segment of the video lasted 25~35 seconds and stopped at an irregular interval, which ended with 4~6 words, including the target word (easy or difficult case). Irregular pauses were made manually to maintain real life listening and avoid word-by-word decoding. The participants were not aware of when the videos were going to stop or which word would be the target word. They could watch each video only once and were supposed to type the last few words they heard immediately after the pause. Limited time was set to avoid overthinking and analyzing, thereby allowing the participants to input what they recognized. The test was made using iSpring Quiz Maker and was launched online. Spelling errors were ignored, unless affecting the meaning.

4.   Results

The results of this experiment include the scores of the participants on transcribing the easy segments of the videos versus the difficult parts that included minimal pairs, homophones, negative forms, and breached boundaries. As Figure 2 (Right) illustrates, the mean scores of the students on the easy segments (*M*=0.85, *SD*=0.08) is much higher compared to the difficult segments (*M*=0.16, *SD*=0.18).

Figure 2. (left) Overall average scores on 'easy' vs. 'difficult' segments. (right) Detailed result on four subcategories of ASR errors vs. respective easy segments

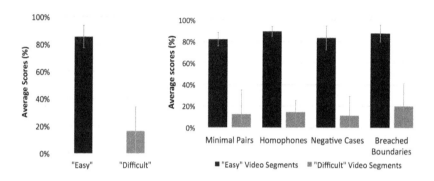

The results of a t-test indicate that this difference is statistically significant (*t*(19)=18.131; p<.05). Figure 2 (left) also suggests that participants' average scores on each of the categories of errors, i.e. minimal pairs (*M*=.12; *SD*=.22), homophones (*M*=.14, *SD*=.11), negative cases (*M*=.11, *SD*=.18) and breached boundaries (*M*=.20, *SD*=.21) were statistically lower than their average scores on respective easy segments of the videos. Interestingly, similar mistakes were found in participants' transcriptions and ASR generated transcript (e.g. "make a new ear" was transcribed as "make a new year" by both ASR and the participants).

5.   Conclusion

The study investigated the use of ASR errors in detecting challenging speech segments of TED talks and improving the word selection criteria in PSC. Following a thorough root-cause analysis, it was found that several categories in the ASR errors suggest the difficulties for L2 listeners. These categories included homophones, minimal pairs, negative forms, and breached boundaries. An experiment with L2 listeners confirmed the feasibility of using these ASR errors to predict L2 speech recognition difficulties. This finding can provide means for future advances of the PSC system by exploiting ASR clues to optimize the choice of words in the caption. In this view, the enhanced version should be compared with the current one to investigate any improvement. Furthermore, discovering challenging speech segments allows the learners to identify their listening problems and provide the teachers with useful information to better scaffold the learners.

References

Bloomfield, A., Wayland, S. C., Rhoades, E., Blodgett, A., Linck, J., & Ross, S. (2010). *What makes listening difficult? Factors affecting second language listening comprehension.* Maryland University.

Cutler, A. (1990). Exploiting prosodic probabilities in speech segmentation. In G. T. M. Altmann (Ed.), *Cognitive models of speech processing: psycholinguistic and perceptional perspectives* (pp.105-121). Cambridge: MIT Press.

Field, J. (2003). Promoting perception: lexical segmentation in L2 listening. *ELT journal, 57*(4), 325-334. https://doi.org/10.1093/elt/57.4.325

Field, J. (2009). *Listening in the language classroom.* Cambridge University Press. https://doi.org/10.1017/cbo9780511575945

Gilmore, A. (2007). Authentic materials and authenticity in foreign language learning. *Language Teaching, 40*(2), 97-118. https://doi.org/10.1017/S0261444807004144

Mirzaei, M. S., Meshgi, K., Akita, Y., & Kawahara, T. (forthcoming) Partial and synchronized captioning: a new tool to assist learners in developing second language listening skill. *ReCALL.*

Révész, A., & Brunfaut, T. (2013). Text characteristics of task input and difficulty in second language listening comprehension. *Studies in Second Language Acquisition, 35*(1), 31-65. https://doi.org/10.1017/S0272263112000678

Rost, M. (2005). L2 listening. In E. Hinkel (Ed.), *Handbook of research in second language teaching and learning* (pp. 503-527). Lawrence Erlbaum Associates, Inc., Publishers.

Weber, A., & Cutler, A. (2004). Lexical competition in non-native spoken-word recognition. *Journal of Memory and Language, 50*(1), 1-25. https://doi.org/10.1016/S0749-596X(03)00105-0

Investigating the affective learning
in a 3D virtual learning environment:
the case study of the Chatterdale mystery

Judith Molka-Danielsen[1], Stella Hadjistassou[2],
and Gerhilde Messl-Egghart[3]

Abstract. This research is motivated by the emergence of virtual technologies and their potential as engaging pedagogical tools for facilitating comprehension, interactions and collaborations for learning; and in particular as applied to learning second languages (L2). This paper provides a descriptive analysis of a case study that examines affective learning outcomes. We present an extension of an Affective Learning Model (ALM) in light of gaming in a 3D Virtual Learning Environment (VLE) in support of an L2 course. We identify affordances while applying an example of a serious game within the selected VLE. The findings of this case investigation give evidence that the gaming activities supported affective learning outcomes. This finding aligns with prior research of the ALM. Our research is based on a set of data collected during a case study as part of Euroversity, a three-year European Commission Project (2011-2014).

Keywords: virtual learning environments, OpenSim, affective model of learning, affordances, gaming.

1.   Introduction

In education and language learning, the main arguments for the use of virtual technology are that 3D environments are engaging as media; facilitating comprehension, interaction, and collaboration by the means of situating learning materials in an immersive context (Roussou, Oliver, & Slater, 2006). Research

1. Molde University College, Molde, Norway; j.molka-danielsen@himolde.no
2. University of Cyprus, Nicosia, Cyprus; stella1@asu.edu
3. Talkademy, Vienna, Austria; gerhilde@talkademy.org

How to cite this article: Molka-Danielsen, J., Hadjistassou, S., & Messl-Egghart, G. (2016). Investigating the affective learning in a 3D virtual learning environment: the case study of the Chatterdale mystery. In S. Papadima-Sophocleous, L. Bradley, & S. Thouësny (Eds), *CALL communities and culture – short papers from EUROCALL 2016* (pp. 319-324). Research-publishing.net. https://doi.org/10.14705/rpnet.2016.eurocall2016.582

shows that learning in VLEs is an emerging trend and can provide a more effective, motivating way of learning than traditional classroom practices (Duncan, Miller, & Jiang, 2012; Monahan, McArdle, & Bertolotto, 2008). However, VLEs on their own cannot serve as effective learning aids. Pedagogical tools and training in the use of such tools within those contexts need to be developed to meet learners' needs. More recently, the application of serious games has been studied as the use of the 'game mechanism' to facilitate the structured delivery of the learning objectives to the targeted groups of learners. Gee (2007), for instance, identified 36 principles of well-designed games that foster learning. These include fostering an environment for practice, transfer of formerly learned skills, and scaffolding of skills. In this paper, we propose these principles are expressed in the affordances of VLEs. We present an extension of an ALM in light of gaming in 3D VLE. We show evidence that the game in the VLE may offer support for affective learning outcomes for learning a second language.

2.   Method

This research stems from a three-year funded network project entitled Euroversity. The Pan European multidisciplinary project (2011-2014) was comprised of 18 partners, including educators, foreign language instructors, and researchers in various fields across Europe. Practitioners strove to develop a set of supportive resources and guidelines for educators in the process of devising productive and immersive learning experiences in VLEs. Data in this paper were collected during an interview (2011) and follow-up interview (2012) on Skype with the Austrian teacher of the case study course and was recorded using the screen recording software Camtasia. Evidence in this study is identified from these interviews. We apply a descriptive analysis, examining the course of 'Chatterdale', using Robbins et al.'s (2004) ALM. We select this model because as O'Neil, Wainess, and Baker (2005), although he identified classification schemes of learning outcomes according to the cognitive learning outcomes that they support (e.g. repetitive task, memory, and exploration), speculates that research is needed on models of learning that include the affective learning outcomes. In particular, it is suggested that game elements that interact with the instructional environment may support learning outcomes. In Robbins et al.'s (2004) AML, the learning outcomes are based on constructs of *academic goals, self-efficacy, effort, play* and *test anxiety*.

The serious game here is also identified as an epistemic game; an epistemic game relates gameplay objectives and constructs to knowledge or the formalisation of certain cognitive concepts within an epistemological L2 context. The game construct was an alien mystery designed to unfold in the virtual village of Chatterdale in the multi-user VLE of OpenSim. The teacher designed the virtual village by combining elements from the students' imagination and a suburban community setting. The Austrian teacher and her Norwegian colleague invited groups of thirteen-year-old Austrian and Norwegian students to explore the virtual community of Chatterdale and become acquainted with the resources of this virtual setting.

Twelve students were assigned to three groups of size four. Each group had two Austrian students and two Norwegian students. During their visit to Chatterdale, students only encountered their peers and instructors and no other persons in the VLE. This prompted them to raise the question: what happened to the residents of Chatterdale? Inspired by students' inquiries about the local residents, the teacher utilised the semiotic resources of this game-mediated setting to design game-play driven quests where students would interact and collaborate by asserting the role of local investigators baffled by the disappearance of the Chatterdale residents.

As investigators of a potential crime scene, students would collaboratively piece together clues about the disappearance of the Chatterdale residents. We extend the ALM model by introducing the third column (Table 1), proposing that affordances enacted in 3D VLEs can support the Affective Learning Constructs (ALC).

Table 1.   Extending Robbins et al.'s (2004) ALM

ALC	Meaning	Proposed affordances of serious games in virtual environments that support ALC
Academic goals	Learner's actions or goal-directed behaviour	Ability to repeat training (persistence of the virtual learning context)
Self-efficacy	Learner's view of their own abilities to succeed	Dynamic view of abilities through real-time interaction with others in VLEs
Effort	Learner's extent of work on a task	Support of scaffolding through recordings of virtual sessions (e.g. machinima)
Play	Learner's actions without fear of consequences (for fun)	Control over virtual profile (e.g. supports possible actions with consequence to real-self)
Test anxiety	Learner's cognitive concern (e.g. on performance) and emotional reaction (e.g. panic)	Safe learning environment (e.g. no risk or physical harm, ability to leave emotionally stressful virtual situations)

3.   Results

We identify affordances that were evident in the actual case of learning in Chatterdale and the affective constructs, as extracted from the interview data, see Table 2. We find that the VLE enacted support of affective learning outcomes in L2. The interview data for this case is described in greater detail in Hadjistassou and Molka-Danielsen (2016).

Table 2.   Affordances perceived in a case example that support ALC

ALC	Affordances perceived by the instructor of the Chatterdale case study that support ALC
Academic goals	Students' persistence in enhancing their oral skills in L2 by participating in an epistemic game to solve an alien mystery and discover the events that had transpired and that had led to the Chatterdalers' disappearance
Self-efficacy	Austrian and Norwegian high school students' capacity to succeed in solving the mystery and enhancing their oral skills in L2
Effort	Extent to which Norwegian and Austrian students strove to uncover clues and solve the alien mystery while engaging in oral interactions in L2
Play	An intriguing and entertaining game play scenario involving an alien mystery, the disappearance of the Chatterdalers. Students were invited to become private investigators to solve the mystery without any trepidation or fear
Test anxiety	Eliminated test anxiety and emotionality through the use an epistemic game and a final reflective written assignment rather than promoting other assessment techniques that would have enhanced students' anxiety

4.   Discussion and conclusions

This study demonstrated that the game-play nature of the Chatterdale village generated multiple and complex affordances that contributed towards students' enhancement of oral proficiency in the target language, English. Aligning with Zheng (2012) and Haines (2015), new affordances emerged as L2 educators integrated this game-play in the VLE and students engaged and participated in constructive game-oriented interactions. The students' aim to solve the mystery pursued shared *academic goals* to complete the goal-driven task. *Self-efficacy* of students was evident in commitment in solving the mystery, and enhancing oral skills warranted their need to engage in deductive thinking, and explore and interact with the semiotic resources. In terms of *effort*, affordances were enacted during students' attempt to uncover the mysterious conditions that had led to the

Chatterdale residents' disappearance, mediated by their oral exchanges and goal-driven tasks. The *play* was based on students' personal interests, and inquiries involved imagination, mystery, crime, and private investigation in a VLE. The game-play scenario and the multiple semiotic resources, including the goal-directed tasks, enacted affordances for promoting learning outcomes, i.e. promoting oral interactions in English among students. Students did not experience any *test anxiety* since the emphasis was placed on the collaborative nature of the activity and the need to compose a collaborative reflective letter or report instead of introducing formative or summative assessment techniques that would have contributed to enhancing students' level of anxiety.

The findings of this study can guide language educators in framing and investigating the complex web of affordances within the lens of the ALM model. Educators could explore further how affordances are enacted during game-based language learning activities in VLEs based on students' *academic goals, self-efficacy, effort, play*, and *test anxiety*. Above all, the five constructs of Robbins et al.'s (2004) AML can guide language educators in developing a better understanding on how the affordances realised can enhance students' language learning experiences during their participation in epistemic games in VLEs. Future studies need to expand further on the complex role of ALC and address them within the situated context of epistemic games, as games are gaining more cultural and social value and popularity. This is especially beneficial in the case of game-play scenarios in VLE in L2 contexts where the game elements can be integrated constructively and effectively to promote or enhance further students' language learning experiences.

5.   Acknowledgements

We thank the students and teachers for participating in the course that took place during the funded period of the Euroversity Network project, as funded by European Commission (2011-2014).

References

Duncan, I., Miller, A., & Jiang, S. (2012). A taxonomy of virtual worlds usage in education. *British Journal of Educational Technology, 43*(6), 949-964. https://doi.org/10.1111/j.1467-8535.2011.01263.x

Gee, J. P. (2007). *Good video game and good learning: collected essays on video games, learning and literacy*. NY: Peter Lang.

Hadjistassou, S., & Molka-Danielsen, J. (2016) Designing alien mysteries in Chatterdale: an instructor's perspective. In D. Russell & J. M. Laffey (Eds), Handbook of research on gaming trends in P-12 education (pp. 222-236). Hershey, PA: IGI Global. https://doi.org/10.4018/978-1-4666-9629-7.ch011

Haines, K. J. (2015). Learning to identify and actualize affordances in a new tool. *Language Learning & Technology, 19*(1), 165-180.

Monahan, T., McArdle, G., & Bertolotto, M. (2008). Virtual reality for collaborative e-learning. *Computers & Education, 50*(4), 1339-1353. https://doi.org/10.1016/j.compedu.2006.12.008

O'Neil, H. F., Wainess, R., & Baker, E. L. (2005). Classification of learning outcomes: evidence from computer games literature. *The Curriculum Journal, 16*(4), 455-474. https://doi.org/10.1080/09585170500384529

Robbins, S., Lauver, K., Le, H., Davis, D., & Langley, R. (2004). Do psychosocial and study skill factors predict college outcomes? A meta-analysis. *Psychological Bulletin, 130*(2), 261-288. https://doi.org/10.1037/0033-2909.130.2.261

Roussou, M., Oliver, M., & Slater, M. (2006). The virtual playground: an educational virtual reality environment for evaluating interactivity and conceptual learning. *Virtual Reality, 10*(3-4), 227–240. https://doi.org/10.1007/s10055-006-0035-5

Zheng, D. (2012). Caring in the dynamics of design and languaging: exploring language learning in 3D virtual spaces. *Language Sciences, 34*(5), 543-558. https://doi.org/10.1016/j.langsci.2012.03.010

Are commercial 'personal robots' ready for language learning? Focus on second language speech

Souheila Moussalli[1] and Walcir Cardoso[2]

Abstract. Today's language classrooms are challenged with limited classroom time and lack of input, and output practice in a stress-free environment (Hsu, 2015). The use of commercial, readily available tools such as Personal Robots (PRs; e.g. Amazon's Echo, Jibo) might promote language learning by freeing up class time, allowing for a more focused personalized instruction, and giving learners more opportunities for input exposure and output practice in a stress-free environment. PRs are pedagogically valuable because of their built-in Automatic Speech Recognition (ASR) software. This feasibility study investigates the pedagogical use of PRs as tools to extend the language classroom by combining it with traditional in-class, teacher-facilitated interactive practices. We evaluated a commercial PRs' ability to comprehend L2 speech, to provide 'easy-to-understand' feedback, and to deliver accurate results for a set of pre-established questions. Using a survey and interviews, the results highlight the benefits of personalized, computer-mediated instruction as an approach to extend the reach of the classroom. As such, our study contributes to this under-studied area of Computer-Assisted Language Learning (CALL): the pedagogical use of personal robots in L2 education.

Keywords: ASR, personal assistants, personal robots, L2 learning, L2 speech.

1. Introduction

The pedagogical use of technologies can be effective in language education as it has the potential to enhance the input (in both quality and quantity), provide authentic means of communication, and provide learners with personalized and therefore more useful feedback. Examples of these technologies include Text to Speech Synthesizers (TTSs) and ASR, the two tools utilized in the technology employed in PRs.

1. Concordia University, Montréal, Canada; so_mouss@education.concordia.ca
2. Concordia University, Montréal, Canada; walcir.cardoso@concordia.ca

How to cite this article: Moussalli, S., & Cardoso, W. (2016). Are commercial 'personal robots' ready for language learning? Focus on second language speech. In S. Papadima-Sophocleous, L. Bradley & S. Thouësny (Eds), *CALL communities and culture – short papers from EUROCALL 2016* (pp. 325-329). Research-publishing.net. https://doi.org/10.14705/rpnet.2016. eurocall2016.583

TTS is a form of speech synthesis that converts text into oral output. It is available and embedded in mobile applications for computers and mobile devices such as smartphones and tablets. ASR, on the other hand, is a technology that, simply put, allows users to speak rather than type in information. As such, ASR transcribes speech and provides information based on spoken questions such as "How is the weather today in Cyprus?". TTS and ASR technologies are seen in products such as GPS and voice-controlled personal assistants such as Siri and Cortana. Their goal is to recognize intelligible speech with accuracy and efficiency, independent of the speaker's accent, background noise, and other variables.

Few research that has examined the pedagogical use of TTS and ASR have found positive outcomes in language performance and oral self-assessment (Dalby & Kewley-Port, 1999; Derwing, Munro, & Carbonaro, 2000). A study by Liakin, Cardoso, and Liakina (2015) showed that the use of a more recent commercial ASR application had a positive effect on the acquisition of the French vowel /y/. Research in mobile technology has shown overall that language students enjoy using their mobile devices to learn vocabulary (e.g. Thornton & Houser, 2005) and pronunciation (Liakin et al., 2015), and it is beneficial to visual and kinesthetic English as a foreign language learners (Hsu, 2015) because it allows them to improve their L2 pronunciation through self-regulated learning.

Interestingly, we are not aware of any study that investigates the pedagogical potential of PRs such as Amazon Echo and Jibo in L2 education. To address this gap, this study investigates L2 learners' perceptions of the personal robot Echo as a pedagogical tool by addressing the following research question: What are learners' perceptions of using a personal robot (Echo) as a pedagogical tool? In the analysis, we considered a number of variables that could affect learners' perceptions: ease of use, options for self-regulation, motivation and, more importantly, opportunities for input and output practice.

2.   Method

2.1.   Participants and design

Four female intermediate-level English learners (equivalent to B1-B2 levels in the Common European Framework of Reference for languages) interacted with Echo in order to assess its pedagogical usefulness in terms of ease of use, options for self-regulation, opportunities for input/output practice, and their motivation to use it. Their interactions, which lasted 30 minutes on average, included asking Echo a pre-established set of questions (to find out the tool's ability to understand different phonemes and stress patterns) as well as learner-generated questions. Later, participants completed a survey about their perceptions and attitudes towards Echo, followed by a semi-structured interview.

Due to its popularity and low cost, we adopted Amazon Echo (Figure 1), a 23.5 cm cylinder speaker that provides oral answers to questions asked and connects to its associated app, the cloud-based voice service Alexa. The Alexa app is the actual voice recognizer that functions as a companion to Echo for setup, remote control, and a set of enhanced features.

Figure 1. A personal robot: Amazon Echo

2.2. Procedure

Participants initially filled out a background questionnaire to report on their language learning experience and personal information. They then interacted with Echo for approximately 30 minutes using a set of questions and commands (n=26, related to general information and games) and learner-generated questions. After their interaction, participants were given a 17-item survey using a 5-point Likert scale (1=strongly disagree and 5=strongly agree) to quantify their responses to a number of statements about their perceptions (e.g. 'Echo is able to understand me'). After the survey, a semi-structured interview was conducted with each participant.

3. Analysis and results

For the survey, means and standard deviations were calculated for each item, as illustrated in abridged format in Table 1.

Table 1. Survey results: learners' perceptions

Statements	MEAN	SD
I felt more comfortable speaking English using Echo than I would in other types of classroom activities	3.75	0.96
I felt more comfortable speaking English while using Echo than I would in front of the teacher	3.75	0.96
I would like to use Echo to learn other languages	4.25	1.50
Echo is a great tool to learn a language	4.00	1.15
Echo is able to understand me	3.25	0.50
Echo's voice is easy to understand	4.25	0.96
I enjoyed using Echo in this project	4.75	0.50

As indicated in Table 1, participants enjoyed their experience using Echo as a pedagogical tool in all of the items included. To summarize the key points, they felt comfortable speaking in this type of computer-mediated communication (3.75), and consider it a great tool to learn languages (4). In addition, they found that Echo was able to comprehend their requests (3.25), was intelligible (4.25), and that their experience was overall enjoyable (4.75).

The transcriptions of the interviews were analyzed and categorized as relating to one of the four topics of the research question: ease of use, autonomy, opportunity for input and output practice, and motivation. We found that participants considered Echo user-friendly, enjoyable, helpful for language learning and fun; as originally written: "It's the first time I talk with the machine, so I found it… c'est amusant [it's fun]"; and "I was very motivated, I want to explore". Participants also found that Echo was helpful for learning pronunciation and vocabulary: "I can hear her to approve my English, so I can hear the way she talk and I learn from her the pronunciation"; "It increase the understanding of pronunciations and some vocabulary". Participants also expressed that they received good implicit feedback that encouraged repetition: "I think it's more encouraging, if you have to repeat, it's like she don't understand you, you can be better the next time". Our findings also revealed Echo as a helpful teacher-facilitated tool to extend the reach of classroom: "I found it very helpful maybe in classrooms, to help teachers maybe". Nevertheless, some participants questioned the use of machine-based interactions, and reported problems with the speech recognizer that sometimes could not understand their requests.

4. Discussion and conclusions

This feasibility study investigated the pedagogical use of a PR (Echo) for L2 education and its potential to provide speaking opportunities outside the classroom and consequently improve one's pronunciation skills. Our results corroborate previous research in terms of ease of use and assisting in pronunciation practice (Liakin et al., 2015), providing opportunities for input exposure and output practice (e.g. Derwing et al., 2000), and motivating students to learn on their own. As such, these results can serve as a starting point to a better understanding of this type of learning environment, one that is able to cater to different learning styles and that can extend the reach of the classroom and thus promote self-regulated learning. We hope that our study will pave the way for this under-studied area of CALL: the use of commercial, readily available personal robots as tools for L2 education.

References

Dalby, J., & Kewley-Port, D. (1999). Explicit pronunciation training using automatic speech recognition technology. *CALICO, 16*(3), 425-445.

Derwing, T. M., Munro, M. J., & Carbonaro, M. (2000). Does popular speech recognition software work with ESL speech? *TESOL Quarterly, 34*(3), 592-603. https://doi.org/10.2307/3587748

Hsu, L. (2015). An empirical examination of EFL learners' perceptual learning styles and acceptance: SR-based computer-assisted pronunciation training. *CALL, 28*, 1-20.

Liakin, D., Cardoso, W., & Liakina, N. (2015). The acquisition of French /y/ in a mobile-assisted learning environment. *CALICO, 32*(1), 1-25.

Thornton, P., & Houser, C. (2005). Using mobile phones in English education in Japan. *Journal of Computer Assisted Learning, 21*, 217-228. https://doi.org/10.1111/j.1365-2729.2005.00129.x

The Digichaint interactive game
as a virtual learning environment for Irish

Neasa Ní Chiaráin[1] and Ailbhe Ní Chasaide[2]

Abstract. Although Text-To-Speech (TTS) synthesis has been little used in Computer-Assisted Language Learning (CALL), it is ripe for deployment, particularly for minority and endangered languages, where learners have little access to native speaker models and where few genuinely interactive and engaging teaching/learning materials are available. These considerations lie behind the development of *Digichaint*, an interactive language learning game which uses *ABAIR* Irish TTS voices. It provides a language-rich learning environment for Irish language pedagogy and is also used as a testbed to evaluate the intelligibility, quality and attractiveness of the *ABAIR* synthetic voices.

Keywords: interactive language learning games, text-to-speech synthesis, Irish.

1.   Introduction

This paper describes the development and some of the evaluations carried out of a prototype interactive platform for Irish language learning, *Digichaint,* which uses TTS voices developed within the *ABAIR* initiative (www.abair.ie) at Trinity College, Dublin. *Digichaint* is one of three distinct prototype CALL platforms (see Ní Chiaráin & Ní Chasaide, 2015, 2016) aligned to current task-based language learning/teaching principles, where (incorporating TTS) the spoken language is central. *Digichaint* explores the potential of interactive speech-based games for Irish language pedagogy and serves as a testbed for evaluating the newly developed TTS voices.

Digichaint was adapted from *The Language Trap* (Peirce & Wade, 2010), an online casual educational game for teaching German to students preparing for the

1. Trinity College, Dublin, Ireland; neasa.nichiarain@tcd.ie
2. Trinity College, Dublin, Ireland; anichsid@tcd.ie

How to cite this article: Ní Chiaráin, N., & Ní Chasaide, A. (2016). The Digichaint interactive game as a virtual learning environment for Irish. In S. Papadima-Sophocleous, L. Bradley, & S. Thouësny (Eds), *CALL communities and culture – short papers from EUROCALL 2016* (pp. 330-336). Research-publishing.net. https://doi.org/10.14705/rpnet.2016.eurocall2016.584

Irish pre-university examinations, using diphone synthesis. *Digichaint* used *The Language Trap* graphics and development framework to design a game suited to a similar cohort of Irish language learners.

2. Motivation

2.1. The Irish language context

Using synthetic voices in interactive learning games may be far more important to the pedagogy of an endangered minority language like Irish, than of a majority language. Irish is spoken as a community language only in limited *Gaeltacht* regions in the West of Ireland, but as the country's first national language, is a compulsory subject taught to school leaving age. One major challenge with the teaching of Irish is the lack of exposure to native speaker models (most teachers are L2 speakers), and there has tended to be an overemphasis on written and grammatical competence.

A further major problem concerns motivation. The dearth of modern pedagogical resources makes it difficult to engage the learner. It is clear that the educational process is important to the long-term survival of the language – not only in terms of its transmission through teaching, but also in fostering engagement with the language. The synthesis-based CALL applications being piloted could contribute, not only in facilitating more extensive exposure to the spoken language and in developing aural/oral skills, but should also help to engage learners, complementing current classroom practices.

2.2. TTS synthetic voices in CALL

TTS has not been widely used to date in CALL (Gupta & Schulze, 2012). As mentioned, the need is not as great in the major languages, given the widespread availability of native speaker models. The lack of TTS takeup probably also reflects the fact that many systems yield relatively poor quality speech output, particularly in terms of prosody, clarity and consistency (Sha, 2010). Evaluations on the use of synthetic speech for CALL purposes are scant, pertain to its use in rather restricted settings, and do not include the gaming environments considered here. In the case of the Irish voices, there has been no formal evaluation to date. Therefore, in *Digichaint,* voices for two main dialects (Connaught and Ulster) are incorporated and evaluated for intelligibility, quality and attractiveness

3. Structure and principal features of *Digichaint*

Digichaint is an interactive guided dialogue that allows students to progress through a virtual world of a hotel and its surroundings. The learner selects the gender/dialect for their own character – male: Connaught Irish / female: Ulster Irish – which were the only choices available in ABAIR at the time. The learner is tasked with seeking the missing half of his/her winning Lottery ticket, mistakingly discarded, but held by one of eight characters in the hotel. To converse with other characters the user selects phrases from a menu of up to four possible options shown on the screen and spoken aloud (Figure 1). The goal is not to reveal one's true purpose to avoid being double-crossed. When the holder of the other half of the ticket is eventually identified, the learner must negotiate how the winnings are to be split. The game can take a great number of pathways as the user controls who to speak to at any given point: the choice of conversational turn determines the subsequent options (868 utterances were created for the game). A fragment of the game's structure is shown in Figure 2. The game lasts approximately 25 minutes.

Figure 1.   Screenshot from the virtual learning environment *Digichaint*

Given only two baseline voices in ABAIR, a major challenge was to provide for the extended cast of the game. To differentiate voices, pitch and speed manipulations were carried out. Some manipulations rendered the voice somewhat sinister, however. While this did not harm the story's narrative, it does appear to impact on the TTS evaluations (see Results and discussion below).

As mentioned in Ní Chiaráin (2014),

> "[t]he game features **linguistic adaptivity**[, i.e.] the language level of the game adapts to the user's language level: as the user chooses more complex structures, the options on offer become more complex, accordingly. **Performance feedback and motivational support** are provided through a particular companion character in the game who, when requested, will tell the player that his/her selections are excellent, good, poor, etc. **Meta-cognitive hints** on how well the player is doing appear as thought bubbles linked to the main character" (p. 83, emphasis added).

115 **dictionary entries**, which give the English translation of particular words and phrases, can be accessed by clicking on underlined words in the text. Learners receive **feedback** at the end on their path through the game, their star rating, words/phrases they looked up in the dictionary, etc., and this information is retained for future revision.

Figure 2.   Overview visual representation of a section of *Digichaint* illustrating multiple pathways

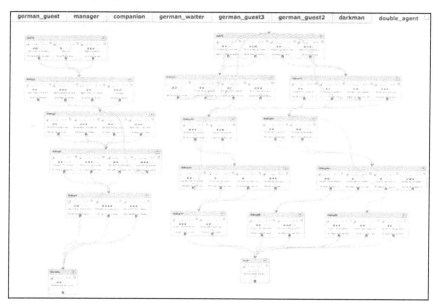

4. Evaluation

Evaluation of the TTS voices was carried out online by 250 16-17 year old pupils (182 female, 68 male) in 13 schools nationwide: these included Gaeltacht (rural), Irish-medium (urban), and English-medium schools (both rural and urban). A pre-game questionnaire elicited background details on individual respondents. Pupils then played the game and gave reactions by way of a post-game questionnaire (Likert 5-point scale).

5. Results and discussion

Pupils' opinions on the TTS voices were elicited in terms of the five questions (Ní Chiaráin, 2014) listed in Table 1. Overall, responses to the quality of the voices were positive. 70% *agreed/agreed completely* that the language level was right (Q1): as pupils differed widely in proficiency one could expect their level to affect intelligibility ratings. Q2 sought to establish specific difficulty with *dialect* variation, and surprisingly low numbers reported difficulty. Intelligibility ratings (Q3) were broadly positive: 56% *agreed/agreed completely* that the voices were sufficiently clear to make the speech intelligible (as against 28% *disagree/disagree completely*). Attractiveness ratings (Q4) were rather low, with only 43% rated as *attractive/very attractive* (what might be considered 'attractive' was left open). As some characters had distorted voice quality the low rating was expected. The quality ratings (Q5) are reasonably high at 62%, although the inclusion here too of distorted voices has impacted. The ratings for attractiveness and quality, and even intelligibility, must be interpreted in conjunction with responses to the other two platforms (not covered here) where no voice distortions were included and ratings were considerably higher: *intelligibility* and *quality* both scored 73% and *attractiveness* scored 57% (Ní Chiaráin, 2014).

Table 1. Questions and results for *Digichaint* evaluation

Q1.1 The overall standard of the Irish used in this game is at about the right level for me		
Completely disagree	4	1.6%
Disagree	40	16%
Neutral	30	12%
Agree	130	52%
Agree completely	46	18.4%
Q1.2 If you feel the Irish used is not at the right level, is this because it was...		
Too difficult	54	48.6%

Too easy	57	51.4%
Q2. Did you experience particular difficulties with the dialects that are used in Digichaint?		
Definitely some difficulty	1	0.4%
Probably some difficulty	75	30%
Neutral	44	17.6%
Probably no difficulty	107	42.8%
Definitely no difficulty	23	9.2%
Q3. The synthesised voices were sufficiently clear to make the speech intelligible		
Completely disagree	14	5.6%
Disagree	55	22%
Neutral	42	16.8%
Agree	115	46%
Agree completely	24	9.6%
Q4. Please give your opinion on the attractiveness of the voices:		
Very unattractive	12	4.8%
Unattractive	75	30%
Neutral	58	23.2%
Attractive	92	36.8%
Very attractive	13	5.2%
Q.5 Please give your opinion on the quality of the synthesised voices: to what extent do you think the voices are adequate for the type of game presented here?		
Completely inadequate	3	1.2%
Inadequate	49	19.6%
Neutral	44	17.6%
Adequate	134	53.6%
Totally adequate	20	8%

6.   Conclusions

Bearing this in mind, there is broadly positive support for the use of the Irish TTS voices in such interactive platforms. Note that evaluations of TTS are highly specific to the quality of the individual voices and there is great variability across systems. Evaluations capture a point in time: even since these tests, the Irish voices have been improved and we expect that a similar evaluation would now yield higher ratings. Importantly, we now know that the voices are adequate for this application and we now have an evaluation method that will serve for testing the TTS voices as development continues.

Furthermore, evaluations of synthesis quality are relative to the context of evaluation. When proposing to deploy TTS in CALL platforms, evaluations should be carried out using multiple real-life platforms and real users, rather than relying on laboratory-based, decontextualized evaluations, as are the norm in TTS evaluation.

7.   Acknowledgements

Sincere thanks to Dr Neil Peirce and Prof. Vincent Wade of KDEG, Trinity College, Dublin. This work was partially funded at different times by SFI/CNGL, the Department of Arts, Heritage and the Gaeltacht (*ABAIR*) and by An Chomhairle um Oideachas Gaeltachta & Gaelscolaíochta (*CabairE*).

References

Gupta, P., & Schulze, M. (2012). *Human language technologies (HLT)*. http://www.ict4lt.org/en/en_mod3-5.htm

Ní Chiaráin, N. (2014). *Text-to-speech synthesis in computer-assisted language learning for Irish: development and evaluation*. Doctoral thesis. CLCS, Trinity College, Dublin.

Ní Chiaráin, N., & Ní Chasaide, A. (2015). Evaluating synthetic speech in an Irish CALL application: influences of predisposition and of the holistic environment. In S. Steidl, A. Batliner, & O. Jokisch (Eds), *SLaTE 2015: 6th Workshop on Speech and Language Technologies in Education* (pp. 149-154). Leipzig, Germany.

Ní Chiaráin, N., & Ní Chasaide, A. (2016). Chatbot technology with synthetic voices in the acquisition of an endangered language: motivation, development and evaluation of a platform for Irish. In *10th edition of the Language Resources and Evaluation Conference, 23-28 May 2016* (pp. 3429-3435). Portorož, Slovenia.

Peirce, N., & Wade, V. (2010). Personalised learning for casual games: the "Language Trap" online language learning. In *Proceedings of the Fourth European Conference on Game Based Learning (ECGBL 2010)* (pp. 306-315). Copenhagen, Denmark: Bente Meyer.

Sha, G. (2010). Using TTS voices to develop audio materials for listening comprehension: a digital approach. *British Journal of Educational Technology, 41*, 632-641. https://doi.org/10.1111/j.1467-8535.2009.01025.x

Mingling students' cognitive abilities and learning strategies to transform CALL

Efi Nisiforou[1] and Antigoni Parmaxi[2]

Abstract. Language researchers have identified a number of elements related to language performance. One of these factors is individual attributes of the language learners or their cognitive ability. In the fall semester 2015, 18 undergraduates of Greek for academic purposes language course of a public university in Cyprus participated in the study. This research work attempts to investigate the relationship between students' Field Dependence-Independence (FDI) cognitive ability and learning strategies within a Computer-Assisted Language Learning (CALL) environment. Students FDI cognitive style was measured on their performance on the Hidden Figures Test (HFT) psychometric tool and classified into Field-Dependent (FD), Field-Mixed or Neutral (FM/FN), and Field-Independent (FI) learners. Statistics and mainly qualitative analyses were used to interpret the data. With the end goal of understanding how learners' FDI cognitive ability intersects in learning within a CALL environment, the article concludes with some directions for further areas of research.

Keywords: FDI cognitive abilities, learning strategies, CALL activities, higher education.

1.   Introduction

There are many aspects to be considered when designing and developing learning environments – physical or digital. The examination of the relationship between individual differences in cognitive styles and learning strategies is one potential area of study that can inform the needs of potential users of these environments and consequently allow for more personalized materials and environments to be developed. Leyu (2001) noted that by taking the cognitive style of language learners' into account,

1. Cyprus University of Technology; efi.nisiforou@cut.ac.cy
2. Cyprus University of Technology; antigoni.parmaxi@cut.ac.cy

How to cite this article: Nisiforou, E., & Parmaxi, A. (2016). Mingling students' cognitive abilities and learning strategies to transform CALL. In S. Papadima-Sophocleous, L. Bradley & S. Thouësny (Eds), *CALL communities and culture – short papers from EUROCALL 2016* (pp. 337-344). Research-publishing.net. https://doi.org/10.14705/rpnet.2016.eurocall2016.585

the instructor could elucidate essential information on learners' characteristics related to the successful learning of a foreign language and consequently relate instructional decisions and teaching methods to learners' individual differences.

As mentioned by Nisiforou and Laghos (2013), "[FDI] is among the most broadly studied of the variety of cognitive style dimensions appearing in the literature (Dragon, 2009)" (p. 81). According to Witkin and his colleagues, the FD and FI dimensions can respond to the different kinds of learning and teaching methods, and they can describe two different ways of processing information (Witkin, Moore, Goodenough, & Cox, 1977). Consequently, the FI learner tends to attain the best success in classroom language learning, in contrary to the FD individual (Chapelle & Heift, 2009). Previous research reported the tendency of FD people to adopt a holistic approach to learning, while FIs revoke the information more analytically (Tinajero, Castelo, Guisande, & Páramo, 2011).

This study consists part of an ongoing project which aims to investigate the relationship between students' FDI cognitive ability and learning strategies within a CALL environment. Hence, the current work attempts to identify students' FDI cognitive ability and learning strategies on a set of language activities. Therefore, the following research question is addressed: what learning strategies do different cognitive groups of learners' exhibit while interacting with a range of language learning environments?

2.   Method

2.1.   Participants

In Fall semester 2015, 18 undergraduates of Greek for academic purposes language course of a public university in Cyprus participated in the study during the 13-week session of their in-classroom instruction. Four participants were excluded from the sample due to non-completion of the HFT psychometric test. The learners' ages range from 19 to 34 years and were recruited from three disciplines; engineering, agricultural studies, and multimedia.

2.2.   Research design

The research design was constructed on the basis of the Task-Based Instruction (TBI) methodological approach. TBI uses tasks or stand-alone activities which require comprehending, producing, manipulating or interacting in the target language (Nunan, 1999).

2.3.   Materials and procedure

The research was conducted in two parts on an individual basis and took place in the classroom. The HFT was administered before the beginning of the classes.

2.3.1.   Psychometric test

The participants were initially categorized by their FDI cognitive style (FD, FN, and FI) on their performance in the HFT (Ekstrom, French, Harman, & Dermen, 1976). The HFT is a psychometric tool that measures the level of an individual's field dependency. It consists of 32 questions, and scores ranged from 1 to 32 (with a maximum of 32 points achievable) on a total completion of 24 minutes. The test presents five simple figures and requests learners to find out which of the five is embedded – with the same size and orientation – in each of the 32 complex patterns (see Figure 1). The testing activity involved in the HFT is a reliable and widely-used approach for determining FDI cognitive dimensions.

Figure 1.   HFT task (Ekstrom et al., 1976)[3]

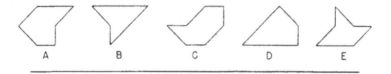

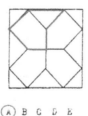

3. The task is to identify which one of the five simpler figures is embedded in the more complex figure. The correct response is the circled letter 'A'.

2.3.2. Learning activities

Students were enrolled in a Greek for academic purposes course which aimed at enhancing their ability to produce language (both oral and written) at an academic level. Throughout this course, students were requested to complete four tasks associated with the four skills:

- Writing: students were tasked to study an academic manuscript and compile it in a short text that can be incorporated in their dissertation.

- Reading comprehension: students were tasked to read an excerpt from an academic manuscript and respond to comprehension questions.

- Speaking: students were tasked to present an academic manuscript related to their dissertation.

- Listening comprehension: students were tasked to listen to an academic lecture and summarize its major points of interest.

Students were requested to elaborate on the process and strategy adopted for completing each of the tasks above, resulting in a list of adopted strategies employed for completing each task. This list consisted of the dataset for capturing students' learning strategies.

3. Results

3.1. Hidden Figures Test

Participants' level of field dependency was measured with the use of the HFT (Nisiforou & Laghos, 2013, 2015). Individuals who scored 10 or below were categorized as FD, those who ranked from 11 to 16 were classified as FN and those who achieved a score of 17 or higher as FI. Participants were classified into their cognitive group as illustrated in Figure 2. The testing activity involved in the HFT is a reliable and widely used approach for determining FDI cognitive dimension. Reliability of the internal consistency of the psychometric test has been validated using Cronbach's alpha coefficient, which is a widely-used index of test reliability. The closer the score is to +1.00, the higher the reliability. In this research study, the

Cronbach's alpha for the HFT was 0.878 (Cronbach, 1977), indicating that items in the psychometric test are correlated to each other.

Figure 2.   Classification and distribution of subjects according to the FDI dimension (N=14)

3.2.   **Learning activities and strategies**

The dataset that consisted of students' learning strategies (see section 2.3.2) was imported into the NVivo qualitative data analysis software version 11. Students' responses were clustered into codes by virtue of thematic coding. The iterative coding approach and the subsequent code saturation elicited a total of 4 main thematic topics which were classified under the four given learning tasks. Figure 3 reflects the thematic categorization of students' learning strategies.

Figure 3.   Students' learning strategies followed for listening comprehension, reading comprehension, presentation skills and production of written text

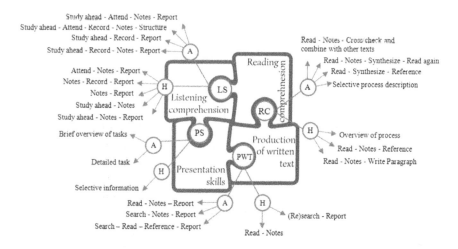

Table 1 demonstrates participants' learning strategies employed for the accomplishment of the four learning tasks by the cognitive group they belong to. Overall, learners' of all three cognitive groups followed a more holistic approach in preference to the analytic approach for the completion of the listening comprehension tasks. The common behavior pattern of solving a listening task is inconsistent with the literature only with regards to the FD and FN group of learners. The results on the FI learners contradict previous studies (e.g. Tinajero et al., 2011) and might have occurred because of the small-scale sample size, seeing that the preferences of the students who adopted a certain learning approach opposed to the other were significantly diverged (only one or two participants).

Table 1. Learning strategies followed by the learners for the completion of the four learning tasks

Participants Code	FDI category	Listening Comprehension (LC)		Reading Comprehension (RC)		Production of Written Text (PWT)		Presentation Skills (PS)	
		AA	HA	AA	HA	AA	HA	AA	HA
P3	FD		✓		✓	✓			✓
P4	FD		✓		✓		✓	✓	
P5	FD		✓	✓			✓	✓	
P9	FD		✓	✓			✓		✓
P14	FD	✓		✓		✓		✓	
P1	FN	✓			✓	✓		✓	
P8	FN		✓	✓		✓		✓	
P10	FN		✓	✓		✓			✓
P12	FN		✓		✓	✓		✓	
P2	FI	✓			✓	✓		✓	
P6	FI	✓			✓		✓		✓
P7	FI		✓	✓		✓			✓
P11	FI		✓	✓			✓		✓
P13	FI		✓	✓		✓		✓	

Notes:
* Listening Comprehension (LC), Reading Comprehension (RC), Production of Written Text (PWT), Presentation Skills (PS); **Analytic approach (AA), Holistic approach (HA)

As for the reading comprehension task, learners applied their analytical skills by extracting detail from its surrounding context. The production of written texts exemplified FDs' and FNs' holistic mode of thought, whereas, strategies adopted by the FNs yielded their ability to analyze info structurally, thus demonstrating their analytic way of thinking. Finally, the speaking ability task revealed individuals' presentation skills. Specifically, those who fall between the FD and FN cognitive dimension revealed a common learning behavior by choosing the analytic pathway, one that identifies the parts of a task and breaks it down into smaller sub-tasks. On the other hand, FIs pursued a holistic mode of thought by seeing each task as a whole and not being able to break it down into smaller parts.

4.   Discussion and conclusion

This work has made progress toward the goal of better understanding the link between individual differences and use of learning activities within a CALL environment. Previous research reported that FD people have a holistic approach to learning, while FIs revoke the information more analytically (Tinajero et al., 2011). The current study found that the capacity to spontaneously shift back and forth between analytic and holistic modes of thought differs according to the nature of the learning task the learner is engaged with.

The data provided additional evidence that more work is needed to provide instructional design principles for the development of learning environments and materials that support different cognitive ability language learners. Awareness of cognitive style may be greatly beneficial for teachers and instructional designers, as they can inform instructional decisions and teaching methods. Future studies of learning strategy usage hold potential for matching learners with appropriate instructions and provide a particularly challenging application for this line of research.

References

Chapelle, C. A., & Heift, T. (2009). Individual learner differences in CALL: the field independence/ dependence (FID) construct. *Calico Journal, 26*(2), 246-266.

Cronbach, L. J. (1977). *Educational psychology* (3rd ed.). New York: Harcourt Brace Jovanovich.

Dragon, K. (2009). *Field dependence and student achievement in technology-based learning: a meta-analysis*. Master thesis. University of Alberta, Alberta.

Ekstrom, R. B., French, J. W., Harman, H. H., & Dermen, D. (1976). *Manual for kit of factor-referenced cognitive tests*. Princeton, NJ: Educational Testing Services.

Leyu, Q. (2001). A consideration of learners' individual differences in classroom language teaching. *Memoires of Fukui University of Technology, 31*(2), 79-86.

Nisiforou, E. A. (2013). Using eye tracking and electroencephalography to assess and evaluate students' cognitive dimensions. *Proceedings of the Doctoral Consortium at the European Conference on Technology Enhanced Learning 2013 (EC-TEL 2013), Paphos, Cyprus, September 17-18, 2013* (pp. 79-86). http://ceur-ws.org/Vol-1093/paper12.pdf

Nisiforou, E. A., & Laghos, A. (2013). Do the eyes have it? Using eye tracking to assess students cognitive dimensions. *Educational Media International, 50*(4), 247-265. https://doi.org/10.1080/09523987.2013.862363

Nisiforou, E., & Laghos, A. (2015). Field dependence–independence and eye movement patterns: investigating users' differences through an eye-tracking study. *Journal of Interacting with Computers, 28*(4), 407-420. https://doi.org/10.1093/iwc/iwv015

Nunan, D. (1999). *Second language teaching and learning.* Boston: Heinle & Heinle Publishers.

Tinajero, C., Castelo, A., Guisande, A., & Páramo, F. (2011). Adaptive teaching and field dependence-independence: instructional implications. *Revista Latinoamericana De Psicología, 43*(3), 497-510.

Witkin, H., Moore, C., Goodenough, D., & Cox, P. (1977). Field-dependent and field-independent cognitive styles and their educational implications. *Review of Educational Research, 47*(1), 1-64. https://doi.org/10.3102/00346543047001001

Taking English outside of the classroom through social networking: reflections on a two-year project

Louise Ohashi[1]

Abstract. In Japan, like most English as a Foreign Language (EFL) contexts, students have few opportunities to use English in daily life, and this limits their ability to develop their language skills. To address this, many teachers provide homework tasks and guide students towards autonomous learning. In an effort to do the latter, a private Facebook group was created for students at a women's university in Tokyo. Through the group, the teacher aimed to provide out-of-class opportunities for English communication; facilitate access to English-language resources; motivate students to study/use English; and create a learning community that had student leaders. This article draws on a small-scale questionnaire, participant interviews, and activity within the Facebook group to examine the extent to which these goals were achieved.

Keywords: independent learning, learning community, Facebook.

1.   Introduction

The Japanese government has described English proficiency as "crucial for Japan's future" (MEXT, 2014, Background to the Reform section, para. 1) and implemented numerous strategies to help students develop it. Despite this, proficiency is still far from reach for most secondary school students (The Japan Times, 2016) and Japanese speakers generally achieve below-average scores on proficiency exams (ETS, 2016). At university level, motivation can be low, particularly among students who are studying English only because it is required, but many students I taught at a women's university in Tokyo expressed the desire to improve their English skills, and some showed a willingness to look beyond coursework. Although students can search for learning opportunities themselves, teachers can also play an important role in supporting autonomous learning (Reinders & Hubbard, 2013; Smith & Craig, 2013). In an attempt to

---

1. Meiji University, Tokyo, Japan; ohashi@meiji.ac.jp

How to cite this article: Ohashi, L. (2016). Taking English outside of the classroom through social networking: reflections on a two-year project. In S. Papadima-Sophocleous, L. Bradley & S. Thouësny (Eds), *CALL communities and culture – short papers from EUROCALL 2016* (pp. 345-350). Research-publishing.net. https://doi.org/10.14705/rpnet.2016.eurocall2016.586

---

do so, I created a Facebook group for my students. The main aims of the group were to provide out-of-class opportunities for English communication, facilitate access to English-language resources, motivate students, and create a learning community that included student leaders.

2. Method

2.1. Managing the Facebook group

I created a private Facebook group in May 2014 and in the following two years invited approximately 400 students from my English classes and a previous Facebook project (Ohashi, 2014) to join. Membership was completely voluntary and had no bearing on homework or grades. Those who wanted to participate sent me a request through the Facebook group, and once approved they could write on the group's 'wall', read other members' posts and comments, and add new members. In the first two years, 145 students joined the group.

2.2. Data collection and analysis

Data collection took three forms. First, posts and comments were tallied, and posts were categorised by type to identify patterns in teacher and student contributions. The number of posts each student made were recorded, the search bar was used to check if each member had commented, and the 'seen by' function was used to check if they had read/seen posts. Second, an online questionnaire (N=30) was used to gather basic information about participation and motivation. Finally, two students were interviewed to obtain more detailed accounts of students' experiences and views.

3. Results and discussion

As outlined above, the Facebook group was created with four aims in mind. These are examined one by one in the sections below.

3.1. Providing opportunities for English communication

There was strong evidence of students taking the opportunity to communicate in English, as shown by their 215 posts and 1000-plus comments. Some of their posts and the 186 that I made sparked lengthy threads involving multiple students, with the longest eliciting over 30 comments. However, although 145 students joined the group within its first two years, only 69 of them posted. Furthermore, posting was not evenly shared by these students, with some posting multiple times (N=37) but others posting only once (N=32). 50% of questionnaire respondents did not post more frequently (or at all) because they lacked time, 23% were deterred by their shyness, and 20% felt under-confident. Confidence was affected by the high level of some contributions, with one student noting, "I feel like I have to write high level, influential posts like [other members] do, so I cannot post much. I feel like it's difficult for me to write motivating posts like that"[2]. While posting was challenging, commenting appeared to be less so, with 90 students writing comments. The remaining 55 students never wrote anything, but they all participated as readers. Questionnaire results (N=30) reflect the patterns shown above, indicating that students were more likely to read posts (100%) and read comments (97%) than write comments (70%) or write posts (60%). The output (writing) figures suggest that the opportunity to communicate was not taken up by some. However, *reading* messages from their teacher and peers was one side of a communicative activity, and feedback from the questionnaire showed that 90% of participants read other students' posts 'often' or more frequently, with even higher figures for the teacher's posts (97%). Therefore, it can be concluded that all students engaged in at least one-way communication, with two-way communication occurring between those who chose to interact by reading *and* writing.

3.2. Assisting students to access English-language resources

This aim was met through a combination of my efforts and those of the students. 41 of my posts had links to educational materials and an additional 26 were provided by the learners. Materials shared ranged from video clips and news articles to quizzes and book recommendations, with the majority primarily useful for developing listening, reading and vocabulary skills. In addition to this, I uploaded 26 posts about English-language competitions and events, and the students posted 30 more. These posts provided information about things like speech competitions, guest lectures, debates, and lunchtime English chat sessions, with most focusing on face-to-face opportunities to listen and speak.

3.3. Motivating students to study and use English

In recent years there have been many studies that highlight the complexity of L2 learner motivation (e.g. Apple, Da Silva, & Fellner, 2013; Dörnyei & Ushioda, 2013;

---

2. Translated from Japanese

Ushioda, 2013). In this study, motivation was addressed in a very limited way by asking students (in the questionnaire and interviews) if and how the Facebook group motivated them. Some students reported being motivated by the efforts of others, with one explaining, "[t]his group motivate[s] me because I feel like studying English harder and harder when I read posts". Members did not need to be good at English to motivate others, with one student noting, "[s]ome are not good at writing English here but they are trying to improv[e] their skills by continuing to write posts. That's impress[ive] and [makes] me feel like studying more". The group could also push students to try when they were unmotivated: "[w]hen I am tired of studying English, I read the posts in this group and they encourage me to keep it up"[3]. Furthermore, there was evidence to suggest that knowing what others were doing was motivating, with one student explaining, "[w]hen I read about other students going overseas I want to go too, and that makes me want to use English more"[4]. Although the impact the group had on each and every member remains unknown, the questionnaire responses, interviews, and comments exchanged within the Facebook group provide some evidence of its motivating effects.

3.4.   Creating a learning community with student leaders

The students in this group took on four different roles, as shown in Figure 1. Those on the fringe were *passive*, only participating as readers (N=55). Those slightly closer to the centre were *responsive*, reacting to what they read by commenting (N=21). The third role, which was more *productive,* involved not only reading and reacting, but also providing posts for others to read (N=56), and those who assumed the fourth role were *leaders* who did all of these things and actively tried to engage others (N=13).

Figure 1.   Roles within the Facebook group

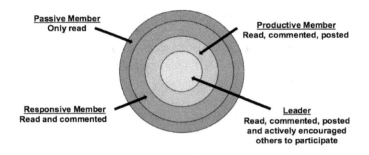

I adopted the leader role, posting 186 times, commenting on all of the students' posts, and responding to their comments. In addition, I prompted members to post and comment, with 34 of my posts devoted to asking new members to post and/ or soliciting contributions from the group. Furthermore, many of my other posts included questions. As noted above, 13 leaders emulated my role, and although their participation was more limited than mine, they were pro-active members who encouraged others in their learning community to participate. When two of the leaders were interviewed, they suggested ways to help passive students into more active roles. One recommended creating opportunities for students to meet face-to-face, as this would make them feel more comfortable writing in the group. The other suggested encouraging students to press 'like' as it shows writers that others have read their posts. This student acknowledged the reciprocal relationship between readers and writers, noting that "writers motivate the reader, but also the reader can motivate the writer to write more" by reacting to them.

4.   Conclusions

The preliminary findings of this investigation suggest that the private Facebook group provided students with opportunities to communicate in English outside of class, gave them access to a wide range of English-language resources, and motivated some of them to study and use English. In addition, there was evidence that the group had evolved into a learning community that was not solely teacher-led, as some students had taken on leadership roles. The benefits reported by students make it worthwhile to continue hosting the group, and may serve as an incentive for those who are considering offering similar opportunities to their students.

5.   Acknowledgements

I would like to thank the students who participated in the questionnaire and interviews for their assistance with this research.

References

Apple, M., Da Silva, D., & Fellner, T. (Eds.). (2013). *Language learning motivation in Japan.* Bristol: Multilingual Matters.

Dörnyei, Z., & Ushioda, E. (2013). *Teaching and researching motivation* (2nd ed.). Oxon: Routledge.

ETS. (2016). *Test and score data summary for TOEFL iBT tests: January 2015 – December 2015 test data.* Educational Testing Service. https://www.ets.org

MEXT. (2014, September 26). *Report on the future improvement and enhancement of English education (outline): five recommendations on the English education reform plan responding to the rapid globalization.* Ministry of Education, Culture, Sports, Science and Technology Japan. http://www.mext.go.jp

Ohashi, L. (2014). Understanding what motivates and deters language learners: an experiment with Facebook groups. *PeerSpectives, 12,* 26-27. http://peerspectives.files.wordpress.com/2010/04/louise-ohashi1.pdf

Reinders, H., & Hubbard, P. (2013). CALL and learner autonomy: affordances and constraints. In M. Thomas, H. Reinders, & M. Warschauer (Eds), *Contemporary computer-assisted language learning* (pp. 359-375). London: Bloomsbury Academic.

Smith, K., & Craig, H. (2013). Enhancing the autonomous use of CALL: a new curriculum model in EFL. *CALICO Journal, 30*(2), 252-278. https://doi.org/10.11139/cj.30.2.252-278

The Japan Times. (2016, February 2). *English skills of Japanese students fail to meet government targets.* http://www.japantimes.co.jp

Ushioda, E. (Ed.). (2013). *International perspectives on motivation: language learning and professional challenges.* Basingstoke: Palgrave Macmillan.

Does the usage of an online EFL workbook conform to Benford's law?

Mikołaj Olszewski[1], Kacper Łodzikowski[2], Jan Zwoliński[3], Rasil Warnakulasooriya[4], and Adam Black[5]

Abstract. The aim of this paper is to explore if English as a Foreign Language (EFL) learners' usage of an online workbook follows Benford's law, which predicts the frequency of leading digits in numbers describing natural phenomena. According to Benford (1938), one can predict the frequency distribution of leading digits in numbers describing natural datasets, e.g. river lengths. In such numbers, the digit 1 occurs most frequently, while the digit 9 occurs least-frequently. This counter-intuitive phenomenon attracted the attention of researchers seeking inconsistencies in data, e.g. false tax claims (Miller, 2015). We show that the practical application of Benford's law could extend to detecting abnormal learner behaviour in online EFL products. First, we show that the distributions of leading digits of the number of online activities submitted by EFL learners on an e-learning platform and the time spent on those activities do indeed follow Benford's law. Then, we show that some learners whose behaviour does not conform to Benford's law show online behaviour that is abnormal relative to their peers – in particular, they submit many activities in a few days, which could suggest, for example, poor time management.

Keywords: Benford's law, EFL, e-learning, time on task.

1.   Introduction

Benford (1938) stated that it is possible to predict the frequency distribution of leading digits in numbers composed of four or more digits describing such natural

1. Pearson IOKI, Poznań, Poland; mikolaj.olszewski@pearson.com
2. Pearson IOKI, Poznań, Poland; kacper.lodzikowski@pearson.com
3. Pearson IOKI, Poznań, Poland; jan.zwolinski@pearson.com
4. Pearson PLC, Boston, United States; rasil.warnakulasooriya@pearson.com
5. Pearson PLC during this research, now at Macmillan Learning, New York City, United States; adam.black@macmillan.com

How to cite this article: Olszewski, M., Łodzikowski, K., Zwoliński, J., Warnakulasooriya, R., & Black, A. (2016). Does the usage of an online EFL workbook conform to Benford's law? In S. Papadima-Sophocleous, L. Bradley, & S. Thouësny (Eds), *CALL communities and culture – short papers from EUROCALL 2016* (pp. 351-357). Research-publishing.net. https://doi.org/10.14705/rpnet.2016.eurocall2016.587

datasets as river lengths or city populations. In such numbers, the digit 1 is expected to be the most frequently occurring leading digit (about 30% of cases), while the digit 9 is expected to occur least-frequently (fewer than about 5% of cases), even though the chance of occurrence is intuitively expected to be the same for all leading digits. In recent years, Benford's law attracted the attention of researchers because of its practical use, e.g. identifying tax or vote frauds (Miller, 2015).

In education, Benford's law has been applied to evaluating the chance of picking the correct answer among distractors on a multiple-choice test (Slepkov, Ironside, & DiBattista, 2015). We know of no previous work exploring the application of Benford's law to e-learning of EFL, hence the present study.

2. Method

2.1. Data

According to Nigrini (2012, pp. 21-22), numbers in a dataset are expected to conform to Benford's law if they describe *natural* events or facts such as city populations (rather than, say, computer-generated bank account numbers) and if the dataset has no inherent limit (which excludes, say, exam scores).

We focused on the number of online learning activities completed by EFL learners and the time spent on those activities. The data comes from MyEnglishLab for Speakout Pre-intermediate 1st edition (henceforth 'MyEnglishLab'), an e-learning platform with exercises accompanying a textbook. The online activities comprise twelve units, each of which contain about thirty activities. The platform is aimed at institutions, so most learners analysed here were enrolled in a course set up by their teacher or instructor. The anonymised dataset contains 3,218,624 first attempts of MyEnglishLab activities from 35,265 learners from 18 different countries (speaking 12 different languages).

2.2. Analysis

To see if the number of MyEnglishLab activities completed by learners conforms to Benford's law, we counted the total number of activities submitted (i.e. attempted) daily by each learner. Days with no learner activity were not included. Resubmitting the same activity did not increase the count. For example: if learner A submits 11 activities on Monday and three activities on Tuesday, and Learner B submits four activities on Tuesday and six on Wednesday, the dataset contains the observations {11, 3, 4, 6}. The frequency distribution of the leading digits of these measurements was plotted and compared with the expected trend according to Benford's law.

To see if time spent on those activities conforms to Benford's law, we listed the time (in seconds) that every learner spent on every first submission of a MyEnglishLab activity. Again, the frequency distribution of the leading digits was plotted and compared with Benford's distribution. We ran a Pearson's Chi-squared Goodness-of-Fit test, which is one of several tests used to evaluate if a dataset conforms to Benford's law. Of several such tests available in the BenfordTests R package (Version 1.2.0; Joenssen, 2015), this one was the fastest. Data processing and visualisation were performed in R (Version 3.2.4; R Core Team, 2016) running in RStudio (Version 0.99.893; RStudio, 2016).

3.   Discussion

A visual inspection of Figure 1 shows that the distribution of leading digits of the number of activities submitted daily per learner on MyEnglishLab follows the Benford's law curve closely, with the exception of the digit 1. This means there were more cases of learners submitting either one or between 11 and 19 activities per day than predicted by Benford's law. Despite this, it could be stated that the number of submitted activities (roughly) conforms to Benford's law.

Figure 1.   Distribution of leading digits of the number of submitted activities compared to Benford's distribution

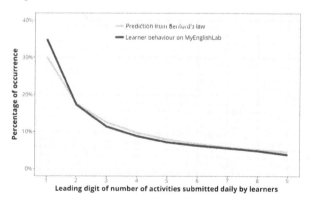

A visual inspection of Figure 2 shows that the distribution of leading digits of time spent on single activities submitted on MyEnglishLab also closely follows Benford's

distribution. Although the digit 1 is an exception again, the fit is better. A similar result was observed for the first two leading digits of time (not shown in this figure).

Figure 2.   Distribution of leading digits of time spent on MyEnglishLab activities compared to Benford's distribution

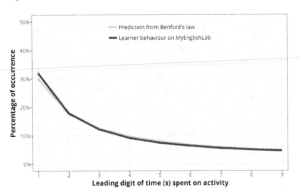

Figure 3 shows learners whose behaviour does not conform to Benford's law. Each thin line represents a learner. Pearson's Chi-squared Goodness-of-Fit test showed that of 12,427 learners who submitted at least 100 MyEnglishLab activities, time on task follows Benford's law for 74% of learners and does not follow Benford's law for 26% of learners ($\alpha = 0.05$).

Figure 3.   Distribution of leading digits of time spent on MyEnglishLab activities by learners whose behaviour does not conform to Benford's law

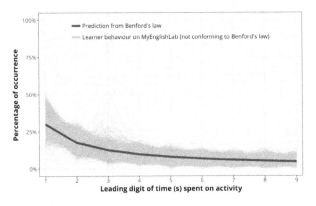

While exploring backend logs of learner interactions with MyEnglishLab, we noticed that some of the 26% of learners whose behaviour does not conform to

Benford's law share three characteristics. First, even if they were enrolled in a course that lasted a couple of months, they used the platform to submit exercises only for a couple of days. Second, on those few days of activity, the learners submitted an unusually high number of activities, often receiving high scores. Third, learners seemed to have worked with these activities simultaneously, i.e. they opened one activity after another in quick succession (probably in separate browser tabs although front-end interactions such as browser focus were not tracked here) and then, after some time, quickly submitted one activity after another. This could be an indication of cramming.

Figure 4 shows an example of one such learner. This learner took part in what seemed to have been an intensive two-month course, judging by the online activity of other participants in that course. While other learners in the course submitted activities relatively frequently, this learner submitted 195 activities on three different days (within a span of 10 days), scoring ~96% per activity, on average. On each such day, the learner opened a number of activities almost at once, spent more time on each following activity, and then submitted them all almost at once. This happened towards the end of the course, so completing online activities might have been a course requirement.

Figure 4.   Distribution of leading digits of time spent on MyEnglishLab activities by a learner whose behaviour does not conform to Benford's law

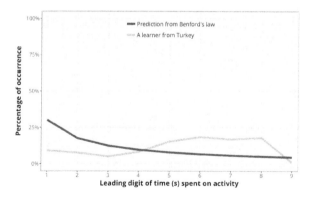

4.   Conclusions

We showed that the distributions of leading digits of the number of online activities completed by EFL learners and the time spent on those activities closely follow Benford's law. The approach used in this paper shows how insights can be revealed in noisy online data, such as the time data, which the standard methods of analysis would not reveal.

Benford's law has been applied for tax fraud detection and our results show that it may also be worth applying it for detection of abnormal learner behaviour. Whereas we do not know if the learners whose behaviour did not conform to Benford's law in this particular study behaved so because of poor time management skills or other factors, Benford's law could help flag such learners to teachers who would then choose the best course of intervention by talking to learners.

Still, our findings are directional and future research should focus on validating such an approach, and its usefulness to teachers. Another strand of research could focus on comparing the computational performance of different tests for evaluating conformity to Benford's law (with operationalising large-scale detection in mind) and comparing this approach to other methods of detection and prediction of learner performance, e.g. those that rely on simpler metrics, such as login frequency.

5.   Acknowledgements

We thank Daniel Roe, Category Director of Pearson English, for granting us permission to share the findings broadly. We also thank Claire Masson and the Pearson English MyEnglishLab team.

References

Benford, F. (1938). The law of anomalous numbers. *Proceedings of the American Philosophical Society, 78*(4), 551-572. http://www.jstor.org/stable/984802

Joenssen, D. W. (2015). *BenfordTests: statistical tests for evaluating conformity to Benford's law* [Computer software]. http://CRAN.R-project.org/package=BenfordTests

Miller, S. J. (Ed.). (2015). *Benford's law: theory and applications.* New Jersey: Princeton University Press. https://doi.org/10.1515/9781400866595

Nigrini, M. J. (2012). *Benford's law: applications for forensic accounting, auditing, and fraud detection.* Hoboken: Wiley. https://doi.org/10.1002/9781119203094

R Core Team. (2016). *The R project for statistical computing* [Computer software]. https://www.R-project.org

RStudio. (2016). *Integrated Development for R* [Computer software]. http://www.rstudio.com

Slepkov, A. D., Ironside, K. B., & DiBattista, D. (2015). Benford's law: textbook exercises and multiple-choice testbanks. *PLoS ONE, 10*(2), 1-13. https://doi.org/10.1371/journal. pone.0117972

Implications on pedagogy as a result of adopted CALL practices

James W. Pagel[1] and Stephen G. Lambacher[2]

Abstract. As part of a longitudinal study on learner and instructor attitudes and patterns of computer and mobile device usage, we have attempted to identify how language instructors and students value their use in L2 learning. During the past five years at Aoyama Gakuin University (AGU) in Tokyo, we have surveyed both students and instructors annually in two separate schools. In the present study, results from the surveys administered to both students and instructors within the two schools are examined and compared, with a focus exclusively on the survey questions corresponding to pedagogically-related issues. Overall, the results show a steady movement on the part of instructors away from a more traditional approach to teaching English, emphasizing grammar and vocabulary memorization, to a more communicative-based approach. Similarly, survey responses from students revealed a clear preference for learner-centered classroom instruction over a traditional grammar-translation and teacher-centered approach.

Keywords: motivation, second language learning, L2, MALL, learner attitudes, instructor practices, grammar translation.

1.   Introduction

Many Japanese undergraduates lack motivation and are often discouraged with their English learning experience, which may be due, in part, to any number of factors, including the emphasis placed on traditional exam-centered or grammar-based English classrooms at a large number of Japanese universities. This lack of motivation and confidence often results in a negative impact on student attitudes and classroom behaviors, leading to long-term and widespread negative learning outcomes (Pagel & Lambacher, 2014). Teachers can often miscalculate their

1. College of Science and Engineering, Aoyama Gakuin University, Tokyo, Japan; jwpagel@yahoo.com
2. School of Social Informatics, Aoyama Gakuin University, Tokyo, Japan; steve.lambacher@gmail.com

How to cite this article: Pagel, J. W., & Lambacher, S. G. (2016). Implications on pedagogy as a result of adopted CALL practices. In S. Papadima-Sophocleous, L. Bradley, & S. Thouësny (Eds), *CALL communities and culture – short papers from EUROCALL 2016* (pp. 358-362). Research-publishing.net. https://doi.org/10.14705/rpnet.2016.eurocall2016.588

students' needs and the targeting of their curriculum, so that it is either too easy or too difficult, which also results in negative outcomes on student motivation and performance (Dörnyei & Ushioda, 2011).

During the past five years at AGU in Tokyo, we have surveyed both our students and instructors annually within two schools – the College of Science and Engineering and the School of Social Informatics. A key motivating factor for this research has been the total revamping of one of our school's English curriculum, which went into effect in April 2012. The surveys were thus developed to serve as part of a faculty development endeavor to evaluate instructor reactions to the new curriculum, which required all classes be held in Computer-Assisted Language Learning (CALL) classrooms and for instructors to adapt their teaching methods to take full advantage of the available facilities and technology. The total number of student respondents from both schools has averaged nearly 350 annually. Our 'in-house' teaching faculty has been comprised of nine full-time and 26 part-time instructors across the two schools.

At the past two EUROCALL conferences, we reported on patterns and changes in teacher and student attitudes and motivation towards the adoption of CALL/Mobile-Assisted Language Learning (MALL) or L2 learning, which is part of an ongoing study. The overall results revealed both students and faculty preferred the use of MALL and CALL, and found it more motivating and valuable for learning English than traditional practices (Pagel & Lambacher, 2014; Pagel, Lambacher, & Reedy, 2015). In the present study, we focus exclusively on survey questions of the study that corresponded to pedagogically-related issues. The main purpose of the study is on identifying how students and teachers assess resultant changes to language teaching pedagogy. Its primary goal is to better understand the motivation and attitudes of English as a Foreign Language (EFL) students consistent with a move to more communicative-based classes held in CALL classrooms.

2. Methods

The teacher and student surveys consisted of 32 and 47 questions, respectively, which involved Likert scale items measured using a six point semantic scale reporting agreement with the affective items ranging from one (strongly disagree) to six (strongly agree). SurveyMonkey® was used to collect and analyze the survey responses. Instructor questions focused on gauging attitudes on a wide range of pedagogical issues, including learning theory, student learning styles, and general teaching practices. Student questions pertaining to pedagogy were likewise broad, and ranged from attitudes and perceptions of learning styles and outcomes, teaching methodology and materials, as well as motivation and goals for studying English.

2.1.   Student survey

The student survey was administered once annually during a five-year period (2012-2016). On average, each year a total of approximately 350 students from the two schools participated in the study. All participants were native speakers of Japanese mostly from the Kanto region, which includes the nearby prefectures of Saitama, Chiba, and Kanagawa. These were primarily 1st and 2nd year students ranging in age from 19 to 23. The percentages of other demographic variables within this population were as follows: female 33%, male 67%; Science and Engineering majors 50%, Social Informatics majors 50%; freshmen 46%, sophomores 36%, juniors 14%, seniors 4%.

2.2.   Instructor survey

Following Pagel et al.'s (2015) approach, the instructor survey was administered four times during a four-year period (2012-2015). To ensure anonymity, all questions regarding personal information, such as age and nationality, were eliminated. The number of English instructors of the two faculties currently totals 34. While the total number of respondents participating in the study during the first three years averaged only 17, this number increased in 2015 due to an increase in the number of instructors employed within both faculties as a result of an expanded English curriculum.

3.   Results

Due to space limitations, we present here just a brief sampling of the results from both surveys. A higher response rating indicated an increase in agreement and a lower rating indicated an increase in disagreement with the survey items.

3.1.   Students

Student survey responses, in general, revealed relatively low mean ratings for questions dealing with traditional classroom practices, such as the grammar-translation method and vocabulary memorization (3.45 and 3.19, respectively). These results helped to confirm that students felt it was not being emphasized by their instructors in their classrooms. On the other hand, for items that related to perception of the level (3.67), pace (3.69), and understanding (3.77) of classroom activities, students exhibited an overall increasing pattern of agreement during the five-year period.

In response to questions related to learning style preferences (i.e. working alone vs. working in a group), a majority of students preferred the latter (3.46 vs. 3.63, respectively). Also, in response to questions related to extrinsic motivation (e.g. relevancy of English for success in job-hunting) a majority of students agreed that English was vital for their future (3.84). Conversely, an overall decreasing pattern of agreement was observed for the question "studying English *only* to earn course credit for graduation" (3.53), which was encouraging to the authors.

3.2.   Instructors

The instructor ratings were relatively low for survey questions dealing with traditional classroom practices, such as a focus on vocabulary memorization, and grammar mastery, and the use of grammar-translation method as a key component of classroom instruction. For example, the survey question "the use of grammar-translation method as a key component of classroom instruction" received a mean rating of 3.25, while the question "I like to try new things to keep the students motivated" received a mean rating of 5.41, which was considerably high. In general, the results during the four-year period revealed a pattern of steady movement on the part of instructors away from a direction of classroom practice emphasizing a more traditional approach to a greater focus on communicative-based teaching, with a few exceptions.

4.   Discussion and conclusion

A majority of Japanese students feel a reluctance to converse in a foreign language, which may be due to a number of factors. For English educators working as teachers at Japanese universities, it is somewhat rare to find students who go out of their way to hone their English skills. Even Japanese students who have returned to Japan after living and studying overseas for a number of years often feel reluctant to speak out as well, unless they are isolated with other fluent speakers of English. We question the reason for this hesitation to learn a language and unwillingness to use what students have mastered through their language learning experiences. That being said, our students have proved to be interested, motivated learners when having encountered a new pedagogy with the incorporation of information and communications technology both in and out of the classroom. Likewise, our instructors have shown a willingness to be flexible and embrace the new technologies and resultant changes into their teaching pedagogies.

The internal reform incorporating the extensive use of CALL into our school's English curriculum has been the motivating factor behind this research, which has attempted to determine whether technology is being embraced in the classroom, and beyond (i.e. MALL). However, the curriculum reform has not only affected students' study habits, but also placed a burden on the part of instructors, many of whom were unfamiliar with using technology in their instruction and more comfortable with traditional lecture style classes focusing on the grammar-translation method. We found the instructors' general movement away from a direction of classroom practice emphasizing a more traditional approach to a focus on communicative-based teaching, as well as student preferences for it, to be extremely positive – and promising. As language educators are exposed to new technologies and teaching approaches (e.g. the implementation of CALL practices), it is evident that their adaptation is possible, even among traditionally-trained native speakers of Japanese serving as EFL teachers.

We will next turn our attention to a critical yet relatively new area of research in language learning and teaching that relates to the adaptation of the Common European Framework of Reference for languages (CEFR) in Japan (CEFR-J), with the goal of ascertaining to what extent CEFR-J is being understood, adapted, and embraced by CALL educators at universities throughout Japan and Asia, and to compare it with European practices.

References

Dörnyei, Z., & Ushioda, E. (2011). *Teaching and researching motivation* (2nd ed.). Harlow: Longman.

Pagel, J. W., & Lambacher, S. G. (2014). Patterns and effectiveness of mobile device usage by Japanese undergraduates for L2 acquisition purposes. In S. Jager, L. Bradley, E. J. Meima, & S. Thouësny (Eds), *CALL Design: Principles and Practice - Proceedings of the 2014 EUROCALL Conference, Groningen, The Netherlands* (pp. 284-289). Dublin Ireland: Research-publishing.net. https://doi.org/10.14705/rpnet.2014.000232

Pagel, J. W., Lambacher, S., & Reedy, D. W. (2015, August). Instructors' attitudes towards CALL and MALL in L2 classrooms. In F. Helm, L. Bradley, M. Guarda, & S. Thouësny (Eds), *Critical CALL – Proceedings of the 2015 EUROCALL Conference, Padova, Italy* (pp. 458-463). Dublin Ireland: Research-publishing.net. https://doi.org/10.14705/rpnet.2015.000375

Exploring the benefits and disadvantages of introducing synchronous to asynchronous online technologies to facilitate flexibility in learning

Salomi Papadima-Sophocleous[1] and Fernando Loizides[2]

Abstract. This article examines the impact of online synchronous tutorials on eight second language (L2) practitioners enrolled in a Master of Arts (MA) in Computer-Assisted Language Learning (CALL) L2 Curriculum Development and Evaluation module. The module is delivered asynchronously and synchronously (lecture). To accommodate immediate interaction to the instructor and the students, weekly synchronous online tutorials were also included. These tutorials aimed to give the opportunity to learners to get their questions answered immediately and receive instant feedback, reinforce their understanding of the content covered and the assigned tasks, discuss issues of concern, share ideas and knowledge, and interact with the instructor for questions or problems. A mixed-method data collection approach was used (records of student participation, online interviews in the middle of the course and online interviews at the end of the 13-week module). The data analysis indicated a positive attitude towards tutorials, improvement in clarity in participants' understanding of the material studied and development of a sense of comfort and reassurance.

Keywords. e-learning, online synchronous tutorials, CALL teacher-training.

1. Introduction

According to literature, synchronous learning gives the opportunity to participate in meaningful face-to-face online interactions (Harris, Mishra, & Koehler, 2009; Hrastinski, 2008; Simonson, Smaldino, Albright, & Zvacek, 2012). It allows students to ask and teachers to answer questions instantly, and students to interact

1. Cyprus University of Technology Language Centre, Limassol, Cyprus; salomi.papadima@cut.ac.cy
2. University of Wolverhampton Emerging Interactive Technologies, Wolverhampton, UK; fernando.loizides@wlv.ac.uk

How to cite this article: Papadima-Sophocleous, S., & Loizides, F. (2016). Exploring the benefits and disadvantages of introducing synchronous to asynchronous online technologies to facilitate flexibility in learning. In S. Papadima-Sophocleous, L. Bradley, & S. Thouësny (Eds), *CALL communities and culture – short papers from EUROCALL 2016* (pp. 363-368). Research-publishing.net. https://doi.org/10.14705/rpnet.2016.eurocall2016.589

with fellow students and instructors, rather than learning in isolation (Hrastinski, 2008). Synchronous e-learning takes place through lectures, discussions, online tutorials, etc. It offers different ways of interaction, sharing and collaboration, flexibility and personalised learning opportunities (Lorenzo & Ittelson, 2005) in real time online (Higley, 2013). However, it requires setting aside a specific time slot in participants' busy schedule in order to be present (Hrastinski, 2008).

In practice, few instructors incorporate synchronous sessions in their online programmes. There are two reasons for this: (1) the large enrolments in online programmes reduce the chance of effective online interactions, and (2) instructors tend to believe that asynchronous forms of communication such as access to course material by simply clicking on course website links are enough as provision of communication (Wang & Newlin, 2001).

Online courses rely primarily on asynchronous communication for course information delivery; chat rooms are usually the only synchronous communication. This is not organised regularly, because most such courses have large enrolments; also, instructors believe it is enough for students to have access to course material through links on the course website. Moreover, instructors believe they already spend more time preparing web-based than conventional courses.

In earlier modules of our MA in CALL, it was noted that students needed synchronous contact with their instructor, not only during online lectures, but in additional synchronous forms, which would support them in their learning, giving them opportunities to ask questions and clarify issues on a more individual and direct level. Therefore, synchronous tutorials were introduced.

2. Method

This exploratory research focusses on the merits of regular scheduled online synchronous communication between the instructor and students. We hypothesise that such interaction constitutes an important component of the course and enhances and clarifies the information accessed in asynchronous ways.

2.1. Participants

The intervention of online weekly tutorials was implemented for an online MA in CALL 13-week module. Eight students took part with ages ranging from early 20s to 50s. Their teaching experience also varied from 20 years to complete novice.

2.2.   Instrumentation and data analysis procedures

Three techniques were used to collect data: (1) a 13-week record of students' tutorial participations, (2) end of week 5 online interview questions on synchronous learning, and (3) a 23-question (5-point Likert scale) online survey on synchronous learning collected at the end of the module in the form of a Google Form survey.

3.   Results

3.1.   Student tutorial participation

Student weekly tutorial participation was systematically recorded for all 13 weeks.

Figure 1.   Student weekly tutorial participation

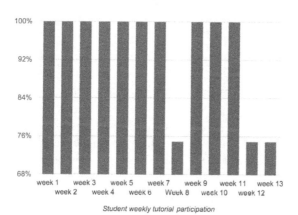

Student weekly tutorial participation

According to participation records, most students participated in the tutorials on a regular basis: all during ten weeks and six during three weeks. When students could not attend during scheduled times, arrangements were made to make up for them. This was indication of the value students put to tutorials.

3.2.   End of week 5 online interview

An online interview was carried out at the end of the week 5 tutorial by the instructor. It aimed at finding out how the eight students valued the tutorials after five weeks. The study revealed the following.

All students found the tutorials beneficial and liked the fact they had the opportunity to meet in real time online to ask questions and have points clarified. Three out of seven felt motivated by the tutorials and found that they made them keep up to date and kept them on their toes.

Students liked the fact that they were not working in isolation. Five of the seven students who had the tutorial with other students liked the fact they had the opportunity to exchange ideas with them. Two students said the tutorials suited their audio/video learning style. Four students liked having the tutorials on a fixed date and time which suited them, particularly halfway through the week; that gave them time before the tutorial to go over the material and be ready during tutorials to ask questions and go over tasks, and have the rest of the week to complete them.

3.3. End of module online survey

Further information regarding student attitudes towards the tutorials was collected at the end of the module with the use of a Google Form. These data revealed the following.

Overall, seven students were satisfied with the tutorials. All students felt very satisfied and four were satisfied with the tutorials' value in helping them improve their professional effectiveness. Seven students found the tutorials a very motivational experience.

Seven students felt the amount of time dedicated to the tutorials met their needs. Regarding the duration of the tutorials, students' opinion varied from 60, 45, 30 to 15 minutes. Two students said "as long as needed". Five students said the tutorials should take place once a week, two students said once a fortnight, and another said they should take place on demand. Six students said they did not find anything they disliked about the tutorials. One said not all tutorials were effective; another said they were sometimes too long. Five students said the addition of the tutorials helped them in their overall performance enhancement, two said very probably and one said probably. All students said they recommend the tutorial to future students.

The conclusions drawn from this survey supported the end of week 5 interview results. All students felt the weekly tutorials helped them in the construction of their weekly knowledge, skills and experiences in the topics covered each week. All the students valued the tutorials. On the whole, students were in favour of regular tutorials and felt a sense of comfort and reassurance.

4.   Discussion and conclusions

The success of e-learning is associated with effective asynchronous and synchronous communication with the materials and the participants. This study examined the impact of online synchronous tutorials with eight second language practitioners enrolled in an MA in CALL Second Language Curriculum Development and Evaluation module. The results suggest that the incorporation of online synchronous tutorials gave the opportunity to students to participate in meaningful face-to-face real time online learning and interaction, share their understanding of the materials studied, both with the instructor and other fellow students, discuss and clarify issues, and achieve a better awareness of the topics studied. They were also given the opportunity to engage in flexible and personalised learning opportunities, in other words to share their learning and not work in isolation. This developed a sense of comfort and reassurance, since the module was delivered online. The tutorials seemed to give an opportunity to students to reassure themselves in their understanding of the concepts covered and the tasks they were required to work on. In some way, the tutorials allowed many students to revisit the content of each week, to clarify concepts discussed in the lectures or presented in the e-learning area, and to clarify what they had to do in terms of tasks. The results support the arguments presented in the literature about the benefits of synchronous learning (Harris et al., 2009; Higley, 2013; Hrastinski, 2008; Lorenzo & Ittelson, 2005; Simonson et al., 2012).

This study has several limitations. The number of participants was only eight students. Students in this study chose to do the MA in CALL, knowing that participation in this course would require synchronous mode. Students in this module may have different abilities and motivation levels than other course populations, which may limit the generalisability of this study.

In conclusion, there are meaningful benefits associated with the inclusion of weekly tutorials in e-learning courses. This module tutorial inclusion allowed the instructor to perceive the level of awareness of new knowledge of students and cater for it during the tutorials and the students to have online face-to-face interaction with their instructor and clarify any misconceptions or difficulties they had with the module.

5.   Acknowledgements

We would like to thank the module students for their participation in this research.

References

Harris, J., Mishra, P., & Koehler, M. (2009). Teachers' technological pedagogical content knowledge and learning activity types: curriculum-based technology integration reframed. *Journal of Research on Technology in Education, 41*(4), 393-416. https://doi.org/10.1080/1 5391523.2009.10782536

Higley, M. (2013). Advantages of using both synchronous and asynchronous technologies in an online learning environment. *eLearning Industry.* http://elearningindustry.com/benefits-of-synchronous-and-asynchronous-e-learning

Hrastinski, S. (2008). Asynchronous & synchronous e-learning. *EDUCAUSE Quarterly, 31*(4), 51-55. http://net.educause.edu/ir/library/pdf/eqm0848.pdf

Lorenzo, G., & Ittelson, J. (2005). An overview of e-portfolios. *EDUCASE Learning Initiative.* http://www.case.edu/artsci/cosi/cspl/documents/eportfolio-Educausedocument.pdf

Simonson, M., Smaldino, S., Albright, M., & Zvacek, S. (2012). *Teaching and learning at a distance: foundations of distance education* (5th ed.). Boston: Pearson.

Wang, A. Y., & Newlin, M. H. (2001). Online lectures: benefits for the virtual classroom. *T.H.E Journal (Technological Horizons in Education), 29*(1), 17-18.

A CALL for evolving teacher education
through 3D microteaching

Giouli Pappa[1] and Salomi Papadima-Sophocleous[2]

Abstract. This paper describes micro-teaching delivery in virtual worlds. Emphasis is placed on examining the effectiveness of Singularity Viewer, an Internet-based Multi-User Virtual Environment (MUVE) as the tool used for assessment of the student teacher performance. The overall goal of this endeavour lies in exploiting the opportunities derived from such an immersive environment in order to provide better distance education. To this end, a total of eight language teacher practitioners from different parts of the world took part in this study and engaged in peer-microteaching as part of their Master of Arts (MA) in Computer Assisted Language Learning (CALL) programme. Data acquisition involved screen recordings of the peer microteaching sessions, statements in participants' reflective journals and both debriefings and written communication within the virtual world. Our results indicated the positive potential of using MUVE platforms as instruments in the assessment of student teacher performance.

Keywords: CALL, teacher education, microteaching, virtual worlds, singularity viewer, MUVE.

1.   Introduction

Recent research reveals that L2 teachers who completed online methodology instruction demonstrated less confidence in their abilities to teach L2 learners (Kissau & Algozzine, 2015). In spite of efforts to better prepare teachers and provide support with emphasis on new technologies, there is a claim that there is need for "better professional development opportunities in the CALL area" (Beaven et al., 2010, p. 7). It is only recently that virtual technology for training in the simulation field has been applied in FL/L2 teacher preparation and education programmes

1. Cyprus University of Technology, Limassol, Cyprus; gp.pappa@edu.cut.ac.cy
2. Cyprus University of Technology, Limassol, Cyprus; salomi.papadima@cut.ac.cy

How to cite this article: Pappa, G., & Papadima-Sophocleous, S. (2016). A CALL for evolving teacher education through 3D microteaching. In S. Papadima-Sophocleous, L. Bradley & S. Thouësny (Eds), *CALL communities and culture – short papers from EUROCALL 2016* (pp. 369-374). Research-publishing.net. https://doi.org/10.14705/rpnet.2016.eurocall2016.590

(Judge & Katsioloudis, 2011). This paper attempts to shed light on how foreign and second language (L2) teaching practices within an MA in CALL online teacher education programme can be extended through virtual worlds. Since the virtual technology for training in the simulation field has only been recently applied in L2 teacher preparation and education programmes (Judge & Katsioloudis, 2011), the use of microteaching techniques, supported by the use of Singularity Viewer environment, are explored for the development of 3D microteaching, as part of the online microteaching component of the programme. Questions regarding the effectiveness of Singularity Viewer as a tool for microteaching delivery and the extent to which microteaching in virtual worlds raises student teacher awareness of the complexity of language teaching through innovative technologies are analysed.

1.1.   Microteaching technique

Microteaching is frequently conducted as a group activity in teacher-training courses. It includes the planning and delivery of a short lesson plan or part of the lesson plan amongst peers, followed by feedback both from the trainees and the instructor (Richards & Farrell, 2011). It is defined as "a scaled down realistic classroom training context in which teachers, both experienced and inexperienced, may acquire new teaching skills and refine old ones" (McKnight, 1980, p. 214). The benefits of this technique have long been discussed and thus it is often used in various teacher preparation programmes.

Student teachers in this project engaged in 3D peer-microteaching, as part of the online microteaching component of the programme. Their teaching was screen recorded on a desktop device for formative assessment purposes. Thus, their "performance skills, cognitive processes and affective learning" (Wallace, 1991, p. 98) were determined in order to assess the extent to which participants' technological abilities to create, design and implement a lesson in a new technological environment had been developed.

1.2.   Virtual worlds use in teacher education

According to Meritt, Gibson, Christensen, and Knezek (2013), digital simulations "provide low-risk, high-touch, scalable and efficient methods for microteaching and pedagogical experimentation combining elements of fantasy and play within realistic dynamics and authentic actions into the pre-service classroom" (p. 412). Although promising alternative ways to provide a practice environment, it is only currently that they have been explored in teacher preparation practice and even less in an online training CALL context. Indeed, two alternative MUVE technologies,

Second Life and OpenSim were used as the simulation field to prepare teachers on how to manage the classroom and anticipate real-life classroom problems in a pre-defined context (Meritt et al., 2013). The results were rather encouraging in relation to the pedagogical knowledge gained.

1.3. Singularity Viewer as the simulation field

Singularity Viewer, a client programme for Second Life and OpenSim, is a private space owned partly by the Cyprus University of Technology. To this end, only its members can have access to the land, i.e. the ten locations, at any given time. As a private space, there is more control over what happens and who is present, thus diminishing the distractions while enhancing the engagement and attention of the participants. In Singularity Viewer, there are some public and private combinations, for instance teleporting from one location to the other. This provides access to a wider range of environments while permitting the flexible design and deployment of a scenario for microteaching according to their needs. A significant limitation is that students are allowed to construct and modify a location provided they were primarily given the appropriate rights to change some properties of the provided objects.

2. Method

2.1. Participants

Eight practicing language teachers (three males and five females) from different parts of the world (Europe and Africa) enrolled in the online MA in CALL programme of the Cyprus University of Technology (CUT) participated in this study. The participants were part-time and full-time students who had no previous experience in creating, designing and delivering microteaching in a Singularity Viewer virtual world. Only one of them had previous experience of designing a virtual serious game.

2.2. Procedure

The use of Singularity Viewer, and its sandbox location in particular, allows users to undertake the detailed configuration of their personal teaching place, i.e. the tools to be used and the knowledge resources to be provided on the subject of interest. Hence, the content can be specifically selected to suit the needs of any specific language subject.

In this particular study, different locations were implemented, while some students preferred to customise their avatars, taking advantage of the tools provided. For example, in one of the microteaching instances, they customised their avatars in colorful cubes and formed different towers according to their fellow students' instructions in order to learn the colours. The learners thus created connections and collaborated with their peers by forming a new virtual learning process. The possibility of reusing the entire set of tools and creating a new environment for a different subject, simply by changing the resources, demonstrates the richer context of the virtual world over any other traditional e-learning platform.

Teaching sessions lasted 20 minutes: five minutes of preparation and settlement in the environment; ten minutes of scenario implementation, predominantly in the sandbox area of Singularity Viewer virtual world; and five minutes of debriefing at the participants' (in the form of avatars) home area. In turns, they shared their experiences and impressions of the use of virtual worlds and conducted self and peer evaluation of their microteaching performance in this environment. After the students had finished all their virtual microteaching, reflective journals were used to establish the participants' feelings regarding the whole experience.

2.3.   Data collection

This study adopted a qualitative approach with a case study design. The virtual classroom performance of the participants and their debriefing were screen recorded with the use of Atube Catcher, an online free screen recording tool, both by the participants and the researcher. Students were instructed to screen record the whole procedure in order to evaluate their performance later in their reflection journals. Hence, the data were gathered through the observations and the participants' utterances or written communication within the virtual world, along with their reflections in their reflective journals. They were further analysed qualitatively through a transcribing and coding process (Creswell, 2008). In the data analysis process, the emerging themes were categorised.

3.   Results and discussion

The multi-user virtual worlds were overall considered by the participants as a powerful medium for instruction and education as well as a good source of user feedback. In addition, analysis of these data provided evidence of students' integrated knowledge of teaching from the perspective of either the actors (as avatars) or the audience. According to students' responses, the easy-to-use affordances of virtual worlds for designing and building enabled them to carry out tasks otherwise physically impossible in the real world. For example, students designed and created contextualised settings such as a travel agency, a gym, a clothes shop and a disco night, where students could simulate the real-life-like roles as avatars in appropriate clothes, for specific contextualised purposes, following real-life scenarios. According to students' comments, this enabled them not only to participate in specific contextualised situations but also to enjoy interaction with each other. This was also observed by the researchers through the screen recorded data.

Analysis of transcripts of the debriefings and student reflections also revealed some common themes that participating student teachers felt teachers should have. These include organisation, class management, student engagement, attention to positive/negative behaviours, time management, misbehaviour management, and proactive teacher behaviours. Some other common themes were related to the limited choice of customisation of the avatars and the locations or even the use of resources of the private space.

There were, of course, some limitations in this project that have influenced the validity of this study. The relatively small number of the participants – eight overall – was one of them. Some technical problems that occurred during the microteaching session, such as sound buzzing and echoing were tackled by the participants themselves, while some others needed the observers' further assistance. Indeed, although immediate assistance was offered to them, there were some distractions and some annoyance.

4.   Conclusions

This study focuses on the opportunities Singularity Viewer, a MUVE could offer in L2 Teacher Education. The data analysis indicated that the use of virtual world desktop applications in microteaching was beneficial for the participants. Student teachers explored ways of extending the use of new technologies in their teaching beyond the Web 2.0 technologies by actually using the 3D virtual world for teaching purposes. Although its limitations need to be addressed, the positive and profitable findings of this programme need to be taken into account and further research carried out in the use of this technology with a larger number of participants.

5.   Acknowledgements

We would like to thank the students who participated in the project.

References

Beaven, T., Emke, M., Ernest, P., Germain-Rutherford, G., Hampel, R., Hopkins, J., Stanojevic, M. M., & Stickler, U. (2010). Needs and challenges for online language teachers – the ECML project DOTS. *Teaching English with Technology: Developing Online Teaching Skills, 10*(2) 5-20.

Creswell, J. W. (2008). *Educational research: planning, conducting, and evaluating quantitative and qualitative research* (3rd ed.). Upper Saddle River, New Jersey: Pearson Education.

Judge, S., & Katsioloudis, P. (2011). The use of virtual environments in teacher preparation. *Lisbon: World Conference on Educational Multimedia, Hypermedia and Telecommunications* (p. 5). EDMEDIA.

Kissau, S., & Algozzine, B. (2015). The impact of mode of instructional delivery on second language teacher self-efficacy. *ReCALL, 27*(2), 239-256. https://doi.org/10.1017/S0958344014000391

McKnight, P. C. (1980). Microteaching: development from 1968-1978. *British Journal of Teacher Education, 6*(3), 214-227. https://doi.org/10.1080/0260747800060305

Meritt, J., Gibson, D., Christensen, R., & Knezek, G. (2013). Interactive technologies for teacher training: comparing performance and assessment in Second Life and simSchool. *International Association for Development of the Information Society*, 411-415

Richards, J. C., & Farrell, T. S. C. (2011). *Practice teaching: a reflective approach*. New York: Cambridge University Press. https://doi.org/10.1017/CBO9781139151535

Wallace, M. J. (1991). *Training foreign language teachers*. Cambridge: Cambridge University Press.

Physicality and language learning

Jaeuk Park[1], Paul Seedhouse[2], Rob Comber[3], and Jieun Kiaer[4]

Abstract. The study draws on the digital technology which allows users to be able to learn both linguistic and non-linguistic skills at the same time. Activity recognition as well as wireless sensor technology, similar to a Nintendo Wii, is embedded or attached to the equipment and ingredients, allowing users to detect and evaluate progress as they carry out their cooking tasks in a real world kitchen. 48 adult participants from 20 countries in total cook, both in a digital kitchen by using real objects and in the classroom by looking at typical pictures/photos in the textbook. These learners from diverse cultural background pose a great potential to the generalizability of the current study. Research questions are: does using real objects to cook in the digital kitchen help students learn vocabulary items better than looking at photos of the objects in the classroom? If so, to what extent? This study attempts to see the effect of physicality in combination with digital technology on foreign vocabulary learning by a experimental design. This project not only helps address well-known problems in relation to classroom teaching and learning, but supports the development of innovative information and communications technology for language learning across the world.

Keywords: CALL, human-computer interaction, task-based learning and teaching, vocabulary learning, digital kitchen.

1.   Introduction

With state-of-the-art technology evolving at an impressive rate, educators in a number of countries are keeping up with the times and waking up to global-language learning; a good command of English and one or more other languages are must-have skills for social and economic, and political purposes (Brecht &

1. Newcastle University, Newcastle upon Tyne, United Kingdom; j.u.park@ncl.ac.uk
2. Newcastle University, Newcastle upon Tyne, United Kingdom; paul.seedhouse@ncl.ac.uk
3. Newcastle University, Newcastle upon Tyne, United Kingdom; robert.comber@ncl.ac.uk
4. Oxford University, Oxford, United Kingdom; jieun.kiaer@orinst.ox.ac.uk

How to cite this article: Park, J., Seedhouse, P., Comber, R., & Kiaer, J. (2016). Physicality and language learning. In S. Papadima-Sophocleous, L. Bradley & S. Thouësny (Eds), *CALL communities and culture – short papers from EUROCALL 2016* (pp. 375-379). Research-publishing.net. https://doi.org/10.14705/rpnet.2016.eurocall2016.591

Ingold, 1998). The world-languages other than English include Spanish, French, German, Chinese, Japanese and Korean, all of which have more than 50 million native speakers, according to the report by Lewis, Gary, and Charles (2016). New methods and technologies have opened up incredible opportunities of learning these popular languages, giving access to real-connection in real-world environments.

This study used the digital kitchen as a real-world digital learning environment (Seedhouse, forthcoming) because the space provides learners with a chance to carry out a real world activity: cooking (see Figure 1). The kitchen also provides a tangible connection to both what Nattinger (1988) claims as a 'situational set' of cooking items by which learners can employ physical object for learning and to what Skehan (1998) referred to as "real world activities" (p. 95) during which learners use authentic language for communicative purposes. Cooking in kitchens is an important part of daily life for many, and an activity with a clear goal, providing helpful tasks in relation to learning; Trubek and Belliveau (2009) suggest that "cooking engages students at an almost instinctive level; the smells, sounds, sights, textures and tastes excite senses and intellect" (p. 16). Considering the nature of the kitchen and its relevance to learning, it is significant to understand the impact of cooking on vocabulary learning in using kitchen environments as learning platforms.

Figure 1.   The Korean digital kitchen

Computer technology has allowed for a wide range of learning platforms for language teaching and learning, one of which is Computer-Assisted Language Learning (CALL) in combination with Task-Based Learning and Teaching (TBLT) (Hinkelman & Gruba, 2012; Salmon, 2011). However, most studies have used TBLT principles just to focus on tasks carried out in the classroom to develop language skills, and few studies have drawn on the real-world tasks out of the classroom, such as asking for directions in the street. Research is therefore needed in which learners carry out the real world task of cooking in a digital kitchen to see the difference in learning from when doing tasks in a conventional setting. This is the research gap the current study attempts to bridge, using a computer and TBLT to examine its effect on vocabulary learning.

2.   Method

There were 48 adult participants from 20 different countries in Newcastle. A total of 24 pairs were chosen to a group. This experimental study was designed to find out which environment, a classroom or a digital kitchen is more effective than the other in promoting vocabulary gain, and which specific aspect contributes to language learning.

Six pairs (Group A) made the dish using Recipe 1 in the classroom and then Recipe 2 in the digital kitchen, while another six pairs (Group D) made Recipe 2 in the digital kitchen and then Recipe 1 in the classroom. Similarly, Group C performed the task using Recipe 2 in the classroom and Recipe 1 in the digital kitchen while Group D carried out its tasks, Recipe 2 in the digital kitchen and Recipe 1 in the classroom. It is thus possible to compare the four Groups. Two recipes have different sets of vocabularies and the same level of difficulty.

The difference between the two settings is that participants in the kitchen use real objects to cook, whereas they simply use photos of objects in the classroom. So, the kitchen users could have all five senses, while classroom learners only accessed a few senses. In the two different settings, learners went through exactly the same test and task procedures in each cooking session; the pre-test assessed ten noun vocabulary items; the exercise pre-task required users to collect each item; the during-task exercise asked them to manipulate items to cook; the post-task exercise requested evaluation; and the post-tests tested their knowledge. Given the nature of the classroom, learners did simulate cooking by interacting with a teacher using the computer, which was not sensor-based, but they were given the same feedback as in the kitchen on their request.

3.   Results

The mean difference for four tests were higher in a digital kitchen than in a classroom and turned out to be statistically significant: immediate receptive test $MD=1.58$, $p<.00$, immediate productive test $MD=1.78$, $p<.00$, delayed receptive test $MD=0.83$, $p<.04$, and delayed productive test $MD=2.12$, $p<.00$. Furthermore, in the kitchen, learners used the real objects to the point where they understood the form and meaning of a target word, whereas in the classroom, simple images of the objects seemed to keep them relatively away from learning.

4.   Discussion

The statistical analyses showed a clear distinction between the two different learning environments. Overall the digital kitchen users scored significantly higher than the classroom ones. In both settings, we could observe that learners used not only each other, but also a computer as learning resources. However, being able to manipulate physical objects in a digital kitchen plays an instrumental role in linking linguistic knowledge to their memory. Nattinger (1988) argues that physical movements help make memory connections, while in a classroom participants may simply rely on their own imagination. The way learners performed the task in the digital kitchen demonstrated more interaction in terms of negotiation, repetition, information transfer and autonomy between peers, compared to the one in the classroom. This might cause different learning outcomes.

The findings of this study suggest that being able to manipulate real objects in the digital kitchen environment can help students obtain vocabulary knowledge. In contrast, learners in the classroom simply used photos, which allowed them to use a few senses. This might keep them from internalizing the memory, thereby resulting in less successful learning. Moreover, being able to manipulate real objects using multi-senses was found to aid vocabulary learning, lending support to former studies (Nattinger, 1988; Trubek & Belliveau, 2009). Thus, using concrete objects provided learners with more vivid and meaningful experiences. Our findings show that physicality enriches vocabulary learning. This study broadened the research scope of the vocabulary learning in TBLT and CALL by using the real world environment of a kitchen.

5.   Conclusions

The answer to the research question is that learners were able to learn foreign vocabulary in the digital kitchen better than in the classroom, because of the different levels of physicality and interactional features in the two separate settings. Yet, the digital kitchen did not suit all learning styles. Nevertheless, the majority of learners preferred the digital kitchen to learn foreign language. Given a range of affordances such as self-organizability, motivation, and meaningful tasks in the digital kitchen, it is however not yet clear exactly which factor resulted in the contrasting outcome. Therefore, recommended future research would be to undertake more controlled experiments.

The findings of the present study implies not only an additional value in the literature of TBLT and CALL, but also a need for potential changes in school curricula and practices in second language teaching and learning as this technology will be able to complement the main learning activities.

References

Brecht, R. D., & Ingold, C. W. (1998). *Tapping a national resource: heritage languages in the United States*. Washington, DC: Center for Applied Linguistics.

Hinkelman, D., & Gruba, P. (2012). Power within blended language learning programs in Japan. *Language Learning & Technology, 19*(2), 46-64.

Lewis, M. P, Gary, F. S., & Charles, D. F. (Eds). (2016). *Ethnologue: languages of the world* (19th ed.). Dallas, Texas: Summer Institute of Linguistics.

Nattinger, J. (1988). Some current trends in vocabulary teaching. In R. Carter & M. McCarthy (Eds), *Vocabulary and language teaching* (pp. 62-82). London: Longman.

Salmon, G. (2011). *E-moderating: the key to online teaching and learning* (3rd ed.). New York: Routledge.

Seedhouse, P. (forthcoming). *Task-based language learning in an immersive digital environment: the European digital kitchen*. London: Bloomsbury.

Skehan, P. (1998). *A cognitive approach to language learning*. Oxford: Oxford University Press.

Trubek, A. B., & Belliveau, C. (2009). Cooking as pedagogy: engaging the senses through experiential learning. *Anthropology News, 50*(4), 16-16. https://doi.org/10.1111/j.1556-3502.2009.50416.x

Designing strategies for an efficient language MOOC

Maria Perifanou[1]

Abstract. The advent of Massive Open Online Courses (MOOCs) has dramatically changed the way people learn a language. But how can we design an efficient language learning environment for a massive number of learners? Are there any good practices that showcase successful Massive Open Online Language Course (MOOLC) design strategies? According to recent research findings (Perifanou & Economides, 2014; Perifanou, 2015) there is not an ideal MOOLC platform that can offer a successful massive open online interactive language learning environment. Most of the current MOOLCs are following the traditional model of xMOOCs that is based on a cognitive behavioral pedagogical model, but there are also few examples that embrace the connectivist version, i.e. the cMOOC model (like Instreamia, Mixxer, OpenLearning, etc.). This paper aims to facilitate the work of language teachers and language and training providers who wish to design and create successful massive open online and interactive language courses for all. First, it presents the Massive Open Online Interactive Language Learning Environment (MOILLE) questionnaire analyzing the key steps in order to design a successful LangMOOC[2]. Next, it showcases specific examples of successful LangMOOC activities and other platforms' features. In the end, the paper provides few useful and practical tips for the MOOLCs designers.

Keywords: MOOCs, MOOLCs, foreign language learning, language education.

1. Introduction

Nowadays, language competence and intercultural skills are more than ever before key qualifications for every citizen in every part of the world. Professional development, cultural awareness, mobility facilitation and social skills building are only a few of the benefits that language literacy can bring. According to

1. University of Macedonia, CONTA Lab, Thessaloniki, Greece; mariaperif@gmail.com
2. More information on the EU funded project LangMOOC can be found at https://www.langmooc.com/; the LangMOOC project is also discussed in Perifanou (2016, this volume)

How to cite this article: Perifanou, M. (2016). Designing strategies for an efficient language MOOC. In S. Papadima-Sophocleous, L. Bradley & S. Thouësny (Eds), *CALL communities and culture – short papers from EUROCALL 2016* (pp. 380-385). Research-publishing.net. https://doi.org/10.14705/rpnet.2016.eurocall2016.592

Perifanou, Holotescu, Andone, and Grosseck (2014), "the main barriers to learn a language are lack of time and motivation, and [the] expense of language courses" (n.p.; see also Andrade et al., 2011). But how easy is it to cover the linguistic needs of a big number of people taking under consideration the above language learning barriers? For the past few years, open education initiatives, such as MOOCs and Open Educational Resources (OERs), have brought about a turning point in the field of language learning as they can easily provide free language education at a large scale with no time and space limitations. MOOCs could be characterized as an innovative educational movement with promising potential but it is still in the middle of an ongoing process. Open education initiatives such as MOOLCs seem to be a promising solution as they give the opportunity to a massive number of learners to learn for free the language of their choice with no space and time limitations.

Research has shown that the key to successful language learning lies in interaction, co-creation, community building and networking (Beaven et al., 2013; Rubio, 2015). The pedagogical philosophy of MOOLCs is connected ideally to the original MOOC, connectivist MOOC (cMOOC), which was built on peer-to-peer learning, autonomy, social networking diversity, openness, emergent knowledge, and interactivity (Mackness, Mak, & Williams, 2010). Research has shown that there is an increasing need for MOOLCs but there are no designing formulas for the creation of efficient language courses for massive number of learners (Perifanou & Economides, 2014). In the following sections this paper aims to propose a questionnaire that can be used as a guide by MOOLC developers, designers and teachers who wish either to create or to evaluate their own MOOC platforms or courses. A few examples and useful tips are also provided.

2. MOILLE framework and questionnaire

The MOILLE questionnaire (Table 1) was created based on the MOILLE framework in accordance to its six key criteria: (1) content, (2) pedagogy, (3) assessment, (4) communication, (5) technical infrastructure, and (6) financial issues (Perifanou & Economides, 2014; Perifanou, 2015). The questionnaire can guide developers, instructive designers or language teachers who plan to design and create an interactive online learning environment for language learners at a massive scale. This questionnaire can be also used as an evaluation tool simply with the addition of a four-point rating scale (high, medium, low, none degrees) to the end of each question or subquestion.

Table 1.　The MOILLE questionnaire

CONTENT
Does the MOOC platform/course:
Q1. support the use and creation of authentic language resources?
Q2. allow user generated content and OER integration/production?
Q3. support textual and highly interactive (multimedia) material?
Q4. support a variety of activities (individual, group, networked) with clear goals that can promote all basic language skills and cultural awareness?
PEDAGOGY
Does the MOOC platform/course:
Q1. support (technically/pedagogically) different types of communication (peer-peer, student-teacher, group-group, open community-natives)?
Q2. promote collaboration and collective intelligence (group projects, forums, etc.)?
Q3. support autonomous and personalized learning activities (autonomous/ self paced/self regulated/personal skills based/reflective learning)?
Q4. increase motivation and engagement via interesting, playful, interactive and often updated activities (playful/game based learning)?
Q5. provide teachers' support during the learning process (number of teachers)?
ASSESSMENT
Does the MOOC platform/course:
Q1. support multiple levels of assessment (peer-peer, student-teacher, open, automated) during the whole learning process (pre/ongoing/final assessment)?
Q2. support 'open' ongoing assessment actions such as comments, reviews, 'likes', shares in social media, or an award automated system for badges and karma?
Q3. support visualization of the learning progress (evidence-based improvement with data mining, learning analytics)?
COMMUNICATION
Does the MOOC platform/course:
Q1. offer social community building features (social media, forums, my personal network, third party tool integration and other tech tools, etc.) that can ensure massiveness and openness?
Q2. promote communication with native speakers?
TECHNICAL INFRASTRUCTURE
Does the MOOC platform/course:
Q1. provide tech infrastructure for asynchronous (private messaging, email, etc.) and synchronous (chat, video conference, etc.) communication?
Q2. support technically OER integration/production?
Q3. support interoperability with other devices (tablet, mobile)? and social media/social network integration (blog, wiki, Facebook, etc.)?
Q4. have a good technical performance with a massive number of participants?
Q5. provide a high security system in many levels (identification system, clear copyright and intellectual property ownership and usage, payment system for concrete services such as certification, ECTS, etc.)?
Q6. offer good usability/personal dashboard (bookmarking, notes, friends, messages, my SM, my content, my grades, etc.)?

Q7. support technologically a multi-level assessment/award system (peer-peer, automated self evaluation, badges, karma, learning analytics, etc.)?
FINANCIAL ISSUES
Does the MOOC platform/course:
Q1. have low costs for its development, implementation and maintenance?
Q2. support certification/accreditation solutions or extra services at low cost?
Q3. potentially have chances to lead to a successful business plan?

3. MOOLC practices: successful examples, useful tips

3.1. Examples of successful LangMOOC activities and interesting features of MOOLC platforms

MOOLC instructional designers should explore successful MOOLC activities that could inspire them to create their own courses. For example:

- Thematic chats or face-to-face instant communication among language peers and teachers using Google Hangouts in groups of ten maximum: the activity should have a predefined topic, time and type of communication such as a self-presentation activity using text, live video or audio. This can be used in combination with general discussion forums. News feeds and an email notification system on all important class activities are also proposed just like in a social network in order to personalize the learning schedule (EdX MOOC platform, Instreamia).

- Authentic oral communication with native speakers via the free voice over IP phone program Skype (Mixxer platform).

- Creation and use of OER's rich content (Eliademy platform).

Interesting features of MOOC platforms that may facilitate the language learning process are the following:

- *Personal study calendar* where each student can find all assigned courses, quizzes and deadlines (Eliademy), *visualization of daily learning progress* based on different language skills and *progress report* that presents all activities and rates (Instreamia).

- Gamification of the learning process and assessment: the learner earns a variety of badges for every completed task, participation, peers' support, etc. (UNED coma).

- Interoperability of the MOOLC platform with other devices.

- Strong community features: social media, third party tool integration, etc.

3.2. Useful tips for MOOLC designers

A promising MOOLC platform should promote a cMOOCs' pedagogy via a variety of tech functionalities that can support collaboration, communication, and authentic and autonomous learning (Perifanou & Economides, 2014). It is though highly recommended that language teachers as well as private educational institutions collaborate with instructional designers and developers in order to find the most adequate MOOC platform for their needs. Another important issue that needs to be considered is the choice of a platform which can offer a multiple and open assessment tools' system (computer-based assessment, teacher-based assessment, automated peer-peer assessment engine, automated award system) that facilitates a multi-level assessment peer-peer, student-teacher, group-group, and student-'open communities' during the whole learning progress.

4. Conclusions

Designing an efficient language learning environment for a massive number of learners is not an easy task. It needs a joint effort of instructive designers, developers and language teachers who will design, implement and evaluate different MOOLC scenarios in order to achieve this goal. Sharing good ideas, practices and examples of these initiatives is a starting point. This paper envisages to start an open discussion about MOOLCs design proposing the MOILLE questionnaire and showcasing good practices.

5. Acknowledgements

This research is an output of the LangMOOC project[3] which has been funded from support of the European Commission within the framework of the Erasmus+ program.

---

3. https://www.langmooc.com/

References

Andrade, A., Ehlers, U.-D., Caine, A., Carneiro, R., Conole, G., Kairamo, A., & Holmberg, C. (2011). *Beyond OER: shifting focus from resources to practices: the OPAL report*. University Duisburg-Essen. http://www.oerup.eu/fileadmin/_oerup/dokumente/Beyond_OER._ Shifting_Focus_to_Open_Educational_Practices__OPAL_Report__2011.pdf

Beaven, T., Comas-Quinn, A., Hauck, M., De Los Arcos, B., & Lewis, T. (2013). The open translation MOOC: creating online communities to transcend linguistic barriers. *Journal of Interactive Media in Education, 3*(18). https://doi.org/10.5334/2013-18

Mackness, J., Mak, S., & Williams, R. (2010). The ideals and reality of participating in a MOOC. In L. Dirckinck-Holmfeld, V. Hodgson, C. Jones, M. De Laat & D. McConnell (Eds), *Proceedings of the 7th International Conference on Networked Learning 2010* (pp. 266-275). Lancaster: University of Lancaster. https://researchportal.port.ac.uk/portal/en/ publications/the-ideals-and-reality-of-participating-in-a-mooc(067e281e-6637-423f-86a5-ff4d2d687af1).html

Perifanou, M. (2015). Research report on the current state of language learning MOOCs worldwide: exploration, classification and evaluation. *LangMOOC project*. http://www. langmooc.com/?cat=7

Perifanou, M. (2016). Worldwide state of language MOOCs . In S. Papadima-Sophocleous, L. Bradley & S. Thouësny (Eds), *CALL communities and culture – short papers from EUROCALL 2016* (pp. 386-390). Research-publishing.net. https://doi.org/10.14705/ rpnet.2016.eurocall2016.593

Perifanou, M., & Economides, A. (2014). MOOCs for language learning: an effort to explore and evaluate the first practices. In *Proceedings of the INTED2014 Proceedings. IATED conference held in Valencia, Spain 8-12 March 2014* (pp. 3561-3570). http://library.iated. org/view/PERIFANOU2014MOO

Perifanou, M., Holotescu, C., Andone, D., & Grosseck, G. (2014). Exploring OERs and MOOCs for learning of EU languages. *SMART Conference 2014 - Social Media in Academia; Research and Teaching, At Timisoara, Romania*. http://www.docfoc.com/exploring-oers-and-moocs-for-learning-of-eu-languages

Rubio, F. (2015). The role of interaction in MOOCs and traditional technology-enhanced language courses. In E. Dixon & M. Thomas (Eds), *Researching language learner interaction online: from social media to MOOCs*. CALICO Monograph 2015. http://calico. org/LearnerInteractionsOnline.pdf

Worldwide state of language MOOCs

Maria Perifanou[1]

Abstract. In the age of globalization, the need for language learning is greater than ever before. "Globalization is a process by which the people of the world are unified into a single society and [function] together" (Chomsky, 2006, cited in Ivan, 2012, p. 81). As global citizens we need to be able to work in settings characterized by linguistic and cultural diversity and that means that "language competencies and intercultural skills [are] more than ever a part of the key qualifications needed to successfully work and live in this new reality" (Perifanou & Economides, 2014, p. 3561). Even though many prestigious universities offer open language courses at a large scale, choosing well known Massive Open Online Course (MOOC) providers, the body of research on mapping existing language learning MOOC initiatives worldwide is rather poor. This paper aims to partially fill this research gap presenting the research contribution of the Erasmus+ KA2 project entitled LangMOOC project. More specifically, the paper first presents the main findings of the background research (Perifanou, 2014; Perifanou & Economides, 2014) of the LangMOOC project that has explored the first language learning MOOC initiatives and evaluated them based on the Massive Open Online Interactive Language Learning Environment (MOILLE[2]) framework. Next, the paper analyzes the overall aims of the LangMOOC project and in the end, it discusses its first research findings as well as its future research steps.

Keywords: MOOLCs, Foreign Language Learning, OER.

1.   Introduction

In the age of globalization, open access to language courses and resources is needed more than ever before in order to meet the needs of linguistically and culturally diverse learners who live and work in a global society. Nowadays, the levels of

1. University of Macedonia, CONTA Lab, Thessaloniki, Greece; mariaperif@gmail.com
2. The MOILLE framework is also discussed in Perifanou (2016, this volume)

How to cite this article: Perifanou, M. (2016). Worldwide state of language MOOCs. In S. Papadima-Sophocleous, L. Bradley & S. Thouësny (Eds), *CALL communities and culture – short papers from EUROCALL 2016* (pp. 386-390). Research-publishing.net. https://doi.org/10.14705/rpnet.2016.eurocall2016.593

multilingualism and multiculturalism have increased. The challenge of offering free language education worldwide and at a large scale is huge. Massive Open Online Language Courses (MOOLCs) is a recent educational phenomenon of online learning that can promote linguistic diversity and language learning, breaking all linguistic barriers (Colas, Sloep, & Garreta-Domingo, 2016). In fact, in the last four years there is a really growing interest for MOOCs and Open Educational Resources (OERs) connected to foreign language learning. For example, over 370,000 students have enrolled in the #FLEnglishIELTS course that prepared them for the English language proficiency test IELTS[3]. This course was offered by the FutureLearn MOOC provider, making it the biggest MOOC so far in the world (Coughlan, 2015).

The first attempt not only to map but also to evaluate the situation of MOOLCs worldwide was made in 2014 (Perifanou & Economides, 2014). More concretely, the researchers proposed the MOILLE framework in order to evaluate all the MOOLCs initiatives offered up to 2014. This framework – also discussed in Perifanou, 2016, this volume – proposes six basic criteria (i.e content, pedagogy, assessment, community, technical infrastructure, and financial issues) that need to be taken under consideration for the successful design and creation of an efficient interactive open and online language learning environment for a massive number of learners.

The MOILLE framework generally embraces a constructivist way of language learning and proposes a "highly interactive [learning] environment where the learners are interconnected to a language learning community building collectively their language skills" (Perifanou & Economides, 2014, p. 3568). The main research aim was to identify if there were MOOLC initiatives that could provide a promising MOILLE. According to the research findings the answer was 'no' because of the following main reasons. Since the beginning of MOOCs up to 2014 there were "more than 16 MOOC platforms that [have offered] more than 50 free [online] language learning courses. More than a half of them were English language MOOCs but there [was] also a great interest for other languages like Arabic, Spanish, Japanese, Chinese, etc." (Perifanou. 2015a, p. 6). Another important research finding was that even though there were some good MOOLC examples, like SpanishMOOC and Mixxer MOOC, most of the evaluated MOOLC initiatives have adopted the traditional model of MOOCs based on a cognitive behavioral pedagogical model (xMOOCs) and did not embrace a more constructivist type (cMOOCs) (for futher reading on a behavioural as opposed to constructivist approach in MOOLCS, see Perifanou & Economides, 2014).

---

3. International English Language Testing System

One of the basic aims of the EU funded project LangMOOC[4] was to repeat the same research methodology with few changes, such as to identify open source and free MOOC platforms, in order to map and evaluate the state of MOOLCs during 2015 but also to compare the latest research results to those of 2014.

2. Research methodology

2.1. LangMOOC basic research steps

The LangMOOC project has adopted the same research methodology adopted by previous research (Perifanou & Economides, 2014; Perifanou, 2014) following 4 concrete research steps:

- First stage: exploration of all the MOOLCs aiming at identifying all MOOC platforms available during 2015 with the support of concrete research tools such as MOOC aggregators, MOOC portals, etc.

- Second stage: classification of the MOOLC initiatives/platforms with respect to the following criteria: (1) use of open source platform/possibility to create a language course individually (i.e. as a teacher), (2) free access to massive online language courses, (3) pedagogy, (4) type of accreditation, and (5) variety of languages and number of courses.

- Third stage: evaluation of six representative MOOLC platforms based on the MOILLE framework.

- Fourth stage: analysis of the research findings and useful conclusions (Perifanou, 2015b).

2.2. LangMOOC implementation

Based on the research findings, the LangMOOC research team aims to propose an improved MOOLC solution that could be implemented by non-academic institutions such as private language schools, language teachers and trainers. In order to achieve this goal the LangMOOC project team has created a toolkit, a step-by-step guideline which includes all the innovative methods and technical tools

---

4. https://www.langmooc.com/

for the creation, management and evaluation of MOOCs and OERs for language learning addressed to non-academic institutions. The LangMOOC project team has also run a series of pilot MOOLCs in order to test the use of OERs in language MOOCs as well as the efficiency of the toolkit promoting at the same time the learning of less 'popular' used European languages (e.g. Greek, Norwegian and Italian).

3.   Main results and discussion

We found 67 different MOOC platforms/providers in total and 29 of those have already offered MOOLCs of 20+ different languages during 2015. Most of them (21 out of 29) were courses for English but there was a big interest for other languages too such as Spanish and Chinese/Mandarin (12 out of 29) but also for less spoken languages such as Greek, Swedish and Irish (1 out of 29). Compared to the research results of 2014, there is an increase of MOOLC initiatives from 16 to 29. Another interesting research finding is that there are 18 out of 29 MOOC platforms (e.g. Open EdX, Moodle, OpenMOOC, WeMOOC, OpenLearning) which use free and open source software. Many of those also give the opportunity to language organizations or to language teachers to build their own MOOLCs (with the possibility to add payment for their services). Almost all of the MOOLCs (24 out of 29) offer accreditation (certifications, badges and/or ECTS credits) after the completion of 70% or 80% of the language course in most cases. Regarding the pedagogy adopted, there are few examples (3 out of 29), such as Mixxer, Instreamia, OpenLearning and TandemMOOC, which support a connectivist way of learning, emphasizing the role of social and cultural context. The results show that the MOOLCs' pedagogy has remained almost the same compared to the one of 2014 despite the total number increase of MOOLCs' initiatives. The third stage of the research evaluating six representative MOOLC platforms (i.e open. EdX, OpenLearning, Instreamia, The Mixxer, UNED, and Eliademy) based on the MOILLE framework have shown another important research finding: there is not one ideal MOOLC platform that can offer a successful MOILLE but there are a few successful cases. In general, most of the evaluated MOOLCs are following the traditional model of xMOOCs (Perifanou, 2015b).

4.   Conclusions

One of the LangMOOC's main goals was to map and evaluate the MOOLCs at a global level. The results described in the previous paragraphs have shown that even though there is an increasing interest for MOOLCs worldwide, the need for the design and creation of successful MOOLCs is high because most of the evaluated MOOLCs still do not offer a successful MOILLE. Furthermore, issues such as the language teachers' new role, time and implementation costs, the empowerment of authentic communication with native speakers, multi-level assessment and accreditation, and MOOC platforms' interoperability remain important and should be considered carefully by all MOOLC teachers/designers.

The LangMOOC project team envisages that the toolkit will facilitate the work of language teachers and language and training institutions across Europe who wish to design and create successful MOOCs.

References

Chomsky, N. (2006, March 24). Chats with Washington Post readers. *The Washington Post.* http://www.chomsky.info/debates/20060324.htm

Colas, J.-F., Sloep, P. B., & Garreta-Domingo, M. (2016). The effect of multilingual facilitation on active participation in MOOCs. *International Review of Research in Open and Distributed Learning, 17*(4). https://doi.org/10.19173/irrodl.v17i4.2470

Coughlan, S. (2015). UK 'biggest online university course'. *BBC news blog.* http://www.bbc.com/news/education-32721056

Ivan, O.-R. (2012). Foreign language learning in the age of globalization. Quaestus Multidisciplinary Research Journal, 1, 80-84. http://www.quaestus.ro/en/wp-content/uploads/2012/02/ivan.oana_.pdf

Perifanou, M. (2014). How to design and evaluate a Massive Open Online Course (MOOC) for language learning. *In Proceedings of the eLSE14 conference held in Bucharest, Romania, 24-25 April 2014.* https://doi.org/10.12753/2066-026X-14-041

Perifanou, M. (2015a). Personalized MOOCs for language learning: a challenging proposal. *eLearning Papers, 45,* 2-16.

Perifanou, M. (2015b). *Research report on the current state of language learning MOOCs worldwide: exploration, classification and evaluation.* LangMOOC project. http://www.langmooc.com/?cat=7

Perifanou, M. (2016). Designing strategies for an efficient language MOOC. In S. Papadima-Sophocleous, L. Bradley & S. Thouësny (Eds), *CALL communities and culture – short papers from EUROCALL 2016* (pp. 380-385). Research-publishing.net. https://doi.org/10.14705/rpnet.2016.eurocall2016.592

Perifanou, M., & Economides, A. (2014). MOOCs for language learning: an effort to explore and evaluate the first practices. *In Proceedings of the INTED2014 conference held in Valencia, Spain 8-12 March 2014.* http://library.iated.org/view/PERIFANOU2014MOO

A Spanish-Finnish telecollaboration: extending intercultural competence via videoconferencing

Pasi Puranen[1] and Ruby Vurdien[2]

Abstract. In language learning today, students from different geographical locations are able to interact online in a more authentic environment, share their views with their partners, create profiles as well as build online communities enjoying common interests. With this in mind, this paper examines and reports on a study about how students from two different countries, Finland and Spain, developed intercultural competence through the use of a videoconferencing platform, Adobe Connect, as a telecollaborative learning context. Eleven Spanish and seventeen Finnish participants were provided with the opportunity to interact with each other outside the classroom with a view to exploring the target culture and, consequently, experiencing intercultural learning. The findings suggest that the students' learning experience was positive and to some extent they had enhanced their knowledge of each other's cultural traits, such as their lifestyle, hobbies and traditions.

Keywords: telecollaboration, videoconferencing, intercultural competence, cross-cultural interaction.

1.   Introduction

In language learning today, students from different geographical locations can interact online with a view to developing language skills and intercultural competence. This online intercultural exchange, which is also known as telecollaboration, enables students to interact outside the classroom situation, exchange their opinions with their peers, give a description of themselves and create online groups who do similar activities. Consequently, Computer-Mediated Communication (CMC) is being increasingly used by language teachers since students can communicate both synchronously and asynchronously

1. Aalto University, Espoo, Finland; pasi.puranen@aalto.fi
2. White Rose Language School, Valladolid, Spain; whiterose_va@yahoo.es

How to cite this article: Puranen, P., & Vurdien, V. (2016). A Spanish-Finnish telecollaboration: extending intercultural competence via videoconferencing. In S. Papadima-Sophocleous, L. Bradley, & S. Thouësny (Eds), *CALL communities and culture – short papers from EUROCALL 2016* (pp. 391-396). Research-publishing.net. https://doi.org/10.14705/rpnet.2016.eurocall2016.594

through a computer with their counterparts in other countries as well as native speakers. With regard to synchronous CMC, chat sessions have been found to be effective communicative tools at intercultural levels (Chun, 2011; Tudini, 2007). Furthermore, research studies, conducted by means of videoconferencing involving sophisticated audiovisual web communication platforms, such as Adobe Connect, Elluminate or Visu (Canto, Jauregi, & Van Den Bergh, 2013; Guichon, 2010; Jauregi & Bañados, 2010), describe experiences contributing to communicative or intercultural development. However, there exists no strong empirical evidence to support the latter and the target of the present study is to make a contribution in this area. Hence, the study aims, firstly, to analyse the development of intercultural competence between students of two different countries, namely Spain and Finland, during their interaction via videoconference on the Adobe Connect platform; and, secondly, to discuss the participants' most important learning outcome of the project. The two research questions that guided the study are as follows:

- To what extent is intercultural competence developed in students' interaction via videoconferencing?

- What do the participants consider to be the most important learning outcome in this intercultural project?

2.   Method

2.1.   The project

The project designed for the present study was task-based and lasted for six weeks. The 11 Spanish participants were preparing for their Cambridge English C1 and C2 levels (based on the Common European Framework of Reference) at a private language school in Spain, whilst the 17 Finnish participants were studying Spanish at a university in Finland. The participants were expected to interact synchronously via videoconferencing on the Adobe Connect platform and the links to the online interactions were then posted on Facebook (an additional tool used) so that they could watch each other's video sessions. Six specific tasks were assigned on a weekly basis. The tasks comprised introducing themselves, talking about leisure activities/sports that are popular at their respective institutions, discussing a newspaper article relating to an important issue in their country, debating a film that they had watched and, finally, exploring stereotyped ideas pertaining to each country. Each student recorded their introductory task on video via Movenote, which they posted on Facebook for their peers to watch.

2.2.   Data collection and analysis

The study adopted a qualitative and quantitative approach and data were collected from various sources, namely videos via Movenote and Adobe Connect. Following Vurdien's (2014) approach, two questionnaires were administered at the beginning and end of the project, and interviews were conducted individually on its conclusion. Finally, a survey in the form of a questionnaire consisting of eight statements was completed by the participants to gather additional data. A five-point Likert scale ranging from one (strongly disagree) to five (strongly agree) was used to gauge the students' reactions to the project.

3.   Results and discussion

The majority of the students had a favourable overview of their experience (Table 1). The survey shows that the students responded positively when asked if they were curious to learn about their peers' culture (statement 2, mean 4.25) and if they felt motivated to interact with their peers online (statement 3, mean 3.68). In general, there were no major differences between the Spanish and Finnish students, although the Finnish students were a little bit more critical in their feedback and assessment. This could be attributed to the fact that most Finnish students had already had experience of the Spanish customs and habits on their frequent visits to Spain and through contact with their Spanish friends. As they also explained in their interview, they felt uneasy while communicating with their Spanish peers due to their speaking level being only B1, and consequently, had some difficulties in expressing their views. Nonetheless, the students found the task and the issues discussed in general interesting (statement 4, mean 3.64).

Table 1.   Students' appraisal of their learning experience

Statement	Mean	Median	Standard Deviation
1. I enjoyed exchanging views with my peers via video conferencing.	4.04	4	0.64
2. I was curious to learn about my peers' culture.	4.25	4	0.70
3. I felt motivated to interact with my peers online.	3.68	3.5	0.86
4. I found the issues we discussed interesting.	3.64	4	0.78
5. I enjoyed working in groups.	3.93	4	0.83

6. I felt happy to share knowledge with my peers.	4.04	4	0.64
7. I have a better understanding of my peers' customs and habits.	3.68	4	0.90
8. I found my peers' comments to be very helpful and informative.	3.68	4	0.90

In their interviews, the students perceived certain similarities and differences between their cultural traits through their willingness to learn about each other's customs and habits, and share knowledge with each other. They mentioned differences in customs, such as Spain being a more family-centred country, whilst in Finland people tend to adopt a more independent attitude. Another difference mentioned is that many Spanish university students live with their parents, whereas the Finnish students generally live by themselves. Nevertheless, many students reported that there were surprisingly many similarities in customs, values and hobbies as well as in lifestyles and thoughts. As for the outcome of their learning experience, the Finnish students claimed that, due to the short duration of the project, the issues were not explored deeply enough to understand each other's cultural traits fully. Some Spaniards, on the other hand, were satisfied with their online interaction and believed that they had enhanced their knowledge about some Finnish cultural traits due to immediate explanation and clarification being given during their online engagement. In some participants' view, videoconferencing can assist in developing friendship since they can see each other, and body language facilitates interaction. A genuine interest in each other's culture plays a crucial role in building friendship, as mentioned by others. However, a few reported that online relationships seem too distant compared with face-to-face interactions which tend to foster friendship better.

The students' appraisal of the issues they discussed exhibited the lowest mean (3.64). This could be explained by the fact that, although they were generally interested in exchanging views on the different subjects they debated, they found the task regarding watching the film and talking about it quite insignificant. The students did not all watch the same films and, as a result, could not follow the thread of discussion. Therefore it would be vital for teachers to select the film they consider appropriate for such a task.

Judging from the students' responses in their questionnaires, videoconferencing can be deemed a useful tool for meaningful learning to take place. Students can feel stimulated to develop curiosity to learn about each other's lifestyle and, as a result, can develop intercultural learning. Because of the synchronous nature of videoconferencing, students are able to spontaneously exchange information and clarify any misunderstanding without any delayed response, thereby facilitating their understanding of each other's cultural traits. Yet the findings from the interviews suggest that the time factor plays a role in exploring issues leading to intercultural development. Therefore, the length of the study should be taken into consideration, as intercultural learning is a long term process and students need time to reflect on their own views prior to reflecting on those of their peers. With regard to developing relationships online, it might surmise that tasks should be carefully chosen and geared towards that aim to benefit students. For example, activities related to students' interests in terms of their age group and their area of studies might be useful for this purpose.

4. Conclusion

This study has given some insight into how videoconferencing can foster intercultural learning by means of tasks that aided students to discover information about each other's cultural traits. The main aim was to examine how intercultural competence is developed in students' interaction via videoconferencing and what the students considered to be the most important learning outcome. Surprisingly, similarities concerning customs, habits, hobbies and even lifestyle were noted. In terms of their learning outcome, some students thought that they did not have sufficient time to explore the issues deeply enough since the project was of a short duration. However, others believed that they had enhanced their knowledge of their counterparts' culture. Videoconferencing seems to be an appropriate tool to assist students in discussing and sharing their thoughts with a view to understanding each other's culture as well as developing friendship. Yet sufficient time should be provided for students to attain this goal since it is an on-going learning process. However, due to the small scale of this study, the data cannot be generalised and, hopefully, further research in this area will benefit the learning process.

References

Canto, S., Jauregi, K., & Van Den Bergh, H. (2013). Integrating cross-cultural interaction through video-communication and virtual worlds in foreign language teaching programs: is there an added value? *ReCALL, 25*(1), 105-121. https://doi.org/10.1017/S0958344012000274

Chun, D. M. (2011). Developing intercultural communicative competence through online exchanges. *CALICO Journal 28*(2), 392-419. https://doi.org/10.11139/cj.28.2.392-419

Guichon, N. (2010). Preparatory study for the design of a desktop videoconferencing platform for synchronous language teaching. *Computer Assisted Language Learning, 23*(2), 169-182. https://doi.org/10.1080/09588221003666255

Jauregi, K., & Bañados, E. (2010). An intercontinental video-web communication project between Chile and The Netherlands. In S. Guth & F. Helm (Eds), *Telecollaboration 2.0: language, literacies and intercultural learning in the 21st century* (pp. 427-436). Bern: Peter Lang.

Tudini, V. (2007). Negotiation and intercultural learning in Italian native speaker chat rooms. *Modern Language Journal, 91*(4), 577-601. https://doi.org/10.1111/j.1540-4781.2007.00624.x

Vurdien, R. (2014). Social networking: developing intercultural competence and fostering autonomous learning. In S. Jager, L. Bradley, E. J. Meima, & S. Thouësny (Eds), *CALL Design: Principles and Practice - Proceedings of the 2014 EUROCALL Conference, Groningen, The Netherlands* (pp. 398-402). Dublin Ireland: Research-publishing.net. https://doi.org/10.14705/rpnet.2014.000252

Developing oral interaction skills with a digital information gap activity game

Avery Rueb[1], Walcir Cardoso[2], and Jennica Grimshaw[3]

Abstract. This study introduces the digital game Prêt à négocier, an information gap digital game, and investigates language learners' perceptions of its use in a French as a Second Language (FSL) context. In the game, students negotiate orally and synchronously with a partner for items like cars, houses, and even pirate ships. Inspired by Larsen-Freeman and Long's (1991) information gap activity, game players exchange information to solve a common problem (e.g. to buy a car within certain conditions imposed by the game). As a competitive game, the pairs must use their oral interaction skills in a comprehensible and persuasive manner to win (e.g. to obtain the best final price on a product). In addition to describing Prêt à négocier, this study examines 28 students' perceptions of its pedagogical use in a standard FSL classroom via a triangulation of methods that include a survey, interviews with participants, and focus group discussions. Based on our findings, we conclude that students' perceptions of the game are highly positive in most aspects of our analysis and that Prêt à négocier is well-positioned to help students improve oral interaction skills in a fun, comfortable, and interactive manner.

Keywords: computer-assisted language learning, mobile technology, digital gaming, L2 education, learner perceptions.

1. Introduction

Oral interaction is a second language (L2) competency that is required in everyday tasks like talking on the phone with a colleague or having a face-to-face conference with a teacher (Hall, 2003). Developing oral interaction skills has many benefits for second language acquisition as students not only practice listening and speaking, but also become motivated to give feedback on what the interlocutor is saying (Gass, 1997).

1. Vanier College, Montréal, Canada; rueba@vaniercollege.qc.ca
2. Concordia University, Montréal, Canada; walcir.cardoso@concordia.ca
3. Concordia University, Montréal, Canada; jennica.grimshaw@gmail.com

How to cite this article: Rueb, A., Cardoso, W., & Grimshaw, J. (2016). Developing oral interaction skills with a digital information gap activity game. In S. Papadima-Sophocleous, L. Bradley, & S. Thouësny (Eds), *CALL communities and culture – short papers from EUROCALL 2016* (pp. 397-402). Research-publishing.net. https://doi.org/10.14705/rpnet.2016.eurocall2016.595

Information gap activities develop interaction skills by requiring learners to engage in dialogue with one another in order to exchange partial information sets so that the team can solve problems that require knowledge of the entire information set. Through the 'forced output' generated by these types of activities, learners become aware of and fill in gaps in their L2 linguistic knowledge through negotiation with their interlocutors (Swain & Lapkin, 1995). However, oral interaction frequently goes underdeveloped in language classrooms. A recent study by Zuniga and Simard (2016), for example, reported that out of 64 hours of classroom observation, Quebec high school language teachers spent 8% of the time developing these interactive skills.

The current study introduces and examines the game Prêt à négocier as a digital information gap activity whose aim is to help students develop oral interaction skills. Developed by Rueb, Cardoso and Affordance Studio[4], the game can be played on mobile devices, desktops and laptops, both in the classroom through face-to-face conversations or at home through an audio chat solution. In the game, students earn points for achieving two objectives: exchanging information about the product and arriving at a final price (see Figure 1). Specifically, the product information must be exchanged in terms of the players' roles criteria (i.e. what the buyer is looking for and what the seller is offering). After the item information has been exchanged, students must continue talking to agree on a final price below the maximum price of the buyer and above the minimum price of the seller.

Figure 1.   Prêt à négocier interface (buyer's view)

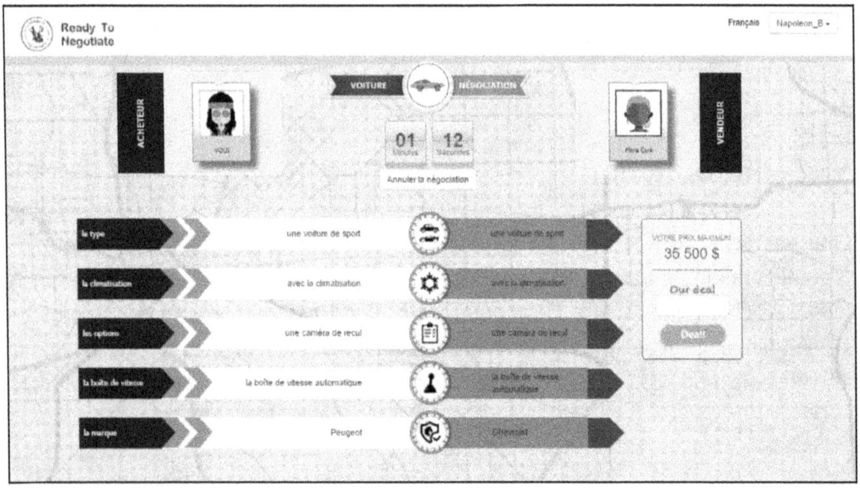

---

4. Visit http://app.readytonegotiate.com for a demo version of the game and email avery@affordancestudio.com for a free teacher trial account

We believe that Prêt à négocier has the potential to help students develop oral interaction skills in a fun, engaging and immersive environment, not only in the classroom under the teacher's supervision, but also outside of the classroom on the learner's own schedule. The goal of our study is to examine students' perceptions of and attitudes toward Prêt à négocier via the use of a survey, interviews, and focus group sections, as will be discussed below.

2. Method

2.1. Participants

The participants were 28 post-secondary students enrolled in an intermediate-level FSL class in a post-secondary institution (a *cégep*) in Québec, Canada. The goal of the course was to develop writing, listening, reading and speaking skills to prepare students for credit classes at the post-secondary level. The participants had various native languages including Vietnamese, Spanish, Chinese, Arabic and English, and their average age was approximately 20 (range 17-25).

2.2. Design and procedure

Participants met with the classroom teacher two-times a week for 100 minutes each class. The treatment consisted of game-playing during 25-minute sessions, twice a week, over a four-week period for a total of approximately 200 minutes of game play. The study was completed using an early version of the Prêt à négocier game with four different negotiation scenarios: buying a car, renting an apartment, buying a pirate ship, and purchasing a trip to space.

After the last treatment session, participants completed the survey and participated in interviews. Select participants also gave feedback in a focus group. The survey contained 16 statements using a 6-point Likert scale ranging from strongly disagree (1) to strongly agree (6) with numerical values indicating degrees of agreement, and asked questions about how the game contributed to learning (e.g. "Prêt à négocier helped me improve my vocabulary"). The research team also conducted interviews and a focus group session with participants in order to delve deeper into some of their answers and to expand on their understanding of the tool's usefulness. In this study, we report the results from the analysis of the data collected from the survey, focus group, and individual interviews with the participants.

3.   Results and discussion

Based on the descriptive statistics from the survey as well as the analysis of the interview and focus group transcripts, our results indicate that participants found Prêt à négocier to be enjoyable and helpful for language learning. Due to space constraints, only the most relevant data are reported here.

Firstly, the participants said to have found the game fun: "It's a fun learning, like, it's not boring or something, we enjoy it. We don't feel like we're learning, but we're learning". Warschauer and Healey (1998) describe this as the 'fun factor' in second language games. This 'fun factor' could be one reason that participants reported really enjoying using the Prêt à négocier game (Mean: 5.29/6; SD: 1.12).

Secondly, students found that the game helped them improve their French (Mean: 5.25/6; SD:0.97) and that Prêt à négocier is a great tool to learn a language (Mean: 5.11/6; SD: 0.99). One possible reason for these results might be the competitive quality of the game where using the language effectively can lead to better game outcomes (see Vandercruysse, Vandewaetere, Cornillie, & Clarebout, 2013 for different results). One student commented in an interview that "the competition is good I think. It makes us know more words to say what we mean".

Another student stated that the game helped to increase her Willingness To Communicate (WTC), a result supported by related studies (Reinders & Wattana, 2014): "It helped me to want to be able to talk more, uh… More open, in a sense, it made me want to talk instead of being – I'm a very shy person when it comes to talking in French, I tend to hold back, so it kinda (sic) made me want to open up and to expose myself". There was a similar trend in the survey, where students felt more comfortable talking in French after playing the game (Mean: 4.46/6; SD: 1.09).

Finally, some students enjoyed the collaborative aspect of the game: "Some of my favourite things are, just getting to talk to other people, that not only helps you but you get to help them too. I always find it rewarding when you get to help somebody else too. So along with improving yourself, others improve too and it just makes everything better".

The relationship between cooperative learning and WTC has been shown in past research (Montasseri & Razmjoo, 2015) and might be one reason why participants felt more comfortable speaking during gameplay than in other oral activities in previous French classes (Mean: 5.25/6; SD:0.97).

In terms of feedback on how to improve the game, students found that the pre-established three minute time limit to reach deals was too short. They also suggested that the tutorial and game onboarding needed to be made more user-friendly. All suggestions will be implemented in the new version of the game, to be released in fall, 2016.

4. Conclusions

Based on students' perceptions of the game, Prêt à négocier appears to be well-positioned to help students improve oral interaction skills in a fun and interactive way. Participants reported a higher level of comfort with this type of game interaction than with other oral activities. They also enjoyed both the collaborative and competitive aspects of the game, which played a role in helping students to feel more motivated to learn French and improve their language skills. This also seems to bear out in the (unpublished) preliminary results from a longitudinal study on the effects of game play on vocabulary acquisition, where we see that the game-playing experimental group outperformed the control group in recalling vocabulary items that they had practiced in oral interactions with their peers via Prêt à négocier.

5. Acknowledgements

The research team would like to thank Vanier College for allowing us to conduct this study and the students who agreed to participate in our study.

References

Gass, S. M. (1997). *Input, interaction, and the second language learner.* Hillsdale, NJ: Erlbaum.

Hall, J. K. (2003). Classroom interaction and language learning. *Ilha do Desterro, 44,* 165-188.

Larsen-Freeman, D., & Long, M. (1991). *An introduction to second language acquisition research.* New York: Longman.

Montasseri, Z., & Razmjoo, S. (2015). The effect of using competitive and cooperative teaching on the WTC of Iranian EFL learners. *International Journal of Language and Applied Linguistics, 1*(3), 54-61.

Reinders, H., & Wattana, S. (2014). Can I say something? The effects of digital game play on willingness to communicate. *Language Learning & Technology, 18*(2), 101–123

Swain, M., & Lapkin, S. (1995). Problems in output and the cognitive processes they generate: a step towards second language learning. *Applied Linguistics, 16*(3), 371-391. https://doi.org/10.1093/applin/16.3.371

Vandercruysse, S., Vandewaetere, M., Cornillie, F., & Clarebout, G. (2013). Competition and students' perceptions in a game-based language learning environment. *Educational Technology Research and Development, 61*(6), 927-950. https://doi.org/10.1007/s11423-013-9314-5

Warschauer, M., & Healey, D. (1998). Computers and language learning: an overview. *Language Teaching, 31*(2), 57-71. https://doi.org/10.1017/S0261444800012970

Zuniga, M., & Simard, D. (2016). Observing the interactive qualities of L2 instructional practices in ESL and FSL classrooms. *Studies in Second Language Learning and Teaching, 6*(1), 135-158. https://doi.org/10.14746/ssllt.2016.6.1.7

Using WebQuests as idea banks for fostering autonomy in online language courses

Shirin Sadaghian[1] and S. Susan Marandi[2]

Abstract. The concept of language learner autonomy has influenced ComputerAssisted Language Learning (CALL) to the extent that Schwienhorst (2012) informs us of a paradigm change in CALL design in the light of learner autonomy. CALL is not considered a tool anymore, but a learner environment available to language learners anywhere in the world. Based on a work-cycle as a practical framework for implementing autonomy in online courses (Legenhausen, 2003), the current study introduces WebQuest to be used as ideas and an activity bank. Work cycle design takes several principles of learner autonomy such as goal setting, content and format choice, self-evaluation and reflection in action and is defined as a learner-based approach that emphasises metacognitive knowledge that raises students' awareness to become more conscious of their own language learning process, strengths and weaknesses (Ter Haseborg, 2012). The idea and activity bank at the top of a work cycle provides learners with the opportunity to plan and negotiate, make decisions, do project work and evaluate their learning in a cyclic mode. Thus, the current article argues that because of its flexibility and accessibility, WebQuests lend themselves to the work cycle approach in online courses aimed at fostering autonomy. Moreover, the findings of the current study indicate that WebQuests contribute to the development of learner autonomy by encouraging critical thinking among learners.

Keywords: CALL, language learner autonomy, WebQuest, online language courses.

1. Alzahra university, Tehran, Iran; shirin_sadaghian@yahoo.com
2. Alzahra university, Tehran, Iran; susanmarandi@alzahra.ac.ir

How to cite this article: Sadaghian, S., & Marandi, S. S. (2016). Using WebQuests as idea banks for fostering autonomy in online language courses. In S. Papadima-Sophocleous, L. Bradley & S. Thouësny (Eds), *CALL communities and culture – short papers from EUROCALL 2016* (pp. 403-407). Research-publishing.net. https://doi.org/10.14705/rpnet.2016.eurocall2016.596

1.   Introduction

Technology offers many opportunities for language learners to learn independently from teachers and interdependently with peers. By providing learners with collaborative authentic contexts, technology helps the improvement of learners' autonomy through developing a "capacity for reflection and analysis, which is central to the development of learner autonomy" (Little, 1996, p. 210). Recently, the spread of the concept of autonomy in the field of CALL has resulted in a paradigm change (Schwienhorst, 2012), defining CALL as an environment or virtual community of learners influenced by pedagogy instead of a tool.

Learner autonomy is defined as "the ability to take charge of one's own learning" (Holec, 1979, p. 3). Holec (1979) believes that autonomy is not inborn but must be acquired either by 'natural' means or formal learning. Based on Holec's (1979) definition, the autonomous learner is able to set goals, select tools and methods to follow and evaluate his/her own progress. Schwienhorst (2008) claims that technology is capable of assisting a learner autonomy-based pedagogy that supports reflection, interaction, experimentation, and participation of learners.

The current study used the concept of work-cycle approach (Legenhausen, 2003) to introduce language learner autonomy in online English as a Foreign Language (EFL) courses. The study was part of a larger autonomous language learning programme conducted in a virtual language institute in Iran and the principles of language learner autonomy were applied using work-cycle approach. The cycle started with planning and negotiation on the learning goals and moved to decision making for the learners' projects. Two important features of the decision making stage were *responsibility* and *accountability*. Learners then moved to the working stage in which they researched, documented and published their project. Finally, the evaluation stage, included learners and teacher's evaluation of the project.

However, the focus of the present study was on using WebQuests as the idea and activity bank in a work-cycle aimed at fostering autonomous language learning. According to Godwin-Jones (2004), "Webquests tend to be student-oriented and collaborative, with students engaged in constructivist activities resulting in shared learning experiences and new knowledge based on enquiry-oriented language use and Web research skills" (p. 9). WebQuests cater for different student learning style needs and are appropriate for collaborative learning (Hopkins-Moore & Fowler, 2002). A WebQuest is comprised of six components, namely introduction, task, process, evaluation and conclusion.

2. Method

2.1. Participants

The participants were 18 Iranian EFL language learners (both male and female), enrolled in virtual language courses. The course was a synchronous online course held twice a week and delivered through a Moodle-based course management system with additional features of Adobe Acrobat Connect and synchronous video and voice interaction. The learners were totally familiar with the features of online classes as they were enrolled in the online English courses and E-zaban virtual university for almost two years and were completing their intermediate-level at the time of the study. However, learners didn't have the experience of learning English through work-cycles and using other online tools such as WebQuest beside the facilities of their virtual university.

2.2. Instrumentation

The WebQuest for the current study was created in zunal.com. Each work-cycle had a WebQuest[3] that included the sources from the web for the completion of the work-cycle. All students were interviewed about the possible effects of using the WebQuest as the idea and activity bank in an online autonomous language course. All the interviews were done in a virtual classroom by the teacher-researcher in English language.

2.3. Procedure

The present study was carried out during three months. Learners had completed six work-cycles during this period, and each work-cycle started with a WebQuest as its idea bank. At the beginning of each work-cycle, learners chose their favorite subject and the subject was chosen in a collaborative whole-class decision making process. The suggested sources were then collected in the work-cycle by the course instructor.

3. Discussion

Based on the data from learners' interviews, WebQuests were reported as a very useful online tool for providing learners with ideas and activities available online.

---

3. http://zunal.com/webquest.php?w=311179

The WebQuest also fit work-cycle approach in that it was open for change during the whole cycle. Moreover, the sections of a WebQuest, namely introduction, task, process and evaluation provided learners with clear guidelines for the rest of the work-cycle.

Learners reported many advantages of using a WebQuest. The codes extracted from learners' interviews regarding the advantages and disadvantages of using the WebQuest as an idea and activity bank are presented in Table 1.

Table 1. Learners' perceptions about using WebQuest

Theme	Code	Example
Positive perceptions	Fast	It was faster than searching on my own.
	Easy to find learning material	Everything is ready but we can add too.
	Variety of material	I could choose to read, or listen to the chosen topic.
	Related parts	There is no irrelevant material like the internet.
	Cooperation	I liked it when the teacher added my choice to the WebQuest.
Negative perceptions	Not fixed like a syllabus	I was worried about missing the recently added materials. Pdf files are fixed.

Our results suggest that the positive features of using the WebQuest as an idea and activity bank outperformed its negative points. The interview results revealed that WebQuest was found useful as it helped learners save the time of their inquiries from the web. It also helped the development of critical thinking abilities as learners reported on the possibility of having variety of related material and synthesising the available information for optimal learning. However, some learners still preferred a pre-planned structured syllabus presented at the beginning of the course to avoid the dynamicity of using the WebQuest as an idea and activity bank. The findings of the current study were in line with the study of Torres (2007), who found WebQuest useful in learning because of its ability to promote the effective use of time and structuring learners' search for information. Moreover, as students were engaged with reading, thinking, synthesising, and evaluating the existing information in the WebQuest to manage their work-cycles, they could gain critical thinking abilities (Halat & Peker, 2011). In line with the findings of the current study, Cai (2005) asserts that using WebQuest helps students become better learners by increasing their autonomy level and providing a sense of fulfilment.

4. Conclusions

The results of the present study showed the potential of WebQuest to be used as the idea and activity bank in online autonomous language courses. As flexible and dynamic idea banks, WebQuests be adapted according to the need of learner throughout a cycle.

References

Cai, S. L. (2005). WebQuest: usage of WebQuest in web-based foreign language teaching. *Computer-Assisted Foreign Language Education, 103*, 41-45.

Godwin-Jones, B. (2004). Emerging technologies: language in action. From WebQuests to virtual realities. *Language Learning & Technology, 8*(3), 9-14.

Halat, E., & Peker, M. (2011). The impacts of mathematical representations developed through WebQuest and spreadsheet activities on the motivation of pre-service elementary school teachers. *TOJET: The Turkish Online Journal of Educational Technology, 10*(2), 259-267.

Holec, H. (1979). *Autonomy and foreign language learning.* Strasbourg, France: Council for Cultural Cooperation.

Hopkins-Moore, B., & Fowler, S. (2002). WebQuests: changing the way we teach online. In *CHI'02 Extended Abstracts on Human Factors in Computing Systems* (pp. 832-833). ACM. https://doi.org/10.1145/506443.506620

Legenhausen, L. (2003). Second language acquisition in an autonomous learning environment. In D. Little, J. Ridley, & E. Ushioda (Eds), *Learner autonomy in the foreign language classroom* (pp. 65-77). Dublin, Ireland: Authentik.

Little, D. (1996). Freedom to learn and compulsion to interact: promoting learner autonomy through the use of information systems and information technologies. In R. Pemberton, E. S. L. Li, W. W. F. Or, & H. D. Pierson (Eds), *Taking control: autonomy in language learning* (pp. 203-218). Hong Kong: University Press.

Schwienhorst, K. (2008). CALL and autonomy: settings and contexts variables in technology-enhanced language environments. *Independence, 43*, 13-15.

Schwienhorst, K. (2012). *Learner autonomy and CALL environments.* Routledge.

Ter Haseborg, H. E. (2012). *Principles of learner autonomy in action: effects and perceptions in a college-level foreign language class.* West Virginia University.

Torres, I. P. (2007). *WebQuest: a collaborative strategy to teach content and language.* University of Granada.

Integrating mobile technologies into very young second language learners' curriculum

Gulnara Sadykova[1], Gulnara Gimaletdinova[2], Liliia Khalitova[3], and Albina Kayumova[4]

Abstract. This report is based on an exploratory case study of a private multilingual preschool language program that integrated a Mobile-Assisted Language Learning (MALL) project into the curriculum of five/six year-old children whose native language(s) is/are Russian and/or Tatar. The purpose of the study was to reveal teachers' and parents' perceptions of the educational value of mobile language learning in English as a Foreign Language (EFL) classroom and explore the case of MALL integration into the curriculum of young language learners. To collect the data, the researchers surveyed eight teachers, including a teacher who introduced the MALL project into her class of 12 children, as well as 12 parents whose children participated in this project. The results speak for the growth of MALL enthusiasts among teachers and the lack of MALL supporters among parents.

Keywords: mobile-assisted language learning, MALL, early childhood education, EFL.

1. Introduction

The educational value of mobile devices for young learners has been questioned by many educators and parents. While many instructors demonstrate a positive attitude to the usage of mobile technologies in the adult classroom (AL-Maagb, 2016; Tai & Ting, 2011), educators have less enthusiasm towards their educational value with younger students (Shuler, 2009). Parents, in turn, allow children to use

---

1. Kazan Federal University, Kazan, Russia; gsadykova2015@mail.ru
2. Kazan Federal University, Kazan, Russia; gim-nar@yandex.ru
3. Kazan Federal University, Kazan, Russia; lilia_khalitova@mail.ru
4. Kazan Federal University, Kazan, Russia; alb1980@yandex.ru

How to cite this article: Sadykova, G., Gimaletdinova, G., Khalitova, L., & Kayumova, A. (2016). Integrating mobile technologies into very young second language learners' curriculum. In S. Papadima-Sophocleous, L. Bradley & S. Thouësny (Eds), *CALL communities and culture – short papers from EUROCALL 2016* (pp. 408-412). Research-publishing.net. https://doi.org/10.14705/rpnet.2016.eurocall2016.597

---

mobile devices even when they do not recognize their educational benefits (Chiong & Shuler, 2010).

This report is based on a case study built around a MALL program that was designed and integrated into the curriculum of five/six year-old children. The report focuses on the instructors' and parents' perception of MALL educational value for very young foreign language learners.

2. Method

This exploratory case study was designed to document and analyze efforts of a private multilingual kindergarten and preschool that enhanced the language curriculum with iPad tasks. Located in Kazan, a Russian city with a multicultural population, this school for children from ages two to six emphasizes the importance of early multilingual education and promotes a curriculum that enriches native (Russian and Tatar) language developmental programs with English, Spanish and Chinese language classes. In late 2015, teaming up with experts in English teaching and educational technologies, the school designed a small-scale program with mobile English language activities for a group of preschoolers (N=12) who had previously studied English for two and a half years. In spring 2016, Reading Eggs™ (http://readingeggs.co.uk/), an internationally recognised Australian program with online reading games and activities for children aged three to 13, was selected as an appropriate mobile application introduced into the curriculum of 12 children whose native language(s) is\are Russian and\or Tatar.

The leading teacher of the class that participated in the study reviewed the Reading Eggs™ application and redesigned her regular English language curriculum to integrate activities suggested by the program. Due to the lack of mobile equipment in school, the Reading Eggs™ activities were suggested for homework to enhance language skills developed in class. The leading teacher registered each child to the mobile application and modeled learning tasks in class to children and after class to each parent individually. As the school promotes active parent-to-child learning, parents were encouraged to supervise and guide their children when they were on the mobile device. The children completed activities at home on their iPads for 30 days (the period of free trial of this commercial application). The activities suggested by the Reading Eggs™ application included picture recognition, word comprehension and voiced books with reading/listening comprehension questions. The application was used to enhance reading and listening comprehension skills in support of the content material covered in the classroom. The leading teacher regularly checked if students completed homework activities and evaluated their progress by incorporating Reading Eggs™ tasks into class work. She also administered a test after the 30-day project.

While the case study collected data to get in-depth understanding of the conditions and results of the MALL activities integrated into the curriculum of young language learners, for the purpose of this report the following research question is selected as focal point: What are the teachers' and the parents' perceptions of integrating MALL into very young second language learners' curriculum?

Parents of 12 children who participated in the MALL activities, as well as all English teachers of the multilingual school, including the leading teacher of the target children group, were asked to complete paper-based questionnaires consisting of one open- and four closed-ended questions. 12 parents and eight teachers responded to the questionnaires.

3.   Results and discussion

Responses from Question 1 of both questionnaires established that the survey was completed by school teachers who worked with children from ages two to seven and by parents of five/six year olds.

Question 2 of the teacher questionnaire stated *"Do you use any educational mobile applications for English language teaching? If yes, please, name these applications"*. The responses indicated that three teachers (37.5%) used mobile applications for language learning and five (62.5%) had not yet adopted MALL for their teaching practices. When parents were asked the same question in regards to their own children, all 12 of them named Reading Eggs™ as the application in use by their children.

Question 3 in both questionnaires stated *"Do educational mobile applications facilitate kindergarteners' language learning?"*. The question referred to teachers' and parents' general perceptions of MALL effectiveness and no additional guidance was given. However, as the questionnaire was administered after the 30-day project was completed, it was assumed that parents would base their answers on observations of their children learning with the Reading Eggs™ application. The teachers' responses demonstrated that they shared the belief in the high educational value of MALL; none of them questioned language learning potential of mobile applications irrespective of whether they used them or not. Parents, in their turn, did not demonstrate unanimity. One parent (8.3%) fully agreed that mobile applications enhance language learning among kindergarteners, 66.7% were not so certain and others (25%) expressed their doubt that mobile applications can assist in language learning. These results were later clarified in the interview with the leading teacher of the target children group. She explained that while all 12 parents were aware of the Reading Eggs™ application and were encouraged to support their child's MALL experience, only seven parents did so and only four children participated in mobile language activities on a regular basis. This indicates that not all parents whose children were supposed to be involved into the project did have a chance to experience MALL benefits and therefore they might have based their opinion on unjustified common beliefs.

Question 4 asked the teachers and parents to characterize language learning applications by selecting one or more answers from a list of ten options. The majority of the teachers found language-learning applications beneficial since they entertain, teach, motivate and enable teachers to diversify their lessons. Still, more than half of the teachers thought that mobile applications might cause addiction (62.5%), while a quarter of respondents (25%) believed that they did not teach at all and limited social interaction. One teacher believed that mobile phones increased the risk of eye damage.

In contrast to the teachers, the parents turned out to be technology pessimists. Most parents found language-learning applications harmful and causing problems such as eye damage (66.6%) and addiction (58.3%). 33% of parents agreed that mobile applications limit social interaction, 8.3% of parents believed that mobile applications distract children from studies and are of no benefit in general. However, half of the parents admitted that mobile applications entertain, teach and motivate, 25% of parents believed that mobile applications may diversify lessons, and 8.35% of parents described apps as 'effective'.

Question 5 of the parents' questionnaire, which aimed at examining overall children's involvement into the digital culture, stated *"Does your child use any mobile applications (games etc.)?"*. Out of 12 parents, the majority (91.6%) reported that their children used mobile applications. One parent answered that his/her child did not use mobile devices. However, when cross-checking with Question 2, it became evident that the child did use one mobile application – Reading Eggs™.

In the teachers' questionnaire, Question 5 stated *"What difficulties can arise/arose when using mobile technologies in EFL classrooms in a group of kindergarteners?"*. The teachers could select answers from a list of 5 options or give their own answer.

All the teachers thought that using mobile applications was challenging because they might lack access to a mobile device. Another problem that was noted was teachers' inability to use mobile applications with certain groups of students; particularly learners' very young age was seen as an obstacle. The teachers were also concerned about their insufficient knowledge of methodology of using mobile technologies for educational purposes and their inexperience in the sphere of mobile technologies in general.

4.   Conclusions

MALL projects gradually find their place in the curriculum of young language learners. The study indicates that most parents may not share enthusiasm of teachers about high educational potentials of modern mobile applications for developing literacy skills, including foreign language literacy. Moreover, the findings suggest that while integrating MALL activities into homework can sometimes solve the problem with the lack of appropriate mobile devices in schools, some parents may not be ready to assist their children with mobile language learning tasks. Further research is needed to provide evidence-based recommendations on the effective ways of integrating mobile activities into the curriculum of very young foreign language learners. While each case has unique MALL integration conditions, projects similar to the one described in this report, may assist researchers and practitioners in building an understanding of the *hows* and *whys* MALL projects could work in a given educational context. It is our hope that school teachers' enthusiasm about MALL will help to overcome some parents' apparent disinvolvement and skepticism about MALL benefits discussed in this study.

References

AL-Maagb, I. F. F. (2016). Pre-service EFL teachers' perceptions of the role of Ipad in language learning. *Research on Humanities and Social Sciences, 6*(2), 10-19.

Chiong, C., & Shuler, C. (2010). *Learning: is there an app for that? Investigations of young children's usage and learning with mobile devices and apps.* New York: The Joan Ganz Cooney Center at Sesame Workshop.

Shuler, C. (2009). *Pockets of potential: using mobile technologies to promote children's learning.* New York: The Joan Ganz Cooney Center at Sesame Workshop.

Tai, Y., & Ting, Y. L. (2011). Adoption of mobile technology for language learning: teacher attitudes and challenges. *The JALT CALL Journal, 7*(1), 3-18.

Investigating commercially available technology for language learners in higher education within the high functioning disability spectrum

Georgia Savvidou[1] and Fernando Loizides[2]

Abstract. This work presents the assistive use of a combination of technologies in language learning to individuals with high functioning disabilities within a higher education environment. The primary aim of this research is to introduce the initial findings of a pilot exploratory user test which aims to facilitate a better understanding of the suitability and user preference of technological tools in language learning; specifically of children with disabilities. In this article, we present a case study of ten young adults with different levels of needs and abilities, including dyspraxia, dyslexia, dysgraphia, attention deficit disorder, articulation, learning difficulties and psychological problems. The learners, engaged in different disciplines in higher education, were exposed to bespoke and off the shelf solutions as assistive technologies.

Keywords: language learning, learning difficulties, technology.

1. Introduction and motivation

This paper presents a case study of young adults with different levels of needs and abilities undertaking different disciplines in higher education. The students attend an English language course in which certain technologies such as educational softwares and devices are utilized in order to facilitate their learning and enhance their motivation. The instructor is faced with the challenge of designing an English for specific purposes course and at the same time tailor it with the individual needs of students (Bocanegra-Valle, 2010). The course effectiveness depends on the content attractiveness in combination with the feeling of achievement on the part of the students.

1. Cyprus University of Technology, Limassol, Cyprus; georgia.savvidou@cut.ac.cy
2. University of Wolverhampton, Wolverhampton, United Kingdom; fernando.loizides@wlv.ac.uk

How to cite this article: Savvidou, G., & Loizides, F. (2016). Investigating commercially available technology for language learners in higher education within the high functioning disability spectrum. In S. Papadima-Sophocleous, L. Bradley & S. Thouësny (Eds), *CALL communities and culture – short papers from EUROCALL 2016* (pp. 413-417). Research-publishing.net. https://doi.org/10.14705/rpnet.2016.eurocall2016.598

The teaching and learning process becomes challenging when this involves students with learning difficulties (Lackaye, Margalit, Ziv, & Ziman, 2006). Strategic planning and curriculum adaptations are thus considered essential, and making necessary changes in the curriculum enhances the learning of students with special educational needs (Ainscow et al., 2006). Based on anticipated learning outcomes, educators need to make the correct decision-making in terms of the teaching material and tools implementation (Marek, 2014). Technology has proven to be an assistive tool due to the fact that it offers students with special educational needs the ability to engage in ways in which adapts to their individual needs and abilities (Edwards, Blackhurst & Koorland, 1995 mentioned in Fernandez-Lopez, Rodriguez-Fortiz, Rodriguez-Almendros, & Martinez-Segura, 2013, p. 22). Educating students with special needs can utilize technology to increase their focus on tasks to be performed (Fernandez-Lopez et al., 2013, p.78). Kukulska-Hulme and Traxler (2007) suggest that mobile technologies amplify all kinds of learning including "personalized, situated, authentic and informal learning" (cited in Jones et al., 2013, p. 22). That is to say, mobile technology learning has been successfully implemented in location based inquiries where learners were asked to explore their educational environment and take an active role in their own learning.

However, what needs to be taken into consideration for students with special needs is that educators should seek for technological devices or softwares which are simple and user-friendly (Marek, 2014). It has been found that 'text-based synchronous activities' may disadvantage those with disabilities due to their difficulties in reading, writing and spelling (Woodfine, Nunes, & Wright, 2008). In contrast, the findings highlight that the specific learners are more comfortable in composing a text due to the nature of an asynchronous environment than in not immediately having to respond, which enables them to both prepare better as well as feel less rushed to provide a response (Woodfine et al., 2008). Technology and the internet have also been applied in teaching Languages for Specific Purposes (LSP) in a way that they have generated tools which assist in providing students with a realistic experience in terms of their social perspective of things (Arno-Macia, 2012).

2.   Methodology

The course lasted for one or two academic years (nine month period per year) with students in groups of two to four receiving two sessions a week, between one to two hours. The course began with one-to-one meetings with the students, after a liaison with the educational psychologist, where they were assessed by being asked to write about themselves. This assessment includes an evaluation of their abilities such as handwriting, spelling, structure and language level. After completing the individual assessment, a discussion is initiated between the professor and the student which enables the professor to gather further information concerning the students' English language experience, diagnoses, level of support they have received as well as its effectiveness and difficulties they would like to report on. This material is then used to match the students' individual requirements with their learning expectations and also match appropriate technologies to each group. In order to engage the students and improve the learning process, a series of technologies are implemented in the classroom environment to involve the students in individual activities.

The assistive technology tools adopted by the instructor included Google Drive and Google Sites for uploading and sharing classroom material and assignments, PowerPoint and Prezi which served as presentation tools, Wordle, QR codes and Instagram for reading and vocabulary purposes, Glogster for producing written work, Kahoot software for revising the course material before the midterm and final exams and Pathbrite for creating an E-Portfolio at the end of the semester. It should be noted that the Bring Your Own Device (BYOD) system was followed in class through which learners accessed the lecture work and material via their laptops, iPads or smartphones. In order to gather data from our participants, a questionnaire was implemented with questions relevant to the course design. The questionnaire was handed out to the students at the completion of the semester. It comprised of fifteen questions including both open and close-ended questions. The questions revolved around three main themes: (1) the learnability of the technologies, (2) the usefulness of the technologies, and (3) the usability and user satisfaction of the technologies. Likewise, also examined was whether they feel their English had improved during the semester.

3.   Findings and discussion

3.1.   The learnability of the technologies

Most of the learners (seven out of ten) commented on both the Google Drive and Google Sites being user-friendly and practical since by the end of the course they became accustomed to their use. However, Wordle seemed to have had a negative impact on the students who expressed their difficulty in tracing the words and explained that the jumbled characters were really hard to recall. Likewise,

Glogster was deemed 'user unfriendly', thus learners found it extremely difficult to experiment with its format and tools. Nevertheless, there was an agreement among students (eight out of ten) in the ease the Pathbrite E-Portfolio provided them with.

3.2. The usefulness of the technologies

This theme revolves around the idea of utilizing technologies with effective learning tools. There was a consensus in the participants (nine out of ten) who stressed the significance of PowerPoint during the lecture due to the fact that it contains all the keywords and important details in combination to audiovisual material (pictures, videos, etc.). Based on the learners' comments, QR codes turned the whole learning experience into an enjoyable moment through which students became more motivated to learn. Surprisingly enough, Instagram was thought to be quite monotonous and six out of ten students stated their lack of interest in using lecture-related hashtags. Conversely, all learners showed a great preference towards Kahoot which they stressed had boosted their memory and therefore developed their learning. Generally, the results interpretation highlights that the use of mobile devices and computer software increased the participants' confidence; both their linguistic knowledge and technology skills have been developed.

3.3. The usability and user-satisfaction of the technologies

This category was created to refer to the pleasure the technologies offered the participants. The majority of the students (eight out of ten) found Google Drive and Google Sites extremely convenient even though at the beginning of the course only a few of them used a Google account. For this reason, they expressed their preference for using Google Drive for storing documents and files in general. Prezi undoubtedly outweighed PowerPoint since, according to eight out of ten students, "it is more attractive and memorable". Equally, QR codes were awarded as the most enjoyable and effective technology medium and all learners were engaged in the activity. Finally, a great number of students (seven out of ten) enjoyed creating the Pathbrite E-Portfolio due to the fact that they could gather all their assignments and course work in one folder.

4. Conclusions and future work

In this paper we presented a series of technologies to students with disabilities and encouraged their use throughout a language learning course. We report on initial findings which provide us with evidence of usage and user satisfaction of the technology's use. We aim to build from these findings an initial framework of technologies that can be promoted for language learners with disabilities through longitudinal and larger scale structured testing.

References

Ainscow, M., Booth, T., Dyson, A., Farrell, P., Frankham, J., Gallannaugh, F., Howes, A., & Smith, R. (2006). *Improving schools, developing inclusion.* London: Routledge. Apple Bonjour Technology. http://www.apple.com/bonjour

Arno-Macia, E. (2012). The role of technology in teaching languages for specific purposes courses. *The Modern Language Journal, 96*(1), 89-104. https://doi.org/10.1111/j.1540-4781.2012.01299.x

Bocanegra-Valle, A. (2010). Evaluating and designing materials for the ESP classroom. *Utrecht Studies in Language and Communication, 22*, 141-165.

Edwards, B. J., Blackhurst, A. E., & Koorland, M. A. (1995). Computer-assisted constant time delay prompting to teach abbreviation spelling to adolescents with mild learning disabilities. *Journal of Special Education Technology, 12*(4), 301-311.

Fernandez-Lopez, A., Rodriguez-Fortiz, M. J., Rodriguez-Almendros, M. L., & Martinez-Segura, M. J. (2013). Mobile learning technology based on iOS devices to support students with special education needs. *Computers and Education, 61*, 77-90. https://doi.org/10.1016/j.compedu.2012.09.014

Jones, A. C., Scalnon, E., & Clough, G. (2013). Mobile learning: two case studies of supporting inquiry learning in informal and semiformal settings. *Computers and Education. 61*, 21-32.

Kukulska-Hulme, A., & Traxler, J. (2007). Designing for mobile and wireless learning. In H. Beetham & R. Sharpe (Eds), *Rethinking pedagogy for a digital age: designing and delivering e-learning* (pp. 180-192). London, UK: Routledge.

Lackaye, T., Margalit, M., Ziv, O., & Ziman, T. (2006). Comparisons of self-efficacy, mood, effort, and hope between students with learning disabilities and their non-LD-matched peers. *Learning Disabilities Research & Practice, 21*, 111-121. https://doi.org/10.1111/j.1540-5826.2006.00211.x

Marek, M. W. (2014). *The integration of technology and language instruction to enhance EFL learning.* http://eric.ed.gov/?id=ED545477

Woodfine, P. B., Nunes, B. M., & Wright, J. D. (2008). Text-based synchronous e-learning and dyslexia: not necessarily the perfect match! *Computers and Education, 50*(3), 703-717. https://doi.org/10.1016/j.compedu.2006.08.010

Learning languages in 3D worlds with Machinima

Christel Schneider[1]

Abstract. This paper, based on the findings of the EU funded CAMELOT project (2013-2015), explores the added value of Machinima (videos produced in 3D virtual environments) in language learning. The project research evaluated all stages, from developing to field testing Machinima. To achieve the best outcome, mixed methods were used for the research, including quantitative and qualitative techniques of data collection, such as questionnaires, interviews and focus group discussions. The data were provided by teachers and learners using Machinima in their classroom, as well as by learners participating in web based language courses of which all results were well documented in the form of case studies.

Keywords: language learning with Machinima, 3D virtual environments, video production.

1.   Introduction

Considering that more and more videos are utilised for educational purposes to enhance users' learning experiences, the EU-funded project 'Cre**A**ting **Machinima** to **E**mpower **L**ive **O**nline Language **T**eaching and Learning' (CAMELOT[2]) assesses the design and usability of video captures, which are film recordings of 3D virtual experiences (Machinima). Based on the CAMELOT project (2013-2015) which aims to promote learning in 3D virtual worlds and trigger interest in teaching and learning in these immersive environments, my study investigated two Machinima Open Online Training courses (MOOT) designed for language educators to learn how to create videos (Machinima). The term Machinima is a neologism, derived from merging the words '**machin**e + **cinema**', first used in the late 1990s (Marino, 2004). In the context of language learning, Machinima are closely related to independent filmmaking as they follow a similar process, which includes design, storyboarding,

---

1. CSiTrain, Hamburg, Germany; chris.schneider@csitrain.net

2. http://camelotproject.eu/

filming and editing. The study results indicate that learners involved in the creation of Machinima gain a better understanding of the impact immersion in 3D virtual worlds has on the learning process and learning outcomes.

2.   Method

For the research, a mixed method approach was chosen, composing several case studies triangulating participating observation with qualitative and quantitative data. This appeared to be particularly useful in cases where questions could not be answered by one method alone (Creswell, 2014). Core areas of the study were carried out in the form of participating observation during the MOOT courses, including synchronous training sessions in Second Life® (SL) and in Adobe Connect™, as well as asynchronous session observations on Moodle. The sessions on Moodle prepared the learners to create their own Machinima with a specific focus on grammar, a narrative, or instructions for the level and language required in the physical or virtual language classroom. The activities on Moodle included discussions, feedback, self-assessment and surveys. The skill practice for creating and editing Machinima took place in SL and Adobe Connect™. Additionally, expert interviews with Machinimatographers and teachers using Machinima with their learners were conducted via Skype or in SL. For the field testing research, a series of Machinima of different styles, formats, language levels and languages, created for the CAMELOT project, were piloted at the University of Istanbul, the National Defence University in Warsaw, the University of West Bohemia, a Secondary Content and Language Integrated Learning School in the Netherlands and by LinguaTV, a video based online language course provider. Of all the courses piloted, 726 learners from higher education, adult education, secondary education, primary schools and one class of students with special needs in a secondary school responded to the survey. The field testing research was based on focus group discussion reports using guided questions, teachers' reports, and questionnaires completed by teachers and students (CAMELOT, 2015).

3.   Discussion

3.1.   Creating Machinima – benefits and challenges

During the two facilitated MOOT courses, enough space was provided for developing social presence, essential for successful collaboration and group activities, such as creating a storyline or exploring different roles and outfits of avatars. It was observed how the activities in SL encouraged interaction and bonding and thus increased mutual support and motivation among the participants, which resulted in a high attendance level and course completion (Wheeler, 2005). Apart from the technical skill set needed to create Machinima, the MOOT courses provided space for discussing challenges and advantages of learning in 3D environments. Some of the benefits discussed were that the learners were not just consumers of content, but became actively involved in the production process (Corrigan, 2014). Further shared advantages were that learners perceived as shy in the physical classroom opened up and became more confident when performing in the virtual environment (De Jong Derrington, 2013).

3.1.1. Time and effort

Experts and practitioners had very opposing experiences in regards to the time needed for creating Machinima. Hancock and Ingram (2007) state that creating Machinima is much faster than shooting real life films, whereas Morozov (2008) argues that the whole process of Machinima production can be quite challenging as it requires a complex set of skills. The actual time spent on the creation of Machinima on the MOOT varied quite a bit, depending on people's skills, technical barriers, personal commitments and goals (Schneider, 2016).

3.1.2. Quality of Machinima

The quality of Machinima was discussed in regards to the expected outcomes of Machinima productions and the way they were perceived by users. None of the Machinima created during the MOOT could be expected to be highly professional. However, teachers accepted their self-created Machinima more easily if they conveyed the learning content in a suitable way (Schneider, 2016). Their learners did not care about the quality of Machinima as long as the content triggered their interest, and the fact that their teacher had created them was especially appreciated. Yet, the evaluation of field testing surveys showed that some Machinima were considered to be of poor quality, because of the lack of non-verbal expressions and the unnatural looks and movements of avatars.

The findings imply that the quality of Machinima is often determined by the user (Schneider, 2016). Discussions with practitioners revealed that regardless of imperfections, quality is secondary as long as the Machinima are relevant, include a fun element and are used as a learning tool, involving learners in the production process. Nonetheless, other examples showed that the quality of

Machinima did matter when using other people's video productions. Teachers and learners unfamiliar with virtual environments or 3D games tended to critique ready-made Machinima because they could not identify with the avatars or even rejected them. Perceptions of avatar aesthetics and the lack of seriousness also had an effect on some learners in their engagement with ready-made Machinima (Schneider, 2016). The following excerpts from the CAMELOT MOOT course 2015 demonstrate the different stages of Machinima productions and skill sets: https://youtu.be/GopJmoH3-s4.

3.1.3.   Learners' involvement

Various language facilitators who were interviewed about teaching in 3D virtual worlds all shared the experience that engaging learners in the process of making Machinima is significantly more important than the actual Machinima. Some were even convinced that their students learn better and even faster by being involved in the production process. Considering that active involvement in Machinima production is essential for successful language learning, the value of including learners in the reflection and feedback discussion appears even more important. Machinima recordings allow learners to review their interactions by reflecting on their performance, and make improvements by re-shooting the scenes they are not satisfied with. Watching the recordings of their activities in a role-play, for example, helps learners to review and analyse their performance and develop an awareness of the language used.

3.2.   Field testing Machinima

The Machinima piloted were ready-made, including teaching guides and materials. As the focus group discussions revealed, people's opinion about advantages and disadvantages of ready-made Machinima were quite different. Some teachers benefitted from ready-made Machinima as it saved them preparation time, whereas others criticised that the language level did not suit their students' needs. The option of creating their own Machinima was considered too demanding in regards to the required skills, equipment and lack of institutional support. It was agreed that ready-made Machinima that focused precisely on what was needed in the lesson were most efficient.

It is remarkable that of the 726 students piloting ready-made Machinima in their lessons, 75% felt comfortable about the learning experience, though the majority preferred traditional videos (CAMELOT, 2015). Issues addressed by the learners were the missing facial expressions and gestures of avatars and their artificial appearance. In some cases, poor sound quality and bad graphics added to the critical assessment (Schneider, 2016, p. 41). Regardless of all critical comments, most piloting teachers reported that their learners felt inspired and attracted by the novelty of using Machinima in the classroom on top of learning something new; they also had fun and enjoyed the lesson. Younger students did not seem to have problems with the avatars or environment as they were used to virtual characters from computer games (Jauregi et al., 2011).

4.   Conclusions

It can be determined that the most effective and rewarding Machinima were the ones that involved the learners in the production process, which none of the students experienced as a 'waste of time'. It is essential for the learning process to immerse in 3D virtual environments to understand the benefits of this kind of learning. Positive experiences through active participation, interaction, mutual support and community building have proven to have a great impact on teaching and learning with Machinima.

As far as the study revealed, it could not be foreseen whether a particular Machinima appealed to a specific group of students or not and whether learners achieved more than they would have done without the use of Machinima. To find out more about the influence of Machinima on language learning, additional and long term research would be necessary to examine which genre of Machinima appeals to different types of learners.

5.   Acknowledgements

The CAMELOT project has been funded with support from the European Commission. This publication reflects the views only of the author, and the Commission cannot be held responsible for any use which may be made of the information contained therein.

References

CAMELOT. (2015). Creating Machinima empowers live online language teaching and learning: 5.3 evaluation of field testing. *Language learning with Machinima*. http://camelotproject.eu/wp-content/uploads/2014/11/WP5.3_EvaluationofFieldTesting.pdf

Corrigan, S. (2014, February 22). Learn it town ESL/EFL students: how to improve pronunciation through performance. *YouTube* [video]. https://youtu.be/Ib2aQKanXKQ

Creswell, J. W. (2014). *A concise introduction to mixed methods research* [Kindle ed.]. Thousand Oaks, California: SAGE Publications.

De Jong Derrington, M. (2013). Second language acquisition by immersive and collaborative task-based learning in a virtual world. In M. Childs & A. Peachey (Eds), *Understanding learning in virtual worlds, human-computer interaction series* (pp.135-163). London: Springer. https://doi.org/10.1007/978-1-4471-5370-2_8

Hancock, H., & Ingram J. (2007). *Machinima for dummies.* Indianapolis, Indiana: Wiley Publishing.

Jauregi, K., Canto, S., De Graaff, R., Koenraad, T., & Moonen, M. (2011). Verbal interaction in Second Life: towards a pedagogic framework for task design. *Computer Assisted Language Learning, 24*(1), 77-101.

Marino, P. (2004). *3D game-based filmmaking: the art of Machinima.* Scottsdale, Arizona: Paraglyph Press.

Morozov, A. (2008). Machinima learning: prospects for teaching and learning digital literacy skills through virtual filmmaking. In J. Luca & E. Weippl (Eds), *Proceedings of EdMedia: World Conference on Educational Multimedia, Hypermedia and Telecommunications, 2008* (pp. 5898-5907). AACE

Schneider, C. (2016). *Exploring the added value of Machinima in language teaching and learning. A case study.* MA thesis, University of the West of England.

Wheeler, S. (2005). Creating social presence in digital learning environments: a presence of mind? *Featured Paper for the TAFE Conference, Queensland, Australia, 11 November 2005.* http://citeseerx.ist.psu.edu/viewdoc/download?doi=10.1.1.99.7721&rep=rep1&type=pdf

What are more effective in English classrooms: textbooks or podcasts?

Jaime Selwood[1], Joe Lauer[2], and Kazumichi Enokida[3]

Abstract. In the 21st century it has become clear that more and more language-learning pedagogical materials have begun to shift to a digital mobile-access format and away from being a textbook and classroom based one. High quality language-learning podcasts can provide a cheap, beneficial and portable technology that allows learners the freedom to access useful materials whenever and wherever convenient – especially through smartphones. However, despite the low cost involved in producing and accessing podcasts, educational institutions still seem reluctant to fully utilise them as an integral part of the language-learning process. This presentation will outline the structure of a comprehensive study that analysed the communicative abilities of 102 university freshmen students undertaking a compulsory English oral communication course. The study was divided into a traditional model that was centred-around a paper textbook and digital model where no textbooks were used and the course was structured around a series of high-quality, pedagogically sound English language podcasts. It was found that students progressed in similar ways during the course, regardless of the pedagogical materials used.

Keywords: podcasts, mobile assisted language learning, authentic materials, smartphones.

1. Introduction

In a comprehensive study, the English communicative abilities of 102 university freshmen at a Japanese university were analysed in detail during one semester. Two instructors each taught two classes; the first being a traditional model which was structured around a textbook, whilst in the other course a digital model was

1. Hiroshima University, Hiroshima, Japan; jselwood@hiroshima-u.ac.jp
2. Hiroshima University, Hiroshima, Japan; lauer@hiroshima-u.ac.jp
3. Hiroshima University, Hiroshima, Japan; kenokida@hiroshima-u.ac.jp

How to cite this article: Selwood, J., Lauer, J., & Enokida, K. (2016). What are more effective in English classrooms: textbooks or podcasts? In S. Papadima-Sophocleous, L. Bradley & S. Thouësny (Eds), *CALL communities and culture – short papers from EUROCALL 2016* (pp. 424-428). Research-publishing.net. https://doi.org/10.14705/rpnet.2016.eurocall2016.600

implemented which utilised high-quality, pedagogically strong English language-learning podcasts. Following Lauer, Selwood, and Enokida (2016), a series of communicative language-learning tests were administered at the beginning, middle and end of the semester to assess the student's progress. The experimental model used in this study partially mirrored an influential study published by Gilmore (2011), which concluded that utilising *authentic materials* – which were mostly Internet-based – seemed to be more effective than traditional English-language learning textbooks. Thus, the goal of this study was to confirm Gilmore's (2011) findings by determining which pedagogical materials were more effective in improving students' oral abilities: textbooks or podcasts.

This paper will outline how the study was implemented, state the benefits that can be found through using non-authentic language learning materials, and report on the results of the tests administered.

2.   Background

The study attempted to determine if podcasts are more effective than textbooks in improving students' English communicative abilities. Significantly, podcasts can be accessed through mobile digital devices such as smartphones or tablets. The potential of podcasts as a language-learning tool is that pedagogically strong podcasts can provide high-quality 'authentic' materials. As Bishop, Amankwatia, and Cates (2008) explain, "podcasts have the power to focus attention and assist language learners to acquire useful and authentic language" (pp. 467-486).

English Language Teaching (ELT) textbooks, on the other-hand, often provide learners an impoverished or distorted view of the native language (Gilmore, 2007). The dialogues in textbooks are often centred-around contrived utterances, with the goal often being to illustrate a particular grammar point whilst highlighting frequent, easy to understood but unnatural vocabulary.

Podcasts also have the potential to motivate because they are often published weekly or monthly and so students are provided with information as events unfold, whilst textbooks can often include language that has been specially adapted, thus losing its authenticity whilst often containing information and facts that soon become out-of-date. Another factor that is often undervalued is that most language-learning podcasts are free, so podcasts can offer a more egalitarian method to language-learners as the materials can be accessed free of charge.

The ultimate aim of a language-learning course should be to improve students' language abilities and communicative competence. Traditionally in Japan, ELT textbooks are the go-to *authentic material* used on language-learning courses. Yet, in a prominent study, Gilmore (2011) concluded that students at a university in Japan significantly improved their communicative competence over a ten month period when they used web-based materials compared to a similar group of students who used only textbooks. The authors wanted to evaluate how successful podcasts could be when used as an essential tool in an English communicative course. By using Gilmore's (2011) study as a starting point, they wished to contrast and evaluate the effectiveness of podcasts in comparison with textbooks.

3.   Method

Two of the authors – Selwood and Lauer – each taught one podcast-centred course and one textbook-centred course. Each author chose different textbooks and podcasts to be used in the study. The podcasts selected by Selwood were *English News Weekly*, *English News Students*, *BBC Six Minute Podcast* and *BBC The English We Speak*. Lauer chose four different podcasts and these were *Hiroshima University's English Podcast*, *VOA Podcast*, *Daily English Show* and *ECC Podcast*. Selwood selected *English Speak* (Selwood, 2014) as his textbook whilst Lauer chose *Slumdog Millionaire* (Close, 2010). All the materials were selected because of their high pedagogical quality and their usage of authentic language.

Each course lasted for one 15-week-semester and each class was 90 minutes in length and held once-a-week. Both the textbook and podcast courses were compulsory first year English communication classes. The students were assigned to each class depending on their faculty and their university entrance exam score and the TOEIC test (the standard English language test used in Japan – the highest score is 900 points). Lauer's textbook class had an average score of 540/900 whilst his podcast class was 419/900. In contrast Selwood's podcast class was 629/900 whilst his textbook class was 467/900. This meant that each author had a 'weaker' and 'stronger' ability class and so the study could be measured amongst students of differing abilities.

To assess students' progress, three sets of tests were included in the survey – at the beginning, middle and end of the semester. The tests focused on grammar, listening and speaking because according to Canale and Swain (1980), these are the essential parts in measuring and analysing communicative competence. The three tests were:

- **Communicative Vocabulary-Grammar Test**. This measured students' vocabulary and grammar skills. This test contained 49 questions, taken from a standard TOEIC test and the same 49 questions were used in all three tests, albeit with the question order changed from test to test.

- **Communicative Listening Test**. This measured general listening ability through 21 questions taken from a TOEIC practice test. Again the question order was re-arranged for each test.

- **Three Minute Recorded Speaking Test**. For this test students were placed in pairs and for three minutes the students entered into a dialogue recorded using smartphones. The audio was then emailed to their teacher for analysis.

4.   Results

The Communicative Vocabulary-Grammar Test results showed only a tiny improvement in both courses. In the textbook classes the average score increased from 69% to 72% whilst the podcast courses showed a tiny increase from 69% to 70%. However, the stand-out result from the study was the improvement in Communicative Listening Test results in both courses. The textbook students improved their listening scores from an average, per student, from 43% to 54%. The podcast students also improved from an average score of 39% to 51% by the end of the semester.

The Three Minute Recorded Speaking Test also showed small improvements in both courses. In the podcast course, each student, on average, increased their word count by 15 words per three minutes. However, in the podcast courses students only increased, on average, by seven words per three minutes.

5.   Conclusions

The study found that, disappointingly, there were no differences in which authentic materials were used. The textbook courses worked just as well as the podcast ones. However, there were mitigating factors to why these results occurred. Firstly, the length of the study was only four months. Secondly, each class met just once a week for 90 minutes. Thirdly, the testing method used to assess the project was hindered by using the TOEIC test as this measures listening ability, vocabulary knowledge and speaking skills. However the test is limited in how it measures students' sociolinguistic abilities, discourse and strategic skills. The authors used this testing method as it had been used in Gilmore's (2011) study as well as being the pre-eminent English language test used in Japanese universities.

In the future, researchers wishing to investigate the merits of podcasts should focus on correcting the problems encountered by the authors on this study, namely expanding the length of time the study runs for.

References

Bishop, M. J., Amankwatia, T. B., & Cates, W. M. (2008). Soound's use in instructional software: a theory to practice content analysis. *Educational technology Research & Development, 56*(4), 467-486. https://doi.org/10.1007/s11423-006-9032-3

Canale, M., & Swain, M. (1980). Theoretical bases of communicative approaches to second language teaching and testing. *Applied Linguistics, 1*(1), 1-47.

Close, B. (2010). *Slumdog millionaire.* Tokyo: RIC Publications.

Gilmore, A. (2007). Authentic materials and authenticity in foreign language learning. *Language Teaching, 40*(2), 97-118. https://doi.org/10.1017/S0261444807004144

Gilmore, A. (2011). "I prefer not to text": developing Japanese leaners' communicative competence with authentic materials. *Language Teaching, 61*(3), 786-819. https://doi.org/10.1111/j.1467-9922.2011.00634.x

Lauer, J., Selwood, J., & Enokida, K. (2016). Which are more effective in English conversation classrooms: textbooks or podcasts? *Hiroshima Studies in Language and Language Education, 19*, 129-140.

Selwood, J. J (2014). *English speak.* Self-published textbook. http://www.jaimeselwood.com/communication-ia

Mind the gap: task design and technology in novice language teachers' practice

Tom F. H. Smits[1], Margret Oberhofer[2], and Jozef Colpaert[3]

Abstract. This paper focuses on the possibilities/challenges for English as a Foreign Language (EFL) teachers designing tasks grounded in Task-Based Language Teaching (TBLT) and taking advantage of the affordances of technology – Interactive WhiteBoards (IWBs). Teachers have been shown to confuse tasks with exercises or activities. The interactive Technologies in Language Teaching (iTILT) projects revealed that when it comes to IWB use the focus often shifts from interactive teaching to interactive technology. To better prepare novice EFL teachers for their future teaching practice, an 'IWB for TLBT' training programme introduced the affordances of IWBs. Our analysis of how (un)successful they were at marrying TBLT and Information and Communication Technology (ICT) operationalised TBLT criteria from Nunan (2004) and Erlam (2016). Supporting evidence of the participants' aptitude in TBLT practice is provided by a traditional, non-IWB-oriented task each individual had designed earlier. Combining both elements in the analysis, our study answers the question: to what extent are pre-service teachers able to design a TBLT environment involving modern technology that adheres to iTILT principles and current theories of TBLT methodology?

Keywords: TBLT, task design, EFL, IWB, teacher education.

1. Introduction

The objective of the European interactive Teaching In Languages with Technology (iTILT2) project, launched in 2014, is to explore the affordances of devices like smartphones and IWBs. More specifically, it investigates the effective use of

1. Universiteit Antwerpen, Antwerp School of Education, Antwerpen, Belgium; tom.smits@uantwerp.be
2. Universiteit Antwerpen, Antwerpen, Belgium; margret.oberhofer@uantwerp.be
3. Universiteit Antwerpen, Antwerpen, Belgium; jozef.colpaert@uantwerp.be

How to cite this article: Smits, T. F. H., Oberhofer, M., & Colpaert, J. (2016). Mind the gap: task design and technology in novice language teachers' practice. In S. Papadima-Sophocleous, L. Bradley & S. Thouësny (Eds), *CALL communities and culture – short papers from EUROCALL 2016* (pp. 429-434). Research-publishing.net. https://doi.org/10.14705/rpnet.2016. eurocall2016.601

these interactive technologies within a TBLT approach. iTILT2 builds on, and extends, the EU project iTILT, focusing on IWBs for teaching foreign languages. However, iTILT2 moves beyond IWBs and includes effective educational design for foreign language learning with a wider range of new interactive technologies (tablets, laptops, mobile phones, videoconferencing software). The educational contexts vary from primary and secondary schools to vocational colleges and universities.

TBLT theory is central to ITILT2 and requires students to do meaningful tasks in the target language, having to choose for themselves the linguistic means for task completion. A task is "an activity in which people engage to attain an objective and which involves the meaningful use of language" (Van den Branden, Van Gorp, & Verhelst, 2007, p. 1). An objective can be anything from producing a poster or website to expressing opinions or writing song lyrics. As learning the target language means making use of it, learners are primarily seen as language users.

Research shows that many language teachers find it difficult to distinguish tasks from simple grammar exercises or activities for vocabulary practice. To help teachers, Shintani (2013) discussed the principles behind TBLT and outlined the main features of language learning tasks:

> 1. activity focus is on meaning, i.e. learners encode/decode messages, no grammar or vocabulary drilling;

> 2. communicative/information gap, e.g. learners need to ask for information they do not have (= gap) or need to express their opinion;

> 3. learners draw on their own (linguistic/non-linguistic) resources to complete tasks. They are not 'taught' the language nor the form to use to complete the task but are free to choose their 'means', although they could for example borrow from the input, use dictionaries/online resources, ask the teacher, etc.);

> 4. clearly defined outcomes other than mere language use, e.g. poster, form, handout, opinion, or reaching a compromise in discussions. While "performing a task, learners are not primarily concerned with using the language correctly but rather achieving the goal stipulated within the task" (Ellis, 2003, p. 35).

2. Method

2.1. Dataset

Our study goes beyond Erlam's (2016) by not limiting itself to applying criteria for task design (e.g. from Ellis, 2003, in Erlam's (2016) study) to evaluate foreign language teachers' self-made TBLT materials in a professional development programme; we also consider the conception of a task in the minds of (postgraduate) pre-service foreign language teachers (N= 28) by analysing a design task that had them formulate a *taaltaak* (integrated language/assessment task). Consequently, the dataset exists of (1) materials designed for use with the IWB, part of (the evaluation of) a series of lessons on TBLT, and (2) the somewhat more traditional *taaltaken*.

The latter tasks the participants designed before the IWB technology was introduced had to contain a step-by-step description with process and product requirements for one or more open-ended B1 tasks fostering the autonomous use of (a) language skill(s) in an authentic context. The choices student teachers made when designing these tasks revealed what they consider meaningful language use for learning and/or open communicative contexts.

Each set of IWB TBLT materials (i.e. the aforementioned (1)) consisted of a lesson plan and the TBLT materials for the IWB (Smarttech Notebook®). The assignment required student duos to plan a lesson on a cultural topic with B1 TBLT activities involving the IWB and to develop accompanying materials.

2.2. Data analysis

The criteria to analyse the pre-service teachers' TBLT approach and materials against were inspired by Nunan's (2004) aspects of qualitative task design: task objective, input quality, quality of activities, classroom setting, and teacher and learner roles.

Given our study's affinities with Erlam (2016), an evaluation grid was used that is based on the central features of TBLT in Nunan's (2004) paradigm and includes some of Erlam's (2016) task criteria (Table 1). The lesson material suits (min. three task slides) were independently evaluated by the first and second author (inter-rater reliability).

Table 1.   Task evaluation grid

1. Meaning versus form	(yes) 1/0.5/0 (no)	Comments/ Justifications
Are pupils acting as language users (rather than learners)?		
Are pupils mainly concerned with expressing/comprehending meaning (not focusing on form)?		
2. Information gap		
Do pupils close an information gap as a result of communication taking place?		
Do pupils find out something they did not know as a result of the communication?		
3. Learner resources		
Has not all language needed for the task been specially pre-taught?		
Does the task allow learners to use language learnt on other, unrelated occasions?		
4. Result/outcome		
Do pupils use English to achieve an outcome (not as an end in itself)?		
Do pupils have to achieve a result to demonstrate task completion?		
5. Technology use		
Is the use of technology integral to the task design? (Is it impossible to do the task without technology, not just more difficult?)		
Does the technology have added pedagogical value (not just motivational)?		

3.   Discussion

With an M score of 6.375/10 (SD=1.398), it cannot be claimed that all participants were successful at applying the programme's input in practice. Of the 14 IWB lesson designs, two were rated unsatisfactory, two achieved the highest score of 9/10. Zooming in on the task design criteria, the trainee teachers struggled most with the TBLT 'Information gap' element (No. 2 in the grid): utilising communication to close an information gap (M=0.429) and allowing pupils to find out something new (M=0.571). 'Meaning vs form' (No. 1) and 'Learner resources' (No. 3) were the aspects they performed best on. Having learners mainly concerned with expressing and comprehending meaning (instead of focusing on form) appears to have been easiest to achieve (M=0.833). Discussing further results would go beyond the scope of this short paper, but the study's practice-based output allows for fine-tuning of the criteria (within the iTILT2 project) so that researchers will have better tools to analyse the TBLT approach of (novice) teachers, and the teachers themselves a clearer idea of what sound TBLT requires.

A Pearson's r hypothesis test did not reveal a (significant) correlation between the IWB group assignment and the individual classic task design ($r=-0.105$, $n=7$, $p=0.6084$) that was to demonstrate causality between TBLT comprehension and task design quality. This does imply, however, that the pre-service teachers benefited from the collaborative aspect of the IWB assignment (and/or from the 'IWB for TBLT' programme itself) and – we would like to think – from the affordances of technology to facilitate meaningful, realistic tasks in class.

4.   Conclusions

The effect of TBLT can be increased considerably, but besides specific affordances, using new technologies like IWBs also entails constraints. From our study and our broader experience with technology, we infer four hypotheses.

> 1. Tasks should be made more motivating by focusing on their mental acceptability and students' willingness to carry them out. Meaningfulness ('What's in it for me?') and usefulness ('What's in it for others?') are key concepts in this respect.

> 2. Tasks should be seen within a wide range of possible activities, from simple drill-and-practice exercises to co-construction of knowledge. Bloom's Digital Taxonomy (Churches, 2009), the SAMR model (Romrell, Kidder, & Wood, 2014) or 21st Century Skills can be inspiring in this respect.

> 3. There is too much focus on the properties of the task as a product, and not enough on task design as a process: how to select and adapt tasks to the specific and variable context of language learners and teachers.

> 4. Tasks should always be seen as hypotheses. The validation of these hypotheses should be carried out by comparing the expected outcome with the actual outcome.

5. Acknowledgements

iTILT2, funded by Erasmus Plus programme (2014-17), focuses on mobile technologies and language learning; http://www.itilt2.eu. iTILT, funded by Lifelong Learning Programme (KA2 Languages, 2011-13), focused on IWBs for FLT; www.itilt.eu.

References

Branden, K. Van den, Gorp, K. Van, & Verhelst, M. (2007). Tasks in action: task-based language education from a classroom-based perspective. In K. Van den Branden, K. Van Gorp, & M. Verhelst (Eds), *Tasks in action. task-based language education from a classroom-based perspective* (pp. 1-6). Newcastle: Cambridge Scholars Publishing.

Churches, A. (2009). *Bloom's digital taxonomy; educational origamy.* http://edorigami. wikispaces.com/Bloom's+Digital+Taxonomy

Ellis, R. (2003). *Task-based language learning and teaching.* Oxford: Oxford University Press.

Erlam, R. (2016). 'I'm still not sure what a task is': teachers designing language tasks. *Language Teaching Research, 20*(3), 279-299. https://doi.org/10.1177/1362168814566087

Nunan, D. (2004). *Task-based language teaching.* Cambridge: Cambridge University Press. https://doi.org/10.1017/CBO9780511667336

Romrell, D., Kidder, L. C., & Wood, E. (2014). The SAMR model as a framework for evaluating mLearning. *Journal of Asynchronous Learning Networks, 18*(2), 1-15.

Shintani, N. (2013). Using tasks with young beginner learners: the role of the teacher. *Innovation in Language Learning and Teaching, 8*(3), 279-294. https://doi.org/10.1080/17501229.2013.861466

Language immersion in the self-study mode e-course

Olga Sobolev[1]

Abstract. This paper assesses the efficiency of the 'Language Immersion e-Course' developed at the London School of Economics and Political Science (LSE) Language Centre. The new self-study revision e-course, promoting students' proficiency in spoken and aural Russian through autonomous learning, is based on the Michel Thomas method, and is focused primarily on lexical work, which students commonly consider to be one of the biggest challenges in language studies. The course, targeted at the intermediate (A2/B1) level of proficiency in Russian (with a specific focus on language for Social Sciences) was incorporated into students' guided revision programme. The package is downloadable as a mobile application offering more flexibility for the users. This paper focuses on the pedagogical evaluation of the project (through students' feedback and their exam performance), and analyses the learning implications of such e-courses as a valuable alternative and added value to classroom teaching. Given that lexical command plays a fundamental role both in fluent language production (speaking and writing) and efficient comprehension (listening and reading), the paper asserts the benefits of such e-courses for blended learning programmes, as well as for improving overall efficiency of students' second language acquisition.

Keywords: mobile application, Michel Thomas method, lexical work, autonomous learning.

1. Introduction

A new self-study revision e-course was designed to develop students' proficiency in spoken and aural Russian and to enhance their skills as autonomous language learners. The Russian Language Course discussed here is offered to LSE undergraduates within their Degree programme. The project was based on the Michel Thomas communicative method (see below) and draws on several related areas of language, pedagogical research and practice. Firstly, it was designed to increase the number

1. London School of Economics and Political Science, London, United Kingdom; O.Sobolev@lse.ac.uk

How to cite this article: Sobolev, O. (2016). Language immersion in the self-study mode e-course. In S. Papadima-Sophocleous, L. Bradley & S. Thouësny (Eds), *CALL communities and culture – short papers from EUROCALL 2016* (pp. 435-439). Research-publishing.net. https://doi.org/10.14705/rpnet.2016.eurocall2016.602

of language immersion hours, especially during the Easter break in the lead-up to students' examinations. The absence of language practice during the four-week break may impair students' fluency and language command acquired over term time; this is largely the case for beginners/low intermediate level students, whose proficiency in Russian has not yet been consolidated by years of continuous tuition and practice.

Secondly, the project addresses difficulties associated with aural and lexical work in language learning. These areas of language acquisition are traditionally perceived by students as the most problematic (Rivers, 1992), and require significantly more practice to reach the same level of mastery as other modules. The issue becomes of particular pedagogical relevance in light of the fact that listening comprehension plays a major role (40-50%) in the overall process of language communication (Gilman & Moody, 1984).

Finally, the course reflects specialised Social Sciences focus of the LSE Language programme. The intention was to provide students with tailor-made language materials within a socio-political context (the relevant spectrum of topics is rare among commercial on-line materials), and to enhance their experience in language learning through a resource adaptable to the variety of learning abilities and individual needs.

2.   Method

The project is grounded in the Michel Thomas method, aimed at developing cognitive fluency through oral and aural practice by way of contextual reiteration of vocabulary and linguistic structures (Solity, 2008; Woodsmall & Woodsmall, 2008). The latter is combined with the 'inductive' mode of critical apprehension (grammatical concepts are derived from a series of examples rather than from traditionally 'pre-packed' explanations). The strength of the method lies in progressive accumulation of ready-to-use lexemes, allowing learners to retain vocabulary, while gaining a deeper understanding of how the language actually works. Every new lexical set is introduced topically within an exchange context. This, together with the interactive aspect (there is constant pressure to recall and reconstruct from the previously acquired lexical bank), provides an effective mode of multidimensional learning from internalising intonation and pronunciation to embedding contextual memory prompts.

The unique feature of the course is its subject-specific content, purposely designed for the LSE Language for Social Sciences programme. The development of this course ties in well with the general framework of applied research carried out by the Russian Section, which is focused on cognitive fluency study (Bershadsky, 2012; Sobolev & Nesterova, 2013).

The course was targeted at the intermediate (A2/B1) level of proficiency in Russian, and was incorporated into students' guided revision programme outside term-time classroom teaching (a group of 12 students used the resources for a continuous period of four weeks). The course was available as a mobile application (iPhone/ iPad/android devices), so that students could have some extra flexibility for the hours spent on their daily language routine (a full written transcript of the recording was accessible on-line).

The project's learning outcome and pedagogical impact were evaluated in two ways: informally, through students' feedback obtained through a short questionnaire; and formally, through students' performance in the end of year examinations. The questionnaire was paper-based, and circulated to students taking the course before examination results were published, and thus functions as an arguably more accurate gauge of the e-course as preparation for the examination.

3.   Results and discussion

The survey contained questions related to the academic values of the project: its pedagogical worth (i.e. increasing students' confidence as language users) and presentation. Students rated each aspect on a scale of one to five (with five being the highest rating). The overall feedback was highly rewarding: all aspects of the project were rated over 80% positive by 92% of students. No negative aspects were specified. In their written comments, students specifically mentioned that the course was extremely helpful for the exams and increased their confidence as language users. The latter was particularly noticeable in oral examinations: according to the external examiner's comments, students' ability to take initiative in conversation was outstanding for an *ab-initio* level group.

Students' performance in exams was compared to their average Continuous Assessment (CA) grade throughout the year; this grade is based on weekly assignments in all four language skills: oral, listening, reading and writing. The cohort was a mixed ability group of students, who had started learning Russian *ab initio* at the beginning of the year (with A2/B1 exit level). The average CA grade for the group (74.2%) corresponds to the average CA grade recorded for the last five years, showing that this was not an exceptionally able group of Russian learners.

The standard of students' performance in the exam was noticeably high: the average final grade was 2% higher than the CA grade obtained throughout the year. This was a positive improvement on the predicted result, reversing the trend for the last five years: the CA grade used to be 2% higher than the exam grade.

The breakdown of exam results in four language skills is presented in Figure 1, showing manifest improvement in all modules as compared to previous years. Given that these results cannot be attributed to the exceptional linguistic ability of the learners, this allows us to link the higher level of students' proficiency in Russian to the benefits of the revision e-course. Although it would perhaps be over-hasty to draw firm conclusions in this area on the strength of a single pilot exercise, the results indicate the key role of vocabulary work in advancing students' proficiency in the second language. The better outcome in reading and writing as compared to listening can be attributed to the generally acknowledged fact that improving aural skills is one of the most difficult tasks for language learners and teachers alike (Rivers, 1992).

Figure 1.   The breakdown of students' exam results in four language skills

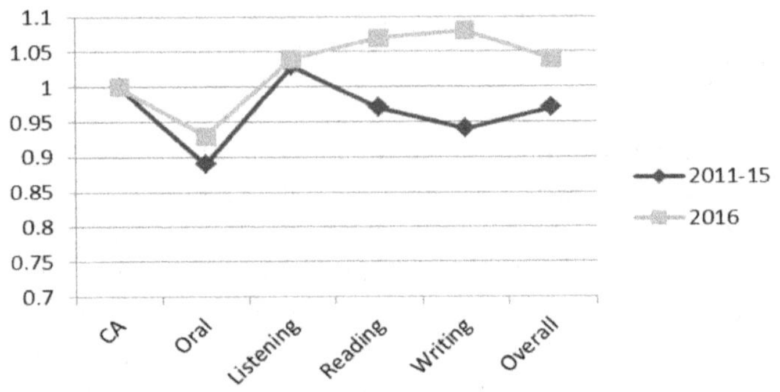

4.   Conclusions

A new self-study downloadable revision e-course had a proven positive impact on students' language learning experience and performance. Apart from a noticeable improvement in their competence in Russian, the course enhanced students' transferable skills as autonomous learners and, through its routine mode of active exchange, increased their self-esteem as confident language users. As regards teaching practice, the use of mobile applications can provide a valuable model for the development of language packages in blended learning – a balanced mix of traditional and digital technologies, which enhances the productiveness of language acquisition. The course can be easily expanded to supplement routine classroom teaching. Topically based modules can be created to enhance and develop students' language skills throughout the year, increasing the number of contact hours of language immersion, ensuring the continuity of the learning cycle, and giving scope for certain activities to be 'flipped'. The preparation of this particular e-course was definitely facilitated by access to the skills available from a Russian language team built up over many years, and with a proven track record shared by all its members. The members of staff involved were, overall, highly encouraged by the outcome of the exercise, and, more generally, LSE are already looking to replicate e-courses along these lines with other languages taught as part of undergraduate degrees.

5.   Acknowledgements

I would like to thank Natasha Bershadsky for the collaborative work in creating this course; as well as the LSE Language Innovation and Technology Unit for funding the project (especially Sarah Ney for all her support).

References

Bershadsky, N. (2012). *Complete Russian Michel Thomas course*. London: Hodder Education.

Gilman, R., & Moody, R. L. (1984). What practitioners say about listening. *Foreign Language Annals, 17*(4), 331-334. https://doi.org/10.1111/j.1944-9720.1984.tb03236.x

Rivers, V. M. (1992). *Communicating naturally in a second language*. Cambridge: Cambridge University Press.

Sobolev, O., & Nesterova, T. (2013). Oral communication in the framework of cognitive fluency. *Language Learning in Higher Education, 3*(2), 271-282.

Solity, J. (2008). *The learning revolution, revealed: secrets of the Michel Thomas method*. London: Hodder Education.

Woodsmall, M., & Woodsmall, W. (2008). *The future of learning: the Michel Thomas method*. Great Falls: Next Step Press.

Aligning out-of-class material with curriculum: tagging grammar in a mobile music application

Ross Sundberg[1] and Walcir Cardoso[2]

Abstract. The time available for classroom language learning is often insufficient for attaining reasonable levels of proficiency in the target language. For this reason, optimising time in the classroom is contingent upon what students are able to do outside of class time. In this paper, we introduce Bande à Part, a mobile application (app) that uses music as a pedagogical tool, developed for learners of French as a second or foreign language. As an out-of-class tool, the proposed app has the potential to increase the quantity (and possibly the quality) of the exposure to the target language, thus addressing the time constraint mentioned above. Specifically, we describe the recent addition of grammatical information to the app, which is now tagged to individual songs. With this addition, songs can be better aligned with curricula and individual needs. Aligning the application to a curriculum helps bring continuity between the classroom and learning outside of the classroom.

Keywords: French as a second language, mobile-assisted language learning, grammar.

1.   Introduction

As any language learner knows, it is not difficult to find target language input online. Nevertheless, as one begins learning a new language, the majority of the available material is incomprehensible and is not appropriate to one's level of proficiency. To demonstrate how access to these materials can be facilitated, we developed a mobile music application for L2 French learners called *Bande à Part* (BàP). This web-based application was realised by drawing on research on the effects of L2 language input (and its relation to output and interaction; e.g. Nation, 2013). BàP heeds Engh's (2013) recommendation to incorporate music into

1. Concordia University, Montréal, Canada; ross.sundberg@concordia.ca
2. Concordia University, Montréal, Canada; walcir.cardoso@concordia.ca

How to cite this article: Sundberg, R., & Cardoso, W. (2016). Aligning out-of-class material with curriculum: tagging grammar in a mobile music application. In S. Papadima-Sophocleous, L. Bradley, & S. Thouësny (Eds), *CALL communities and culture – short papers from EUROCALL 2016* (pp. 440-444). Research-publishing.net. https://doi.org/10.14705/rpnet.2016.eurocall2016.603

language learning, and adapts the concept of graded readers (wherein vocabulary is controlled in 'grade' levels to make content accessible to learners). This student-centred application allows learners to choose material based on a number of criteria which enable them to learn according to their interests and proficiency level, in an effort to extend learning beyond the classroom.

During the pilot testing of the app, French teachers (and students) asked for the ability to choose songs based on grammatical features. Their rationale for this suggestion was to align the application with their current curriculum and to allow students to receive extra practice with the features with which they struggled. This echoes the principles outlined by Doughty and Long (2003), who recommend that new language learning technologies be aligned with L2 learning curricula and student needs. The current study reports these developments in the design of BàP in which songs are organised in terms of grammatical categories. Figure 1 illustrates the new version of the song selection database that displays the 'Grammar' column and some of the searchable criteria that learners can use to select music.

Figure 1.   BàP: song selection

Song	Artist	Country Of Origin	Gender of Singer	Genre	Vocabulary Difficulty	Grammar
Est-que tu le sais?	Les Chats Sauvages	France	Male	Retro	Easy	1st/2nd person pronouns, Verbs in 1st/2nd person, Clitic pronouns
Je T'aime	Françoise Hardy	France	Female	Retro	Easy	
Je Le Savais	Julie Doiron	Canada	Female	Indie	Easy	Adverbs, 1st/2nd person pronouns, Verbs in 1st/2nd person
Si Tu Es Un Homme	Alizée	France	Female	Pop	Medium	1st/2nd person pronouns, Auxiliary verbs in 1st/2nd person, Negation participle 'ne', Connector subordinate conjuctions 'si, quand, etc.'
Tous Les Mêmes	Stromae	Belgium	Male	Rap	Medium	Number invariate nouns, Special adjectives in singular
Laisse Tomber Les Filles	France Gall	France	Female	Retro	Medium	Plural determiners, Special invariate adjectives

In the next section, we introduce BàP and outline the procedures adopted for tagging the grammatical categories in the corpus. The method for creating the app and the grading of vocabulary have been reported in Sundberg and Cardoso (2015).

2.   BàP: the addition of grammatical categories

BàP is a database of songs consisting of a variety of genres (so that learners can select songs according to their interests), and artists from a variety of regions (to expose students to different accents). Once the database was compiled and the lyrics analysed by frequency bands (for details about this process, see Sundberg &

Cardoso, 2015), videos were created and uploaded onto a website so that learners could access them via a mobile device or computer.

To contextualise the current study, Figure 2 illustrates the interactive screen used by learners to play a song in BàP once they have made a selection. This interactive video-based interface allows learners to slow down the music, navigate at a phrase level to repeat troublesome lines, read along to the lyrics of the song and display a translation if they are struggling to understand a word or a sentence. In addition, textual enhancements are present to increase the saliency of language features (e.g. liaison, gender, the subjunctive form).

Figure 2.   BàP: the interface

For tagging the grammatical categories in the corpus, Open Xerox's 'Part of Speech Tagging (Standard)' tool was used, which is part of their linguistic tools web app (Open Xerox, 2016). By 'grammatical category', we refer to the part of speech categories set out by Open Xerox, which include parts of speech as well as further delimitations such as number and person agreements.

The grammar in the lyrical content of the songs was analysed in three ways with the goal of tagging each song with at least three prominent features. For the first analysis, the entire corpus was analysed as a whole. This enabled us to calculate the percentage at which each of the grammatical features occurred in the corpus. The percentage served as the average that each of the songs could later be compared to.

So, for example, in the corpus, adverbs made up 5.4% of the total words, whereas, in a particular song such as 'Le Slow' (by Granville), they made up 15% (a total of 42 adverbs in the song); nearly 10% more than the average, including all songs. By comparison, the song 'Jeans Troués', by the same artist, includes only three adverbs in the whole song (or 1.9% of that song's grammatical content). Based on these results, we conclude that the song 'Le Slow' is a more fitting candidate for exposing learners to adverbs (and their positioning) in French. A song was tagged for a particular grammar feature only if that feature occurred 5% or more than in the corpus as a whole (the inclusion of less frequently occurring items would generate too many tags, diminishing the impact of the most frequently occurring grammatical features).

One issue that arose was that certain parts of speech are more susceptible to variation between songs. For example, it is very unlikely that the conjunction *que* will appear 5% more in one song compared to another and so, using the above procedure, no song would be tagged as being a good exemplar for the conjunction. For that reason, we used a second procedure to analyse the grammar. For many of the categories that never varied by 5% or more, we tagged the top 10% of the songs with the highest percentage of a given feature. For example, the song 'Si tu es un homme' by Alizee contains the negative participle *ne* 3.7% more than the average and this turns out to be far more than what is typically found in the data set (only three of the total songs vary positively or negatively by more than 2% with this feature).

The last way the grammar in the songs was analysed was by looking at the number of occurrences (rather than percentages) of the target grammatical feature. Songs differ considerably in length (total number of words), so a longer song could still have many instances of any one element without boosting the percentage – suggesting that it should be tagged with that feature. An example of this is found in the song 'Les Passants' by Zaz. This song includes 19 plural determiners, more than any other song in the corpus; however, due to its length, this does not account for 5% more than the average (it is close at 4.2%), nor place it in the top 10% when looking at plural determiners alone (there are other songs that have higher percentages).

3. Discussion and concluding remarks

The intent of this paper was to demonstrate how out-of-class, student-centred material such as BàP can be aligned with current curriculum with respect to grammar in L2 French. To do so, we have provided users with practical and useful information about grammatical categories in songs in order to expand the means by which the learning process can be regulated. With ample material available online, music is but one form of input. A lot of potential exists for curating online material for learners according to established research. This can be done through flexible programs such as BàP, which have the potential to meet the needs of independent learners, and fulfill the curriculum requirements for language teachers.

There are still some issues that will need to be addressed in future developments of the app, following usability tests. One of these concerns has to do with how the grammatical categories are displayed in the app. As illustrated in Figure 1, some of the information provided is complex and/or lengthy. A possible solution to this problem is to make the relevant and complex grammatical feature/s clickable or 'hyperlinked' so that learners can access definitions or examples on their own.

4.   Acknowledgements

We would like to thank the Social Sciences and Humanities Research Council (SSHRC), the Concordia School of Graduate Studies, and the students who have provided us with feedback on their experience using Bande à Part.

References

Doughty, C., & Long, M. (2003). Optimal psycholinguistic environments for distance foreign language learning. *Language Learning & Technology, 23*, 35-73.

Engh, D. (2013). Why use music in English language learning? A survey of the literature. *English Language Teaching, 6*(2), 113-127. https://doi.org/10.5539/elt.v6n2p113

Nation, I. S. P. (2013). *Teaching & learning vocabulary.* Boston: Heinle Cengage Learning.

Open Xerox. (2016). *Linguistic tools.* Xerox Corporation. https://open.xerox.com/ Services/ fst-nlp-tools/Consume/Part%20of%20Speech%20Tagging%20(Standard)-178

Sundberg, R., & Cardoso, W. (2015). A musical application to aid second language learners' development of pronunciation features. In J. Volín (Ed.), *Proceedings of the international conference on English pronunciation: issues & practices* (pp. 135-138). Prague, Czech Republic: Charles University.

Meeting the technology standards
for language teachers

Cornelia Tschichold[1]

Abstract. The starting point for this project was the question in how far a Computer-Assisted Language Learning (CALL) module in a Teaching English to Speakers of Other Languages (TESOL) course can bring the students up to the required level of being confident CALL users. The teachers' part of the TESOL Technology Standards Framework was chosen as evidence for the level of training required. Each standard was first matched against the components of an existing CALL module. Standards that were not met were then filtered for achievability in a pre-service teacher training situation. Next, all remaining standards were examined to find out whether they could be incorporated into the module, either by modification of an existing element or the introduction of new elements. A second step involved the evaluation of components of the CALL course that did not seem to contribute to helping the students reach any of the technology standards. One of the goals of this procedure was to give more structure to the process of regular updates of the module content, beyond simply updating the software used in the module, and to allow for a more principled improvement of the module over the years.

Keywords: teacher education, TESOL, technology standards framework, normalization of CALL.

1.   Introduction

While computers of various types are increasingly common in classrooms, CALL itself cannot be said to be entirely normalized yet, partly because many language teachers are reluctant to use much technology in their classes. The need for more systematic integration of CALL in teacher training has been pointed out by Hubbard (2008) and He, and Puakpong, and Lian (2015), amongst others. Hong (2010) states that the aim of such training is teachers knowing about and

1. Swansea University, Wales, United Kingdom; c.tschichold@swansea.ac.uk

How to cite this article: Tschichold, C. (2016). Meeting the technology standards for language teachers. In S. Papadima-Sophocleous, L. Bradley & S. Thouësny (Eds), *CALL communities and culture – short papers from EUROCALL 2016* (pp. 445-449). Research-publishing.net. https://doi.org/10.14705/rpnet.2016.eurocall2016.604

being confident with CALL in their classrooms, something that probably cannot be achieved with just a few workshops. Teachers, and also trainee teachers, vary widely not just in their knowledge of potential CALL tools, but also in their confidence and attitude towards them. O'Reilly (2016) attempts to address this kind of variation among teachers by a needs analysis in the form of a survey that includes a range of answers for a whole series of dimensions. If we only look at trainee teachers rather than in-service teachers, we might assume that these digital natives would be a more homogeneous group, but there is still considerable variation in their skills level.

2.   Method

The starting point for this project was the question in how far a CALL module in an undergraduate TESOL/Applied Linguistics course (i.e. not an actual teacher training course) can bring the students up to the required level to give them the skills and the confidence to use CALL once they start teaching. A large proportion of the students go on to some form of teaching; some already have a CELTA. The module is based around a multimedia CALL project that the students create over the course of ten weeks, using either free or very commonly used software (mostly Microsoft PowerPoint, Google Forms, Hot Potatoes).

The *Technology Standards for Language Teachers* (part of the TESOL Technology Standards Framework, Healey et al., 2008) was chosen as evidence for the level of training required. The TESOL Technology Standards includes sets of standards for both learners and their teachers; here only the teachers' set was considered. The teacher standards are structured into a basic and an expert level and have further specifications for various teaching contexts, e.g. English for Specific Purposes (ESP), young learners,and high-tech or low-tech classrooms (cf. Kessler, 2016 for a discussion of this set of standards). In a first instance, each standard was matched against one or more components of an existing CALL module. Standards that were not met were then filtered for achievability in a pre-service teacher training situation, and those that were deemed not to be achievable or relevant in the given context were eliminated. All remaining standards were then examined to find out whether they could be incorporated into the module, either by modification of an existing element or the introduction of new elements. A second step involved the evaluation of components of the CALL course that did not seem to contribute to helping the students reach any of the technology standards. One of the goals of this procedure was to give more structure to the process of regular updates of the module content, beyond simply updating the software used in the module, and to allow for a more principled improvement of the module over the years.

The given technological context was relatively high-resource and high-access; the course took place in a computer lab with internet access at a British university. Students also had access to networked PCs in the university library, and also typically their own laptops and smartphones. Resources going beyond this were limited however, and students would more likely use their mobile phones for recording their own video material than borrow a video camera. Table 1 gives an overview of the TESOL technology standards for teachers and whether each one was deemed to be met in the CALL module or not, followed by a brief comment. Only abbreviated titles are given for the individual goals; for the full version, along with examples and vignettes, see Healey at al. (2008).

Table 1. Overview of standards (E: expert level)

Goal 1	Foundational knowledge & skills	Met?	Comment
1.1	Basics	Yes	Students normally come to the course with this level of knowledge already present.
1.2	Understand the range	Yes	Students have at least a basic knowledge and can easily deal with the extra width and depth as covered in the course.
1.3	Expand the knowledge base	Yes	Some of this standard is met via the lectures and the reading material, some via the group assignment.
1.4	Culture and ethics	In part	Much of this is covered in other courses and is not particularly specific to CALL.
Goal 2	Integration		
2.1	Identify suitable technology	Yes	The assignment is used as a 'teaching context' and students choose from technology presented in class or found elsewhere.
2.2	Integrate technology	Yes	An undergraduate programme for pre-service teachers allows for limited coverage of this standard, mainly through the group assignment.
2.3	Design tasks using technology	Yes E: no	The assignment is the main element to meet this standard, albeit to a surprisingly limited extent. The expert level can only be said to be met on one element due to time restrictions.
2.4	Use research findings	In part E: no	In a pre-service environment, the principles can be covered via the readings. The expert level standard is not achievable.

Goal 3	Application in assessment		
3.1	Evaluate and implement	No	Students experience these technologies from the learners' perspective mainly.
3.2	Collect and analyse data	No	This is not achievable in a pre-service environment.
3.3	Evaluation	No	This is not achievable in a pre-service environment.
Goal 4	Technology for improvement		
4.1	Contact and collaboration	No	Some of the students' other courses cover some of these issues.
4.2	Reflection	No	This is not achievable in a pre-service environment.
4.3	Efficiency	No	This is not achievable in a pre-service environment.

3.   Discussion and conclusion

No elements of the course were found that did not contribute is some way to help the students reach one of the technology standards, but the balance of elements in the course could be changed to bring it more in line with the set of standards. On the whole, it was surprising to the module coordinator how few of these standards occur in a semester-long CALL course. For the next student cohort, standard 2.3 in particular should receive more attention; while students will happily try out a variety of tools, their critical evaluation of these tools is often quite superficial. One reason for this relatively low coverage is clearly the limited amount of time available; the notional 200 hours of work for a student for a module with 25 contact hours do not allow for much more than a taste of CALL.

The other important issue is the fact that the students by and large have no teaching experience and no simple access to learners, so a number of the standards are basically out of reach for them. While the standards are a useful element for curriculum planning, a further structuring into pre-service and in-service training could be helpful for teacher trainers in their endeavour to improve and update their courses. Kessler (2012) pointed out the need for teacher trainers to raise their language teacher trainees' awareness of the complexities of CALL tools, while also showing them the potential such technologies hold, in order to avoid early disappointment when something goes wrong. In addition to the TESOL standards, this may be a good general guideline to follow when updating a module on CALL.

References

He, B., Puakpong, N., & Lian, A. (2015). Factors affecting the normalization of CALL in Chinese senior high schools. *Computer Assisted Language Learning, 28*(3), 189-201. https://doi.org/10.1080/09588221.2013.803981

Healey, D., Hegelheimer, V., Hubbard, P., Ioannou-Georgiou, S., Kessler, G., & Ware, P. (2008). *TESOL Technology Standards Framework*. TESOL Inc.

Hong, K. H. (2010). CALL teacher education as an impetus for L2 teachers in integrating technology. *ReCALL, 22*(1), 53-69. https://doi.org/10.1017/S095834400999019X

Hubbard, P. (2008). CALL and the future of language teacher education. *CALICO Journal, 25*(2), 175-188.

Kessler, G. (2012). Preparing tomorrow's second language writing teachers. In G. Kessler, A. Oskoz, & I. Elola (Eds.), *Technology across writing contexts and tasks*. CALICO Monograph.

Kessler, G. (2016). Technology standards for language teacher preparation. In F. Farr & L. Murray (Eds.), *The Routledge handbook of language learning and technology* (pp. 57-70).

O'Reilly, E. (2016). Developing technology needs assessments for educational programs: an analysis of eight key indicators. *International Journal of Education and Development using Information and Communication Technology, 12*(1), 129-143.

Mobile-assisted language learning community and culture in French-speaking Belgium: the teachers' perspective

Julie Van de Vyver[1]

Abstract. This paper focuses on the perceptions and uses of mobile technologies by 118 Belgian teachers in foreign language teaching and learning in secondary education. The purpose of the study is to analyze the teachers' attitudes towards the use of mobile technologies in- and outside the classroom via an online questionnaire. The preliminary findings presented in this paper establish that the concept of a 'Mobile-Assisted Language Learning (MALL) community' does not yet exist in our context as the use of mobile devices is still limited. Nevertheless, it can also be stated that teachers' attitudes and behavioral intention towards the use of tablets are slightly more positive than towards the use of smartphones, and that a vast majority of the teachers are interested in being trained to MALL.

Keywords: MALL, teacher education, attitudes, usage patterns.

1.   Introduction

The Computer-Assisted Language Learning (CALL) culture has been developing for several decades thanks to individual initiatives, scientific research and reflective practices from CALL practitioners. New teaching designs have subsequently emerged – such as Puentedura's (2013) SAMR model or Liu et al.'s (2014) TPACK model – and new tools have been created (e.g. interactive whiteboards, educational apps). Mobile learning in general, and MALL in particular, are more recent manifestations of CALL and before integrating the technology in Belgium, there is a need to observe and discuss the current situation (Davie, 2015) and the readiness to adopt these tools in education as was done in other contexts (Fujimoto, 2012 for the Australian

1. Université catholique de Louvain, Louvain-la-Neuve, Belgium; julie.vandevyver@uclouvain.be

How to cite this article: Van de Vyver, J. (2016). Mobile-assisted language learning community and culture in French-speaking Belgium: the teachers' perspective. In S. Papadima-Sophocleous, L. Bradley & S. Thouësny (Eds), CALL communities and culture – short papers from EUROCALL 2016 (pp. 450-455). Research-publishing.net. https://doi.org/10.14705/rpnet.2016.eurocall2016.605

context and Pieri & Diamantini, 2014 for the Italian one). Several projects have been implemented in the Federation Wallonia-Brussels (FWB), which is, in short, the French-speaking part of Belgium. They include the Plan Cyberécole in 1999, Plan Cyberclasse in 2005, Ecole Numérique in 2011, and Plan du Numérique in 2015 (see www.ecolenumerique.be for more details) and were meant to equip educational environments with, among others, computers and tablets. Surveys have then been regularly conducted to evaluate the access to technologies in our secondary schools (Agence wallonne des télécommunications, 2013). However, mobile technologies per se and their use have not yet been much investigated in this context.

2. Method

2.1. Design and distribution of the study

This present study concentrates on the perceptions and uses of mobile technologies by teachers in language learning in the FWB. Data was collected through an online survey conducted in 2016 and distributed in schools via e-mail lists and social networks. 87 male teachers and 31 female teachers, who teach the last three years of secondary education, completed the 15-minute questionnaire in French. The survey, which is part of a wider project on the acceptance of technologies for language learning, sought to answer the following research questions:

- When and how (often) do these teachers use their computer, tablet and smartphone for educational purposes?

- What are the teachers' attitudes towards the use of the tablet and the smartphone in foreign language learning?

- What is the teachers' behavioral intention of use of these mobile devices in their teaching?

The questionnaire mainly consisted in closed questions with items based on Davis's (1989) Technology Acceptance Model (TAM) and extended TAM categories (Davis, Bagozzi, & Warshaw, 1992) and used a Likert-scale response format. They addressed teachers' perception of ease of use, usefulness and enjoyment of mobile technologies, viz. tablets and computers in language learning. Another set of questions included teachers' behavioral intention to use these technologies in the classroom and their actual use of the system.

2.2. Participants' profile

Out of the 118 respondents, the vast majority teach English (n=101) and/or Dutch (n=80) while some others are German (n=11), Italian (n=11) or French (n=1) teachers. As illustrated in Table 1, they are aged between 21 and 59 with nearly two-thirds (64%) of them above 40, 24% aged between 31 and 40 and 12% aged between 21 and 30.

Table 1.   Age of the respondents

Age range	Frequency	%
21-30	14	12
31-40	28	24
41-50	44	37
51-60	32	27
Total	118	100

The subjects come from nearly 60 schools throughout the federation. We collected 4 to 35 answers per province, mainly from rather experienced teachers, which correlates with the participants' age groups. Although all the respondents possess a computer, only 70% of them own a smartphone and 43% report having a tablet. Besides, 38% possess two devices out of the three aforementioned, and 37% own the three devices.

3. Results

3.1. Teachers' educational uses of mobile technologies

The teachers were asked to select their different types of use of the computer, tablet and smartphone. Illustrated in Table 2 are their educational uses of each device. We can see that these uses are quite limited on mobile technologies. Indeed, whereas 82% of the computer users consult a translation dictionary on their computer, only 34% of the tablet users use one on a tablet and 27% of the smartphone users check words on a translation dictionary on their phone. Similarly, most teachers use websites for language learning and teaching on their computer. Although the use of a school platform or Open Educational Resources (OERs) is not so common among teachers, it is more common on a computer than on mobile devices. Regarding the use of educational applications, which are only available on mobile devices, we can see that only 4 smartphone users report using them.

Table 2. Educational uses of the three devices

	Computer	Tablet	Smartphone
Translation dictionaries	82%	34%	27,50%
Websites for language teachers	76%	2,50%	10%
Websites for language learning	76%	2,50%	8%
Use of school platform	38%	6%	6%
Use of OERs	23%	0%	4%
Use of educational apps	N/A	0%	5%
Total users	118	82	51

3.2. Teachers' use of technology in the classroom

The following set of questions dealt with the use of the three devices for language learning. According to the subjects, 83 teachers (70%) use the computer with their pupils during languages classes, among which 39 (33%) use it *rarely*, 33 (28%) use it *sometimes* and the remaining 11 (9%) from *often* to *all the time*.

Regarding the use of mobile devices in the classroom, 18 teachers (15%) report using a tablet, among which 11 (9%) of them use it *rarely*. 20 teachers (16%) use a smartphone in the language classroom.

3.3. Teachers' perception of ease of use, usefulness and enjoyment of mobile devices

In order to find out about teachers' perceptions of the use of the mobile devices in language learning, the participants were asked to answer the following question using a seven-point Likert scale with 12 opposite adjectives (e.g. useful vs useless): "Using the tablet (Q1)/the smartphone (Q2) to learn languages in secondary education is according to you...".

Illustrated in Table 3 are the means obtained for each category of adjectives. These scores establish that the teachers' Perceived Ease of Use (PEoU), Perceived Usefulness (PU) and Perceived Enjoyment (PE) are all slightly higher for the tablet than for the smartphone. However, the PU and PEoU results are quite close to the neutral position (4) and should therefore neither be considered as highly positive nor as highly negative perceptions. Furthermore, the only score below the neutral position (4) reflects the teachers' perception of usefulness of the smartphone.

Table 3. PEoU, PE, and PU for mobile devices

T PEoU	4,32	S PEoU	4,28
T PE	5,1	S PE	4,88
T PU	4,29	S PU	3,86

3.4. Teachers' behavioral intention of use of mobile devices

According to nearly all the participants (n=116), teachers should use mobile devices in language classes in secondary education. As shown in Figure 1, 56% (n=66) of them think that these devices should be used *occasionally* to *sometimes* and 42% (n=50) believe they should be used *regularly* to *very often*. Nevertheless, when asked about their wish to use a tablet or a smartphone in their classroom, about 50% of the respondents answer negatively. Still, 77% (n=91) of them are interested in some MALL training.

Figure 1. Teachers' opinion on the use of mobile devices in the language classroom

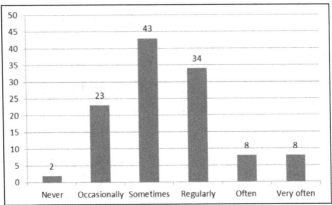

4. Discussion and conclusions

The results regarding the use of technologies by the teachers for educational purposes show that most activities are performed on computers as opposed to mobile technologies, which are used by only a third of the population, mainly for looking up words in a dictionary. As for the use of mobile technologies in the language classroom, less than 20% of the respondents report using a tablet or a smartphone in this context. With regards to the teachers' attitudes towards the use of the tablet and the smartphone in the classroom, the survey establishes that, although the perceptions of ease of use, usefulness and enjoyment of both devices are neither very positive nor very negative, the tablet receives slightly higher scores. According to the teachers, it is a more enjoyable, more useful and somewhat easier to use tool. Dealing with our last research question, the teachers show some inconsistency in their answers as the overwhelming majority stand for the use of mobile technologies in the language classroom and as, on the other hand, half of them do not wish to use tablets or smartphones in their classroom. Still, most of the subjects report being interested in knowing more about MALL.

In conclusion, it seems important to take these perceptions into consideration when implementing MALL in the context. Although deeper analyses will be needed to detect the most influential factors that lead to the usage of the technology, it can already be stated that the use of MALL in schools is at an early stage of development in French-speaking Belgium and that we should develop the field of MALL in teacher education, taking the cultural specificities of the context into account.

References

Agence wallonne des télécommunications. (2013). *Baromètre TIC 2013 : l'usage des technologies de l'information et de la communication en Wallonie*. Retrieved from: http://www.awt.be/contenu/tel/dem/AWT-Barom%C3%A8tre_g%C3%A9n%C3%A9ral.pdf

Davie, N. (2015). *Considerations before introducing mobile learning*. Technical report, South-Westphalia University of Applied Sciences, Meschede, Germany. https://www.researchgate.net/publication/271201264_Considerations_before_introducing_mobile_learning.

Davis, F. D. (1989). Perceived usefulness, perceived ease of use, and user acceptance of information technology. *MIS quarterly, 13*(3), 319-340. https://doi.org/10.2307/249008

Davis, F. D., Bagozzi, R. P., & Warshaw, P. R. (1992). Extrinsic and intrinsic motivation to use computers in the workplace. *Journal of Applied Social Psychology, 22*(14), 1111-1132. https://doi.org/10.1111/j.1559-1816.1992.tb00945.x

Fujimoto, C. (2012). Perceptions of mobile language learning in Australia. How ready are learners to study on the move? *JALT CALL Journal, 8*(3), 165-195.

Liu, S., Liu, H., Yu, Y., Li, Y., & Wen, T. (2014). TPACK: a new dimension to EFL teachers' PCK. *Journal of Education and Human Development, 3*(2), 681-693.

Pieri, M., & Diamantini, D. (2014). A new Italian survey about university students' readiness for mobile learning. In P. Bonfils, P. Dumas & L. Massou (Eds), *Numérique et Education Dispositifs, jeux, enjeux et hors jeux*. Editions universitaires de Lorraine.

Puentedura, R. R. (2013, May 29). *SAMR: moving from enhancement to transformation* [Web log post]. http://www.hippasus.com/rrpweblog/archives/000095.html

Classification of Swedish learner essays by CEFR levels

Elena Volodina[1], Ildikó Pilán[2], and David Alfter[3]

Abstract. The paper describes initial efforts on creating a system for the automatic assessment of Swedish second language (L2) learner essays from two points of view: holistic evaluation of the reached level according to the Common European Framework of Reference (CEFR), and the lexical analysis of texts for receptive and productive vocabulary per CEFR level. We describe the data and resources that our experiments were based on, provide a short introduction to the algorithm for essay classification and experiment results, present the user interface we developed for testing new essays, and outline future work.

Keywords: automatic online L2 essay classification, lexical complexity assessment, productive and receptive vocabulary by CEFR levels.

1. Introduction

Learner essay grading presents a lot of challenges, especially in terms of manual assessment time and assessors' qualification. Evaluating learner writing quality can be very time-consuming since it stretches along different linguistic dimensions and thus might need several iterations of re-reading. Human assessment is precise and reliable provided that assessors are well trained. However, their judgements may also be subject to different outside factors, such as hunger or a negative attitude to a learner. To avoid misjudgements and to ensure objectivity, certain institutions have started to complement human grading with automatic assessment as a more objective reference point, e.g. Educational Testing Services (Burstein & Chodorow, 2010).

1. Språkbanken, University of Gothenburg, Gothenburg, Sweden; elena.volodina@svenska.gu.se
2. Språkbanken, University of Gothenburg, Gothenburg, Sweden; ildiko.pilan@svenska.gu.se
3. Språkbanken, University of Gothenburg, Gothenburg, Sweden; david.alfter@svenska.gu.se

How to cite this article: Volodina, E., Pilán, I., & Alfter, D. (2016). Classification of Swedish learner essays by CEFR levels. In S. Papadima-Sophocleous, L. Bradley & S. Thouësny (Eds), *CALL communities and culture – short papers from EUROCALL 2016* (pp. 456-461). Research-publishing.net. https://doi.org/10.14705/rpnet.2016.eurocall2016.606

Developing a data-driven Automatic Essay Grading (AEG) system is a non-trivial task which needs to rely on (1) *data* consisting of essays manually graded by human assessors, (2) a *set of rules* or specific *features* relevant for the assessment, and (3) a *classification algorithm* based on the example data provided and the specified features that can predict the grade or level of previously unseen essays. AEG tasks have been addressed previously in a number of projects, e.g. Hancke and Meurers (2013) for German, Burstein and Chodorow (2010) for English, and Vajjala and Lõo (2014) for Estonian. For Swedish, Östling, Smolentzov, Tyrefors Hinnerich, and Höglin (2013) have looked at Swedish upper secondary school essays, i.e. first language (L1) learner essays, and evaluated them in terms of performance grades (pass with distinction, pass, fail). In contrast to them, our main aim has been to assess the reached proficiency levels in essays written by L2 learners of Swedish.

The system presented here uses CEFR levels (Council of Europe, 2001). The CEFR framework has been selected since it is very influential in both Europe and outside with numerous projects targeting its interpretation (e.g. Hancke & Meurers, 2013; Vajjala & Lõo, 2014), however, very little work has been done for CEFR-based L2 Swedish.

2. L2 essay classification

2.1. Essay corpus

The availability of data is critical for AEG experiments. Our experiments are based on SweLL (Volodina et al., 2016), a corpus consisting of L2 Swedish learner essays, linked to proficiency levels as defined by CEFR. Essays cover five of the six proficiency levels (see Table 1) with varying amounts of essays per level.

All essays contain information on learners' mother tongue(s), age, gender, education level, and at which CEFR level the essay is. Essays have been used to extract features based on available annotation, such as level, dictionary forms, word classes, syntactic annotation.

Table 1. Overview of SweLL corpus

	A1	A2	B1	B2	C1	Unknown	Total
Nr essays	16	83	75	74	89	2	339
Nr tokens	2 084	18 349	29 814	32 691	60 095	360	144 087

2.2. Feature selection

Feature selection is the most important and time-consuming part of an AEG project. Features can be language independent, such as n-grams, sentence- and word-length, or language specific, such as out-of-vocabulary words (where vocabulary is defined as some lexicon or word list). Our experiments included an empiric analysis of data, the extraction of relevant features in machine learning experiments and experimentation with those to select the most predictive ones. Our complete set of 61 features (Pilán, Vajjala, & Volodina, forthcoming) extracted from the linguistic annotation available in SweLL include count-based, lexical, syntactic, morphological, and semantic features.

2.3. Essay classification experiments and results

Using SweLL as training data, we created a classification system which predicts which CEFR level the writer of an essay has performed at. We used the Sequential Minimal Optimization (SMO) machine learning algorithm available in WEKA (http://www.cs.waikato.ac.nz/~ml/weka/), which based on the linguistic features observed in hand-annotated essays is able to learn how to automatically assign a CEFR level to a previously unseen essay. Table 2 presents results obtained using different types of features, where F1 is the harmonic mean of precision and recall, and accuracy expresses the amount of correctly classified texts. The number of features per sub-group is also indicated since it may influence performance.

Table 2.   Classification results

	Nr features	F1	Accuracy (%)
All	61	0.66	66.96
Count	7	0.45	51.48
Lexical	11	0.58	59.52
Morphological	30	0.53	55.35
Syntactic	11	0.51	53.86
Semantic	2	0.28	36.90

Our system with the complete feature set (ALL) classified essays with 67% accuracy, i.e. making correct assessments about seven out of ten times. However, almost all (98.5%) classification errors were minor, within one CEFR level distance from the teacher-assigned level, a very encouraging result which compares well to the human performance of 45.8% reported in Östling et al. (2013) and systems for other languages using three times more annotated data, e.g. 61% for German (Hancke & Meurers, 2013) and 79% for Estonian (Vajjala & Lõo, 2014). Lexical features were the most informative, and the most useful single features included the number of tokens per CEFR level and word-list based frequency information.

3. Lexical complexity analysis

Both previous research and our experiments have indicated lexical features as one of the most predictive ones (Pilán et al., forthcoming). For this reason, we experimented with a stand-off (i.e. separate from essay classification in section 2) lexical analysis of the essays for giving insights into the lexical complexity of a text, seen from receptive and productive perspectives. Similar efforts have been taken for other languages, e.g. English (http://www.englishprofile.org/wordlists/text-inspector) and French (http://cental.uclouvain.be/flelex/), however, our resources allow us to identify receptive versus productive lexical items per level, whereas only productive vocabulary is targeted in the English system and only receptive in the French one. To be able to perform lexical analysis of texts, two lists have been employed: SVALex (François, Volodina, Pilán, & Tack, 2016) and SweLL-list (Llozhi, 2016).

SVALex is a frequency-based list derived from reading comprehension texts used for teaching CEFR courses, thus representing lexical items that L2 learners are exposed to while reading or listening, i.e. receptive vocabulary. The *SweLL list* is derived from the SweLL corpus, showing the distribution of lexical items over CEFR levels based on frequency information. Since SweLL-list items come from essays, they indicate the productive use of vocabulary. Each item in the two lists, a combination of a dictionary form (lemma) and parts of speech, has associated information on levels at which it appears. We preliminarily consider frequency peaks as an indication of the target level for that item. Refinement of the strategies for identifying target levels are under development.

For analysis of *lexical complexity,* each word (i.e. its lemma in combination with its part of speech) in an essay is tested against the two resources and is associated with the CEFR level for receptive or productive knowledge.

4. User interface

The described work has resulted in an online service for testing arbitrary new essays written in Swedish. This is the first prototype of our system, where natural language processing tools are combined to deliver a user-friendly analysis of essays. Initially, essays undergo automatic linguistic analysis which generates dictionary forms, parts of speech and syntactic annotation. Then, depending upon user choices, a holistic assessment (i.e. reached CEFR level) as well as lexical analysis of an essay are generated using resources and techniques described above.

Figure 1. User interface for L2 text classification

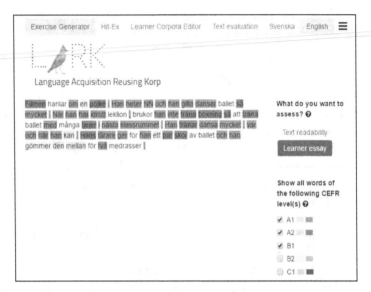

Figure 1 shows available choices on the right, the feedback statement below the input and colour-coded lexical analysis of the pasted texts. Users have a choice to evaluate either L2 learner essays or reading comprehension texts. However, since classification of reading comprehension texts is outside the scope of this paper, we do not go into details. Words from the selected CEFR levels are highlighted showing receptive ones in a lighter color and productive ones in a darker color.

The SweLL-based online system is not yet released for public use, however an experimental version is already available through the Swedish Language Bank at the university of Gothenburg, Sweden (https://spraakbanken.gu.se/larkalabb/).

5.   Concluding remarks

Our classification experiments showed that, even though the presented system is an initial prototype and more work needs to be invested to make it fully functional and useful in the language learning context with regards to evaluation of learner-written texts, essay classification results are promising. We found that considering the lexical dimension is particularly effective for CEFR level classification. Further work on refining the SweLL-AEG algorithm would include, among others, adding error annotation to the essays, linking error types to CEFR proficiency levels, and employing error types as a feature in our algorithm. Availability of error annotation would also facilitate a more instructive feedback to learners.

6. Acknowledgements

We thank the Swedish Language Bank (Språkbanken) and Department of Swedish at the University of Gothenburg, Sweden for supporting our work and providing necessary financing.

References

Burstein, J., & Chodorow, M. (2010). Progress and new directions in technology for automated essay evaluation. In R. B. Kaplan (Ed.), *The Oxford handbook of applied linguistics* (2 ed.). Oxford University Press. https://doi.org/10.1093/oxfordhb/9780195384253.013.0036

Council of Europe. (2001). *The common European framework of reference for languages: learning, teaching, assessment.* Cambridge University Press.

François, T., Volodina, E., Pilán, I., & Tack, A. (2016). SVALex: a CEFR-graded lexical resource for Swedish foreign and second language learners. *Proceedings of LREC 2016, Slovenia.*

Hancke, J., & Meurers, D. (2013). Exploring CEFR classification for German based on rich linguistic modeling. *LCR 2013.*

Llozhi, L. (2016). *SWELL LIST. A list of productive vocabulary generated from second language learners' essays.* Master Thesis. University of Gothenburg.

Pilán, I., Vajjala, S., & Volodina, E. (forthcoming). A readable read: automatic assessment of language learning materials based on linguistic complexity. *To appear in International Journal of Computational Linguistics and Applications (IJLCA).*

Vajjala, S., Lõo, K. (2014). Automatic CEFR level prediction for Estonian learner text. *Proceedings of the third workshop on NLP for computer-assisted language learning.* NEALT Proceedings Series 22 / Linköping Electronic Conference Proceedings 107.

Volodina, E., Pilán, I., Enström, I., Llozhi, L., Lundkvist, P., Sundberg, G., & Sandell, M. (2016). SweLL on the rise: Swedish learner language corpus for European reference level studies. *Proceedings of LREC 2016, Slovenia.*

Östling, R., Smolentzov, A., Tyrefors Hinnerich, B., & Höglin, E. (2013). Automated essay scoring for Swedish. *The 8th Workshop on Innovative Use of NLP for Building Educational Applications, US.*

Mobile assisted language learning and mnemonic mapping – the loci method revisited

Ikumi Waragai[1], Marco Raindl[2], Tatsuya Ohta[3],
and Kosuke Miyasaka[4]

Abstract. This paper presents the prototype of a Mobile Language Learning Environment (MLLE) allowing learners of German at a Japanese university to map classroom learning content onto the pathways of their everyday lives, turning places they come by into mnemonic *loci*, and thus changing their daily commute into a learning trail. Even though the evaluation based on learners' self-reports could not confirm the assumption that this type of MLLE supports the use of the loci method for all learners, it allows the conclusion that at least for some learners mnemonic mapping with mobile devices might lead to changes in learning awareness and an expansion of strategy knowledge.

Keywords: MALL, memory strategies, context awareness, informal learning.

1.   Introduction

Learners of German at Japanese universities face difficult learning conditions: they start late; class hours are few; their language learning biographies have been shaped by a school system mainly dedicated to making them pass entrance exams, leading to learning focussing on grammar rules, rote memorization of word lists and test taking strategies. A survey about learning habits conducted in the context of this study revealed low diversity of strategy use and showed that lots of learning happens on public transport, during often hour-long commutes.

1. Keio University, Tokyo, Japan; ikumi@sfc.keio.ac.jp
2. Dokkyo University, Sōka, Japan; raindl@dokkyo.ac.jp
3. Nanzan University, Nagoya, Japan; FZE00305@nifty.ne.jp
4. Keio University, Tokyo, Japan; mikko@sfc.keio.ac.jp

How to cite this article: Waragai, I., Raindl, M., Ohta, T., & Miyasaka, K. (2016). Mobile assisted language learning and mnemonic mapping – the loci method revisited. In S. Papadima-Sophocleous, L. Bradley & S. Thouësny (Eds), *CALL communities and culture – short papers from EUROCALL 2016* (pp. 462-467). Research-publishing.net. https://doi.org/10.14705/rpnet.2016.eurocall2016.607

The authors assume that, in order to foster successful learning in this context, a push for expanding learning times and trying out new learning approaches can be effective. They set out to support out-of-class learning, and to help learners create links between out-of-class learning and formal learning through mobile learning.

It is often argued that mobile learning has the potential to bridge formal learning and informal learning experiences (Kukulska-Hulme & Sharples, 2016). One of the toeholds that mobile devices offer for connecting our learners' out-of-class experiences and their formal learning is context awareness, the focus on *place* (Kukulska-Hulme, 2010, p. 11). As learners move through the real world, learning opportunities can (be made to) arise that prompt learners to revisit what they learnt in the classroom.

The authors have been exploring different ways of connecting places in German speaking countries and classroom learning contents, by designing MLLEs that supplied learners with learning materials according to (1) situations experienced in specific places (in public transport, in restaurants, etc.), offering on-the-spot help for oral interaction (Waragai, Ohta, Raindl, & Kurabayashi, 2013), or (2) the places that learners had visited during the day, providing them with scaffolding for writing SNS-entries about their experiences (Waragai et al., 2014).

The MLLE *2d-radio* presented in this paper follows a different approach to the notion of place: *place* does not figure as site of supported contact with the target language, but as a mnemonic *locus*. In the loci method, a mnemonic technique dating back to Greek and Roman orators and beyond, contents to be memorized is associated with places along a pathway and then depicted in an image (Moè & De Beni, 2005).

Users of *2d-radio* can register geolocational positions they come by regularly, such as train stations, on their mobile devices, and use them as *loci* for revision of classroom contents: they create images for each learning item and mentally link those images to *loci* on their pathway – and then review the items when travelling along the pathway again, or retrieve the memorized items when revisiting the different places in their minds.

The authors developed, implemented and evaluated the MLLE in order to find out, if an MLLE linking places on learners' commute to learning content can successfully support learners in applying the loci method.

2. Design of the learning environment

2.1. The learning context

2d-radio was designed as a platform for out-of-class learning, targeting participants of a German intensive course at Keio University, a 3-semester-program covering Common European Framework of Reference for Languages (CEFR) levels A0 up to A2. Instruction in the course is based on video-centered courseware that presents interaction in situations closely related to students' daily lives. Functions, grammar and vocabulary introduced in each chapter are summed up into seven to 16 key phrases excerpted from the video dialogues.

2.2. Concept of the application

Figure 1. Concept of the application

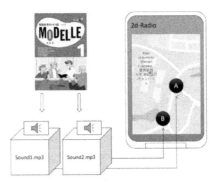

2d-radio was built on four principles: it (1) supports out-of-class reviewing of learning content, (2) offers learning incentives for commuting times, (3) encourages learners to link learning content to specific places and thus to try out a new mnemonic strategy (the survey of learning habits revealed that learners hardly employed memory strategies such as using sounds, images or emotions), and (4) focuses on aural input (Figure 1). The decision to provide aural input was informed by several considerations: the survey showed that learners tended to review key phrases by reading, pronouncing and writing rather than by listening; aural input might allow flexible use in different situations of commute; it can easily be linked to oral output; and there is evidence that the loci method leads to better memory results with aural than with written input because of the absence of visual interference (Cornoldi & De Beni, 1991).

Figure 2.   Functions of the application

2.3.   Functions of the application

2d-radio was developed as a web-application. Users can place content onto locations on a map (Figure 2). They can post comments about the content (accessible by other users) and evaluate how well they have learnt each item by assessing retention with one out of three performance levels, which are represented by pins of different colors.

3.   Evaluation of a test run

A two month test run was carried out in the spring semester 2016. For some chapters, the placement of the learning items was left to the learners; for other chapters, the administrator arranged the items on the maps. At the beginning of the term, *2d-radio* was presented to all 52 learners in the course. 15 of them showed interest in using the learning environment. Ten students took part in the online survey. It could not be reconstructed how many learners used *2d-radio* in the first half of the test run; in the second half, when log data were collected, only three learners were found to have used the application. The log data of all three participants (subjects A, B and C) showed low average using times (ranging from ten to 21 minutes), even though subjects A and B had rather long commutes.

At the end of the trial use, one of the authors interviewed the three subjects. The interviews were semi-structured, touched on the subjects' general learning habits, with a focus on media use and strategies for reviewing classroom content, and on their use of the application. The interviews were partially transcribed and analysed exploratively. Major findings were:

1. Subjects A and B used *2d-radio* in public transport, but reported that they found it difficult to create mental links between places on their commute and learning items, stating that they did not know much about the places on their way to school, whereas subject C, who commutes by bicycle or walking, noted that she found it easy to link places along her path to key phrases.

2. Subjects A and B described learning routines (such as reading, writing and using the textbook) they had developed and were not inclined to change. Subject C remarked she had used listening for reviewing for the first time and expressed surprise about how aspects of vocal expression remained in her memory together with the places and items.

3. Subjects A and C preferred the learning items to be mapped by the administrator to having to do the mapping themselves. Subject C stated that she felt motivation when finding learning items in unexpected places.

4. Subject A expressed tolerance about leisure and learning interlocking (e.g. by having her player shuffle between music and learning items). Subjects B and C stated that they preferred to keep both domains separate. At the same time, subject C noted that she appreciated that *2d-radio* provided her with an activity for her commute and thus prompted her to learn.

4.   Discussion and conclusion

The first test run of *2d-radio* could not confirm that this type of MLLE can support learners in using the loci method successfully: too few learners used the application for too little time. The example of subject C though, who did report learning success and stated that she had discovered new learning approaches (reviewing by listening), might allow the conclusion that for some learners an MLLE like *2d-radio* can lead to broader strategy knowledge and changes in learning awareness (finding 2).

Subject A and B did not perceive their mnemonic pathways as meaningful, whereas subject C did (finding 1). So, contrary to the assumption that *2d-radio* would work well for long commutes in a big urban conglomeration, the idea of meaningful pathways has to be reconsidered when designing similar MLLE.

The subjects showed different preferences as to the amount of control about the arrangement of learning content (finding 3). Whereas in the test run mapping was done either by learners or by the administrator, it seems advisable to offer learners both options at the same time and allow them to choose their preferred level of control.

On a more general level, it could be reconfirmed that the modulation between leisure and learning is a sensitive issue for MLLE (finding 4). As already suggested by other researchers (Stockwell & Hubbard, 2013, p. 9), providing learners with control over how much they want to be pushed for learning might be a solution to this problem.

The conclusions that can be drawn from the evaluation of the first test run, based on data of only three subjects, are certainly limited. They do, however, allow insight into factors to consider when working with mnemonic mapping on mobile devices.

References

Cornoldi, C., & De Beni, R. (1991). Memory for discourse: loci mnemonics and the oral presentation effect. *Applied Cognitive Psychology, 5*(6), 511-518. https://doi.org/10.1002/acp.2350050606

Kukulska-Hulme, A. (2010). Learning cultures on the move: where are we heading? *Journal of Educational Technology and Society, 13*(4), 4-14.

Kukulska-Hulme, A., & Sharples, M. (2016). Waypoints along learning journeys in a mobile world. In W. Ng & T. M. Cumming (Eds), *Sustaining mobile learning: theory, research and practice* (pp. 43-56). New York: Routledge.

Moè, A., & De Beni, R. (2005). Stressing the efficacy of the loci method: oral presentation and the subject-generation of the loci pathway with expository passages. *Applied Cognitive Psychology, 19*(1), 95-106. https://doi.org/10.1002/acp.1051

Stockwell, G., & Hubbard, P. (2013). *Some emerging principles for mobile-assisted language learning*. Monterey, CA: The International Research Foundation for English Language Education. http://www.tirfonline.org/english-in-the-workforce/mobile-assisted-language-learning

Waragai, I., Kurabayashi, S., Ohta, T., Raindl, M., Kiyoki, Y., & Tokuda, H. (2014). Context-aware writing support for SNS: connecting formal and informal learning. In S. Jager, L. Bradley, E. J. Meima & S. Thouësny (Eds), *CALL design: principles and practice. Proceedings of the 2014 EUROCALL Conference, Groningen, The Netherlands* (pp. 403-407). Dublin: Research-publishing.net. https://doi.org/10.14705/rpnet.2014.000253

Waragai, I., Ohta, T., Raindl, M., & Kurabayashi, S. (2013). An experience-oriented language learning environment supporting informal learning abroad. *Educational technology research, 36*(1), 179-189.

CALL and less commonly taught languages – still a way to go

Monica Ward[1]

Abstract. Many Computer Assisted Language Learning (CALL) innovations mainly apply to the Most Commonly Taught Languages (MCTLs), especially English. Recent manifestations of CALL for MCTLs such as corpora, Mobile Assisted Language Learning (MALL) and Massively Open Online Courses (MOOCs) are found less frequently in the world of Less Commonly Taught Languages (LCTLs). While some resources exist, there is not the range and variety of CALL resources available for these languages compared with the MCTLs. The vast majority of CALL literature refers to learning English in many different contexts and there is a limited amount of publications on LCLTs in the CALL domain. There are many reasons for this, including economic, political, cultural and historical ones as well as the fact that English is the *de facto* global lingua franca at the moment. It is important that CALL researchers working with LCTLs utilise the knowledge gained from CALL for the MCLTs. CALL researchers working with LCTLs can also learn from other LCTL CALL researchers and aim to be pragmatic and efficient when designing, developing and deploying CALL resources for learners.

Keywords: CALL, less commonly taught languages, CALL challenges.

1. Introduction

Most of the recent developments in CALL mainly apply to MCTLs, especially English (Gamper & Knapp, 2002). Indeed, most of the presentations at CALL related conferences and journals report on CALL research for English. This is to be expected as English is by far the most popular language for learners to study due to its prominence as a language of global communication (Nunan, 2001). The popularity of languages for learners is influenced by a variety of factors, including how useful it will be for learners, how potentially beneficial it will be for their career and if it is

1. Dublin City University, Ireland; monica.ward@dcu.ie

How to cite this article: Ward. M. (2016). CALL and less commonly taught languages – still a way to go. In S. Papadima-Sophocleous, L. Bradley & S. Thouësny (Eds), *CALL communities and culture – short papers from EUROCALL 2016* (pp. 468-473). Research-publishing.net. https://doi.org/10.14705/rpnet.2016.eurocall2016.608

relevant to them for cultural or religious reasons. The term LCTLs (CARLA, 2016) refers to languages that are not the most commonly studied in a particular region or country. Languages such as French, German and Spanish are also considered MCTLs, although the classification can vary depending on geographical location. For example, from a European perspective, French, German and Spanish are considered MCTLs while Chinese is not. However, Chinese could be considered as a MCTL in the Asian and Oceania contexts and is certainly not a 'lesser used' language.

2. CALL and LCTLs

The list of recent and not so recent manifestations of CALL such as the use of corpora, MALL, MOOCs and telecollaboration in CALL (Beatty, 2013) are found less frequently in the world of LCTLs. It is easy to see why this might be the case as CALL development is difficult (Ward, 2015). With telecollaboration, at least one group, but preferably both groups, of participants have to be studying or have the ability to use the languages involved in the telecollaboration (e.g. English-French). For LCTLs it can be difficult to find matching language pairs of L1-L2 speakers for unusual combinations of LCTLs (e.g. Polish-Arabic learners).

Many of the LCTLs are under-served by CALL resources and artefacts. In many cases, the knowledge of the worldwide CALL community has not spread out to researchers and teachers working in LCTLs and this is a pity as sometimes mistakes made in the MCTL context is repeated in the LCTL one. It takes time for the normalisation of CALL to occur and often the teachers and learners of LCTLs go through the (potentially painful) CALL normalisation cycle rather than avoiding pitfalls and arriving at normalisation quicker. Lack of awareness of strategies that have been successful in the MCTL context mean that this knowledge is not leveraged in the LCTL context. Sometimes the CALL assessment developers did not even speak the language for which they were developing resources (Ryan & Brunfaut, forthcoming). Godwin-Jones (2013) provides a good overview of technology and LCTLs.

3. Extra CALL challenges for LCTLs

There are several extra CALL challenges for LCTLs – these include motivation, limited access to suitable resources and pedagogical issues. Motivation is very important in the language learning context and perhaps even more so in the LCTL context. There are several extrinsic motivational reasons for learning an MCLT (e.g. potential economic benefits) but perhaps fewer for LCTLs. Some learners learn an

LCTL for pragmatic reasons, (e.g if you are living in the Czech Republic it is useful to learn Czech). Some learners learn an LCTL for heritage reasons, perhaps as adults or 'encouraged' by their parents (e.g. children of Greek heritage learning Greek in the UK). However, learners of an LCTL may need more motivational help if there is a smaller pool of peer learners for them to interact with and learn from (e.g. Japanese students learning Russian).

With the advent of the internet, in theory, learners of an LCTL can also have access to a wide range of written, spoken and video resources in the target learning language. However, the mere existence of these materials does not imply that they are useful for language learners if they are too advanced for the learner or outside the learner's zone of proximal development (Vygotsky, 1987). The materials need to be filtered and adapted to the learner's needs. Learners whose L1 is written using a Latin or extended Latin alphabet often learn a new language using a Romanised version of that language and this can hinder their language learning progress (Reichelt, 2011). Van Aacken (1999) reports on the difficulties learners have with character-based languages. Japanese is one of the most spoken languages in the world and Japanese has overtaken German as the third most used language on the web (W3Techs, 2016). However, this does not automatically imply that it is useful for learners. For example, if a learner of Japanese is learning the language using romaji, the application of the Latin script to write Japanese, material written in kanji, hiragana and katakana will be unintelligible to the learner. For MCTLs, especially English, there is a wealth of pedagogical knowledge on how to teach the language, including how to teach to different groups of L1 learners. However, there is a lot less research into the pedagogical issues involved in teaching many of the LCTLs. For some languages, e.g. Russian (Rodgers, 1967), there is a history of research into the difficulties students face when learning the language, but for others there are gaps. For example, what are the different challenges faced by L1 Greek speakers compared with L1 Thai speakers when learning Finnish? CALL design should draw on second language acquisition as well as language specific acquisition research in the case of LCTLs, as that research may not be very extensive and this could hamper the design of good CALL resources.

4.   Examples of LCTLs

Arabic, Irish and Nawat are three LCTLs with different profiles and challenges. There are approximately 400 million Arabic speakers, and yet, until recently, it was an LCTL. Recent geo-political events have seen in increase in student numbers.

Learners of Arabic face challenges when learning to read and write in Arabic (Aliakbari, 2002). They often learn the language with short vowels marked by diacritics which are generally not used in written texts for native speakers and this can make it challenging for these learners to read authentic materials. Arabic is an example of a language with a large number of speakers that does not have the corresponding quantity of CALL resources available to learners.

Irish is one of the two official languages in Ireland, the other one being English. English, however, is the L1 of the vast majority of the population. Most of the teachers are L2 speakers and there are continued improvements in the pedagogy of Irish. There are some high quality CALL resources for Irish (e.g. Abair, 2016; Gramadóir: a grammar-checking framework, Scannell, 2008) but there is a lack of awareness amongst learners about their existence. Other CALL resources are aimed at linguists or may be developed by enthusiasts (and may contain errors) and are thus unsuitable for learners.

Nawat is an Endangered Language (EL) spoken in Western El Salvador. There are approximately 150 remaining L1 speakers. In recent years, there have been some CALL resources available for the language, but there are either fairly basic (Ward, 2001) or comprehensive (King, 2016) but lack interactivity. However, even though the resources are basic, they are of use to learners. Nawat is an example of an extremely EL that shares many characteristics with other ELs (limited number of native speakers, mainly elderly in poor circumstances) but has managed to develop CALL resources that can provide a starting point for other CALL and non-technological resources.

5. Conclusions

There are fewer CALL resources available for LCTLs compared with the MCTLs, one reason, as suggested by Wang (2009), might be related to the smaller pool of expertise available to LCTL CALL researchers. The CALL community can liaise with university teaching departments and teacher training colleges to make the future generation of teachers aware of CALL and how it can help in the learning process of LCTLs. It may seem that the difficulties may preclude the development of CALL resources for LCTLs, and there is no denying that it is more challenging in the LCLTs context. However, there are examples of CALL resources for LCTLs that can provide inspiration for LCTL CALL researchers, for example for Icelandic (IcelandicOnline, 2014) and Dutch (Rubens, 2014).

While such resources may lack the coverage and depth of other CALL artefacts, they can provide valuable resources for language learners.

References

Abair. (2016). Abair – the Irish language synthesiser. www.abair.ie

Aliakbari, M. (2002). Writing in a foreign language: a writing problem or a language problem? *Journal of Pan-Pacific Association of Applied Linguistics, 6*(2), 157-68.

Beatty, K. (2013). *Teaching & researching: computer-assisted language learning*. Routledge.

CARLA. (2016). Less commonly taught languages. *Center for Advanced Research on Language Acquisition* (CARLA). http://carla.umn.edu/lctl/index.html

Gamper, J., & Knapp, J. (2002). A review of intelligent CALL systems. *Computer Assisted Language Learning, 15*(4), 329-342. https://doi.org/10.1076/call.15.4.329.8270

Godwin-Jones, R. (2013). Emerging technologies: the technological imperative in teaching and learning less commonly taught languages. *Language Learning & Technology, 17*(1), 7-19.

IcelandicOnline. (2014). *Icelandic online*. http://icelandiconline.is/index.html

King, A. (2016). *Timumachtikan!* http://tushik.org/timumachtikan/

Nunan, D. (2001). English as a global language. *TESOL quarterly, 35*(4), 605-606. https://doi.org/10.2307/3588436

Reichelt, M. (2011). Foreign language writing: an overview. *Foreign language writing instruction: Principles and practices*, 3-21.

Rodgers, T. S. (1967). *Measuring vocabulary difficulty: an analysis of item variables in learning Russian-English and Japanese-English vocabulary pairs*. Doctoral dissertation, Committee on Linguistics, Stanford University.

Rubens, W. (2014). Four years of Dutch experience with MOOCs. *Checkpoint.eLearning, Special-Edition, 6.*

Ryan, E., & Brunfaut, T. (forthcoming). When the test developer does not speak the target language: the use of language informants in the test development process. *Language Assessment Quarterly.*

Scannell, K. P. (2008). An Gramadóir: a grammar-checking framework for the Celtic languages and its applications. In *14th annual NAACLT conference.*

Van Aacken, S. (1999). What motivates L2 learners in acquisition of Kanji using CALL: a case study. *Computer assisted language learning, 12*(2), 113-136. https://doi.org/10.1076/call.12.2.113.5723

Vygotsky, L. S. (1987). *Mind in society: the development of higher psychological processes*. Harvard University Press.

Wang, S. C. (2009). Preparing and supporting teachers of less commonly taught languages. *The Modern Language Journal, 93*(2), 282-287. https://doi.org/10.1111/j.1540-4781.2009.00860_8.x

Ward, M. (2001). *Nawat language program*. https://www.computing.dcu.ie/~mward/nawat/general/html/intro_eng.html

Ward, M. (2015). Factors in sustainable CALL. In A. Gimeno Sanz, M. Levy, F. Blin & D. Barr (Eds),. *WorldCALL: Sustainability and Computer-Assisted Language Learning* (p. 132). Bloomsbury Publishing

W3Techs. (2016). Usage of content languages for websites. https://w3techs.com/technologies/overview/content_language/all

Demystifying pronunciation with animation

Monica Ward[1]

Abstract. The orthographical depth of a language impacts on a learner's ability to learn a language (Katz & Frost, 1992). If it is easier for learners to read the language as it is written, it will make the learning process easier. One way to address the problem of orthographically deep or opaque languages where the pronunciation is not very easy to determine is to demystify its pronunciation by using animation. This involves showing learners graphically how a combination of certain letters or diacritics produces a particular sound. This is particularly useful when the combination is different to what might be expected given the learner's knowledge of how those letters or symbols sound individually. This is also important when two orthography systems may appear similar on a superficial level but are actually different. This paper provides an overview of the animation component of the CALLIPSO system – a CALL resource for Irish orthography and pronunciation. Irish uses the same letters as the English alphabet but there are differences in the letter-sound correspondences. In the animation component, words are passed to the animation tool which demonstrates how each combination of letters gives rise to the overall pronunciation of the word. The tool is language independent and can be used for languages other than Irish.

Keywords: orthography, pronunciation, animation, Irish.

1.   Introduction

Languages have different levels of depth or transparency; this refers to the degree to which the written language follows a one-to-one letter-phoneme correspondence. The orthographical depth of a language impacts on the learners' ability to learn as well as their motivation. For example, in terms of a beginner's ability to read and pronounce words in a language, an orthographically shallow (or transparent) language like Spanish is less challenging than an orthographically deep (or opaque) language such as English. For instance, learners with a knowledge of the Latin alphabet can give

1. Dublin City University, Dublin, Ireland; monica.ward@dcu.ie

How to cite this article: Ward, M. (2016). Demystifying pronunciation with animation. In S. Papadima-Sophocleous, L. Bradley & S. Thouësny (Eds), *CALL communities and culture – short papers from EUROCALL 2016* (pp. 474-478). Research-publishing.net. https://doi.org/10.14705/rpnet.2016.eurocall2016.609

at least an approximate pronunciation of Spanish even if they cannot understand the language. However, in the case of orthographically deep languages, learners can struggle to read words and this can lower their motivation levels. Orthographically shallow languages include Spanish, Italian and Finnish, whereas English, French and Hungarian are considered to have deep orthographies (Katz & Frost, 1992).

Irish is the official first language of Ireland, but the vast majority of the population are L1 English speakers. Most learners of Irish are compulsory learners as Irish is a core subject on the national curriculum. Motivation is especially important for compulsory learners who have to learn the language, as opposed to voluntary learners who choose to learn the language.

Animation is an approach to demystify the pronunciation of a language. This involves graphically showing learners how a combination of certain letters or diacritics produces a sound combination. This is particularly useful when the combination is different to what might be expected given the learner's knowledge of what those letters or diacritics sound like individually. For example, in English the combination 'th' sounds different to that what a learner might expect when a 't' and a 'h' are combined, based on their sound as standalone letters. This is particularly important when two orthography systems may appear similar superficially but are actually different.

Animation has been used in many domains for teaching and learning purposes (Ainsworth, 2008). Animation is useful for showing learners the transitions from one state to another and has been used in medical learning for many years (Grange, Bunker, & Cooper, 1997), but was not used extensively in the area of language learning, though there are many potential uses in the language learning context, such as showing word formation in morphologically rich languages or sentence structures in languages with different types of word order. Research in the area of visualisation and learning suggests that key pieces of past information should be visible to the learner and that users can control the speed of animation, although the issue of potential cognitive overload has to be taken into consideration.

2. Method

2.1. Overview of Irish orthography and pronunciation

An animation component has been added to the CALLIPSO system (CALLIPSO, 2016), which is a CALL resource for Irish orthography and pronunciation. Irish uses the same letters as the English alphabet, with the letters 'j, k, q, v, w, x, y, z' only found in loanwords. However, there are differences in the letter-sound correspondences. Vowels present a particular challenge for L1 English learners of Irish, that is, the vast majority of Irish learners. They often ignore the accent and pronounce the letters the same way as its corresponding non-accented vowel. In the animation component, annotated words are passed to the animation tool which demonstrates to the learner how each combination of letters gives rise to the overall pronunciation of the word. For example, the popular Irish first name *Seán* is pronounced *Shawn* [ʃ aː ɲˠ], but ab-initio learners may pronounce it as *Say-an* [seɪ- æn]. The animation tool explains the correct pronunciation of the word as a series of steps. Firstly, the learner is shown that 'á' is the key vowel to pronounce and that the other vowels are ignored. Then the tool explains that 'á' has an 'aw' [aː] (as in 'raw') sound. The 's + e' combination means that the 's' is pronounced as 'sh' [ʃ]. At the end of the animation process, the learner can see the steps involved in arriving at the correct pronunciation of the word. The tool uses a combination of colours and movements to demonstrate these steps (see Figure 1).

Figure 1.   Screenshot of the animation of 'Seán'

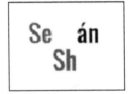

3.   Discussion

From a pedagogical perspective, some would question the synthetic phonics approach to teaching orthography and pronunciation (see Torgerson, Brooks, & Hall, 2006 for an overview of analytic and synthetic phonics). However, a similar approach has been used for teaching English to young L1 learners and it has been quite successful (Johnston & Watson, 2005). Children can pronounce previously unseen words comfortably and feel more confident in their reading. The CALLIPSO animated visualisation tool was originally designed for autonomous adult learners – with two specific groups in mind. The first group consists of parents of children learning Irish in school. Most parents will have studied Irish themselves in school, but a large cohort would have limited mastery of the language (e.g. immigrant parents who have never studied Irish). Given that Irish is a compulsory subject in primary and secondary schools in Ireland, parents may struggle while helping their children with their Irish homework – especially when checking their spelling and reading skills. A parent cannot ask a child to spell a word such as 'teach' (house) if s/he pronounces it like the English word *teach* as opposed to the correct pronunciation [tʲ a x].

The second group of learners consists of trainee teachers. Hickey and Stenson (2011) highlighted the need for a systematic approach to the teaching of Irish orthography. They argued that children struggled with reading in Irish because they did not know the rules of Irish pronunciation and there was an incorrect transfer from English, the L1 of the vast majority of the learners. They did not know the rules because they were not taught to them. This was because the teachers were not explicitly taught the rules themselves, which in part may be due to the fact that the rules were never fully defined. Hickey and Stenson (2011) have worked to address this issue and have published the rules of Irish pronunciation, which is indubitably a complex area. Ongoing research is required, but their work to date provides a basis for the tool discussed in this paper, which could be used by trainee teachers themselves to 'confirm' their intuitions about Irish pronunciation or as a way of familiarising themselves with the patterns without having to expose their lack of knowledge to their peers or lecturers.

4. Conclusions

In recent years, research in CALL has tended to focus on Web 2.0 resources such as wikis, blogs and mobile learning. These resources could be classified as CALL tools on Levy's (1997) CALL tool-tutor spectrum. They are computer-based tools that facilitate the teaching and learning of a language, but were not specifically designed for the purpose of language learning. The development of CALL specific artefacts, such as the CALLIPSO animated visualisation tool presented in this paper, is difficult and requires more time and resources than using an already existing technology, which is perhaps why there are generally less reported on in the CALL literature. However, there is room and a need for such resources. It is important that such resources are built using good software engineering techniques and incorporate reusability and sustainability concepts in their design to try to ensure that the resources can be used in other contexts and with other languages where possible, as in the case of the CALLIPSO animated visualisation tool, which can be used for languages other than Irish.

References

Ainsworth, S. (2008). How do animations influence learning. In D. H. Robinson & G. Schraw (Eds), *Current perspectives on cognition, learning, and instruction: recent innovations in educational technology that facilitate student learning* (pp. 37-67). Charlotte, NC: Information Age Publishing.

CALLIPSO. (2016). *CALLIPSO – CALL for Irish for Parents, Students and Others*. http://callipso.computing.dcu.ie

Katz, L., & Frost, R. (1992). The reading process is different for different orthographies: the orthographic depth hypothesis. *Orthography, phonology, morphology and meaning, 94*, 67-84. https://doi.org/10.1016/S0166-4115(08)62789-2

Grange, S., Bunker, T., & Cooper, J. (1997). Virtual reality, a training world for shoulder arthroscopy. *The Journal of Bone & Joint Surgery-British, 79*(2), 159-168.

Hickey, T., & Stenson, N. (2011). Irish orthography: what do teachers and learners need to know about it, and why? *Language, Culture and Curriculum, 24*(1), 23-46. https://doi.org/10.1080/07908318.2010.527347

Johnston, R., & Watson, J. (2005). *The effects of synthetic phonics teaching on reading and spelling attainment: a seven year longitudinal study*. http://www.gov.scot/Publications/2005/02/20688/52449

Levy, M. (1997). *Computer-assisted language learning: context and conceptualization*. Oxford University Press.

Torgerson, C., Brooks, G., & Hall, J. (2006). *A systematic review of the research literature on the use of phonics in the teaching of reading and spelling*. Nottingham: DfES Publications.

The effects of utilizing corpus resources to correct collocation errors in L2 writing – Students' performance, corpus use and perceptions

Yi-ju (Ariel) Wu[1]

Abstract. Data-Driven Learning (DDL), in which learners "confront [themselves] directly with the corpus data" (Johns, 2002, p. 108), has shown to be effective in collocation learning in L2 writing. Nevertheless, there have been only few research studies of this type examining the relationship between English proficiency and corpus consultation. The current study intends to fill the gap by investigating how 140 learners of three different levels of English proficiency from Taiwan utilized Corpus of Contemporary American English (COCA) to correct eight different types of collocation errors adapted from their writing. Data was obtained from three aspects: learners' collocation performance, learners' COCA use, and learners' evaluation toward COCA. A mixed-methods approach that included quantitative statistics and qualitative interviews was used. The results showed that even though learners of higher English proficiency performed better when using corpus, learners across all proficiency levels have improved collocation performance by 30%. Nevertheless, even though lower proficiency learners have received the same amount of assistance from corpus consultation, they did not think corpus as helpful as their higher proficiency fellows did. Teachers should not restrict the use of corpus to higher proficiency learners only because lower proficiency can also benefit from corpus use.

Keywords: data-driven learning, L2 writing, corpus linguistics, collocation teaching, collocation learning.

---

1. Chinese Culture University, Taipei, Taiwan; yjarielwu@gmail.com

How to cite this article: Wu, Y. J. (2016). The effects of utilizing corpus resources to correct collocation errors in L2 writing – Students' performance, corpus use and perceptions. In S. Papadima-Sophocleous, L. Bradley & S. Thouësny (Eds), *CALL communities and culture – short papers from EUROCALL 2016* (pp. 479-484). Research-publishing.net. https://doi.org/10.14705/rpnet.2016.eurocall2016.610

---

1.   Introduction

DDL, originated from Johns (1990), in which learners approach linguistic data and induce patterns, has shown to be effective in collocation learning. Learners are able to consult a corpus, induce patterns, and correct collocation errors in their L2 writing (e.g. Kennedy & Miceli, 2010; O'Sullivan & Chambers, 2006). While most researchers have argued that student-led corpus consultation can benefit advanced learners the most (Lin, forthcoming; O'Sullivan & Chambers, 2006), there has been little empirical evidence to support that claim (e.g. Boulton, 2009; Tono, Satake, & Miura, 2014).

The current study intends to fill the gap by investigating how 140 learners of three different levels of English proficiency from Taiwan utilized COCA to correct eight collocation errors adapted from their writing. The research questions addressed are as follows:

- How are the collocations enhanced after learners of three different levels of English proficiency consult COCA?
- How do learners of three different English proficiency levels utilize COCA?
- How do the students reflect on their COCA use?

2.   Method

2.1.   Participants

The participants were non-native English speakers whose first language was Mandarin Chinese. Before taking part, the students had learned English for about eight to ten years, and their English proficiency levels spanned mostly the B1 to B2 levels in the Common European Framework of Reference for language (CEFR). Students were divided into three levels as Group A (46 students, lower-intermediate level, B1 in the CEFR), Group B (47 students, intermediate level, B1+ in the CEFR) and Group C (47 students, upper-intermediate level, B2 in the CEFR).

2.2.   Research instrument and materials

First, after the corpus tutorial and collocation instruction, learners completed the paper-based test in which they corrected eight collocation errors and provided three correct answers for each error. Table 1 shows the eight collocation errors adapted from their writing and were chosen based on three sets of variables: L1 congruency, level of difficulty, adjective+noun collocation and verb+noun collocation (e.g. Nesselhauf, 2003; Sun & Wang, 2003). Learners were not allowed to use any reference tools, which helps researchers to evaluate their original collocation knowledge. Afterwards, learners completed the COCA-based test, in which they corrected the same eight collocation errors by consulting COCA. In the study, learners used the 'LIST' function of COCA which showed the 100 most frequent collocates of the searched word. Learners were allowed to check other reference tools such as dictionaries, and they reported how many collocates they had clicked when checking COCA LIST functions. Learners completed the questionnaire regarding their corpus use after the COCA-based test. Ten students from three proficiency levels out of 140 subjects were chosen to videotape their corpus consultation and be interviewed at the end.

Table 1.   Eight collocation errors in the paper-based and COCA-based tests

	Collocation errors and three sample answers	Verb+noun collocation or adjective+noun collocation	Easy or difficult collocation	L1 congruency
Q1.	*tall salary :high, good, nice	Adj.+noun	Easy	L1 congruent
Q2.	*produce money: make, earn, get	Verb +noun	Easy	L1 congruent
Q3.	*appropriate reason :legitimate, justifiable, compelling	Adj.+noun	Difficult	L1 incongruent
Q4.	*destroy attempt :defeat, foil, thwart	Verb +noun	Difficult	L1 incongruent
Q5.	*good desire: genuine, sincere, real	Adj.+noun	Easy	L1 incongruent
Q6.	*talk concern: express, show, convey	Verb +noun	Easy	L1 incongruent
Q7.	*unsatisfying desire : insatiable, unquenchable, overwhelming	Adj.+noun	Difficult	L1 congruent
Q8.	*cancel taxes : reduce, eliminate, abate	Verb +noun	Difficult	L1 congruent

2.3.   Data analysis

First, the scores from both paper-based and COCA-based tests were analyzed using Stata's descriptive statistics and a regression analysis to investigate the differences in the learners' scores to answer research question one about learners' performance and improvement in collocation knowledge. To answer research question two regarding subjects' COCA use, the use record from the 140 subjects, regarding the number of collocates they had clicked on in COCA, was analyzed by using descriptive statistics and a regression analysis in Stata to see how the number of collocates checked on the COCA LIST correlated with learners' performance and improvement. Also, the videotaped videos and interview were analyzed qualitatively to understand the qualitative corpus behavior. In addition, the third question regarding learners' attitudes toward corpus use was answered by analyzing questionnaire results and interview results.

3.   Discussion

In total, 140 subjects corrected eight collocation mistakes in the paper-based and COCA-based tests, so in total, 1120 question hits were produced in each test. First, as shown in Table 2, subjects of higher proficiency have better collocation performance in the COCA-based test (Chan & Liou, 2005). Likewise, when learners utilize corpus to learn lexico-grammatical patterns, advanced learners perform the best (e.g. Johns, 1991; Lin, forthcoming).

The current study further shows that the key point which makes learners of higher proficiency level outperform learners of lower proficiency levels is their better analytical and linguistic skills, rather than the better query skills (e.g. O'Sullivan & Chambers, 2006) or more corpus searches, because the behavior log showed that learners of all proficiency levels had no problem conducting corpus query and the frequency of corpus consultation does not differ among learners of different proficiency levels.

Nevertheless, Table 2 also indicates that although learners of higher English proficiency outperformed learners of lower English proficiency in the COCA-based test, learners of all three proficiency levels improved the same amount in collocation by 30%. This shows that to assist learners of lower proficiency in DDL, student-led corpus consultation can be made easier through the following ways, such as giving learners access to a dictionary, providing sufficient corpus training (e.g. Kennedy & Miceli, 2010) and offering adequate teacher support such as underlining the errors (e.g. Mueller & Jacobsen, 2015; Tono et al., 2014) to help them conquer the difficulties in corpus consultation, such as inadequate skills in corpus query (e.g. Charles, 2011) and unfamiliar vocabulary and grammar in concordance lines (e.g. Chang, 2014), as the questionnaire data also showed that learners of lower proficiency did not think corpus use more difficult compared with their high proficiency classmates in the current study.

Nonetheless, even though subjects of lower English proficiency improved the same amount compared to the higher proficiency fellows, they gave corpus use lower evaluation compared with learners of higher proficiency. This also aligns with previous studies that except for advanced learners in Yoon and Hirvela (2004) who showed lower motivation toward corpus use, learners of higher proficiency generally showed more positive feedback to DDL compared to subjects of lower proficiency (O'Sullivan & Chambers, 2006; Tono et al., 2014).

Table 2. Distribution of number and percentage of answers from subjects of various levels in the paper-based and COCA-based test

		Performance
Group A	Paper-based	124 (33.96%)
	COCA-based	240 (65.28%)
	Improvement	116 (31.32%)
Group B	Paper-based	168 (44.7%)
	COCA-based	285 (76.1%)
	Improvement	117 (31.4%)
Group C	Paper-based	173 (46.88%)
	COCA-based	293 (77.97%)
	Improvement	120 (31.09%)

4. Conclusions

This paper showed that corpus consultation is beneficial for learners' collocation enhancement, for both higher and lower proficiency learners, because learners of low proficiency have improved the similar amount as their fellows of higher English proficiency; but they were not aware of the efficacy corpus use has brought to them, as their evaluation toward the utility of COCA was statistically lower. This can be implied rather than restricting the corpus consultation use to learners with high English proficiency, as many researchers have suggested, teachers should, instead, be more open-minded about allowing all learners with different levels of English proficiency to obtain assistance from this resource.

5. Acknowledgements

I would like to thank the Ministry of Education in Taiwan for funding my PhD dissertation writing in which this paper has been adapted from.

References

Boulton, A. (2009). Testing the limits of data-driven learning: language proficiency and training. *ReCALL, 21*(1), 37-51. https://doi.org/10.1017/S0958344009000068

Chan, T. P., & Liou, H. C. (2005). Effects of Web-based concordancing instruction on EFL students' learning of verb–noun collocations. *Computer Assisted Language Learning, 18*(3), 231-251. https://doi.org/10.1080/09588220500185769

Chang, J. Y. (2014). The use of general and specialized corpora as reference sources for academic English writing: a case study. *ReCALL, 26*(2), 243-259. https://doi.org/10.1017/S0958344014000056

Charles, M. (2011).Using hands-on concordancing to teach rhetorical functions: evaluation and implications for EAP. In A. Frankenburg-Garcia, L. Flowerdew, & G. Aston (Eds), *New trends in corpora and language learning* (pp. 26-43). London: Continuum.

Johns, T. (1990). From printout to handout: grammar and vocabulary teaching in the context of data driven learning. *CALL Austria, 10*, 14-34.

Johns, T. (1991). Should you be persuaded? Two samples of data-driven learning materials. *English Language Research Journal, 4*, 1-16.

Johns, T. (2002). Data-driven learning: the perpetual challenge. In B. Kettemann & G. Marko (Eds), *Teaching and learning by doing corpus analysis* (pp. 107-117). Amsterdam: Rodopi. https://doi.org/10.1163/9789004334236_010

Kennedy, C., & Miceli, T. (2010). Corpus-assisted creative writing: introducing intermediate Italian learners to a corpus as a reference resource. *Language Learning & Technology, 14*(1), 28-44

Lin, M. H. (forthcoming). Effects of corpus-aided language learning in the EFL grammar classroom: a case study of students' learning attitudes and teachers' perceptions in Taiwan, *TESOL Quarterly* (Early View). https://doi.org/10.1002/tesq.250

Mueller, M., & Jacobsen, N. D. (2015). A comparison of the effectiveness of EFL students' use of dictionaries and an online corpus for the enhancement of revision skills. *ReCALL, 28*(1), 1-19.

Nesselhauf, N. (2003). The use of collocations by advanced learners of English and some implications for teaching. *Applied Linguistics, 24*(2), 223-242. https://doi.org/10.1093/applin/24.2.223

O'Sullivan, Í., & Chambers, A. (2006). Learners' writing skills in French: corpus consultation and learner evaluation. *Journal of Second Language Writing, 15*(1), 49-68. https://doi.org/10.1016/j.jslw.2006.01.002

Sun, Y. C., & Wang, L. Y. (2003). Concordancers in the EFL classroom: cognitive approaches and collocation difficulty. *Computer Assisted Language Learning, 16*(1), 83-94. https://doi.org/10.1076/call.16.1.83.15528

Tono, Y., Satake, Y., & Miura, A. (2014). The effects of using corpora on revision tasks in L2 writing with coded error feedback. *ReCALL, 26*(2), 147-162. https://doi.org/10.1017/S095834401400007X

Yoon, H., & Hirvela, A. (2004). ESL student attitudes toward corpus use in L2 writing. *Journal of Second Language Writing, 13*(4), 257-83. https://doi.org/10.1016/j.jslw.2004.06.002

A social constructionist approach to teaching and learning vocabulary for Italian for academic purposes

Eftychia Xerou[1], Salomi Papadima-Sophocleous[2], and Antigoni Parmaxi[3]

Abstract. This study presents the way Parmaxi and Zaphiris's (2015) social constructionist framework was used in order to teach and learn vocabulary in an Italian for Specific Academic Purposes (ISAP) tertiary course. The participants (beginner students) were guided to build in groups an artifact, i.e a specific academic vocabulary collection. To do so, they used *Quizlet*; this online learning tool allows the creation of digital artifacts, such as vocabulary flashcards, games and quizzes, and the sharing of the collections created. The purpose of the creation of the artifact was the learning and sharing of vocabulary in Italian used in the specific area of the students' university fields of study. The data revealed that the social constructionist approach facilitated a more engaged and motivating attitude towards learning, allowing students to work constructively and collaboratively and share their knowledge with the use of new technologies.

Keywords: vocabulary, Italian for specific purposes, constructionism, Quizlet.

1.   Introduction

Constructionism is a theory of learning, teaching and design which supports that knowledge is better gained when students construct it by themselves while they construct artifacts that can be shared and probed to the world. The student activities were framed according to a social constructionist framework which highlights three important activities: the exploration of ideas, the construction of an artifact and the

1. Cyprus University of Technology, Limassol, Cyprus; eftychia.xerou@cut.ac.cy
2. Cyprus University of Technology, Limassol, Cyprus; salomi.papadima@cut.ac.cy
3. Cyprus University of Technology, Limassol, Cyprus; antigoni.parmaxi@cut.ac.cy

How to cite this article: Xerou, E., Papadima-Sophocleous, S., & Parmaxi, A. (2016). A social constructionist approach to teaching and learning vocabulary for Italian for academic purposes. In S. Papadima-Sophocleous, L. Bradley & S. Thouësny (Eds), *CALL communities and culture – short papers from EUROCALL 2016* (pp. 485-489). Research-publishing.net. https://doi.org/10.14705/rpnet.2016.eurocall2016.611

evaluation of an artifact (see Parmaxi et al., 2013; Parmaxi & Zaphiris, 2014, 2015; Parmaxi, Zaphiris, & Ioannou, 2016). In this study, this triptych was used for the group and collaborative construction of an artifact, an ISAP vocabulary collection, with the use of *Quizlet* for the learning of vocabulary in a mixed fields class. *Quizlet* is an online learning environment as well as a mobile application which permits the creation of vocabulary, flashcards, games and quizzes and the sharing (through Facebook or other applications) of the collections created by the users.

2.   Method

In this study a qualitative approach was adopted in order to observe the use of *Quizlet* under the social constructionist approach. The main research question that guides this study is: How a social constructionist approach can guide the use of technology, in this case *Quizlet*, to support the learning of ISAP?

2.1.   The setting

The *Italian language and Culture I* course is a four-hour per week, six-credit ISAP course. Its primary goal is to provide the basic communicative skills to students and to enable them to respond to basic daily needs, socially and for specific academic purposes, both orally and in writing. The use of new technologies is an integral part of the learning process.

2.2.   Students

The participants were 16 students (13 female and three male), four students were 17-19 years old, nine students 20-22 years old and two students 23-25 years old. Students had Greek as their mother tongue and English as their second language. None of them had any prior knowledge of Italian. They studied different fields: Management and Economics (three students); Communication and Internet Studies (six); Engineering and Technology (three); Geotechnical Sciences (two); and Environmental Management (two).

2.3.   The activities

Based on Parmaxi and Zaphiris's (2015) social constructionism framework, students worked and constructed new knowledge through continuous interaction, ideas sharing, and cooperation in groups. The result of this interaction was a vocabulary collection for each group which summarises their knowledge of ISAP.

Parmaxi and Zaphiris's (2015) social constructionist framework involves three dimensions and nine actions:

- exploration of ideas: orientation, brainstorming, material exploration;

- construction of artifacts: outlining, editing material;

- evaluation of artifacts: revising, peer reviewing, instructor reviewing, presenting/publishing.

Students were divided in subgroups based on their field of study (Management and Economics, Communication and Internet Studies, Engineering and Technology, Geotechnical Sciences, and Environmental Management). The five sub-groups contributed to the building of the learning process; they created academic vocabulary collections related to their field of study and related profession using *Quizlet*. One 90-minute lesson was fully dedicated for each one of the five different academic fields of study groups.

Following the constructionist aspirations, knowledge was not presented and imposed to the students by an expert, such as a teacher (Parmaxi & Zaphiris, 2014), instead, students created and co-constructed collaboratively their knowledge in the form of an artifact, an ISAP vocabulary collection. After being introduced to the tool (*Quizlet*) and the activity, they were prompted to brainstorm in groups, explore relevant material (online and/or offline), collaboratively outline and edit the material, and conclude in revising, reviewing and presenting their artifact to the group, following the social constructionist framework.

2.4. The instruments

The instruments used were two focus groups and a final questionnaire.

3. Results

For the construction of their artifact, students initially met to decide which words were important to be included in their ISAP vocabulary collection, searched terms and then found their meaning in Google Translator and other online dictionaries; finally, they inserted the terms in *Quizlet*. The groups consisted of two to six students. This was based on their field of study. Two groups followed the procedures given to them. However, some differentiations were noted in the rest of the groups:

in the three member groups, only one person of the group inserted the words in *Quizlet* (in other groups all students added words in their *Quizlet* online collection); in the six member group, due to its size, each student conducted a smaller research in order to reach the word limit for the creation of the vocabulary. One group used Google Docs as well before inserting the terms in *Quizlet* just to keep a record of each person's contribution. The three dimensions and how they were applied in combination with *Quizlet* are presented in Figure 1.

Figure 1.   The three dimensions and how they were applied in the present research using *Quizlet*

Exploration of ideas 1. Orientation 2. Brainstorming 3. Material exploration	1. *Quizlet* was introduced to the students during a tutorial. Students were divided into 5 groups; they created accounts in *Quizlet*. 2. Students engaged in an initial brainstorming; its outcome was the gathering of some important terms. 3. Students collected more terms with the use of the web, books, etc. In that way, they were engaged in a more in depth research.
Construction of an artifact 1. Outlining 2. Editing Material	1. Students gathered all the terms (80 per group) and started organising the material, using other tools as well (Google Translator, Google Docs). 2. Students inserted the terms in *Quizlet*. They created a full version of their vocabulary and they continued editing their material.
Evaluation of an artifact 1. Revising 2. Peer reviewing 3. Presenting/Publishing	1. Students revised their artifacts: they corrected their terms, used vocabularies and correctors. 2. The instructor revised every vocabulary in *Quizlet* by correcting, deleting terms before the publication. 3. The vocabularies were published through a link in facebook and then in *Quizlet*.

With regards to the difficulties that students encountered during the social constructionist approach, two out of the five teams reported that they only found difficult translating ISAP terms; the two member team stated that because they were only two, they had to do more work regarding the material they had to gather, and the terms they had to find; two teams reported that they faced no problem at all. Two teams stated that due to the fact that they were smaller groups (two or three persons), it was more convenient for them – even though they worked more, they worked better.

Overall, students replied positively to the activity as it allowed them to find the words themselves and construct their knowledge of the vocabulary. This fostered students' knowledge in their specific fields of study; students found conducting the specific research with this method and the use of technology more interesting. The knowledge of the ISAP vocabulary made the student's learning of the specific fields easier. Students also highlighted the importance of the intervention of the instructor at the end of the group work. Finally, students valued the cooperation between the members of the team and the group work as a way to improve themselves in ISAP.

4. Discussion and conclusion

This study presented the implementation of a social constructionist approach for developing an artifact with the use of *Quizlet* that aimed to develop students' vocabulary in ISAP through sharing ideas, constructing and evaluating knowledge. The findings regarding students' attitude towards the implementation of the social constructionist framework (i.e. exploration, construction, and evaluation) indicated positive results. According to students' responses, they appreciated the three-step process, the independent learning nature of the activity, the collaborative group work, and the use of the particular technology (*Quizlet*). Students stated that their learning was motivated by this activity. Moreover, they stated that they did not only understand the vocabulary related to their field of study better, but also that of other academic fields. Finally, the findings were consistent with those of Parmaxi and Zaphiris (2015), demonstrating that the students appreciated the process and the steps followed.

References

Parmaxi, A., & Zaphiris, P. (2014). The evolvement of constructionism: an overview of the literature. In *Learning and Collaboration Technologies. Designing and Developing Novel Learning Experiences* (pp. 452-461). Springer International Publishing. https://doi.org/10.1007/978-3-319-07482-5_43

Parmaxi, A., & Zaphiris, P. (2015). Developing a framework for social technologies in learning via design-based research. *Educational Media International, 52*(1), 33-46. https://doi.org/10.1080/09523987.2015.1005424

Parmaxi, A., Zaphiris, P., & Ioannou, A. (2016). Enacting artifact-based activities for social technologies in language learning using a design-based research approach. Computers In Human Behavior, *63*, 556-567. https://doi.org/10.1016/j.chb.2016.05.072

Parmaxi, A., Zaphiris, P., Michailidou, E., Papadima-Sophocleous, S., & Ioannou, A. (2013). Introducing new perspectives in the use of social technologies in learning: social constructionism. In P. Kotzé et al. (Eds), *Proceedings of INTERACT 2013, Lecture Notes in Computer Science* (Vol. 8118, pp. 554-570). Springer. https://doi.org/10.1007/978-3-642-40480-1_39

Flip-J: development of the system for flipped jigsaw supported language learning

Masanori Yamada[1], Yoshiko Goda[2], Kojiro Hata[3],
Hideya Matsukawa[4], and Seisuke Yasunami[5]

Abstract. This study aims to develop and evaluate a language learning system supported by the 'flipped jigsaw' technique, called 'Flip-J'. This system mainly consists of three functions: (1) the creation of a learning material database, (2) allocation of learning materials, and (3) formation of an expert and jigsaw group. Flip-J was developed as the plugin of the learning management system Moodle, and the formative evaluation for its improvement was conducted in a language learning class. Learners were required to answer an open-ended questionnaire on the usability of Flip-J after three weeks of flipped jigsaw classes, and the instructor was interviewed by the researcher. The results highlighted several areas for improvement, such as 'unfriendly interface of discussion plugin' and 'translation function', which will be incorporated in forthcoming classes. The instructor pointed out issues such as the learners seemed to face difficulties in using the discussion plugin and role management in Flip-J.

Keywords: flipped learning, jigsaw method, open educational resources, instructional design.

1.   Introduction

The flipped class has gained international attention as an effective method of language teaching; it uses a blended learning design with online learning materials to enhance learning engagement in face-to-face classes (Sams & Bergmann,

1. Kyushu University, Fukuoka, Japan; mark@mark-lab.net
2. Kumamoto University, Kumamoto, Japan; ygoda@kumamoto-u.ac.jp
3. Otemae University, Nishinomiya, Japan; k-hata@otemae.ac.jp
4. Tohoku University, Sendai, Japan; matukawahideya@tohoku.ac.jp
5. Kumamoto University, Kumamoto, Japan; yasunami@kumamoto-u.ac.jp

How to cite this article: Yamada, M., Goda, Y., Hata, K., Matsukawa, H., Yasunami, S. (2016). Flip-J: development of the system for flipped jigsaw supported language learning . In S. Papadima-Sophocleous, L. Bradley & S. Thouësny (Eds), *CALL communities and culture – short papers from EUROCALL 2016* (pp. 490-495). Research-publishing.net. https://doi.org/10.14705/rpnet.2016.eurocall2016.612

2013). It has been employed in English as a Foreign Language (EFL) learning with positive results (e.g. Engin, 2014; Fraga & Harmon, 2015). In language learning, it is desirable that instructors and learners acquire the necessary knowledge and vocabulary prior to face-to-face classes. However, several issues with the implementation of flipped classes have been pointed out. For example, learners do not watch the required video prior to the class (Sams & Bergmann, 2013). Therefore, a flipped class design that enhances learning engagement should be considered for effective and efficient face-to-face classes.

The jigsaw collaborative learning approach can be one of effective instructional approach for the enhancement of learning responsibility and interaction. The jigsaw collaborative learning approach consists of two phases; expert and jigsaw phases. First, the discussion topic was presented to students. For expert phase, students are divided into several groups, with each group assigned a different perspective of critical points of the discussion. Students usually study the material individually. Therefore, students confirm their understanding of each other, and discuss the theme in order to deepen their idea as 'experts' of the theme. After the expert phase, they move to the jigsaw phase. Students discuss the theme with different members of the expert group. They first introduce the contents that they studied, and discuss the topic. After the jigsaw phase, they are required to share their idea with all classmates. When the jigsaw collaborative learning approach was used to encourage quality interactions and promote higher-order thinking to improve the students' learning engagement, positive effects on learning were reported in different subjects, from elementary to graduate school (Aronson & Patnoe, 2011). This is a helpful method for EFL students who lack confidence in speaking in English; this method helps them develop enough confidence to discuss their assigned expert topic with a jigsaw group and speak in English successfully. In this study, the flipped class and jigsaw approaches were merged to create the flipped jigsaw collaborative learning approach (or 'flipped jigsaw').

Goda et al. (2015) reported on the practice of employing flipped jigsaw activities in EFL education. The results showed that many students found the study for English practice taxing with this learning approach, although their expectations of their English skill improving were also high in general. However, preparing for this approach seems to take a lot of time and instructors feel that the workload, which includes preparing for group formation and re-formation in case the learners are absent and/or do not submit their homework, is high. This study aims to develop a language learning support system called Flip-J that supports the flipped jigsaw class design, and to evaluate its usability in language learning classes.

2. System functions

The system is a web-based application that uses the plugin for the learning management system Moodle. Flip-J has three functions: creation of a learning material DataBase (DB), allocation of learning materials, and formation of an expert and jigsaw group. First, using the learning material DB, instructors can register information (URL, starting time, description, and metadata) on open educational resources such as YouTube and Voice of America videos that are free to use for teaching. They can reuse and share these learning materials with other instructors. Second, under allocation of learning materials, instructors can set the homework as an expert group activity. The instructor sets the number of expert groups (topic) and team members in each expert group. If the instructor sets three expert groups and there are four team members in each group, the instructor has to prepare for three types of learning materials in the DB. The instructor provides information about the homework using the learning material DB. Thirdly, in the formation of an expert and jigsaw group, students are automatically assigned to expert and jigsaw groups for both virtual and face-to-face classes, based on their homework for the expert group activity submitted to Flip-J and the number of members set by the instructor. The instructors can change the members assigned to a group even after the automatic group formation. When an instructor finds that students are absent or identifies students who do not complete their homework, he/she can modify the group by using the drag-and-drop function on the user-friendly interface. Students who did not finish homework are required to study their homework for expert phase, because they cannot explain their ideas, and contribute to expert and jigsaw discussion without the accomplishment of their homework. Sample interfaces are shown in Figure 1.

Figure 1.   Interface of Flip-J: learning process and task submission deadline

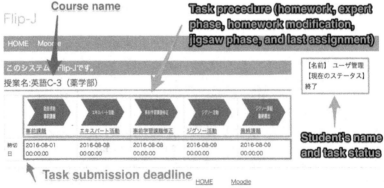

3. Methods

94 university students (female: 7, male: 87; all students were in the second year, and belonged to the School of Engineering) and one professor participated in the formative evaluation. The instructor designed the class for language learning using Flip-J. After the classes were over, students were required to answer the open-ended questionnaire on the usability of Flip-J, and researchers interviewed the instructor in order to identify areas for improvement.

The design and implementation of the flipped jigsaw approach followed the study by Goda et al. (2015). Three in-class and two out-of-class activities were embedded in the design for three weeks. In the first week, students received instructions regarding the procedure and the purpose of the activities. One of the three video clips was randomly assigned to each student, and the students would then act as experts on the content assigned to them. The students were required to submit Assignment 1, wherein they answered four open-ended questions regarding the video, through Flip-J.

Assignments were due the day before the next class. This forced each student to prepare for the expert discussion – and, further, for the jigsaw discussion – during the next class session. The discussion topic in the jigsaw group was as follows: 'What skills, knowledge, and attitudes should be acquired in the 21st century? How can we effectively and efficiently learn new things in our modern society? Compare and contrast the traditional and new education methods'. The video clips had been selected by the instructor from open educational resources such as YouTube. These videos showed content pertinent to the jigsaw discussion.

In an expert group discussion, three to four students who watched the same video were assembled, and confirmed their understanding of the video content for 20 minutes with each other.

Following this, students were asked to revise their answers in Assignment 1. Then, three students from different expert groups were organized into jigsaw groups. The students in the jigsaw groups were instructed to share their findings and understanding of the assigned video content and were asked to discuss the topic for 40 minutes. They were then instructed to submit Assignment 2, a report of the topic in third class, via Flip-J by the next class session. During the class in the third week, reports submitted as Assignment 2 were peer reviewed, and the students presented their thoughts on the topic to the class.

4.   Results

31 out of 94 students answered the questionnaire about Flip-J after the third class. They understood the flow of the learning activity and completed the tasks via Flip-J. Above all, learners recognized that the Flip-J interface was highly accessible (ten learners) and user-friendly overall (six learners). 15 learners answered that they enjoyed communicating with acquaintances. The learners identified several areas for improvement to this system: (1) feature to adjust speech speed on embedded movie players (seven learners), (2) the function of the caption translation into native language (three learners), and (3) the interface of a discussion plugin, which was installed as a default Moodle plugin (19 learners). The instructor also suggested improvements in function: adding role management, which allows instructors to check the learning materials assigned to learners, and improving a discussion forum that was installed as a Moodle plugin and which the learners found difficult to use. In the latter, the learners could see the discussion forum of all groups, but had to reload the forum board when other learners posted.

5.   Conclusions

In this study, we developed a language learning system supported by the flipped jigsaw technique, called Flip-J. We also conducted a formative evaluation of the technique using an open-ended questionnaire and an interview with the instructor. The results of the formative evaluation indicated that Flip-J can support learning behaviors in language learning, but has several areas for improvement, such as discussion forum and role management. We will improve the functions identified in this formative evaluation and re-evaluate the effects of this system from the viewpoint of the learning community (Yamada & Goda, 2012).

6.   Acknowledgements

This research is supported by Grant-in-Aid for Scientific Research (B) No. JP26280120 from the Japan Society for the Promotion of Science.

References

Aronson, E., & Patnoe, S. (2011). *Cooperation in the classroom: the jigsaw method* (3rd ed.). London, UK: Pinter & Martin Ltd.

Engin, M. (2014). Extending the flipped classroom model: developing second language writing skills through student-created digital videos. *Journal of Scholarship of Teaching and Learning, 14*(5), 12-26. https://doi.org/10.14434/josotlv14i5.12829

Fraga, L. M., & Harmon, J. (2015). The flipped classroom model of learning in higher education: an investigation of preservice teachers' perspectives and achievement. *Journal of Digital Learning in Teacher Education, 31*(1), 18-27. https://doi.org/10.1080/21532974.2014.967 420

Goda, Y., Yamada, M., Matsukawa, H., Hata, K., & Yasunami, S. (2015). Practical report on flipped jigsaw collaborative learning of English as a foreign language. *Proceedings of the 23rd International Conference on Computers in Education* (pp. 591-595).

Sams, A., & Bergmann, J. (2013). Flip your students' learning. *Educational Leadership, 70*(6), 16-20.

Yamada, M., & Goda, Y. (2012). Application of social presence principles to CSCL design for quality interactions. *Educational stages and interactive learning: From kindergarten to workplace training* (pp. 31-48). https://doi.org/10.4018/978-1-4666-0137-6.ch003

"Check your Smile", prototype of a collaborative LSP website for technical vocabulary

Nadia Yassine-Diab[1], Charlotte Alazard-Guiu[2],
Mathieu Loiseau[3], Laurent Sorin[4], and Charlotte Orliac[5]

Abstract. In a design-based research approach (Barab & Squire, 2004), we are currently developing the first prototype of a collaborative Language for Specific Purposes (LSP) website. It focuses on technical vocabulary to help students master any field of LSP better. "Check Your Smile" is a platform aggregating various types of gameplays for each of which games are generated, based on the content of a collaboratively-constructed/user-generated multilingual dictionary. To this day the platform integrates six lexical games. In addition, "Check your Smile", as a prototype of a new platform itself, has been selected as an Initiative of Excellence Project from the University of Toulouse in France. In a context of digital game-based learning, and as games, gaming and playing have become one of the main trends in educative innovation, we first justify the choice of a digital game-based learning solution. Then, we present the methodology followed for the development of "Check your Smile" and describe the linguistic and collaborative objectives. Finally, we conclude by presenting the potential future evolutions of our platform, as the release candidate version will be accessible from early 2017 onwards.

Keywords: language service provider, game-based digital learning, collaboration, technical vocabulary, Web 2.0, user-generated content, vocabulary learning.

1. LAIRDIL, University of Toulouse, Toulouse, France; nadia.yassine-diab@univ-tlse3.fr
2. OCTOGONE-LORDAT, University of Toulouse, Toulouse, France; alazard@univ-tlse2.fr
3. LIDILEM, University of Grenoble Alpes, Grenoble, France; mathieu.loiseau@univ-grenoble-alpes.fr
4. IRIT, University of Toulouse, Toulouse, France; laurent.sorin@irit.fr
5. IRIT, University of Toulouse, Toulouse, France; charlotte.orliac@irit.fr

How to cite this article: Yassine-Diab, N., Alazard-Guiu, C., Loiseau, M., Sorin, L., & Orliac, C. (2016). "Check your Smile", prototype of a collaborative LSP website for technical vocabulary. In S. Papadima-Sophocleous, L. Bradley & S. Thouësny (Eds), *CALL communities and culture – short papers from EUROCALL 2016* (pp. 496-501). Research-publishing.net. https://doi.org/10.14705/rpnet.2016.eurocall2016.613

1. Context and choice of a digital game-based solution

In France, it is mandatory to study at least one foreign language at university, whatever the student's major might be. This may directly impact how students view language learning and how (un)motivated they are to learn a foreign language (Dornyei, 2009). The recent literature shows the positive impact of digital game-based solutions on motivation (e.g. Oblinger, 2004; Papastergiou, 2009; Sharples et al., 2013), hence our choice to develop a game-based collaborative platform. Besides, university language teaching for students is not always adapted to their future linguistic needs in the professional world, which sometimes also contributes to a lack of motivation, hence our choice to focus on technical vocabulary learning. For the past 20 years in France, several LSP teacher associations and research groups (such as the GERAS research group for English for specific purposes, www.geras.fr/) have promoted research in LSP and have contributed to the development and teaching of LSP, showing the positive impact it has on students' motivation and students' preparation to their professional life (Van Der Yeught, 2014). The construct of LSP didactics and in particular of a theoretical framework is still being developed in France (see Sarré & Whyte, 2016). This reveals an increasing concern for LSP which is of course not limited to terminology but also involves a specific syntax, abbreviations and neologisms for instance. However, in order to both facilitate the professional integration of French students and potentially help increase their motivation to learn LSP vocabulary which is linked to their field of study, we have decided to focus on specialized vocabulary learning as a complementary tool to LSP classes. Indeed, vocabulary is seen as a basic but essential tool without which a specialized technical discourse cannot be built. In a context where Web 2.0 has set the ground for large scale collaborative work, we are currently developing the first multidisciplinary and multilingual platform in France called "Check your Smile" which harnesses the scientific and academic terms of all specific purposes to be acquired by the students. Furthermore, as games, gaming and playing have become one of the strong trends in educative innovation in general (Sharples et al., 2013) and in language learning in particular (Cornillie, Thorne, & Desmet, 2012), we have adopted a digital game-based learning approach to hopefully trigger and/or sustain the motivation of our students, which is one of the effects of using games in learning (Oblinger, 2004; Papastergiou, 2009). To do so, we have adapted Thiagi's (n.d.) recent Four Door model[6] and designed three different spaces on the platform: (1) the library (we called it *Dictionary*)

---

6. For a visual presentation of Thiagi's Four Door model, see https://liquidinteractive.files.wordpress.com/2013/02/four-doors1.jpg

which is an online user-generated dictionary; (2) the playground (we called it *Games*) where all the games are; and (3) the social interactions part which is what we called *Community*: this is the space where you can vote on (i.e. assess) other players' submissions and/or complete other players' submissions. The six current games range from audio crosswords to a taboo-like game[7] or a hangman-like game; our objective is to allow the student to work on listening and reading, as well as on writing and speaking which are traditionally more difficult to assess in a digital context. However, the integration of games into the learners' activity is not the sole object of our system. Based on the works of Kim (2008), who stresses the importance of collaborative tasks to promote the acquisition of L2 vocabulary, we assume that students will be more involved, as they take part in the content generation process, which in itself can also be motivating (Kessler, 2013). This hypothesis will be tackled during the user tests and after the release of Version 1 next January, using Rabardel's (1995) concept of 'Instrumental genesis' to consider this platform in the context of its future use.

2.   History, methodology and objectives

"Check your smile" was originally designed in a specific Content and Language Integrated Learning (CLIL) set of classes from a computing department where students had to take computing, maths and economics classes in English, in 2013. Its name stems from this original CLIL experience then called SMILE. It was initially an extra tool in this learning environment. Today, even though the scope has changed as it is meant to be both multidisciplinary and multilingual, the name remained the same. In 2014 and 2015, an interuniversity and interdisciplinary team was set up to rethink a new version of "Check your Smile". It comprised 11 schools and universities, four sites and about 80 people from the University of Toulouse, in addition to national and international collaborations. Then, "Check your Smile" was selected in late 2015 as an Initiative of Excellence Development Project from the University of Toulouse in France (http://www.univ-toulouse.fr/node/11538). The budget granted early 2016 allows us to redevelop the former 2013 prototypal version in a more professional way, and to experiment with it on our students.

Our international team now collaborates in gathering lexical corpora for specific purposes in different languages (such as French, English, Spanish, or Chinese) and in different fields (such as mechanical engineering, law or design). We first

---

7. For a presentation of the game 'Taboo', see https://en.wikipedia.org/wiki/Taboo_(game)

started by breaking down into categories and subcategories the different fields and subfields studied at the University, using both universities' online courses presentations and teachers' feedback.

Our categorization currently comprises more than 400 subfields or technical specialties (e.g. databases) for about 40 fields of study (e.g. computer science). Our team then used this material in the process of providing lexical entries, for its categorization. This step of the project is particularly important in order to obtain a first lexical corpus rich enough to play on the platform at its release, before any further vocabulary can be collaboratively built. This first version of the platform database will then contain entries submitted by our team, as well as science vocabulary from an online corpus called *Lexico-Science* (http://lexico.unisciel.fr/) whose owners generously agreed for us to use in our project.

3.   Future work

User tests have already started and the platform will soon be available at the following address: www.checkyoursmile.fr. In the long term, we hope to develop new games, some of which in collaboration with the Innovalangues 2012-2018 IDEFI Project (Masperi & Quintin, 2014). More generally, we are currently aiming at developing new sets of games based on mimes, gestures and imitation through the use of a webcam. We are for instance exploring the possibility of integrating gesture recognition in the platform as it has been demonstrated that hand gestures facilitate the acquisition of L2 vocabulary (e.g. Pavelin, 2002).

4.   Conclusion

Cognitive ergonomics literature has taught us that no matter how innovative a tool is, it only starts to exist when it is used, i.e. to properly analyze a tool (or instrument), one needs to consider it in the context of its actual use (Rabardel, 1995). As a follow-up research study, we have assumed so far that students will be more involved and thus more motivated: as we said, this is a user-generated content database. Given that the use of the platform is part of the teaching scenario, the students will have to take part in the generation process of the content. This hypothesis will be tested in the near future, once the new version platform is up and running. Following research questions are thus inherent to computer assisted language learning; not whether an invention works but rather in which contexts it works or does not, and how and why (e.g. Bétrancourt, 2011).

5. Acknowledgements

We would like to thank all the language teachers, colleagues from different fields, interns who made and are still making this project both a wonderful scientific and human experience. We would also like to thank the team of *Lexicosciences* for their collaboration and exchange of corpus data.

References

Barab, S., & Squire, K. (2004). Design-based research: putting a stake in the ground. *Journal of the Learning Sciences, 13*(1), 1-14. https://doi.org/10.1207/s15327809jls1301_1

Bétrancourt, M. (2011). *Réflexion sur les technologies dans l'éducation et la formation: quelles pistes pour la recherche?* (Rapport de Prospective pour la Recherche: éducation et Apprentissage à l'horizon 2030 (PREA 2K30)). Agence Nationale de la Recherche. http://tecfa.unige.ch/perso/mireille/papers/Techno-Conditions.pdf

Cornillie, F., Thorne, S., & Desmet, P. (2012). Editorial. Digital games for language learning: challenges and opportunities. *ReCALL, 24*(3), 243-256. https://doi.org/10.1017/S0958344012000134

Dornyei, Z. (2009). *The psychology of second language acquisition.* Oxford University Press.

Kessler, G. (2013). Collaborative language learning in co-constructed participatory culture. *CALICO Journal, 30*(3), 307-322. https://doi.org/10.11139/cj.30.3.307-322

Kim, Y. (2008). The contribution of collaborative and individual tasks to the acquisition of L2 vocabulary. *The Modern Language Journal, 92*(1), 114-130.

Masperi, M., & Quintin, J.-J. (2014). L'innovation selon Innovalangues (E. D. Col, Éd.) *Lingua e nuova didattica*, (1/2014), 6-14.

Oblinger, D. G. (2004). The next generation of educational engagement. *Journal of Interactive Media in Education, 2004*(1). https://doi.org/10.5334/2004-8-oblinger

Papastergiou, M. (2009). Digital game-based learning in high school computer science education: impact on educational effectiveness and student motivation. *Computers and Education, 52*(1), 1-12. https://doi.org/10.1016/j.compedu.2008.06.004

Pavelin, B. (2002). *Le geste à la parole.* Toulouse : Presses Universitaires du Mirail.

Rabardel, P. (1995). *Les hommes et les technologies: approche cognitive des instruments contemporains. U. Série Psychologie.* Paris: Armand Colin.

Sarré, C., & Whyte, S. (2016). Research in ESP teaching and learning in French higher education: developing the construct of ESP didactics. *Asp, 69*, 139-164. https://doi.org/10.4000/asp.4834

Sharples, M., McAndrew, P., Weller, M., Ferguson, R., FitzGerald, E., Hirst, T., & Gaved, M. (2013). *Innovating pedagogy 2013: exploring new forms of teaching, learning and assessment, to guide educators and policy makers* (No. 2). United Kingdom: The Open University. http://www.open.ac.uk/iet/main/sites/www.open.ac.uk.iet.main/files/files/ecms/web-content/Innovating_Pedagogy_report_2013.pdf

Thiagi. (n.d.). The 4Door™ eLearning approach. *The Thiagi Group.* http://www.thiagi.com/games/2015/7/31/the-4door-elearning-approach

Van Der Yeught, M. (2014). Développer les langues de spécialité dans le secteur LANSAD – Scénarios possibles et parcours recommandé pour contribuer à la professionnalisation des formations. *Recherche et pratiques pédagogiques en langues de spécialité, 33*(1), 12-32. https://doi.org/10.4000/apliut.4153

Author index

www.ingramcontent.com/pod-product-compliance
Lightning Source LLC
LaVergne TN
LVHW012326060326
832902LV00011B/1738